# Rebuilding Sustainable Communities after Disasters in China, Japan and Beyond

# Rebuilding Sustainable Communities after Disasters in China, Japan and Beyond

Edited by

Adenrele Awotona

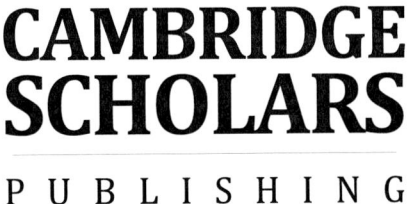

Rebuilding Sustainable Communities after Disasters in China, Japan and Beyond,
Edited by Adenrele Awotona

This book first published 2014

Cambridge Scholars Publishing

12 Back Chapman Street, Newcastle upon Tyne, NE6 2XX, UK

British Library Cataloguing in Publication Data
A catalogue record for this book is available from the British Library

Copyright © 2014 by Adenrele Awotona and contributors

All rights for this book reserved. No part of this book may be reproduced, stored in a retrieval system, or transmitted, in any form or by any means, electronic, mechanical, photocopying, recording or otherwise, without the prior permission of the copyright owner.

ISBN (10): 1-4438-5814-5, ISBN (13): 978-1-4438-5814-4

# TABLE OF CONTENTS

List of Figures ................................................................................. ix

List of Tables .................................................................................. xi

Acknowledgments ........................................................................ xiii

Introduction ................................................................................... xv
Adenrele Awotona

### PART I
#### CULTURAL, ETHICAL AND PHILOSOPHICAL DIMENSIONS OF NATURAL DISASTERS AND ENVIRONMENTAL SUSTAINABILITY

Chapter One ..................................................................................... 3
Natural Disaster as an Ontological Event
Charles Bonner

Chapter Two .................................................................................. 17
International Protocols to Ameliorate the Effects of Environmental Disasters
John H. Dreher

### PART II
#### POST-DISASTER RECONSTRUCTION IN CHINA

Chapter Three ................................................................................ 45
Reconstruction after Reconstruction: A Study of the Post-Earthquake Reconstruction of Taoping Village, a Traditional Qiang Settlement in Sichuan, China
Wang Yu with Hans Skotte

Chapter Four .................................................................................. 61
Post-Earthquake Recovery Planning in Chengduo County, Tibetan Region: An Analysis from Visionary and Pragmatic Approaches
Gui Yanli, Qin Bo, and Hao Kai

Chapter Five ............................................................................................. 81
Post-Disaster Reconstruction in Education from the Perspective
of the Social Support System: The Case of the Wenchuan
Earthquake in China
Yumei Han, Wenfan Yan, Ling Li, Haifeng Li, Xinzhi Liu,
and Yuping Han

Chapter Six ............................................................................................ 111
Ecosystem Services in the Context of Rapid Urbanization in China:
Towards Sustainable Land Use Planning Mechanisms
Xinyue Ye and Hao Zhang

Chapter Seven ....................................................................................... 131
Disaster Risk Reduction: A Comparative Assessment of Policies
in the U.S. and China
Bandana Kar

PART III
POST-DISASTER REBUILDING IN JAPAN

Chapter Eight ........................................................................................ 173
NGOs, International Philanthropy, and Disasters in Developed Countries:
The U.S. Response to Japan's 3.11 Disaster
James Gannon

Chapter Nine ......................................................................................... 203
The Language of Leadership in the Aftermath of the Japanese Earthquake
Shoji Azuma

PART IV
A GLOBAL SURVEY OF SUSTAINABLE DEVELOPMENT
IN AREAS OF SOCIAL VULNERABILITY

Chapter Ten .......................................................................................... 227
Prison Labor, Education, and Recidivism: A Study of the Bolivian Prison
System as a Possible Model for Effective Prisoner Rehabilitation
Cristal Downing

Chapter Eleven ................................................................................... 251
The Seywiaka Project: Expanded Territory and Access to Education
in a Displaced Indigenous Community in Colombia
Cristal Downing

Chapter Twelve ................................................................................... 283
Empty Lots: Success or Failure of Sustainable Urbanization
and Development against Flooding?
Jennifer Trivedi

Chapter Thirteen ................................................................................. 309
Indicators of Social Vulnerability and Sustainable Development
Oluwatoyin Olatundun Ilesanmi

Chapter Fourteen ................................................................................ 339
Social Vulnerability and Resilience in Lagos Megacity and Ibadan
Urban Fringe, Nigeria
Adetokunbo Oluwole Ilesanmi

Chapter Fifteen ................................................................................... 371
Beyond the Code of Silence: Finding a Better Path to Rebuilding
and Reconciliation in Post-Independence Namibia
Ndumba J. Kamwanyah

Contributors ........................................................................................ 405

Index ................................................................................................... 413

# LIST OF FIGURES

Figure 4.1. Natural Landscape; Cultural Activities ...................................................62
Figure 4.2. The Renmin Planning Crew; the Researchers at the Site .....................64
Figure 4.3. An Evaluation Map of Safety Conditions in Post-Earthquake Chengduo ..................................................................................................................65
Figure 4.4. Introduction for the Locals; Residents in Discussion ............................68
Figure 4.5. Spatial Textures in Different Types of Land. ........................................76
Figure 4.6. An Aerial View of the Urban Design .....................................................76
Figure 4.7. A Panoramic View of the Post-Earthquake Reconstruction in Chengduo, Taken June 8, 2012 .....................................................................................78
Figure 5.1. Conceptual Framework of the Social Support System for Post-Disaster Reconstruction in Education ...................................................................84
Figure 7.1. Number of Natural Hazards/Induced Disasters Worldwide ...............132
Figure 7.2. Number of People Killed by Natural Hazards/Induced Disasters Worldwide ..................................................................................................................133
Figure 7.3. Number of People Affected by Natural Hazards/Induced Disasters Worldwide ..................................................................................................................133
Figure 7.4. Estimated Damage Due to Natural Hazards/Induced Disasters Worldwide ..................................................................................................................134
Figure 7.5. Number of Natural Hazards/Induced Disasters in the U.S. ................138
Figure 7.6. Number of People Killed by (Natural) Disasters in the U.S., 1980–2012. ..................................................................................................................139
Figure 7.7. Number of People Affected by (Natural) Disasters in the U.S., 1980–2012. ..................................................................................................................139
Figure 7.8. Total Financial Damage Caused by (Natural) Disasters in the U.S., 1980–2012. ..................................................................................................................140
Figure 7.9. Number of Natural Hazards/Induced Disasters in China, 1980–2012 ..................................................................................................................145
Figure 7.10. Number of People Killed by Natural Hazards/Induced Disasters in China, 1980–2012 ..................................................................................................146
Figure 7.11. Number of People Affected by Natural Hazards/Induced Disasters in China, 1980–2012. ..................................................................................................146
Figure 7.12. Total Financial Damage Caused by Natural Hazards/Induced Disasters in China, 1980–2012. ..................................................................................147
Figure 8.1. U.S. Giving in Response to Major Disasters .........................................174
Figure 8.2. Types of Groups with Large-Scale "Japan Funds" ..............................179
Figure 13.1. Boko Haram Members ........................................................................310
Figure 13.2. SEI / Clark University Vulnerability Framework ..............................311
Figure 13.3. The Risk-Hazard (RH) Model ............................................................313
Figure 13.4. The Pressure and Release (PAR) Model ............................................314
Figure 14.1. Map of Nigeria Showing the States ....................................................346

Figure 14.2. Floods in an Apete Neighborhood in Ibadan..................................358
Figure 14.3. Wreckage of Connecting Bridge and Queue on a Temporary
    Timber Bridge............................................................................................359

# List of Tables

Table I.1. An Overview of Natural Disasters that Occurred in China from 1980 to 2010 ............ xvii
Table I.2. Number of People Killed in Natural Disasters that Occurred in China from 1980 to 2010 ............ xvii
Table I.3. Economic Damage Due to Natural Disasters that Occurred in China from 1980 to 2010 ............ xvii
Table I.4. Laws, Regulations, and Plans for Natural Disaster Reduction, Relief and Recovery in the People's Republic of China (PRC) ............ xx
Table I.5. An Overview of Natural Disasters that Occurred in Japan from 1980 to 2010 ............ xxi
Table I.6. Number of People Killed in Natural Disasters that Occurred in Japan from 1980 to 2010 ............ xxi
Table I.7. Economic Damages Due to Natural Disasters that Occurred in Japan from 1980 to 2010 ............ xxi
Table 8.1. Largest U.S. Fundraising Campaigns for the 3.11 Response ............ 184
Table 10.1. Income and Profit from Each Item Sold by Prisoners of San Pedro de Sacaba ............ 234
Table 13.1. Indicators of Vulnerability and Capacities ............ 318

# ACKNOWLEDGMENTS

In November 2012, the Center for Rebuilding Sustainable Communities after Disasters (CRSCAD), in collaboration with the College of Advancing and Professional Studies' China Program Center and the Ritsumeikan Research Center for Sustainability Science, Kyoto, Japan, organized an international conference on *Rebuilding Sustainable Communities after Disasters in China and Japan: Best Practices and Lessons Learned*. Similarly, in November 2011, CRSCAD organized an international workshop on *Innovation, Diversity and Sustainable Development in Areas of Social Vulnerability* in partnership with the Chair in Multiculturalism at the University of São Paulo, Brazil. This edited book is based predominantly on papers that were initially presented at these two events.

I would like to begin by expressing my gratitude to the co-sponsors of the 2012 conference and 2011 workshop for their contributions to the successful outcome of the events. They were the China Program Center at the University of Massachusetts Boston, and its Director, Wanli Hu; Shanghai Jiaotong University, Shanghai, China; Dalian University of Technology, Dalian, China; Ritsumeikan Research Center for Sustainability Science, Kyoto, Japan; and the Chair in Multiculturalism at the University of São Paulo, Brazil.

I would also like to recognize the following people and organizations for their efforts to make the events a success: all the program participants; Fran Berger, Director of Marketing, College of Advancing and Professional Studies, University of Massachusetts Boston; Christopher Brindley, Computer Specialist and Domain Administrator, John W. McCormack Graduate School of Policy and Global Studies, University of Massachusetts Boston; Angela Castillo, Research Assistant, Center for Rebuilding Sustainable Communities after Disasters (CRSCAD), University of Massachusetts Boston; Philip DiSalvio, Dean of the College of Advancing and Professional Studies, University of Massachusetts Boston; Candyce Carragher, Business and Grants Manager, John W. McCormack Graduate School of Policy and Global Studies, University of Massachusetts Boston; Carol Darcy, Vice President for the World Organization for Early Childhood Education, United States National Committee and Acting Secretary of the UNICEF NGO Committee on the Working Group on Education; Barbara Graceffa, Director, Marketing and

Communications, John W. McCormack Graduate School of Policy and Global Studies, University of Massachusetts Boston; Yimin Li, Program Assistant to the Director, Center for Rebuilding Sustainable Communities after Disasters (CRSCAD), University of Massachusetts Boston; Gary Lowell, Research Assistant to the Director (Intern), Center for Rebuilding Sustainable Communities after Disasters (CRSCAD), University of Massachusetts Boston; J. Keith Motley, Chancellor, University of Massachusetts Boston; Winston Langley, the Provost and Vice Chancellor for Academic Affairs, University of Massachusetts Boston; Jane O'Brien Friederichs, Dean, Division of Social Sciences and Professional Studies, MassBay Community College, Wellesley, Massachusetts; Shaleah Rather, Administrative Assistant, John W. McCormack Graduate School of Policy and Global Studies, University of Massachusetts Boston; Gislene Aparecida dos Santos, Public Policy Management Undergraduate Program and Human Rights Graduate Program, University of São Paulo, Brazil; Qian Xuepeng, Ritsumeikan Research Center for Sustainability Science, Japan; and William "Russ" Webster, Federal Preparedness Coordinator, Region 1, Federal Emergency Management Agency.

In addition to these people, there were many others who worked tirelessly on these events. I thank all of them as well.

*Adenrele Awotona*
*Center for Rebuilding Sustainable Communities after Disasters*
*(CRSCAD)*
*John W. McCormack Graduate School of Policy and Global Studies*
*University of Massachusetts Boston*
*USA*

# INTRODUCTION

## A SYNOPSIS OF EXPERIENCES AND RESPONSES TO DISASTERS IN CHINA AND JAPAN

### ADENRELE AWOTONA

This volume consists of papers which were presented at two international conferences that were held at the University of Massachusetts Boston in 2011 and 2012, as well as some invited contributions from leading scholars on community rebuilding after disasters in China and Japan.

According to the United Nations Office for Disaster Risk Reduction, Asia continues to be the world's most disaster-prone continent, with floods and storms as the foremost dangers "affecting the greatest number of people" and causing the most economic damages in the region, particularly China, where the economic toll in 2012 exceeded US$10 billion. In 2011, Asia recorded a stunning US$300 billion loss, in large part because of Japan's earthquake and tsunami and Thailand's floods.[1] Debby Sapir, director of the Brussels-based Center for Research on the Epidemiology of Disasters, has been reported by Ron Corben as saying that

> Asia's share [of disasters] in the last ten years is also extremely important. About 90 percent of the total affected population in the world is in Asia and almost all of the other deaths, the economic losses and the numbers of events are all rather high in Asia.[2]

Similarly, Corben quoted Vinod Thomas, a director-general at the Asian Development Bank, as noting that

> going forward, what we are looking at is not an interruption to economic growth and development but a systematic threat that could potentially derail economic development in the region.[3]

In 2012, floods were the most common disasters occurring in Asia, accounting for 54 percent of the death toll and 56 percent of all economic damages. In June to July only, floods in China affected over 17 million people and caused the greatest economic losses (US$4.8 billion). Jerry Velasquez, head of the UN Office for Disaster Risk Reduction for Asia Pacific, is reported as saying that the

> number of people living in flood-prone regions in Asia has more than doubled, in the past forty years, to more than 60 million. About 120 million people live in areas exposed to cyclones.[4]

Furthermore, UNISDR notes that

> in Southern, South-Eastern and Eastern Asia, eighty-three disasters (earthquakes, storms and other natural catastrophes) caused 3,103 deaths, affected a total of 64.5 million people and triggered US$15.1 billion damages from January to October 2012. Globally, these three regions accounted for 57 percent of the total deaths, 74 percent of the affected people and 34 percent of the total economic damages caused by disasters in the first ten months of 2012. Worldwide, 231 disasters caused 5,469 deaths, affected a total of 87 million others, and caused US$44.6 billion economic damages.[5]

Consequently, one of the themes that this book explores is the extent to which flood hazard has been methodically incorporated into all the urban and development management plans of China and Japan in order to ensure sustainable post-disaster reconstruction of its communities and vulnerable populations.

Indeed, on November 8, 2011, the Special Representative of the United Nations Secretary-General for Disaster Risk Reduction, Margareta Wahlström, observed that China "experienced more major reported disasters" in 2010 than any other country.[6] They included successions of severe droughts and dust storms in Yunnan, Guizhou, Guangxi, Sichuan, Shanxi, Henan, Shaanxi, Chongqing, Hebei, and Gansu; the Yushu earthquake; and floods and landslides in Guizhou and Gansu, which in total affected more than 230 million people in twenty-eight provinces, municipalities and regions, as well as the evacuation of 15.2 million people.[7]

Tables I.1–I.3 provide data related to human and economic losses from disasters that occurred in China between 1980 and 2010.[8]

Table I.1. An Overview of Natural Disasters that Occurred in China from 1980 to 2010.[9]

| Overview | |
|---|---|
| No. of events: | 597 |
| No. of people killed: | 155,563 |
| Average killed per year: | 5,018 |
| No. of people affected: | 2,815,051,215 |
| Average affected per year: | 90,808,104 |
| Economic Damage (US$ X 1,000): | 342,833,162 |
| Economic Damage per year (US$ X 1,000): | 11,059,134 |

Table I.2. Number of People Killed in Natural Disasters that Occurred in China from 1980 to 2010.[10]

| Disaster | Date | No. of People Killed |
|---|---|---|
| Earthquake* | 2008 | 87,476 |
| Flood | 1980 | 6,200 |
| Flood | 1998 | 3,656 |
| Earthquake* | 2010 | 2,968 |
| Flood | 1996 | 2,775 |
| Flood | 1989 | 2,000 |
| Drought | 1991 | 2,000 |
| Mass Movement Wet | 2010 | 1,765 |
| Flood | 1991 | 1,729 |
| Flood | 2010 | 1,691 |

* Including tsunami

Table I.3. Economic Damage Due to Natural Disasters that Occurred in China from 1980 to 2010.[11]

| Disaster | Date | Cost (US$) |
|---|---|---|
| Earthquake* | 2008 | 85,000,000 |
| Flood | 1998 | 30,000,000 |
| Extreme temperature | 2008 | 21,100,000 |
| Flood | 2010 | 18,000,000 |
| Drought | 1994 | 13,755,200 |
| Flood | 1996 | 12,600,000 |
| Flood | 1999 | 8,100,000 |
| Flood | 2003 | 7,890,000 |
| Flood | 1991 | 7,500,000 |
| Flood | 1995 | 6,720,000 |

* Including tsunami

## CRSCAD's 2012 International Conference

Subsequently, the Center for Rebuilding Sustainable Communities after Disasters (CRSCAD) at the University of Massachusetts Boston organized an international conference on *Rebuilding Sustainable Communities after Disasters in China and Japan: Best Practices and Lessons Learned* from November 15 to 16, 2012.[12]

### Reconstruction in China

The central goal of the first part of the conference was to examine best practices and lessons learned in reducing the socio-economic impact of various forms of disasters on vulnerable communities in China and to share these with the international community. For example, UNICEF has noted that children usually represent over

> 50 to 60 percent of those affected by disasters, whether through loss of life or from diseases related to malnutrition and poor water and sanitation—conditions that are exacerbated by disasters.[13]

Indeed, McCurry reported that

> as many as 100,000 children may have been displaced by the March 2011 earthquake and tsunami that devastated Japan.... About 25 percent of the 1,200 people sleeping on cardboard mats at one shelter in Sendai are children, many of them with disabilities.[14]

Presentations at the event, therefore, focused on the themes listed below with a view to providing insight into what has worked in China under specific post-disaster conditions that could be improved upon and appropriately applied to reconstruct safe and sustainable communities in other parts of the world. Recommendations from the conference aimed to provide policy advice and practical assistance, which should improve the efficiency and effectiveness of reconstruction policies as well as the monitoring of implementation processes and outcomes everywhere.

Here are some of the themes of the conference:
- Sustainable land-use planning mechanisms, traditional mitigation practices, and public policies for managing floods and floodplains.[15]
- Culture-based post-disaster support mechanisms for the poor.
- The role of public/private sector partnerships in reducing the impact of natural hazards and other types of disasters on vulnerable communities in China.

- The role of Chinese entrepreneurs, commerce, industry and community participation in disaster-risk reduction and the improvement of local disaster resilience.
- The role of local governments in disaster-risk reduction.[16]
- Post-disaster reconstruction and the role of the media.[17]
- Strategies for integrating disaster-risk reduction into planning and physical risk management practices in China.[18]
- The role of Chinese policy-makers and community-based grassroots organizations in pre- and post-disaster urban and rural development and the reconstruction of infrastructure, public health, and schools.
- Housing finance instruments before and after disasters.
- Women and children during and after disasters.[19]
- The elderly and the disabled in post-disaster reconstruction.
- Post-disaster urban reconstruction policy formulation and implementation processes.
- Assessments of mitigation, preparedness, response and recovery efforts by multilateral agencies.[20]
- Reinforcement of existing building design and regulations in China's cities and towns in order to make the buildings earthquake-proof.
- The response of international humanitarian agencies to disasters.
- International case studies of best practices in post-disaster reconstruction.
- Post-disaster participatory planning, housing, and community reconstruction programs and projects.

In their publication, *Disaster Management in China and Taiwan: Models, Policies, and Programs for Social Recovery*, Ngoh Tiong Tan, Yunong Huang, and Lihrong Wang have identified a number of laws and regulations that have been enacted to provide a legal basis for the emergency management system and to ensure its operation in China since the 1990s.[21] Table I.4 highlights some of the laws, regulations and plans for natural disaster reduction, relief and recovery of the People's Republic of China (PRC).

## *Reconstruction in Japan*

The second part of the 2012 International Conference surveyed case studies of best practices in post-disaster reconstruction efforts after the March 11, 2011 Great East Japan Earthquake struck, triggering a devastating tsunami,[22] and the response of the U.S. Nuclear Regulatory

Commission (NRC) to the meltdown of the nuclear reactors in Fukushima.[23] The *Asia-Pacific Disaster Report 2012* by the United Nations Office for Disaster Risk Reduction (UNISDR) reported that

> this compound disaster caused a record $210 billion in losses and damage, representing 3.8 percent of Japan's GDP. Production sites in the affected coastal areas experienced one and half times as much damage as inland areas…While many sectors suffered severe damage, the manufacturing and chemical industries were particularly badly affected with the potential for long-lasting impacts on companies' production and delivery of services.[24]

**Table I.4. Laws, Regulations, and Plans for Natural Disaster Reduction, Relief and Recovery in the People's Republic of China (PRC).[25]**

| *Laws* (by the Standing Committee of the National People's Congress of PRC) | *Regulations* (by the State Council) | *Plans* (by the State Council) |
|---|---|---|
| Law of PRC on Protection Against and Mitigation of Earthquake Disasters (adopted in 1997) | Flood Control Regulations of PRC (adopted in 1991 and amended in 2005) | The Disaster Reduction Plan of PRC (1998–2010) (issued in 1998) |
| Flood Control Law of PRC (adopted in 1997) | Regulations on Handling Major Animal Epidemic Emergencies (adopted in 2005) | The General State Emergency Response Plan for Unexpected Public Emergencies (issued in 2005) |
| Meteorology Law of PRC (adopted in 1999) | Regulations on the Handling of Destructive Earthquake Emergencies (adopted in 2005) | The State Emergency Relief Plan for Natural Disasters (issued in 2006) |
| Law of PRC on the Prevention and Treatment of Infectious Diseases (adopted in 1989 and amended in 2004) | Regulations on post-Wenchuan Earthquake Restoration and Reconstruction (adopted in 2008) | The State Emergency Plan for Earthquakes (issued in 2006) |
| The Emergency Response Law of PRC (adopted in 2007) | Drought Control Regulations of PRC (adopted in 2009) | The Eleventh National Five-Year Plan on Comprehensive Disaster Reduction (issued in 2007) |
| Fire Control Law of PRC (adopted in 1998 and amended in 2008) | Regulations on the Prevention and Control of Geological Disasters (adopted in 2003) | |

There have been written records of strong earthquakes in Japan since 412 A.D.[26]

**Table I.5. An Overview of Natural Disasters that Occurred in Japan from 1980 to 2010.**[27]

| Overview | |
|---|---|
| No. of events: | 157 |
| No. of people killed: | 8,568 |
| Average killed per year: | 276 |
| No. of people affected: | 3,361,979 |
| Average affected per year: | 108,451 |
| Economic Damage (US$ X 1,000): | 208,230,800 |
| Economic Damage per year (US$ x 1,000): | 6,717,123 |

**Table I.6. Number of People Killed in Natural Disasters that Occurred in Japan from 1980 to 2010.**[28]

| Disaster | Date | No. of People Killed |
|---|---|---|
| Earthquake* | 1995 | 5,297 |
| Flood | 1982 | 345 |
| Earthquake* | 1993 | 239 |
| Storm | 1983 | 131 |
| Mass Movement Wet | 1983 | 117 |
| Earthquake* | 1983 | 102 |
| Storm | 1982 | 100 |
| Storm | 2005 | 100 |
| Storm | 2004 | 89 |
| Storm | 2004 | 88 |

* Including tsunami

**Table I.7. Economic Damages Due to Natural Disasters that Occurred in Japan from 1980 to 2010.**[29]

| Disaster | Date | Cost (US$) |
|---|---|---|
| Earthquake* | 1995 | 100,000,000 |
| Earthquake* | 2004 | 28,000,000 |
| Earthquake* | 2007 | 12,500,000 |
| Storm | 1991 | 10,000,000 |
| Storm | 2004 | 9,000,000 |
| Flood | 2000 | 7,440,000 |
| Storm | 1999 | 5,000,000 |
| Storm | 1990 | 4,000,000 |
| Storm | 1998 | 3,000,000 |
| Storm | 2006 | 2,500,000 |

* Including tsunami

Tables I.5–I.7 provide data related to human and economic losses from disasters that occurred in Japan between 1980 and 2010. In March 2013, the Japan Center for International Exchange reported that since Japan was struck by the "triple disaster" in March 2011, the U.S. has donated US$712.6 million to help with relief and recovery efforts, "the largest ever for a disaster in another developed nation and the fifth most generous U.S. response to any disaster in history."[30]

## CRSCAD's 2011 International Workshop

Earlier, from November 17–18, 2011, CRSCAD organized an International Workshop on *Innovation, Diversity and Sustainable Development in Areas of Social Vulnerability* in collaboration with the Chair in Multiculturalism at the University of São Paulo, Brazil, a country where floods claimed over 600 lives in January 2011, its deadliest single-day natural disaster.[31] Takeshi Hikihara, the Consul General of Japan in Boston and one of the keynote speakers at this workshop, provided a detailed analysis of Japan's preparedness and rebuilding process following its 9.0 magnitude earthquake and tsunami of March 2011.[32]

The workshop furthermore addressed the following main issues:
- Strategies for sustainable development in areas of social vulnerability.
- Strategies for population empowerment and the elimination of humiliations connected to social vulnerability and/or gender, age, ethnicity, race, sexual orientation, and disability.
- Children and youth care and empowerment in areas of social vulnerability.
- Strategies for sustainable urbanization against flooding and other kinds of disasters due to climate change or lack of public policies.
- Establishing indicators of social vulnerability and sustainable development.
- Strategies for fundraising to assist in the development of vulnerable areas before and after disasters.

Both the 2011 workshop and 2012 conference brought together specialists and stakeholders from around the globe to share information and experiences and to develop strategies around some of the core issues concerning the place of vulnerable people in local, regional, national and international post-disaster reconstruction policies, plans and programs. These professionals included: disability community leaders; gerontologists; officials of governmental, non-governmental, international, and grassroots agencies; disaster-preparedness professionals; crisis managers; emergency response workers and managers; employees of humanitarian relief organizations; academics and students; leaders of industry and the private sector; physical medicine and rehabilitation physicians; geriatric rehabilitation professionals; architects; healthcare workers; law enforcement officers; engineers; environmental risk managers; epidemiologists; hazard experts; transport providers; and community leaders, organizers, experts, attorneys, and advocates.

## Structure of the Book

This volume is divided into four parts. Part I examines the cultural, ethical and philosophical dimensions of natural disasters and environmental sustainability, and consists of two chapters. Part II, which comprises five chapters, analyses the challenges of post-disaster reconstruction in China, while Part III, with two chapters, explores post-disaster rebuilding in Japan. Part IV, with six chapters, is a global survey of sustainable development in areas of social vulnerability.

In Chapter One, Charles Bonner looks at natural disaster as an ontological event. A natural disaster—flood, tsunami, earthquake or hurricane—has the potential, in itself and in its aftermath, to radically alter the fundamental structure of the *world* inhabited by its victims. A community of human beings inhabits a world, the basic understanding of reality that constitutes a meaningful whole in which human activity is situated. Our political and economic systems, our social, psychological and personal contexts of meaning are shaken, undermined, perhaps shattered by the forces of nature unleashed in natural disasters. Conceived of in this way as an ontological event—an event that affects the basic layout of a world order for the community—the importance of a *philosophical* perspective on natural disaster becomes evident. In the experience of disaster, the coherent structure of the world breaks down; the basic and shared understanding of "being itself" that normally holds a community together is called into question in profound and urgent ways. Everyday life, personal and professional relations, and perspectives on past and future, are distorted and torn apart with the same violence that reduces buildings to piles of rubble and twists roads and bridges into grotesque and dysfunctional masses of metal and concrete.

To reflect on *the ontological meaning of disaster* is not to distract consciousness from the urgent needs of victims—rather, the philosophical dimension reveals what is ultimately at stake: the basic structure of "the world" no longer holds together. Our response to natural disasters can be oriented toward this philosophical or ontological dimension. Attempting to rebuild sustainable communities in the wake of a tsunami, hurricane, flood or earthquake can be understood as a task of rethinking and reconstituting the basic structures of meaning that make the world livable for a community of human beings.

In Chapter Two, John H Dreher argues for international standards and protocols for ameliorating and responding to environmental catastrophes. Those catastrophes may be due to human error (e.g., Three Mile Island), to natural causes (e.g., earthquakes and tsunamis), or to a combination of the two (e.g., Fukushima). The basic idea is that the protection of the environment is both a planetary issue and an issue affecting the welfare of individual human beings. The chapter argues for international protocols and guidelines to ensure the construction of safe facilities (e.g., from nuclear power plants to apartment houses) and to guarantee timely and effective response to disasters. Nations subscribing to those standards would enjoy the benefits of technical and economic assistance in developing resources, and would also be indemnified and entitled to assistance in cases of disaster. The chapter argues from both moral and prudential perspectives.

Chapter Three, by Yu Wang with Hans Skotte, is a study of the post-earthquake reconstruction of Taoping village, a traditional Qiang settlement in Sichuan, China. The fieldwork in the Taoping Village uncovered that two sequential reconstructions had taken place, the official government reconstruction and a locally driven "re-reconstruction". The authors call it "voluntary restoration". This chapter describes and explains why those two reconstructions were not coordinated and presents the consequences of the processes not overlapping. The Chinese Government's official reconstruction was organized and directed by the State Administration of Cultural Heritage of China. Cultural heritage conservationists, guided by The Venice Charter and its updates, stood responsible for the planning, design, and implementation. The subsequent local voluntary restoration took place without any professional or technical support. It was an individual, unorganized and unexamined activity, mainly focused on reinforcing the buildings' structures, changing of interior spaces, façades and roofs, etc. This uncoordinated, double reconstruction of Taoping stemmed from two different understandings of the challenge, which were apparent from the very beginning. Reconstruction authorities simply regarded Taoping as a damaged cultural heritage site like any other heritage site damaged by the earthquake. For the local inhabitants, on the other hand, the village was the existential pivot of their lives. The reconstruction was a means of "returning to life"; to recover their homes, their livelihoods, but also improve their living standards, as was the case for most of the victims in the quake zone. The official reconstruction was conducted in a top-down manner excluding local inhabitants. This official approach was further exacerbated by the social disengagement of the heritage conservationists. These differences in conceptualizing the task at hand and the embedded processes sustained a constant conflict between the official reconstruction and the local population. Out of this conflict, fueled by anger, emerged a "social energy" that underpinned and sustained the individual, uncontrolled "voluntary restoration" which in fact damaged part of both the official reconstruction—and the cultural heritage value of Taoping as a "living monument".

In Chapter Four, Gui Yanli, Qin Bo and Hao Kai analyze post-earthquake recovery planning in Chengduo County, Tibetan Region. The magnitude 7.1 earthquake on April 14, 2010, caused tremendous damage to Yushu Autonomous Prefecture, Qinghai Province in China. A team made up of faculty members and students from the Department of Urban Planning and Management at Renmin University of China undertook the task of Post-Earthquake Recovery Planning in Chengduo, one of the six counties in Yushu. The recovery planning project was a formidable challenge due to the unfamiliar location, climatic conditions, and unique characteristics of the high Tibetan mountainous region. Its Tibetan culture, stock-raising-dependent economy, small population, and fragile ecological system all put pressure on the planning process. Based on intensive field reconnaissance, several rounds of interviews, and a large scale household survey, the team analyzed the county from both visionary and pragmatic perspectives and proposed a planning scheme which combined both the long-term vision and pragmatic measures. From a visionary perspective, the scheme emphasized preserving cultural resources, facilitating social development, upgrading the industrial structure, and protecting the ecological system; from a pragmatic perspective, the scheme focused on the difficulties in constructing buildings in Chengdu due to its high altitude, cold weather and distinctive culture. Thus the planning project provided feasible solutions for realizing the scheme itself.

Chapter Five, co-authored by Yumei Han, Wenfan Yan, Ling Li, Haifeng Li, Xinzhi Liu and Yuping Han, adopts the perspective and framework of the social support theory to introduce and analyze the function of the social support system in the post-disaster educational reconstruction. The co-authors set up a conceptual framework for the social support system for post-disaster reconstruction in the Chinese context, which is composed of all levels of government, non-government organizations, research institutes, entrepreneurs, and volunteers from all walks of society, who participate in reconstructing the school building and facilities, the psychological restoration of students and teachers, and the reconstruction of the teaching force. This chapter takes Wenchuan earthquake in China as a case to demonstrate the unique collectivist culture and ideology and the unified power of the centralized government-led social support system when faced with disasters and post-disaster reconstruction. The mandatory one-on-one partnership model is especially emphasized as a unique and effective policy in the Chinese context to combat disasters and facilitate reconstruction.

Chapter Six, by Xinyue Ye and Hao Zhang, examines ecosystem services in the context of the rapid urbanization in China. The rapid urban development and pervasive "land use and land cover" (LULC) change have been significant in stimulating economic prosperity in China. However, unprecedented urban growth has triggered drastic land use conversion, either replacing the wild lands with semi-natural lands, or changing the use of semi-natural lands to urban development. Inevitably, this land use process has altered the structure, pattern and functionality of the ecosystems that provide vital support to human society. Therefore, sustainable development policies must address the decline of ecosystem services to reduce the impact of disasters on vulnerable communities in China. This chapter reviews the substantial recent literature on ecosystem services in China, emphasizing Sustainable Land Use Planning Mechanisms. It attempts to assess critically the progress and changes in the structure of such research, highlighting the important role of institutions and geography, as well as emerging geospatial technologies. Ye identifies intriguing and important questions that remain insufficiently studied and highlights concepts deserving further development. In so doing, he raises questions relating to future research and explores avenues for moving the field forward.

In Chapter Seven, by Bandana Kar, the risk-reduction policies used in the U.S. and China are compared and contrasted to determine best practices for building sustainable communities after a disaster. The occurrence of natural hazards is not uncommon. Over the years, with rapid population growth and urbanization, the financial losses, and in some cases fatality rates, from these hazards have increased in every country. Risk-reduction approaches are implemented by each country to reduce these losses. However, the effectiveness of these policies still remains to be seen. The U.S. is the largest economy in the world and ranks third in terms of world population. China has the highest population in the world and is the world's second-largest economy. While building codes, land-use regulations, flood insurance, and other risk-reduction techniques have been used for centuries to minimize potential losses from natural hazards in the U.S., the current financial loss record reflects the lack of success of these measures and policies. China, on the other hand, does not have a long-standing history of emergency management and suffers from a myriad of governance problems, resulting in slow recovery and increased financial losses and fatalities from these hazards. It is pertinent to develop preparedness and mitigation policies for early recovery and subsequent increase in resilience and sustainability of communities in the event of future disasters. To reduce disaster risk, the take home points are: 1) both structural and non-structural mitigation measures should be taken; 2) preparedness and mitigation policy intervention is pertinent, although relief and response are essential for returning impacted communities to normalcy; 3) the socio-cultural characteristics of impacted communities need to be considered during the formulation and implementation of preparedness and mitigation policies; and 4) education and outreach programs are essential to increase the knowledge base of at-risk communities.

Chapter Eight, by James Gannon, investigates American philanthropy and Japan's 3/11 Disaster. The apocalyptic images that streamed out of Japan after its massive 2011 earthquake and tsunami elicited an unprecedented outpouring of support from around the world. In the U.S., new information technologies and strong grassroots ties with Japan sparked $666 million in donations to aid groups responding to the disaster—the fifth most generous U.S. response to any disaster in history and the largest outpouring of support ever for another developed country. This highlighted new trends in disaster giving, but it also exposed many of the challenges of responding to overseas disasters in our globalized era, particularly ones in other developed countries. Coordination mechanisms for overseas aid organizations were lacking. American groups that raised funds struggled to disburse them to Japanese nonprofit organizations and large differences in institutional capacity, work cultures, and communications styles made partnerships between Japanese and overseas organizations difficult to sustain. Nevertheless, the American outpouring of support has played an important role in helping Japan recover, and it offers numerous lessons for future disaster responses.

*The Great Eastern Japan Earthquake Disaster* which occurred on March 11, 2011, was the most powerful earthquake known to have hit Japan. How did the Japanese leadership deal with the national crisis? Chapter Nine, by Shoji Azuma, is a contrastive discourse analysis between the political leadership (i.e., the Prime Minister) and the symbolic leadership (i.e., the Emperor). The Prime Minister's language was largely unsuccessful in consoling and encouraging the people of Japan due to his traditional *report talk*, whereas the language of the Emperor was *rapport talk* filled with compassion.[33] In particular, the conceptual metaphor of *family* was communicatively powerful. People were deeply moved and encouraged by his language of affection. This chapter argues that the language of solidarity, or rapport talk, is crucial for any leadership when offering people encouragement and hope in the most difficult times.

Chapter Ten, by Cristal Downing, is a study of the Bolivian prison system as a possible model for effective prisoner rehabilitation. Few communities are as socially vulnerable as prisoners, particularly in a developing country like Bolivia. This chapter examines the relationship between two phenomena concerning Bolivian prisons. First, inmates must pay to live in prison. They rent or buy their cells and are responsible for almost all living expenses. These individuals therefore establish small businesses within the prisons. Second, recidivism rates in Bolivia are unusually low compared to the international average. This chapter analyzes the organization of the Bolivian prison. It describes activities related to prison labor and education in the prisons of Cochabamba, Bolivia and assesses the efficiency of the Bolivian prison in terms of rehabilitation and preparation for reintegration. The chapter hypothesizes that the prison environment, by necessitating prison labor and educational programming, empowers Bolivian prisoners to lead stable lives both inside prison and when they return to society outside. The prisons thereby provide an unexpected yet effective solution to problems of social vulnerability in the previously incarcerated community.

Chapter Eleven, also by Cristal Downing, examines the Seywiaka Project, an expanded territory and access to education program in a displaced indigenous community in Colombia. The Seywiaka village project is an indigenous-requested, state-funded development initiative in the Sierra Nevada de Santa Marta, Colombia. The project has three goals: to restore ancestral lands to the indigenous people who were forcibly displaced to remote regions due to armed conflict; to create sustainable villages where indigenous people can maintain their traditions and access state-provided services such as education; and to facilitate a move away from coca production. This chapter first argues that this project was selected for government support because the Kogi people possess ecological and other types of legitimacy, demonstrate high levels of social cohesion despite their vulnerability as a displaced people, and presented the government with an opportunity to establish a peaceful presence in a rural conflict-affected setting without diminishing indigenous sovereignty there. The chapter goes on to discuss potential outcomes of the Seywiaka project, particularly in the area of education, and examines external limitations that may be detrimental to the project's potential as a scalable model.

Chapter Twelve, by Jennifer Trivedi, investigates the success or failure of sustainable urbanization and development against flooding. In Biloxi, Mississippi, recovery from Hurricane Katrina and related preparations for future hurricanes have been shaped by both the rising costs associated with rebuilding in flood zones and social and political debates related to new construction in non-flood zones. Both aspects are shaped by external and internal decisions and have led to the underdevelopment of East Biloxi. In addition to East Biloxi's underdevelopment, the issues of rising rebuilding costs and debates about new construction have had an effect on the city as a whole and its residents. By considering an example like Biloxi, subject to repeated disasters and recoveries, we can better understand influences on urbanization and development against flooding and the potential success or failure of this development. We may also be able to understand better how we can measure this success or failure.

Chapter Thirteen, by Oluwatoyin Olatundun Ilesanmi, examines the indicators of social vulnerability and sustainable development in developing areas like Nigeria, which are susceptible to disasters. The fragility of the human condition in relation to disaster centers on the idea that disasters are simply unavoidable extreme physical events produced by the complex mix of social, political and economic forces that make people vulnerable to hazardous environments. Depending on the nature of the hazard and the socio-cultural context, different groups are more vulnerable than others. Important here is the focus on human agency as expressed in culturally reinforced social practice. That is, the specific things people do, situated in time and space, affect their vulnerability to various kinds of natural hazards. Therefore, in order to address issues of sustainable development effectively in areas that are susceptible to disaster, it is necessary to identify factors that are indicative of social vulnerability (SV) in such societies.

Chapter Fourteen, by Adetokunbo Oluwole Ilesanmi, frames the issues of vulnerability and resilience within two case-study contexts: the megacity of Lagos and the urban fringe of Ibadan, Nigeria. Megacities, as contemporary products of global urbanization, represent both spaces of opportunity and of risk and potential disasters. Megacities in developing nations are particularly critical, given their size, pace of growth, high population density, social inequality, poverty and complexity. The first analysis examines the historical, physical and social characteristics of Lagos, illustrating how Lagos reflects and is positioned within the coordinates of three tensions related to social vulnerability in megacities: the global-local; the formal-informal; and the social-ecological. The second analysis examines the vulnerability implications of urbanization on the urban fringe of Ibadan—which refers to the border zone between urban and rural landscapes. It traces the changing morphology of the Ibadan metropolis, identifying the factors of vulnerability associated with the sprawling trend of urbanization. The study concludes by stressing the need to appropriate the diversity and human scale of megacities and urban fringes, and the necessity for integrated and participatory approaches to urban planning, development, and governance in order to reduce vulnerability, increase resilience, and improve quality of life. It stresses the value of social capital in transforming these cities into more resilient systems with sustainable futures.

Chapter Fifteen, by Ndumba J. Kamwanyah, examines Namibia's efforts at rebuilding and reconciliation in its post-independence era. In order to reverse the course of the divisive colonial past, just like the stuff of the tower of Babel in the ancient city of Babylon as told in the Book of Genesis, the South West Africa People's Organization (SWAPO)-led government introduced the policy of national reconciliation to rebuild and unify Namibia under the rubric of *one Namibia, one nation* at the dawn of independence in March 1990.[34] Understandably, this distinction is important for post-independence Namibia because colonialism and the national liberation struggle divided and segregated Namibians along geographical, economic, political, gender and sociocultural boundaries.

However, what is the implication of this one national identity for diversity and pluralism? Does unity imply silence over differences, especially unpopular or dissenting views? Put differently, is racial, ethnic and political diversity a curse in the sense that Namibia's heterogeneity is too great a barrier for the country's reconciliation and national unity, thus posing a danger for nation-building? Or, the other way around, is reconciliation being used by SWAPO, the ruling party, as a fig leaf for manipulation through the slogan of *one Namibia, one nation* to control politics in Namibia?

Focusing on the detainee issue (the people detained, tortured and some killed by the then-liberation movement, SWAPO, in exile during the war of national liberation), this article examines the impact of the Policy of National Reconciliation in Namibia at the national and individual levels. The analysis reveals that if the apartheid regime of South Africa used Namibia's diversity to divide and rule by making racial, ethnic and political groups compete against each other, the SWAPO government is using its national reconciliation policy to control and rule. The chapter concludes that not only is Namibia's policy of reconciliation being poorly implemented, but it is also being used as a political tool for censorship and political domination. Consequently, instead of valuing differences and critiques as resources for building an inclusive *one Namibia, one nation*, the Namibian reconciliation approach of national unity, with its cult-like discourse of a single Namibian nationhood script, not only treats reconciliation as an end (as opposed to viewing it as a means to an end), but also fixes the meaning of national identity to the exclusion of other alternative modes of identifications and interpretation.

## Notes

[1] UNISDR, *Reducing Vulnerability and Exposure to Disasters: The Asia-Pacific Disaster Report 2012* (Bangkok, Thailand: UN ESCAP / UNISDR, 2012), 10.

[2] Ron Corben, "UN: Natural Disasters Pose Serious Economic Threat to Asia," *Voice of America News / Asia*, December 11, 2012, para. 4.

[3] Ibid., para. 10.

[4] Ibid., para. 8.

[5] "Flood Deaths Down but Economic Losses Significant," UNISDR Web site, para. 5. http://www.unisdr.org/archive/30026

[6] Margareta Wahlström, the Special Representative of the United Nations Secretary-General for Disaster Risk Reduction, November 8, 2011 (UNISDR). As observed by Jeffrey Hays,

figures for natural disasters are not always accurate. In July 2008, officials in Shanxi Province announced that eleven people had been killed in a natural landslide. An investigation after an Internet-lodged complaint discovered that forty-one villagers had been buried under a torrent of rocks and waste from an iron mine. (Jeffrey Hays, *Natural Disasters in China: Landslides, Mudslides and Forest Fires*, 2011)

[7] China is exposed to almost every type of natural hazard. Ye lists the great natural catastrophes that happened from 1954 to 1998:

- 1954 severe flooding affecting the middle reaches of Yangtze River killed more than 30,000 people;
- 1959–1961 continual great droughts caused large-scale famine and disaster over an area of 153,346 km$^2$;
- 1975 a heavy rainstorm in Henan Province caused 26,000 deaths;
- 1976 the Great Tangshan Earthquake caused 242,000 deaths;
- 1987 the Daxinganling Mountain forest fire destroyed 80 million cubic meters of forest;
- 1991 flooding in Anhui and Jiangsu Provinces caused 5,000 deaths and 77.9 billion RMB of direct economic losses;
- 1998 flooding in the Yangtze, Songhuajiang and Nen river basin caused the collapse of more than 6 million dwelling units and direct economic losses of 200 billion RMB.

According to Jeffrey Hays:
> In 2003, floods, droughts, earthquakes, hail storms, wind storms, landslides, mud flows, and other natural disasters killed about 2,000 people, destroyed 2.62 million homes, damaged 6.8 million homes and damaged crops on 50.7 million hectares of land. More than 6.3 million people had to be evacuated.
> 
> In 2006, natural disasters killed more than 2,000 people. In 2005 they killed almost 2,500 people and left 15.7 million people homeless. That year there were thirteen earthquakes measuring 5 or higher and eight typhoons that made landfall. Natural disasters in 2001 killed over 2,500 people. Natural disasters—namely the massive Sichuan earthquake—cost China $110 billion in 2008.
> 
> 2010 was a bad year for natural disasters, particularly droughts and floods which caused extensive crop damage and food prices rises. An estimated 80 million people needed food relief in the winter of 2010–2011 as a result of food shortages. (Hays)

China's natural disasters can be classified into the following seven types based on their characteristics, management and mitigation system. According to Ye, the most important disasters are:

- Floods and waterlogs;
- Earthquakes;
- Meteorological disasters, including droughts, rain waterlogs, rainstorms, tropical cyclones (typhoons, hurricanes), cold waves, damage to plants caused by sudden drops in temperature, freeze injuries, windstorms, hail, snowstorms, tornados, thunderstorms, etc.;
- Geological disasters, including avalanches, landslides, mud-rock flows, ground ruptures, collapses, volcanic eruptions, freezing and thawing, ground settling, land desertification, soil and water loss, salinization, etc.;
- Ocean disasters, including wind-driven tides, tsunamis, sea waves, sea ice, seawater intrusion, red tides, tide disasters, positive movement, seawater encroachment, etc.;
- Crop disasters, including crop and plant diseases, insect pests, plagues of rats, agricultural meteorological disasters, agricultural environment disasters, etc.;
- Forest disasters, including forest plant diseases, insect pests, plagues of rats, forest fires, etc.

Ye reports that:

- Damaging earthquakes have occurred in almost every province of the country. About one half of China's population lives in earthquake-prone areas with a seismic intensity of VII and above, which covers 3,120,000km$^2$ and comprises 32.5 percent of the total territory. Earthquakes in China from 1950 to 1999 resulted in at least 281,706 deaths, damaged 20,223,989 dwelling units and caused direct economic losses of 107.627 billion RMB.

- With regards to flood disasters in mainland China from 1950 to 1999, the annual flood-affected areas and consequent disaster areas amounted to 7,804,000 km$^2$ and 4,308,000 km$^2$ respectively; on average, 5,500 people died annually.

The Council on Foreign Relations has noted that China suffered its most catastrophic rainstorm in four decades in July 2012, a deluge that brought 16 to 18 inches of rain to some areas, killing thirty-seven people and causing US$1.6 billion in damage. Some Chinese researchers attributed the storm's power to the effects of urbanization (Council on Foreign Relations, "Man-Made Cities and Natural Disasters: The Growing Threat," *Devex*, August 16, 2012, https://www.devex.com/en/news/man-made-cities-and-natural-disasters-the-growing/78936 Retrieved February 27, 2013). See also "Beijing Chaos after Record Floods in Chinese Capital," BBC, July 27, 2012, http://www.bbc.co.uk/news/world-asia-18949777 (retrieved March 1, 2013).

[8] The preliminary 2012 data on natural disasters in twenty-eight Asian countries, released by UNISDR and the Belgian-based Centre for Research on the Epidemiology of Disasters (CRED) on December 11, 2012, show that from 1950 to 2011, nine out of ten people affected by disasters worldwide were in Asia; that of the top five disasters that created the most damage in 2012, three were in China (the other two were in Pakistan and Iran); that cumulatively, these events resulted in an estimated $13.3 billion in damage; that China led the list of most disasters in 2012 (eighteen), followed by Philippines (sixteen), Indonesia (ten), Afghanistan (nine) and India (five); that China was the only "multi-hazard"-prone country; and that the June–July 2012 floods in China affected over 17 million people and caused the greatest economic loss in the region—US$4.8 billion.

[9] UNISDR, "China—Disaster Statistics," *PreventionWeb* 2013, http://www.preventionweb.net/english/countries/statistics/?cid=36

[10] Ibid.

[11] Ibid.

[12] On January 7, 2013, the Government of the People's Republic of China issued the following press release:

Recently many departments including the Ministry of Civil Affairs and General Office of National Committee for Disaster Reduction organized meetings to analyze the conditions of natural disasters of China in 2012. Disasters affected 290 million people, destroyed 906,000 houses, severely damaged 1.46 million houses and caused direct economic losses of 418.55 billion yuan (66.55 billion U.S. dollars) on the Chinese mainland, according to a joint statement from the Ministry of Civil Affairs and the office of the National Committee for Disaster Reduction. In 2012, the main disasters included floods, geological disaster, typhoon and hail. Drought, earthquake, snowstorm, sandstorm and forest fire also hit. The features of the natural disasters were as follows:
- First, the distribution of disasters was large. In some regions, the disasters were quite serious. Thirty-one provinces and over 2,600 counties (regions and cities) suffered disasters.

- Second, spring and summer floods in southern China were remarkable and floods in northern China were severe. Spring floods in many provinces of southern China were earlier. In summer, twenty-one rainstorm processes hit.
- Third, typhoons frequently landed with large-scale influences. Ten typhoons struck mainland China, of which seven landed in the coastal areas.
- Fourth, in some places, hail disaster was serious while drought disaster was remarkably light.
- Fifth, earthquakes hit western China frequently and low temperature and snow disaster hit northern China. The mainland China suffered sixteen earthquakes whose magnitudes were above 5. All these were in western China. In winter of 2012, the average temperature of China was lower than the long term average. From November, China has got seven remarkable temperature drop processes.
- Sixth, poor regions frequently suffered severe disasters.

Kong Yan, "Natural Disasters in China Showed 6 Features in 2012," China Meteorological News Press, reprinted on *Reliefweb*, http://reliefweb.int/report/china/natural-disasters-china-showed-6-features-2012. See also Olivia Boyd, "China Faces a Flooding Crisis as Natural Disasters Triple in 30 Years," *Chinadialogue*, January 1, 2013, http://www.chinadialogue.net/article/show/single/en/5510-China-faces-a-flooding-crisis-as-natural-disasters-triple-in-3-years

[13] According to Wisner, as noted in the discussion paper "Children and Disaster—Risk Reduction in Asia and the Pacific: A Way Forward" (2006) prepared for the High-Level Meeting on Cooperation for Child Rights in the Asia-Pacific Region, Beijing, China, November 4–6, 2010,

> the National Textbook Authorization Committee for Primary and Middle Schools of China agreed in 2004 to the production of a textbook for senior middle schools on natural hazards. By 2006, a copy was reported to be on every senior middle school student's desk. The book is a thorough introduction to natural hazards in the world, including in China, and has a separate chapter on preparedness and Disaster Risk Reduction. The book also features a list of Chinese websites that students and teachers can consult for further information. (Catherine Cameron and Gemma Norrington-Davies, 2010, Agulhas, http://www.unicef.org/eapro/AsiaPacific_DRR_final.pdf)

For a study of children's vulnerability immediately after major disasters as well as their mental health needs in China, see Louise Edwards and Chen Minglu, *Protecting Children in Disasters Project, Evaluator's Report, Stage One (April 2007–March 2008)* (Broadway, NSW: University of Technology Sydney China Research Centre, 2008). The project, by Australian and Chinese mental health practitioners, aimed to enhance knowledge within Chinese communities

> of key intervention strategies by providing simple, step-by-step approaches that can be implemented immediately by teachers, community leaders and parents.

¹⁴ Justin McCurry, "Japan Earthquake: 100,000 Children Displaced, Says Charity," *The Guardian*, March 15, 2011, paras. 1, 9, http://www.theguardian.com/world/2011/mar/15/japan-earthquake-children-displaced-charity. For a report of the progress made by Save the Children in the response and recovery effort two years after the earthquake, please see Save the Children, *Japan Two Years On: Save the Children's Response and Recovery Program*, March 2013, http://www.savechildren.or.jp/jpnem/jpn/pdf/two_year_later/two_year_on.pdf. The report covers the following aspects of post-disaster recovery: Community Grants Initiative, Creating Child-Friendly Communities/Child Participation, Education, Child Protection, Fukushima, Beneficiary Numbers (net numbers from January 2012 through January 2013), Disaster Risk Reduction, Stories from The Field, Kesen Koryo Special Needs School, Future Directions, and Resource and Financial Status.

¹⁵ According to Global Water Partnership (GWP),

> inappropriate land use management has been a shortcoming of past flood management in China due to the unprecedented pace of socioeconomic development and the increase in population densities. To apply land use planning as a flood management is required especially at local government level where most land use planning is practiced. (*China: From Flood Control to Integrated Flood Management* (#420), Author, 2013)

In 1997, the government passed the Flood Control Law in order to ensure a

> more integrated flood management approach... necessary to adapt to changing social, hydrological, and environmental conditions along the nation's major waterways; (Ibid.)

and, in 2005, the Ministry of Water Resources prepared a national flood management strategy. GWP observes that

> this strategy reflects a shift from dependence on structural measures to a balanced approach using both structural and non-structural measures. (Ibid.)

The Flood Control Law remains the centerpiece legislation supported by regulations guiding the implementation of flood management policies.

UNISDR's *Asia-Pacific Disaster Report 2012* noted that

> in the developed countries of the Asia-Pacific region, where prosperity should be used to address the many downsides of economic growth, disaster losses are growing most rapidly (because) land use and urban planning, ecosystem management and disaster recovery—the very tools devised to deal with exposure to risks—are not yielding the desired results. (UNISDR)

It goes on to report that there are, however, some outstanding efforts being made to reverse these trends in China, and its 2011–2015 Comprehensive Disaster Prevention and Reduction Plan aims to reduce disaster losses annually to less than 1.5 percent GDP through investment measures across government sectors.

¹⁶ As at February 23, 2013, the following were China's participating local governments in UNISDR's *The Making Cities Resilient: "My City is Getting Ready!"* campaign, launched in May 2010 by the Global Platform for Disaster

Risk Reduction: Baofeng County, Chengdu, Luoyang, Mianyang City, Sanya City, Xianyang City, and Xining. The campaign addresses issues of local governance and urban risk (http://www.unisdr.org/campaign/resilientcities/about).

[17] In 2012, there were 385 natural disasters globally. These killed more than 297,000 people worldwide and affected over 217 million others. According to Jurgita Balaisyte, Maria Besiou, and Luk N. Van Wassehove,

> although more than five times more people were affected by China's floods than by the earthquake in Haiti and the floods in Pakistan combined, China's floods received far less media attention than either Pakistan or Haiti. (*The Media and Disasters*, INSEAD Humanitarian Research Group, May 2011, para. 1)

They also cited the following examples to illustrate the fact that "media attention does not necessarily depend on the number of casualties and the size of the disaster"—

> The web-portal Reliefweb, administered by the United Nations Office for the Coordination of Humanitarian Affairs (OCHA), posted only 243 entries on the Chinese floods in comparison with 2,500 entries on the flooding in Pakistan.
>
> Another disaster that was well mediatised was the Tohoku disaster in Japan. Despite the scale of the devastating 2011 Tohoku earthquake and tsunami disaster, it caused only one-tenth of Haiti's casualties. This disaster also received broader media coverage, followed by higher fundraising, than China's floods. (Ibid., paras. 3–4)

[18] The Global Assessment Report on Disaster Risk Reduction 2011 notes that public awareness of risks and of how to address them is a key to strengthening accountability and ensuring that disaster risk management [DRM] is implemented. (United Nations, 2011, 4.7.2 para. 1.)

According to this report, China has made a

> substantial and comprehensive progress on the availability of risk information, on developing a countrywide public awareness strategy, and on integrating DRM into school curricula (from primary to tertiary levels). China is also one of the countries that have included DRM in the national educational curriculum and university and professional training, as well as conducting research on improved multi-risk assessments and cost-benefit analyses of disaster risk reduction. (Ibid., para. 2)

[19] For all relevant UN Security Council resolutions on children and armed conflict, see Security Council resolutions 1325 (October 31, 2000), 1820 (June 19, 2008), 1888 (September 30, 2009), 1889 (October 5, 2009), 1960 (December 16, 2010), 1882 ( August 4, 2009), and 1998 (July 12, 2011), as well as Human Rights Council Resolutions 17/11 (June 17, 2011) (on accelerating efforts to eliminate all forms of violence against women, ensuring due diligence in protection), 20/6 (July 5, 2012) (on the elimination of discrimination against women), and 20/12 (July 5, 2012) (on accelerating efforts to eliminate all forms of violence against women and remedies for women who have been subjected to violence). (United Nations, "The Elimination and Prevention of All Forms of Violence against Women and

Girls: Agreed Conclusions," Advance unedited version, Commission on the Status of Women, Fifty-Seventh Session (New York, NY: Author, 2013).

[20] For the United Nations' contribution to post-disaster recovery efforts in China, especially in the areas of coordination and technical support, recovery appeal, training and raising awareness of environmental and ecological considerations within the overall state planning processes, see, for example,

- UN Environment Program (UNEP), *Disasters and Conflicts: China*, n.d., http://www.unep.org/disastersandconflicts/UNEPsActivities/China/tabid/54634/Default.aspx
- *United Nations in China* website for reports on the UN's two-day workshop in July 2008 with China's Ministry of Commerce, which brought together international experts and Chinese Government officials to discuss recovery and sustainable development practices for the affected areas following the devastating Wenchuan earthquake of May 12, 2008. http://reliefweb.int/report/china/un-china-launches-appeal-assist-wenchuan-earthquake-victims
- UNESCO International Research and Training Centre for Rural Education (INRULED), First Dujiangyan International Forum, Education for Sustainable Development, *Policy Framework, Professional Standards, Innovative Practices. Final Report* (Chengdu, China: Author, 2010), http://www.inruled.org/a/soft/101217/1stDujiangyanInternationalForumFinalReport.pdf

[21] Ngoh Tiong Tan, Yunong Huang, and Lihrong Wang, "Disaster Management in China and Taiwan: Models, Policies, and Programs for Social Recovery," *Journal of Global Social Work Practice*, 4(1).

[22] For reports and conference proceedings on *One Year after the 2011 Great East Japan Earthquake*, see, for example:

- *Proceedings of the International Symposium on Engineering Lessons Learned from the Giant Earthquake: One Year after the 2011 Great East Japan Earthquake*, Kenchiku-Kaikan, Tokyo, Japan, March 1–4, 2012, http://www.jaee.gr.jp/event/seminar2012/eqsympo/proceedings.html
- Hiroko Tabuchi, "An Anniversary of 'Heartbreaking Grief' in Japan," *New York Times*, March 11, 2012, http://www.nytimes.com/2012/03/12/world/asia/a-year-later-effects-of-japans-disaster-are-still-unfolding.html?_r=1&ref=world&pagewanted=all
- Yuka Hayashi, Daisuke Wakabayashi, and Mitsuru Obe, "An Altered Japan Marks a Year After Quake," *Wall Street Journal*, March 12, 2012, http://online.wsj.com/article/SB10001424052970204781804577273302704771354.html?mod=googlenews_wsj
- "Japan Marks Quake and Tsunami Anniversary," *BBC News Asia*, March 11, 2012, http://www.bbc.co.uk/news/world-asia-17326084
- "Japan Marks Year Since Tsunami, Earthquake Disasters," *Fox News*, March 11, 2012, http://www.foxnews.com/world/2012/03/10/japan-marks-year-since-tsunami-earthquake-disasters/?test=latestnews

- "Japan Post Disaster," *Architectural Record*, March 9, 2012, http://archrecord.construction.com/features/humanitarianDesign/Japan/Japan-Post-Disaster.asp
- Danielle Demetriou, "A Whole Year Wasted Since Tsunami Disaster, Says Japan Red Cross," *The Telegraph*, March 8, 2012, http://www.telegraph.co.uk/news/worldnews/asia/japan/9130259/Japan-earthquake-and-tsunami-anniversary-a-whole-year-wasted-since-tsunami-disaster-says-Japan-Red-Cross.html
- "One Year Later, 'Inside Japan's Nuclear Meltdown'," *National Public Radio (NPR)*, February 28, 2012, http://www.npr.org/2012/02/28/147559456/one-year-later-inside-japans-nuclear-meltdown

[23] The following constitutes a summary of actions taken by the U.S. Nuclear Regulatory Commission (NRC) in response to the nuclear disaster at Fukushima in Japan.

- On Friday, March 11, when the earthquake and tsunami struck in Japan, the NRC's headquarters Operations Center began operating on a twenty-four-hour basis to monitor and analyze events at the nuclear power plants in Japan.
- At the request of the Japanese government, and through the United States Agency for International Development (USAID), the NRC sent a team of its technical experts to provide on-the-ground support, and the NRC maintained continual contact with them.
- Within the United States, the NRC worked closely with other Federal agencies as part of our government's response to the situation.
- The Chairman of NRC traveled to Japan over the weekend of March 26–27 to convey a message of support and cooperation to our Japanese counterparts and to assess the current situation. During the time he was there, he also met with senior Japanese government and TEPCO officials and consulted with the NRC team of experts who were in Japan as part of NRC's assistance effort.
- The decision to recommend a fifty-mile radius evacuation of U.S. citizens near the Fukushima Daiichi site was based on limited information and the best assessment of conditions as the NRC understood them at the time. Four of the six plants at the site were facing extraordinary challenges, including hydrogen explosions and the possibility of overheating in a spent fuel pool containing a recent full core offload of fuel. In addition, radiation monitors were showing very high levels of radiation on the plant site, which would impede workers trying to stabilize the reactors.
- The NRC began systematically and methodically to evaluate the lessons being learned at Fukushima Daiichi as they might apply to the safety of reactors in the United States and relay important information to our country's nuclear power plants. In communicating this information to licensees, the NRC sought to

assist them in considering the ramifications of a similar event for their facilities and to take site-specific actions, as appropriate.
- In addition to communicating information to licensees, the NRC also focused and enhanced its oversight on issues highlighted by its observations of the events at Fukushima. It issued instructions to NRC inspectors, calling for immediate, independent assessments of each plant's level of preparedness. The instructions covered Extensive Damage Mitigation Guidelines, station blackout and seismic and flooding issues, as well as Severe Accident Management Guidelines. Our resident inspector program, which stations NRC inspectors at all operating U.S. nuclear plants, enabled the NRC to take prompt oversight action.
- The Commission undertook a systematic and methodical review of its nuclear safety program. On March 21, the Commission established a senior-level Task Force, made up of some of the agency's most experienced and expert staff. Collectively, the Task Force members have more than 135 years of regulatory experience. They were asked to conduct a short-term review, to assist the Commission to better understand the events in Japan and determine the implications for domestic nuclear safety.
- In line with the overall agency approach to nuclear safety, the Task Force took a defense-in-depth approach focused on prevention, mitigation and emergency response. They examined a broad range of issues, including seismic, flooding and other natural hazards, how to maintain power during these types of events, how to mitigate the potential loss of power and emergency preparedness. In working through these issues, the Task Force relied on information and analysis from the NRC Operations Center, the NRC's site team in Japan and dozens of other agency experts. They also called on experts from throughout the federal government, including the Federal Emergency Management Agency, which engaged the Task Force in discussions of offsite emergency preparedness and provided insights on the U.S. National Response Framework; the Institute of Nuclear Power Operations which shared information on the industry's post-Fukushima actions; and other groups and individuals who shared their views with the Task Force.
- The time constraints of the short-term review understandably placed limitations on the extent of stakeholder involvement, but in line with the NRC commitment to openness and transparency, three public meetings—at the thirty-day, sixty-day and ninety-day marks—were held by the Commission, and the final short-term Task Force Report and recommendations were provided to the Commission on July 12 and made public on July 13.
- The NRC safety review examined a broad range of events and risks. Those included hazards specifically contemplated in the

design basis and others beyond the design basis. Specifically, it evaluated the requirements and safety margins for seismic and flooding events, and other external events that might inflict widespread damage to the plant and lead to an extended station blackout. Its review was not limited to the type of seismic/tsunami event experienced by Japan. It also looked at risks posed by other types of flooding (including dam failures and river flooding), fires and combinations of different events. (Gregory B. Jaczko, Chairman of the U.S. Nuclear Regulatory Commission, to Senator Jeff Sessions, September 14, 2011, http://pbadupws.nrc.gov/docs/ML1125/ML112580085.pdf)

For the findings of Independent Investigation Commissions on the Fukushima Daiichi Nuclear Accident, see, for example:

- Mark Holt, Richard J. Campbell and Mary Beth Nikitin, *Fukushima Nuclear Disaster*, Congressional Research Service Report R41694, January 18, 2012, http://www.fas.org/sgp/crs/nuke/R41694.pdf
- Yoichi Funabashi and Kay Kitazawa, "Fukushima in Review: A Complex Disaster, A Disastrous Response," *Bulletin of the Atomic Scientists*, 68(2), 9–21. This article concludes that the March 11, 2011 earthquake and tsunami that crippled the Fukushima Daiichi Nuclear Power Station was

    exacerbated by communication gaps between the government and the nuclear industry;...[that] the government, the Tokyo Electric Power Company (Tepco), and other relevant actors were thoroughly unprepared on almost every level for the cascading nuclear disaster; [that] this lack of preparation was caused, in part, by a public myth of "absolute safety" that nuclear power proponents had nurtured over decades and was aggravated by dysfunction within and between government agencies and Tepco, particularly in regard to political leadership and crisis management; [and] that the tsunami that began the nuclear disaster could and should have been anticipated and that ambiguity about the roles of public and private institutions in such a crisis was a factor in the poor response at Fukushima.

[24] UNISDR, 89.
[25] After Tan, Huang, and Wang.
[26] Major earthquakes in Japan from 1703–2011 (David Bressan, "A Short History of Earthquakes in Japan," *Scientific American*, March 11, 2012):

- December 31, 1703: Japan was hit by a strong earthquake with a reconstructed intensity of 8 after the Mercalli scale. In Edo (Tokyo), most of the wooden buildings collapsed. The earthquake and the floods and fires that occurred in its aftermath killed an estimated 150,000 people. More than 6,500 people were killed by a flood wave, which caused havoc in the bay of Sagami and on the peninsula of Boso.
- November 11, 1855: One of the most important historic earthquakes hit Tokyo, killing 16,000 to 20,000 people.

- October 28, 1891: The agricultural region of Nobi experienced a magnitude 8 earthquake. Many houses were damaged or collapsed, thousands of people lost their homes and 7,000 people were killed.
- September 1, 1923: The cities of Yokohama and Tokyo were hit again by an earthquake. More than 99,000 people were killed by the collapse of buildings, a 10- to 12-meter-high tsunami, and fires. The bodies of more than 40,000 victims were never found.
- January 1995: The industrial city of Kobe was hit by a magnitude 7.2 earthquake, the strongest earthquake in Japan since 1923. More than 6,000 people were killed and more than 300,000 people lost their homes.
- March 11, 2011: The devastating tsunami was triggered by the strongest earthquake ever recorded.

[27] UNISDR, "Japan—Disaster Statistics," *PreventionWeb* 2013, http://www.preventionweb.net/english/countries/statistics/?cid=87
[28] Ibid.
[29] Ibid.
[27] Japan Center for International Exchange (JCIE), 1, http://jcie.org/researchpdfs/311/JCIE_USGivingReport3.pdf
[31] Subir Ghosh, "Brazil Floods: Worst Single-Day Natural Disaster in its History," *Digital Journal*, January 16, 2011, http://digitaljournal.com/article/302622. In 2010, floods and landslides killed over eighty in January, 246 people near Rio de Janeiro in April, and more than forty people in the northeastern part of the country in June.

Patricia Knebel, in her report for *Infosurhoy.com* on March 9, 2011, wrote that

> for every R$10 (US$6.08) that's spent on natural disasters in Brazil, R$9 (US$5.47) goes toward dealing with a disaster's aftermath, and just R$1.00 (US$0.61) is spent on prevention, according to the Integrated Financial Administration System (SIAFI). In addition, for every R$4 (US$2.43) allocated to disaster prevention, less than R$1 (US$0.61) is spent. In 2010, Brazil spent R$2.3 billion (US$1.4 billion) on reconstruction and R$137 million (US$83.3 million) on prevention. The state of Bahia received 50.5 percent of the federal funds budgeted for disaster prevention…Of the R$450 million (US$273.6 million) set aside for disaster prevention in the federal budget, only R$137 million (US$83.3 million) was spent. (http://infosurhoy.com/cocoon/saii/xhtml/en_GB/features/saii/features/society/2011/03/09/feature-02)

In 2011, Brazil was placed third on the list of countries where the world's deadliest catastrophes occurred—behind Japan, which experienced a 9.0 magnitude quake in March, and the Philippines, which endured massive flooding in December.

[32] The Consul General of Japan in Boston, Takeshi Hikihara, was one of the keynote speakers at the international workshop on "Innovation, Diversity, and Sustainable Development in Areas of Social Vulnerability", November 17–18, 2011, which was organized by CRSCAD. Drawing participants from five

continents, the workshop examined lessons from Japan as well as social vulnerabilities in specific populations worldwide.

As part of his frank assessment of Japan's preparedness and rebuilding process following its 9.0 magnitude earthquake and tsunami to an international audience of the workshop, Consul Hikihara noted that

> preparation made all the difference for the Tohuku schools when the 3/11 earthquake and tsunami struck Japan.
>
> In most schools, staff had agreed on an evacuation route in advance, and that careful planning saved nearly 3,000 students in Kamaishi City. But at the Okawa Elementary School in Miyagi, valuable time was lost as teachers tried to agree on where to go. As a result, sixty-eight of the school's 108 pupils died.
>
> Our temperament and our mindset are an important part of preparedness. (Killingback, paras. 1–2, 5.)

He further told the audience that

> the safe evacuation of most schools was the result of careful disaster preparation. All organized emergency drills in the first week of September. This careful planning also ensured the successful automatic shutdown of the Shinkansen, bullet trains that run at speeds up to 200 miles per hour, that resulted in zero derailments, fatalities, or injuries to those on board. (Ibid., para. 6)

Continuing, Consul Hikihara informed the workshop participants that

> the budget for Japan's reconstruction is $228 billion over the next five years and a government agency for reconstruction will be launched to oversee the process. "Easy to use" grants for local governments to implement their own rebuilding plans and working with the private sector are two strategies. Overarching policies will also ensure that rebuilding responds to the longer-range challenges of an aging society and population decline. (Ibid., para. 7)

[33] Tannen.

[34] Note that after independence the acronym SWAPO was changed to Swapo Party to denote the transition from a liberation movement to a political party, but I am using the acronym SWAPO to place my study in the broader historical context.

# Bibliography

Balaisyte, Jurgita, Maria Besiou, and Luk N. Van Wassenhove. *The Media and Disasters.* INSEAD Humanitarian Research Group, May 2011. http://www.insead.edu/facultyresearch/centres/isic/humanitarian/the_media_and_disasters.cfm

Bressan, David. "A Short History of Earthquakes in Japan." *Scientific American,* March 11, 2012 http://blogs.scientificamerican.com/history-of-geology/2012/03/11/a-short-history-of-earthquakes-in-japan/

Corben, Ron. "UN: Natural Disasters Pose Serious Economic Threat to Asia." *Voice of America News / Asia*. December 11, 2012. http://www.voanews.com/content/un-says-natural-disasters-pose-serious-economic-threat-to-asia/1562550.html

Edwards, Louise, and Chen Minglu. *Protecting Children in Disasters Project: Evaluator's Report, Stage One (April 2007–March 2008)*. Broadway, NSW, Australia: University of Technology Sydney China Research Centre, 2008. http://www.aamh.edu.au/__data/assets/pdf_file/0013/415210/Final_Evaluators_Brief_Edwards.pdf (retrieved March 14, 2013).

Global Water Partnership (GWP). *China: From Flood Control to Integrated Flood Management* (#420). Author, 2013. http://www.gwptoolbox.org/index.php?option=com_case&id=308

Hays, Jeffrey. *Natural Disasters in China: Landslides, Mudslides and Forest Fires*. 2011. http://factsanddetails.com/china/cat10/sub65/item397.html

Japan Center for International Exchange. "US Giving for Japan Disaster Exceeds $710 Million—Record Amount for Overseas Disaster in a Developed Country." JCIE Special Report, March 2013. http://jcie.org/researchpdfs/311/JCIE_USGivingReport3.pdf

Killingback, Muna. "International Workshop Examines Post-Disaster Rebuilding in Japan and Global Social Vulnerabilities." *UMass Boston News*, December 12, 2011. http://www.umb.edu/news_events_media/publications/the_point/international_workshop_examines_post_disaster_rebuilding_in_japan_and_globa

Tan, Ngoh Tiong, Yunong Huang, and Lihrong Wang. "Disaster Management in China and Taiwan: Models, Policies, and Programs for Social Recovery." *Journal of Global Social Work Practice*, 4(1), http://www.globalsocialwork.org/vol4no1/Tan.html

Tannen, Deborah. *You Just Don't Understand*. New York, NY: Ballantine, 1990.

United Nations. "Strengthening Institutional and Legislative Arrangements." *Global Assessment Report on Disaster Risk Reduction, 2011*. 2nd ed. Geneva, Switzerland: Author, 2011. http://www.preventionweb.net/english/hyogo/gar/2011/en/hfa/regional.html#4.8

United Nations Office for Disaster Risk Reduction (UNISDR). *Reducing Vulnerability and Exposure to Disasters: The Asia-Pacific Disaster Report 2012*. Bangkok, Thailand: UN ESCAP / UNISDR, 2012. http://www.unisdr.org/files/29288_apdr2012finallowres.pdf

United Nations. "The Elimination and Prevention of All Forms of Violence against Women and Girls: Agreed Conclusions." Advance unedited version. Commission on the Status of Women, Fifty-Seventh Session. New York, NY: Author, 2013. http://www.un.org/women watch/daw/csw/csw57/CSW57_agreed_conclusions_advance_unedited _version_18_March_2013.pdf

Wisner, Ben. *Let Our Children Teach Us! A Review of the Role of Education and Knowledge in Disaster Risk Reduction.* Geneva, Switzerland: UNISDR, 2006.

Ye, Yaoxian. *Chinese Experience with Post-Natural-Disaster Reconstruction.* Beijing, China: China Architectural Design and Research Group, n.d. http://www.grif.umontreal.ca/pages/i-rec%20 papers/Ye%20Yaoxian.pdf

# Part I

# Cultural, Ethical and Philosophical Dimensions of Natural Disasters and Environmental Sustainability

# CHAPTER ONE

## NATURAL DISASTER AS AN ONTOLOGICAL EVENT

### CHARLES BONNER

Natural disasters are empirical events, to be sure, but their impact and significance, their "meaning" for the affected community, cannot be measured solely in empirical terms. The following pages outline an *ontological* approach to natural disaster, which recognizes that "the world" affected by disaster includes dimensions that cannot be reduced to material, economic and social consequences. The lives of individuals and communities are affected by natural disasters, but not only in terms of objective measures (death and injury, disorientation, post-traumatic stress, etc.): the structure of *the world as a meaningful and livable whole* is undermined and undone by floodwaters and tectonic shifts. The ontological structures that constitute a world as a meaningful whole—concepts of time, of order, of "man's place in nature"—can be devastated by earthquakes and tsunamis just as surely as buildings collapse and croplands are ruined. These ontological structures lie beyond the realm of calculation and technological intervention, but the tasks of response and preparation for disaster must take into account the devastation inflicted on *the inhabited world* as such—as a world of meanings and motivations, structures that allow human beings to make sense of their individual lives and collective activities.

Historical events—wars, famines, revolutions—mark turning points, critical moments or periods in which fundamental change occurs. Migrations of peoples are driven by economic developments, ethnic tensions, or subtle shifts in climate. Technological developments, epidemics, and the spread of religious ideas can bring about fundamental change for communities and nations. Terrorist attacks and nuclear disasters can affect the historical fate of nations and peoples. Natural disasters such as volcanoes, hurricanes, and tsunamis can radically disrupt the way of life of individuals and communities. Such events have devastating effects on infrastructure and material culture. Political regimes and economic systems may be blown away by gale-force winds or washed away with floodwaters. "Human costs" are measured in numbers of dead and injured, psychological trauma of survivors, losses in productivity, declines in GNP. The breakdown of social institutions and social services, chaos, disorientation, and mass hysteria can all result from natural events that take place in the Earth's atmosphere, the oceans, or the tectonic plates in the Earth's crust.

To designate such occurrences as "ontological events" is to recognize their capacity for altering the fundamental structure of reality—*the world*—of the affected community. In recent decades we have been faced with the foreseeable possibility, perhaps the inevitability, of a natural event that could alter the structure of reality for all of mankind: a global upheaval whose impact would fundamentally disrupt the international economic relations and the geopolitical order that structure our world. It is no longer adequate to think of these developments in terms of natural events whose impacts can be measured (that is, calculated and predicted) in terms of economic, political, social, or "humanitarian" costs. To recognize that natural disasters have the capacity to fundamentally alter the world we live in—to disrupt radically the structures that make the "reality" we inhabit meaningful, structures that make our lives and activities meaningful, structures that allow us to make sense of our lives—is to conceive of natural disaster as an ontological event.

## Ontology and Environmentalism

Our current attempts to think about *ontology* ("theory of being" or understanding of the ultimate nature of reality) are derived from the work of Martin Heidegger. In *Being and Time* he attempted to revive the "question of being" through the project designated as *fundamental ontology*.[1] The starting point for radical inquiry into being (being itself, as opposed to entities) was the interrogation of a particular entity or type of being, namely the being that "I"—the one who inquires—have special access to: human being. The inquiry into the type of being that I am discloses human existence as a particular way of being *in time*, and a particular relation to *other beings*. My own being is structured by *care* (*Sorge*) for my own future existence (since human existence essentially projects itself into the future) and by *concern* or solicitude (*Fursorge*) for the other beings that make up *the world* around me.[2] The "world", for Heidegger, is not the sum total of atoms and molecules and physical forces that make up the universe as determined by the natural sciences; the world is the meaningful order in which I come to understand my own existence. This meaningful order constitutes a whole, a totality of relations in which other entities and other human beings are disclosed along with my own self-disclosure (that is, along with my own existence in time, as a being essentially concerned for its own future being). *The world*, in this phenomenological-existential conception, is the meaningful whole in which human beings understand their own existence, in relation to other human beings and other types of beings, as meaningful.

It is this meaningful totality that constitutes "our world" whose fundamental structure is threatened, as we now understand, by global natural disaster. ("Global" should be understood here in two senses, as planetary in scope and all-encompassing in depth.) The foundations of the world we inhabit can be shaken by earthquakes and shattered by the powerful forces of nature. The "reality" we inhabit is investigated and conceptualized by the natural sciences, to be sure, but is also determined by economic and political structures, by art and religion, by friendship and love. A tsunami shatters the world of the affected community, not just by destroying buildings and ruining crops: social order and rule of law may also break down, basic patterns of orientation and structures of motivation are also blown away by hurricane winds, or are turned to chaos by forces emanating from the Earth's crust. Collective and individual identities, motivations and goals that give meaning to our actions and lives constitute the fundamental contours of the world we inhabit, fundamental structures of a reality whose stability is now seen to be vulnerable to elemental forces of nature. The order of our world and the ultimate nature of the reality we inhabit are constituted by the laws of nature, to be sure, but also by the demand for economic growth, for example, by political principles, and by relations of aesthetic or religious transcendence. The concept of human rights plays a role in shaping the meaningful totality that is our world, just as the law of gravity and the force of the hydrogen bond constitute fundamental aspects of the universe disclosed by the natural sciences. Modern science itself is a distinctive and fundamental feature—with economic, political, and philosophical preconditions and implications—of our reality.

In his later thinking, Heidegger abandoned the project of fundamental ontology, realizing that being human as such could serve as no special point of access to "being itself". Reflecting instead on the ontological role played by language and especially by *technology* in disclosing the being of all entities (including the entities we are, as human beings), the inquiry into *being itself* now takes its point of departure not in philosophical anthropology, but in an attempt to clarify our relation to technology. It is this later period of Heidegger's thinking that holds special relevance for understanding the essence of modern environmentalism—and more specifically, for our problem of natural disaster as ontological event.[3]

Environmentalism emerged in the 1960s and -70s as a response to the growing awareness of potentially catastrophic (if unintended) consequences of our modern agricultural, industrial and technological activities. Inspired originally by fears of nuclear radiation and pesticide contamination, the early environmental movement expanded its concerns from local issues to a regional and eventually a planetary scope. At the essential core of this new "ecological consciousness"—beyond the political, economic, and social dimensions—is a fundamental ontological shift in contemporary humanity's self-understanding. "Man's place in nature" has been conceptualized in radically new ways over the course of the past half-century: no longer steward with divine sanction, "Western man" has come to understand his own dangerously destructive tendencies as inevitable byproducts of the scientific and technological advances that drive economic growth. Philosophically speaking, the status of contemporary technological humanity has shifted: our relation to the ordered totality of beings (our world) has undergone radical revision such that our *ontologically privileged status* as masters of nature and insatiable consumers of resources is now seen to constitute the core of our ecological and environmental problems.

Both theoretically and pragmatically, the question of our relation to the ordered and meaningful whole which is "our world"—that is to say, inquiry into the ontological status of human being as such—now plays a crucial role in our attempt to re-think our economic and biological needs and to re-configure the fundamental ontological set-up of the world we inhabit. Environmentalism, thus construed, takes on a philosophical significance and a philosophical task beyond the very real, indeed urgent, concerns with pollution, habitat loss, climate change, etc. In addition to habitat destruction, species extinction, rising temperatures and projected flooding of coastal areas, we are concerned with the question of *the place of the human being* in the new configuration of our ontological order. How do we situate ourselves (assuming it is up to us to do so) in the emerging totality of a world order that recognizes its essential vulnerability to catastrophic change? To be sure, we see ourselves as both agent and victim of such change; but can we envision the shape of a world in which human activity will have adjusted itself, re-oriented and reformed itself in response to—or in preparation for—global catastrophic change? To pose this question another way: what pragmatic implications ensue from recognizing natural disaster as ontological event? Our reflections here are intended merely to formulate this line of inquiry: to pose the "ontological question" in a new way and to suggest the relevance of this approach for the general problem of preparation and response to natural disaster. The attempt to articulate the "pragmatic implications" mentioned above lies beyond the scope of this paper and will have to be relegated to a separate study.

## Technology, Ontology, and Natural Disaster

In recent decades, historians have increasingly looked to natural events—the "Little Ice Age" that shaped early modern Europe, the role of infectious disease in the "Columbian Exchange", the collapse of non-Western civilizations due to ecological catastrophes—for causal explanations of broad historical developments and sudden historical shifts. It is inevitable, to some extent, that we project our own assessment, our contemporary understanding of the ontological situation we find ourselves in, back onto earlier epochs and other civilizations. And yet, if we wish to grasp the "meaning" of a natural disaster such as the volcanic eruption that buried the Roman city of Pompeii in 79 CE or the earthquake that destroyed Lisbon in 1755, it would be necessary to situate the event in its proper ontological-historical context. How was the eruption of Vesuvius understood and experienced by Roman citizens who believed in a divine "natural providence" (via the prevailing "state philosophy" of Stoicism)? Why was the disaster in Lisbon so troubling to rationalist philosophers and Enlightenment thinkers such as Kant, Rousseau and Voltaire? (The devastating tsunami of 2004 did not provoke philosophical or theological debate.) To question the meaning of a natural disaster is not to measure it quantitatively in terms of forces of nature, nor to calculate its "human costs". The meaning of a disaster, like the meaning of any event, can only be adequately grasped or comprehended by first gaining some understanding of the ontological context in which the event occurred. This implies that the significance of a natural disaster in our own time can only be adequately grasped if we first comprehend the ontological order in which the event occurs—the ontological order which is at the same time threatened by the disaster. But what does it mean to *comprehend* an ontological order: to gain insight into the fundamental contours of a world—our own or that of an earlier epoch, another civilization?

Heidegger's later thinking recognized that our contemporary experience of reality is essentially determined by technology; that is to say, modern technology plays an ontological role in shaping our basic understanding of being. Every other epoch and every other civilization or culture had its distinctive form of technology, of course, but ours is the first ontological configuration to be fundamentally shaped, not by metaphysics or religion, but by the modern scientific worldview and its corresponding technological capacities and practices. At the beginning of his famous essay on "The Question Concerning Technology", Heidegger writes:

> We shall be inquiring into technology, and in doing so we would like to prepare a free relationship to it. The relationship will be free if it opens our human existence to the essence of technology.[4]

The phrase "essence of technology" is crucial for understanding the intention here: the German word *Wesen* does not designate "essence" in the medieval scholastic (or metaphysical) sense. What Heidegger intends here, rather, is an "opening" of human existence to the *way of being* that corresponds to technology. This distinction is important for understanding the difference between ontological inquiry and metaphysical speculation. As this essay tries to show (along with other later works), there is a distinctive *relation to being* that corresponds to our technological epoch. It is not merely the idea that the use of machines or of technologically advanced equipment brings about a certain understanding of being and a particular "technological" relation to the totality of all beings ("the world"). Rather, Heidegger's insight here recognizes that the use of our distinctively modern technological apparatus is possible only on the basis of a certain ontological ground: the use of modern technology is possible only on the condition that "being itself" manifests itself in such a way that technological mastery of the totality is an inherent feature of our reality. (Information technology, for example, is possible—and necessary—for the epoch in which being itself manifests itself *as* information.)

This feature—the susceptibility of our world to total technological mastery—is the distinctive ontological feature of our epoch. Obviously, the "world of antiquity" was not experienced in this way; the world of medieval Christendom was not susceptible to total technological manipulation—not because humans had not yet developed powerful machines, but because the fundamental ontological-religious conception of the world did not allow, in principle, for total technological mastery by human beings. Only if we recognize the essence of our technological epoch and "open ourselves" to the distinctive ontological configuration of the world we inhabit, only if we grasp the implications of the *way of being* that corresponds to our modern technological apparatus, can we prepare for what Heidegger calls a *free relationship to technology*. The meaning here is made clear in the very next sentence (continuing the remarks cited above): "When we can respond to this essence [*Wesen*], we shall be able to experience the technological within its own bounds."⁵

Now, all of this is intended here as an approach to the ontological context of a world—our own—in which the looming threat of planetary natural disaster provokes reflection on the fundamental instability of the reality we inhabit. Our brief commentary on the starting point of Heidegger's inquiry into the essence of modern technology has served to posit an understanding of our epoch in ontological terms as one in which the prevailing fundamental understanding of reality is essentially technological. In order to "situate" natural disaster—qua ontological event—within its given epochal context (ancient, medieval, modern, etc.), it is necessary, we argued, to gain insight into the ontological configuration which the disaster event occurs in and threatens to disrupt. Our present configuration is essentially technological.

Before trying to "situate" natural disaster ontologically, in order to determine adequately its "meaning" or significance, and to grasp what is ultimately at stake in preparing for and responding to disaster, it will be necessary to reflect on what Heidegger means by the goal of experiencing the technological *within its own bounds*. It is here that the profound *inadequacies* of our technological epoch's prevailing ontological framework will emerge—specifically, in our inability adequately to grasp the ontological significance of natural disaster insofar as we remain within the bounds of the technological determination of our world. Whatever else may be implied by Heidegger's formulation (and no attempt is made here to work out a full exegesis), his stated intention of preparing for a free relation to the technological essence of our contemporary epoch suggests that our starting point—that is, prior to the inquiry opened up in his essay—is somehow constrained or "unfree". Only, presumably, by *experiencing the technological within its own bounds*, can our theoretical and practical engagement adequately take into account the distinctive ontological configuration that shapes our world. Again, by opening human existence to the technological essence of our epoch, we prepare a "free relation"—that is, no longer constrained by that technological essence itself—to our current ontological arrangement. In this free relation we come to experience the technological way-of-being within its proper limits. In opening ourselves to reflection on the technological way of being, we step outside this technological-ontological framework in order to recognize its proper domain. That is to say, we come to recognize, first of all, that the technological framework in which all beings are subject to calculation and manipulation—*has* limits. It is this motif, discerned here in a preliminary way, which is important for the task of approaching natural disaster as an ontological event.

To recognize the limits of the technological-ontological framework that shapes our prevailing conception of reality is to recognize that the "ultimate foundations" of our epoch (or any other epoch) are finite, unstable and fragile. The ontological importance of natural disaster now becomes apparent: the event of disaster reveals the essential fragility of "the world" of the affected community. It is, once again, not only a matter of calculating costs and damages to the infrastructure, agriculture, economic productivity, and psychological well-being of the affected community: what is at stake in the event of disaster is the *structure of the world* as a meaningful, inhabited totality. In the wake of a massive earthquake or devastating hurricane, the need for mourning is just as "real" as the need for food and shelter. The need for maintaining some form of cultural continuity—that the community, its values and traditions, its gods, its artworks, and its distinctively human ways of being—not be eradicated by violent forces of nature becomes imperative. The need to maintain or reconstruct the integrity of the world is a fundamental aspect of the "big picture" (i.e., the ontological framework), and is no less important than the need for emergency medical supplies or rule of law. One advantage of the ontological perspective sketched out in these pages is that it allows for consideration of all dimensions of the problematic (important both for preparation and response to disaster), including those aspects that lie *beyond* the technological framework.

In our technological epoch the event of natural disaster is understood technologically. That is, like all other events and entities in the totality of our world, including birth and death, life itself, natural phenomena and human existence, it is understood in terms of basic processes which are, in theory, reducible to relations between matter and energy and information—thus rendered calculable, predictable, manipulable. Thought itself is reduced to functions and processes of neural networks, cognitive modules and brain chemistry. All beings and all events, all developments can be, in principle, mathematically modeled and technologically manipulated. The Earth itself becomes an object for manipulation via geo-engineering. The event of a natural disaster, with all its ramifications in the economic and social spheres, with its human costs and ecosystem damages (all calculable, in theory, in monetary terms), emerges into the reality of the technological-ontological configuration of our world as a phenomenon whose causes and effects can be rigorously and objectively determined: a phenomenon whose likelihood (or inevitability) can be calculated in advance. The event—any event—is subject to prediction, calculation and control.

The essence of our technological-ontological arrangement, according to Heidegger, is that all entities (including human beings) have the status of *resources*. The world itself is determined as a total stockpile of potential resources, whose value and usefulness are determined according to the totality of human wants and needs. Entities are valued according to strictly "technical" criteria: as potentially useful or marketable materials, as energy reserves to be preserved or exploited, as biological material with potential medicinal value. "Technology", understood in this ontological way of thinking, is not a category that includes machines, tools and calculating apparatus; it designates instead a particular *mode of being*, the way in which entities "come to be", enter into reality, emerge as phenomena in a world—our own—in which all entities and events and phenomena exist as potential resources for human use and consumption. "Technology" is the name for the world in which consciousness reveals being itself in such a way that the totality of all beings is available, in principle, for exploitation.

> Everywhere everything is ordered to stand by, to be immediately at hand, indeed to stand there just so that it may be available for further ordering. Whatever is ordered in this way [i.e., all beings in the epoch determined by technology] has its own standing. We call it the stockpile [*Bestand*].[6]

It is hardly surprising, then, to recognize that the event of natural disaster, experienced within the framework of our technologically determined world, can itself be exploited. This is the insight articulated in the important book by Naomi Klein, *The Shock Doctrine: The Rise of Disaster Capitalism*.[7] The final section of this paper turns to this work in order to point to the pragmatic implications of the seemingly "abstract" reflections in the preceding pages.

If a certain ontological conception of reality determines the shape of a world inhabited and experienced by human beings as a meaningfully ordered whole, this ontological arrangement is in no way a matter of "ideology" or abstract speculation. A world is a concrete structure in which human beings find meaning and motivation for their lives; whatever *grounds* it (religion or metaphysics or modern science), a particular configuration of reality includes the relations between human beings and nature—that is, the means of fundamental human activities and institutions such as agriculture and architecture, medicine and law. *A world* is neither a set of ideas nor a collection of things; it is a concrete ordered whole in which human existence finds meaning—or not—in its relations to nature, to the gods (or God), relations to art and history and language. In the epoch in which Western rationality reaches planetary dominance via technological mastery over being itself, the event of natural disaster takes on an essentially technological meaning: it can be calculated, predicted, manipulated and exploited. Its meaning, in this regard, is thoroughly determined within the bounds of the technological determination of reality.

## Disaster Capitalism: Technological Preparation, Ontological Response

As outlined above (very schematically), from the ontological perspective adopted here, natural disasters cannot be adequately understood if considered strictly as "natural phenomena" with "human costs". What is at stake, rather, is the total structure of the world as a meaningful whole: the world of the affected community is shaken to its foundations, meaningful human reality is disrupted. The disaster brings about cataclysmic upheaval in the structure of the world. Social, political, and economic structures, features of the stable world in which human existence had hitherto thrived—or subsisted—are thrown into chaos and tragic confusion. By taking into account this dimension of *the world*, as conceived phenomenologically (in Heidegger's thought, for example), we are pointing to aspects or consequences of disaster that cannot, strictly speaking, be *accounted* for—that is, cannot be reduced to utilitarian cost-benefit calculus, cannot be planned or programmed, cannot be manipulated by political, financial, or technological intervention.

In a chapter analyzing the political and economic responses to the devastating tsunami of 2004, focusing on Sri Lanka—particularly hard-hit, but only one part of the widespread destruction wrought by the tsunami—Klein brings out the horrific details, not of human suffering or destruction of infrastructure, but of the "second wave of the tsunami" brought on by economic vultures waiting to pounce on opportunity, aided and abetted by local politicians and international financial organizations:

> Any country hit by a disaster on the scale of the 2004 tsunami needs a comprehensive plan for reconstruction, one that will make the wisest use of the influx of foreign aid and ensure that the funds reach their intended recipients. But Sri Lanka's president [Chandrika Kumaratunga], under pressure from Washington lenders [i.e., the IMF and the World Bank], decided that reconstruction could not be entrusted to her government's elected politicians. Instead, just one week after the tsunami leveled the

coasts, she created a brand-new body called The Task Force to Rebuild the Nation.[8]

Klein goes on to explain that this non-democratically elected task force was made up of the country's wealthiest business leaders, representing banking and industry—in particular the tourism industry, which was in a position to take advantage of the devastation for its own aims and profits. In reflecting on this development, it is important to keep in mind that we are dealing here with just one instance of what this author has called *disaster capitalism*. What we see here is a certain "technological response"—broadly construed so as to include political and economic intervention via technical manipulation of the institutional weaknesses in the aftermath of disaster. What Klein points to is a will to manipulate the objective situation of institutional breakdown in the wake of disaster: the human tragedy approached as an opening for political, social and economic regime change, catastrophe recognized as a potential economic goldmine. The task force appointed by fiat to manage the billions of dollars of international aid and foreign investment in reconstruction represented the industries poised to cash in on the disaster.

> There was no one from the fishing or farming sectors on the task force, not a single environmentalist or even a disaster-reconstruction expert.[9]

There were no representatives from the survivors of small fishing villages, actual victims of the tsunami, no social scientists or doctors or religious leaders.

> The creation of the task force represented a new kind of corporate coup d'état, one achieved *through the force of natural disaster*. As in so many other countries, in Sri Lanka, Chicago School [economic] policies had been blocked by the normal rules of democracy…. But with the country's citizens pulling together to meet a national emergency, and politicians desperate to unlock aid money, the express wishes of voters could be summarily brushed aside and replaced with *the direct unelected rule by industry*—a first for disaster capitalism.[10] (emphasis added)

We see here an example of the type of impact of which "the force of natural disaster" is capable. In ways that are not measurable on the Richter scale or any other quantitative or empirical index, natural disaster also wreaks havoc on the affected community's political and economic systems. When the "normal" rules and patterns of life are suspended, when whole communities are in disarray, in mourning, in shock, an opening arises for those who would rebuild the world in their own interests. Instead of programs for sustainable agriculture and maintaining local culture and tradition, disaster capitalists pounce on valuable coastal land, now available for resort hotels and high-end tourism.

Klein's informed and lucid analysis of this and other cases document the rise of disaster capitalism. In the lead-up to Hurricane Sandy last fall, cable news programs tracked the movement of the "superstorm" along with the movements of stock prices for corporations in position to gain from the disaster. The essence of the technological-ontological framework that shapes our reality is the combined calculability, predictability and manipulability of the event of disaster that recognizes political and economic consequences—and opportunities—in the devastation of a world, the collapse of meaningful structures inhabited by a community of human beings. In our present ontological configuration, the flow of capital seeking high-yield investment opportunity is as fundamental as the law of gravity, as inexorable as the shift of tectonic plates in the Earth's crust. Disaster capitalism and sensationalist media coverage constitute the event of disaster as a particular type of phenomenon—"breaking news" with potential for large-scale profiteering—in a world (our own) in which economic interests and media spectacles constitute fundamental structures that shape our experience and understanding of reality.

We have mentioned natural disasters as relatively isolated events that affect particular communities. Disasters may well elicit global response, but no natural disaster has heretofore in human history affected the entire planet or disrupted the world of the entire international community. Even in the case of the 2004 tsunami that devastated Sri Lanka, Indonesia, and parts of Southeast Asia, the disaster was limited in scope to a certain (albeit enormous) geographical region. Do we not have a growing awareness of a potential disaster that would affect mankind on a planetary scale? Predicted consequences of global climate change include an increase in frequency and magnitude of violent storms and hurricanes. Can we not conceive of the total ramifications of climate change, from sea level rises to mass migration—with political, economic and social consequences that can hardly be imagined—as constituting a global and protracted natural disaster? Is it not in the preparation and planning for response to this planetary disaster, the onset of which is already palpable in some parts of the planet, that we come up against the incalculable and unforeseeable impacts that will alter the very structure of the world we inhabit?

Without pursuing the type of approach outlined in these pages to its end, we can nevertheless catch a glimpse of the *ontological stakes of global disaster*. The economic and political forces that would "capitalize" on opportunities opened up on a planetary scale would not be merely a quantitative extension of the phenomenon of disaster capitalism described by Klein. It is in our vision of global disaster in which mathematical models and computer simulations no longer allow for a coherent or "manageable" picture that ontological inquiry becomes crucial.

No one contemplates "the question of being" in the midst of an emergency, where the need for medical aid and for human solace demand the energy and attention of survivors and aid workers. Yet we can now foresee with disturbing lucidity a situation in which our human reality defies calculation, modeling and control. Here we see that what is at stake cannot be rendered numerically or projected via computer screens. What is at stake is the "meaning of being" and the structure of the world (or worlds) that will have to emerge from the ruined foundations of buildings, institutions and civilizations. We have sought to contemplate this ontological dimension—already "visible" and already palpable even for disasters of limited scale—in order to focus attention on the need for preparation and response to global disaster that defies empirical measurement and calculation. In approaching natural disaster as an ontological event we recognize the task of thinking as one of preparing a change in mankind's fundamental position vis-à-vis "being itself". This approach points to a quasi-religious or transcendental dimension, beyond the empirical phenomena that can be mapped and measured, which will be crucial for orienting preparation for and response to the natural disasters we know to be inevitable and for the global disaster that now seems imminent.

## Notes

[1] Martin Heidegger, *Being and Time*, trans. John Macquarrie and Edward Robinson (New York, NY: Harper and Row, 1962).
[2] Heidegger 1962, Part I, Chapter VI.
[3] Martin Heidegger, *The Question Concerning Technology*, trans. William Lovitt (New York, NY: Harper and Row, 1977).
[4] Heidegger 1977, 3.
[5] Heidegger 1977, 4.
[6] Heidegger 1977, 17.
[7] Naomi Klein, *The Shock Doctrine: The Rise of Disaster Capitalism* (New York, NY: Henry Holt and Company, 2006).
[8] Klein, 396.
[9] Klein, 396–7.
[10] Klein, 397.

## Bibliography

Heidegger, Martin. *Being and Time*. Translated by John Macquarrie and Edward Robinson. New York, NY: Harper and Row, 1962.
—. *The Question Concerning Technology*. Translated by William Lovitt. New York, NY: Harper and Row, 1977.
Klein, Naomi. *The Shock Doctrine: The Rise of Disaster Capitalism*. New York, NY: Henry Holt and Company, 2006.

# CHAPTER TWO

# INTERNATIONAL PROTOCOLS TO AMELIORATE THE EFFECTS OF ENVIRONMENTAL DISASTERS

## JOHN H. DREHER

### Introduction

This chapter takes a broad view of disasters. In the first place, it sees disasters from a global point of view, and argues that the benefits of avoiding and relieving disasters redound to the good of all, indeed to the global good, and not merely to those immediately affected. The global good is conceived both geographically and diachronically. Natural disasters like enormous volcanoes (e.g., Krakatoa) or even man-made disasters (e.g., Fukushima or the BP oil spill) have direct consequences for climate and indirect economic consequences of global significance. Moreover, schemes to deal with disasters need to take a longer view, far into the future. For example, preventing and ameliorating the effects of collisions with asteroids require the development of innovative technologies to be available worldwide. Assuring the continuity of oxygen-producing life, both in tropical rainforests and (more importantly) in the seas, is essential in maintaining an atmosphere that can support advanced neurological systems. Seeing disasters as threats to the global good and conceiving the global good broadly are critical in developing schemes that are likely to be implemented.

There are essentially two ways of justifying other-regarding behavior. The first is to argue that the behavior is required morally; in other words, that it is a matter of justice. The second way is to argue that other-regarding behavior is ultimately rational in that it serves self-interest. These issues are extraordinarily complicated and controversial, and are among the most difficult in moral, social and political philosophy. Indeed, it is especially difficult for nation-states to adopt policies on the basis of the requirements of global justice.[1] That is because the leaders of nation-states have generally sworn to promote the interests of their own constituents. It is therefore natural for them to conduct diplomacy on the basis of national interests rather than to take a global view of national policy. This means that there is a tendency to allow less fortunate states to look after themselves in times of trouble. Indeed, dealing with disasters appears to present a perfect case of a *practical* dilemma. It appears that the common good is best served if all come to the aid of those in distress, but unfortunately it appears to be in the interest of each to contribute at little as possible to the common good while encouraging others to contribute as much as possible. Let us call this the principle *MAXIMIN: Maximal contribution from you; minimal contribution from us.* Many (e.g., Kantians) have argued that MAXIMIN is an example of an unethical principle of behavior, and surely it is. Even so, this paper argues that it is very difficult to believe that the Kantian approach will be likely to lead to the cooperative action that is necessary to prevent disasters and ameliorate their consequences. Conceptions of justice drawn from Kant (and followers like Rawls) tend to be "procedural", seeing justice as a fair distribution of burdens and benefits while avoiding questions of substantive good or considering them to be merely secondary. Indeed, justice undeniably involves a fair distribution of burdens and benefits, but this paper argues that there is more to justice than fairness and that it essentially involves the common good of those to whom burdens and benefits are distributed. In this sense, justice by its very nature redounds to the good of all who subscribe to its principles.

Based upon a conception of justice that incorporates the common good as an essential element, this chapter seeks to identify principles that can now be adopted on a rational basis as part of a world-wide effort by the community of nations to deal with disasters, including principles for assessing the likelihood of certain classes of disasters; principles for assigning economic weight to disasters; and principles for distributing the costs of dealing with disasters. Finally, the chapter argues that it will be in the interest of every nation-state to adopt the principles of global justice in dealing with catastrophes and even mere environmental threats.

## **Preliminaries: Practical Dilemmas**

Above I referred to a "practical dilemma". Indeed there is an enormous amount of literature dealing with practical dilemmas and their consequences for moral judgment and rational deliberation. The *locus classicus* of philosophical literature on practical dilemmas occurs in Parfit.[2] In his discussion, Parfit defines several varieties of practical dilemmas, including the "Prisoner's Dilemma" and the "Samaritan's

Dilemma". These dilemmas have come to be interpreted in many, sometimes incompatible, ways. So, it will be useful to review them with a view to their consequences for theories about the common good in general and disasters in particular.

The practical dilemmas that we shall take up are a species of what Parfit calls "collectively self-defeating dilemmas". These dilemmas share an important characteristic, which is that if we all pursue our individual aims identified by a certain theory "T", we shall cause ourselves to be worse off than if none us had tried to realize the aims of T. So, if nation-states wish to industrialize, and all follow the most aggressive policies, which (we suppose) lead to severe pollution, all nation-states will be worse off despite the best efforts of each to the contrary. It will be helpful to distinguish the varieties of collectively self-defeating behaviors.

## *The Prisoner's Dilemma*

The most familiar of the collective self-defeating dilemmas is the one-to-one dilemma familiar to us as the Prisoner's Dilemma. The set-up of the dilemma is this: A and B are accused of a crime. Each is interrogated, and each is ignorant of the content of the other's interrogation. Each knows the following from the set-up of the crime scene: if each keeps silent, there will be insufficient evidence to get a conviction for a *heinous* crime, and each is likely to suffer a moderate sentence (say two years), for a total of four years' imprisonment. If each confesses, then each will receive ten years' imprisonment, for a total of twenty years imprisonment. But if one keeps silent and the other goes state's evidence, the one who keeps silent gets twelve years and the other goes free, in which case their combined punishment is twelve years. We assume that each knows the set-up. Now suppose A reasons that what is best for the collective is to remain silent and does remain silent. B hypothesizes that A will reason the matter through in just that way; knowing A, B concludes that A will choose to remain silent. But B reasons that if he goes state's evidence and confesses, implicating A, he (B) will go free (instead of receiving two years) and A will yet twelve years. The collective disvalue in this case is twelve (just as it would be if A had turned on B). But, now suppose that just as B knows A, A knows B. *Mutatis mutandis* each concludes that the other will remain silent and hence (as B did above) that it would be best to confess, that is, to go state's evidence. In that case, as we have supposed, each will get ten years, in which case the total collective negative value is twenty years. Each would be better off remaining silent and getting a minimum sentence, but calculations of self-interest lead to at least one getting a very long sentence and perhaps lead both to sentences that add up to the worst possible collective outcome.

Notice that in this case it is crucial that the prisoners are not allowed to collaborate, for example, to consult and to deny criminal wrongdoing. In the event that the first knew that the other would confess, the first would surely confess as well. On the other hand, assuming that there is no honor among thieves, if the first knew that the other would keep silent, the first surely would confess. However, if each *knew* that the other would remain silent and not turn state's evidence no matter what, each surely would choose the course that is disadvantageous, though minimally, from an individual standpoint, but that is maximally advantageous from the collective standpoint. This is the type of situation that arises in bilateral negotiations where each side forswears certain behaviors *that can be hidden*—for example, in agreements to renounce the enrichment of uranium or in faithless intimate relations. What is to be learned from this example, the simplest of the practical dilemmas, is that *just* bilateral agreements (and indeed multilateral agreements) need to be transparent, that is, that (principle [P] 1) *all international agreements should be open and verifiable.*

## *Moral Hazard and the Samaritan's Dilemma*

Multilateral agreements give rise to more complicated practical dilemmas. Among those is the so-called Samaritan's Dilemma. This dilemma has come to be interpreted in a variety of ways. For example, conservative politicians worry that aid to the poor will be self-defeating because it "enables dependence". Still others think that the fact (and especially the guarantee) of aid given to relieve disaster will be a disincentive to preventive action, like taking out insurance against disasters.[3] Strictly speaking, these are not examples of the Samaritan's Dilemma but rather of examples of "moral hazard", where charity or indemnification has the unintended consequence of disincentivizing prudence. That is why it is that many states require drivers to purchase liability insurance and it is the source of doubts about government programs to indemnify relatively wealthy people against flooding and earthquakes. It may be thought that moral hazard is a serious impediment to concluding international agreements to deal with disasters, but this is generally not true. The reason is that those who are in greatest need of support are typically those with the least to lose and therefore are the least expensive to support. At the international level, those with the least to lose are often underdeveloped nations or regions.

Moreover, in many cases the very fact of underdevelopment should be counted as an outsized premium for the disaster insurance. As recently reported in the popular press,[4] a "lost tribe" of natives was discovered in the Colombian Amazon. Robert Caneiro of the American Museum of Natural History in New York theorizes that the tribe is likely to be descended from the Yuri, who were thought to be extinct. The newly discovered tribe live primitively "off the land", doing virtually nothing to disrupt the valuable ecology of the Amazon, which is vital in both the processes of evolution[5] and in maintaining a resource, oxygen, which is essential to the "health" of the atmosphere and survival of creatures with advanced neurological systems. The Colombian government has wisely decided to protect these natives who keep ancient ways alive. Whatever benefits the natives receive are *more than repaid by the mere fact that they do not disturb the jungle in which they live.*

The Samaritan's Dilemma, *strictly construed*, arises in large groups *where it is unlikely that aid to others will be reciprocated in time of need.* For example, in small faith communities, it is likely that assistance to a fellow believer in time of need will be repaid to benefactors who fall on hard times. However, in very large groups, acts of generosity are not likely to be repaid (or perhaps even acknowledged). In large groups it will be in each individual's interest to help out as little as possible, although ultimately everyone will be worse off for it. This situation also arises where we are expected (that is, there is social pressure) to contribute to the common good. For example, as Parfit observes, each is better off driving to work, although we are all worse off if everyone drives to work and no one takes public transportation. Each soldier is better off to run away unnoticed, but all will be likely to be captured or killed if everyone runs away.[6]

These examples of moral hazard and the Samaritan's dilemma suggest that international protocols dealing with disaster prevention and relief need to (P2) *guarantee reciprocity for those nation states that are asked to help others*, and (P3) *acknowledge that merely maintaining valuable ecological resources and foregoing industrial development is itself a contribution to disaster relief.*

## Justice and the Common Good

Political philosophy in the Anglo-American tradition has been dominated for some time by conceptions of justice that purport to be independent of substantive goods. This is a view that has been vigorously defended by Rawls in *Political Liberalism.* Just relations among nations,

Rawls insists, do not involve substantive conceptions of the good, but merely involve schemes for the distribution of burdens and benefits that each nation freely and reasonably accepts under the famous "veil of ignorance". Now, if the point is that systems of distribution adopted under Rawlsian conditions are independent of substantive conceptions of the good, but that substantive conceptions of the good are nonetheless relevant to political obligation, my complaint about Rawls would merely be a complaint about his conception of justice, because justice would then not establish political obligation. On the other hand, if Rawls believes that just relations among states are sufficient to establish the legitimacy of the scheme of distribution, then my complaint is that any satisfactory conception of justice must include the common good. All this is neatly illustrated, I think, by a famous story. It is widely reported (though I cannot prove it is true) that a distinguished philosopher was asked by the press to comment on the student riots at Columbia University in 1968 and in particular on whether or not the police had been fair. His response was that the police had been fair, because they beat up everyone, but that the beatings were nonetheless unjust. In other words, if fairness makes justice, then justice does not establish political obligation or right. On the other hand, if justice does establish political obligation, it must amount to more than the fair distribution of burdens; it must also justify the imposition of burdens by reference to the good of those burdened.

The conception of justice that I am advancing here involves a conception of the common good. This view derives from Plato and on my account is carried on by Hume, Montesquieu and Rousseau.[7] Hume makes a similar point in a nice metaphor.[8] Consider a canoe or a row boat that is bound for a certain destination. Each member of the "crew" will have a particular assignment, and justice requires the fair distribution of benefits and burdens. But the assignment of burdens will not be justified, even if it is fair, if it does not promote the common good, which is to reach the boat's destination in good time and good order. I would not complain if someone wants to say that the distribution of burdens and benefits can be just, even if it does not promote the common good, *provided that we then agree that a just arrangement is not sufficient to establish a legitimate obligation*. In other words, unless the common good is promoted (or at least respected), no one is under an obligation to accept a burden, even if the burden would otherwise be "fair". This point is extremely important if we hope to develop protocols for dealing with disasters that nations are *obligated* to follow. In any case, viewing the common good as an integral part of justice, I claim that (P4) *a scheme of distributing burdens and benefits is just only if the scheme promotes the common good.*

Suppose that someone (or more likely a whole nation) claims that there should be a worldwide effort to promote a certain religion or to advance socialist or libertarian forms of government, or democratic "bourgeois" republics or welfare states. The chance of cooperative action in these cases would be approximately zero. The reason is that there isn't agreement that any particular religion is a common good (or indeed that religion itself is a good). There is deep disagreement about what forms of government are good for people. It would be somewhat more likely to achieve broad agreement that art is worth pursuing, but it is difficult to believe that there would be agreement about what precisely constitutes art. It is significant that we do better with sports, say through the Olympic movement. Perhaps that is because human beings all have bodies, and perfecting them resonates universally. It is significant that there aren't any countries that have withdrawn from the Olympics because they disapprove of athletic excellence.

Identifying a common good involves identifying a common interest, and we are on firm ground in identifying Earth itself as an interest humans have in common. Earth itself is a comfortable home, a virtual paradise, by comparison with neighboring venues (planets and their satellites, asteroids, neighboring stars and their solar systems). The very material of life, water, rains down from the sky; Earth's atmosphere is rich in oxygen and is otherwise filled with benign or inert gasses; the temperature at the surface of the Earth is generally greater than 0°C but less than 45°C; the stuff of organic compounds is everywhere. The twenty or so miles of terrestrial earth and its atmosphere that surround Earth are so rich in life, and conducive to life, that life is ubiquitous. And it is clear that there is nothing at all like Earth within light years of the Solar System. All humans agree that Earth is home and that it is precious.

To be sure, there are occasional disruptions in our benign environment, including tornadoes, earthquakes, tsunamis and "megastorms". These disruptions, viz. ordinary disasters, remind us of our dependence upon nature and how even minor disturbances—that is, minor from the cosmic point of view—can wreck our lives. Humans, even eccentric humans, value and respect Earth and they fear and respect disruptions to its otherwise benign environment. Maintaining our benign environment is a common good because it supports our lives, including our bodily integrity and general health. When our benign environment is threatened, we seek to restore it or to find artificial ways to re-create it—in shelters, for example.

Ordinary disasters are not the only or even the main threats to our common interests; indeed the concept of "disaster" that is relevant here is very broad. It also includes extraordinary events like climate change, disruption of evolution, epidemics, and even cosmic events. Forestalling or coping with extraordinary events is also a matter of the common good. Indeed, Earth itself is like Hume's canoe or rowboat, and keeping it afloat is just about as obvious a common good as there could be.

To be sure, that does not mean that justice itself is something about which humans agree. Indeed, we may all agree that it is in our common interest to preserve our home but disagree about the assignment of burdens and benefits associated with it. As I have pointed out elsewhere, we are hardly in agreement about whether justice is individual or collective.[9] What then are the standards by which we should evaluate schemes for the distribution of burdens and benefits associated with the maintenance of Earth and coping with ordinary and extraordinary disasters? Perhaps the first step is to think about ways of analyzing the severity of the threats that we face. It may be that the limitations of resources and human energy and intelligence require us to set priorities as we respond to disasters and threats. I shall urge a holistic approach to this problem.

## Holistic Approaches

One way to establish priorities as we respond to threats and disasters is by a conventional cost/benefit analysis. This is especially common in dealing with ordinary disasters (like hurricanes or earthquakes) and in assessing possible schemes to anticipate and deal with them. One standard approach is to quantify value in terms of money. Suppose that an average earthquake will damage or destroy, say, 10 percent of the buildings in its area and that the average damage done will be 25 percent of the structure's replacement cost. Thus, anticipating the damage (D) that an earthquake would cause to structures in the area is $D = (.1 * .25 * V)$, where V is the replacement costs of buildings in the area. We can then quantify the economic value of various projects to reinforce buildings to withstand earthquakes and charge premiums accordingly. As difficult as it will be to determine replacement costs and to establish the pertinent probabilities, determining the economic value is easy compared to determining what might be called "human" value.[10]

Human value can also be viewed, coldly, from a purely economic point of view. We might anticipate the average cost of medical treatment and the average income lost due to a disaster. This might be a way of calculating the human cost of an earthquake from a purely economic point of view. Yet, the economic value of a human being is not the same as the value of a human being, and assigning a value to a human life, or a single human limb, is, to say the least, a matter of controversy.

In addition to assessing the costs of dealing with natural disasters, we need to ask ourselves how those costs are to be distributed. Even in the case of natural disasters, we immediately encounter both conceptual and practical difficulties. When people are bound together by natural ties of affection (parents for children, spouses for each other), no effort is spared to ameliorate the effects of any misfortune. But when it comes to strangers, it is a different matter entirely. Generally, we think of helping strangers as a matter of charity, and while most approve of charity in principle, nearly all are wary of the moral hazard it can involve and doubtful that charity will be repaid. As observed earlier, in the case of nation-states, whose leaders are bound to advance the interests of their own populations, charity may go unnoticed or at least unacknowledged. In fact, the very characterization of assistance as "charity" suggests that it is optional, not something that justice requires. We seem to have run into a wall of trouble.

It is at this point that we may need to take a broader, holistic approach to make progress, and the key element of a holistic approach is (P5) *to broaden our conception of the common good both geographically and diachronically*. Rather than beginning by considering threats to individuals and the obligations of individuals to each other, let us begin by considering the common good and turn our attention from ordinary natural disasters to threats to entire populations or to Earth itself, not only immediate threats but those that extend far into the future. *The main argument for a holistic approach turns on economies of scale.* Suppose that the international community were to invest heavily in managing the climate and protecting Earth from cosmic assault (for example, from collisions with asteroids or from cosmic radiation) and in controlling threats from the disruption of evolutionary processes, which, for example, may result in potentially lethal microbes resistant to antibiotics and vaccines. It is reasonable to suppose that part of the infrastructure and science developed in response to long-term threats to the planet would also be useful in preventing and coping with damage due to ordinary, garden-variety disasters. The existence of the necessary tools would lower the costs of supporting those in need from ordinary disasters. This in turn would facilitate a response to the Samaritan's Dilemma, because the level of sacrifice required would be lower and the prospect of reciprocity would be greater.

To be sure, there are costs and benefits to be carefully assessed in setting the priorities for development of the necessary infrastructure, keeping in mind that the opportunity cost of long-term planning is the possibility of inadequate response to short-term needs. I have argued elsewhere that the principal difficulty in setting priorities is the tendency to assign very high prior probabilities (or "priors", as they are called by probability theorists) to low-frequency, high-value outcomes.[11] A prior probability (i.e., a "prior") is a subjective measure of probability assigned by an individual on the basis of a personal assessment of the likelihood of an outcome at a given time. How to assign this original measure of probability is virtually a matter of personal taste or intuition. According to the Bayesian model of probability, probabilities (including priors) are rationally revised on new evidence. Each new probability measure is essentially a revision of the existing probability measure on the basis of all old "evidence" plus new evidence.

When priors are assigned to outcomes that are discrete events that can be determined with virtual certainty (like the outcomes of coin tosses), very high and low priors can be corrected in straightforward ways by relatively few further experiments.[12] When, however, probabilities concern relatively low-frequency events, it is virtually impossible to correct imprudent, outlier prior probabilities. For example, the probability of the release of harmful radiation from a nuclear power plant is not something can be calculated by anything analogous to tosses of a coin. Calculating the probability of an unfavorable outcome is more nearly analogous to validating a scientific theory.[13] Much depends upon the particulars of the construction of the plant and on the cooling methods that are used. The conclusion to draw from all this is that (P6) *it is wise to be conservative in assigning priors that cannot be corrected easily and inexpensively, especially when dealing with high-value outcomes.*

## Main Argument and Recapitulation of Principles

To this point I have urged us to consider disasters within a wider context that includes not only clean-up and remediation but also prevention and management. This means that climate change, cosmic events, and man-made disasters of global significance are to be considered along with ordinary disasters like storms and earthquakes. To be sure, the distinction between local and global disasters is blurred at the edges. The terrestrial damage done by earthquakes diminishes as shock waves travel further from their epicenters, although the tsunamis generated have global consequences. As a general rule I have suggested that international planning concerning disasters should be undertaken from the top down rather than the bottom up. There is a deep philosophical reason for looking at the matter in this broader, more holistic way. The need to manage threats to the entire planet, or threats like epidemics or nuclear radiation, are of significance to all people and something about which there is universal agreement. This, however, does not mean that local consequences of disasters are to be ignored. Rather, it is to be hoped that provision to deal with global threats will put into place an infrastructure, both financial and physical, that will encourage worldwide responses to all disasters. There is little point in trying to argue in the abstract for the pertinent principles (P1–P6) that characterize this holistic approach. It will be more helpful to envision what the world would look like were those principles adopted.

To recapitulate, the holistic approach to Disaster Management (Prevention and Response) is characterized by the following principles:

P1) to ensure that all international agreements will be open and verifiable;

P2) to guarantee reciprocity to those nation-states that are asked to support disaster prevention and relief;

P3) to acknowledge that merely maintaining valuable ecological resources and foregoing industrial development is itself a contribution to disaster relief;

P4) to deem a scheme of distributing burdens and benefits to be *just* (and therefore to create an obligation to satisfy its demands only if the scheme promotes the common good;

P5) to broaden our conception of the common good both geographically and diachronically;

P6) to be conservative in assigning priors that cannot be corrected easily and inexpensively, especially when dealing with high-value outcomes.

(P1) is designed to maximize the probability of defeating calculations of self-interest based upon MAXIMIN. (P2) is important in confronting the Samaritan's Dilemma and assuring that highly developed nations have an interest, and therefore a motive, to cooperate in schemes that in the short run benefit less-developed nations and peoples. As we shall see, it also recognizes the fact that rich nations may be challenged by environmental change and therefore may be in need of aid themselves at some point in the future. (P3) recognizes the fact that forestalling a threatening development is in itself a contribution to a healthy environment. It therefore argues that less-developed nations in effect do much of their share of disaster prevention by leaving the environment largely undisturbed. (P4) is the key philosophical principle on which the main argument rests: it claims that we are justified in imposing burdens only if they serve the common good. Otherwise, schemes of justice will be unmotivated; that is, it will not be rational for every party to subscribe to accept.[14] (P5) is the cornerstone of the argument, that it is reasonable to take the common good as one's own, if it is broadly construed and projected into the indefinite future. (P6) is a fundamental epistemological and methodological principle: we cannot expect others to sacrifice unless a careful analysis of the burdens and benefits show that the sacrifice is warranted in the long run. On the other hand, unless a reasonable assessment of risk shows that sacrifice is necessary, it is unreasonable to expect others to respond to the need it purports to address.

The next part of this project is to see just how these six principles can be applied to some of the familiar and difficult issues that we face in connection with disasters. We first consider the extraordinary global threats where the common good is easily identified, and then consider how responses to the wider global threats will facilitate effective, collective responses to ordinary disasters. These topics include: climate change, evolutionary disruption, cosmic threats, and finally ordinary disasters.

## Climate Change

In their landmark paper, Schipper and Pelling identify "three communities of practice", including "disaster risk reduction, climate change, and development."[15] Their work begins by focusing on the United Nations Millennium Declaration[16] and the subsequent Millennium Declaration Goals.[17] They acknowledge the widely shared view that climate change is at least in part a consequence of industrialization, and in particular of industrial gasses. Elsewhere I have argued against the assumption that industrial pollution is the only or even the primary source of climate change; on the other hand, there can be little doubt that industrial pollution is a significant factor, and that we ignore it at our peril.[18] Schipper and Pelling endorse the plausible injunction that the "polluter pays" and concludes that the North needs to take financial responsibility for reducing industrial pollution.[19]

The polluter pays principle is undoubtedly just, but the polluters of the world do not seem to have acknowledged it, or at least not to have accepted the responsibilities that follow from it. One may cynically (and perhaps correctly) conclude that the reluctance to accept that the polluter pays simply follows from a crude calculation of self-interest, but I believe that the issue is much deeper. The Western understanding of right to common goods derives from Locke, and it is a cardinal principle of

Lockean political theory that each has a *right* to utilize the common good provided that as much and as good is left for everyone else.[20] Of course, by ruining or diminishing the quality of the environment, polluters do not leave as much and as good for everyone else. But that does not address the question of redress. Just what are developed nations supposed by Lockean theory to do to compensate others for the harm of industrial pollution? Shall we destroy all that has been built, return to the cave, and exponentially decrease the human population?

I believe the best way to think about this problem is to first consider relatively undeveloped economies. We have already observed that native tribes in the Colombian rainforest have foresworn industrial development for a simpler lifestyle. Many cultures contribute to planetary health by accepting lifestyles that would be unappealing to most Westerners. This is itself an important contribution that warrants compensation, at least to the extent of receiving generous support, especially in the case of disasters that are partially, even if not wholly, attributable to industrial pollution. This means that primitive islanders who are about to lose their homes to rising tides have a legitimate expectation of relocation at the expense of those nation-states responsible for the climate change that has led to the inundation of low-lying islands.

There are various proposals for the imposition on industrial enterprises of excise taxes that are proportioned to the level of industrial pollutants expelled into the atmosphere which abuse the common good and certainly leave neither as much nor as good for others. However, these proposals, as difficult as they are to implement, do not begin to address the underlying societal need to change attitudes concerning pollution. Communities need to provide incentives to those who pollute less than average and disincentives to those who pollute more than average.[21] Many communities in California already have taken steps in the right direction: San Jose, for example, has long since adopted plans to recycle all waste.[22]

For present purposes, the most important point is that our duties to preserve the environment lie deep within the ideology of Western culture. That is why it is possible to change putatively backward views about the practices that contribute significantly to climate change. Apart from changing attitudes, there is also the need to change the practices of heavy industry, particularly in the production of electrical energy. This is of course a project for central governments. It involves not only regulation but also standards of excellence to which nation-states commit themselves worldwide.

There are, for example, quite a number of interesting proposals concerning the generation of electricity; policy is now fluid. The disaster at Fukushima initially horrified the international community as well as Japan itself. Part of the horror derived from the direct effects of the tsunami, which took thousands of lives. Radiation leaks led to widespread calls to de-commission nuclear plants, and Japan itself responded by shutting virtually all its nuclear facilities. It may very well be, however, that the dreadful situation itself prompted a miscalculation of the actual dangers from radiation. Indeed, as we have seen, (P6), there is an unfortunate tendency to assign outsized probabilities to low-frequency, high-value events. This tendency affects both the assignment of priors and recalculations of probabilities on the basis of new evidence.

There has been excellent work done to identify alternative sources of power for Japan.[23] It may very well be that the horror of Fukushima prompted a miscalculation of the actual dangers from *radiation*. Indeed, there has recently been some re-thinking about the consequences of Fukushima reported in both the popular and academic press. Compared to the disaster envisaged during the panicky days after the meltdown, there so far appears to be relatively little damage to health from radiation. Fortunately, people living near the disaster were promptly evacuated. Beyond that, approximately 80 percent of the radiation was blown out directly to sea. Because nature has deposited much radioactive material in the sea, the additional radioactive material from Fukushima has been relatively "miniscule".[24] The fact that so much radiation from Fukushima harmlessly drifted to the east and into the sea suggests the importance of relatively simple measures to ameliorate disasters, for example to locate nuclear sites only on shores to the leeward.

Admittedly, nuclear power production has a checkered record. It is hardly necessary to recount its failures. On the positive side, we find the experiences of France, where AREVA (a consortium of enterprises managed by the government of France) has played a leading role in making use of a mixture (called MOX) of uranium and plutonium oxides. This in effect is an attempt to recycle nuclear by-products by producing yet more energy from them. The residual of this process, about 4 percent of the original material, is vitrified and stored in what amounts to glass logs.[25]

Taking all this together, it may well be that the future of nuclear energy is brighter than anyone could have imagined just three years ago, at the height of the Fukushima tragedy. Moreover, since that time, enormous quantities of natural gas have been found in both the U.S. and China. Although the reserves in China are somewhat more difficult to extract by fracking than those in the U.S., it now appears that the world's two economic behemoths may well become self-sufficient in the use of a relatively clean fuel within several years. Of course, just as it would have been wrong just a few years ago to conclude that nuclear energy hasn't a future, it would now be wrong to conclude that the world's energy problems are over. There is still the threat of climate change from both natural gas and nuclear energy, and there is still is a need to conserve energy and to make use of alternative sources in localities that are especially well-suited to generate power from self-renewing sources like the wind and the sun.

## Evolutionary Disruption

I believe that the potential for disaster due to evolutionary disruption is generally underestimated. Worries about evolutionary disruption may seem to overestimate the dangers of global integration, but those dangers are nonetheless real. Recently there is has been considerable press given to the invasion of the Burmese python in the Everglades. This sensational story, filled with spectacular images, apparently arose from the release into the Everglades of small juvenile pythons that had been imported by enthusiasts and kept as pets. Unfortunately, the python does not have natural enemies in the Everglades, and pythons are capable of killing virtually every other in creature in the protected area. Pythons grow to approximately 20 feet and weigh 200 pounds. Surely they are formidable intruders, which may prove difficult to control.[26] Of course there have been other imports, less intimidating than the Burmese python, that have also managed to take an unwelcome place in foreign ecological systems, for example kudzu in the southeast of the U.S.

Evolutionary disruptions that are of greatest concern include changes at the *microbial* level. Indeed, the enemies that evoke the greatest fear are viruses and bacteria that may be immune to vaccines and antibiotics currently in production. So far, international medical science has remained one step ahead of the danger. But there are constant warnings, including scares involving new strains of tuberculosis and influenza. The consequences of unrestrained microbial mutations that threaten human beings are truly horrific and might well rival other plagues such as AIDS.

Just as the recent tsunami in East Japan, Hurricane Sandy, and the earthquake in Haiti required immediate life-saving aid that was not always available in good time and sufficient quantity, genuine attacks of unstoppable viruses or bacteria would require massive responses rivaling military operations. Later, in (9) we'll consider possible innovative systems to respond to disasters that occur despite our best intentions to avoid them, either by anticipating and deflecting them or by preparing ourselves as best we can.

## Cosmic and Geological Threats

As frightening as disruptions to the course of evolution may be, they are dwarfed by genuine cosmic threats, perhaps the ultimate in low-frequency, high-value events. Asteroids and even large meteors cause destruction at levels that are comparable to the devastation of nuclear warfare. Cosmic disasters are so formidable that the thought of preparation for them seems almost laughable. But the sobering thought is that in the fullness of time, perhaps extending for hundreds or even thousands of years, cosmic events appear to be almost inevitable. Because the large majority of meteors and asteroids have not been charted, trouble at some level may be closer than we might have imagined. It is tempting to think that collisions could be averted by exploding unwanted intruders, like comets and asteroids. Unfortunately, exploding the intruders would fragment them but would not necessarily alter their courses. At this point, it would appear that there is virtually nothing that human beings can do to prevent large-scale disruptions of these sorts; perhaps all the more reason to begin thinking more creatively now about how to face them.

## Ordinary Disasters

Ordinary disasters include earthquakes, tornadoes, hurricanes, floods, shortages of food and outbreaks of uncontrollable diseases. Sometimes these events can be dealt with at the local level; other times they require a national or even international effort. Some people living at the margin in primitive societies are unable to deal with ordinary disasters. The question is whether or not it is possible to reach a consensus about how to mount international responses to ordinary disasters. I think that the community of nations can respond to those in distress by developing structures that will not only ameliorate the effects of ordinary disasters but also have the potential to prevent or ameliorate the effects of mega-disasters like war, cosmic change, evolutionary disruptions and climate change induced by ordinary causes—as opposed to cosmic events.

I will begin by reviewing what I shall call "The Standard Model" for risk management. We shall see that this model, as ordinarily conceived, is completely inadequate to deal with the risks associated with ordinary disasters, much less extraordinary ones. This will lead us to an alternative vision of risk management, which will involve a commitment to new models of risk sharing and infrastructure. The type of infrastructure that I have in mind requires some imagination and a re-conception of the roles that we play in each other's lives.

### *The Standard Model*

The standard model of risk management involves the pooling of risks. Each insured entity contributes a premium which is added to a pool that is available to indemnify the insured against a well-defined set of negative outcomes. In other words, we are talking about standard health insurance, life insurance, property insurance, and liability insurance.

Now it is obvious that this model cannot deal even with ordinary disasters at the international level. The reason for this is that the nation-states and regions that are least able to cope with disasters are also least able to pay premiums to indemnify the risks associated with them. This is also true for individuals even in highly developed countries where risk management is a personal responsibility. For example, purchasing earthquake insurance in California or flood insurance in Louisiana is extremely expensive.

### *Measuring Contributions to the Common Good*

To my way of thinking, P2, P3 and P4 are the keys to a better understanding of what would constitute a just scheme for dealing with disasters. First of all, whatever scheme of distribution of burdens and benefits is adopted, it must be designed to promote the common good, and P4, that common good includes not only the well-being of individual people but also the health of the planet as a whole. One way to contribute to the common good, which includes preventing man-made disasters and ameliorating the effects of man-made and natural disasters, is to provide the infrastructure and perishables necessary for disaster prevention and response. Nation-states and wealthy regions are obviously in the best position to contribute the necessary resources. They are also under a greater obligation to provide those resources. That is because wealth depends to a great extent upon the materials that are extracted from the Earth as well as the physical infrastructure necessary to turn those materials into the products associated with highly developed economies. On other hand, we have already suggested that poorer, underdeveloped economies that have made but modest demands upon Earth have already contributed to the common good. *This new model for risk sharing associates more advanced development with an obligation to provide proportionately more in the way of infrastructure to deal with disasters and to promote the common good.* But this is not *because* those with more, *for that reason alone*, have a greater obligation (which may be true); it is rather that those who have more have obtained more by extracting more from the Earth. Inversely, those who have taken less from the Earth have a greatly reduced obligation to contribute to provide further resources to restore the Earth's ecology. The argument for this is Lockean and is deeply embedded in the ideology of the most advanced nations. In fact, *under this new model, the contributions of all will be roughly equitable (as in the Standard Model) because the "premium" to defray the risk will include not only direct payments that provide necessary infrastructure and perishables, but will also take account of the fact that those with less to contribute will have taken less from the Earth, which is precisely why it is that they have less to contribute to the common effort.*

Working out this model will not be nearly as tricky as it might initially seem. That is because the underlying assumption is that that those who have taken the most from the Earth have a duty to give back the most. Those who have taken the most (plausibly, though not necessarily) will have just that much more to give back.[27] Those who have taken the least and have exploited the Earth to the least degree therefore have already paid (plausibly, though not necessarily) the premium that entitles them to relief in times of distress. Of course, international agreements to determine the levels of contributions to the common good of all will need to be transparent (P1), and more developed economies will in fact justify extracting more from the Earth and making relatively greater demands on its ecology by the fact that they give back in exact proportion to what they have taken (P2). This new method of calculating contributions to the common good is obviously meant to be worldwide, but it is also meant to be viewed diachronically (P5). Whatever one generation takes from the Earth must in some form be repaid to the common good—not only of those in other regions of the Earth but also to future generations.

## *Immediate Steps*

A serious criticism of the current theory is that it is merely visionary and will depend upon complicated agreements and disclosures about the details of economic development that many nations may be unwilling to provide. Moreover, it is unreasonable to think that more fortunate nations will make large sacrifices unless a fair distribution of burdens and benefits has been established. Is there anything that is available at this point to address issues concerning disaster prevention and relief and the just use of resources? Is there anything that could be done now that would be a catalyst for further progress? Here we are thinking of ways to provide leadership that might change people's perspectives from narrow self-interest to the welfare of people who are in need now and ultimately to the future of Earth itself.

Elsewhere[28] I have suggested that there may be more cost-effective opportunities than we think. For example, the U.S. has decided to de-commission the *USS Enterprise*. The *Enterprise* is a huge nuclear-powered aircraft carrier that has been in service for half a century. The U.S. Navy plans to dismantle the ship and reduce it to scrap for recycling. It might be worth considering whether or not it would be feasible to re-purpose this great warship as a disaster relief, supply and hospital ship. It has an immense flight deck that would be suitable for large helicopters that could evacuate people in danger zones and to provide relief in disaster areas.

Although it would be unreasonable to think that the gigantic ship would not remain under the control of the U.S. Navy, it might be possible to staff the re-purposed Enterprise with young volunteers from all over the world. This would mean that there would be a resource at the ready to respond to both natural and man-made disasters. Obviously the envisioned resources would be available to all people and regions in need. Indeed, they might have been welcomed in recent disasters even by the most advanced industrial countries, for example in response to Fukushima and Hurricanes Sandy and Katrina. Obviously there would be considerable expense associated with re-purposing the *Enterprise*. On the other hand, it is already built, and it is inconceivable that a new ship of its magnitude would be built and dedicated to disaster relief at any time soon. Finally, de-commissioning and scrapping the *Enterprise* would also be hugely expensive, perhaps more expensive than re-purposing it.

There are other economical projects that also come to mind, projects that might provide relief to those in need. For example, much of the U.S. is plagued by fierce forest fires. Perhaps in some regions it would be possible to harvest trees that have "matured" and are subject to infestations by beetles and termites. The trees might be harvested by volunteers or perhaps even by non-violent prisoners who would welcome an opportunity to work outdoors in exchange for a reduction in their sentences. The harvested trees could then be distributed to regions where trees are scarce.[29]

These suggestions may (or may not) be practical. But they illustrate possibilities that could have positive effects at relatively low cost, which might inspire other nations to adopt similar programs. Contributions of this sort not only materially benefit humankind but also are of great *symbolic* importance, in that they show a commitment to preserve Earth and to contribute to the common good of humanity.

## War

Aside from a potential collision with a gigantic asteroid, there is perhaps no greater disaster than nuclear war. Why then is nuclear war threatened or seriously entertained? Indeed, "Why", as the psalmist pondered, "do the nations rage so furiously together; and why do the people imagine a vain thing?" (Psalms 2:1). Perhaps these two questions are related. Perhaps the nations rage so furiously together *because* the people imagine a vain thing. And what is the vain thing they imagine, or more generally, what form does their imagining take? The answer, possibly, is that the people imagine that their own good should have been the good of all, and that if their benighted neighbors refuse to embrace that "obvious" fact, they should be *compelled* to accept it.

The idea that the common good begins with me, or my people or my religion or my ideology or my country, is to identify the common good of humanity and of Earth as a merely provincial good. *That a merely provincial good should be forced upon all is perhaps the ultimate vanity.* It is one thing, of course, to try to convince others by argument of one's conception of the good or even by modeling it to make it appealing to others. But it is something else entirely to force it upon others by acts of violence, that is, by war. Possibly it is this insight that leads some of the great twentieth-century philosophers, like Rawls, to the view that liberal democracies can tolerate anything except "outlaw states" that violate "human rights", which may be justifiably opposed militarily.[30] *Of course* Rawls has a point. Even those who do not affirm any substantive good will acknowledge that it is not good at all to be forced to live by someone else's conception of substantive good. Surely if violence is ever justified, it is justified in response to those who would forcibly impose their own conception of the good upon others. However, perhaps Rawls goes too far when he suggests that liberal democracies intervene militarily to "protect" others. It is hardly obvious that the idea that we'll tolerate anything but intolerance justifies an otherwise unprovoked violent response to intolerance.

In any event, perhaps it is not too naïve to think that a global system to respond to disasters could tend to bring people and their nations together in service of the common good. Indeed, other human activities, including the international space effort, the advance of science, particularly astrophysics and medical science, as well as endeavors like orchestral music (unlike representational art) and causes like the Olympic movement have had a unifying effect. Perhaps all these activities can reinforce each other and thereby defang one of the greatest sources of human misery and pollution: war itself.

## Summary and Conclusion

The basic idea underlying this paper is that there really are substantive goods that all humans hold in common, but that those goods are not theological, philosophical or ideological. On the contrary, the goods that we hold in common are (a) the Earth itself, the only place within light years that we have to live, and (b) the goods that are the basis of universal sympathetic response, not only of humans for each other but also of humans for animals. Those goods are familiar, universal, and include bodily integrity as well as release from pain, hunger and disease, all of which are threatened by man-made and natural disasters. That is why it is reasonable to think that *in the long run* it is in the interests of all to work for the common good; indeed, how could it be otherwise?

This paper is philosophical in that it offers a conception of justice that is essentially linked to an undeniably common good. It argues that a system of benefits and burdens to promote that good should require equitable sacrifice by nation-states and regions (and hence their populations). However, it sees equity rather differently from what is seen on the standard model of risk assessment and management. We have a need to promote and restore the common good in proportion to what we have taken from it. Because our ability is plausibly correlated with what we have extracted from the common good, those with more will need to contribute more. Agreements that instantiate this system of justice will need to be transparent and to recognize that all have a duty to contribute as well as a right to receive. In calculating what is required of each, we must take into account the damage that is done to the Earth and its ecology by industrial development and acknowledge that the mere act for refraining from that development is, in a way, a positive contribution to the common good. Because the scheme envisioned focuses on the common good of humankind, it is applicable across the world and to future generations. In all our calculations, however, it will pay us to promote epistemological modesty in assessing benefits and burdens. That is because it is very easy to miscalculate the probability of low-frequency, high-value outcomes. Miscalculations can lead to unnecessary and unreasonable burdens as well as reckless dismissal of possible dangers. Perhaps one can say that in a world that is globally integrated economically, technologically, and even biologically, the only rational course is to identify what is undeniably good and to pursue it together on an equitable basis. That is especially true given that the world we have is the only world we have, and is very likely the only world we'll ever have.

## Notes

[1] See Michael A. Smith, *The Moral Problem* (Oxford: Blackwell, 1994) for a lucid and accessible introduction to the issues concerning the distinction between motivating and justifying reasons for other-regarding behavior, especially pp. 1–15, 92–98.
[2] Derek Parfit, *Reasons and Persons* (Oxford, UK: OUP, 1983).
[3] Lisa Schipper and Mark Pelling, "Disaster Risk, Climate Change and International Development," *Disasters*, 30(1), p. 25
[4] Joshua Hammar, "The Lost Tribes of the Amazon," *Smithsonian.com*, February 22, 2013.
[5] Perhaps the main metric by which ecological policies should be measured is the extent to which they disrupt the processes of evolution. I have discussed this at length in John H. Dreher, "Evolution and the Goal of Environmentalism," *Forum on Public Policy*, 2011(2), special section p. 1.
[6] Parfit, p. 61f.
[7] John H. Dreher, "Implementing Standards of Global Justice and the Common Good (A Theoretical Perspective on Global Responsibility)," paper presented at Ethics and Practices of Responsibility, November 19–20, 2012, Paris, France (revised January 2013), p. 5f.
[8] David Hume, *A Treatise of Human Nature*, eds. Lewis Amherst Selby-Bigge and P. H. Nidditch, 2nd ed. (Oxford, UK: OUP, 1978[1739–40]), III II:II:5.
[9] Dreher, 2013, p. 3f.
[10] For a very helpful analysis of these issues, see Charles Kenny, "Disaster Risk Reduction in Developing Countries: Costs, Benefits and Institutions," *Disasters* 36(4), pp. 563–9.
[11] John H. Dreher, "Environmental Sustainability as a Culturally Invariant Value," *Forum on Public Policy*, 2012(1), special section p. 1, pp. 3–11.
[12] Dreher, 2012, pp. 4–6, esp. fn. 5.
[13] Colin Howson, *Hume's Problem* (Oxford, UK: OUP, 2000), p. 179.
[14] Of course Kantians and other "deontologists" may claim that justice will be its own motivating reason. But this theory appears to be based upon an internalization of morality to which few subscribe. It is unreasonable to expect others to accept conclusions of arguments based upon premises they do not believe.
[15] Schipper and Pelling, p. 19.
[16] United Nations, "Millennium Declaration," Doc A/RES/55/2 (New York, NY: Author, 2000).
[17] United Nations, "Road Map toward the Implementation of the United Nations Millennium Declaration," Doc A/56/326 (New York, NY: Author, 2001).
[18] Dreher, 2012, pp. 2–4.
[19] Schipper and Pelling, p. 26.

[20] John Locke, *Second Treatise of Government*, ed. Thomas Peardon (Indianapolis, IN: The Library of the Liberal Arts/Bobbs-Merrill, 1983[1689]), §36.

[21] Aregai Tecle, "Sustainable Management of Natural Resources in an Era of Global Climate Change," in Reck, 2010, pp. 419–32.

[22] City of San Jose, *Environmental Services Department Integrated Waste Management, Zero Waste Strategic Plan* (San Jose, CA: Author, 2008).

[23] See, for, example, Ryuji Matsuhashi, Kae Takase, Koichi Yamada, and Yoshikuni Yoshida, "Study of Scenarios after the Great East Japan Earthquake to Create a Secure, Affluent and Low-Carbon Society," *Forum on Public Policy*, 2012(1), special section p. 1, pp. 12–4.

[24] Robert Peter Gale and Eric Lax, "Fukushima Radiation Proves Less Deadly than Feared," *Bloomberg.com*, March 3, 2013, paras. 1–5.

[25] Katherine Ling, "Is the Solution to the U.S. Nuclear Waste Problem in France?" *New York Times*, May 19, 2009.

[26] Matt Sedensky, "Huge Burmese Python Caught in Florida Everglades," Associated Press, reprinted in *USA Today*, August 14, 2012.

[27] Some economies are more efficient than others. Those that are more efficient will be in a stronger position to give back than those that are less efficient. Although they will be required to give more back than the inefficient, they will have more to give back. The present theory therefore takes into account the idea that efficiency is properly rewarded.

[28] Dreher, 2013, p. 10.

[29] A possible objection to this scheme might be that the ashes from forest fires serve to replenish the soil. On the other hand, it might well be possible to mill the harvested trees and to return the residual bark and associated celluloid material to the soil. In any event, there must be something to be said in favor of reducing the fuel that produces enormous air pollution and endangers valuable structures, which required resources to construct in the first place.

[30] John Rawls, *The Law of Peoples* (Cambridge MA: HUP, 1999), p. 82ff.

# Bibliography

Batteen, Mary Louise, Timothy Peter Stanton, and Wieslaw Maslowski. "Climate Change and Sustainability: Connecting Atmospheric, Ocean and Climate Science with Public Literacy." In Reck, *Climate Change and Sustainable Development*, 79–88.

City of San Jose. *Environmental Services Department Integrated Waste Management, Zero Waste Strategic Plan.* San Jose, CA: Author, 2008. www.sanjoseca.gov/Document Center/View/1020.

Dreher, John H. "Evolution and the Goal of Environmentalism." *Forum on Public Policy*, 2011(2), special section p. 1.

—. "Environmental Sustainability as a Culturally Invariant Value." *Forum on Public Policy*, 2012(1), special section p. 1.

—. "Implementing Standards of Global Justice and the Common Good (A Theoretical Perspective on Global Responsibility)." Paper presented at Ethics and Practices of Responsibility, November 19–20, 2012, Paris, France. Revised January 2013. Available at www.labtop.univ-paris8.fr/?p=451

Gale, Robert Peter, and Eric Lax. "Fukushima Radiation Proves Less Deadly than Feared." *Bloomberg.com*, March 3, 2013. www.bloomberg.com/news/2013-03-10/fukushima-radiation-proves-less-deadly-than-feared.html

Hammar, Joshua. "The Lost Tribes of the Amazon." *Smithsonian.com*, February 22, 2013. www.smithsonianmag.com/ideas-innovations/The-Lost-Tribes-of-the-Amazon-192124351.html

Howson, Colin. *Hume's Problem*. Oxford, UK: OUP, 2000.

Hume, David. *A Treatise of Human Nature*. Edited by Lewis Amherst Selby-Bigge and P. H. Nidditch. 2nd ed. Oxford, UK: OUP, 1978[1739–40].

—. *A Treatise of Human Nature*. Edited by David Fate Norton and Mary J. Norton. Oxford, UK: Oxford University Press, 2000[1739–40].

Justice, Jeff William, Ryan Cheek and Brandon Buckman. "Ideological Impacts upon Environmental Problem Perception. *Forum on Public Policy*, 2012(2), special section p.1. http://forumonpublicpolicy.com/vol2011.no2/archivevol2011.no2/justice.pdf

Kenny, Charles. "Disaster Risk Reduction in Developing Countries: Costs, Benefits and Institutions." *Disasters* 36(4), 559–588. DOI: 10.1111/j.1467-7717.2012.01275.x

Ling, Katherine. "Is the Solution to the U.S. Nuclear Waste Problem in France?" *New York Times*, May 19, 2009. http://www.nytimes.com/cwire/2009/05/18/18climatewire-is-the-solution-to-the-us-nuclear-waste-prob-12208.html?pagewanted=all

Locke, John. *Second Treatise of Government*. Edited by Thomas Peardon. Indianapolis, IN: The Library of the Liberal Arts/Bobbs-Merrill, 1983[1689].

Matsuhashi, Ryuji, Kae Takase, Koichi Yamada, and Yoshikuni Yoshida. "Study of Scenarios after the Great East Japan Earthquake to Create a Secure, Affluent and Low-Carbon Society." *Forum on Public Policy*, 2012(1), special section p. 1. http://forumonpublicpolicy.com/vol2012.no1/archive/matsuhashi.pdf

Parfit, Derek. *Reasons and Persons*. Oxford, UK: OUP, 1983.

Rawls, John. *The Law of Peoples*. Cambridge MA: HUP, 1999.

Reck, Ruth, ed. *Climate Change and Sustainable Development*. Yarton, UK: Linton Atlantic Books, 2010.

Schipper, Lisa, and Mark Pelling. "Disaster Risk, Climate Change and International Development." *Disasters*, 30(1), 19–38. DOI: 10.1111/j.1467-9523.2006.00304.x

Sedensky, Matt, "Huge Burmese Python Caught in Florida Everglades." Associated Press, reprinted in *USA Today*, August 14, 2012. http://usatoday30.usatoday.com/news/nation/story/2012-08-13/burmese-python-florida/57039860/1

Smith, Michael A. *The Moral Problem*. Oxford: Blackwell, 1994.

Snow, Mary M., and Richard K. Snow. "Climate Change and Challenge for Coastal Communities." In Reck, *Climate Change and Sustainable Development*, 383–89.

Tecle, Aregai. "Sustainable Management of Natural Resources in an Era of Global Climate Change." In Reck, *Climate Change and Sustainable Development*, 419–34.

Thorpe, H. R. "Habitat Restoration: Aspect of Sustainable Management." In Reck, *Climate Change and Sustainable Development*, 239–46.

United Nations. "Millennium Declaration." Doc A/RES/55/2. New York, NY: Author, 2000.

—. "Road Map toward the Implementation of the United Nations Millennium Declaration." Doc A/56/326. New York, NY: Author, 2001.

# Part II

# Post-Disaster Reconstruction in China

# CHAPTER THREE

# RECONSTRUCTION AFTER RECONSTRUCTION: A STUDY OF THE POST-EARTHQUAKE RECONSTRUCTION OF TAOPING VILLAGE, A TRADITIONAL QIANG SETTLEMENT IN SICHUAN, CHINA

## WANG YU
## WITH HANS SKOTTE

My fieldwork in Taoping Village revealed that two sequential reconstructions had taken place, the official government reconstruction and a locally driven "re-reconstruction", which I refer to herein as "self-restoration". This chapter will describe and explain why these two reconstruction efforts were not coordinated and present the consequences of the efforts not overlapping.

The government's official reconstruction was organized and directed by the State Administration of Cultural Heritage of China. Cultural heritage conservationists, guided by the Venice Charter and its updates, were responsible for the planning, design, and implementation. The subsequent local "self-restoration" took place without any professional or technical support. It was an individual, unorganized, and unexamined activity, mainly focusing on reinforcing the buildings' structure, changing of interior spaces, façades, roofs, etc.

This uncoordinated double reconstruction of Taoping stems from two different understandings of the challenge, which were apparent from the very beginning. Reconstruction authorities simply regarded Taoping as a damaged cultural heritage site like any other heritage site damaged by the earthquake. For the local inhabitants, on the other hand, the village was the existential pivot of their lives. The reconstruction was a means of "returning to life", recovering their homes and livelihoods, but also to improve their living standards, as was the case for most of the victims in the Sichuan quake zone. The official reconstruction was conducted in a top-down manner, excluding local inhabitants. This official approach was further exacerbated by the social disengagement of the heritage conservationists. These differences in conceptualizing the task at hand and the embedded processes sustained a constant conflict between the official reconstruction and the local population. Out of this conflict, fueled by anger, emerged a "social energy" that underpinned and sustained the individual, uncontrolled "self-restoration" which in fact damaged part of both the official reconstruction and the cultural heritage values of Taoping as a "living monument".

## Introduction

Involving communities in the conservation of cultural heritage has recently attracted greater attention in the heritage conservation arena. The importance of community to heritage protection is reflected in the recent key documents approved by the World Heritage Convention (WHC) of UNESCO. In the 2002 Budapest Declaration, WHC stated four strategic objectives: Credibility, Conservation, Capacity-building, and Communication, in order to enhance implementation of the declaration.[1] Five years later, in 2007, this "four-C" strategy became a "five-C" strategic objective, as it was joined by Community. In line with New Zealand's proposal, WHC now holds that "heritage protection without community involvement and commitment is an invitation to failure."[2]

The issue of community involvement has been widely discussed in the community of heritage conservation since it became the fifth C, as shown by the chosen theme for the fortieth anniversary of the WHC in 2012: "World Heritage and Sustainable Development: The Role of Local Community." Through these discussions, a series of relevant questions about this issue have arisen, such as how to raise local awareness of the unique values of cultural heritage, how to secure local benefits from heritage, and how to enhance development of the local community based on its heritage values.

This chapter is an attempt to join this ongoing discussion through a case study of the post-Sichuan earthquake[3] reconstruction in Taoping,[4] a traditional Qiang settlement, by reviewing and analyzing the phenomenon of two uncoordinated reconstructions, the official reconstruction and the local self-restoration, which happened in the process of reconstructing Taoping. My research addresses this observed reconstruction phenomenon: after the "official" expert-driven reconstruction was completed, a second reconstruction took place. Community members made substantial changes to their heritage properties. How can this be explained and what is there to learn from this when reconstructing what I call Lived-in Cultural Heritage[5] settlements?

In this research I divide the reconstruction program into four periods: 1) the very beginning; 2) policy formulation; 3) experts' practice; and 4) the second reconstruction. The purpose of this "periodization" is to identify the events which occurred during each period and, through that, uncover those events' impact on the relationship between government reconstruction policies, the conservation experts, and the local community. This is necessary in order to explain the final outcome.

## The Very Beginning

This refers to a very brief period, approximately half a month long, beginning about two weeks after the quake and ending when the Sichuan Earthquake Reconstruction Regulations were published. In this period there was a major shift in focus from emergency rescue of survivors to forging a policy for building refugee resettlement and for post-disaster reconstruction. During this period, quake victims started to return to their damaged dwellings and some even started to rebuild.

China's State Council reconstruction efforts were officially underway on May 25, 2008, thirteen days after the quake, when Prime Minister Wen announced to the public that quake relief was shifting to reconstruction.[6] The Policy Bureau of China's Communist Party, the top leadership of China, confirmed Wen's announcement in a meeting the day after. At the same time a number of ministries, directly under the State Council, launched their own reconstruction measures, e.g., the Ministry of Housing and Urban-Rural Development pledged to build 1.5 million temporary housing units for more than 11 million homeless people in the quake-hit areas.[7]

The State Council launched Regulations on Post Sichuan Earthquake Restoration and Reconstruction on June 8, 2008. This is the legal document that defined Taoping as a Qiang heritage village and thus defined the reconstruction strategy to be employed, all according to Chapter V, Article 39, stating that

> Relevant authorities shall take effective measures to protect earthquake ruins…
> Protected sites of cultural relics shall be preserved in-situ.
> …structures of historic value and ethnic characteristics and historic architecture that may be preserved….[8]

The reason for Taoping's reconstruction following this article is that since 2007 Taoping has been included in the list of Major Historical and Cultural Sites Protected at the National Level, which is the highest level of heritage protection in China, recognized by the State Administration of Cultural Heritage (SACH). Furthermore, the importance SACH placed on the reconstruction of Taoping was made evident by the official Chinese press agency, *Xinhua News*, when the village was mentioned alongside the reconstruction of the Erwang Temple, a site on UNESCO's World Cultural Heritage list. The reason for Taoping's high profile was SACH's plan to make the reconstruction of this village a model for the reconstruction for other Qiang settlements, in spite of the fact that the quake left most of the conservation zone of Taoping intact. That was not the case for the region as a whole.

There were no records of destroyed buildings within the Taoping historic conservation zone, whereas a good number of newer buildings adjacent to the old town were severely damaged by the quake, leaving some fifty inhabitants homeless. Within the village proper, however, the quake did cause substantial damage to the old building stock.

Quake survivors living beside the ruins of their dwellings were confronted by crucial questions of survival after the disaster, particularly those living in rural areas. This required the quake refugees to rebuild their livelihoods spontaneously. For example, a report in *The Guardian*, a UK newspaper, reported on Mr. Zhang who, after burying his wife, rushed back to his fields because he was really concerned about planting his seeds in time for September's harvest. In the end he said he is alive and could use his hands to rebuild his house.[9] Similarly, a group of Taoping farmers who lived in the worst quake-hit area had similar priorities pertaining to the reconstruction of livelihoods and housing.

Inhabitants perceive Taoping in a different way from government agents and conservation experts. To the people who live there, Taoping is a settlement of nearly 100 families, in which they live and are going to live in the future. Officials and experts regard Taoping as a place of cultural value containing traditional historical residential buildings representing the Qiang nation's history and cultural symbols. Consequently, the government's reconstruction plan for Taoping was to preserve its heritage value and repair quake-damaged heritage properties, a standard approach to cultural heritage reconstruction. Meanwhile inhabitants also expected to rebuild the same buildings, but the reason for rebuilding is primarily for living, i.e., rebuilding their homes. Therefore, a conceptual difference existed from the very beginning between the conservation authorities and the inhabitants of Taoping as to the purpose of the reconstruction.

## Formulating the Reconstruction Policy

The reconstruction regulations as formulated by the State Council stated in general terms how to treat quake-damaged cultural heritage properties in its Article 39. It was left to SACH to develop these policies into a plan for reconstruction activities. For this mission SACH mobilized itself quickly and positively by undertaking extensive efforts to assess heritage damage, composing reconstruction plans, channeling financial support, etc.

On May 14, 2008, two days after the quake, SACH launched an emergency notification about the requirements of heritage protection and disseminated it to the lowest levels of the hierarchy, the local Culture and Sports Offices. Two days after this notification, the first sixteen sets of reports on heritage sites damage were fed back to SACH. These primary reports basically gave photographic documentation of the damage. Because of the general urgency of the reconstruction these constituted the principal background material for the subsequent reconstruction plans.

SACH assembled the reports of quake-damage assessments rapidly and in June 2008 released the document "Sichuan Earthquake Damage Assessment on Cultural Relics of Sichuan Province," which classified all the quake-hit zone's heritage properties into four levels of damage. This assessment was a necessary reference for the reconstruction plans for cultural heritage properties.

On July 20, 2008, five weeks after the quake, SACH released a fairly detailed document, "Post-Quake Reconstruction Planning on Cultural Heritage." The SACH document is a comprehensive scheme for reconstructing cultural heritage sites in the quake-hit zone. It determines the number of heritage properties in need of repair; how to rebuild those heritage sites; how long the whole program should take; and the reconstruction budget for each property. According to the SACH document, Taoping was assessed as category B, "Building Structure Seriously Damaged", which called for immediate structural repair. SACH also indicated that around 12.4 million CNY (US$1.9 million) would be invested in Taoping heritage reconstruction over a period of three years.[10]

SACH also gave instructions on the management approach to the implementation of the reconstruction projects. This approach applied a three-level hierarchical structure with designated roles and responsibilities. SACH was the senior inspectorate and the principal planning, coordinating, and overseeing body. The second tier was the provincial heritage administration, which was required to set up a heritage reconstruction office that was to take full responsibility for the implementation of all reconstruction projects within the province. The Cultural and Sport Office at the regional level was the "ground agency" directly conducting the physical projects within its own county, instructed by the provincial level of administration and SACH.

The cultural heritage reconstruction was organized to ensure efficient and fast reconstruction according to China's State Council instructions, as were all reconstruction sectors. This meant organizing management hierarchies where authority and responsibilities were clearly defined from top to bottom, which, by the way, is the way the Chinese society is organized, i.e., in a traditional "top-down" manner. Donovan describes this as when

> a political elite makes public policies that are implemented through a stable, strict and sequential chain of command by bureaucrats and service providers.[11]

In terms of a speedy reconstruction they succeeded. In their report on the reconstruction, the FAFO Institute for Applied International Studies was openly impressed.[12]

However, this time-efficient, top-down approach had certain crucial weaknesses. It contributed to serious grievances on the part of the local community. The approach adopted did not accept any participation or contribution from the victims. They remained—in the name of efficiency—bystanders to their own homes and means of livelihoods being reconstructed according to plans on which they had no influence. This exclusion stands out as the main reason for the "second reconstruction".

## Experts' Practice

Experts were answerable for the reconstruction implementation, relying on their technical and professional knowledge and skills informed by administrative frameworks and reconstruction policies. In the case of Taoping, most experts came from the Chinese Architectural History Research Institute (CAHRI), a highly regarded institute in the field of cultural heritage conservation in China. They carried out the design planning, while the Dalong Construction Group (DCG), an experienced builder of Chinese traditional architecture, took on the actual (re)construction work.

CAHRI, after the initial four-day field assessment in June, published the "Planning of Post-Quake Cultural Heritage Conservation of Taoping" at the beginning of July 2008. Two months later they presented their "Design for Rescuing, Repairing and Protecting the Historical Buildings of Taoping." These two documents presented CAHRI's methods and plans for Taoping's cultural heritage reconstruction. Their methodological approach relied on the theories of cultural heritage conservation as presented in the "2004 Principles for Conservation of Heritage Sites in China," issued by China ICOMOS.[13] CAHRI's plan aimed at preserving what they held to be Taoping major heritage values, its outstanding defense system,[14] the quality of the village location, the distinctive construction technologies applied, the typical Qiang building style and the magnificent landscape.

CAHRI's documents on planning and design assessed every historical building in Taoping on the basis of its heritage value and level of damage. This was done according to professional standards as applied in international heritage conservation.

Based on the outcomes of these assessments, all 115 buildings of the core district of Taoping were classified into four categories, and each level had a set of related treatments with specified measures for repairing and rebuilding. Meanwhile, CAHRI experts also formulated the underlying principles to be applied in the overall repair and rebuilding process. Here they particularly highlighted the principle of adopting traditional construction technology, employing local craftsmen to repair and rebuild the damaged buildings, and using local materials such as yellow mud, stone, and timber as much as possible. Besides traditional skills, advanced modern technologies in construction were also allowed, but were to be used cautiously, according to its guidelines on planning and design.[15]

The experts' practice in the reconstruction of Taoping could thus be defined as a process of applying general expert skills and knowledge irrespective of context. It is an example of applying single-solution thinking where

> problem-seeking and problem-solving is linear and predictable: diagnose the problem, search out for opportunities, assess your risk, assemble the team, sort out the budget, draw up the plans, design a response and deliver whatever.[16]

However, in CAHRI's expert approach, several provisions of their plan were incompatible with the realities of the Taoping reconstruction challenges. Some of the generalized approaches were deemed inappropriate in the context of Taoping. The village inhabitants expressed difficulty in understanding the results of the assessments and CAHRI's professional analysis:

I don't think the repair work is finished in only twenty-five days when only the east and the west walls are fixed as long as the two other walls are still unsecured. Besides, the workers [have spent] more time repairing someone else's house which does not have [as] high [a] ranking as mine.

This was stated by Mr. Yang, a local resident aged thirty, whose dwelling was assessed as one of the eleven most valuable buildings in Taoping. He and his family refused to move back into their house.

Likewise, experts' fundamental strategy, applying traditional technology, employing local craftsmen, and using ordinary local materials, did not sit well with the reconstruction realities. Repairing the housing stock for the ninety-five families of the village required nearly 900 workers, twice the number of people living in Taoping. Only about eighty of the 900 were craftsmen, and only a few of those were experienced in building traditional Qiang stone housing. Before the quake most of the local stonemasons and carpenters had lost their knowledge and skills because no one had built a traditional-style building for the previous twenty years. Consequently, a few local inhabitants rejected the proposal of the experts to repair their dwellings because they simply did not trust the construction skills of the local craftsmen.

Similarly, the prescribed approach of using local materials proved inappropriate in that such a vast amount of local construction material could not be provided in a mere three-year period. For instance, yellow mud, the traditional adhesive material for stone walls, should be dug only in autumn, when it contains the appropriate level of moisture to serve as an adhesive, according to the older experienced local craftsmen. That in turn meant it might take far more than three years to finish Taoping reconstruction projects, if this traditional method of only constructing housing in autumn was followed.

Also, some of the modern construction technologies applied to the reconstruction could not be adapted to traditional construction systems. A number of buildings in Taoping developed leaks in their roofs during the rainy season after reconstruction. Here the roofs were built with a modern waterproof layer widely used in modern concrete roof structures, which works very well against water and snow when connected to a flat and smooth surface such as a concrete slab, but in the Taoping buildings it was used inappropriately on flat roofs; it was layered and glued sloppily to rough surfaces made of wood or mud, which resulted in leaks that were difficult to detect and repair.

The result of Taoping's official reconstruction was that the inhabitants were not satisfied; instead its various deficiencies caused anger. Meanwhile, in the course of their practice, the experts focused their attention only on cultural heritage repair rather than seeing that this was the reconstruction of people's homes and part of the livelihood of the Taoping population. They seem to have missed the perspective of Taoping as a lived-in cultural heritage. Furthermore, the experts, being limited in their practice perspective, were unable to listen to the demands of the inhabitants, thereby losing the opportunity to establish a platform for communication between the reconstruction authority and the local community, a critical chance to fill the gap between them. They lost the chance to acquire essential knowledge and skills for reconstruction from local people as well. On the contrary, due to the experts not meeting the expectations of the local community through the applied reconstruction approach, local inhabitants were angered by their practice, which in turn fueled the locals' misunderstanding of the official reconstruction objectives.

## The Second Reconstruction

After the official reconstruction, a large number of Taoping's inhabitants spontaneously started to carry out their own renovations of their newly repaired and rebuilt houses. These "self-restoration" projects were driven by personal and local needs and aspirations. This stands in paradoxical contrast to the official Taoping reconstruction being awarded a prize as one of the ten best-reconstructed cultural heritage sites in China in 2011.

Most of Taoping residents' self-restoration projects could be regarded as adaptation to the local economic changes after the quake, in which Taoping people were forced to leave their agricultural life because their farm land had been taken over by new commercial and public buildings and housing. The most obvious economic alternative after the quake was to move into the booming tourist business, which explains the need for physical alterations to the reconstructed building stock.

Due to the economy shifting to tourism, many people in Taoping redecorated their houses in order to adapt to this significant change. For example, Mr. Yu, aged forty, whose dwelling was near the village square, converted his house after the official repair was completed in order to catch up with the new lifestyle and thus prepare for the anticipated wave of tourists. "We enlarged former windows and also added some windows on the external walls to bring more sunlight into our rooms," Mr. Yu's wife said. Bringing more sunshine into the house meant enlarging the former window openings of approximately 20 x 20 cm to 80 x 100 cm, which fundamentally changed the original façade pattern and the proportions between windows and wall.

Because Mr. Yu decided to give up his previous career as farmer, rooms on the ground floor, which had been the space for livestock, were redecorated as guestrooms with big windows and flush toilets. Likewise, the attic, a space used previously for storing harvests and farm tools, was also changed into another guestroom, which Mr. Yu expected to rent to tourists during the holiday season. In the interior, the Yu family also changed the living room, which was once a traditional Qiang space with a square fire-pit in the center. Now the room has been converted into a modern-style living room with a three-person sofa, a square tea table and an entertainment center.

> We also installed a flush toilet next to the living room instead of the traditional pit latrine because a flush toilet is more hygienic. It will also prevent the stink of feces, which used to bother the tourists,

Mrs. Yu said.

Besides the approach applied by Mr. Yu in his self-restoration, there are two other much more radical examples of conversions and changes to the official reconstruction. In 2011 Mr. Zhou, aged fifty, practically demolished the entire internal structure of his house. Only the external walls and the roof were left standing. His ambition was to build a unique high-standard hotel in this village. So he hired construction workers to build a new three-story concrete structure to replace the former traditional structure within the old external walls.

The other conversion was initiated by the Long family. They are pioneers in the tourist business in Taoping, having started up twenty years ago. After the quake, they successfully persuaded three neighboring families whose houses connect to theirs to sell to them. Shortly afterward, the Longs combined all four houses into the biggest building in Taoping. Meanwhile they rearranged the rooms of this new giant building with antique furniture and vintage decorations collected from the neighboring villages and named it "The Qiang Palace".

Besides conversions due to alternative modes of livelihood, changes were also justified by acts of appropriation, i.e., changes stemming from the strong emotion people invest in their houses as homes, or "housing as [a] symbol of home," as claimed by Skotte.[17] Because a house "becomes a symbol of home by representing the system of activities with a system of settings" and "is not only an area for everyday life [it also] provides meaning to life."[18] These activities in themselves entail, or may entail, physical changes to one's "officially repaired, culturally appropriate heritage property."

"Security and control" could be one highlighted attribute among those multiple meanings associated with home, according to a 1995 American study.[19] The purpose of post-disaster reconstruction would then be about regaining that control. However, this dimension of the reconstruction was neglected during the official reconstruction because government officials and experts only focused on the issue of cultural heritage conservation and ignored other dimensions of the complex meanings of buildings to the local community.

The second reconstruction could therefore be considered the Taoping inhabitants' self-adaptation of livelihood change and restoration of the lost attributes that recreated their dwellings as symbols of home. Unfortunately, in Taoping, the official reconstruction modified their way of life, and moreover failed to provide a platform for the inhabitants to accomplish the mission of "going home". The inhabitants were not able perceive the official rebuilding as a recreation of home. Therefore they began their other reconstruction as a "home reconstruction". The "second reconstruction" instigated by the village inhabitants negated the officially defined cultural heritage reconstruction by acting on livelihood prospects and the need to appropriate their property as a home space. Hence the second reconstruction fundamentally changed the results of the official reconstruction and diminished the cultural heritage value of the village of Taoping.

## Conclusion and Recommendation

The post-Sichuan earthquake reconstruction of Taoping was divided into an uncoordinated two-stage reconstruction effort: an official reconstruction and a local self-restoration effort. This paper argues that this situation is due to the implementation of inappropriate post-disaster reconstruction planning practices. Because of this split, the reconstruction effort failed or at least diminished the cultural heritage properties of the village, and failed to accommodate a transition toward the new livelihood challenges of the post-quake era.

The reason for this double reconstruction stems from the fact that the officials and the experts on the one hand, and the local inhabitants on the other, applied irreconcilable concepts as to what the reconstruction was about. This was apparent at the very beginning. The official approach was grounded in the urge to preserve the cultural heritage of the Qiang minority; the inhabitants, themselves of Qiang stock, saw the reconstruction as a means of accommodating the changes in livelihoods caused by the quake and as a process of rebuilding their homes. Policymakers seemed not to have acknowledged the locals' understanding. They were at no stage invited to participate in deciding on reconstruction issues. Experts moreover rejected the wishes of Taoping inhabitants to take charge of rebuilding their own dwellings, and as a result the locals rejected the official reconstruction because of the experts' tendency to provide and apply their expert knowledge rather than to communicate with the community and listen to their aspirations. This was particularly damaging to the reconstruction process, as such communication could well have provided a useful source of contextualized expert knowledge. Instead the local residents of Taoping seemed to have retaliated against this process by venturing into a series of self-restoration projects to respond to the livelihood challenges as they perceived them and as a way of reclaiming control of their dwellings. Without any inspection and technical advice, locals' self-restoration has seriously changed the achievements of official reconstruction and ultimately damaged the cultural values of the heritage properties of Taoping.

There seems to be one principal lesson from the Taoping case: reconstructing a lived-in cultural heritage site requires a negotiated approach. The absolute, almost abstract, way the reconstructions efforts focused on the formal "cultural heritage" values seemed not to recognize the difference between a lived-in cultural heritage and, say, that of a "cultural heritage monument". The local community living in the heritage environment harbors its own expectations, aspirations and interests. Without these being recognized in the reconstruction phase and respected by the conservation authorities and experts, any reconstruction efforts might prove useless. The heritage values may be damaged and/or the site might be deserted. To secure a sustainable post-disaster reconstruction of a cultural heritage site where heritage values are honored and communities may prosper requires a different approach than the one applied in Taoping. If nothing else, this study is field-based evidence that confirms in full the WHC claim that "heritage protection without community involvement and commitment is an invitation to failure."[20] Indeed.

## Notes

[1] UNESCO, *Convention Concerning the Protection of the World Cultural and Natural Heritage, Item 9: The Budapest Declaration on World Heritage*, WHC-02/CONF.202/5 (Paris, France: Author, 2002), 1.

[2] Ibid., *Convention Concerning the Protection of the World Cultural and Natural Heritage, Item 13: Evaluation of the Results of the Implementation of the*

*Committee's Strategic Objectives*, WHC-07/31.COM/13B (Paris, France: Author, 2007), 2.

[3] On the afternoon of May 12, 2008, a 7.9 magnitude earthquake hit Sichuan Province, a mountainous region in Western China, killing about 70,000 people and leaving over 18,000 missing. The worst-hit zone, an area nearly the size of Greece or Iceland, was confronted with severe damage which completely destroyed 5.46 million residences and severely damaged another 5.93 million, leaving 11 million people homeless, 5 million of them in immediate need of relocation.

[4] Taoping, representing the Qiang minority traditional settlement, is right in between the foot of Dabao Mountain and the Zagunao River, a branch of the Min Jiang River. The people of Taoping have lived in this place for several centuries. Remarkably skilled local craftsmen built the houses of Taoping centuries ago using local materials such as stones, yellow mud, and timber.

[5] *Lived-in cultural heritage* is a term coined by myself (with Dr. Skotte) referring to a cultural heritage site or settlement where people live and whose cultural properties are used to sustain their livelihoods.

[6] Xinhua News Agency, "Premier says Quake Relief Shifting to Reconstruction," *China Daily*, May 25, 2008.

[7] Ibid., "China to Build 1.5 Million Make-Shift Houses," *China Daily*, May 25, 2008.

[8] State Council of the People's Republic of China, "Regulations on Post-Wenchuan Earthquake Restoration and Reconstruction," Order of the State Council of the People's Republic of China no. 526, June 8, 2008.

[9] Tania Branigan, "Survivors Look to Rebuild Their Homes and Lives," *The Guardian*, May 21, 2008.

[10] 中国国家文物局，中国建筑研究院建筑历史研究所 [State Administration of Cultural Heritage (SACH), China, and the Chinese Architectural History Institute (CAHRI)], 《国家汶川地震灾后重建划文物救保修复划大纲》 ["2008 Post-Sichuan Earthquake Reconstruction Planning on Cultural Heritage"], unpublished paper on architectural design, 2008.

[11] Claire Donovan, "Top-Down Approach," *Encyclopedia of Governance*, vol. 2, ed. Mark Bevir (Thousand Oaks, CA: Sage, 2007), 14.

[12] Kristin Dalen, Hedda Flatø, Liu Jing and Zhang Huafeng, *Recovering from the Wenchuan Earthquake—Living Conditions and Development in Disaster Areas 2008–2011* (Oslo, Norway: Fafo, 2012).

[13] 中国建筑研究院建筑历史研究所 [The Chinese Architectural History Institute (CAHRI)], "桃坪羌寨抢险维修保护工程——灾后保护工程规划" ["2008 Post Sichuan Earthquake Reconstruction Planning of Taoping"], unpublished paper on Urban Planning, 2008, "桃坪羌寨抢险维修保护工程——抢险维修工程方案" ["2008 Post Sichuan Earthquake Reconstruction Design of Taoping"), unpublished paper on Urban Planning, 2008.

[14] In order to prevent the robbers' invasion, hundreds of years ago the Taoping people designed a defense system by building watchtowers to spy on would-be attackers, constructing a water supply system both for daily life and agriculture,

and creating a complex road system in the village to confuse robbers when they went into the village.

[15] CAHRI, "2008 Post Sichuan Earthquake Reconstruction Planning…", "2008 Post Sichuan Earthquake Reconstruction Design…".

[16] Nabeel Hamdi, *The Placemaker's Guide to Building Community* (London, UK: Routledge, 2010), 142.

[17] Hans Skotte, "Theoretical Foundation and Current Practice," in "Tents in Concrete," PhD dissertation, Norwegian University of Science and Technology, 2004, 36.

[18] Irwin Altman and Setha M. Low, *Place Attachment* (New York, NY: Plenum Press. 1992), 109.

[19] A. Rapoport, "A Critical Look at the Concept of 'Home'," in *The Home: Words, Interpretations, Meanings and Environment*, ed. David N. Benjamin, 25–52 (Aldershot, UK: Avebury, 1995).

[20] UNESCO, 2007.

# Bibliography

Altman, Irwin, and Setha M. Low. *Place Attachment*. New York, NY: Plenum Press. 1992.

Branigan, Tania. "Survivors Look to Rebuild Their Homes and Lives." *The Guardian*, May 21, 2008. http://www.theguardian.com/world/2008/may/22/chinaearthquake.china

中国建筑研究院建筑历史研究所 [The Chinese Architectural History Institute (CAHRI)]. "桃坪羌寨抢险维修保护工程——灾后保护工程规划" ["2008 Post Sichuan Earthquake Reconstruction Planning of Taoping"]. Unpublished paper on Urban Planning. 2008.

—. "桃坪羌寨抢险维修保护工程——抢险维修工程方案" ["2008 Post Sichuan Earthquake Reconstruction Design of Taoping"). Unpublished Paper on Urban Planning. 2008.

Donovan, Claire. "Top-Down Approach." *Encyclopedia of Governance*, Vol. 2. Edited by Mark Bevir. 971–2. Thousand Oaks, CA: Sage, 2007.

Dalen, Kristin, Hedda Flatø, Liu Jing, and Zhang Huafeng. *Recovering from the Wenchuan Earthquake—Living Conditions and Development in Disaster Areas 2008–2011*. Oslo, Norway: Fafo, 2012. http://www.fafo.no/pub/rapp/20266/20266.pdf

Hamdi, Nabeel. *The Placemaker's Guide to Building Community*. London, UK: Routledge, 2010.

Rapoport, A. "A Critical Look at the Concept of 'Home'." In *The Home: Words, Interpretations, Meanings and Environment*. Edited by David N. Benjamin. 25–52. Aldershot, UK: Avebury, 1995.

Skotte, Hans. "Theoretical Foundation and Current Practice." In "Tents in Concrete." PhD dissertation. 36–42. Norwegian University of Science and Technology. 2004.

中国国家文物局，中国建筑研究院建筑历史研究所 [State Administration of Cultural Heritage (SACH), China, and the Chinese Architectural History Institute (CAHRI)].《国家汶川地震灾后重建划文物救保修复划大纲》["2008 Post-Sichuan Earthquake Reconstruction Planning on Cultural Heritage"]. Unpublished Paper on Architectural Design. 2008.

State Council of the People's Republic of China. "Regulations on Post-Wenchuan Earthquake Restoration and Reconstruction." Order of the State Council of the People's Republic of China no. 526. June 8, 2008. http://www.sc.gov.cn/10462/10758/10759/10764/2012/7/26/10219700.shtml

UNESCO. *Convention Concerning the Protection of the World Cultural and Natural Heritage, Item 9: The Budapest Declaration on World Heritage.* WHC-02/CONF.202/5. Paris, France: Author, 2002. http://whc.unesco.org/archive/2002/whc-02-conf202-5e.pdf

—. *Convention Concerning the Protection of the World Cultural and Natural Heritage, Item 13: Evaluation of the Results of the Implementation of the Committee's Strategic Objectives.* WHC-07/31.COM/13B. Paris, France: Author, 2007. http://whc.unesco.org/archive/2007/whc07-31com-13be.pdf

Xinhua News Agency. "Premier says Quake Relief Shifting to Reconstruction." *China Daily*, May 25, 2008. http://www.chinadaily.com.cn/business/2008-05/25/content_6709999.htm

—. "China to Build 1.5 Million Make-Shift Houses." *China Daily*, May 25, 2008. http://www.chinadaily.com.cn/bizchina/2008-05/25/content_6709814.htm

—. "文物局表示将尽快开展地震灾区文物抢救工作" ["Cultural Relics Bureau Says it Will Carry Out Work as Soon as Possible to Rescue Cultural Relics from Earthquake Disaster."] *China News*, May 19, 2008. http://news.xinhuanet.com/newscenter/2008-05/18/content_8199391.htm

# CHAPTER FOUR

# LONG-TERM VISION AND PRAGMATISM IN POST-EARTHQUAKE RECOVERY PLANNING: THE CASE OF CHENGDUO, TIBETAN REGION

## GUI YANLI, QIN BO,[1] AND HAO KAI

## Background of the Post-Earthquake Recovery Planning in Chengduo

*Brief Introduction to Chengdu*

A place in the east of the Qinghai-Tibet Plateau, and also in the south of Qinghai Province and the northeast of Yushu Prefecture, Chengduo County is one of the counties located in the Sanjiangyuan National Nature Reserve, or the Three Rivers Nature Reserve. It measures 160.25 km from east to west and 209.5 km from north to south covering a total area of 15,400 km$^2$, which is 7.8 percent of the entire prefecture and 2.2 percent of the province. Standing at an average altitude of 4,100 m above sea level, the county features a total population of 58,021, a GDP of RMB 276 million, and an RMB of 4,758 per capita; the ratio of the primary, secondary and tertiary industries' output value is 58:22:21.[2] Chengduo County is comprised of the five towns of Chengwen, Qingshuihe, Xiewu, Zhenqin and Zhaduo, the two townships of Gaduo and Labu, as well as fifty-seven villages and 253 other settlements.

Chengduo County possesses a unique natural, political and cultural environment. The location of the Sanjiangyuan Nature Reserve makes it one of China's most important water sources. The average altitude of 4,100m creates an elevated, oxygen-poor plateau environment and the naturally beautiful landscape and magnificent scenery of the Tongtianhe River (Figure 4.1, left), provides unique biological resources. Chengduo County is also an ethnic minority area in which 90 percent of the locals are

---

[1] Corresponding author, qinbo@vip.sina.com

of Tibetan nationality and maintain a rich Kangba culture (Figure 4.1, right). In addition, the long history of Tibetan Buddhism contributes to the unique folk culture and the temple culture of the county, all constituting an extraordinary cultural environment. Despite the prominence of its farm and pasture products that depend on the special plateau environment, its overall economic development is still behind the times, with poor educational resources and outdated municipal facilities. It is now confronted by a number of challenges associated with economic development: the tension between the vulnerable ecosystem and a booming population; between the need to protect the core areas of the Sanjiangyuan water source and the development of modern farming, animal husbandry and tourism; and between the need to curb the overexpansion of township enterprises and the growth of migration and employment.

Figure 4.1. Natural Landscape (left); Cultural Activities (right).

## *Background of the Plan*

On April 14th, 2010, a 7.1 magnitude earthquake hit Yushu Prefecture, Qinghai Province, causing the collapse of many buildings and seriously damaging local facilities. Responding to this devastating disaster, the Central Government of China and relevant governmental departments extensively mobilized all kinds of resources, supporting the recovery and reconstruction of the quake-hit areas, helping restore the devastated region to its normal productivity and daily life, and laying a solid foundation for future economic and ecological improvement. When an earthquake strikes, the harm done often cannot be rectified. It could be a fatal disaster or a chance for regional development, depending on how we respond to it. Therefore, the first priority should be the comprehensive, systematic, and scientific planning of the entire area based on a forward-looking vision. This should optimize the spatial structure of the city, deepen the exploitation of cultural resources, boost development in social sectors, incorporate urban and rural construction and industrial transformation, and strengthen ecological and environmental protection.

In order to help reestablish the vitality of the quake-hit area, the Department of Urban Planning and Management of the School of Public Administration and Policy, Renmin University of China, and China Urban Construction Design and Research Institute were jointly commissioned by the Housing and Urban-Rural Construction Bureau of Qinghai Province to develop a whole set of post-earthquake recovery plans for Chengduo County, including a master plan, an urban design, and a detailed plan for certain key areas. The faculty members and postgraduate students promptly formed a team and started off on May 20, 2010, for the quake-hit areas. After two months' intensive work, the proposal passed the expert and official reviews on July 22. These were organized by the Department of Housing and Urban-Rural Development of Qinghai Province, which announced the approval and implementation of the post-earthquake recovery plan.

The planning for post-earthquake recovery was launched when the CCP Central Committee set requirements for building a new Socialist Yushu. At this point the local authorities appealed to expand their current role in order to accelerate development. The local population expressed their hopes of retaining their original property rights and lifestyle. However, the planning is in reality restricted by complex local terrains and landforms, uneven hydrological conditions and irrigation works, and a severe shortage of infrastructure such as an underground piping network. With limited time, the planning project suffered from deficient communication with local authorities and residents. Given its remote location, rebuilding Chengduo County after the earthquake had to overcome this time constraint for construction work on the plateau to be carried out and to satisfy the long-term demands for urban development. The current situation had to be accommodated and longer-term goals were taken into consideration. Citizens' daily difficulties had to be addressed, and the systematic development of the whole city planned. That is why post-earthquake reconstruction must stick to the combination of present recovery and reconstruction, of enhancing the local culture and living standards, and of respecting the collective will while protecting the ecological environment. It should conform to guidelines that respect nature, value resources, culture, and tradition, and focus on people. It should start with facts, maintain a pragmatic spirit and encompass appropriate planning which is both far-sighted and practical.

The outcomes of the post-earthquake recovery planning in Chengduo County include overall planning guidelines, planning maps, research reports on specific issues, urban design schemes and detailed plans, all sent from local authorities in the provincial municipality for review and approval, after which the package was formally published and applied in guiding the post-earthquake reconstruction in Chengduo and its future urban planning. In the letter of thanks sent by the local government of Chengduo County, appreciation was expressed for the planning, which

> shows an exhilarating blueprint for the recovery and reconstruction of a post-earthquake Chengduo County and for its sound and rapid development in the future,

a great effort for which they felt cordially grateful to the faculty and students of Renmin University. The research and formulation for the planning of Chengduo was successfully completed.

Figure 4.2. The Renmin Planning Crew (left); the Researchers at the Site (right).

## Field Surveys for Planning

*Field Surveys*

In such exceptional circumstances, the post-earthquake recovery planning of Chengduo County was finished within a short period of time and was to be implemented within three years, according to national requirements. In order to gain a full understanding of the current conditions and the locals' actual needs, the project team gave out a large number of questionnaires and held many interviews with local residents, in addition to collecting materials and conducting on-site investigations in the conventional sense. In the end, as many as 250 questionnaires were issued, in both Chinese and Tibetan languages, so as to reach inhabitants from different parts of the community. We issued fifty questionnaires targeting the staffs of the County's authorities, enterprises and institutions and 100 each for Shangzhuang and Xiazhuang villagers. Altogether, 143 questionnaires were finally collected, fifty-one (36 percent) from Shangzhuang and fifty (35 percent) from Xiazhuang, twenty (14 percent) from the local government, enterprises and institutions and the remaining 12 (15 percent) from other sources, e.g., merchants and tourists from other places. The questionnaire consisted of five sections relating to ecology, landscape, transportation, culture, and people's livelihoods. It involved important issues concerning the most urgent post-earthquake work: how residences were rebuilt, which public facilities the County prioritized for improvement, how to renovate religious sites of the most importance, how to preserve and improve the desired public open spaces and agricultural land, landmark urban buildings in Chengduo County, and so on. It aimed to elicit a set of opinions from governmental departments and ordinary people that would provide the basis for deciding the final planning proposals.

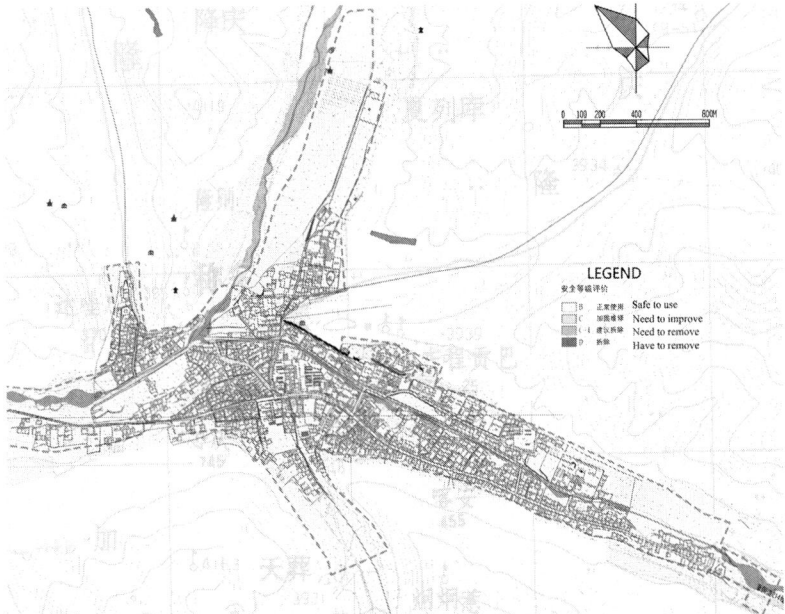

Figure 4.3. An Evaluation Map of Safety Conditions in Post-Earthquake Chengduo.

As a county in the east of Yushu Prefecture, Chengduo was hit by the disaster but did not lose as many buildings as Jiegu Town, home to the Prefecture government, though cracks were found in most of the buildings. Because of the particular architecture found in Chengduo and the structural features of Tibetan vernacular housing, no engineering technique was suitable for repairing the damage caused by the earthquake. There is no analogous situation with which the damage that occurred in Chengdu can be compared. To ensure the safety of residents, the project crew suggested to local officials that a professional agency be engaged to evaluate and identify the safety of different buildings. On the basis of the result, a safety evaluation map was drafted (Figure 4.3, above). The map in Figure 4.3 shows that 99 percent of the county's residences and roughly 59 percent of the public buildings needed to be demolished and rebuilt, and so this was the starting point for the plan.

## *Scientific Research*

To guarantee that the planning was scientific, proper and feasible, and to provide a yardstick for deciding the final version of the post-earthquake plan, the team carried out four complementary areas of research on strategic issues: population and land use estimation; industrial development; policies to protect the Sanjiangyuan Reserve and ecologically friendly migration; and the mechanism to implement the plan. Taking the example of population and land use estimation, by the end of 2009, Chengduo County was estimated to have 14,895 households, equivalent to 58,021 persons. Statistics show that the area's population increased by 44 percent annually between 2000 and 2009. Designed objectively, acknowledging the recent rapid population growth, this research estimated that the total population of Chengduo County should be curbed at 70,000, 80,000 and 90,000 respectively in 2015, 2020 and 2025. The research suggested that the limit of the regional population growth should be set at 80,000, and its total size should decline in the long term.

As for the research on the policies protecting the Sanjiangyuan Reserve and ecologically friendly migration, the reality is that in China, most of the areas at high risk for natural disasters such as earthquakes are located in insecure east-to-west terraced zones. These belong to the mountainous areas that support a mix of agriculture and animal husbandry, which are ecologically fragile. They feature distinctive qualities in strata, geography and terrains, and play a prominent role in ecological functions such as biodiversity and conservation of water resources, soil, and the eco-landscape. Currently, the ecological environment in Chengduo County faces numerous challenges: severe vegetation degradation, lack of coordination in the planning of water resource exploitation, an increasing number of meteorological disasters, serious pollution caused by domestic waste, inadequate awareness of modern environmental protection, and a shortage of scientifically based, universally applied environmental monitoring systems. This situation was aggravated by the earthquake. In order to achieve effective ecological management, this plan proposed implementing control of the ecological environment by dividing the county into three ecological zones.

Of the three zones, the populous urban zone will become the key central city with the highest population density in Chengduo County. In accordance with the environmental features and building conditions of different lands for use, four land types—"no construction", "limited construction", "construction-favorable", and "constructed"—have been identified, so as to effect space management in varying degrees as well as ecological and environmental protection measures in informed and sensitive ways. The core zone of ecological protection, mainly consisting of a nature reserve and a headwaters conservation area, is essential to the protection of the entire ecosystem in Chengduo. Within the core zone, there should be a strict limit to the number of construction projects, while the protection of the original environment should remain the primary concern. The plan designates the central areas along the Tongtianhe River, the marshes near the rivers, and the lakes within the district into the core zone for ecological protection. The ecologically vulnerable zone is subject to adverse environmental conditions and is unsuitable for exploitation and utilization. Planning focuses largely on ecological conservation and environmental improvement.

Meanwhile, the plan also endeavors to launch ecologically friendly migration by improving education and industrial capacity to create favorable prerequisites for farmers and herdsmen to make a living outwith agriculture. By promoting ecologically friendly migration and settlement projects, farmers and herdsmen, especially those among the younger generation, can be encouraged to work in non-agricultural sectors. A ban on grazing or the introduction of stable breeding to transform the traditional stocking methods will eventually help to decrease the total number of livestock and achieve a balance between grass supply and livestock needs. A decrease in population and livestock will help to alleviate the heavy demand for the vulnerable grassland and, after years of natural recovery, will help to restore the current environment to its original state of blue mountains and green waters.

### *Public Participation and Support*

Since being commissioned with the planning task, the project team has visited Chengduo County six times and Qinghai Province six times, overcoming tight deadlines, altitude stress, and other unfavorable factors to carry out the planning and organizing work. During the process, the team sought opinions from all around and invited extensive public participation. To be specific, the first time the staff visited Chengduo was for six days, from May 20 to 25. They investigated the disaster scene and conceived the initial version of the plan, seeking opinions and suggestions from local government officials and citizens. On June 3, the outline of the draft was presented to the Department of Housing and Urban-Rural Development of Qinghai Province and to local experts and specialists experienced in post-earthquake reconstruction in order to get their comprehensive suggestions. The team visited Chengduo for a second time between June 21 and 25, presenting the preliminary plan and seeking more opinions (Figure 4.4); a third visit was made between July 2 and 15, when the final plan was shown to the entire local community, in accordance with the *Urban and Rural Planning Law*, so as to guarantee that the local residents' views were taken into consideration throughout the organizing and implementing process of the planning.[3]

Figure 4.4. Introduction for the Locals (left); Residents in Discussion (right).

## Long-Term Vision in the Planning

### *Exploring Patterns for Industrial Development*

Shaped jointly by primitive, agricultural and nomadic civilizations, Chengduo County's development was shaped by the endowments of both human and animal natural resources. Its development arose spontaneously from its original ecological and natural conditions. So any natural disaster, such as a serious earthquake, results in a complex conflict between man and nature.[4] As an area of complex geological conditions vulnerable to ecological changes, the county has constantly suffered a wide range of problems: grassland deterioration and blackening soil desertification; water and soil loss; shrinkage of wetlands; prolonged population growth; and the gradual decrease, fragmentation and degeneration of pasture lands, all of which have contributed to the undermining of the local primary industry.

In this sense, the foundation for post-earthquake urban development lies in continuous industrial development. To this end, it requires, in a down-to-earth fashion, the establishment of solutions to the following prevailing difficulties and restrictions: high altitude and extreme cold, limited resources, poor communication, costly transportation, different cultural ideas and understandings, and a meager population. These restrictions call for appropriate action, suitable for local circumstances, to be taken to develop ecological civilization, while preventing further geological calamities from recurring and further environmental deterioration. In doing this, the utmost priority must be to develop a distinctive civilization. This requires intelligence and all-round excellence, so as to embark on a harmonious development track and promote the transformation of the industrial structure that will support rapid urban development.

In light of the industrial development trend of Chengduo County and the importance of protecting the Sanjiangyuan Reserve's ecology, Chengduo County should actively transform the development pattern of its farming and animal husbandry into an economic strategy that optimizes different industries and involves the entire municipality. This needs to guarantee that priority is given to the development of eco-friendly animal husbandry, animal product processing, and trade. Cultural-oriented eco-tourism, the Tibetan packing industry, and Tibetan Mastiff breeding must be encouraged, as these measures would gradually downsize the proportion of traditional farming and animal husbandry in the economy. It should also boost ecological migration in order to return farmlands to forestry and rangeland to grassland with the growing of green industries. It should reduce the damage to ecology caused by traditional agriculture and livestock breeding and advance the protection of Sanjiangyuan Reserve. All these efforts will raise the locals' living standards and buttress the urbanization of Chengduo County. In the short run steps must be taken to cultivate the construction and building materials industry, as well industries and services related to the cascade hydropower station project at Tongtianhe River. Such programs will spur a substantial momentum within a short period and give time for the eco-tourism to grow and the typical Tibetan packing and circulating industry of animal products to prosper.[5]

## *Readjusting Urban Development Configuration*

The restructuring of Chengduo's urban area aims at an orderly concentration of population and the directing of rural populations into cities and towns or central villages. It also requires the removal of population from the zones of frequent seismic activity to relatively safe places and from uphill to downhill, so as to achieve a normal population distribution. To all these ends, the plan should work with the specifics of the settlements' distribution, population size, and long-term development features. It should dismantle and merge the villages and towns which are small or have inadequate public services. As a result, the seven villages and towns of Chengduo County are to be reorganized into a central county of three key towns, two specialized towns and a general township. Thus, the focus of the development has been highlighted and its features clearly defined. This calls for the formation of the spatial development strategy to develop a dominant center in a zonal arrangement. Only by resetting the development configuration of Chengduo County in a scientific way can it adapt to long-term and sustainable development for the region.

It is also stated in the plan that the central county of Chengduo must turn into a national ecological protection base for the Tongtianhe River core area at Sanjiangyuan. At the same time it must develop a culture-oriented tourist city with Kangba specialties with a processing trade base for Tibet's modern agriculture and farming industry, a comprehensive provider of hydropower and electricity, and an indispensable component of Chengduo's urbanization. Hence, the nature of the central county is defined as the political, economic and cultural center of Chengduo County. It will also be the ecologically friendly migration base in Tongtianhe River's core region of the Sanjiangyuan Nature Reserve, and the base for the processing trade of modern agricultural and farming products in Yushu Prefecture.

Of Chengduo's three key towns established in the plan, Qingshuihe Town, the northeastern portal to Yushu Prefecture, will serve as Chengduo's key trade market for agricultural and farming products and a center for transportation service; Xiewu Town, a hub connecting Yushu Prefecture and the western part of Sichuan Province, will figure as a transit depot for the transportation and trade of agricultural and farming products; Zhaduo Town will become a hub for entering Qumalai County from Xining, through Chengduo County, and it will also serve as an important market for the worm grass trade in Yushu Prefecture as well as a major provider of economic and social services in the northwestern part of Chengduo County and southeastern areas of Qumalai County. The blueprint establishes two specialized towns that are to embark on specific development tracks. Among them, Labu Town will develop into a center for folk dance and songs in Yushu and a historical and cultural tourist town mainly renowned for its temple culture and natural scenery. Gaduo Town will become the service center for agriculture and farming in nearby areas and a tourist reception center for Gaduojuewu parkland. As for the general township, Zhenqin Township, it will turn into a significant transportation and food processing area in Chengduo. According to the nature of the urban areas, adjustment should be added to the layout of infrastructure and public service facilities, with the central county to be equipped with complete public service facilities. Appropriate and established techniques should be adopted in the reconstruction process, and environmentally friendly reconstruction methods should be strictly adhered to. Apart from this, the plan should be strictly observed in all rebuilding projects, except where it is appropriate to adopt higher construction standards.

During the optimization of the urban spatial structure, the selection of settlement sites should be based on the guarantee of residential security, with a respect for the inhabitants' true feelings and the maintenance of conventional social structure; it should also take future development and employment into consideration, involve industrial restructuring in population redistribution and migration, and consequently form an urban configuration which is rational in distribution, advanced in structure, and complete in function. This plan will improve the overall human settlement and encourage the harmonious coexistence of man and nature.

### *Optimizing Urban Spatial Structure*

The central county in Chengduo is the gathering locus for the local population and also the center of Chengduo's industrial development and public services. Since the devastating earthquake struck, the central county has undergone a tremendous transformation in its urban structure and spatial form. Simultaneously, it has also been confronted by a series of challenges, such as the limited size of land and population, the shortage of urban facilities, the incompetence of supportive public facilities, and restricted space for future development. In a nutshell, the absence of planning has posed great difficulties for readjusting its organization and structure. During the post-earthquake reconstruction, Chengduo County has put planning in the first place, has observed the guidance and restriction of planning from higher authorities, and has incorporated the development between urban and rural areas and in various regions. On the premise that the capacity of resources and the environment are respected, local authorities should properly determine the scope, the arrangement and the shape of the urban reconstruction and the scope and standard for all the projects to be rebuilt.

*(1) Identifying the urban population/land use scale.* Estimates indicate that the population of Chengduo's central county will reach 12,000, 17,000 and 25,000 by 2015, 2020, and 2025 respectively. The land use scale will be altered from the current construction norm of 296.45 m$^2$ per capita to (but no more than) 150 m$^2$. By the end, the entire construction land use will reach 369 hectares and the area per capita 149 m$^2$, which will leave plenty of room for further urban expansion.

*(2) Improving the disaster mitigation system.* In the post-earthquake construction planning, experience has been gained and lessons learnt from the disaster.[6] Full consideration has been given to the disaster mitigation and relief system, the effort to build a lifeline system and an evacuation passageway network, improving the urban spatial pattern of Chengduo County (especially by increasing the density of roads), standardizing road grades, decreasing the standard of occupancy density, and to building an open and flexible spatial framework.

*(3) Upgrading service capability.* In order to upgrade public service facilities, the recovery plan creates greater space for traditional transactions and, with the reconstruction in place, relocates the administration building and alters its original site into public service facilities conveniently accessible to all citizens.

## *Exploiting Cultural Resources*

The post-earthquake recovery plan should further exploit the distinctive resources and adopt acceptable forms that showcase the folk, religious, plateau, and water cultures of Chengduo County.[7] The plan attaches great significance to the protection and excavation of historical remains, includes the expression of the features of different cultures in the spatial arrangement, and creates small towns and rural settlements with unique specialties, thus laying the foundation for future renovation and development of tourism in the region. For instance, it will build a center for folk dancing and singing, and a Tongtianhe River cultural square that represents the regional culture; in order to promote the religious culture and to preserve the original religious facilities, it will build religious squares, improve internal apparatus and use sculptures of Buddhist stories as street furniture for the city, all contributing to a greater cultural atmosphere.

To promote a "water culture", it was planned to incorporate the water system into urban life, to encourage travelers and citizens to come closer to and dabble in the water, to enjoy the sight of it, listen to it, love it, to connect natural features and cultural elements by "water". A cultural square was also proposed, with the theme of "Source of Sangjiangyuan and Valley of Kangba culture", surrounded by a series of sculptures and street furniture that are all Sangjiangyuan-oriented. A Sanjiangyuan Museum (Folk Culture Museum) was planned, as well as a 500-meter-long wall of water-related stories that display the rich connotations of the region's water culture.

To reflect the special culture of the Tibetan minority, it will be built using Tibetan techniques, based on the authentic features of traditional Tibetan architecture. It will redesign the indoor structure to achieve better anti-seismic stability and use local materials to develop a landscape that is integrated with the natural environment.

## Applicable Short-Term Responses in the Planning

### *Comprehensive Arrangement of Construction Projects*

After the Yushu Earthquake hit, national authorities planned to complete the major reconstruction within three years and to help the areas involved to regain or surpass the basic living standards and economic development standards which existed before the disaster. Considering the work in high-altitude regions and the time limit, which demanded stricter requirements to make the plan feasible, Chengduo County had to coordinate the sequence, investment and scope of different reconstruction and renovation projects. It had to ensure that a proper and balanced arrangement between urban and rural infrastructure was in place, and that the advance of both urban and rural construction was synchronous, with highest priority given to the rebuilding of residences, public facilities like schools and sanitary services, infrastructure, and industrial workshops.

It was essential that the recovery plan should fully consider people's vital interests and rights, guarantee their basic property and land-use rights, and give ample importance to their independence, creativity, and initiative in rebuilding their homes. In combination with scientific planning, this could form a virtuous mode of employment and industrial development. It could also actively create the advantages of producing a larger number of jobs, encouraging earthquake-stricken victims to help themselves by taking to production and seeking employment, increasing the training of migrant workers and engaging them in tourism, community management and services, business management, and logistics transportation. All these methods would perfectly link victims' employment and the county's post-earthquake reconstruction.

The major geological hazards facing the central county of Chengduo include flooding and earthquake-induced disasters like collapses, landslips, unstable slopes, and mudslides. Therefore, the central county needed first to build and upgrade the disaster-resistant infrastructure, which covers the three major types of exit and rescue passageways, shelters and lifeline projects. Some construction projects associated with Chalalong River and Xiqu River were needed, such as repairing the river beds and readjusting the river routes, in accordance with road construction and landscape alternation regulations. The flood control standard should be raised to the grade necessary to cope with once-in-twenty-years flooding and the community ground in the central county should be strictly defined as a planned region where livestock grazing is forbidden, but conservation of soil and water is encouraged so as to prevent natural disasters such as mudslides. The post-earthquake reconstruction should build fire stations to higher standards and ensure security against fire disasters.

## *The Priority of Constructing Public Facilities*

The focal points and difficulties of the post-disaster reconstruction lie in how to stabilize people's livelihoods rapidly and boost the development of social undertakings; how to build a new homeland in which people can live and work in peace and contentment, where an ecological balance is realized and security and harmony are achieved; and how to lay a solid foundation for sustainable economic and social development. In accordance with Chengduo's existing situation in its social development and in keeping with the requirements of relevant national policies, the plan has adopted the strategy of public service development by centralizing the functions and improving the development of services, and concentrating the population in central areas.

It also planned that a day school will be built in the west of the central county, a primary school and two kindergartens in the east; each town and township would have another boarding primary school, and each administrative village a new kindergarten. The plan for medical and health facilities, combining the principles of concentration and distribution where necessary, requires each administrative village or natural settlement to have a health center and each town and township a central hospital. The central county should expand the Tibetan hospital and reconstruct the people's hospital so as to improve overall health services.

Social welfare facilities should be strengthened, with full importance given to the functions of residences for the elderly, including expansion in scale and improvement in efficiency. Based on this, more homes are to be added to satisfy the current demand. The plan should enlarge the schools for orphans and set standards for teaching. The neighborhood committees in farming and pastoral areas and in cities and townships should build a number of cultural outlets for communities, while the central county should plan to construct a Tianhe cultural square, a Dongcheng cultural square, an exhibition hall named the Sanjiangyuan Museum for Folk and Religious Culture, and a gymnasium, so as to increase the number of local cultural and sports facilities.

In regard to business services and facilities, the emphasis should be placed on the planning of business services and specialized markets, as well as business outlets in different cities and towns. Chengduo County should upgrade its business facilities and give priority to the planning of the specialized trade market for agricultural and farming products in Qingshuihe, the specialized trade market for the worm grass trade in Zhaduo, and the center for transportation of goods in Xiewu, according to the demand of industrial development.

## *Respect for Original Spatial Fabric*

In the post-earthquake recovery planning and architecture design, the "low-impact/high-respect" mode was implemented regarding the natural environment. "Low-impact" means that Chengduo County should, in its reconstruction, correspond to the historical landscape of the towns and villages; that is, to build alongside the mountain shape, to create small clusters of houses, and to reconstruct in the original places. "High-respect" means that much respect should be paid to the geo-spatial identity of the Tibetan people's production, living and ecology in the high, cold mountain region. Such high respect should also be paid to the recycling of resources used in agricultural production and to the original spatial texture (see Figure 4.5).

Buildings and structures should be renovated wherever possible, with certain parts being improved and upgraded, while the indigenous people rebuild their own houses on their original sites and retain the layouts as they were prior to the earthquake. For them, building materials and workers should come from local areas, which, in combination with modern earthquake-resistant techniques, can contribute to numerous buildings and houses maintaining the local and traditional culture. They also need to use various renewable energy sources as much as possible, adjust road networks in certain places, highlight the valley landscape, and increase green spaces.

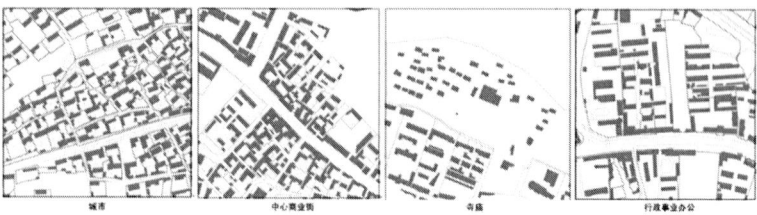

Figure 4.5. Spatial Textures in Different Types of Land.

Figure 4.6. An Aerial View of the Urban Design.

In order to adapt to the current implementation of construction projects, it is planned that the indigenous villagers will maintain 420 square meters for each household and rebuild the majority of sites. Furthermore, more public support facilities will be put in place and reasonable policies should be formulated for land replacement and relocation. Changes should also be made to the architectural structure of the original buildings.

## *Formulation and Implementation of Follow-Up Policies*

The post-earthquake reconstruction plan endeavors to address a number of economic, social, environmental, and spatial issues within a short period of time. It recognizes that many of the emerging social phenomena and problems unrelated to physical planning and projects are not within the scope of space-oriented reconstructive solutions. Thus, supporting policies have been introduced in the plan to target potential problems and long-term development goals.

In relation to economic development, particular emphasis is placed on the instructions for the relevant industries that set strict constraints on environmental destruction and pollution. The post-earthquake plan is intended to advance the transformation of traditional agriculture and animal husbandry; to increase the protection of and support for Tibetan folk customs, religious culture, and heritage; and to provide financial subsidies for local people's participation in competitive industries. It also incorporates a plan for Chengduo's tourism development into the integrated planning of tourism development in Yushu Prefecture. It increases support for the development of infrastructure for appropriate industries, and provides financial aid for the development of potential regional industries.

For development in the social sectors, the plan proposes strict controls on population growth and scientific policies for population conditions. Particularly, it sets reasonable standards for population size, mechanisms to establish and strengthen educational development, active promotion of culture and sports projects, the increase of employment, the perfection of the social security system, the advance of urban information management and the enhancement of urban public security. It should also get rid of the institutional barriers in the dual administration between urban and rural sectors and incorporate the development of cities and countryside.

For ecological and environmental protection, the plan suggests a package of policies such as the exploitation of water resources, protection of eco-greenbelts, efficient utilization of energy and renewable resources, and the economized and intensified use of land resources. Priority should be given to conserving the Sanjiangyuan Reserve. This calls for special funds from the central government and for a survey network of the ecosystem to be set up, with enhanced promotion of and education in ecological and environmental protection. In addition, policies to support ecological migration should be improved. As estimated in *The Conservation Planning of Sanjiangyuan Reserve*, the area contains 16,234 persons, or 2,952 households, a figure that makes up 44.9 percent of the 36,109 now living in the natural reserve. Among these, as many as 19,875 persons are to be transferred elsewhere, and hence the enactment of basic ecological compensation and resettlement compensation strategies will provide practical help to raise the migrants' living standards.

To facilitate implementation of the plan, it is proposed that legal obligations be strengthened to uphold the authority of the overall post-earthquake scheme. In other words, it should increase the supervision of construction in the regions covered by the plan, standardize the inspection and approval procedures, improve the land management system (especially to tighten up the inspection and control of land), and arrange a scientific schedule for all construction. It should guarantee the building of key projects while avoiding the illusion of localized prosperity, so as to build up more effective management and supervisory systems for construction and land utilization. The plan proposes an idea of stage-by-stage investment and financing for urban and ecological constructions in Chengduo. Borrowing the "city marketing" concept, it presents a marketing strategy tailored for Chengduo: to introduce market mechanisms, activate the land market and set up a land reserve center, to introduce the advanced build-operate-transfer (BOT) mechanism, raise funds in various ways, and ensure sufficient capital for construction. Moreover, it entails the participation of the public, to whom subsequent technical guidance and service are to be given throughout the rebuilding process, for the sake of publicity, equity, and high efficiency.

To date, the post-earthquake recovery plan has been in full operation in Chengduo, and it is greatly improving the services and the landscape of the area. During the implementation, however, there also appeared a certain degree of mismatch between the recovery plan and the actual selection of sites, a problem that largely resulted from the provincial headquarters' numerous readjustments and from local habitants' carelessness, especially in their excess occupation of land or illegal constructions. So, there is still a long way to go before the reconstruction goals are fully achieved.

Figure 4.7. A Panoramic View of the Post-Earthquake Reconstruction in Chengduo, Taken June 8, 2012.[8]

## Notes

[2] Chengduo Statistics Bureau (CSB), "Chengduo tongji baogao" ["Chengduo Statistical Report"], unpublished report, 2011.
[3] Sheng Ying, "Post-Earthquake Reconstruction: Towards a Much More Participatory Planning," *Theoretical and Empirical Researches in Urban Management*, 4(1S), 27–37.

[4] Mohsen Ghafory-Ashtiany and Mahmood Hosseini, "Post-Bam Earthquake: Recovery and Reconstruction," *Natural Hazards* 44(2), 229–41.
[5] Jen-Hung Huang and Jennifer C. H. Min, "Earthquake Devastation and Recovery in Tourism: The Taiwan Case," *Tourism Management* 23(2), 145–54.
[6] James Schwab, Kenneth C. Topping, Charles D. Eadie, Robert E. Deyle, and Richard A. Smith. *Planning for Post-Disaster Recovery and Reconstruction* (Chicago, IL: American Planning Association, 1998).
[7] Teddy Boen and Rohit Jigyasu, "Cultural Considerations for Post-Disaster Reconstruction Post-Tsunami Challenges." 2005.
[8] Image provided by the Planning Agency of the Government of Chengduo County. Reprinted by permission.

# Bibliography

Boen, Teddy, and Rohit Jigyasu. "Cultural Considerations for Post-Disaster Reconstruction Post-Tsunami Challenges." 2005. Available at http://www.adpc.net/irc06/2005/4-6/TBindo1.pdf

Chengduo Statistics Bureau (CSB). "Chengduo tongji baogao" ["Chengduo Statistical Report"]. Unpublished report, 2011.

Ghafory-Ashtiany, Mohsen, and Mahmood Hosseini. "Post-Bam Earthquake: Recovery and Reconstruction." *Natural Hazards*, 44(2), 229–41.

Huang, Jen-Hung, and Jennifer C. H. Min. "Earthquake Devastation and Recovery in Tourism: The Taiwan Case." *Tourism Management* 23(2), 145–54.

Schwab, James, Kenneth C. Topping, Charles D. Eadie, Robert E. Deyle, and Richard A. Smith. *Planning for Post-Disaster Recovery and Reconstruction* (Chicago, IL: American Planning Association, 1998).

Ying, Sheng. "Post-Earthquake Reconstruction: Towards a Much More Participatory Planning." *Theoretical and Empirical Researches in Urban Management*, 4(1S), 27–37.

# CHAPTER FIVE

## POST-DISASTER RECONSTRUCTION IN EDUCATION FROM THE PERSPECTIVE OF THE SOCIAL SUPPORT SYSTEM: THE CASE OF THE WENCHUAN EARTHQUAKE IN CHINA[1]

### YUMEI HAN, WENFAN YAN, LING LI, HAIFENG LI, XINZHI LIU, AND YUPING HAN

### Introduction

The severe earthquake that took place in May 12, 2008 in Wenchuan and many other counties in Sichuan Province and peripheral provinces of China (known as the "Wenchuan Earthquake" or the "5.12 Earthquake") was a devastating disaster and is even now a terrible memory for people of the whole nation. Among all the damage, the loss and destruction of schools, students, and teachers are the most heartbreaking part of the crisis. More than five years have passed since the disaster. Reconstruction work, including educational reconstruction, has been ongoing as one of the primary missions of the whole of Chinese society. Central and local government organizations and institutions, mass media, people from all walks of life, as well as people from the earthquake-stricken areas, have been constantly contributing their efforts to the reconstruction process in one way or another. This chapter focuses on the case of educational reconstruction after the Wenchuan earthquake in China to demonstrate the collaborative roles and efforts of different participants and agents in the reconstruction process from the perspective of the social support system, and to explore experiences and lessons of the pattern of such a social support system in post-disaster educational rebuilding in the Chinese socialist context.

## Post-Disaster Reconstruction in Education

There is plenty of literature on post-disaster reconstruction. However, surprisingly, post-disaster reconstruction in the field of education has not been a priority focus, although educational reconstruction is regarded as one of the most important parts of post-disaster reconstruction.[2] More often, educational reconstruction has been touched upon as just one aspect when scholars address post-disaster reconstruction.[3] Among the research related to post-disaster educational reconstruction issues, scholars mainly focus on two domains either entirely or partially: first, tangible or infrastructural reconstruction, indicating the restoration and reconstruction of school buildings and teaching facilities;[4] and second, intangible reconstruction, indicating the rebuilding of the teaching force and students' and teachers' psychological recovery from the trauma.[5]

Scholars also point out that educational reconstruction should be achieved in two phases: the meeting-basic-needs phase and the sustainable development phase.[6] The meeting-basic-needs phase of recovery refers to the initial goal and step of restoring a certain amount of educational resources, including funding, school buildings, teaching facilities, the teaching force, and class restoration rate, according to the basic needs of the surviving students in earthquake-stricken areas.[7] The sustainable phase of reconstruction means the long-term goal and strategy of sustaining and improving the quality of education in earthquake-stricken areas. This should be measured by students' academic achievement, attainment level, and psychological status, as well as teachers' professional development, school administration and management, and the educational output of human capital suitable for the society.[8]

Educational reconstruction can be seen as an opportunity after disaster as a way rebuilding a better educational system and landscape, as shown in the cases of Indonesia, Japan, the U.S., as well as in China.[9] This chapter focuses on the educational reconstruction in China after the Wenchuan earthquake, inquiring into the devastating damage done to school buildings and infrastructure, the teaching force, and students' state of mind, and how these are being addressed by various contributors across society.

## Social Support System

Social support is a definition more often used in the disciplines of psychology, medicine, public health, nursing, and social work. Although it is hard to achieve a consensus on defining social support as a concept, it generally means assistance, companionship, or other types of supportive action provided by individuals or groups of people, such as families, friends, community, and organizations to an individual recipient or group.[10] It is often regarded as synonymous with social networks.[11] In this sense, social support is usually linked to benefits for both physical and mental health.[12]

Social support mainly falls into four types based on its functions.[13] Emotional support indicates the offering of empathy, concern, condolence, care, love, and trust.[14] Tangible or instrumental support indicates the provision of financial aid, material supplies, services, or other concrete acts of help and support.[15] Informational support indicates the provision of guidance, instruction, advice, suggestions, or other useful information.[16] Companionship support, as the name suggests, indicates the provision of companionship, which gives the recipient a sense of social belonging.[17]

Combined together, the social support system refers to the collected pattern of diverse types of support by various providers, with each provider playing a different role and having ties to each other through certain relationships and interaction patterns.[18] The components of a social support system mainly include families, friends, coworkers, communities, and organizations.[19] Some scholars insist that governments should be an indispensable part in the system,[20] while others regard governments as providing public aid rather than social support.[21]

Currently, the definition of "social support system" is widely accepted in academic circles in China and the rest of the world as sociology, public policy, and education. Some scholars define the social support system from the perspective of public policy studies, contending that it is comprised of the collected factors and powers that support and help public policy making and implementation. They argue that the components of the system include public, non-governmental organizations and the mass media.[22] Some scholars have explored how the social support system applies to education, especially for beginning urban teachers,[23] university transfer students,[24] individual students,[25] rural migrant laborers' children,[26] and children who are left home alone while their parents work far away.[27] Some scholars have also applied the social support system concept to post-disaster reconstruction studies, such as social support systems for disaster-stricken women,[28] adolescents,[29] college students,[30] and post-disaster reconstruction in general.[31] These scholars mainly address the issues of the recipients, the components of the social support systems for these recipients, and how the social support system works and affects the recipients.

## *Domains of Social Support System for Post-Disaster Educational Reconstruction*

Based on previous research, in this chapter we define the social support system as the joint assistance, guidance, resources, and other forms of support provided to people affected by earthquakes. Due to the distinctive characteristics of the top-down administrative model in the Chinese political and social context, and taking into consideration the findings of the literature discussed above, we include governments as a major part of the social support system for post-disaster educational reconstruction. The components of this system thus include: a) central and local governments, non-governmental organizations and enterprises; b) organizations, enterprises and institutes; c) members of the public in society; and d) people from earthquake-stricken areas, with the governments being the leader, the center, and the collective power of the whole support system. As for the major missions of educational reconstruction, the Central Institute of Education Sciences in China has proposed six aspects of reconstruction: psychological rehabilitation, school reconstruction, restoration of teaching, restoration of campuses, restoration of teaching staff, and the summarizing of past quake recovery efforts.[32] In this chapter, we mainly address three critical issues among these six: i) school building and facilities reconstruction; ii) psychological recovery; and iii) restoration of the teaching force. With all these issues solved, a brand new educational landscape will be established. The role of each component of the social support system in solving the three issues,

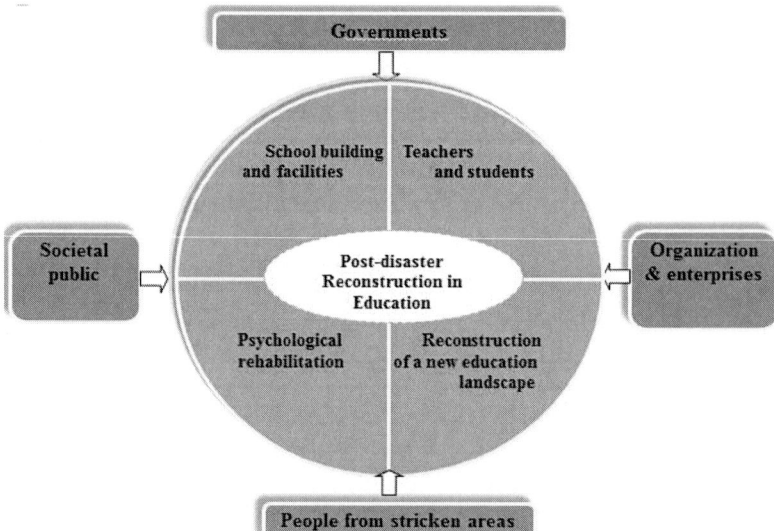

Figure 5.1. Conceptual Framework of the Social Support System for Post-Disaster Reconstruction in Education.

as well as the relationship and interaction between these components, will be analyzed in this chapter. The achievements of the social support system will also be examined.

Figure 5.1 above shows the conceptual framework of the social support system for post-disaster reconstruction in education based on these domains chosen in the context of the Wenchuan earthquake.

## Damages and Issues: The Case of the Wenchuan Earthquake in China

The Wenchuan earthquake was devastating for the population of the affected areas. According to the National Bureau of Statistics, in Sichuan province the Wenchuan earthquake reached a magnitude (M) of 8.0, claiming 68,712 lives, along with 17,921 missing and 375,000 injured, and causing direct economic losses as high as RMB 845.1 billion.[33] The loss in education was also vast in terms of infrastructure, human lives, and psychologically. The grave situation posed a great challenge to the post-quake reconstruction of education; how to successfully implement post-earthquake reconstruction of education became a pressing issue.

### *Loss of School Buildings and Infrastructure*

The earthquake caused the collapse of many school buildings and houses, killing a great number of students; 13,768 schools were damaged, resulting in a direct economic loss of more than RMB30 billion.[34] Data sourced from the Construction Department of Sichuan Province revealed that in severely damaged regions, the total number of collapsed schools covered an area of 1,997,228 $m^2$, comprising 1.3 percent of the area of the collapsed houses and buildings, which covered an area of 148,893,000,000 $m^2$.[35]

As of the end of April 2009,[36] according to official statistics in the thirty-nine most severely damaged counties (cities and regions), as many as 3,340 schools of all levels were in need of restoration and reconstruction. Of these, 2,455 schools needed partial reconstruction or repair and reinforcement. Preliminary estimates of the cost of partial reconstruction or repair and reinforcement were as much as RMB48.75 billion. Meanwhile, among the twelve most severely damaged counties identified in Sichuan province, more than 1,213 schools needed reconstruction and restoration, requiring an estimated RMB3.7 billion. Among the ninety-one more generally damaged counties (including three earthquake-stricken counties in Panxi, where the shock measured 8.3), a total of 4,592 schools were in need of restoration and reconstruction, requiring an estimated RMB10 billion. In this way, the reconstruction and restoration of all schools in the earthquake-stricken areas of Sichuan province was expected to cost a total of about RMB62.5 billion.

## *Loss of Life among Students and Teachers*

As of May 26, 2008, the Wenchuan earthquake had claimed 4,737 students' lives, and more than 16,000 students were injured in Sichuan province alone; the student deaths accounted for 7 percent of the total 67,000 deaths in Sichuan.[37] According to the statistics for 2009, a total of 5,335 students were reported dead or missing.[38]

Although specific statistical data on teacher deaths or injuries were not found in the official statistics (as these were counted in the total population of victims), a great many teachers were known to have lost their lives or were badly injured during the earthquake. Many of them sacrificed their lives when they tried to save their students rather than escape themselves. There are many shocking and moving stories told throughout the nation about how Ms. Wenting Yuan, Ms. Qian Xiang, Mr. Jijun Liu, and many other great teachers saved many students and were themselves finally killed in the process of saving others left in classrooms, and how students survived or were rescued in time because they had been shielded by their teachers' bodies.[39]

## *Psychological Trauma*

Due to the loss of families, homes, possessions, and the stunning shock from the disaster, teachers and students who survived the earthquake have been suffering from tremendous psychological trauma.[40] As a catastrophic event, an earthquake is likely to cause various mental disorders, of which post-traumatic stress disorder (PTSD) is the most prevalent. The Institute of Psychology of the Chinese Academy of Sciences (CAS) conducted a survey of about 6,000 students as part of its psychological assistance program in the quake-battered areas. They found that six months after the quake, the prevalence of PTSD was up to an after quake range of 12.7 to 22.1 percent, the prevalence rate with significant depressive symptoms was at a range of 13.2 to 21.5 percent. and the prevalence rate with marked anxiety reached a range of 20.2 to 29.9 percent; one year after the quake, students suffering from PTSD still represented approximately 13.4 percent of the whole population, those with significant depressive symptoms represented 16.1 percent, and those with marked anxiety 22.7 percent.[41]

# Post-Earthquake Educational Reconstruction: The Social Support System and its Functions

As mentioned above, the term "social support system" in this research specifically indicates the collected assistance, resources, and all other means of help and support provided by the system, comprising all levels of governments, social agents, and the public. In this section we will demonstrate how each agent of the support system functioned in the process of educational reconstruction, what role each played, how they interacted and collaborated to make a stronger contribution, and overall how they coordinated their efforts for post-disaster reconstruction in education. Hopefully, this model, with its unique Chinese socialist characteristics, will generate beneficial implications for other societies.

### *Government: Top-Down Leadership and Public Aid*

As China is a single-party state governed by the Communist Party (CPC), and the Central Government directly controls the whole educational system through the Ministry of Education, in the process of post-earthquake educational reconstruction, the Central Government serves as a leader in uniting the whole nation into one family, formulating strategic planning, legislation and polices, allocating and redistributing resources and funds, and collecting and coordinating other agents of the support system. In response to the summons from the Central Government, provincial governments, especially those from the more developed eastern and central regions of China, united to provide various forms of support to local governments in the disaster-stricken areas. In this sense, the social support system in the Chinese context is essentially government-led.

### *Leadership and United Power: The "Whole Nation System"*

Immediately after the earthquake, Chinese President Hu Jintao, Chinese Premier Wen Jiabao hurried to the front line of quake-hit areas frequently, and personally directed disaster relief and reconstruction work, demonstrating the great concern of CPC Central Committee.[42] On many occasions during the reconstruction process, the top leaders of the nation went to visit the survivors and supervise the reconstruction work in the affected regions. They put great emphasis on the health of the students and teachers, their psychological state, the conditions in which classes were being resumed, and the progress of school restoration and rebuilding. One high-priority common concern was to ensure the health of teachers and students; another was to ensure suitable capacity and high quality of the buildings where education was to take place. As Premier Wen said, the goal is:

> to build the schools into the safest, strongest and most reliable places which can withstand the test of history and disasters, and which can protect students and teachers from any harm.[43]

Under the leadership of the CPC, the Chinese Central Government fully demonstrated the advantages of socialist characteristics by initiating "the whole nation system", which means that the whole nation unites as one single power, with all people participating in and prioritizing post-disaster salvage and reconstruction work under the leadership of the CPC.[44] Immediately after the earthquake, the Chinese government made a large-scale allocation and delivery of the whole nation's human, material, and financial resources, and implemented a series of measures such as the one-on-one partnership aiding system, showing a unique institutional strength.

In general, the whole nation system is regarded as an ideological framework and practical operation system at critical crisis times with unique Chinese characteristics, which takes the Communist Party as the core leadership, aims to serve the people's fundamental interests, and is dominated by the Central People's Government and social unity and harmony. It is supported by great national material and spiritual resources, and is based on scientific and democratic decision-making. Such a system and mechanism executes centralized, unified, and coordinated work on a national scale through legislation, policy-making and administrative procedures.[45] Under the universal value that "human life is the first priority,"[46] the whole nation system in China's unique socialist context demonstrates immense power. With its powerful whole-nation system, from 2008–2010 the government allocated a total of RMB301.894 billion for reconstruction; all sectors of the government were prepared to allocate resources to support reconstruction projects and related policy implementations, and set up the so-called "green passages" for post-disaster reconstruction, which is a mechanism of unconditional support that prioritizes all tasks related to post-disaster reconstruction.[47]

### *Legislation and Policy Making: Mandatory Partnership Support*

Immediately after the Wenchuan earthquake, the State Council set up Headquarters for Earthquake Fighting and Disaster Relief (HEFDR) and consecutively issued policies and legislations to summon the united power of the whole nation and organize the salvage and restoration work.

The first legislation released was "The Notice of Approving and Forwarding the Current Progress in Earthquake Relief and the Missions for Next Phase: From the HEFDR Headquarter of the State Council" on May 28, 2008.[48] This notice summarized the "ordered, effective and influential" earthquake relief work of the previous phase, and planned deployment for the next phase. To be human-oriented was the primary value emphasized throughout the policy. As for education, the first requirement was that the provision of suitable spaces for teaching was to be prioritized, and that classes should be resumed as soon as possible.

Most distinctively in this law, a strategy for establishing and improving a one-on-one partnership-aiding mechanism was put forward. This required the unaffected provinces to help the severely damaged counties; several safe provinces were commissioned to help one severely damaged city under this bond partnership, and the whole nation's resources were reallocated in a short period to save the vulnerable as fast as possible. This strategy was given more operational details in subsequent legislation issued on June 11, 2008, "Notice from the State Council Office on Implementing the One-on-One Partnership Aiding System for Wenchuan Earthquake Restoration and Reconstruction."[49] According to the economic levels and regional development strategies of different provinces (cities), the Central Government set up the overall planning and designated nineteen eastern and central provinces (including autonomous municipalities like Beijing and Shanghai) to support twenty earthquake-stricken counties (one developed province helped two counties). Specifically, within the partnership bond, the provincial government supplying support had the autonomy to make plans as to what and how to provide the support for the affected county. They mainly targeted the financial, resource, school reconstruction, student placement and teaching force rebuilding needs of the stricken areas.

On June 29, 2008, the State Council issued another document, "Strategies for Supporting the Post Wenchuan Earthquake Restoration and Reconstruction,"[50] which focused more specifically on education reconstruction. It proposed to prioritize the reconstruction of public service facilities and required that reconstruction funds for public facilities be dominated by Government money, supplemented by social donations and other contributions.

On July 3, 2008, the State Council issued the "Guidance of the State Council on Wenchuan Post-Earthquake Restoration and Reconstruction."[51] In this document, the principles and guidelines of the reconstruction work were emphasized. These include the demand that scientific rules of development and people-oriented values were to be adhered to, and that nature was to be respected. A scientific model of reconstruction was to be adopted. The reconstruction of schools and other public facilities was again made the top priority, along with strict enforcement of mandatory construction standards so as to build schools in the safest and most secure places. Meanwhile, the opportunity for school reconstruction would also take into consideration the current rural and urban educational integration reform background, and adjust rural and urban school layouts to meet the requirement of integrating educational resources. For instance, high schools and secondary vocational schools originally in rural areas should be rebuilt in towns, and elementary school layouts should be relatively more concentrated and consolidated.

On September 19, 2008, the State Council issued the "Notice of the State Council on Printing and Distributing the Overall Project of Post Wenchuan Earthquake Restoration and Reconstruction."[52] This document primarily focused on reconstruction work in the educational field. Items included: a) to focus on compulsory education infrastructure reconstruction and to make overall arrangements for reconstructing enterprise-supported educational institutions and non-governmental educational institutions; b) to ensure the high-quality restoration and reconstruction of schools; c) to expand boarding schools and the registration ratio; d) to implement a volunteer teaching assistant project with the support of excellent teachers from elementary and secondary schools; e) to allocate the reconstruction sites of rural high schools, secondary vocational schools in towns, and elementary schools in rural areas; f) to create a reasonable distribution of the reconstruction sites of kindergartens and schools for special education; and g) to restore and reconstruct damaged universities and research institutions.

## *Initiating Collaboration between Different Sectors*

China's Ministry of Education, the Ministry of Construction, and other sectors also closely followed the Central Government's guidance and issued related policies to guarantee the implementation of educational reconstruction. On May 26, 2008, the Ministry of Education printed and distributed the "Plan on the Placement of Earthquake-Stricken Teachers and Students and the Preparation for Restoration and Reconstruction in Education."[53] This was the first legislation dealing specifically with educational reconstruction after disasters. It put forth ten missions and set up a detailed and specific agenda for educational reconstruction, such as strengthening students' psychological counseling, resuming classes as soon as possible, preparing the partnership-supporting resources, and intensifying the quality control of school buildings. On October 24, 2008, the Ministry of Education, the Ministry of Construction, and the National Development and Reform Commission jointly issued the "Guide of School Layout and Design in Post Wenchuan Earthquake Reconstruction." The sectors were to collaborate to build schools in the safest and most suitable places. In addition, the Ministry of Education also developed the "Reconstruction Plan for Post Wenchuan Earthquake Education" and the "Blueprint of School Layout and Design for the Post Wenchuan Earthquake Reconstruction," providing a scientific basis for post-quake reconstruction.

In the process of education reconstruction, the Central Government exhibited the most impressive and powerful leadership, which effectively and efficiently minimized the damaging effects on teachers and students arising from the crisis, and maximized the powers, assistance and support needed for post-disaster reconstruction. Under the leadership of the Central Government, the top-down cooperation between different levels of provincial and local government, as well as the collaboration between different sectors of the government, work was done quickly to support the affected students and teachers both physically and emotionally. Due to the leadership of the government, the victims received strong, tangible support in the form of rebuilt or new school buildings and facilities and financial resources, as well as strong intangible support, such as guidelines, advice, assistance and encouragement on how to recover from the worst conditions. The government designed a framework and laid a solid foundation for a powerful support system for the vulnerable education system after the disaster.

### *Organizations, Institutions, Enterprises and Other Social Public Forces*

At the start of the disaster relief, a large number of volunteers, psychological workers, and social workers travelled to the quake-hit areas, giving psychological comfort to teachers and students and helping them cope with their difficulties. Some professional psychological teams were already on hand, having always been stationed in the quake-hit areas to give psychological treatment to teachers and students. Finally, in the partnership aiding projects, enterprises and social organizations, in the form of social capital, also participated in aid projects and providing one-to-one assistance to schools. All of this support helped to boost the reconstruction of education in quake-hit areas.

### *Public Donations*

Making donations are one important way that the general public can participate in supporting post-disaster reconstruction. According to the

National Audit Report (2010), as of September 30, 2009, the total amount donated by the public nationwide reached RMB79.70 billion, including RMB68.79 billion in monetary donations and RMB10.91 billion in material/resource donations such as clothes, food, water, medicine, etc. RMB52.77 billion of the total amount donated has been spent, including RMB17.38 billion used for emergency assistance and RMB35.39 billion for post-disaster reconstruction. Of the total spent from donations, about RMB7.93 billion was spent on educational reconstruction, mainly restoring and reconstructing school buildings and facilities. The sources of these donations were sixteen charity foundations as well as organizations and individuals from provinces throughout the country.

A large number of private entrepreneurs who comprise a big part of the national economy also participated in the immediate post-disaster salvage work and the reconstruction process. Some with expertise in the educational and mass media industries, such as Mr. Yifu Shao from Hong Kong Television Broadcast Limited, donated RMB100,000,000, and Mr. Hongmin Yu from New Oriental Education and Technology Group donated RMB15 million especially to help the reconstruction of schools and facilities in the stricken areas. These entrepreneurs demonstrated their strong sense of social responsibility at the most critical time for the people.

*Volunteering*

According to the statistics from the Sichuan government,[54] in total about 1.18 million registered individual volunteers and 180,000 thousand group-based volunteers participated as volunteers in the salvage and reconstruction work after the disaster, amounting to 1.78 million interventions. This number does not include the innumerable volunteers who donated blood and came to help without registering. These volunteers risked their own lives in locating and rescuing survivors and retrieving bodies from the buildings damaged during the earthquake, and they contributed their efforts and expertise to provide voluntary assistance in terms of psychological counseling, teaching, medical assistance, and other services for reconstruction. These volunteers not only donated their physical efforts, resources and financial support, but the more importantly, they provided companionship to people who have lost their families, friends, even parts of their own bodies. These altruistic actions contribute the most powerful support to the victims and are helping greatly with the reconstruction process.

Besides, research institutes and universities either close to the stricken areas or from other provinces also provided strong support through the provision of professional knowledge and skills, especially in the form of psychological support and counseling, which greatly helped the stricken people to deal with the trauma. This will be expanded upon in more detail below. The counties which were severely hit by the disaster and their people were greatly and positively motivated by all the support from the government and from people from all walks of life in society. The victims of the disaster also took part themselves in the rescue and reconstruction process. This will also be looked at in more detail in the following section.

## Achievements Made and Lessons Learned

Under the mechanism of the joint efforts of the social support system led by the visible hand of the Central Government and with the cooperation of other social forces, the restoration work has been accomplished as efficiently and as quickly as possible.

*School Reconstruction*
The key to the rapid implementation of post-quake education reconstruction, especially with regard to school reconstruction, is the One-on-One Partnership Aiding System mentioned in last part of this chapter, which refers to the system set up for nineteen provinces to partner with twenty quake-stricken regions in order to provide help and to contribute to all aspects of restoration. Immediately after the disaster, students from the affected schools were temporarily transferred to other schools in the supporting provinces for schooling until their own schools were restored or rebuilt. Through the government-allocated funds, the provincial revenues, and funds donated by the public, these supporting provinces directly financed 62,552 students and provided free schooling to 7,904 students from quake-hit areas. Each supporting province also promptly developed an overall agenda to implement the reconstruction plans, and each was required to contribute no less than 1 percent of their revenue from the previous fiscal year towards restoring or reconstructing schools in their partner county, abiding by the safety standards stated by the State Council.

Thanks to the nineteen provinces' companionship, support, and assistance, together with the donations from local communities, enterprises, and social organizations, the post-quake school reconstruction proceeded quickly and in an orderly fashion, and was a remarkable achievement. According to the report from China Education Daily (2011), at the end of October 2011, of the 8,323 schools which needed to be rebuilt throughout 142 earthquake-hit counties in Sichuan province, 8,283 were completed— a completion rate of 99.52 percent. Among them, there were 3,001 schools to be rebuilt in the thirty-nine worst damaged counties, cities, and districts, and the severely damaged counties, as confirmed by national surveys. Of these, 2,978 schools were completed, a completion rate of 99.23 percent. The main structures of these schools were designed to withstand magnitude 8 earthquakes or stronger disasters, and the structural standard was set at fortifications capable of withstanding a magnitude 9 earthquake. The quality of the teaching facilities was also much higher than ever before.[55]

The reconstruction under the one-on-one partnership aiding system motivated the enthusiasm of the supporting provinces, and each province was permitted to create an autonomous reconstruction supporting plan in accordance with the specific environmental requirements of each affected county. For the partnership between Guangdong Province and Wenchuan County, the "New School, New Future" Project was initiated in Wenchuan County. In around fifteen months, Guangdong invested RMB870 million to complete building sixteen schools, including two secondary schools, ten elementary schools, and four kindergartens, with a total building area of 222,550 m$^2$, and sports areas of 160,000 m$^2$, benefiting a total of 15,080 students. This is 67,543 m$^2$ larger than the combined area of the eighty-three schools destroyed by the earthquake, and accommodates 1,000 more students than the previous student population. These buildings were tested to meet the national school building standards, are able to withstand severe disasters in excess of a magnitude 8.0 earthquake, and enable better and more equal allocation of educational resources.[56]

## *Psychological Rehabilitation*

How to intervene effectively to treat the psychological problems of teachers and students in earthquake-stricken areas to help them recover normal psychological well-being has been among top the priorities of education reconstruction since the earthquake. As mentioned above, social support is key to the psychological health of those who have survived a disaster. The role of the government-led social support system should therefore have the most potential and should generate the greatest effort in post-disaster reconstruction.

The Ministry of Education of the Central Government and the Department of Education of Sichuan Province both organized an expert psychological service group to provide professional psychological recovery assistance for teachers and students in the earthquake-stricken areas. Besides on-site visits, medication service, and a counseling clinic, the expert group also compiled pamphlets, guidelines, and handbooks to help disaster victims take advantage of companionship, courage, comfort, and recovery techniques by reading books on psychological self-recovery skills. Teachers, school administrators, and communities were also able to gain skills to provide psychological assistance to their students through reading the books.

The Department of Education of Sichuan Province initiated a series of teachers' rehabilitation plans. In 2008 and 2009, the Department organized and implemented the "Special Training Program of Supporting Teachers in Sichuan Earthquake-Hit Areas" and the "Training Program of Psychological Health Education to Elementary and Secondary School Teachers in Sichuan Earthquake-Hit Areas." Both programs provided group-based psychological rehabilitation training to schoolteachers who suffered serious trauma such as the loss of families or who were severely injured or disabled as a result of the disaster.

In order to help forget the trauma by being immersed in a brand-new environment, the Department of Education of Sichuan Province organized the earthquake-stricken teachers and students to go abroad or visit other provinces for recuperation. From 2008 to 2009, it was arranged that a total of 1,570 students from quake-hit areas visited Russia for recuperation. In August 2008, approximately 100 elementary and secondary students from quake-hit areas were sent to Hungary and Bulgaria for recuperation. In June 2008, eighty-nine students from quake-hit areas were sent to receive music therapy in Haikou, Hainan Province.

Apart from the centralized assistance from the government, all other social forces, including university research institutes such as the Institute of Psychology of Chinese Academy of Sciences, Beijing Normal University, Sichuan University, and Southwest University, NGOs such as the Chinese Red Cross, the Federation of Non-Governmental Organizations, the Children's Foundation of China, and the China Charity Federation, and many other organizations and individual volunteers participated in the whole process of psychological aid and companionship from the beginning to the present. These social organizations, either group- or individual-based, built temporary shelters and provided services in quake-hit areas by being fully involved in the lives of the victims and greatly helping the relief of mental suffering experienced by the students and teachers. For instance, the Institute of Psychology of China Academy of Sciences and the Chinese Psychological Society established a "Mianyang Service Station" to provide voluntary professional psychological assistance, which was well recognized by the recipients in the area and effectively helped with the local people's sufferings.

Based on the fully immersed participation by the government-led social support system, the project of psychological rehabilitation of students and teachers has experienced long-term combat success. According to a large-scale test launched by the Department of Education of Sichuan Province in late December 2009 on 7,962 students and 1080 teachers from five most badly affected areas, the total prevalence rate of PTSD is relatively low, at a range of 3.83 to 5.27 percent, which means that most of the sample population had recovered to a quite stable state of psychological health, although some teachers and students still displayed obvious PTSD symptoms.[57] Owing to the effective measures and overall support from all kinds of participants, the post-quake psychological rehabilitation of teachers and students is to date a success.

Challenges ahead include the recruitment and placement of more qualified psychology teachers for the reconstructed schools, ongoing professional training for the psychological health of teachers, adjustment of the curriculum to include post-disaster psychological relief for the students, and long-term follow-up on the students' and teachers' mental health conditions through research programs and scientific measurement techniques.

*Reconstruction of the Teaching Force*

Teachers being the most critical human capital of schools, the reconstruction work focusing on individual teachers and the whole teaching force of schools is regarded as the most important post-disaster mission. Such reconstruction is regarded as intangible intelligence reconstruction. The sources of support for this come mainly from the partner provinces that provide financial and logistical support, which were called "blood transfusions", and also from within the affected areas themselves, which was called "automatic blood generation".[58]

*Reconstruction of the Teaching Force: The Blood Transfusion Model*

The supporting provinces within the partnership program supported the affected teachers by assisting them with high-quality educational resources, establishing school partnerships, providing teaching assistance, initiating exchange programs for them to come and teach in the supporting provinces, and providing professional training services to the teachers in quake-hit areas. In this process, the nineteen partner provinces established a total of 411 school partnership programs, sent 2,380 excellent teachers to assist teaching in affected areas, and received 5,907 teachers from affected areas to receive training in the sponsored provinces.

In the case of the partnership between Beijing and Shifang, which was launched on March 25, 2009, Beijing Education Board mainly assisted in four aspects of teaching force development: on-site teaching assistance, professional training of teachers and school administrators on a regular basis, long-term one-on-one school partnership, and establishment of a long-distance training and resource-sharing platform between Beijing and Shifang teachers.[59]

As of September 2011, Beijing had sent three groups of education experts to Shifang, one in March 2009, one in November 2009, and one in May 2010 to attend local teachers' classes and assist with their teaching. These expert teachers also demonstrated lessons for students and discussion-based seminars for the local teachers. Almost 3,000 teachers of different subjects in Shifang received systematic training and guidance from the Beijing experts. These were regarded as beneficial and helpful in broadening their knowledge and enhancing their teaching skills. Besides, from April 2009 to 2010, 147 school administrators and 179 common core subject teachers received specially designed training in Beijing. These teachers will then help train and lead other local teachers and administrators upon completion of the training programs.

All thirty-five public schools in Shifang have found partners in Beijing and established one-on-one partnerships with them, through which the Beijing schools will be responsible for providing companionship and assistance in terms of teaching and instruction, school management, teachers' professional development, and educational quality enhancement. Such partnerships lay solid foundations for a long-term mutual support mechanism.

Currently, the "Shifang Long-Distance Education Training Network" is being put into practice. This website integrates the highest-quality online education resources of the Beijing schools, which include demonstration lessons, class design templates, and customized resources based on the needs of Shifang teachers. The 3,500 teachers from Shifang have all been given a learning card which enables them to visit the website and share all the resources therein free of charge. They can learn from and communicate with expert teachers and receive immediate instruction, making professional development possible at any time, in any place.

***Reconstruction of the Teaching Force: Automatic Blood-Generation Model***

Since the Departments of Education of local governments are directly in charge of teacher recruitment and placement, apart from the assistance provided by supporting provinces, Sichuan province, together with the local county-level governments, also initiated programs to restore and enhance their own teaching forces.

In response to teachers' demands after the disaster, the Department of Education of Sichuan Province recruited about 7,780 new teachers to schools in the affected areas. These new teachers include 5,242 of the official quota, 1,509 from the "Special Post Project" (a special teacher education program that sends graduates to teach in areas of greatest need), and 1,030 within and outside of the province as volunteer teachers. These teachers promptly fulfilled the immediate requirements, allowing students to resume classes and school activities.

In addition, Sichuan Province implemented a series of schemes such as the "Training Program of Assisting Elementary and Secondary School Teachers in Earthquake Stricken Areas", the "Training Program of Psychological Recovery to Teachers in Earthquake Stricken Areas", and the "Training Program for Principals to Enhance School Management in Earthquake Stricken Areas". All of these provide customized professional training designed for teachers and staff in schools in the stricken areas. These programs directly benefited 4,119 teachers and principals in the local elementary and secondary schools.

As compensation and for comfort, Sichuan Province also sponsored teachers from stricken areas by paying better welfare, providing material resources, and ensuring on-time distribution of salaries.

As some scholars hold, disasters can sometimes give rise to good opportunities for new developments.[60] Such is the case with the Wenchuan earthquake. A brand-new educational landscape has been created from the destruction as a result of the efficient and effective efforts of the government-led social support system.

## Conclusion

Post-Wenchuan-earthquake reconstruction in the educational sector achieved great success with the highly efficient and high-quality help of the government-led social support system. It was a matter of great concern to the leadership of the CPC Committee of the Central Government and the active collaboration between the ministries and commissions that related policies on education reconstruction after the Wenchuan earthquake were instantly formed and implemented. With the full participation of all the social forces in the system, the government-led program made it possible for original and subsequent reconstruction work to be carried out in a prompt, orderly and organized way, and the school reconstruction program was completed successfully in three years as planned (May 2008–May 2011).

The one-on-one partnerships established between the eastern and central provinces and the disaster-stricken provinces introduced an innovative and effective support model for vulnerable individuals and groups through the provision of direct companionship, material assistance, and physical and emotional care. This model demonstrates the unique collectivist culture and centralized political system of China, which generates tremendous united power and intelligence in crises through an effective and efficient top-down decision-making system. The leadership and decisiveness demonstrated by the Central Government, the implementation of Central Government policies and responsiveness of provincial and local county governments, the participatory actions of and fundamental supporting roles played by all other organizations, institutes, enterprises and individual volunteers, and the independent recovery efforts made by the strong-minded people from the stricken areas, together made the education reconstruction happen in a short time. However, the experience is particularly representative of the socialist and collectivist culture and context of China, while it may not be suitable in other contexts. Yet useful implications may be drawn from the successful experience of the Wenchuan earthquake reconstruction for other societies in the way that the whole nation united as one family, and that the government-led, top-down social support system functioned as a mechanism to help the post-disaster educational reconstruction.

# Notes

[1] This chapter is sponsored by research grants, including the MOE's major 2010 philosophy and social sciences research and development project, "Research on Building Mechanisms for an Integrated Urban-Rural Education System" (10JZD0041); the Municipality of Chongqing's 100 Leading Scholarly Academic Talents project; and the excellent doctoral dissertation nurturing project "Research on the International Educational Reform Patterns based on the Rural and Urban Regional Relations" (kb2011003).

[2] Fei Yuan, "On the Periodic Evaluation of the Post-Disaster Reconstruction of Education: A Theoretical Analysis on the Education Development," *Journal of Qingdao Technical College*, 24(3), 44–47; Shi-yong Jiang and Li-sheng Dai, "Oversea Reconstruction of Education after Disasters: Summary and its Enlightenment," *Journal of Changchun University of Science and Technology* (Social Sciences Edition), 23(6), 45–7.

[3] Priscilla Dass-Brailsford, "After the Storm: Recognition, Recovery, and Reconstruction," *Professional Psychology: Research and Practice*, 39(1), 24–30; Yan Chang, Suzanne Wilkinson, David Brunsdon, Erica Seville, and Regan Potangaroa, "An Integrated Approach: Managing Resources for Post-Disaster Reconstruction," *Disaster*, 35(4), 739–65; Toshihiko Hayashi, "Japan's Post-

Disaster Economic Reconstruction: From Kobe to Tohoku," *Asian Economic Journal*, 26(3), 189–210.

[4] Yan Chang, Suzanne Wilkinson, Regan Potangaroa, and Erica Seville, "Resourcing Challenges for Post-Disaster Housing Reconstruction: A Comparative Analysis," *Building Research & Information*, 38(3), 247–64; Paul K. Freeman, "Allocation of Post-Disaster Reconstruction Financing to Housing," *Building Research and Information*, 32(5), 427–37; Y. Q. Huang, "Allocation of Education Technology Facilities for the Rural Schools in Earthquake-Stricken Areas," *China Modern Educational Equipment* 2011, no. 14, 8–9.

[5] Jiqing Liu and Ming Li, "Post-Disaster Education: Developmental and Sustainable Reconstruction," *Journal of National Academy of Education Administration*, 2008 no. 11, 60–63; N. B. Zeng and C. C. Lai, "Teachers and Students Psychological Recovery after Disasters," *Education Science Forum*, 2009 no. 9, 59–68.

[6] Yuan.

[7] Yuan.

[8] Shi-yong Jiang and L.C. Kong, "Rebuilding of Teacher Identity and Professional Development: Values of Post-Disaster Restructuring of Teacher Professional Development," *Education Exploration*, 2011 no. 1, 106–7.

[9] Joy Lesnick and Katherine Schultz, "Out of Disaster Comes Opportunity: Initial Lessons from Teacher Mentoring in Banda Aceh, Indonesia," *Penn GSE Perspectives on Urban Education*, 4(2), 1–13; Hayashi; Southern Education Foundation, *New Orleans Schools Four Years after Katrina: A Lingering Federal Responsibility* (Atlanta, GA: Author, 2009); B. Zhou, "Turning Disaster into Opportunities for a Better, Modern, and More Equal Educational System." *Chengdu Daily*, August 12, 2010.

[10] Gerald Caplan, *Support Systems and Community Mental Health: Lectures on Concept Development* (New York, NY: Behavioral Publications, 1974), "The Family as Support System," in *Support Systems and Mutual Help: Multidisciplinary Explorations*, eds. Gerald Caplan and Marie Killilea, 19–36 (New York, NY: Grune and Stratton, 1976); M. Barrera Jr., "Distinctions between Social Support Concepts, Measures, and Models," *American Journal of Community Psychology*, 14(4), 413–45.

[11] Catherine A. Heaney and Barbara A. Israel, "Social Networks and Social Support," in *Health Behavior and Health Education: Theory, Research, and Practice*, eds. Karen Glanz, Barbara K. Rimer, and K. Viswanath, 4th ed. 189–210 (San Francisco, CA: Jossey-Bass, 2008).

[12] Sheldon Cohen and Thomas Ashby Wills, "Stress, Social Support, and the Buffering Hypothesis," *Psychological Bulletin*, 98(2), 310–57;Ross M. G. Norman, Ashok K. Malla, Rahul Manchanda, Raj Harricharan, Jatinder Takhar and Sandra Northcott, "Social Support and Three-Year Symptom and Admission Outcomes for First-Year Psychosis," *Schizophrenia Research*, 80(2–3), 227–34; Bert N. Uchino, "Social Support and Health: A Review of Physiological Processes Potentially Underlying Links to Disease Outcomes," *Journal of Behavioral Medicine*, 29(4), 377–387; Brian Lakey and Arika Cronin, "Low Social Support and Major Depression: Research, Theory, and Methodological Issues," in *Risk Factors for*

*Depression*, eds. Keith S. Dobson and David J. A. Dozois, 385–408 (San Diego, CA: Academic Press, 2008); Po Sen Chu, Donald A. Saucier, and Eric Hafner, "Meta-Analysis of the Relationships between Social Support and Well-Being in Children and Adolescents," *Journal of Social and Clinical Psychology*, 29(6), 624–45; Juliane Holt-Lunstad, Timothy B. Smith, and J. Bradley Layton, "Social Relationships and Mortality Risk: A Meta-Analytic Review," *PLoS Medicine*, 7(7), e1000316.; Shelley E. Taylor, "Social Support: A Review," in *The Handbook of Health Psychology*, ed. H. S. Friedman, 189–214 (New York, NY: OUP, 2011).

[13] Thomas Ashby Wills, "Supportive Functions of Interpersonal Relationships," in *Social Support and Health*, eds. Sheldon Cohen and S. Leonard Syme, 61–82 (Orlando, FL: Academic Press, 1985), "Social Support and Interpersonal Relationships," in, *Prosocial Behavior*, Review of Personality and Social Psychology, vol. 12, ed. Margaret S. Clark, 265–89 (London, UK: Sage, 1991); Bert N. Uchino, *Social Support and Physical Health: Understanding the Health Consequences of Relationships* (New Haven, CT: Yale University Press, 2004).

[14] Catherine Penny Hinson Langford, Juanita Bowsher, Joseph P. Maloney, and Patricia P. Lillis, "Social Support: A Conceptual Analysis," *Journal of Advanced Nursing*, 25(1), 95–100; M. L. Slevin, S. E. Nichols, S. M. Downer, P. Wilson, T. A. Lister, S. Arnott, J. Maher, R. L. Souhami, J. S. Tobias, A. H. Goldstone, et al., "Emotional Support for Cancer Patients: What Do Patients Really Want?" *British Journal of Cancer*, 74(8), 1275–9.

[15] Catherine A. Heaney and Barbara A. Israel, "Social Networks and Social Support," in *Health Behavior and Health Education: Theory, Research, and Practice*, eds. Karen Glanz, Barbara K. Rimer, and K. Viswanath, 4th ed. (San Francisco, CA: Jossey-Bass, 2008); James S. House, *Work Stress and Social Support* (Reading, MA: Addison-Wesley, 1981); Langford et al.

[16] Wills, 1991; Neal Krause, "Social Support, Stress, and Well-Being among Older Adults," *Journal of Gerontology*, 41(4), 512–9.

[17] Wills, 1991; Uchino, 2004.

[18] S. D. Yin and M. S. Zhu, "Construction of Social Support System for Rural Left-Home Children's Education: A Survey of the North Anhui Province in China," *Journal of the Chinese Society and Education*, 2006 no. 2, 14–16.

[19] Taylor.

[20] Yin and Zhu; P. Lei et al., "Construction of Social Support System Intervention Model for Rural Migrant Laborers' Left-Home Children." *Journal of Education*, 2010 no. 12, 30–33; L. G. Zhou and J. H. Feng, "A Review of Theories of Social Support," *Journal of Guangxi Teachers College* (Social Science Edition), 2005 no. 3, 11–14, 20.

[21] X. C. Yuan et al., "Components and Factors of Social Support System," *Shanghai Psychic Medical Journal*, 6(1), 38–42.

[22] B. Ruan, "Social Support System for Public Policies" *Theory Discussion*, 2011 no. 6, 16–9.

[23] Kira J. Baker-Doyle, "Circles of Support: New Urban Teachers' Social Support Networks," PhD dissertation, University of Pennsylvania, 2008.

[24] S. V. Burdette, "Social Support and Persistence among University Transfer Students Attending a Community College: A Grounded Theory Study," Ph.D. dissertation, Clemson University, 2009.
[25] Millicent Nelson and C. Douglas Johnson, "Individual Differences in Management Education: The Effect of Social Support and Attachment Style," *Academy of Educational Leadership Journal*, 15(1), 65–76.
[26] T. T. Zhuang and Y. J. Wang, "Survey on Factors of Social Support to Preschool Education of Migrant Children in the Urban and Rural Joint Areas in Shanghai," *Studies in Preschool Education*, 2010 no. 3, 24–27; David Scott McLaughlin, "Leveraging Relationships: Social Networks and the Education of Burmese Migrant Children," PhD dissertation, Michigan State University, 2010, ProQuest ID 815440467.
[27] Lei et al.; Yin and Zhu; X. Liu, X. Fan, and J. Shen, "Relationship between Social Support and Problem Behaviors of the Left-Home Students in Junior Middle School," *Psychological Development and Education*, 23(3), 98–102.
[28] H. Y. Wang, "The Study on Social Support for Rural Females of 5.12 Earthquake-Devastated Areas," Graduate thesis, Lanzhou University, 2010.
[29] L. Y. Zhao, "The Study of the Social Support Networks Provided for Adolescents from the Wenchuan Earthquake Area," Graduate thesis, China Youth University for Political Sciences, 2010.
[30] L. Chen, "The Study on Social Support System for College Students' Psychological Rebuilding after the Earthquake," Graduate thesis, Chengdu Technology and Engineering University, 2010.
[31] Ai-ying Geng, "The Role of Social Support in Post-Disaster Psychological Crisis Intervention," *Journal of Shandong University (Philosophy and Social Sciences)*, 2008 no. 6, 44–9; H. Guo, "Reconstructing Spiritual Home by Social Support System after Disaster," *Forum on Chinese Culture*, 2010 no. 3, 26–27; Yandong Zhao, "The Role of Social Network in Disaster Governance: An Example of Wenchuan Earthquake," *China Soft Science*, 2011 no. 8, 56–64.
[32] B. Gong and X. Yang, "Post-Disaster Reconstruction in Education," *Journal of Chinese Education*, 2008 no. 11, 9–12; National Institute of Education Sciences, "A Survey of Post-Disaster Educational Reconstruction in Sichuan," *Journal of Sichuan Administration College*, 2010 no. 3, 19–22.
[33] Post-Wenchuan Earthquake Education Reconstruction Research Project Team, *Post-Disaster Educational Reconstruction: The Case of 5.12 Wenchuan Earthquake in Sichuan China* (Beijing, China: Education and Science Press, 2011); National Bureau of Statistics of China, "2008 National Economic and Social Development Statistics Bulletin," National Bureau of Statistics of China Website, February 26, 2009.
[34] Post-Wenchuan Earthquake Education Reconstruction Research Project Team, *Post-Disaster Educational Reconstruction: The Case of 5.12 Wenchuan Earthquake in Sichuan China* (Beijing, China: Education and Science Press, 2011).
[35] H. W. Zhang, X. M. Hao, and H. T. Zhu, "A Review of Policy Studies about School Building Capacity in the Past Thirty Years," *Journal of Tsinghua University* (Social Science Edition), 2009 no. 1, 146–58.

[36] S.Y. He, "Adhering to Scientific Reconstruction and Reviving Sichuan Education," *Educational Research*, 2009 no. 12, 95–9.
[37] Zhang et al.
[38] Ibid.
[39] "Teachers Who Sacrificed Their Lives to Save Students during the Earthquake", Baidu Web site, May 27, 2009.
[40] He, 2009.
[41] Post-Wenchuan Earthquake Educational Reconstruction Research Team.
[42] L. H. Xu and G. S. Dai, "Experience of and Implications from the Post-Wenchuan Earthquake Reconstruction," *Journal of Technology and Science University* (Social Science Edition), 2010 no. 5, 16–9.
[43] Ministry of Education, "Report on Post-Wenchuan Earthquake School Restoration and Reconstruction by Ministry of Education," The Central People's Government of the People's Republic of China Website, May 11, 2009.
[44] Y. X. Lan, "Wenchuan Earthquake: A Literature Review," *China Nonprofit Review*, 3(2), 3–6.
[45] Ibid.
[46] D. C. Ye, "Human Life Priority and the National System," *Theory*, 2008 no. 6, 4.
[47] Xu and Dai.
[48] State Council, "The Notice of Approving and Forwarding the Current Progress in Earthquake Relief and the Missions for Next Phase: From the HEFDR Headquarter of the State Council (#16)," The Central People's Government of the People's Republic of China Website, May 28, 2008.
[49] State Council, "Notice from the State Council Office on Implementing the One-on-One Partnership Aiding System for Wenchuan Earthquake Restoration and Reconstruction (#53)," The Central People's Government of the People's Republic of China Web site, June 30, 2008.
[50] State Council, "Strategies for Supporting the Post Wenchuan Earthquake Restoration and Reconstruction (#21)," The Central People's Government of the People's Republic of China Web site, June 30, 2008.
[51] State Council, "Guidance of the State Council on Wenchuan Post Earthquake Restoration and Reconstruction (#22)," The Central People's Government of the People's Republic of China Web site, July 4, 2008.
[52] State Council, "Notice of the State Council on Printing and Distributing the Overall Project of Post Wenchuan Earthquake Restoration and Reconstruction (#31)," The Central People's Government of the People's Republic of China Web site, September 23, 2008.
[53] Ministry of Education, "Plan on the Placement of Earthquake-Stricken Teachers and Students and the Preparation for Restoration and Reconstruction in Education," People's Republic of China Ministry of Education Teach to Do Document #20084. May 26, 2008.
[54] Y. Jiang et al., "The Chinese Power from Millions of Volunteers for Post-Wenchuan Earthquake Reconstruction," *Xinhua Agency Chengdu Branch News*, May 15, 2009.
[55] L. Liu, "Achievements of the Post-Disaster School Reconstruction in Sichuan," *China Education Daily*, November 12, 2011.

[56] H. H. Deng and J. Lin, "Guangdong Province Supporting Reconstruction of 16 Schools in Wenchuan," *China Youth Daily*, August 28, 2009.
[57] Post-Wenchuan Earthquake Education Reconstruction Research Project Team, 2011.
[58] He, 2009.
[59] L. Y. J. Lian, "Post-Wenchuan Earthquake Reconstruction in Education Sector and the Related Model Research: An Example of Shifang City, Sichuan Province," Graduate thesis, Southwest Jiaotong University, 2011.
[60] Lesnick and Schultz.

# Bibliography

Baker-Doyle, Kira J. "Circles of Support: New Urban Teachers' Social Support Networks." PhD dissertation, University of Pennsylvania. 2008.

Barrera Jr., M. "Distinctions between Social Support Concepts, Measures, and Models." *American Journal of Community Psychology*, 1986, 14(4), 413–45.

Burdette, S. V. "Social Support and Persistence among University Transfer Students Attending a Community College: A Grounded Theory Study." PhD dissertation, Clemson University. 2009.

Caplan, Gerald. *Support Systems and Community Mental Health: Lectures on Concept Development*. New York, NY: Behavioral Publications, 1974.

—. "The Family as Support System." In *Support Systems and Mutual Help*: *Multidisciplinary Explorations*. Edited by Gerald Caplan and Marie Killilea. 19–36. New York, NY: Grune and Stratton, 1976.

Chang, Yan, Suzanne Wilkinson, David Brunsdon, Erica Seville, and Regan Potangaroa. "An Integrated Approach: Managing Resources for Post-Disaster Reconstruction." *Disaster*, 35(4), 739–65.

Chang, Yan, Suzanne Wilkinson, Regan Potangaroa, and Erica Seville. "Resourcing Challenges for Post-Disaster Housing Reconstruction: A Comparative Analysis." *Building Research & Information*, 38(3), 247–64.

Chen, L. "The Study on Social Support System for College Students' Psychological Rebuilding after the Earthquake." Graduate thesis, Chengdu Technology and Engineering University. 2010.

Chu, Po Sen, Donald A. Saucier, and Eric Hafner. "Meta-Analysis of the Relationships between Social Support and Well-Being in Children and Adolescents." *Journal of Social and Clinical Psychology*, 29(6), 624–45.

Cohen, Sheldon, and Thomas Ashby Wills. "Stress, Social Support, and the Buffering Hypothesis." *Psychological Bulletin*, 98(2), 310–57.

Dass-Brailsford, Priscilla. "After the Storm: Recognition, Recovery, and Reconstruction." *Professional Psychology: Research and Practice*, 39(1), 24–30.

Deng, H. H. and J. Lin. "Guangdong Province Supporting Reconstruction of 16 Schools in Wenchuan." *China Youth Daily*, August 28, 2009.

Freeman, Paul K. "Allocation of Post-Disaster Reconstruction Financing to Housing." *Building Research and Information*, 32(5), 427–37.

Geng, Ai-ying. "The Role of Social Support in Post-Disaster Psychological Crisis Intervention." *Journal of Shandong University (Philosophy and Social Sciences)*, 2008 no. 6, 44–9.

Gong, B., and X. Yang. "Post-Disaster Reconstruction in Education." *Journal of Chinese Education*, 2008 no. 11, 9–12.

Guo, H. "Reconstructing Spiritual Home by Social Support System after Disaster." *Forum on Chinese Culture*, 2010 no. 3, 26–27.

Hayashi, Toshihiko. "Japan's Post-Disaster Economic Reconstruction: From Kobe to Tohoku." *Asian Economic Journal*, 26(3), 189–210.

He, S.Y. "Adhering to Scientific Reconstruction and Reviving Sichuan Education." *Educational Research*, 2009 no. 12, 95–9.

—. Sichuan Practice of Post-Wenchuan Earthquake Reconstruction in Education. 2011. http://www.nier.go.jp/06_jigyou/kyouiku_sympo_h23/25_siryou.pdf

Heaney, Catherine A., and Barbara A. Israel. "Social Networks and Social Support." In *Health Behavior and Health Education: Theory, Research, and Practice*. Edited by Karen Glanz, Barbara K. Rimer, and K. Viswanath. 4th ed. 189–210. San Francisco, CA: Jossey-Bass, 2008.

Holt-Lunstad, Juliane, Timothy B. Smith, and J. Bradley Layton. "Social Relationships and Mortality Risk: A Meta-Analytic Review." *PLoS Medicine*, 7(7), e1000316. DOI: 10.1371/journal.pmed.1000316.

House, James S. *Work Stress and Social Support*. Reading, MA: Addison-Wesley, 1981.

Huang, Y. Q. "Allocation of Education Technology Facilities for the Rural Schools in Earthquake-Stricken Areas." *China Modern Educational Equipment*, 2011, no. 14, 8–9.

Jiang, Shi-yong, and Li-sheng Dai. "Oversea Reconstruction of Education after Disasters: Summary and its Enlightenment." *Journal of Changchun University of Science and Technology* (Social Sciences Edition), 23(6), 45–7.

Jiang, Shi-yong, and L.C. Kong. "Rebuilding of Teacher Identity and Professional Development: Values of Post-Disaster Restructuring of Teacher Professional Development." *Education Exploration*, 2011 no. 1, 106–7.

Jiang, Y. et al. "The Chinese Power from Millions of Volunteers for Post-Wenchuan Earthquake Reconstruction." *Xinhua Agency Chengdu Branch News*, May 15, 2009. http://www.gov.cn/jrzg/2009-05/15/content_1315960.htm

Krause, Neal. "Social Support, Stress, and Well-Being among Older Adults." *Journal of Gerontology*, 41(4), 512–9.

Lakey, Brian, and Arika Cronin. "Low Social Support and Major Depression: Research, Theory, and Methodological Issues." In Dobson, Keith S. and David J. A. Dozois. *Risk Factors for Depression*. 385–408. San Diego, CA: Academic Press, 2008.

Lan, Y. X. "Wenchuan Earthquake: A Literature Review." *China Nonprofit Review*, 3(2), 3–6.

Langford, Catherine Penny Hinson, Juanita Bowsher, Joseph P. Maloney, and Patricia P. Lillis. "Social Support: A Conceptual Analysis." *Journal of Advanced Nursing*, 25(1), 95–100. DOI: 10.1046/j.1365-2648.1997.1997025095.x

Lei, P., et al. 2010. "Construction of Social Support System Intervention Model for Rural Migrant Laborers' Left-Home Children." *Journal of Education*, 2010 no. 12, 30–33.

Lesnick, Joy, and Katherine Schultz. "Out of Disaster Comes Opportunity: Initial Lessons from Teacher Mentoring in Banda Aceh, Indonesia." *Penn GSE Perspectives on Urban Education*, 4(2), 1–13.

Lian, L. Y. J. "Post-Wenchuan Earthquake Reconstruction in Education Sector and the Related Model Research: An Example of Shifang City, Sichuan Province." Graduate thesis, Southwest Jiaotong University. 2011.

Liu, Jiqing, and Ming Li. "Post-Disaster Education: Developmental and Sustainable Reconstruction." *Journal of National Academy of Education Administration*, 2008 no. 11, 60–63.

Liu, L. "Achievements of the Post-Disaster School Reconstruction in Sichuan." *China Education Daily*, November 12, 2011.

Liu, X., X. Fan, and J. Shen. "Relationship between Social Support and Problem Behaviors of the Left-Home Students in Junior Middle School." *Psychological Development and Education*, 23(3), 98–102.

McLaughlin, David Scott. "Leveraging Relationships: Social Networks and the Education of Burmese Migrant Children." PhD dissertation. Michigan State University. 2010. ProQuest ID 815440467

Ministry of Education. "Plan on the Placement of Earthquake-Stricken Teachers and Students and the Preparation for Restoration and Reconstruction in Education." People's Republic of China Ministry of Education Teach to Do Document #20084. May 26, 2008. http://baike.baidu.com/view/2945469.htm#2

—. "Guide of School Layout and Design in Post Wenchuan Earthquake Reconstruction." 2008. http://www.moe.gov.cn/publicfiles/business/htmlfiles/moe/moe_1892/201001/xxgk_77147.htm

—. "Report on Post-Wenchuan Earthquake School Restoration and Reconstruction by Ministry of Education." The Central People's Government of the People's Republic of China Website, May 11, 2009. http://www.gov.cn/gzdt/2009-05/11/content_1311034.htm

National Audit Office, People's Republic of China. "The Audit Report of Monetary and Material Social Donation for Wenchuan Earthquake." *China News*, January 6, 2010. http://www.chinanews.com/gn/news/2010/01-06/2056700.shtml

National Bureau of Statistics of China. "2008 National Economic and Social Development Statistics Bulletin." National Bureau of Statistics of China Web site, February 26, 2009. http://www.stats.gov.cn/tjgb/ndtjgb/qgndtjgb/t20090226_402540710.htm

National Institute of Education Sciences. "A Survey of Post-Disaster Educational Reconstruction in Sichuan." *Journal of Sichuan Administration College*, 2010 no. 3, 19–22.

Nelson, Millicent, and C. Douglas Johnson. "Individual Differences in Management Education: The Effect of Social Support and Attachment Style." *Academy of Educational Leadership Journal*, 15(1), 65–76.

Ning, Wei-wei, and Jian Xu. "Post-Disaster Psychological Recovery and Psychology Education." *Journal of Southwest Jiaotong University* (Social Sciences Edition), 2008(4), 1–4.

Norman, Ross M. G., Ashok K. Malla, Rahul Manchanda, Raj Harricharan, Jatinder Takhar and Sandra Northcott. "Social Support and Three-Year Symptom and Admission Outcomes for First-Year Psychosis." *Schizophrenia Research*, 80(2–3), 227–34.

Ruan, B. "Social Support System for Public Policies." *Theory Discussion*, 2011 no. 6, 16–9.

Post-Wenchuan Earthquake Education Reconstruction Research Project Team. *Post-Disaster Educational Reconstruction: The Case of 5.12 Wenchuan Earthquake in Sichuan China*. Beijing, China: Education and Science Press, 2011, 47–64.

Slevin, M. L., S. E. Nichols, S. M. Downer, P. Wilson, T. A. Lister, S. Arnott, J. Maher, R. L. Souhami, J. S. Tobias, A. H. Goldstone, et al.

"Emotional Support for Cancer Patients: What Do Patients Really Want?" *British Journal of Cancer*, 74(8), 1275–9.

Song, Chun. "The System of Social Support: The Construction of the External Environment of Migrant Children's Education." *Journal of Education Institute of Taiyuan University*, 28(4), 39–42.

Southern Education Foundation. *New Orleans Schools Four Years after Katrina: A Lingering Federal Responsibility*. Atlanta, GA: Author, 2009.

State Council. "The Notice of Approving and Forwarding the Current Progress in Earthquake Relief and the Missions for Next Phase: From the HEFDR Headquarter of the State Council (#16)." The Central People's Government of the People's Republic of China Website, May 28, 2008. http://www.gov.cn/zwgk/2008-05/30/content_999288.htm

—. Notice from the State Council Office on Implementing the One-on-One Partnership Aiding System for Wenchuan Earthquake Restoration and Reconstruction (#53)." The Central People's Government of the People's Republic of China Website, June 30, 2008. http://www.gov.cn/zwgk/2008-06/30/content_1031467.htm

—. Strategies for Supporting the Post Wenchuan Earthquake Restoration and Reconstruction (#21)." The Central People's Government of the People's Republic of China Website, June 30, 2008. http://www.gov.cn/zwgk/2008-06/30/content_1031467.htm

—. "Guidance of the State Council on Wenchuan Post Earthquake Restoration and Reconstruction (#22)." The Central People's Government of the People's Republic of China Website, July 4, 2008. http://www.gov.cn/zwgk/2008-07/04/content_1036351.htm

—. "Notice of the State Council on Printing and Distributing the Overall Project of Post Wenchuan Earthquake Restoration and Reconstruction (#31)." The Central People's Government of the People's Republic of China Website, September 23, 2008. http://www.gov.cn/zwgk/2008-09/23/content_1103686.htm

Taylor, Shelley E. "Social Support: A Review." In *The Handbook of Health Psychology*. Edited by M. S. Friedman. 189–214. New York, NY: OUP, 2011.

"Teachers Who Sacrificed Their Lives to Save Students During the Earthquake." Baidu Web site, May 27, 2009. http://zhidao.baidu.com/question/99009980.html

Uchino, Bert N. *Social Support and Physical Health: Understanding the Health Consequences of Relationships*. New Haven, CT: Yale University Press, 2004. 16–17.

—. "Social Support and Health: A Review of Physiological Processes Potentially Underlying Links to Disease Outcomes." *Journal of Behavioral Medicine*, 29(4), 377–387.
Wang, H. Y. "The Study on Social Support for Rural Females of 5.12 Earthquake-Devastated Areas." Graduate thesis, Lanzhou University. 2010.
Wang, Z. D. "A Report on the Survey of Teacher Force Reconstruction in the 5.12 Earthquake Stricken Areas of Sichuan." *Education Science Forum*, 2009 no. 3, 66–76.
Wills, Thomas Ashby. "Social Support and Interpersonal Relationships." In *Prosocial Behavior. Review of Personality and Social Psychology*, vol. 12. Edited by Margaret S. Clark. 265–89. London, UK: Sage, 1991.
—. "Supportive Functions of Interpersonal Relationships." In *Social Support and Health*. Edited by Sheldon Cohen and S. Leonard Syme. 61–82. Orlando, FL: Academic Press, 1985.
Xu, L. H. and G. S. Dai. "Experience of and Implications from the Post-Wenchuan Earthquake Reconstruction." *Journal of Technology and Science University* (Social Science Edition), 2010 no. 5, 16–9.
Ye, D. C. "Human Life Priority and the National System." *Theory*, 2008 no. 6, 4.
Yin, S. D. and M. S. Zhu. "Construction of Social Support System for Rural Left-Home Children's Education: A Survey of the North Anhui Province in China." *Journal of the Chinese Society and Education*, 2006 no. 2, 14–16.
Yuan, Fei. "On the Periodic Evaluation of the Post-Disaster Reconstruction of Education: A Theoretical Analysis on the Education Development." *Journal of Qingdao Technical College*, 24(3), 44–47.
Yuan, X. C., et al. "Components and Factors of Social Support System." *Shanghai Psychic Medical Journal*, 6(1), 38–42.
Zeng, N. B., and C. C. Lai. "Teachers and Students Psychological Recovery after Disasters." *Education Science Forum*, 2009 no. 9, 59–68.
Zhang, H. W., X. M. Hao, and H. T. Zhu. "A Review of Policy Studies about School Building Capacity in the Past Thirty Years." *Journal of Tsinghua University* (Social Science Edition), 2009 no. 1, 146–58.
Zhao, L. Y. "The Study of the Social Support Networks Provided for Adolescents from the Wenchuan Earthquake Area." Graduate thesis, China Youth University for Political Sciences. 2010.

Zhao, Yandong. "The Role of Social Network in Disaster Governance: An Example of Wenchuan Earthquake." *China Soft Science*, 2011 no. 8, 56–64.

Zhou, B. "Turning Disaster into Opportunities for a Better, Modern, and More Equal Educational System." *Chengdu Daily*, August 12, 2010.

Zhou, L. G., and J. H. Feng. "A Review of Theories of Social Support." *Journal of Guangxi Teachers College* (Social Science Edition), 2005 no. 3, 11–14, 20.

Zhuang, T. T., and Y. J. Wang. "Survey on Factors of Social Support to Preschool Education of Migrant Children in the Urban and Rural Joint Areas in Shanghai." *Studies in Preschool Education*, 2010 no. 3, 24–27.

# Chapter Six

## Ecosystem Services in the Context of Rapid Urbanization in China: Towards Sustainable Land Use Planning Mechanisms

### Xinyue Ye and Hao Zhang

**Introduction**

With the ongoing trend of urbanization, it is estimated that more than half of the world's population resides in urban areas, and this percentage is predicted to rise to 69.6 percent by 2050. The growth of urban areas and the impact of human activities on ecosystems have been leading issues of ecological interest. The impact of LULC (land use/land cover) change raises growing concerns about the processes and functions of ecosystems. Urbanization is considered the most important driver of climate change, though total urban area only accounts for a small proportion of the earth. As addressed in previous studies, intensive and rapid urbanization generates human-induced LULC change, which exacerbates impacts on the climate system. Changes due to multi-scale factors such as microclimatology, biophysical features, urban form, urban size, and population density play a key role in modifying the local and regional climate. Thus, understanding the role of the impact of urban land-use dynamics on the climate system is of interest in the context of global warming. Rapid urbanization and pervasive LULC change have significantly stimulated economic prosperity worldwide. However, unprecedented urban growth has triggered drastic land use conversion, either replacing wild lands with semi-natural lands or using semi-natural lands for urban development. Inevitably, such land use processes have altered the structure, pattern, and functionality of the ecosystems which provide vital services supporting human society.

In the post-war era, population growth and economic expansion have been the primary drivers of LULC change worldwide, especially in developing countries that prioritize economic prosperity, which has been encouraged, admired, and pursued by government agencies and individuals. Seventy percent of the world's largest cities can now be found in the developing world. The rapid urbanization and pervasive LULC change occurring in fast-growing developing countries such as China, India, Pakistan, Turkey, and the countries of Latin America have been attracting increasing attention.

China is the largest urbanizing nation in the world.[1] Over the past three decades, economic expansion has stimulated unprecedented urbanization in China due to its open-door policy and the process of globalization. As the preferred destination for investment, coastal provinces have been spearheading phenomenal national growth and serving as engines of China's economic growth. This dramatic transition has led to accelerated urban expansion and has attracted millions of domestic migrants and overseas investors. Meanwhile, huge areas of arable land, scrub land, waterways, and marshland, as well as other wild lands have been rapidly developed to meet strong demand stemming from urbanization and industrial development. Consequently, these regions face pronounced environmental pollution, ecological deterioration and associated economic loss, which inevitably impair the sustainability of regional development. Given the important role of coastal regions in China's economy, there is an urgent need to address these emerging environmental challenges, because the increasing demand for land use will place heavy pressure on natural and semi-natural ecosystems.

Ecosystem services refer to the vital benefits from ecosystem functions that underlie the foundation of human society. Ecosystem services and their value have received much attention in scholarly research on the relationship between natural resources and the human environment. However, it is still a great challenge to incorporate an ecosystem services valuation (ESV) approach into land use and urban planning, although the concepts of ecosystem services, natural capital, and ESV techniques have provided new perspectives for a better understanding of the value of the survival of our environment and the roots of human-environment conflict.

## China in Transition

After China's economic reforms began in the late 1970s, economic growth has been its top policy concern and the paramount political issue in this transitional country. In addition, China has experienced unprecedented development since 1978, the year that the country's radical economic reforms were launched. Today China has the second-largest national economy in the world. Many analysts thus speculate that if China's current rate of development continues, the economic hegemony of the U.S. will be displaced by that of China in this century. Such dramatic economic growth has been a hallmark of China's development and rise, generating escalating demands for energy and resources, which has resulted in environmental damage stemming from the widespread exploitation of natural resources. This environmental damage is due to economic growth driven by a single-minded focus on GDP.

From local to national levels, China's dramatically growing economy and ambitious regional development plan have been increasingly accompanied by a variety of serious and catastrophic negative outcomes, such as the loss of biodiversity, degradation/depletion of natural resources, and mounting environmental pollution. To make matters worse, the environmental impact of the quickly expanding economy has not only been concentrated in China, but also affected the status of the environment in Asia and the whole world. At the same time, China's industrial growth and fast urbanization have caused a mounting broad environmental concern because the fortunes of regions and nations have been tightly woven. China's booming economy is generating an intense and unparalleled request for energy and resources beyond its own land. Disastrous effects on health and the environment will gradually rise if China's economic development style is not adjusted and actions are not carried out to address this challenge. Unless emissions are significantly curtailed within a reasonable timeframe, global warming will be sooner or later both irreversible and exacerbated, leading to stronger hurricanes, higher sea levels, and other types of environmental and climate disasters. Such situations contribute to a cycle of continued warming and accumulated environmental disaster, thus limiting both the short- and long-term sustainability of the global environment.

It is an alarming fact that sixteen of the world's twenty most polluted cities are in China. It is estimated that about 14,000 new cars appear on the roads per day in China. The present rate of energy consumption is generating immeasurable consequences, and environmental damage will eventually yield unimaginable and terrible outcomes.

Since 1978, China has enjoyed unprecedented economic growth and undergone remarkable social restructuring. The dramatic transition in this continuing dynamic economic system has led to accelerated urban expansion and has driven more people, especially those who have lost their land, to seek employment opportunities and residency in urban areas.

The number of cities in China has rapidly increased from 193 in 1978 to 660 in 2008. Meanwhile, the total urban population increased from 172.45 million to 606.67 million over the same period. In the past three decades, rapid economic and population growth have triggered these trends in the developing regional and international metropolitan areas of China. China's twenty fastest-growing metropolitan areas (including Beijing, Tianjin, Suzhou, Shanghai, Hangzhou, Guangzhou, and Shenzhen) are located primarily in the coastal region. These major metropolitan areas are the preferred destination for millions of domestic migrants and overseas investors, and have been the engines of China's economic growth.[2] Unfortunately, only 26 percent of land in China is suitable for urban development. Inevitably during the unprecedented transition from a largely agricultural society to a modern and industrialized society, huge areas of arable land, forest, and grassland, as well as numerous bodies of water, have been used in new ways to meet the strong demand stemming from urbanization and industrial development. With the rapid development of the economy and urban expansion, these areas have suffered environmental pollution, ecological deterioration, and economic loss.[3] Given the important role of these metropolitan areas in China's economy, there is an urgent need to address these emerging environmental challenges and develop policies for sustainable development.

China's unprecedented and multifaceted growth has generated many fascinating issues for scholarly research. Understanding the urban changes in China would allow appropriate strategies and policies to be formulated to facilitate future sustainable development in China. As the world's largest developing country with nearly three decades of almost double-digit economic growth, the cost of China's systemic shift from state socialism to a market economy has been environmental deterioration. With growing demand and policy support, the urban transformation has also caused various land use and environmental problems, including reductions in rural and agricultural land, landscape fragmentation, loss of wetland and biodiversity, water and air pollution, threats to urban health and safety, and traffic congestion. Severe resource constraints and increased environmental stress have brought the environment to a tipping point.

Rapid urbanization continues to generate a profound environmental impact through the nexus of political, economic and technological access and control. The overall environmental quality is worsening in China, with environmental pollution equivalent in monetary terms to an estimated annual loss of 3 to 8 percent of GDP. In addition, environmental pollution has caused serious health issues. These pressures are likely to jeopardize economic development and sustainability. The pro-growth and resource-intensive strategy has certainly led to environmental deterioration and thus has raised environmental awareness in the nation.

The accelerated growth of cities has attracted considerable attention from scholars, planners, and policy makers. Rapid urban growth of cities is usually accompanied by an increased burden on the urban environment due to growing energy use. This in turn causes increasing deterioration of air and water quality and gives rise to noise pollution and the loss of agricultural and natural land to urban land. Urban population growth, its consequent real estate development and urban land transformation, as well as urban production and consumption activities, have demanded more resources and exerted more burdens on the environment, from air and water to land, thereby affecting the environment in various ways. As a result of the urbanization process, dramatic LULC change has taken place in most of China's territory. Land use patterns have been diversified as a response to the increased demand for urban land for industrial, residential, and infrastructural uses, as well as for ecological conservation. LULC change, as a consequence of rapid urbanization, can have environmental impacts on hydrologic, climatic, and socio-economic systems.[4] Rampant urban growth/sprawl and massive encroachment on agricultural land have led to severe environmental problems in China.[5] Urban sprawl in China is also related to many economic factors, such as globalization, rural industrialization, improvements in transportation, and the lack of land management or a monitoring system.[6]

China has achieved significant economic development, reaching an annual GDP growth rate of 10 percent since the initiation of economic reform and the open-door policy in 1978. Economic reforms have liberalized and globalized the Chinese economy. At the same time, urbanization has led to the destruction of sensitive ecosystems and has altered the hydrology of urban areas and their immediate vicinities. Hence, urbanization has not only a local environmental impact but also leaves a significant "ecological footprint" further afield.[7] Many scholars are exploring a wide range of associated topics, including the characteristics of environmental problems and how this is related to China's urban transition. This paper also discusses the dynamics of the land use patterns and environmental issues at all levels in China. Finally, the consequences of this growth are explored, as well as the challenges Chinese cities face and how this can inform future public policies and management strategies.

However, in planning for sustainability, we need to move beyond city limits and consider the entirety of the human-dominated system, which depends on natural ecosystem services. These services refer to vital benefits from ecosystem functions that underlie the foundation of human society.[8] Scholarly research also included new explorations in both concepts and ESV techniques.[9] This emerging literature offers a new perspective for better understanding the value of our environment and the roots of human-environment conflicts.[10] A number of recent case studies also focused on China, which has witnessed an impressive rate of urban growth during the last three decades. Despite this analytical progress, however, due to constraints inherent in the methods and techniques of ESV, it remains a difficult task to examine quantitatively the relationship between changes in ESV and the sustainability of the human-dominated ecosystem. It is especially difficult to characterize the relationship between urban growth patterns, changes in ESV, and the consequent loss of ecological capacity supporting the human-dominated ecosystem.

China's dramatic urban growth and changing environmental dynamics since the reform have generated many intriguing issues and challenges for scholarly research and policy-making. Historically and politically, Chinese cities have developed into modern metropolitan areas in very different ways from those in Western countries and other developing countries. In China, private land ownership is prohibited and the government supervises the allocation and development of land resources. The government therefore plays the key role in guiding urban planning and regional development and in ensuring an orderly transition from the old planned economy to the current market-oriented economy. With growing public awareness of sustainability issues with regard to the environment, society, and the economy, any government plan should maximize the benefit of land use and minimize potential risks, effectively balancing conflicts between land use and environmental deterioration, establishing the necessary urban infrastructure and providing services. The importance of ESV as a useful tool in enhancing land use planning has been widely recognized.[11] Unfortunately ESV is seldom used in practice, despite the clear advantages of this approach and the growing number of case studies that point to its usefulness. However, given China's robust economic growth and the rapid expansion of built-up land, it seems that the alarming level of ESV deterioration was not taken into consideration, nor did it influence the government's land use policy.

The following facts may explain why little attention has been paid to the ESV approach in the policy-making sphere. First, due to the underlying uncertainties and constraints in present models of ESV,[12] it is still difficult to persuade policy-makers that ESV is a useful tool in practice. This may be because, in most of the case studies, the basis for the ESV calculation is the simple method developed by Costanza et al.[13] This means that uncertain factors such as temporal and spatial scale effects, landscape heterogeneity, and numerous evaluation models inevitably lead to conflicting and doubtful results, despite the fact that the coefficients of ESV associated with land cover types are usually adjusted to reflect the characteristics of a given study area.[14] For instance, a recent criticism is that in most existing studies, the ESV of built-up land is usually set as zero, regardless of any positive or negative effects of the built-up land on the environment.[15] However, in a fast-growing metropolitan area with millions of inhabitants, ignoring the effects of the built-up land may lead to biased estimates of regional ESV and may mislead decision-makers and planners. Moreover, trade-offs will occur when the provision of one ecosystem service is reduced as a consequence of the increased use of another ecosystem service. According to our estimate, however, the ESV for all forms of land cover declined over the study period. We did not detect such trade-offs. In the face of rapid population growth and urban expansion, the roles of urban green space and traditional cultural resources are limited because these spaces occupy a very small proportion of the human-dominated ecosystem.

Secondly, knowledge gaps on how to quantify ESV accurately, how to apply it in practice, and how to communicate information to policy-makers and the general public are still thorny issues for scholars and urban/environmental planners. Thirdly, the government agencies responsible for land use planning tend to focus on land price and compensation for land requisition and relocation. Although the ESV approach of measuring regional ecosystem services in monetary value is an important and easy tool for managing land resources and development, there are very few skilled and qualified ESV auditors working in government agencies. Due to the complexity and uncertainty of assigning monetized value, ESV has not been officially adopted and therefore serves only an ancillary role, without any support from laws or regulations. Consequently, local authorities tend to allow the conversion of low-return lands into high-return developmental land when facing trade-offs between urban expansion and non-urban land use.[16] In fact, an ESV approach integrated with land use and urban planning can yield both visual and computational outputs, which comprehensively reveal the relationship between gains and losses of vital ecosystem services, land-use intensity, and socioeconomic change in the context of rapid urbanization. Unfortunately, so far, there are no straightforward solutions to address these issues. Thus, to a large degree, these technologies frustrate the stakeholders and decision-makers who are involved in the process of land use planning. Therefore, in future research, more accurate assessment methods and evaluation models for ESV are urgently needed to achieve sustainable land use and regional development.

## Data and Methodology

Many studies combine time series of LULC data, landscape metrics, gradient analysis, and socioeconomic factors, using an integrated approach of remote sensing (RS), geographical information systems (GIS), and statistical analysis. Time series of LULC data sets were produced from multi-spectral Landsat TM/ETM+ imagery. Based on the land use classification system released by the China National Committee of Agricultural Divisions (1984), five land use types are classified in most metropolitan areas as built-up land (including urban area and intensive rural settlement), cropland, fallow land, forest, and water bodies (mainly rivers, channels, ponds, and reservoirs). Thus, these data were available for further study. Furthermore, a cross-tabulation detection method was employed to detect changes in LULC. The land use change matrix which showed quantitative data of the overall LULC changes over a number of years in the study area can be produced. Based on the main types of gains and losses in each category shown by the change matrix, land use transfer images and a land use transfer matrix for each type can also be created.

To measure land fragmentation under the pressure of human activities, especially the recent rapid transition of land use due to urban growth and socioeconomic development, landscape metrics at the class and landscape levels can be selected. Firstly, three class-level metrics—number of patches (NP), mean patch size (MPS), and largest shape index (LSI)—can be employed to measure the average fragmentation. Secondly, three landscape-level metrics—Contagion Index (CONTAG), Landscape Division Index (DIVISION), and Splitting Index (SPLIT)—can be employed to depict the fragmentation distribution along the cross-sections to capture the landscape configuration.[17] The cross-section methodology has been applied to detect fragmentation patterns along the urban-rural gradient.[18]

The landscape indices were computed as follows:

$$NP = N_i \quad (1)$$

where $N_i$ is the patch number of the landscape type (class) $i$. Patch density (PD):

$$PD = \frac{N_i}{A} \quad (2)$$

where $N_i$ is the number of class $i$ and $A$ is the total area size. Mean patch size (MPS):

$$MPS = \frac{A_i}{N_i} \quad (3)$$

where $A_i$ is the area *size* of class $i$ and $N_i$ is the number of class $i$. Largest shape index (LSI):

$$LSI = \frac{e_i}{\min e_i} \quad (4)$$

Where $e_i$ is the total length of the edge (or perimeter) of class $i$ in terms of the number of cell surfaces; $\min e_i$ is the minimum total length of the edge (or perimeter) of class $i$ in terms of the number of cell surfaces. Contagion (CONTAGION):

$$CONTAGION = \left[1 + \frac{\sum_{i=1}^{m}\sum_{k=1}^{n}\left(p_i \times \frac{g_{ik}}{\sum_{k=1}^{m} g_{ik}}\right) \times \left(\ln p_i \times \frac{g_{ik}}{\sum_{k=1}^{m} g_{ik}}\right)}{2\ln(m)}\right] \times 100 \quad (5)$$

where $P_i$ is the proportion of the landscape occupied by patch type (class) $i$, $g_{ik}$ is the number of adjacencies (joins) between pixels of patch types (classes) $i$ and $k$ is based on the double-count method, and $m$ is the number of patch types (classes) present in the landscape, including the landscape border, if there is one. Landscape Division Index (DIVISION):

$$DIVISION = 1 - \sum_{i=1}^{m}\sum_{j=1}^{n}\frac{a_{ij}^2}{A^2} \quad (6)$$

where $a_{ij}$ is the area of patch $ij$ and $A$ is the total landscape area. DIVISION ranges [0, 1] equals 0 when the landscape consists of a single patch, whereas it equals 1 when the landscape in every cell is a separate patch. Splitting Index (SPLIT):

$$SPLIT = \frac{A^2}{\sum_{i=1}^{m}\sum_{j=1}^{n} a_{ij}^2} \quad (7)$$

where the definition of $a_{ij}$ and $A$ are same as above. This index is unitless: it equals 1 when the landscape consists of a single patch, and its upper limit is constrained by the ratio of landscape area to cell size.

The valuation of ESV is a useful tool to better understand the importance of ecosystem services. The estimated ESV across different years can be computed as follows:

$$ESV = \sum_{i=1}^{m}\sum_{j=1}^{n} A_i \times VC_{ij} \quad (8)$$

where $A_i$ is the area (ha) of land cover for type $i$ and $VC_{ij}$ is the value coefficient of ecosystem service function for type $j$ (RMB Yuan/ha) combined with land cover type $i$.

## Discussion

Analysis of ESV as a consequence of LULC change helps quantify environmental costs and benefits of different land planning decisions and thus allows decision-makers to better understand different trade-offs for efficient ecosystem management.[19] In this context, incorporating the ESV approach into land use planning provides a practical means of efficient ecosystem management and rational land use. Given the growth over the past decades, China will face challenges of scarcity of land resources, population growth, and environmental protection. The recent transition has given rise to strong demand for balancing the conflicts between human needs and nature. Recent case studies in China have shown that well-governed policies for urban planning and land use will produce positive results by reinforcing reforestation and promoting land use zoning, as assessed with enhanced regional ESV.[20] This result, in turn, will inspire and encourage decision-makers and planners to seek more rational policies. However, due to China's limited experience in this field, it is regrettable that the ESV approach and land use planning are two independent aspects of development. As a result of this, diagnostic analyses of the shortcomings in present land use policies and implications have been addressed.

Institutionally, according to the Chinese constitution, the government assumes responsibility for any activities related to land allocation, land development, and land marketing. The dynamics of the physical environment reveal the conflicts arising from the fast-growth, resource-intensive, and export-oriented development strategy promoted by the government. Thus, the government plays the key role of "politically correct and economically rewarding" entrepreneurial activities in guiding land use, urban planning, and regional development, including new sites for natural resource extraction and transportation infrastructure. It is a fact that local governments rely heavily for their financial budgets on the granting of land-use rights and land development. How to maximize the economic benefits from land development and marketing is the primary issue influencing decision-makers. As a result, it is very common for local authorities to allow the conversion of low-return lands into high-return developmental land in well-developed regions of the Yangtze River basin when facing trade-offs between urban expansion and non-urban land use.

As the fastest-growing economy in the world, China is seriously challenged and limited by the issues of environmental degradation during its transition from a planned economy to a more profit-seeking entrepreneurial state. In many Chinese cities and regions, regional ESV appears to decrease remarkably in response to dramatic urbanization at a highly variable rate.[21] Unfortunately, it seems that the alarming level of ESV deterioration was not given due attention in many recent urban planning projects. In addition, it did not influence the government's land use policy. Largely due to educational, scientific, legislative and political constraints, citizens are still remote from policy decision-making processes for land development and urban planning,[22] although public participation has been gradually recognized as a necessary element in advancing efficient land use and sustainable land development. The most important and thorny issues are the knowledge gaps between different stakeholders. In practice, how to quantify ESV accurately, how to incorporate the ESV approach into land use planning, and how to communicate information to policy-makers and the general public are still thorny issues. Due to the underlying uncertainties and constraints in present ESV models, it is still difficult to persuade the government agencies responsible for land use planning to look beyond land price and compensation for land requisition and relocation. In addition, there are many debates among researchers, planners, and decision-makers on the complexity and uncertainty of assigning monetary value for different ecosystem services. Consequently, this may mislead the general public and weaken the role of public participation in land development and urban planning. Thus, in the long run there is an urgent need for the ESV approach to be incorporated into land use planning, focusing on the relationship between gains and losses of vital ecosystem services, land-use intensity, and socioeconomic change in the context of rapid urbanization. The notion of sustainable development fully acknowledges the constraints on growth and capacity to cope with transformation, emphasizing the significance of the resources in limiting economic growth.[23]

Given the ongoing trends of urbanization and socioeconomic development in China, it is projected that an increasing demand for land use will place heavy pressure on natural and semi-natural ecosystems. Consequently, ecological functions that support the human-dominated ecosystem will be impaired. Policies that aim to achieve long-term sustainable development must therefore address the environmental effects of rapid urbanization and the loss of semi-natural and natural lands. We suggest developing an integrated RS/GIS decision support system, not only for visually mapping land use dynamics and spatiotemporal patterns of ESV based on retrospective analysis, but also for estimating and modeling population growth trends and evaluating the loss of natural and semi-natural lands and the ecological consequences that accompany the rapid expansion of urban areas. Further research along these lines should be encouraged, as we believe additional studies will be beneficial for the governmental authorities who engage in planning activities at various levels. In addition, more innovative stochastic modeling approaches are needed in regional studies and urban analysis to enrich operational models for implementing sustainable development in urbanization and land development processes, with limited resources and stringent environmental constraints taken into consideration.

## Notes

[1] T. N. Chase, R. A. Pielke, T. G. F. Kittel, R. R. Nemani, and S. W. Running, "Simulated Impacts of Historical Land Cover Changes on Global Climate in Northern Winter," *Climate Dynamics* 16(2–3), 93–105; Eric F. Lambin, B. L. Turner, Helmut J. Geist, Samuel B. Agbola, Arild Angelsen, John W. Bruce, Oliver T. Coomes, Rodolfo Dirzo, Gunther Fischer, Carl Folke, et al., "The Causes of Land-Use and Land-Cover Change: Moving Beyond the Myths," *Global Environmental Change: Human and Policy Dimensions* 11(4), 261–9.

[2] Chase, T. N., R. A. Pielke, T. G. F. Kittel, R. R. Nemani, and S. W. Running. "Simulated Impacts of Historical Land Cover Changes on Global Climate in Northern Winter." Climate Dynamics 16(2–3), 93–105.

[3] Su, Shiliang, Rui Xiao, Zhenlan Jiang, and Yuan Zhang. "Characterizing Landscape Pattern and Ecosystem Service Value Changes for Urbanization Impacts at an Eco-Regional Scale." Applied Geography 2012 no. 34, 295–305.

[4] Robert T. LeBlanc, Robert D. Brown, and John E. FitzGibbon, "Modeling the Effects of Land Use Change on the Water Temperature in Unregulated Urban

Streams," *Journal of Environmental Management* 49(4), 445–69; M. Zhao, A. J. Pitman, and T. Chase, "The Impact of Land Cover Change on the Atmospheric Circulation," *Climate Dynamics* 17(5–6), 467–77; A. Veldkamp and P. H. Verburg, "Modeling Land Use Change and Environmental Impact," *Journal of Environmental Management*, 72(1–2), 1–3.

[5] Qihao H. Weng, "Land Use Change Analysis in the Zhujiang Delta of China Using Satellite Remote Sensing, GIS and Stochastic Modeling," *Journal of Environmental Management* 2002 no. 64, 273–84.

[6] Yehua Dennis Wei and Wangming Li, "Reforms, Globalization, and Urban Growth in China," *Eurasian Geography and Economics* 43(6), 459–75; Jun Luo and Yehua Dennis Wei, "Modeling Spatial Variations of Urban Growth Patterns in Chinese Cities," *Landscape and Urban Planning* 91(2), 51–64.

[7] Masakazu Ichimura, "Urbanization, Urban Environment and Land Use: Challenges and Opportunities," Issue paper for Asia-Pacific Forum for Environment and Development, Guilin, China, January 23, 2003.

[8] Burkhard et al.; Costanza et al.; Daily; de Groot et al.; Wilson et al.; Bolund and Hunhammar; Francisco J. Escobedo, Timm Kroeger, and John E. Wagner, "Urban Forests and Pollution Mitigation: Analyzing Ecosystem Services and Disservices," *Environmental Pollution* 159(8–9), 2078–87; Brendan Fisher, R. Kerry Turner, and Paul Morling, "Defining and Classifying Ecosystem Services for Decision Making," *Ecological Economics* 68(3), 643–53; Vejre et al.; Petteri Vihervaara, Timo Kumpula, Ari Tanskanen, and Benjamin Burkhard, "Ecosystem Services—A Tool for Sustainable Management of Human-Environment Systems. Case Study Finnish Forest Lapland," *Ecological Complexity* 7(3), 410–20.

[9] Rocco Scolozzi, Elisa Morri, and Riccardo Santolini, "Delphi-Based Change Assessment in Ecosystem Service Values to Support Strategic Spatial Planning in Italian Landscapes," *Ecological Indicators*, 2012 no. 21, 134–44.

[10] Jonathan P. Atkins, Daryl Burdon, Mike Elliott, and Amanda J. Gregory, "Management of the Marine Environment: Integrating Ecosystem Services and Societal Benefits with the DPSIR Framework in a Systems Approach," *Marine Pollution Bulletin* 62(2), 215–26; María Paula Barral, and Néstor Oscar Maceira, "Land-Use Planning Based on Ecosystem Service Assessment: A Case Study in the Southeast Pampas of Argentina," *Agriculture, Ecosystems and Environment* 2012 no. 154, 34–43; M. J. Metzger, M. D. A. Rounsevell, L. Acosta-Michlik, R. Leemans, and D. Schroter, "The Vulnerability of Ecosystem Services to Land Use Change," *Agriculture, Ecosystems and Environment* 114(1), 69–85.

[11] Y.-H. Sun, Y-G. Zong, D. Ke, B. Wang, and Y.-J. Wang, "Application of Spatial Ecological Value Assessment for Urban Sprawl Control: A Case Study in the Central Area of Xi'an, China," *Modern Urban Study*, 2011 no. 5, 64–9.

[12] John Harwood and Kevin Stokes, "Coping with Uncertainty in Ecological Advice: Lessons from Fisheries," *Trends in Ecology and Evolution* 18(12), 617–22.

[13] Robert Costanza, Ralph d'Arge, Rudolf de Groot, Stephen Farber, Monica Grasso, Bruce Hannon, Karin Limburg, Shahid Naeem, Robert V. O'Neill, Jose Paruelo, et al., "The Value of the World's Ecosystem Services and Natural Capital," *Nature* 1997 no. 387, 253–60.

[14] Gao-Di Xie, Chun-Xia Lu, Yun-Fa Leng, Du Zheng, and Shuang-Cheng Li,"Ecological Assets Valuation of the Tibetan Plateau," *Journal of Natural Resources* 18(2), 189–96.

[15] Bolund and Hunhammar; Li, Li and Qian; Yong Liu, Jinchang Li, and Hong Zhang, "An Ecosystem Service Valuation of Land Use Change in Taiyuan City, China," *Ecological Modeling* 2012 no. 225, 127–32.

[16] Hualou Long, Guoping Tang, Xiubin Li, and Gerhard K. Heilig, "Socio-Economic Driving Forces of Land-Use Change in Kunshan, the Yangtze River Delta Economic Area of China," *Journal of Environmental Management* 83(3), 351–64

[17] Kevin McGarigal, Sam A. Cushman, and Eduard Ene, FRAGSTATS V. 4: Spatial Pattern Analysis Program for Categorical and Continuous Maps. [Software]. University of Massachusetts, Amherst, 2012.

[18] M. Luck and J. Wu, "A Gradient Analysis of the Landscape Pattern of Urbanization in the Phoenix Metropolitan Area of USA," *Landscape Ecology* 2002 no. 17, 327–39.

[19] Atkins et al.; Barral and Maceira; Fisher et al.; Joshua H. Goldstein, Giorgio Caldarone, Thomas Kaeo Duarte, Driss Ennaanay, Neil Hannahs, Guillermo Mendoza, Stephen Polasky, Stacie Wolny, and Gretchen C. Daily, "Integrating Ecosystem-Service Tradeoffs into Land-Use Decisions," *Proceedings of the National Academy of Sciences* 109(19), 7565–70; Scolozzi et al.; Sun et al.; Vihervaara et al.

[20] S. Chen, Y.-X. Liu, and L.-H. Peng, "Dynamics of Urban Ecological Space Evolution and Policy Responses: A Case Study of Nanjing City," *Acta Ecologica Sinica* 28(5), 2270–8;W.-P. Peng, J.-M. Zhou, H. L. Luo, C.-J. Yang, and J.-F. Zhao, "Estimation on Gain and Losses of Ecosystem Service Value of Urban Land Use—A Case Study of Chengdu City." *Research of Soil and Water Conservation* 18(4), 43–52.

[21] F. Li, Y. Ye, B. Song, and R. Wang, "Spatial Structure of Urban Ecological Land and its Dynamic Development of Ecosystem Services: A Case Study in Changzhou City, China," *Acta Ecologica Sinica* 31(19), 5623–31; Chen, Liu, and Peng; Wu and Zhang.

[22] X.-Y. Cheng and K.-J. Shen, "The Public Participation in the Land Use Law of China," *China Land Science* 24, 31–5; X.-H. Dou, R.-Z. Liu, and X.-Z. Chen, "Thinking on China's Urban and Rural Planning," *Theory Monthly* 2011 no. 2, 173–5; Jing Song, "On Peasants' Participation on the Governance of Rural Homestead in China," *Journal of Fujian Administration Institute* 2010 no. 5, 45–51

[23] A. G. O. Yeh and X. Li, "Sustainable Land Development Model for Rapid Growth Areas Using GIS," *International Journal of Geographical Information Science* 12(2), 169–89.

## Bibliography

Atkins, Jonathan P., Daryl Burdon, Mike Elliott, and Amanda J. Gregory. "Management of the Marine Environment: Integrating Ecosystem Services and Societal Benefits with the DPSIR Framework in a Systems Approach." *Marine Pollution Bulletin* 62(2), 215–26.

Barral, María Paula, and Néstor Oscar Maceira. "Land-Use Planning Based on Ecosystem Service Assessment: A Case Study in the Southeast Pampas of Argentina." *Agriculture, Ecosystems and Environment* 2012 no. 154, 34–43.

Bastian, Olaf, Dagmar Haase, and Karsten Grunewald. "Ecosystem Properties, Potentials and Services—The EPPS Conceptual Framework and an Urban Application Example." *Ecological Indicators* 21(2012), 7–16.

Bolund, Per, and Sven Hunhammar. "Ecosystem Services in Urban Areas." *Ecological Economics* 29(1999), 293–301.

Burkhard, Benjamin, Irene Petrosillo, and Robert Costanza. "Ecosystem Services—Bridging Ecology, Economy and Social Sciences." *Ecological Complexity* 7(3), 257–9.

Chase, T. N., R. A. Pielke, T. G. F. Kittel, R. R. Nemani, and S. W. Running. "Simulated Impacts of Historical Land Cover Changes on Global Climate in Northern Winter." *Climate Dynamics* 16(2–3), 93–105.

Chen, Nengwang, Huancheng Li, and Lihong Wang. "A GIS-Based Approach for Mapping Direct Use Value of Ecosystem Services at a County Scale: Management Implications." *Ecological Economics* 68(11), 2768–76.

Chen, S., Y.-X. Liu, and L.-H. Peng. "Dynamics of Urban Ecological Space Evolution and Policy Responses: A Case Study of Nanjing City." *Acta Ecologica Sinica* 28(5), 2270–8. [Original in Chinese.]

Cheng, J., K. Yang, J. Zhao, and J.-P. Wu. "Impact Assessment of Land Use Change in Center District of Shanghai Based on Ecosystem Services Value." *China Environmental Science* 29(1), 95–100. [Original in Chinese.]

Cheng, X.-Y., and K.-J. Shen. "The Public Participation in the Land Use Law of China." *China Land Science* 24, 31–5. [Original in Chinese.]

China National Committee of Agricultural Divisions. *Technical Regulation of Investigation on Land Use Status*. Beijing, China: Surveying and Mapping Publishing House, 1984. [Original in Chinese.]

Costanza, Robert, Ralph d'Arge, Rudolf de Groot, Stephen Farber, Monica Grasso, Bruce Hannon, Karin Limburg, Shahid Naeem, Robert V. O'Neill, Jose Paruelo, et al. "The Value of the World's Ecosystem Services and Natural Capital." *Nature* 1997 no. 387, 253–60.
Daily, Gretchen C., ed. *Nature's Services: Societal Dependence on Natural Ecosystems.* Washington D.C.: Island Press, 1997.
de Groot, R. S., R. Alkemade, L. Braat, L. Hein, and L. Willemen. "Challenges in Integrating the Concept of Ecosystem Services and Values in Landscape Planning, Management and Decision-Making." *Ecological Complexity* 7(3), 260–72.
Dou, X.-H., R.-Z. Liu, and X.-Z. Chen. "Thinking on China's Urban and Rural Planning." *Theory Monthly* 2011(2), 173–5. [Original in Chinese.]
Ellis, Gregory M., and Anthony C. Fisher. "Valuing the Environment as Input." *Journal of Environmental Management* 25(2), 149–56.
Escobedo, Francisco J., Timm Kroeger, and John E. Wagner. "Urban Forests and Pollution Mitigation: Analyzing Ecosystem Services and Disservices." *Environmental Pollution* 159(8–9), 2078–87.
Feng, X. Y., G. P. Luo, C. F. Li, L. Dai and L. Lu. "Dynamics of Ecosystem Service Value Caused by Land Use Changes in Manas River of Xinjiang, China." *International Journal of Environmental Research* 6(2), 499–508.
Fisher, Brendan, R. Kerry Turner, and Paul Morling. "Defining and Classifying Ecosystem Services for Decision Making." *Ecological Economics* 68(3), 643–53.
Garrod, Guy D., and Ken G. Willis. *Economic Valuation of the Environment.* Cheltenham, UK: Edward Elgar, 1999.
Gibbs, H. K., A. S. Ruesch, F. Achard, M. K. Clayton, P. Holmgren, N. Ramankutty, and J. A. Foley. "Tropical Forests Were the Primary Sources of New Agricultural Land in the 1980s and 1990s." *Proceedings of the National Academy of Sciences* 107(38), 16732–7.
Gillham, O. *The Limitless City: A Primer on the Urban Sprawl Debate.* Washington DC: Island Press, 2002.
Goldstein, Joshua H., Giorgio Caldarone, Thomas Kaeo Duarte, Driss Ennaanay, Neil Hannahs, Guillermo Mendoza, Stephen Polasky, Stacie Wolny, and Gretchen C. Daily. "Integrating Ecosystem-Service Tradeoffs into Land-Use Decisions." *Proceedings of the National Academy of Sciences* 109(19), 7565–70.

Harwood, John, and Kevin Stokes. "Coping with Uncertainty in Ecological Advice: Lessons from Fisheries." *Trends in Ecology and Evolution* 18(12), 617–22.

Ichimura, Masakazu. "Urbanization, Urban Environment and Land Use: Challenges and Opportunities." Issue paper for Asia-Pacific Forum for Environment and Development, Guilin, China, January 23, 2003.

Janssen, Lucas L. F., and Frans J. M. van der Wel. "Accuracy Assessment of Satellite-Derived Land-Cover Data: A Review." *Photogrammetric Engineering and Remote Sensing* 60(4), 419–32.

Kamal-Chaoui, Lamia, Edward Leman and Zhang Rufei. "Urban Trends and Policy in China." OECD Regional Development Working Papers 2009/1. Paris, France: OECD, 2009. DOI: 10.1787/225205036417.

Lambin, Eric F., B. L. Turner, Helmut J. Geist, Samuel B. Agbola, Arild Angelsen, John W. Bruce, Oliver T. Coomes, Rodolfo Dirzo, Gunther Fischer, Carl Folke, et al. "The Causes of Land-Use and Land-Cover Change: Moving Beyond the Myths." *Global Environmental Change: Human and Policy Dimensions* 11(4), 261–9.

LeBlanc, Robert T., Robert D. Brown, and John E. FitzGibbon. "Modeling the Effects of Land Use Change on the Water Temperature in Unregulated Urban Streams." *Journal of Environmental Management* 49(4), 445–69.

Li, F., Y. Ye, B. Song, and R. Wang. "Spatial Structure of Urban Ecological Land and its Dynamic Development of Ecosystem Services: A Case Study in Changzhou City, China." *Acta Ecologica Sinica* 31(19), 5623–31. [Original in Chinese.]

Li, Tianhong, Wenkai Li, and Zhenghan Qian. "Variations in Ecosystem Service Value in Response to Land Use Changes in Shenzhen." *Ecological Economics* 69(7), 1427–35.

Liao, Felix H. F., and Yehua Dennis Wei. "Modeling Determinants of Urban Growth in Dongguan, China: A Spatial Logistic Approach." *Stochastic Environmental Research and Risk Assessment* September 2012. DOI: 10.1007/s00477-012-0620-y

Liu, Yong, Jinchang Li, and Hong Zhang. "An Ecosystem Service Valuation of Land Use Change in Taiyuan City, China." *Ecological Modeling* 2012 no. 225, 127–32.

Long, Hualou, Guoping Tang, Xiubin Li, and Gerhard K. Heilig. "Socio-Economic Driving Forces of Land-Use Change in Kunshan, the Yangtze River Delta Economic Area of China." *Journal of Environmental Management* 83(3), 351–64.

Lu, Jin Deng, and Xiao Mei Lu. "An Appraisal of Environmental Dynamics and the Driving Causes of Surface Water in the Last

Decade of China." *Ecological Science* 21(4), 370–3. [Original in Chinese.]
Luck, M., and J. Wu. "A Gradient Analysis of the Landscape Pattern of Urbanization in the Phoenix Metropolitan Area of USA." *Landscape Ecology* 2002 no. 17, 327–39.
Luo, Jun, and Yehua Dennis Wei. "Modeling Spatial Variations of Urban Growth Patterns in Chinese Cities." *Landscape and Urban Planning* 91(2), 51–64.
McGarigal, Kevin, Sam A. Cushman, and Eduard Ene. FRAGSTATS V. 4: Spatial Pattern Analysis Program for Categorical and Continuous Maps. [Software]. University of Massachusetts, Amherst. 2012. http://www.umass.edu/landeco/research/fragstats/fragstats.html
Metzger, M. J., M. D. A. Rounsevell, L. Acosta-Michlik, R. Leemans, and D. Schroter. "The Vulnerability of Ecosystem Services to Land Use Change." *Agriculture, Ecosystems and Environment* 114(1), 69–85.
Peng, W.-P., J.-M. Zhou, H. L. Luo, C.-J. Yang, and J.-F. Zhao. "Estimation on Gain and Losses of Ecosystem Service Value of Urban Land Use—A Case Study of Chengdu City." *Research of Soil and Water Conservation* 18(4), 43–52. [Original in Chinese.]
Robinson, Lin, Joshua P. Newell, and John M. Marzluff. "Twenty-Five Years of Sprawl in the Seattle Region: Growth Management Responses and Implications for Conservation." *Landscape and Urban Planning* 71(1), 51–72.
Scolozzi, Rocco, Elisa Morri, and Riccardo Santolini. "Delphi-Based Change Assessment in Ecosystem Service Values to Support Strategic Spatial Planning in Italian Landscapes." *Ecological Indicators*, 2012 no. 21, 134–44. DOI: 10.1016/j.ecolind.2011.07.019
Song, Jing. "On Peasants' Participation on the Governance of Rural Homestead in China." *Journal of Fujian Administration Institute* 2010 no. 5, 45–51. [Original in Chinese.]
Su, Shiliang, Rui Xiao, Zhenlan Jiang, and Yuan Zhang. "Characterizing Landscape Pattern and Ecosystem Service Value Changes for Urbanization Impacts at an Eco-Regional Scale." *Applied Geography* 2012 no. 34, 295–305.
Su, Shiliang, Dan Li, Xiang Yu, Zhonghao Zhang, Qi Zhang, Rui Xiao, Junjun Zhi, and Jiaping Wu. "Assessing Land Ecological Security in Shanghai (China) Based on Catastrophe Theory." *Stochastic Environmental Research and Risk Assessment*, 2011 no. 25, 737–46.
Sun, Y.-H., Y-G. Zong, D. Ke, B. Wang, and Y.-J. Wang. "Application of Spatial Ecological Value Assessment for Urban Sprawl Control: A

Case Study in the Central Area of Xi'an, China." *Modern Urban Study* 5(2011), 64–9. [Original in Chinese.]

Taizhou Municipal Government. *The Master Planning for Taizhou City (2010–2020)*. Taizhou, China: Author, 2010.

Tang, Qi-Yi. Data Processing System (DPS)—Experimental Design, Statistical Analysis, and Data Mining. 2nd ed. Beijing, China: Science Press: 2010.

Vejre, Henrik, Frank Søndergaard Jensen, and Bo Jellesmark Thorsen. "Demonstrating the Importance of Intangible Ecosystem Services from Peri-Urban Landscapes." *Ecological Complexity* 7(3), 338–48.

Veldkamp, A., and P. H. Verburg. "Modeling Land Use Change and Environmental Impact." *Journal of Environmental Management*, 72(1–2), 1–3.

Vihervaara, Petteri, Timo Kumpula, Ari Tanskanen, and Benjamin Burkhard. "Ecosystem Services—A Tool for Sustainable Management of Human-Environment Systems. Case Study Finnish Forest Lapland." *Ecological Complexity* 7(3), 410–20.

Wang, Shujun, Jennifer Li, Daqian Wu, Jian Liu, Kai Zhang, and Renqing Wang. "The Strategic Ecological Impact Assessment of Urban Development Policies: A Case Study of Rizhao City, China." *Stochastic Environmental Research and Risk Assessment* 23(8), 1169–80.

Wei, Yehua Dennis, and Xinyue Ye. "Beyond Convergence: Space, Scale, and Regional Inequality in China." *Journal of Economic and Social Geography* 100(1), 59–80.

Wei, Yehua Dennis, and Wangming Li. "Reforms, Globalization, and Urban Growth in China." *Eurasian Geography and Economics* 43(6), 459–75.

Weng, Qihao H. "Land Use Change Analysis in the Zhujiang Delta of China Using Satellite Remote Sensing, GIS and Stochastic Modeling." *Journal of Environmental Management* 2002 no. 64, 273–84.

Wilson, Matthew A., Austin Troy and Robert Costanza. "The Economic Geography of Ecosystem Goods and Services Revealing the Monetary Value of Landscapes through Transfer Methods and Geographic Information Systems." In *Cultural Landscapes and Land Use: The Nature Conservation—Society Interface*. Edited by Martin Dieterich and Jan Van Der Straaten. 69–94. Dordrecht, the Netherlands: Kluwer Academic Publishers, 2004.

Wu, Fulong, and Anthony Gar-On Yeh. "Changing Spatial Distribution and Determinants of Land Development in Chinese Cities in the

Transition from a Centrally Planned Economy to a Socialist Market Economy: A Case Study of Guangzhou." *Urban Study* 34(11), 1851–79.
Wu, Kai-Ya, Xin-Yue Ye, Zhi-Fang Qi, and Hao Zhang. "Impacts of Land Use/Land Cover Change and Socioeconomic Development on Regional Ecosystem Services: The Case of Fast-Growing Hangzhou Metropolitan Area, China." *Cities* 2013 no. 31, 276–84.
Wu, Kai-Ya, and Hao Zhang. "Land Use Dynamics, Expansion Patterns of Built-Up Land, and Driving Forces Analysis of the Fast-Growing Hangzhou Metropolitan Area, Eastern China (1978–2008)." *Applied Geography* 2012 no. 34, 137–45.
Xie, Gao-Di, Chun-Xia Lu, Yun-Fa Leng, Du Zheng, and Shuang-Cheng Li. "Ecological Assets Valuation of the Tibetan Plateau." *Journal of Natural Resources* 18(2), 189–96. [Original in Chinese.]
Ye, Xinyue, and Yichun Xie. "Re-Examination of Zipf's Law and Urban Dynamic in China: A Regional Approach." *Annals of Regional Science* 49(1), 135–56. DOI: 10.1007/s00168-011-0442-8
Yeh, A. G. O., and X. Li. "Sustainable Land Development Model for Rapid Growth Areas Using GIS." *International Journal of Geographical Information Science* 12(2), 169–89.
Yue, Wenze, Peilei Fan, Yehua Dennis Wei, and Jiaguo Qi. "Economic Development, Urban Expansion, and Sustainable Development in Shanghai." *Stochastic Environmental Research and Risk Assessment.* (2012), 1–17. DOI: 10.1007/s00477-012-0623-8.
Zhang, Hao, Li-Guo Zhou, Ming-Nan Chen, and Wei-Chun Ma. "Land Use Dynamics of the Fast-Growing Shanghai Metropolis, China (1979–2008) and its Implications for Land Use and Urban Planning Policy." *Sensors* 11(2), 1794–809. DOI: 10.3390/s110201794
Zhao, M., A. J. Pitman, and T. Chase. "The Impact of Land Cover Change on the Atmospheric Circulation." *Climate Dynamics* 17(5–6), 467–77.

# CHAPTER SEVEN

# DISASTER RISK REDUCTION: A COMPARATIVE ASSESSMENT OF POLICIES IN THE U.S. AND CHINA

## BANDANA KAR

### Hazardousness of Places

Are countries worldwide at higher risk of natural hazards? This has been debated for decades and will probably continue to be for a long time. The question should not be whether countries are at higher risk or not, but should rather be what action each country is taking to reduce its risk. If each country's risk is increasing, should we conclude that no action has been taken, or that the actions taken are ineffective? An exploration of this question is the focus of this paper. However, before discussing this question further, let's define a hazard and a disaster and explore the global trend of hazards. A hazard is a

> potentially damaging physical event, phenomenon or human activity that may cause loss of life or injury, property damage, social and economic disruption or environmental degradation.[1]

Based on their origins, hazards could be natural or human-induced. Human-induced hazards are caused by human forces, while natural hazards are regarded as "elements of the physical environment, harmful to man and caused by forces extraneous to him."[2] Natural hazards may further be classified as geophysical (earthquakes, avalanches, landslides, etc.), hydro-meteorological (floods, tropical storms, hailstorms, etc.) or biological (floral and faunal).[3] Not every hazard has damaging consequences. A disaster is a hazard with devastating consequences, and is defined as a serious disruption of the functioning of society, causing widespread human, material or environmental losses which exceed the ability of the affected society to cope using only its own resources.[4]

Globally, the past fifty years has seen an increase in the loss of human lives, financial losses due to damage to properties, loss of infrastructure, and damage to our ecosystems due to disasters.[5] During the period from 1970 to 2000, the total number of natural hazards worldwide almost tripled.[6] The frequency and severity of disasters significantly increased from 1990 to 2010 (Figure 7.1). Although the past decade (2000–2010) has seen a decrease in disaster numbers, the total number of people impacted and the financial losses incurred have increased (Figures 7.2–7.4). In 2012 alone, 310 disasters of different magnitudes killed more than 9,300 people and cost about U.S. $138 billion worldwide; the majority of these financial losses occurred in the U.S., Italy and China.[7]

As Newton indicated, a natural disaster does not exist; rather, it results from the interaction of two dynamic environments: physical and social.[8] The rising societal exposure to natural hazards due to population growth; movement of populations to hazard-prone areas due either to poverty, as is the case in developing countries, or to affluence, as is the case in the U.S.; increase in property values in hazardous places, as in the U.S.;[9] degradation of ecosystems; and climate change are responsible for the increase in disasters and their subsequent impacts on society and ecosystems.[10]

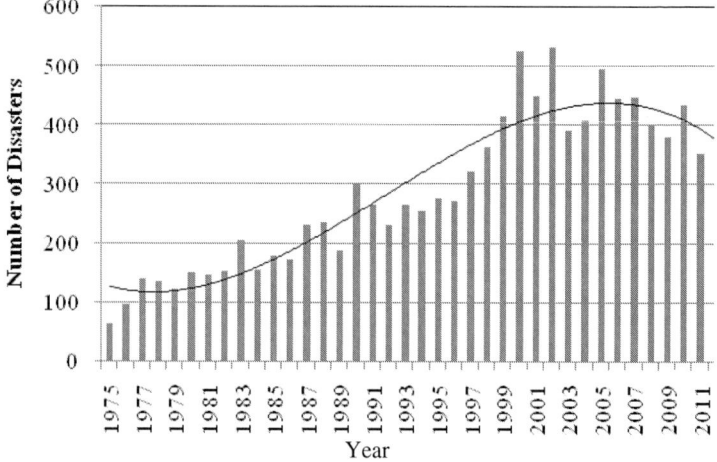

Figure 7.1. Number of Natural Hazards/Induced Disasters Worldwide.[11]

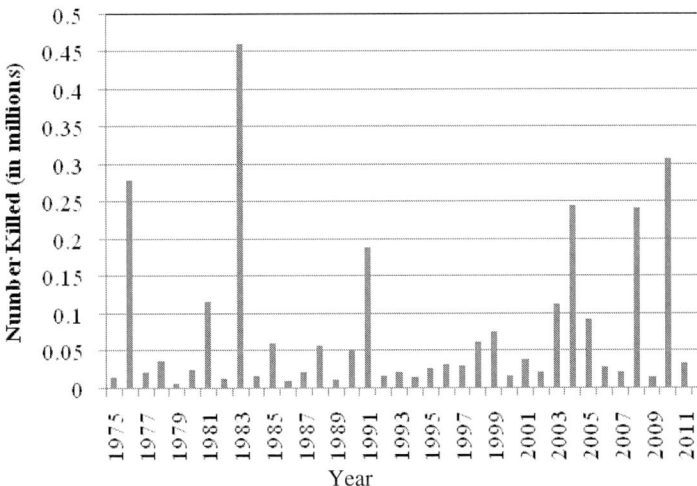

Figure 7.2. Number of People Killed by Natural Hazards/Induced Disasters Worldwide.[12]

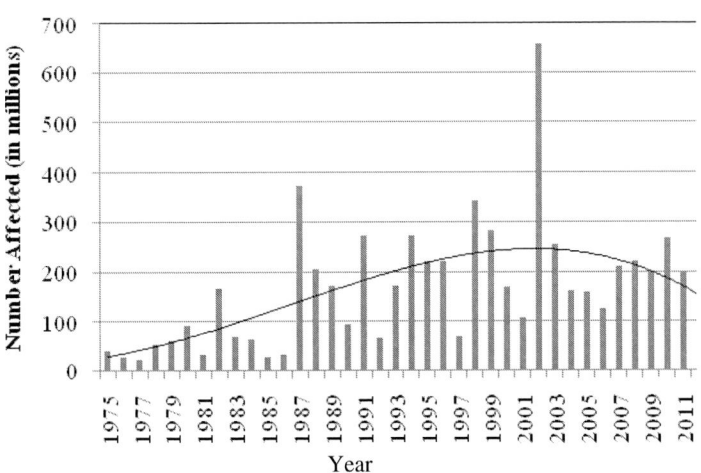

Figure 7.3. Number of People Affected by Natural Hazards/Induced Disasters Worldwide.[13]

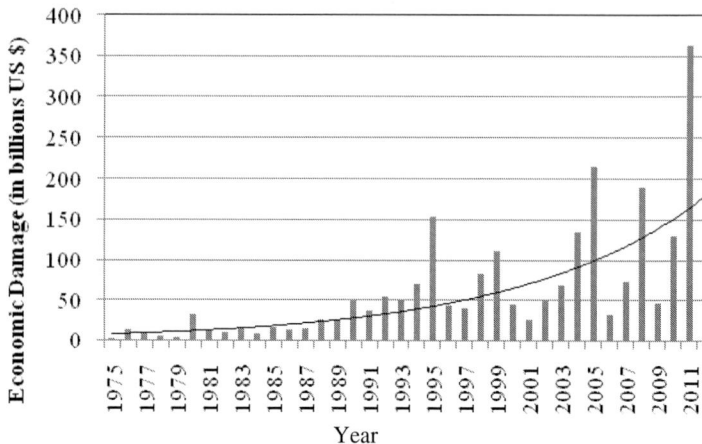

Figure 7.4. Estimated Damage Due to Natural Hazards/Induced Disasters Worldwide.[14]

While it is not possible to prevent or eliminate the occurrence of natural hazards, it is possible to take preventive actions to influence anthropogenic activities that contribute to the vulnerability of communities to such hazards and to improve communities' resilience. For instance, advances in effective warning systems, implementation of mandatory or optional evacuation policies, and the implementation of structural and non-structural mitigation strategies (such as land-use zoning ordinances and building guidelines) have definitely reduced the death tolls from natural hazards over the years in the U.S. and in other countries.[15] In the period from 1973 to 2000, the death tolls from natural hazards fell by 50 percent worldwide.[16] The global increase in financial losses, however, indicates that these policies and plans formulated to reduce the damaging effects of these hazards are not always effective. The mitigation policies to some extent also work as incentives for people to locate themselves in hazard-prone areas, which ultimately results in a disaster.[17] The occurrence of repeat flood losses in the U.S. is an example of the failure of the National Flood Insurance Program (NFIP).

This dichotomy of mitigation approaches necessitates a discussion of the effectiveness of risk-reduction policies. In this paper, two ethnically and culturally diverse countries—the United States of America and the People's Republic of China—were selected for a comparison of their emergency management policies because: 1) China has the highest population in the world and the U.S. is the largest economy in terms of per capita GDP (Gross Domestic Product) as of 2012;[18] and 2) China has a long-standing history and is a growing world power, but is still a developing country, as opposed to the U.S., which is the current foremost world power and is a developed country. Comparing these two countries that are in contrast with each other in terms of population and financial growth will help us identify effective policies and approaches to create resilient communities worldwide.

This paper is organized into four sections. The first section introduces and describes concepts pivotal to risk reduction and the creation of resilient communities. The second section discusses international frameworks that have been in place for decades to increase mitigation efforts in every country. The third section discusses the risk profile and the history of emergency management policies and plans in the U.S. and China. In section four, using a comparative politics approach, the success/failure of risk-reduction programs and policies in the two countries are explored. The concluding section presents a synopsis of the comparative analysis and provides an overview of where we are and where we must go to create sustainable communities after a disaster.

## Definitions and Frameworks of Risk Reduction

An emergency, as defined by the World Health Organization (2013), is a *state that occurs at a specific time and space due to an unforeseen event, has the potential to cause significant financial and environmental damages and/or deaths and injuries, and requires immediate attention and action.*[19] Depending upon the severity of an event, an emergency can exceed the capability of impacted communities to respond to and recover from the event's adverse impacts. Emergency management (EM) involves implementation of precautionary and managerial actions to mitigate emergency situations arising because of a disaster. These actions can be taken before, after, and/or during an emergency in the form of policies, tools/techniques, and plans/programs to provide human and financial resources to aid communities' fast recovery from disasters.

Preparedness, mitigation, recovery, and response are the four phases of the EM cycle responsible for risk reduction.[20] Preparedness, the first phase, involves preparation of plans to determine the specific actions to be taken and the agencies to help with the implementation of these actions before and during a disaster.[21] Though considered a second phase of the EM cycle, mitigation can occur at any time. It entails implementation of structural and non-structural policies/ techniques to reduce the risk of and damage from of a disaster.[22] Response focuses on protecting lives and diminishing damage to properties during a disaster. It may involve mechanisms to increase public awareness (e.g., using alert mechanisms) so that communities are prepared to respond to a disaster and to allocate resources for recovery.[23] Recovery, the last phase, occurs following a disaster: actions are taken to help communities return to normalcy by rebuilding structures and infrastructure. The duration of this phase depends on the severity of the disaster and the resilience of communities to deal with it.[24]

The term *vulnerability* was used by engineers in the 1960s to represent the resistance of structures to environmental impacts.[25] With the broadening of the hazard research discipline in the 1980s, the *physicalist* focus of vulnerability embraced both socioeconomic and environmental characteristics to determine the vulnerability of a place and people.[26] Based on numerous definitions, vulnerability can be defined as

> the potential and degree of susceptibility of an individual, group or community to experience adverse impacts of hazards due to sociocultural, physical, economic and environmental conditions.[27]

Vulnerability is a dynamic condition that changes with time, location, and among social groups.[28]

Resilience, derived from the Latin word *resiliere*, means bouncing back to an original stage.[29] In disaster risk reduction, resilience is perceived as the opposite of vulnerability, which results from a society's external and internal forces.[30] Resilience is also the product of a wide range of socioeconomic, cultural, and political variables, and manifests itself in both the policy framework of a community and the individual actions of its residents.[31]

Sustainability originated from classic twentieth-century environmentalist thought[32] and a wide range of literature calling for a more ecologically sound, socially just society.[33] Historic international events, such as the 1992 UN Earth Summit and the 2002 World Summit on Sustainable Development, have expanded the theoretical scope of sustainability and transformed it into a policy imperative for the global community.[34] Sustainability calls for poverty alleviation, greater social and economic equity, democratization, ecologically sound resource use, and environmental protection,[35] so that global society can meet "the needs of the present without compromising the ability of future generations to meet their own needs."[36]

The UN's International Decade for Disaster Reduction (IDNDR) in 1992 was the first step towards building resilient communities worldwide.

The UN noticed the need to understand the social and physical processes that cause disasters and to use technology to assess vulnerability and the threat these disasters pose to the sustainable development of future societies.[37] *The Yokohama Strategy and Plan of Action for a Safer World* (1994) laid out the principles for risk reduction.[38] These principles emphasized: the need for risk and vulnerability assessment; the integration of mitigation and preparedness policies with relief efforts; capacity-building of communities to mitigate disaster impacts; and protecting the environment.[39] It is obvious that both the strategy and the IDNDR program have made progress, but still there remains an unknown but significant factor responsible for the rising costs of disasters.

The *Hyogo Framework for Action* of 2005 is a recent global initiative for risk reduction.[40] This framework recognizes the strengths and failings of the past UN initiatives and lays out priority actions for every country: the participation of stakeholders in increasing disaster resilience; the implementation of a multi-hazard approach integrating the socioeconomic and cultural characteristics of local communities; the increased participation of local authorities and communities; the use of knowledge, education and innovation to increase awareness and community participation; the sharing among countries of lessons learned; and the implementation of warning systems as a preparedness policy.[41] This framework is the motivator for this study to determine best risk-reduction practices in the U.S. and China.

## Emergency Management

With the growing concern of every country about societal and environmental losses resulting from natural hazards, EM is fundamental to increasing every country's resilience to disasters. The EM agencies and legislation currently in place in the U.S. and China are discussed in the following sections.

### *Risk Profile and EM in the U.S.*
With a land mass of 9.3 million km$^2$, the U.S. is the fourth-largest country in the world by land area.[42] As of 2013, the total U.S. population was about 316 million, an 8.35 percent growth over the population in 2000 (291,421,906).[43] Irrespective of a drop in growth rate from almost 30 percent to 10 percent since 1790, the U.S. is still experiencing positive population growth. From 1790 to 2013, the U.S. urban population has grown from about 5 percent to 82 percent and the rural population has declined from about 95 percent to 18 percent.[44] The 2013 GDP for the first

quarter (~$16.5 trillion) was a 2.5 percent growth over the last quarter of 2012.[45]

The number of disasters in the U.S. has been increasing since 1980 (Figure 7.5). These disasters are caused predominantly by hydro-meteorological events. Despite exposure of coastal communities to coastal hazards, in 2009 about 52 percent of the total U.S. population resided in 675 counties identified as *coastal* by the National Oceanic and Atmospheric Administration.[46] The estimated insured values of coastal counties from Texas to Maine amounted to almost $9 trillion dollars in 2007.[47] Taken together, these factors partly explain the rising costs and severity of impacts from disasters in recent decades (Figure 7.8).[48] In 2012, the country's insured losses reached a total of about $58 billion, which was more than double the insured losses incurred from 2000 to 2011.[49] Contrary to rising financial losses, no significant trend exists with regard to loss of lives and people affected by these natural-hazard-induced disasters (Figures 7.6–7.7). The apparent decrease in death toll in comparison to the total number of people affected alongside the presence of at-risk and high-vulnerability communities necessitates a closer look at the effectiveness of EM actions.

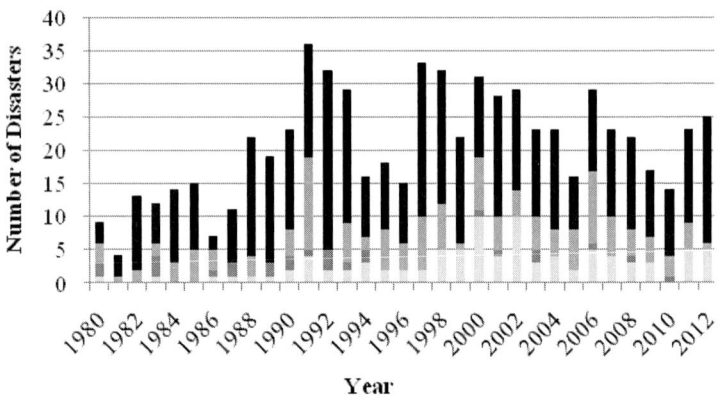

Figure 7.5. Number of Natural Hazards/Induced Disasters in the U.S.[50]

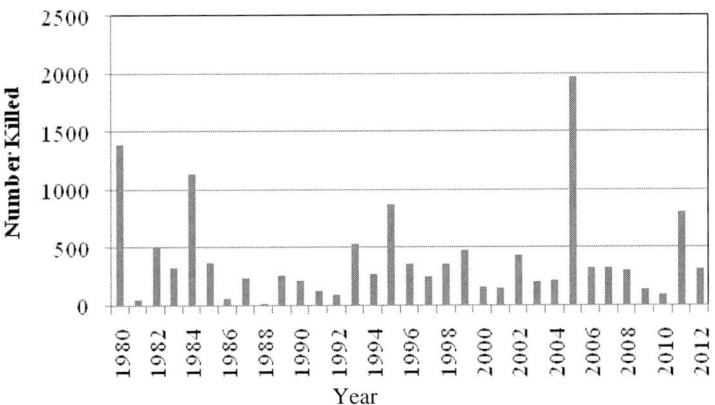

Figure 7.6. Number of People Killed by (Natural) Disasters in the U.S., 1980–2012.[51]

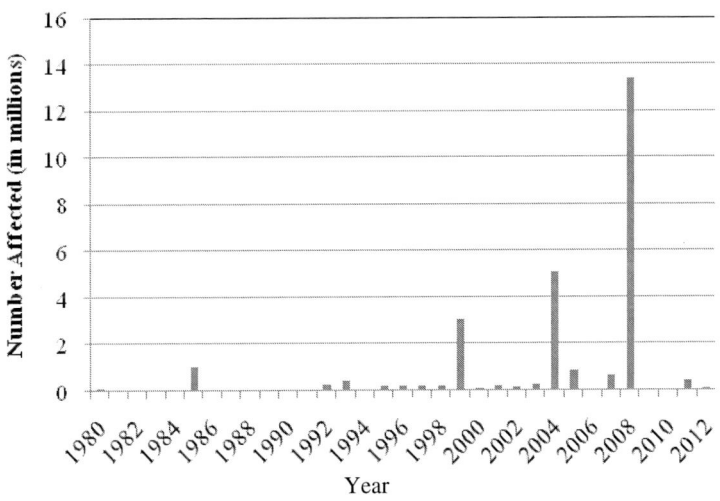

Figure 7.7. Number of People Affected by (Natural) Disasters in the U.S., 1980–2012.[52]

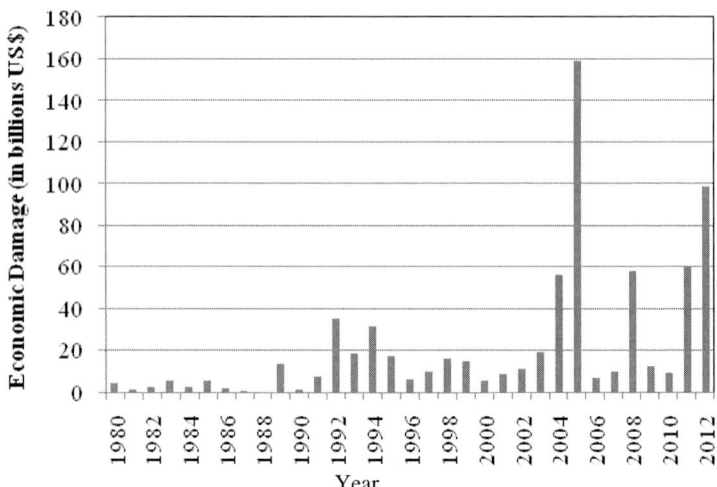

Figure 7.8. Total Financial Damage Caused by (Natural) Disasters in the U.S., 1980–2012.[53]

## History of EM

The growth of EM services in the U.S. can be divided into four distinct periods. The Congressional Act of 1803 that was passed to provide assistance to Portsmouth, New Hampshire to deal with a disastrous fire marked the beginning and first period of EM.[54] For more than a century after the first disaster legislation was passed, ad-hoc legislation was enacted to deal with hurricanes, earthquakes, floods, etc., until the 1930s, when, upon realizing the advantages of federal assistance in responding to disasters, a number of disaster laws were passed and organizations were established.[55] The Reconstruction Finance Corporation was authorized in 1932 to provide loans for repair and reconstruction of public facilities following an earthquake, and later other disasters.[56] The Tennessee Valley Authority (TVA) was established in 1933 to provide support for navigation, flood control and other disaster-prevention and economic development activities.[57] In 1934, the Bureau of Public Roads was created to finance the repair of highways and bridges damaged by natural hazards.[58] Following the large flood events of 1849 and 1850, the Swamp Land Acts of 1849 and 1850 required transfer of federal lands to state authorities for building dams, levees and drainage channels to mitigate flood impacts along the Mississippi River.[59] This act facilitated agricultural use of low-lying areas, thereby intensifying flood damage in the later period of the nineteenth century, which led to the passage of the Flood Control Act of 1936. This comprehensive act established a partnership of federal, state, and local governments, and authorized federal agencies to construct structures along the major rivers to reduce flood impacts.[60]

Unlike the first period, when ad-hoc disaster legislation was the norm, the second period (post-World War II, during the 1940s and 1950s) marked the creation of agencies and legislation to address civil defense activities and reduce Cold War tensions. EM in this period focused on reducing the threat of nuclear attack to the public. During the 1940s, civil defense programs such as air raid warning systems and emergency shelter programs, and agencies such as the Federal Civil Defense Administration and the Office of Defense Mobilization, were created to establish community-based EM strategies for public protection.[61] The Disaster Relief Act of 1950, the first comprehensive federal relief law, authorized federal agencies to support state and local governments after a disaster and to work with the President to regulate EM actions.[62] The Federal Civil Defense Act (1950) created a nationwide system of civil defense agencies.[63] In 1958, the Federal Civil Defense Administration and the Office of Defense Mobilization were combined to create the Office of Civil and Defense Mobilization (1958–1961) to undertake emergency preparedness activities.[64]

The increase in frequency and severity of disasters during the 1960s and -70s, such as the earthquake near Hebgen Lake, Montana (1959) and Hurricanes Donna (1960), Carla (1962), Betsy (1965), Camille (1969), and Agnes (1972), required extensive involvement of federal agencies in recovery and response efforts. This marked the third period of U.S. EM. The Office of Emergency Planning that was created in 1961 by renaming the Office of Civil and Defense Mobilization was again renamed the Office of Emergency Preparedness (OEP) in 1968, and a number of mitigation and preparedness laws were passed in the following years.[65] The National Flood Insurance Act (NFIA) of 1968 created the National Flood Insurance Program (NFIP), which implemented a shared-risk approach to provide financial aid to communities and individual homeowners who are part of the NFIP and have purchased a flood insurance policy.[66] The Flood Disaster Protection Act (1973) mandated flood insurance for properties located within Special Flood Hazard Areas identified by the NFIA.[67] The Disaster Relief Act (1969) created the Presidential disaster declaration process to facilitate the availability of federal aid to state and local governments in case of a disaster with significant societal and environmental impacts. The extension of this Act in 1974 required state and local governments to assist individuals and families after a disaster.[68] To manage coastal developments, protect coastal communities and marine environments, and reduce coastal hazard impacts, the Coastal Zone Management Act was enacted in 1972,[69] along with the National Dam Inspection Act, which mandated periodic inspections of dams to prevent flood impacts. In 1977, the Earthquake Hazards Reduction Act was passed, under which the *National Earthquake Hazards Reduction Program (NEHRP)* was created to reduce losses from earthquakes by coordinating mitigation activities among federal, state, and local governments.[70]

In the 1970s, there were six agencies involved in EM: 1) the National Fire Prevention and Control Administration (NFPCA) was responsible for fire prevention and training; 2) the General Services Administration was responsible for coordinating and mobilizing emergency, military, civilian, and industrial institutions to prepare for mitigating disaster impacts; 3) the Department of Defense was in charge of Civil Defense Programs; 4) the Housing and Urban Development Agency was responsible for disaster assistance and insurance programs; 5) the Nuclear Regulatory Commission was liable for emergency preparedness with regard to nuclear power plants; and 6) the Treasury Department was in charge of providing funding.[71] To reduce the number of agencies involved in EM and increase collaboration and coordination among these agencies, the Federal Emergency Management Agency (FEMA) was created in 1979 as an independent agency through an executive order. The new agency, an amalgamation of the Federal Insurance Administration, the National Fire Prevention and Control Administration, the National Weather Service Community Preparedness Program, the Federal Preparedness Agency of the General Services Administration, and the Federal Disaster Assistance Administration activities from the Department of Housing and Urban Development (HUD), was responsible for Civil defense actions.[72]

Despite their intention to reduce risk, the legislation passed in the period from 1960s to 1980s created a safety net for at-risk communities. In reaction to the rising financial losses from natural hazards in 1980s and 1990s (Hurricanes Hugo and Andrew, the Loma Prieta and Northridge earthquakes) and response to the UN's IDNDR movement (IDNDR), FEMA created a Mitigation Directorate in 1993.[73] In the 1990s, FEMA also embraced an all-hazard, risk-based, collaborative, and coordinated approach requiring participation of public and private stakeholders to implement mitigation and preparedness policies to increase community resilience.[74] The NFIA was reformed to the National Flood Insurance Reform Act of 1994.[75] This reformed Act required the participation of state and local governments in implementing structural and non-structural mitigation measures to reduce flood impacts. The Disaster Relief Act was amended in 1988 as the Robert T. Stafford Disaster Relief and Emergency Assistance Act (Stafford Act).[76] This revised Act played a major role in mitigating disaster impacts at a local level by requiring the federal government to give priority to mitigation and provide assistance to state and local governments to help local communities deal with disasters. The Act also required the local governments to prepare mitigation plans for a place—a city, a county—based on a comprehensive all-hazards approach accounting for the social vulnerability and physical risk of the place to all hazards and identifying EM activities and agencies responsible for coordinating response and recovery efforts. In 2000 this Act was amended to create the Disaster Mitigation Act (DMA),[77] which, besides providing help to prepare mitigation plans, required states to submit a mitigation plan in order to receive federal disaster assistance. The DMA 2000 also provided incentives for coordinating preparedness and mitigation activities among state and local governments. In 1992, the Federal Response Plan was prepared, which assigned roles to twenty-seven federal agencies and the American Red Cross to coordinate emergency actions at every phase of EM following large-scale disasters.[78]

The fourth period of EM started following the 9/11 terrorist attack on the World Trade Center, which contributed to the collapse of the global and the U.S. financial markets. Given the unknown threat presented by terrorism, the focus of EM shifted from mitigation and preparedness activities to protecting the civilian population from the threat of terrorism, and a number of laws were enacted to that effect. The first major Act in the twenty-first century was the Uniting and Strengthening America by Providing Appropriate Tools Required to Intercept and Obstruct Terrorism Act (U.S. Patriot Act) of 2001.[79] By this time, FEMA was criticized for its efforts to mitigate the impacts of Hurricane Hugo and the Loma Prieta and Northridge earthquakes and demands were made for its reform. With the passing of the Homeland Security Act (HSA) of 2002, the Department of Homeland Security was established and FEMA was absorbed into DHS, along with twenty-two other agencies.[80] A number of Homeland Security Presidential Directives (HSPDs) were passed as a result of the HSA. HSPD 5 dealt with the Management of Domestic Incidents and established the National Incident Management System (2003) to enable the collaboration and coordination of agency efforts in building resilient communities to cope with future disasters.[81] The HSPD 8 focused on strengthening preparedness policies and actions to reduce impacts of terrorism and other disasters.[82]

Hurricane Katrina in 2005 caused significant financial, environmental and psychological damage. Apart from losing their homes and relocating to trailers provided by FEMA, many people were forced to leave their pets behind due to lack of space available to shelter the pets or because it was not allowed. Whatever the reason, the sad story was during Hurricane Katrina many pets and service animals were left behind and the welfare of animals was of the least concern of governments. FEMA was again criticized for its failure to coordinate and organize response and recovery efforts immediately after the hurricane's landfall along the Gulf Coast. FEMA's ineffectiveness in dealing with emergency activities, which was the reason the agency had been created, was again brought to the forefront. In 2006, the Post-Katrina Emergency Management Reform Act was enacted to establish FEMA as a separate entity within DHS, and the Stafford Act of 2000 was amended to include the Pets Evacuation and Transportation Standards Act to provide federal assistance to evacuate pets and other animals while undertaking the evacuation of residents.[83] The National Response Framework was created in 2008 to encourage public and private-sector participation in responding to future disasters.[84] As of 2013, the primary mission of FEMA is

> to reduce the loss of life and property and protect the Nation from all hazards, including natural disasters, acts of terrorism and other man-made disasters, by leading and supporting the Nation in a risk-based, comprehensive emergency management system of preparedness, protection, response, recovery and mitigation.[85]

Despite so many changes in the U.S. EM policies, the financial losses from natural hazards keep on increasing. Hurricane Sandy (2012), which impacted the coast of New Jersey, is a very good example of the current state of the U.S. EM, despite its long-standing mission to protect communities and mitigate disaster impacts. In the aftermath of Hurricane Sandy, the Biggert-Waters Flood Insurance Reform Act of 2012[86] was passed to extend the NFIP until 2017 to protect people from floods. Even after amending the specific (e.g. NFIP) and general (e.g. DMA) EM policies, the consistent increase in financial losses due to different hazards requires an evaluation of the effectiveness of EM policies.

## *Risk Profile and EM in China*

China, located in East Asia, is the third-largest country in the world by land area (covering approximately 9.6 million square kilometers).[87] China is also the world's most populous country, with a population of approximately 1.34 billion as of 2012, a 6.8 percent growth since 2000.[88]

In 2008, about 46 percent of China's population (1.3 billion) resided in urban areas.[89] With the introduction of economic reforms in 1978, China has become the world's fastest-growing major economy.[90] As of the first quarter of 2013, China is the second-largest economy based on nominal total GDP and purchasing power.[91]

Not surprisingly, China is impacted by a number of hazards; however, floods, earthquakes, and typhoons are the most frequently occurring hazards with disastrous consequences (Figure 7.9).[92] Since the 1980s, the fatality rate has decreased in comparison with the total number of people affected by disasters, but there is no significant trend in the number of people affected (Figures 7.10 and 7.11). The financial damage does not reflect a specific trend, except that it has been increasing over time (Figure 7.12). Overall, floods and storms (hydro-meteorological events) are responsible for the maximum number of people affected and financial damages, but earthquakes (geophysical events) are responsible for the maximum loss of lives. Like every other country, rapid population growth and high population density in hazardous areas contribute to the continuous increase of the disastrous consequences of these hazards.[93] In the light of this problem, it is imperative to examine the situation of EM within the broader picture of natural hazards.

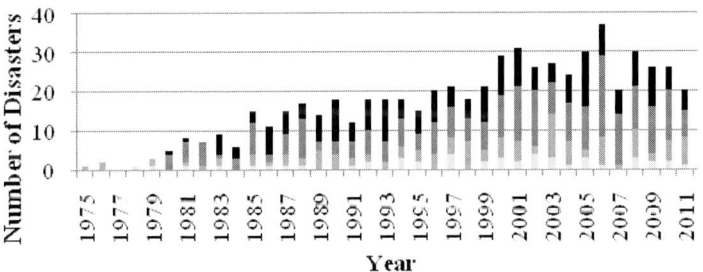

Figure 7.9. Number of Natural Hazards/Induced Disasters in China, 1980–2012.[94]

146 Chapter Seven

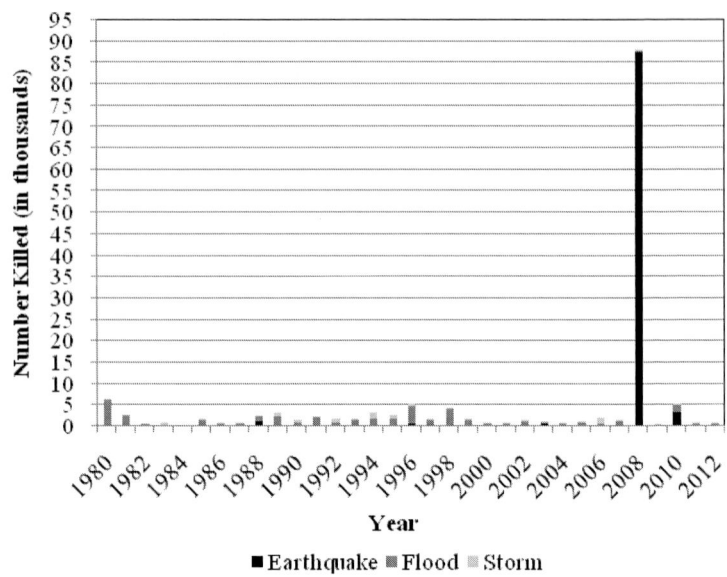

Figure 7.10. Number of People Killed by Natural Hazards/Induced Disasters in China, 1980–2012.[95]

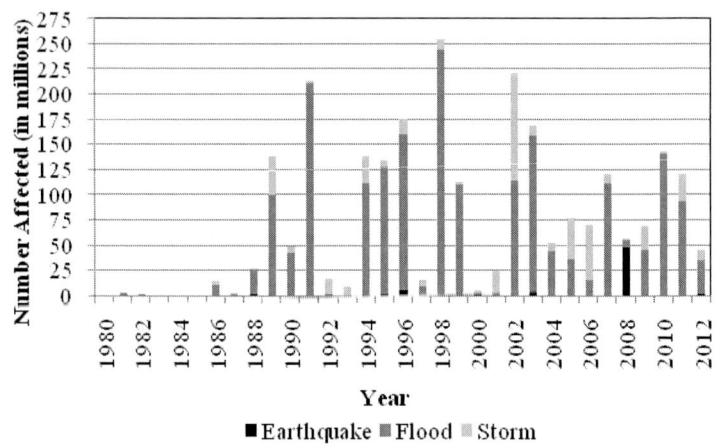

Figure 7.11. Number of People Affected by Natural Hazards/Induced Disasters in China, 1980–2012.[96]

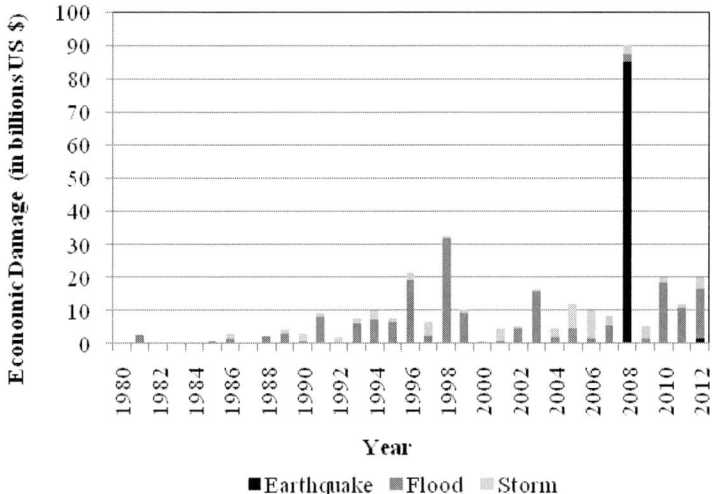

Figure 7.12. Total Financial Damage Caused by Natural Hazards/Induced Disasters in China, 1980–2012.[97]

## *The History of EM*

China is faced with numerous hazards with high mortality risk and which cause significant financial losses. Irrespective of the country's long history, very little was done in terms of EM until the outbreak of Severe Acute Respiratory Syndrome (SARS) in 2003 that raised concern all across the globe because of its serious public health implications.[98] Before 2003, there was a fragmented approach to disaster prevention and risk reduction, which cost a large amount of money; the SARS attack mobilized the Chinese government to establish the Emergency Management Office (EMO) in 2005,[99] the first umbrella agency to implement comprehensive EM activities.

Even with the establishment of the EMO, there remains a myriad of agencies involved in EM activities. The main agency is the Ministry of Civil Affairs (MCA), founded in 1978, which is responsible for natural disaster relief.[100] The National Disaster Reduction Center (NDRC) of the MCA collects and analyzes disaster-related information to assess damage and required emergency relief in the case of a disaster event and provides technical support to disaster-management departments in their decision-making. The State Administration of Work Safety (SAWS) and the National Workplace Emergency Management Center (NWEMC) deal with technological disasters arising from traffic incidents, hazardous materials, mine safety, etc.[101] The National Civil Defense (NCD) deals with aerial defense and hazardous-material-related disasters. The EMO plays a supervisory and coordination role and is responsible for coordinating EM activities among the MCA, SAWS, Ministry of Health (MOH), and Ministry of Public Security (MPS).[102]

Because of the long history of flooding of major rivers, the country has taken extensive steps to protect people from riverine flood impacts. The Ministry of Water Resources (MWR) is the main agency responsible for maintaining water resources and controlling flood disasters. From the 1950s to the 1970s, the ministry established River Basin Commissions (RBC) to implement river basin plans dealing with structural flood control measures such as construction of dikes, dams and reservoirs to reduce flood impacts.[103] The Water Law of 1988, which regulated the use of water resources and control of water-related hazards, was revised in 2002 to focus specifically on development along water bodies, protection and sustainable use of water resources, and prevention of water-related disasters.[104] Because of the high dependence of China's population on rivers, other laws have been passed over the years to protect both water resources and the public from hazards. The Water Pollution Prevention and Control Law of 1984, which was amended in 1996, provides guidelines to reduce the pollution of water bodies. The National Flood Control Law of 1997 provides specific instructions about flood control and flood management through implementing risk-sharing approaches.[105]

China has also enacted legislation and established agencies to respond to earthquake-induced disasters. The National Earthquake Administration of 1971, later known as the China Earthquake Administration (CEA) (1998), monitors and responds to earthquakes.[106] The Earthquake Prevention and Disaster Reduction Act (EPDRA), enacted by China's State Council in 1995, is responsible for mitigating earthquake risk.[107] In the aftermath of the 2008 Wenchuan earthquake, which caused significant financial losses and loss of life (Figures 7.10 and 7.12), the Ministry of Finance and State Administration of Taxation implemented the Earthquake Relief and Reconstruction Tax Policies to provide relief and support to the affected population. These policies use an enterprise income tax, individual income tax, house property tax, resource tax, stamp tax, urban land-use tax, vehicle- and vessel-use tax, and import tax to generate money for relief and response efforts in case of an earthquake.[108]

In the wake of the UN's IDNDR, China published the "China 21st Century Agenda", which emphasized the need for disaster reduction and the creation of sustainable communities.[109] Under this agenda, the "National Disaster Reduction Plan of the People's Republic of China

(1998–2010)" was published to address disaster reduction through policy intervention.[110] This agenda was also responsible for the enactment of the "Fire Protection Law" of 1998 to safeguard citizens from the disastrous consequences of fires and to prevent fires.[111]

The failure of the Chinese government to address health issues during 2003 SARS event also mobilized the government to enact about thirty-five laws and thirty-seven regulations from 2003 to 2007, including the *Regulation on the Urgent Handling of Public Health Emergencies*, which is fundamental for developing EM plans relating to public health and hygiene issues in case of emergency events.[112] The *Master State Plan for Rapid Response to Public Emergencies* was issued in 2006 to help the EMO set up a framework for emergency planning and the *Law of the People's Republic of China on Emergency Responses* went into effect in 2007 to provide legal support to all levels of governments to prepare emergency plans.[113]

In essence, China's disaster-reduction policies appear to be short-term fixes very often enacted to address a specific disaster. The lack of cohesiveness in these policies in the event of a disaster such as an earthquake or a flood also appears to be contributing to an increase in financial loss and an increase in the total number of people affected. As China's population is growing and the majority of people are living in at-risk zones, it is pertinent to discuss what is lacking in the current policies and what actions should be taken to increase their effectiveness and efficiency in reducing future disaster impacts.

## Comparative Politics

Comparing the disaster policies of different countries is not new. Newton conducted an assessment of mitigation policies in the U.S. and Canada;[114] Weiner compared climate change policies in the U.S. and China; and Gemmer et al. compared agencies involved in climate change policy formulation and enforcement in the U.S. and China.[115] Though comparative assessment of disaster policies is not new, the framing of assessment methodology within comparative politics, a sub-discipline of political science,[116] is fairly recent.

Comparative politics is "the study of how, why, and to what effect different governments pursue particular courses of action or inaction"[117] and focuses on "exploring patterns, processes and regularities among political systems."[118] This sub-discipline of political science is concerned with comparing and contrasting policies to identify significant factors contributing to the success/failure of policies.

Because hazards are fairly common and result in disastrous consequences, McEntire and Mathis advocated using comparative politics to explore the effectiveness of disaster policies between countries to garner new knowledge about risk reduction.[119] Using the comparative politics framework, this paper compares the origins of EM and the ability of agencies and legislation to deal with different phases of EM in the U.S. and China. The findings of this comparison are presented in the following section.

*Origins*

U.S. EM has a longer history than that of China. Almost thirty years after independence in 1776, the first ad-hoc disaster legislation was enacted in the U.S. in 1803, but no action was taken until the 1930s when the country seriously considered its position in terms of EM and disaster risk reduction. This laid the foundation for the establishment of agencies and legislation to deal with mitigation, preparedness, response, and recovery efforts. A centralized agency to oversee EM activities (FEMA) was set up in 1979, more than two centuries after independence.

Obviously China does not appear to have a long history of EM. However, unlike the U.S., immediately after the formation of the People's Republic of China (PRC) in 1949, legal action was taken in 1950s to address the devastating impact of natural hazards in the newly formed country. The umbrella agency for EM was established about half a century after the formation of the PRC.

The maturity of the U.S. EM is due its longer existence as an independent country, as opposed to the PRC's short history of independence. In a short span, China has taken impressive action to create disaster-resilient and sustainable communities. The current status of the U.S. EM, on the other hand, is questionable. It seems that the U.S. is lagging behind China in building its communities' resilience. During Hurricane Sandy, almost seven years after Hurricane Katrina, when the U.S. EM failed to provide adequate response and recovery in the wake of a disaster, U.S. EM efforts again came under scrutiny because of its failure to provide timely response and recovery efforts, and the lack of coordination and collaboration between federal and state agencies and local communities. The increased funneling of federal money to respond to and recover from a disaster rather than aiding communities to be resilient by implementing effective mitigation and preparedness policies, as was seen after Hurricane Sandy, also poses a question about the current state of FEMA's core strategy as an EM agency. At the same time, failure of China to cope with SARS in 2003 and the Wenchuan Earthquake in

2008 indicates the weak and ineffective nature of its EM activities. Despite their histories, both countries have a long way to go to create sustainable communities.

*Policies*

Mitigation, the first pillar of the EM cycle, has been the crux of hazard policies in the U.S. Over the years a significant proportion of policies have been enacted in law to mitigate the hazard impacts in response to the rising cost of disasters.

*1. Structural mitigation measures.* The Swamp Land Acts were the first mitigation policies requiring construction of structures to protect communities from riverine flooding. Other structural mitigation policies that have been formulated since 1930s include: the Flood Control Act (1936), the Coastal Zone Management Act (1972), and the National Dam Inspection Act (1972). These three regulations required the building of dams, levees, and dikes along major rivers; regular inspection of these structures; and regulated urbanization along the coastal boundaries to protect communities from future flooding events and reduce flooding impacts.

*2. Non-structural mitigation measures.* The National Flood Insurance Act (1968) and the Disaster Protection Act (1973) are the most prominent non-structural mitigation policies. These Acts made the purchasing of insurance by coastal communities mandatory to protect them from future flooding impacts, especially those residing within flood hazard areas. The amended NFIA of 1994 increased partnerships and collaboration among state and local governments for effective implementation of structural and non-structural flood mitigation actions.

The majority of China's policies are structural in nature. For instance, both the Water Law and the National Flood Control Law regulate developments along water bodies, the use of water resources, and the construction of flood-protective structures. Flood control has been the focus of these laws rather than flood management through the implementation of risk-transfer techniques such as the NFIP, which has taken priority following the Hyogo Framework.[120]

Pre-disaster mitigation or preparedness actions and policies have been central to reducing the death toll in the U.S. The major preparedness action is the Emergency Alert System (EAS), a public warning system designed to provide adequate information about impending hazards to at-risk populations so that effective and efficient mitigation actions can be taken to reduce the adverse impacts of the event.[121] The system originated in 1951 as the Control of Electromagnetic Radiation (CONELRAD) program, which later became the Emergency Broadcast System (EBS) in 1963 and eventually the Emergency Alert System (EAS) in 1994 with the creation of the Federal Communications Commission in 1994.[121] Despite its long-standing history and effectiveness, during Hurricane Katrina the risk communication system was criticized for its failure to reach out to vulnerable communities such as the Vietnamese fishermen residing along the Mississippi Gulf Coast. Following the *Public Alert and Warning System Executive Order* in 2006, FEMA established the Integrated Public Alert and Warning System (IPAWS).[123] IPAWS uses a network of broadcasting systems and technologies such as the Tone Alert Radio (TAR), broadcast stations, cable companies, and the Commercial Mobile Alert System (CMAS) to deliver authentic alert messages from the authorities (e.g., NOAA) to the public in a timely manner.[124] This system is still being developed, as the integration of earthquake warnings is still in progress.

China's current warning system, which is supposed to be a multi-hazard warning system incorporating the monitoring of floods, earthquakes, marine disasters, etc., is still in its infancy. The warning system relies on texts, press conferences, and other means of communication to disseminate information to the public. Compared to the U.S., China's warning system does not appear to be sufficiently advanced to reach a wider audience.

Response and relief steps are taken in the aftermath of a disaster to help communities either return to or better their pre-disaster ways of life. The Disaster Relief Act (1950) was the first comprehensive relief policy of the U.S. federal government. It was amended in 1970 and 1974 to incorporate the Presidential Disaster Declaration process to provide federal assistance to states to deal with severe disasters and required communities receiving aid to assess their mitigation actions to reduce disaster impacts.[125] China's first relief policy was the Earthquake Relief and Reconstruction Tax Policies of 2008, enacted to provide relief support to earthquake-impacted populations.

A number of comprehensive disaster policies are in place in the U.S. The DMA 2000 is a comprehensive policy designed to help communities and local agencies identify structural and non-structural mitigation measures, and to help agencies coordinate mitigation, response, and recovery efforts. This Act requires all levels of government to prepare mitigation plans to determine the contingency fund needed to respond to a Presidential declared disaster. The Earthquake Hazards Reduction Act (1977) is a comprehensive and specific policy designed to reduce earthquake impacts. Under the NEHRP program, agencies such as the U.S. Geological Survey (USGS) prepare predictive models to assess the potential damage of earthquakes. The program also focuses on formulating structural guidelines to reduce structural damage due to an earthquake, and it disseminates information about seismic activities and their potential impacts to stakeholders through outreach and educational programs.[126] The Federal Fire Prevention and Control Act (1974) is another comprehensive policy that regulates fire hazards and was responsible for creating the U.S. Fire Administration (USFA) and the National Fire Academy (NFA).[127] Both agencies implement models to predict potentially disastrous impacts of fires and develop educational programs to increase public awareness of fire. China, on the other hand, does not seem to have any such comprehensive policy at all.

*Agencies and Programs*

The creation of FEMA and the establishment of the Mitigation Directorate paved the way to implementing risk-reduction approaches to reduce fatalities and property losses due to natural hazards in the U.S. The umbrella agency (FEMA) mobilized the creation of similar EM agencies at state and local government levels. Having one agency to oversee every facet of EM aided the creation of the Federal Response Plan to increase coordination among agencies to deal with large-scale disasters and the passing of the *National Mitigation Strategy—Partnerships for Building Safer Communities*.[128] The National Incident Management System (2003) created under HSPD 5 enables the collaboration and coordination of local agencies (local law enforcement agencies, public health agencies, departments of transportation, etc.) during any emergency situation.

In contrast to the U.S., China has a plethora of agencies at different government levels to deal with EM. The Ministry of Civil Affairs, the National Disaster Reduction Center and the National Commission for Disaster Reduction are responsible for coordinating disaster-reduction activities and damage assessment. The State Administration of Work Safety and the National Workplace Emergency Management Center assist with technological disasters. The National Civil Defense and the Emergency Management Office are in charge of EM actions. The Ministry of Water Resources oversees mitigation and preparedness activities related to flooding, and the China Earthquake Administration oversees EM activities in the case of an earthquake. China also has formulated a number of plans and policies, such as the *Regulation on the Urgent Handling of Public Health Emergencies*, the *Master State Plan for Rapid Response to Public Emergencies*, and the *Law of the People's Republic of China on Emergency Responses*, to legalize preparation of emergency plans for all hazards, including those pertaining to public health and hygiene issues.

Having a single agency, such as FEMA, in the U.S. enables coordination and standardization of EM activities to some extent. China, on the other hand, suffers from the lack of coordination and collaboration among so many agencies. The presence of so many agencies in China at all government levels to address different disasters and different aspects of EM also makes the implementation of EM actions at the local level very difficult and ultimately ineffective and weak.

## Conclusion

Both countries have demonstrated their readiness to implement diverse EM techniques and policies to combat the ever-growing financial costs of disasters. Both countries, however, need to face the truth about the current status of their EM policies before they can take the necessary actions to build resilient and sustainable communities, as required by the Hyogo framework.

Mitigation and preparedness have been the cornerstones for the U.S. EM to reduce the impact of and risks from any disaster. The policies have been successful in reducing disaster-related fatalities, but have failed in reducing financial losses, which is essential for the economic growth of the country and the building of resilient communities. The events of the past decade indicate the presence of certain issues that are central for the success of future EM policies in the U.S. Hurricane Katrina (2005) made landfall on the Gulf Coast, where communities have long experience of tropical storms. Because of their extensive experience with storms, some communities were well prepared to implement warnings and evacuation policies on time. Nonetheless, the lingering devastation of Katrina indicates that though Gulf Coast communities are aware of their imminent risk, they are either reluctant to implement mitigation policies due to lack of financial means or are unaware of the risk and/or policies. New Jersey is not new to tropical storms, but the extent of damage along the Jersey shore has not been significant due to storms since the Great Atlantic Hurricane of 1938. When Hurricane Sandy swept over the New Jersey coast in 2012, only a year after Hurricane Irene made landfall in the same region in 2011, it cost the country billions of dollars. Though New Jersey had started emphasizing mitigation actions and policies after Hurricane Irene, the communities appear to be unaware of their risk, which may be due to the lack of damage from past hurricanes. The salient point is that, whether communities are aware or unaware of their risk, they maintain an apathetic attitude towards hazard risk and ignore the significance of mitigation policies.

China has been spending a lot of money on structural measures to mitigate flood and earthquake impacts. At the same time, almost half of the Chinese population live in poverty and do not have access to information as readily as their urban compatriots. The increasing financial loss and falling mortality rates draw attention to the fact that these policies are effective to some extent in reducing direct/indirect losses, but the lack of risk awareness by communities and the fact that some people cannot afford to implement these policies probably play a bigger role in the rising disaster cost.

The NFIP was designed as a risk-transfer mechanism to help flood victims recover with the help of insurance provided by public and private agencies. It appears, however, to have become an incentive for growth in risk-prone areas rather than a deterrent. The guaranteed availability of financial aid leads to repeat losses and relocation of people in the same hazardous places. China, in contrast, does not have any such non-structural mitigation approach. Therefore, the property losses are much higher than insured losses.[129] China is proposing to implement a flood-management approach similar to that of the NFIP. Looking at the situation in the U.S., the lesson to be learned is that unless structural mitigation policies are in place, this technique might very well end up as a response and relief effort rather than a damage-prevention policy.

The U.S. warning system (EAS) is the reason for the reduction in mortality rates; however, the system was criticized during Katrina because of its failure to reach out to culturally and ethnically diverse communities, such as the Vietnamese community. China is still developing a comprehensive warning system. The lesson to be gained from the U.S. experience is that the socioeconomic aspect of communities should be accounted for before using a warning system. The other preparedness policy in place in the U.S. is the evacuation policy, which is specific to a state. Again, these evacuation policies have been criticized for their failure to address the sociocultural aspects of the affected communities that influence their decision to evacuate.

For mitigation efforts to be successful, the role of local communities must be taken into account. If a community is prepared, it is resilient. For EM to succeed, both countries must:

1) Increase awareness through educational and outreach programs. Programs such as those used by the USGS to increase earthquake awareness help communities understand the implications of policies and programs in increasing their sustainability in the long run.

2) Increase participation of public and private stakeholders along with local communities to implement coordinated EM actions. If a

community participates in formulating guidelines and policies, then its trust in such policies will increase, thereby leading the community to take appropriate action.

3) Assess risk and vulnerability as an integral part of preparing mitigation plans. In addition to being quantitative in nature, these assessments require spatial data. Because spatial data are available at multiple scales of analysis, it is essential to identify a scale of analysis for such assessments to get accurate outcomes.[130] The sociocultural, -economic, and -political factors of each community must also be accounted for in assessing their vulnerability and physical risk, which are dynamic in nature.

Policy intervention is the best way to standardize anything, but lack of understanding of a policy by the public seems to be the downfall of the mitigation policies in both the U.S. and China. The fragmented nature of policies and lack of an "all hazards" approach also does not help China's case. The increasing reliance on the response and relief effort evident in FEMA's 2013 budget, in which funding for pre-disaster mitigation programs was eliminated while support for the response and recovery phases of EM increased,[131] along with the lack of public-private partnership, is crippling the U.S. EM system. For countries to succeed in creating sustainable communities after a disaster, the public—the main part of the EM equation—must be part of policy preparation and implementation.

## Notes

[1] United Nations Inter-Agency Secretariat of the International Strategy for Disaster Reduction (UNISDR), *Living with Risk: A Global Review of Disaster Reduction Initiatives* (Geneva, Switzerland: Author, 2004), 4.
[2] Department of Regional Development and Environment Executive Secretariat for Economic and Social Affairs Organization of American States (DRDEES), *Primer on Natural Hazard Management in Integrated Regional Development Planning* (Washington DC: Author, 1991).
[3] Ian Burton, Robert W. Kates, and Gilbert F. White, *The Environment as Hazard* (New York, NY: Guilford Press, 1993).
[4] United Nations, *Terminology on Disaster Risk Reduction* (Geneva, Switzerland: Author, 2009), 9.
[5] Nicole Laframboise and Boileau Loko, *Natural Disasters: Mitigating Impact, Managing Risks*, International Monetary Fund Working Paper, 2012.
[6] UNISDR, 2004.
[7] United Nations, *Economic Losses from Disasters Set New Record in 2012*, UNISDR Web site, 2013.

[8] John Newton, "Federal Legislation for Disaster Mitigation: A Comparative Assessment Between Canada and the United States," *Natural Hazards* 1997 no. 16, 219–41.

[9] AIR-Worldwide Corporation (AIRWC), *The Coastline at Risk: 2013 Update to the Estimated Insured Value of U.S. Coastal Properties* (Boston, MA: Author, 2013).

[10] Daniel Sarewitz and Roger Pielke Jr., "Extreme Events: A Research and Policy Framework for Disasters in Context," *International Geology Review* 2001 no. 43, 406–18; UNEP, "Natural Disasters," in "State of the Environment and Policy Retrospective: 1972–2002," chapter 2 of *Global Environmental Outlook 3*, 270–96 (London, UK: Earthscan, 2002).

[11] Centre for Research on the Epidemiology of Disasters (CRED), *Emergency Events Database (EM-DAT)*, CRED Web site, 2009.

[12] Ibid.

[13] Ibid.

[14] Ibid.

[15] Edward N. Rappaport, "Loss of Life in the United States Associated with Recent Atlantic Tropical Cyclones," *Bulletin of the American Meteorological Society* 81(9), 2065–73; Sarewitz and Pielke Jr.

[16] UNISDR, 2004.

[17] Raymond J. Burby, "Hurricane Katrina and the Paradoxes of Government Disaster Policy: Bringing about Wise Governmental Decisions for Hazardous Areas," *The Annals of the American Academy of Political and Social Science* 2006 no. 604, 171–91; Edward L. Kick, James C. Fraser, Gregory M. Fulkerson, Laura A. McKinney, and Daniel H. De Vries, "Repetitive Flood Victims and Acceptance of FEMA Mitigation Offers: An Analysis with Community–System Policy Implications," *Disasters* 35(3), 510–39.

[18] PwC Economics, *World in 2050: The BRICs and Beyond: Prospects, Challenges and Opportunities*, PwC Website, 2013; U.S. Census Bureau, *U.S. and World Population Clock*, U.S. Census Web site, 2013a.

[19] World Health Organization, *Glossary of Humanitarian Terms* [online], WHO Web site, 2013.

[20] Federal Emergency Management Agency (FEMA), *Principles of Emergency Management*, FEMA Web site, 2007.

[21] Ibid.

[22] Ibid.

[23] Ibid.

[24] Ibid.

[25] United Nations Disaster Relief Organization (UNDRO), *Natural Disasters and Vulnerability Analysis in Report of Expert Group Meeting* (Geneva, Switzerland: Author, 1979).

[26] Burton et al.; Ben Wisner, Piers Blaikie, Terry Cannon, and Ian Davis, *At Risk: Natural Hazards, People's Vulnerability and Disasters* (London: Routledge, 1994).

[27] Burton et al.; Wisner et al.; Terry Cannon, "Vulnerability Analysis and the Explanation of Natural Disasters," in *Disasters, Development and Environment*, ed. Ann Varley, 13–30 (Chichester, UK: John Wiley, 1994); Jeanne X. Kasperson, Roger E. Kasperson, and B. L. Turner, eds., *Regions at Risk: Comparisons of Threatened Environments* (Tokyo, Japan: United Nations University Press, 1995); Susan L. Cutter, "Vulnerability to Environmental Hazards," *Progress in Human Geography* 20(4), 529–39; Kenneth Hewitt, *Regions of Risk: A Geographical Introduction to Disasters* (Essex, UK: Addison Wesley Longman, 1997); Mary B. Anderson, "Vulnerability to Disaster and Sustainable Development: A General Framework for Assessing Vulnerability," in *Storms*, vol. 1, eds. Roger A. Pielke Jr. and Roger A. Pielke Sr., 11–25 (London, UK: Routledge, 2000); B. L. Turner, Pamela A. Matson, James J. McCarthy, Robert W. Corell, Lindsey Christensen, Noelle Eckley, Grete K. Hovelsrud-Broda, Jeanne X. Kasperson, Roger E. Kasperson, Amy Luers, et al., "Illustrating the Coupled Human–Environment System for Vulnerability Analysis: Three Case Studies," *Proceedings of the US National Academy of Sciences* 100(14), 8080–5.

[28] Cutter.

[29] Laurie McCubbin, "Challenges to the Definition of Resilience," Paper presented at the Annual Meeting of the American Psychological Association, August 22–26, 2001, San Francisco, CA; Richard J. T. Klein, Robert J. Nicholls, and Frank Thomalla, "The Resilience of Coastal Megacities to Weather-Related Hazards," in *Building Safer Cities: The Future of Disaster Risk*, eds. Alcira Kreimer, Margaret Arnold, and Anne Carlin, 101–20 (Washington DC: The World Bank Disaster Management Facility, 2003); Douglas Paton and David Johnston, *Disaster Resilience: An Integrated Approach* (Springfield, IL: Charles C. Thomas, 2006).

[30] Dennis S. Mileti, *Disasters by Design: A Reassessment of Natural Hazards in the United States* (Washington DC: Joseph Henry Press, 1999); Adam Rose, "Defining and Measuring Economic Resilience to Disasters," *Disaster Prevention and Management* 13(4), 307–14.

[31] R. Tinch, *Resilience and Resource Management under Risk* (Norwich, UK: School of Environmental Science, University of East Anglia, 1998); Mileti; Rose.

[32] A. Leopold, *A Sand County Almanac* (New York, NY: Ballantine Books, 1949); Wendell Berry, *The Unsettling of America: Culture and Agriculture* (New York, NY: Avon, 1977).

[33] Herman E. Daly, *Steady-State Economics: The Economics of Biophysical Equilibrium and Moral Growth* (New York, NY: W. H. Freeman, 1977); Erik P. Eckholm, *Down to Earth: Environment and Human Needs* (London, UK: International Institute for Environment and Development / Earthscan, 1982); World Commission on Environment and Development (WCED), *Our Common Future* (Oxford, UK: OUP, 1987); United Nations Environmental Program (UNEP), *Global Environmental Outlook 2000* (London, UK: Earthscan / Author, 2000).

[34] William M. Adams, *Green Development: Environment and Sustainability in the Third World*, 2nd ed. (London, UK: Routledge, 2001).

[35] J. MacNeill, "Strategies for Sustainable Economic Development," *Scientific American,* 261(3), 154–65; W. Ruckelshaus, "Toward a Sustainable World," *Scientific American* 261(3), 166–75.
[36] WCED, 8.
[37] UNISDR, 2004.
[38] UN, *The Yokohama Strategy and Plan of Action for a Safer World,* Guidelines for Natural Disaster Prevention, Preparedness and Mitigation presented at the World Conference on Natural Disaster Reduction, Yokohama, Japan, May 23–27, 1994.
[39] UNISDR, 2004.
[40] UNISDR, *Hyogo Framework for Action 2005–2015: Building the Resilience of Nations and Communities to Disasters* (Geneva, Switzerland: Author, 2005).
[41] Ibid.
[42] The World Bank, *World Development Indicators: Size of the Economy,*" The World Bank Web site, 2013.
[43] U.S. Census Bureau, 2013a.
[44] Ibid.
[45] U.S. Department of Commerce Bureau of Economic Analysis, *National Income and Product Accounts: Gross Domestic Product, 3rd Quarter 2013 (Advance Estimate),* Bureau of Economic Analysis Web site, November 7, 2013.
[46] U.S. Census Bureau, *Statistical Abstract of the United States: 2011,* U.S. Census Web site, 2011.
[47] AIR-WC.
[48] H. Kunreuther and E. Michel-Kerjan, eds., *At War with the Weather: Managing Large-Scale Risks in a New Era of Catastrophes* (Cambridge, MA: MIT Press, 2009); Munich Re, *Topics: Annual Review: Natural Catastrophes 2009* (Munich, Germany: Author, 2010).
[49] Insurance Information Institute, *Catastrophes: U.S.,* Insurance Information Institute Web site, 2013.
[50] CRED.
[51] Ibid.
[52] Ibid.
[53] Ibid.
[54] Bruce B. Clary, "The Evolution and Structure of Natural Hazard Policies," *Public Administration Review* 1985 no. 45, 20–8.
[55] Ibid.
[56] Town of Phillipsburg, NJ, *Emergency Management History* (Phillipsburg, NJ: Author, n.d.).
[57] Tennessee Valley Authority, *TVA History,* TVA Web site, 2013.
[58] Town of Phillipsburg.
[59] James M. Wright, *The Nation's Responses to Flood Disasters: A Historical Account* (Madison, WI: Association of State Floodplain Managers, 2000).
[60] Wright; Dan Henstra, and Andrew Sancton, *Mitigating Catastrophic Losses: Policies and Policy-Making at Three Levels of Government in the United States*

*and Canada*, Institute for Catastrophic Loss Reduction Research Paper Series no. 23 (Toronto, Canada: ICLR, 2002).
[61] Town of Phillipsburg.
[62] Henry B. Hogue and Keith Bea, *Federal Emergency Management and Homeland Security Organization: Historical Developments and Legislative Options* (Washington DC: Congressional Research Service / Library of Congress, 2006).
[63] Wilbur J. Cohen and Evelyn F. Boyer, "Federal Civil Defense Act of 1950: Summary and Legislative History," *Social Security Bulletin*, April 1951, 11–6.
[64] Hogue and Bea.
[65] Ibid.
[66] Clary.
[67] Henstra and Sancton.
[68] Clary; Town of Phillipsburg.
[69] Henstra and Sancton.
[70] Clary; Henstra and Sancton.
[71] Hogue and Bea.
[72] FEMA, "The Federal Emergency Management Agency," FEMA Web site, 2010.
[73] Newton.
[74] FEMA, *Principles of Emergency Management*, FEMA Web site, 2007.
[75] Newton.
[76] Henstra and Sancton.
[77] Ibid.
[78] Hogue and Bea.
[79] William C. Nicholson, *Introduction: A Short History of Homeland Security and Emergency Management Law* [PowerPoint Slide], FEMA Web site, 2013.
[80] Michael J. Fagel and Stephen J. Krill Jr., "Introduction: Why Plan for Disasters?" in *Principles of Emergency Management: Hazard-Specific Issues and Mitigation Strategies*, ed. Michael J. Fagel, 1–24 (Boca Raton, FL: CRC Press, 2012).
[81] Ibid.
[82] Ibid.
[83] Francis X. McCarthy, *Federal Stafford Act Disaster Assistance: Presidential Declarations, Eligible Activities, and Funding* (Washington DC: Congressional Research Service, 2011); Fagel and Krill.
[84] Fagel and Krill.
[85] Nicholson, 2013:49.
[86] FEMA, "Flood Insurance Reform Act of 2012," FEMA Web site, 2013.
[87] The World Bank, "World Development Indicators: Size of the Economy," The World Bank Web site, 2013.
[88] U.S. Census Bureau, *U.S. International Programs*, U.S. Census Web site, 2013b.
[89] Kam Wing Chan, "The Problem with China's Urban Population Data," *East Asia Center* Winter 2010, 2–3.
[90] Gregory C. Chow, "Economic Reform and Growth in China." *Annals of Economics and Finance*, 2004 no. 5, 127–52.

[91] The World Bank, *Data: GDP Ranking*, The World Bank Web site, 2013.
[92] UNISDR, *China–Disaster Statistics*, PreventionWeb Web site, 2013.
[93] Jörn Birkmann, "Risk and Vulnerability Indicators at Different Scales: Applicability, Usefulness and Policy Implications," *Environmental Hazards*, 2007 no. 7, 20–31; Aniello Amendola, Joanne Linnerooth-Bayer, Norio Okada, and Peijun Shi, "Towards Integrated Disaster Risk Management: Case Studies and Trends from Asia," *Natural Hazards* 44(2), 163–8.
[94] CRED.
[95] Ibid.
[96] Ibid.
[97] Ibid.
[98] Victor Bai, "Emergency Management in China," in *Comparative Emergency Management: Understanding Disaster Policies, Organizations, and Initiatives from around the World*, ed. D. A. McEntire, Chapter 25 (Emmitsburg, MD: FEMA Emergency Management Institute, 2013).
[99] Ibid.
[100] Ibid.
[101] Ibid.
[102] Ibid.
[103] Hu Xunrun, "Comprehensive Planning," in *Multipurpose River Basin Development in China*, ed. P. Sun, 31–5 (Washington DC: The World Bank, 1994); Seungho Lee, *China's Water Policy Challenges* (Nottingham, UK: University of Nottingham China Policy Institute, 2006).
[104] Lee.
[105] Ibid.
[106] Bai.
[107] Ibid.
[108] Ibid.
[109] China National Committee for International Decade for Natural Disaster Reduction (CNCIDNDR), *China Country Report 1999*, Asian Disaster Reduction Center Web site, 1999.
[110] Ibid.
[111] Ibid.
[112] Bai.
[113] Ibid.
[114] Newton.
[115] J. B. Weiner, "Climate Change Policy and Policy Change in China," *UCLA Law Review*, 2008 no. 55, 1805–26; M. Gemmer, A. Wilkes, and L. M. Vaucel, "Governing Climate Change Adaptation in the EU and China: An Analysis of Formal Institutions," *Advances in Climate Change Research* 2(1), 1–11.
[116] James A. Bill and Robert L. Hardgrave, Jr., *Comparative Politics: The Quest for Theory* (Lanham, MD: University Press of America, 1981).
[117] A. J. Heidenheimer, H. Heclo, and C. T. Adams, *Comparative Public Policy: The Politics of Social Choice in America, Europe and Japan* (New York, NY: St. Martin's Press, 1990), 3.

[118] H. J. Wiarda, *Introduction to Comparative Politics: Concepts and Processes* (Belmont, CA: Wadsworth, 1993), 12.
[119] David A. McEntire and S. Mathis, "Comparative Politics and Disasters: Assessing Substantive and Methodological Contributions," in *Disciplines, Disasters and Emergency Management: The Convergence and Divergence of Concepts, Issues and Trends from the Research Literature*, ed. David A. McEntire, 178–195 (Springfield, IL: Charles C. Thomas, 2007).
[120] Yoshiaki Kobayashi and John W. Porter, *Flood Risk Management in the People's Republic of China: Learning to Live with Flood Risk* (Manila, Philippines: Asian Development Bank, 2012).
[121] B. Reynolds and M. W. Seeger, "Crisis and Emergency Risk Communication as an Integrative Model," *Journal of Health Communication*, 2005 no. 10, 43–55; Hugh Gladwin, J. K. Lazo, Betty Hearn Morrow, Walter Gillis Peacock, and H. E. Willoughby, "Social Science Research Needs for the Hurricane Forecast and Warning System," *Natural Hazards Review* 8(3), 87–95; S. Krimsky, "Risk Communication in the Internet Age: The Rise of Disorganized Skepticism," *Environmental Hazards* 2007 no. 7, 157–64.
[122] New Hanover County, NC, *History of the Emergency Alert System*, News and Information, New Hanover County Web site, n.d.
[123] FEMA, *Integrated Alert and Warning System (IPAWS)*, FEMA Web site, 2013.
[124] J. H. Sorensen, "Hazard Warning Systems: Review of 20 Years of Progress," *Natural Hazards Review*, 1(2), 119–25; FEMA, "IPAWS".
[125] Clary.
[126] FEMA, *National Earthquake Hazards Reduction Program*, FEMA Web site, 2013.
[127] FEMA, *About the U.S. Fire Administration (USFA)*, FEMA Web site, 2013.
[128] FEMA, *National Mitigation Strategy: Partnerships for Building Safer Communities* (Washington DC: Author, 1995).
[129] Swiss Re, 2006
[130] L. Stephen and T. E. Downing, "Getting the Scale Right: A Comparison of Analytical Methods for Vulnerability Assessment and Household-Level Targeting," *Disasters* 25(2), 113–35; Bandana Kar and M. E. Hodgson, "Observational Scale and Modeled Potential Residential Loss from a Storm Surge," *GIScience and Remote Sensing*, 49(2), 202–27.
[131] FEMA, *Fiscal Year 2013 Budget*, FEMA Web site, 2012.

# Bibliography

Adams, William M.. *Green Development: Environment and Sustainability in the Third World.* 2nd Edition. London, UK: Routledge, 2001.
AIR-Worldwide Corporation (AIRWC). *The Coastline at Risk: 2013 Update to the Estimated Insured Value of U.S. Coastal Properties.* Boston, MA: Author, 2013. http://www.air-worldwide.com/_public/images/pdf/AIR2013_Coastline_at_Risk.pdf.

Amendola, Aniello, Joanne Linnerooth-Bayer, Norio Okada, and Peijun Shi. "Towards Integrated Disaster Risk Management: Case Studies and Trends from Asia." *Natural Hazards* 44(2), 163–8.

Anderson, Mary B. "Vulnerability to Disaster and Sustainable Development: A General Framework for Assessing Vulnerability." In *Storms*. vol. 1. Edited by Roger A. Pielke Jr. and Roger A. Pielke Sr. 11–25. London, UK: Routledge, 2000.

Bai, Victor. "Emergency Management in China." *In Comparative Emergency Management: Understanding Disaster Policies, Organizations, and Initiatives from around the World.* Edited by D. A. McEntire. Chapter 25. Emmitsburg, MD: FEMA Emergency Management Institute, 2013. http://training.fema.gov/EMIWeb/edu/CompEmMgmtBookProject.asp

Berry, Wendell. *The Unsettling of America: Culture and Agriculture.* New York, NY: Avon, 1977.

Bill, James A., and Robert L. Hardgrave, Jr. *Comparative Politics: The Quest for Theory*. Lanham, MD: University Press of America, 1981.

Birkmann, Jörn. "Risk and Vulnerability Indicators at Different Scales: Applicability, Usefulness and Policy Implications." *Environmental Hazards* 2007 no. 7, 20–31.

Burby, Raymond J. "Hurricane Katrina and the Paradoxes of Government Disaster Policy: Bringing about Wise Governmental Decisions for Hazardous Areas." *The Annals of the American Academy of Political and Social Science* 2006 no. 604, 171–91.

Burton, Ian, Robert W. Kates and Gilbert F. White. *The Environment as Hazard.* New York, NY: Guilford Press, 1993.

Cannon, Terry. "Vulnerability Analysis and the Explanation of Natural Disasters." In *Disasters, Development and Environment*. Edited by Ann Varley. 13–30. Chichester, UK: John Wiley, 1994.

Centre for Research on the Epidemiology of Disasters (CRED). "Emergency Events Database (EM-DAT)." CRED Web site. 2009. http://www.emdat.be/database

Chan, Kam Wing. "The Problem with China's Urban Population Data." *East Asia Center* Winter 2010, 2–3. http://faculty.washington.edu/kwchan/Chan-article-EACWtr10.pdf

Chow, Gregory C. "Economic Reform and Growth in China." *Annals of Economics and Finance*, 2004 no. 5, 127–52.

China National Committee for International Decade for Natural Disaster Reduction (CNCIDNDR). *China Country Report 1999*. Asian Disaster Reduction Center Web site, 1999. http://www.adrc.asia/countryreport/CHN/CHNeng99/China99.htm

Clary, Bruce B. "The Evolution and Structure of Natural Hazard Policies." *Public Administration Review* 1985 no. 45, 20–8.
Cohen, Wilbur J. and Evelyn F. Boyer. "Federal Civil Defense Act of 1950: Summary and Legislative History." *Social Security Bulletin*, April 1951, 11–6. http://www.ssa.gov/policy/docs/ssb/v14n4/v14n4p11.pdf
Cutter, Susan L. "Vulnerability to Environmental Hazards." *Progress in Human Geography* 20(4), 529–39.
Daly, Herman E. *Steady-State Economics: The Economics of Biophysical Equilibrium and Moral Growth.* New York, NY: W. H. Freeman, 1977.
Department of Regional Development and Environment Executive Secretariat for Economic and Social Affairs Organization of American States (DRDEES). *Primer on Natural Hazard Management in Integrated Regional Development Planning.* Washington D.C.: Author, 1991. http://www.oas.org/dsd/publications/Unit/oea66e/begin.htm
Eckholm, Erik P. *Down to Earth: Environment and Human Needs.* London, UK: International Institute for Environment and Development / Earthscan, 1982.
Fagel, Michael J., and Stephen J. Krill Jr.. "Introduction: Why Plan for Disasters?" In *Principles of Emergency Management: Hazard-Specific Issues and Mitigation Strategies.* Edited by Michael J. Fagel. 1–24. Boca Raton, FL: CRC Press, 2012.
Federal Emergency Management Agency (FEMA). *National Mitigation Strategy: Partnerships for Building Safer Communities.* Washington DC: Author, 1995.
—. "Principles of Emergency Management Supplement." FEMA Web site. September 11, 2007. http://www.iaem.com/documents/PrinciplesofEmergencyManagement.pdf
—. "The Federal Emergency Management Agency." FEMA Web site. 2010. http://www.fema.gov/pdf/about/pub1.pdf
—. "FEMA Fiscal Year 2013 Budget." FEMA Web site. 2012. http://www.fema.gov/fiscal-year-2013-budget
—. "Flood Insurance Reform Act of 2012." FEMA Web site. 2013. http://www.fema.gov/flood-insurance-reform-act-2012
—. "Integrated Alert and Warning System (IPAWS)." FEMA Web site. 2013. http://www.fema.gov/emergency/ipaws/index.shtm
—."National Earthquake Hazards Reduction Program." FEMA Web site. 2013. http://www.fema.gov/national-earthquake-hazards-reduction-program
—. "About the U.S. Fire Administration (USFA)." FEMA Web site. 2013. http://www.usfa.fema.gov/about/

Gemmer, Marco, Andreas Wilkes, and Lucie M. Vaucel. "Governing Climate Change Adaptation in the EU and China: An Analysis of Formal Institutions." *Advances in Climate Change Research* 2(1), 1–11.

Gladwin, Hugh, Jeffrey K. Lazo, Betty Hearn Morrow, Walter Gillis Peacock, and Hugh E. Willoughby. "Social Science Research Needs for the Hurricane Forecast and Warning System." *Natural Hazards Review* 8(3), 87–95.

Heidenheimer, Arnold J., Hugh Heclo, and Carolyn Teich Adams. *Comparative Public Policy: The Politics of Social Choice in America, Europe and Japan.* New York, NY: St. Martin's Press, 1990.

Henstra, Dan, and Andrew Sancton. *Mitigating Catastrophic Losses: Policies and Policy-Making at Three Levels of Government in the United States and Canada.* Institute for Catastrophic Loss Reduction Research Paper Series no. 23. Toronto, Canada: ICLR, 2002. http://www.iclr.org/images/Mitigating_catastrophic_losses.pdf

Hewitt, Kenneth. *Regions of Risk: A Geographical Introduction to Disasters.* Essex, UK: Addison Wesley Longman, 1997.

Hogue, Henry B., and Keith Bea. *Federal Emergency Management and Homeland Security Organization: Historical Developments and Legislative Options.* Washington DC: Congressional Research Service / Library of Congress, 2006. http://www.fas.org/sgp/crs/homesec/RL33369.pdf

Insurance Information Institute. "Catastrophes: U.S." Insurance Information Institute Web site. 2013. http://www.iii.org/facts_statistics/catastrophes-us.html

Kar, Bandana, and Michael. E. Hodgson. "Observational Scale and Modeled Potential Residential Loss from a Storm Surge." *GIScience and Remote Sensing* 49(2), 202–27.

Kasperson, Jeanne X., Roger E. Kasperson, and B. L. Turner, eds. *Regions at Risk: Comparisons of Threatened Environments.* Tokyo, Japan: United Nations University Press, 1995.

Kick, Edward L., James C. Fraser, Gregory M. Fulkerson, Laura A. McKinney, and Daniel H. De Vries. "Repetitive Flood Victims and Acceptance of FEMA Mitigation Offers: An Analysis with Community–System Policy Implications." *Disasters* 35(3), 510–39.

Klein, Richard J. T., Robert J. Nicholls, and Frank Thomalla. "The Resilience of Coastal Megacities to Weather-Related Hazards." In *Building Safer Cities: The Future of Disaster Risk.* Edited by Alcira Kreimer, Margaret Arnold, and Anne Carlin. 101–20. Washington DC: The World Bank Disaster Management Facility, 2003.

Kobayashi, Yoshiaki, and John W. Porter. *Flood Risk Management in the People's Republic of China: Learning to Live with Flood Risk.* Manila, Philippines: Asian Development Bank, 2012. http://reliefweb.int/sites/reliefweb.int/files/resources/PDF_182.pdf

Krimsky, Sheldon. "Risk Communication in the Internet Age: The Rise of Disorganized Skepticism." *Environmental Hazards*, 2007 no. 7, 157–64.

Kunreuther, Howard, Erwann O. Michel-Kerjan, Neil A. Doherty, Martin F. Grace, Robert W. Klein, and Mark V. Pauly, eds. *At War with the Weather: Managing Large-Scale Risks in a New Era of Catastrophes.* Cambridge, MA: MIT Press, 2009.

Laframboise, Nicole, and Boileau Loko. *Natural Disasters: Mitigating Impact, Managing Risks.* International Monetary Fund Working Paper. 2012. http://www.imf.org/external/pubs/ft/wp/2012/wp12245.pdf

Lee, Seungho. *China's Water Policy Challenges.* Nottingham, UK: University of Nottingham China Policy Institute, 2006. http://www.nottingham.ac.uk/shared/shared_cpi/documents/discussion_papers/Discussion_Paper_13_China_Water_Policy_Challenges.pdf

Leopold, Aldo. *A Sand County Almanac.* New York, NY: Ballantine Books, 1949.

MacNeill, Jim. "Strategies for Sustainable Economic Development." *Scientific American*, 261(3), 154–65.

McCarthy, Francis X. *Federal Stafford Act Disaster Assistance: Presidential Declarations, Eligible Activities, and Funding.* Washington DC: Congressional Research Service, 2011. http://www.fas.org/sgp/crs/homesec/RL33053.pdf

McCubbin, Laurie. "Challenges to the Definition of Resilience." Paper presented at the Annual Meeting of the American Psychological Association, August 22–26, 2001. San Francisco, CA.

McEntire, David A., and Sarah Mathis. "Comparative Politics and Disasters: Assessing Substantive and Methodological Contributions." In *Disciplines, Disasters and Emergency Management: The Convergence and Divergence of Concepts, Issues and Trends from the Research Literature*, Edited by David A. McEntire. 178–195. Springfield, IL: Charles C. Thomas, 2007.

Mileti, Dennis S. *Disasters by Design: A Reassessment of Natural Hazards in the United States.* Washington DC: Joseph Henry Press, 1999.

Munich Re. *Topics: Annual Review: Natural Catastrophes 2009.* Munich, Germany: Author, 2010.

Newton, John. "Federal Legislation for Disaster Mitigation: A Comparative Assessment Between Canada and the United States." *Natural Hazards*, 1997 no. 16, 219–41.

New Hanover County, NC. "History of the Emergency Alert System." News and Information, New Hanover County Web site. n.d. http://www.nhcgov.com/News/Pages/EAS_History.aspx.

Nicholson, William C. "Introduction: A Short History of Homeland Security and Emergency Management Law." [PowerPoint Slide]. FEMA Web site. 2013. http://training.fema.gov/

Paton, Douglas, and David Johnston. *Disaster Resilience: An Integrated Approach*. Springfield, IL: Charles C. Thomas, 2006.

PwC Economics. *World in 2050: The BRICs and Beyond: Prospects, Challenges and Opportunities*. PwC Website, 2013. http://www.pwc.com/en_GX/gx/world-2050/assets/pwc-world-in-2050-report-january-2013.pdf

Rappaport, Edward N. "Loss of Life in the United States Associated with Recent Atlantic Tropical Cyclones." *Bulletin of the American Meteorological Society*, 81(9), 2065–73.

Reynolds, Barbara, and Matthew W. Seeger. "Crisis and Emergency Risk Communication as an Integrative Model." *Journal of Health Communication*, 2005 no. 10, 43–55.

Rose, Adam. "Defining and Measuring Economic Resilience to Disasters." *Disaster Prevention and Management* 13(4), 307–14.

Ruckelshaus, William. "Toward a Sustainable World." *Scientific American*, 261(3), 166–75.

Sarewitz, Daniel, and Roger Pielke Jr.. "Extreme Events: A Research and Policy Framework for Disasters in Context." *International Geology Review* 2001 no. 43, 406–18.

Sorensen, John H. "Hazard Warning Systems: Review of 20 Years of Progress." *Natural Hazards Review*, 1(2), 119–25.

Stephen, Linda, and Thomas E. Downing. "Getting the Scale Right: A Comparison of Analytical Methods for Vulnerability Assessment and Household-Level Targeting." *Disasters*, 25(2), 113–35.

Swiss Re. *Natural Hazards in China: Ensuring Long-Term Stability*. Zurich, Switzerland: Author, 2006. http://media.swissre.com/documents/natural_hazards_in_china_en.pdf

Tennessee Valley Authority (TVA). "TVA History." TVA Web site. 2013. http://www.tva.com/abouttva/history.htm

Tinch, R. *Resilience and Resource Management under Risk*. Norwich, UK: School of Environmental Science, University of East Anglia, 1998.

Town of Phillipsburg, NJ. *Emergency Management History*. Phillipsburg, NJ: Author, n.d. http://www.phillipsburgnj.org/pdf/ACF4A8.pdf

Turner, B. L., Pamela A. Matson, James J. McCarthy, Robert W. Corell, Lindsey Christensen, Noelle Eckley, Grete K. Hovelsrud-Broda, Jeanne X.

Kasperson, Roger E. Kasperson, Amy Luers, et al. "Illustrating the Coupled Human–Environment System for Vulnerability Analysis: Three Case Studies." *Proceedings of the US National Academy of Sciences*, 100(14), 8080–5.

United Nations. *The Yokohama Strategy and Plan of Action for a Safer World. Guidelines for Natural Disaster Prevention, Preparedness and Mitigation.* Presented at the World Conference on Natural Disaster Reduction, Yokohama, Japan, May 23–27, 1994. http://unpan1.un.org/intradoc/groups/public/documents/apcity/unpan029311.pdf

—. *Economic Losses from Disasters Set New Record in 2012.* 2013. http://www.unisdr.org/archive/31685

United Nations Disaster Relief Organization (UNDRO). *Natural Disasters and Vulnerability Analysis in Report of Expert Group Meeting.* Geneva, Switzerland: Author, 1979.

United Nations Environmental Program (UNEP). *Global Environmental Outlook 2000.* London, UK: Earthscan / Author, 2000.

—. "Natural Disasters." In Chapter 2, "State of the Environment and Policy Retrospective: 1972–2002," in *Global Environmental Outlook 3*, 270–96. London, UK: Earthscan, 2002. http://www.unep.org/geo/geo3/english/448.htm

United Nations Inter-Agency Secretariat of the International Strategy for Disaster Reduction (UNISDR). *Living with Risk: A Global Review of Disaster Reduction Initiatives.* Geneva, Switzerland: Author, 2004.

—. *Hyogo Framework for Action 2005–2015: Building the Resilience of Nations and Communities to Disasters.* Geneva, Switzerland: Author, 2005. http://www.unisdr.org/2005/wcdr/intergover/official-doc/L-docs/Hyogo-framework-for-action-english.pdf

—. *Terminology on Disaster Risk Reduction.* Geneva, Switzerland: Author, 2009. http://www.unisdr.org/files/7817_UNISDRTerminologyEnglish.pdf

—. "China–Disaster Statistics." PreventionWeb Web site, 2013. http://www.preventionweb.net/english/countries/statistics/?cid=36

U.S. Census Bureau. "Statistical Abstract of the United States: 2011." U.S. Census Web site. 2011. http://www.census.gov/compendia/statab/cats/population.html

—. "U.S. and World Population Clock." U.S. Census Web site. 2013a. http://www.census.gov/popclock/

—. "U.S. International Programs." U.S. Census Web site. 2013b. http://www.census.gov/population/international/data/idb/informationGateway.php

U.S. Department of Commerce Bureau of Economic Analysis. "National Income and Product Accounts: Gross Domestic Product, 3rd Quarter 2013 (Advance Estimate)." Bureau of Economic Analysis Web site. November 7, 2013. http://www.bea.gov/newsreleases/national/gdp/gdpnewsrelease.htm

Weiner, Jonathan B. "Climate Change Policy and Policy Change in China." *UCLA Law Review*, 2008 no. 55, 1805–26.

Wiarda, Howard J. *Introduction to Comparative Politics: Concepts and Processes*. Belmont, CA: Wadsworth, 1993.

Wisner, Ben, Piers Blaikie, Terry Cannon, and Ian Davis. *At Risk: Natural Hazards, People's Vulnerability and Disasters*. London: Routledge, 1994.

World Bank, The. "Data: GDP Ranking." The World Bank Web site. 2013. http://data.worldbank.org/data-catalog/GDP-ranking-table

——. "World Development Indicators: Size of the Economy." The World Bank Web site. 2013. http://wdi.worldbank.org/table/1.1

World Commission on Environment and Development (WCED). *Our Common Future*. Oxford, UK: OUP, 1987.

World Health Organization (WHO). *Glossary of Humanitarian Terms* [online]. 2013. http://www.who.int/hac/about/definitions/en/

Wright, James M. *The Nation's Responses To Flood Disasters: A Historical Account*. Madison, WI: Association of State Floodplain Managers, 2000. http://www.floods.org/PDF/hist_fpm.pdf

Xunrun, Hu. "Comprehensive Planning." In *Multipurpose River Basin Development in China*. Edited by P. Sun. 31–5. Washington D.C.: The World Bank, 1994.

# PART III

# POST-DISASTER REBUILDING IN JAPAN

# CHAPTER EIGHT

## NGOs, International Philanthropy, and Disasters in Developed Countries: The U.S. Response to Japan's 3.11 Disaster

### James Gannon

I was still fumbling with the lock on the office door when the phone started ringing. It was already late but I had spent the first two hours that morning calling around Tokyo to make sure that my brother and my colleagues were safe after the day's massive earthquake. When I finally made it inside and picked up the phone, a Congresswoman was on the line to ask for the latest report from Japan and to express her sympathy for the victims of the unfolding tragedy. She was clearly shaken and struggled to maintain her composure. As soon as I put the receiver back in the cradle, it rang again. This time it was a schoolteacher who saw that our organization's name began with "Japan" and wanted advice on things that her students could do to support relief efforts. By the time that call ended, several of our other lines were lighting up. The ringing was to continue nonstop for weeks to come, with calls from hundreds of concerned people around the country from all walks of life who wanted to help Japan in some way.

In retrospect, it seems remarkable that the trends that became evident that first day—March 11, 2011—would hold true throughout the American public's response to the disaster that became known in Japan simply as "3.11", the 9.0 magnitude earthquake, the towering tsunami and the chilling crisis that unfolded afterward at Fukushima Daiichi Nuclear Power Plant. The response was overwhelming, highly diverse, and largely based on people's personal connections to Japan, whether through travel or work, participation in some Japan-related activity, or memories of a Japanese exchange student they had known as a child. Moreover, the intensity of emotion and the compassion that many Americans felt toward

Japanese victims seemed to be magnified by the shocking footage they saw on television and the Internet and then further amplified by social media.

In a pattern that was to be repeated around the world, Americans in all corners of the country mobilized to demonstrate their solidarity with Japan and raise funds for the disaster response. In the end, they donated nearly three-quarters of a billion dollars for a broad range of rescue, relief and recovery efforts—the greatest outpouring of charitable donations ever for an overseas disaster in another rich country.[1] Remarkably, this ranked as the fifth-most generous incidence of private giving in U.S. history for any disaster, trailing only the responses to Hurricane Katrina, the 9/11 attacks, the 2004 Indian Ocean tsunami, and the 2010 Haiti earthquake. The story of how this extraordinary response played out reveals a great deal about the trends that have been reshaping disaster philanthropy in recent years and yields vital lessons for future responses to megadisasters, especially in other developed countries.

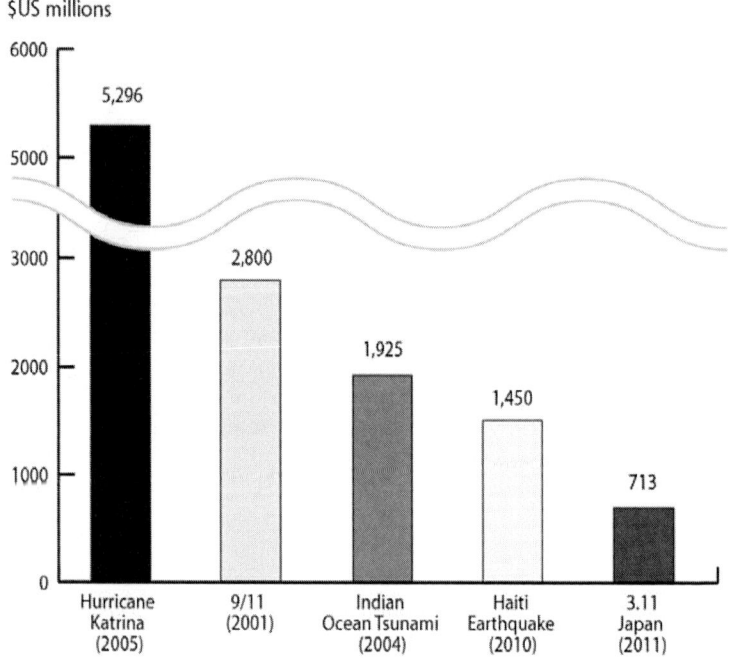

Figure 8.1. U.S. Giving in Response to Major Disasters.[2]

## The Growing Roles of NGOs and International Disaster Philanthropy

The story of the response to the Great East Japan Earthquake is a profoundly human one and one that encompasses the experiences of millions of people. There is the mayor who spent a snowy night stranded on the roof of city hall watching his city being swept away, then felt compelled to work around the clock for weeks to direct rescue operations without taking time to grieve with his two sons or to search for his wife, who went missing in the waves. There is the young woman who accepted her colleague's offer to cut in front of him on the stairs while fleeing the rising waters and now struggles with guilt after being the last person to make it out alive. There is the volunteer who gave up a comfortable job in Tokyo to find new meaning in life running a nonprofit aid center in the disaster zone. There is the California couple who were so moved by the suffering that they decided to refuse wedding gifts and instead urged their guests to make donations in their honor to a relief fund.

But it is also part of a larger story about the globalization of disasters and the growing role of nongovernmental actors in disaster responses. The massive outpouring of U.S. giving for Japan is important not just as a reflection of the goodwill that one country's people harbored toward another's, but also because it signifies how the nongovernmental sector's response increasingly has the capacity to alter the course of a disaster recovery half a world away. While the public perception is that national governments and UN agencies lead the international response to megadisasters, the role of nongovernmental organizations (NGOs) and private donations has been expanding for some time. This trend was already apparent in the international response to the 2004 Indian Ocean tsunami, when nearly 40 percent of the $14 billion in pledged overseas aid came from private donations.[3] Similarly, data from the UN Office for Coordination of Humanitarian Affairs indicates that nearly 40 percent of all overseas pledges after the Haiti earthquake—and 50 percent of commitments disbursed to date—were from private donors, although this likely undercounts total private giving for the disaster.[4] But the role of private giving became even more pronounced in the overseas response to 3.11, as private-sector donations quietly outpaced official government aid for Japan.[5]

Of course, any retelling of the American response to 3.11 must start with the rapid military response, one that was brilliantly named Operation Tomodachi, incorporating the Japanese term for "friend". U.S. forces stationed in Japan began mobilizing within hours; twenty-four naval vessels, including an aircraft carrier, were positioned off the Tohoku coast while U.S. spy planes flew data-gathering missions over the nuclear plant; and 24,000 American service members became involved in the relief efforts, many of them working alongside Japanese Self Defense Force troops in the disaster zone, clearing rubble, transporting emergency supplies, and aiding survivors.[6] Stateside in Washington D.C., a broad range of government agencies sprang into action to coordinate government agencies' provision of aid, support U.S. residents in Japan, and undertake the increasingly critical task of advising the Japanese government—and pressuring it to move more decisively—in its halting response to the nuclear crisis.

Still, the nongovernmental response from the U.S. was equally impressive and in some ways even more astounding. The $712.6 million in U.S. private donations dwarfed the $95 million that the U.S. government is estimated to have spent in helping Japan, although it bears noting that the specialized capabilities that the U.S. military and other government agencies brought to the response cannot be quantified solely in financial terms.[7] The prominence of nongovernmental actors on the donor side was matched by the expanded role that Japanese NGOs played in the response, filling the gaps in the national and local governments' provision of services essential for relief and recovery to an extent that is unprecedented in Japanese history. This helped to make 3.11 one of, if not the, first major disasters in modern history when the nongovernmental sector played as crucial a role in the international response as governments and international organizations.

## The U.S. Nongovernmental Response

In the initial days after 3.11, a diverse range of American groups began weighing how they could help without placing a greater burden than necessary on local authorities and frontline responders. The fact that the disaster had struck such a rich country with considerable resources and extensive experience dealing with large-scale disasters made it even more challenging to identify precisely what they should be doing. While a few of the NGOs that normally respond to disasters scrambled to put staff on the Friday morning flights to Japan—even with little idea of how to proceed once they landed in Japan—most of the major humanitarian assistance organizations took a more restrained posture of monitoring the situation and consulting with Japanese authorities about what gaps they could fill. A handful even debated whether it was appropriate to raise funds for the response: Doctors Without Borders and a few other groups initially declared that they would not accept donations specifically earmarked for Japan until they had a clearer picture of how much need there would be for their assistance. However, for many groups, especially the major humanitarian assistance organizations accustomed to raising large amounts of funds in the immediate aftermath of disasters, the default stance was to start a relief fund. Within the week, hundreds of major organizations were launching fundraising drives, even though many had not decided whether to use them to support their own relief activities or to grant the contributions to Japanese groups.

In those chaotic first days, it became apparent that there were at least three distinct sets of organizations active at the national level in the U.S., and while there was some overlap, by and large the groups that fell into one set had little awareness of what others in different circles were doing. One set consisted of the professional humanitarian assistance and disaster relief organizations that are accustomed to mobilizing rapidly to dispatch assessment teams and deliver aid for crises around the world. These included, for example, the American Red Cross, World Vision, and Mercy Corps. A second, smaller set involved international philanthropic intermediaries, organizations that specialize in collecting donations and then regranting them overseas. This encompassed more traditional groups like United Way, as well as some new, tech-savvy organizations such as Global Giving that have sprung up to facilitate online giving. The third set, meanwhile, consisted of Japan-related organizations in the U.S., ranging from the national network of roughly forty Japan-America Societies to policy-oriented institutes and charitable foundations that support U.S.-Japan exchange.

Each of these groupings had their own particular strengths and shortcomings. The professional humanitarian assistance organizations had a deep understanding of what was required to respond at the different stages of disasters. They had a playbook for what to do on Day 1, Day 3 and Day 10; they knew how to anticipate the transitions from rescue to relief and from relief to recovery; and they had a good feel for how needs were likely to change at each stage. They also had mechanisms in place that allowed them to launch major fundraising appeals on a moment's notice—website templates, lists of major donors, and what can be called brand recognition among the general public.

However, most of these groups also had limited knowledge of Japan and few connections to the Japanese government officials and humanitarian aid groups that were taking the lead in the response. Things proved particularly challenging because these organizations were accustomed to operating in developing countries, where donor coordination mechanisms utilized to share information among groups distributing development aid could quickly be repurposed to facilitate NGO coordination on the disaster response. In Japan, though, there was no natural contact point for overseas organizations that needed both connections to other organizations and a crash course on how to operate in its unique societal milieu; there was also no obvious convener that could facilitate coordination with the dozens of other Japanese and overseas groups that were rushing to help. While two groups, Japan Platform and the Japan NGO Center for International Cooperation (JANIC), eventually took on some of these functions, they remained imperfect vehicles for this purpose.

Meanwhile, the second set of organizations that mobilized—the philanthropic intermediaries—had a strong grasp of what was required to raise funds that could be regranted to overseas organizations and how to do this in a deliberate and sustainable manner. This made them particularly well suited to support the Japanese nonprofit organizations that would be relied upon to play key roles in the long-term recovery process. They also had a good understanding of the often undervalued art of grant-making, meaning that they recognized the importance of working in a collaborative manner with funding recipients to encourage them to formulate viable project plans. They structured the funding process in a way that did not test the limits of already overstretched Japanese groups and insisted on injecting appropriate accountability and transparency requirements into funding proposals and grant agreements.

However, while they had a deep understanding of international grant-making—as well as the intricacies of domestic tax law that pertain to it—they had a much weaker comprehension of the practices commonplace in Japan's nonprofit sector, which was far less professionalized than in other developed countries. Fortunately, though, the three key philanthropic intermediaries that were most active in the disaster response—Global Giving, Give2Asia, and United Way Worldwide—happened to have special ties to Japan. Global Giving, which heretofore had focused on supporting development projects in poor countries, was headed by a dynamic Japanese expatriate, Mari Kuraishi, who had a personal stake in helping her country. Give2Asia, meanwhile, had been spun off from the Asia Foundation and was designed to channel funds to nonprofit initiatives in Asia, so it had historic ties to Japan as well as staff members with experience of living in the country. Meanwhile, United Way Worldwide, the Virginia-based parent organization for the United Way affiliates in the U.S. and around the world, had long cooperated on small-scale initiatives with the Central Community Chest of Japan.

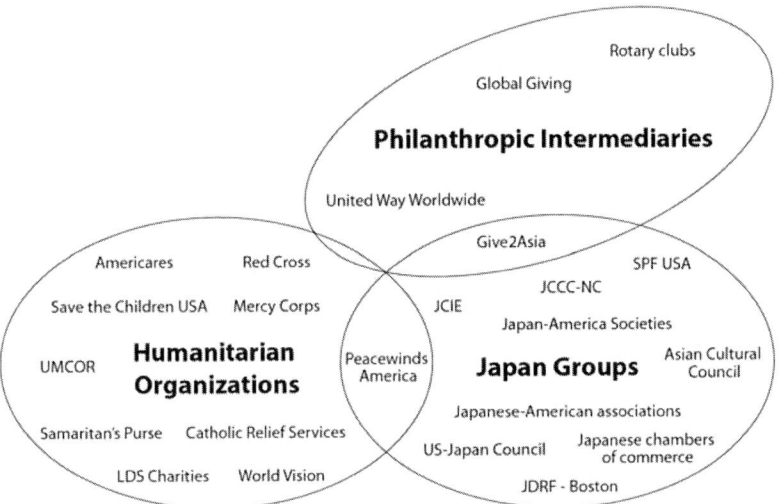

Figure 8.2. Types of Groups with Large-Scale "Japan Funds".

For their part, the third set of organizations that became particularly prominent in the philanthropic response, a broad mélange of institutions dedicated to various aspects of U.S.-Japan exchange, had hard-earned insights into the dynamics of Japanese society and strong networks at the national and local level in the country. Their staff also had a deep personal commitment to working with Japan. They tended to have language skills that enabled them to go beyond English-speaking circles to access a much broader range of information and people, and they often had a base of constituents with a deep interest in Japan and a desire to donate money and time to help.

Yet they too were forced to grapple with serious shortcomings. Their intimate knowledge of some aspects of Japanese society did not necessarily extend to a deep understanding of how Japan's nonprofit sector operated. Moreover, with a few exceptions, they had little experience of international grant-making, and were forced to spend valuable time on basic steps such as learning how to create application forms that would elicit crucial information from potential grantees but avoid burdening them during a time of crisis, consulting with lawyers about how grant agreements could be structured to meet U.S. tax requirements and post-9/11 anti-terrorism mandates, and creating orderly processes to evaluate potential funding recipients. They also had to learn the basics of disaster response on the fly. In some instances, decisions that groups made in the initial hours and days—for example, to announce that they would not set aside management fees from incoming donations and would channel 100 percent of funds raised into the disaster zone—later created significant burdens for them when far more money than anticipated flowed into their coffers. Finally, since they were, by and large, small organizations with tight budgets and limited staff, their institutional capacity was strained by the added burden of managing disaster funds, a particularly ironic development as one of their major concerns in evaluating candidates for funding was the limited institutional capacity of the Japanese NGOs working in the disaster zone.

## Who is Coordinating This Thing?

Even though the disaster dominated national news for weeks and hundreds of groups were launching major disaster responses, there was no concerted effort to forge a coordinated national response in the way that had been done for other recent megadisasters. After the 2004 Indian Ocean tsunami, former presidents Bill Clinton and George H. W. Bush famously stood at a White House press conference alongside President George W. Bush, where they urged Americans to give generously to U.S. humanitarian groups involved in relief efforts. A similar tack was taken for the 2010 Haiti earthquake, when Clinton and George W. Bush were asked by President Barack Obama to play a leading role in mobilizing Americans to support the response, inspiring them to launch the Clinton-Bush Haiti Fund and keep the issue of Haiti relief in the public spotlight by taking several high-profile trips to the country. In the case of Japan, however, no national figures were tapped as focal points for mobilizing the philanthropic response, no real attempt was made to organize a national benefit concert, and no comprehensive information-sharing effort succeeded in reaching the full range of groups operating "Japan funds" and pledging aid.

Part of the reason for the lack of coordination at the national level can be ascribed to the sheer number and diversity of organizations that mobilized in an organic fashion for the response. One stunning statistic that illustrates the diversity of efforts is the fact that forty-five different nonprofit organizations each raised more than $1 million for relief and recovery efforts. More than 100 gathered over $100,000 a piece—notably, only a small portion of them specialized in humanitarian assistance and disaster relief, and over one-third had no prior experience of fundraising for disaster responses.[8]

But the sheer number of players was not the whole story. While American humanitarian groups have considerable experience responding to disasters in developing countries, there was no recent precedent for assisting a developed country with such a massive disaster. This sparked debates over whether it made sense to try to aid another rich country and, if so, how to best do this. A spate of articles penned by commentators who were perhaps well-intentioned but woefully uninformed about Japanese society and the real needs on the ground came out cautioning Americans against donating for the disaster response in a country that arguably had sufficient resources to take care of itself.[9] While this provoked considerable handwringing among the groups working around the clock to support their Japanese compatriots, these arguments ultimately had less impact on the response than the lack of clarity about who, if anybody, should be taking the lead in responding.

Ultimately, the coordination that did take place on the national level ended up happening within the distinct circles of groups and not between them. The U.S. Agency for International Development (USAID), the lead government agency for overseas humanitarian crises, and InterAction, the Washington D.C.-based umbrella organization for U.S. humanitarian assistance and disaster relief NGOs that work internationally, quickly began sharing information with each other as well as with the U.S. Chamber of Commerce Business Civic Leadership Center. These three organizations formed a hub that relayed information among the U.S. government, big business, and the major humanitarian assistance groups. However, there was no effort to reach out to the U.S.-Japan organizations, at least those outside of the Washington D.C. area, or to most of the philanthropic intermediaries.

Simultaneously, there were multiple efforts to share information among U.S.-Japan exchange organizations, Asian-American groups, and a handful of organizations for Japanese expatriates. These included initiatives spearheaded in the first week after the disaster by the Japan Center for International Exchange and by the U.S.-Japan Council to convene meetings and disseminate information online for NGOs involved in the philanthropic response. There were also a number of more discrete efforts: the National Association of Japan-America Societies regularly kept its member organizations informed; the Japan Society of New York periodically convened a small set of New York-based organizations for roundtables to share information; and local initiatives emerged in Seattle, New Orleans, and elsewhere around the country.

Even though some of the efforts among Japan-related groups grew to be quite large, involving dozens of organizations, they tended to operate in an ad hoc manner depending heavily on personal connections. There was no systematic exchange of information with the humanitarian groups that were having separate discussions among themselves, although by chance some of the major philanthropic intermediaries, namely Give2Asia and Global Giving, were eventually brought into the Japan-related organizations' coordination efforts. The lack of communication between the circles of humanitarian assistance organizations and Japan-related groups was not because either side wanted to exclude the other, but simply because each was hardly aware of the other was doing.

Unsurprisingly, this lack of awareness about what other groups were doing extended to the international realm as well. Even before American groups started trying to bring some coordination to their efforts, internationally minded Japanese NGOs in the disaster relief field had started meeting in various forums in Tokyo and elsewhere, most notably under the aegis of Japan Platform and JANIC. Yet most American groups were barely aware that these discussions were taking place, and even after the first several months had passed, there was little flow of information across the Pacific about what was being discussed in the various forums.

## A Grassroots Phenomenon

While the larger humanitarian groups, philanthropic intermediaries and Japan-related organizations were working to formulate their responses, a more organic movement was brewing at the grassroots level. In the initial days and weeks after the disaster, the media had started reporting on the reluctance of Americans to donate generously to help Japan, contrasting it with the outpouring of giving after the 2004 Indian Ocean tsunami and the 2010 Haiti earthquake. *USA Today* blared "US Donations Not Rushing to Japan" and ABC News asked "Americans Less Generous in Disaster Relief?"[10] Of course, the circumstances were very different. Japan was a rich country that was well-prepared to deal with disasters, while Haiti and the Asian countries struck by the 2004 tsunami were much poorer, so it stood to reason that the humanitarian groups and faith-based organizations that normally mobilize for disasters in developing countries would not see the same inflows of charitable donations. But still the headlines did not jibe with what was unfolding around the country.

One of the first hints that something different was happening was the scene that played out in New York City six days after the disaster, on March 17. Naoko Fitzgerald, a young Japanese mother of two, had emailed a call to action urging her other friends, most of them also Japanese expatriates, to join her in Manhattan's Union Square that afternoon to show support for her country's people and collect donations. She expected maybe one or two dozen friends to join her, but was taken aback when the square quickly filled up with hundreds of Japanese and American mothers wearing kimonos, wheeling baby strollers and carrying signs that read "Help Japan" and "Pray for Japan".

As they stood on the sidewalks with donation boxes, green-clad St. Patrick's Day revelers who had been celebrating at the parade farther uptown started to stream down Broadway. That is when the second surprise came. What could have been a recipe for an embarrassing alcohol-fueled display of cultural insensitivity instead turned into a bittersweet spectacle, as passersby walked up to the mothers to offer pocket change, words of comfort and in some cases tearful hugs. When the mothers and children combined the contents of their donation boxes, it turned out they had collected more than thirty pounds in coins and small bills in a matter of three hours—a total of $11,204. Americans really were giving.

Similar scenes played out around the country as thousands of schools, churches and community groups conducted fundraising drives. In many instances, these were inspired by personal ties. Japanese-American organizations, which traditionally had kept low public profiles, took the lead in launching fundraising campaigns in communities around the country. Americans who had lived and worked in Japan, including the 26,000 alumni of the Japan Exchange and Teaching Program, could be found behind the scenes of many of the major fundraising initiatives that were started at corporations and nonprofit organizations that were not normally identified with Japan. Meanwhile, at least ninety-five municipalities with sister cities in Japan launched fundraising drives of their own, collecting a combined total of more than $2.4 million to support relief efforts.[11] Hundreds of anime fan clubs, karate schools, university Japan clubs and other small groups devoted to some aspect of Japanese culture started their own relief funds. It turned out that the grassroots ties between the two countries were deeper and more diverse than most people realized.

However, this upsurge of philanthropy did not register in the early tallies of U.S. donations, giving rise to the media narrative that the U.S. public response was muted. This was because the thousands of small groups that were at the forefront of the fundraising effort were operating below the radar of the national media, which was accustomed to surveying the top ten or fifteen humanitarian organizations that traditionally collect the vast bulk of donations for any given overseas disaster. This time, though, people were donating to a much broader range of groups, often smaller ones close to home, and these groups were taking their time to deliberate over how they could most wisely channel the funds they had collected to Japan. A remarkable number of groups, more than 330 in all, found ways to give funds directly to Japan, mainly to Japanese NGOs working in the disaster zone.[12] The others donated the proceeds of their fundraising drives to other, larger U.S. groups, which in some case fed them to the even larger organizations that eventually disbursed them to Japan. (Table 8.1 shows the organizations with the largest U.S. fundraising campaigns, although in almost all cases they are the beneficiaries of many smaller organizations that re-granted funds to them.)

**Table 8.1. Largest U.S. Fundraising Campaigns for the 3.11 Response.[13]**

| | |
|---|---|
| 1. American Red Cross | $312,000,000 |
| 2. Save the Children, USA | $26,150,000 |
| 3. Samaritan's Purse | $23,290,000 |
| 4. Catholic Relief Services | $23,000,000 |
| 5. Mercy Corps | $16,000,000 |
| 6. World Vision | $14,000,000 |
| 7. Japan Society of New York | $13,130,000 |
| 8. Latter-Day Saints Charities | $13,000,000 |
| 9. United Methodist Committee on Relief | $12,140,000 |
| 10. GlobalGiving | $10,050,000 |
| 11. Salvation Army | $9,900,000 |
| 12. Americares | $8,800,000 |
| 13. Give2Asia | $8,580,000 |
| 14. United States Fund for UNICEF | $7,000,000 |
| 15. International Medical Corps | $6,200,000 |
| 16. Direct Relief International/JACL | $5,980,000 |
| 17. Church World Service | $5,100,000 |
| 18. Japan-America Society of Hawaii | $4,450,000 |
| 19. Sasakawa Peace Foundation USA | $4,400,000 |
| 20. United Way Worldwide | $4,135,000 |
| 21. Japanese Cultural and Community Center of Northern California | $4,000,000 |
| 22. International Rescue Committee | $3,900,000 |
| 23. Operation Blessing International | $3,370,000 |
| 24. Japan Center for International Exchange | $3,280,000 |
| 25. Kids in Distressed Situations (KIDS) | $3,000,000 |

The lag time that resulted from this chain of giving meant that sizeable donations were still coming into organizations playing major roles in the disaster response six months and even one year after the disaster. It also obscured the fact that nearly three-quarters of a billion dollars had been donated, much of it in a spontaneous and organic manner. Fortunately, the grassroots nature of the response had another unintended benefit. The delays in getting funds into the disaster zone meant that a sizeable portion of the donations raised in the U.S. could be used for long-term recovery efforts rather than for immediate rescue and relief. The Japanese government and private sector had sufficient domestic resources to support much of the initial relief activities that were needed, so it was a boon that additional monies would be available for the recovery stage, when funding often dries up.

## The Drivers of American Giving

The sheer amount of donations raised in the U.S. for the disaster, at least $712.6 million over the first two years, indicates that something important has changed in terms of how Americans respond to disaster. Of course, this is not merely an American phenomenon. While the U.S. has been the origin of the most overseas private donations for Japan, there were similarly extraordinary responses from many other countries as well. Taiwanese donors reportedly made roughly $235 million in contributions, making Taiwan the second-largest source of overseas private giving for 3.11.[14] Despite long-standing historical animosities, South Koreans also donated record amounts for the relief and recovery efforts,[15] and Canadians, the British, and people in many other countries had similar reactions.

It was not just the amount raised in aggregate that increased; the funds donated to many individual organizations also far exceeded expectations. For instance, the staff of the Japan Society of New York created a disaster relief fund after the 1994 Great Hanshin Earthquake killed more than 6,400 people in Kobe, raising roughly $75,000. Seventeen years later, when they launched their new Japan Earthquake Relief Fund, they anticipated some increase in giving but never expected to raise nearly 175 times that amount—more than $13.1 million.[16]

One factor that surely contributed to the extraordinary outpouring of charitable contributions is the gradual rise of a culture of disaster giving. In recent years, Americans have become accustomed to making donations to help with disasters that receive prominent media attention. It is easy to see how this can become self-reinforcing, building up expectations that donations should be made after subsequent major disasters. Numerous studies show that disaster giving tends to be made on impulse, so these expectations, combined with the increasing ease with which people can quickly donate online or through text messages and other media, seem to have driven a shift in Americans' thinking about what they should do when they learn of a major tragedy.[17] It should therefore be no surprise that four of the five largest outpourings of U.S. private giving in response to major disasters have all taken place in the last decade and all five have occurred since 2001.

As noted earlier, a second important driver of the Japan response was the strength of people-to-people connections and grassroots ties at different levels of the U.S.-Japan relationship. A third was surely the enormous scope of the disaster, which was by far the most devastating to strike a developed nation. The magnitude of 3.11 and its extraordinary nature—the tsunami waves were higher than people had imagined was possible, the drama surrounding the efforts to prevent a full meltdown at the Fukushima nuclear plant was more chilling than any Hollywood movie —encouraged people to donate who may have been less willing to do so for a large but less shocking disaster.

A fourth major factor appears to have been the advance of communications technology, particularly the Internet, digital technology, and social media. In addition to increasing the ease of giving, these brought an immediacy to the disaster that turbocharged the philanthropic response. While personal ties made the disaster significant, the ubiquity of heartbreaking news and apocalyptic images helped to convince people that they needed to do something to help. Being able to click on YouTube and watch cell phone videos shot from rooftops while the waves rose menacingly from below gave the disaster a raw emotional resonance that was barely conceivable in the era of print media alone.

The disaster response was also different because of Japan's status as another advanced, post-industrial society. On the one hand, this led some to refrain from donating and compelled many humanitarian organizations to hesitate about launching all-out funding appeals. However, on the other hand, it seems to have encouraged donors who might otherwise not have contributed to appeals for funds. One reason is that grassroots ties between the two nations were arguably more robust because of the similar levels of development of both countries. Another equally significant factor is the strong economic relationship that has developed between Japan and the U.S. Thousands of U.S. companies have business ties to Japan by owning subsidiaries there, serving as subsidiaries of Japanese companies, counting Japanese companies as important clients, or depending on Japanese suppliers. The human relationships developed through these business interactions, as well as the desire to be perceived in Japan as aiding in the country's time of need, drove many companies to make the kinds of generous donations that may not have been forthcoming for a similar disaster in a remote, poor country. In the end, more than fifty U.S. companies pledged over $1 million for the disaster response, a remarkable number by any measure.[18]

## Assessing the U.S. Nongovernmental Response

First and foremost, any assessment of the American response needs to weigh how much of a difference U.S. support made on the ground. Considering the key role that the Japanese nonprofit sector has played in the disaster response, the massive amount of U.S. private giving was guaranteed to have a sizable impact if directed effectively. But the nature of the overall flows into the nonprofit sector in Japan has meant that this impact has been even more pronounced and beneficial than one might assume at first glance.

This is because, while the nonprofit sector in Japan has been expanding from a relatively low base, a culture of giving for nonprofit activities has yet to develop deep roots and thus domestic philanthropy has not kept up with the demand from nonprofit organizations. Although domestic giving for the disaster soared to record levels, totaling an estimated 600 billion yen (US$6.7 billion) by September 2012, nearly 85 percent went to local government agencies and the country's traditional *gienkin* funds that distribute cash payments as compensation to disaster survivors and the family members of victims.[19] Japanese companies and individuals are still unaccustomed to supporting nonprofit organizations, so only a small fraction of donations—less than 10 percent by some accounts—went for nonprofit activities.[20]

In contrast, nearly 90 percent of U.S. donations were earmarked for nonprofit activities, a total of roughly $640 million.[21] While it is difficult to get a clear picture of the overall size of the pool of donations available to Japanese nonprofit organizations working on the response, a rough estimate is that, at least for the initial two years, U.S. donors ended up accounting for as much as one-quarter to one-third of total private giving to support the Japanese NGO response to the disaster—a remarkable share by any measure.[22] Considering the key role that Japanese NGOs have played, it seems clear that American contributions have helped to fill an important gap.

Of course, a flood of money to NGOs is not always a good thing. After the Indian Ocean tsunami, the Tsunami Evaluation Coalition criticized the "second tsunami" of aid organizations that rushed to the scene to implement programs despite having little or no experience or capacity to follow through on their commitments.[23] This is always a risk in international crises, but this time almost all of the U.S. donors sought to disburse the funds they raised by regranting them to Japanese organizations or by working in close cooperation with local partners. This was not solely because they had learned from past mistakes, but also because it was much more daunting to parachute into a developed country and try to implement programs directly, especially in a nation like Japan with such high linguistic and cultural barriers. As a result, it seems that U.S. funding gave rise to few of the negative unintended consequences that are often seen in other disaster responses.

In a sense, a "second tsunami" did occur, but this came in the form of the numerous Japanese NGOs with no prior expertise in disaster-related issues that rushed to help and the hundreds of new nonprofit organizations that were established by Japanese volunteers. This had little to do with overseas funding, however. Given the deep desire of ordinary Japanese to do something to help, the surge of unskilled domestic NGOs into the disaster zone would have happened regardless of the availability of overseas funding. While some of these groups launched overlapping, and sometimes marginally useful, activities, on balance most managed to play a positive role in advancing the relief and recovery efforts and many proved to be indispensible. Moreover, being Japanese, they could more easily be brought into local coordination initiatives and had the linguistic and cultural understanding that enabled them to be more responsive to local needs and desires than overseas groups could have been.

Another sign that U.S. funding was being directed wisely was the fact that most donations took the form of cash rather than in-kind goods, which accounted for less than 2 percent of total U.S. giving.[24] In the early days, there was a scramble among some American organizations to ship food, medical supplies, gasoline, and even socks to Japan; however, many of these efforts were quickly aborted after Japanese government authorities and disaster professionals stressed that the issue on the ground was not a domestic shortage of supplies but rather the destruction of the local transportation infrastructure and distribution networks.[25]

## Challenges for Donors and Recipients

While the outpouring of American giving has been overwhelmingly beneficial for Japan and has filled a critical niche, both U.S. organizations collecting funds and Japanese ones utilizing them faced numerous challenges along the way. In the early days, it looked as though one major problem would be the gold rush of concerned groups and individuals that were launching fundraising campaigns with little idea of how to distribute the proceeds effectively. However, this eventually sorted itself out, as many of these groups decided to funnel their funds through organizations with greater capacity to direct them to worthy Japanese NGOs.

But even when these funds were handed over to more professionalized organizations, the lack of understanding about the terrain of the Japanese nonprofit sector and the dynamics of international grant-making was a major hurdle. While each of the major sets of organizations playing prominent roles in the response—the humanitarian assistance organizations, philanthropic intermediaries and Japan-related groups—had a good grasp of their own area of expertise, almost none of them started out with the whole picture; nor was there sufficient coordination across the circles to allow them to remedy their weaknesses easily. Instead, each organization had to learn, largely on its own, how best to go about providing aid in Japan.

One of the major complaints that quickly arose among U.S. organizations trying to support Japanese NGOs involved the difficulties they faced in identifying appropriate institutions and soliciting grant requests from them. In a June 2011 conference convening many of the larger Japan-related organizations and philanthropic intermediaries in the U.S., the head of one major philanthropic intermediary exclaimed that in all of her years of trying to facilitate funding to nonprofit organizations in countries around the world, she had never before seen a situation in which it was so difficult to find organizations willing and able to take their money.[26]

Part of the problem arose from American organizations' lack of familiarity with the Japanese nonprofit sector, as well as large gaps in expectations on both sides. But there were also more complicated issues at play that stemmed from the underdeveloped state of Japan's nonprofit sector, at least relative to what was common in other developed countries. Many U.S. organizations were unwilling to disburse funds—and in fact, they were legally prohibited from doing so—without fully vetting the Japanese recipients, receiving a viable project plan, signing a funding agreement and requiring regular reporting and accountability. In short, they were committed to making professionalized grants (or what is called *joseikin* in Japanese). But many Japanese organizations had little experience with grants, and with so much domestic funding with few strings attached sloshing around the disaster zone in the early days, it was easier to focus on receiving straightforward donations (*kifukin*) that they could use however they wished without sticking to a predetermined project plan or providing detailed reporting.

In almost all instances, the main issue was not that Japanese organizations were irresponsible or trying to avoid accountability; rather, most tended to be overly diligent in respecting the desires of the donors. But they were woefully understaffed and the one or two senior figures who could deal with overseas organizations—and even Japanese funders—were making heroic efforts, working sixteen- to eighteen-hour days, seven days a week for months on end just to keep resources flowing to the people carrying out programs on the ground. The mismatch in capacity with U.S. organizations was stark, even though many Americans were unaware of how just how unbalanced things were.

To take one example, the Central Community Chest of Japan and its annual "red feather" campaign is recognized by practically every ordinary Japanese, and the group fulfills a role in Japanese society that is analogous to that of the United Way in the U.S. It has long played a key role in disbursing funds after domestic disasters and it has historic ties to United Way Worldwide, the U.S.-based umbrella group for the United Way network, so it was natural for United Way Worldwide to channel the funds it raised for the 3.11 response to the Central Community Chest. But even though the Central Community Chest is one of Japan's most established organizations in the nonprofit sector, it operates with just sixteen full-time staff, in comparison with United Way Worldwide's more than 260 staff. If such vast disparities can arise in the relationship between one of the most established organizations in the Japanese nonprofit sector and its longtime partner, it is easy to imagine how dealings between other overseas and Japanese organizations could be even more unbalanced, and how smaller Japanese groups, facing overwhelming demands on their time, would have a preference for the funding with the least paperwork.

The limited institutional capacity of Japanese NGOs was not just an issue of size, and it proved to be one of the most critical challenges for overseas donors trying to support relief and recovery efforts. Most of the staff working at Japanese NGOs have limited experience in program planning, project management, and the other specialized tasks that are essential for major nonprofit organizations' operations. This is a product of the underdevelopment of the country's nonprofit sector and the weak financial base of most of its nonprofit organizations, which obliges senior staff to cover a broad range of duties that might otherwise be left to more junior staff, were there funds to hire them. As a result, the people who could otherwise focus primarily on serving as liaisons with overseas organizations or on devising and drafting sophisticated project plans tend to be spread far too thinly on a broad range of tasks. This problem was further exacerbated by a Japanese work culture that relies heavily on time-consuming, face-to-face meetings, and a lack of awareness on the part of U.S. groups of how much of a disruption requests for even relatively simple documentation could cause for Japanese NGO staff trying to juggle so many other tasks. Going beyond these more immediate issues, the tenuous financial situation of many Japanese NGOs and the overall weakness of the philanthropic sector in Japan also called into question the long-term sustainability of programs, even if they could be launched with overseas money.

In the face of these challenges, one of the keys to the quick and effective disbursement of the funds was the presence of pre-existing relationships between American donors and Japanese NGOs. These made it easier for overseas organizations to disburse funds in a timely manner and also helped smooth over tensions when problems inevitably arose. As one program officer at a major American donor organization remarked, even though their grantee was not providing timely activity reports as promised, "we have faith in their leadership because we have worked with them for so many years and know they will deliver in the end."[27]

However, the number of U.S. donors with prior ties to Japanese organizations involved in the disaster response was surprisingly limited. A number of faith-based organizations, such as Catholic Relief Services, Latter-Day Saints Charities, and the Adventist Development and Relief Agency (ADRA), had longstanding ties to their Japanese counterparts from the same religious traditions (Caritas Japan, the Japanese branch of the Church of Jesus Christ of Latter-Day Saints, and ADRA Japan); also, a handful of humanitarian assistance organizations such as the American Red Cross, Save the Children USA, and World Vision had affiliates in Japan as part of their global networks. But, outside of linkages with groups that were often perceived as Japanese branches of Western organizations, there were few strong ties between independent U.S. and Japanese humanitarian groups. (The relationship between Mercy Corps and Peace Winds Japan, which motivated Mercy Corps to raise funds specifically for Peace Winds Japan in the early days, is perhaps the only prominent exception.) This held true for many of the philanthropic intermediaries, too, and even for the Japan-related organizations, which were generally unfamiliar with the types of Japanese organizations that were skilled enough to carry out relief and recovery activities. This lack of pre-existing ties led Stacey White, an American expert on natural disasters, to lament in a *New York Times* opinion piece five days after the disaster that

> Just yesterday, I found myself on a conference call with a group of smart and well-intentioned people seeking to help Japan at this critical time. At one point during the conversation, someone asked how she might

connect not just with U.S. aid entities and international nongovernment organizations, but directly with Japanese businesses and civil society groups. There was silence. No one seemed to know.[28]

Not only were the networks that could be activated for the disaster response surprisingly thin, but the strains of responding to 3.11 exposed serious fault lines in many of the partnerships that predated the disaster and severely tested the new ones that were forged afterward. Wide expectation gaps, vastly differing communication styles, cultural misunderstandings, a lack of institutional capacity among Japanese NGOs, and the strain of the intense time commitment needed to maintain strong partnerships fed disillusionment on both sides. This compelled many of the U.S. organizations attempting to distribute funding for the disaster response to give up on their initial thoughts of channeling money through Japanese intermediaries or disbursing it solely to one organization, and instead to carve out a more active role in identifying and evaluating grantees. In many instances, they ended up dispatching representatives to Japan on a temporary basis to oversee the distribution of their funds rather than entrusting this to a Japanese partner. In the end, while many U.S. and Japanese organizations involved in the 3.11 response eventually found ways to make partnerships work, the challenge of keeping them effective and balanced has remained a lingering problem.

A final challenge that U.S. organizations and their Japanese partners are starting to face involves the funding bubble that has developed in the disaster zone. In the initial months after the disaster, the outpouring of charitable contributions from home and abroad was stunning. One report found that 77 percent of Japanese adults gave funds, an extraordinary rate for a country said to have a weak culture of giving.[29] Another revealed that 95 percent of major Japanese companies made cash donations, 72 percent provided in-kind contributions and 56 percent had employees who volunteered with relief efforts.[30] But as is common in such cases, the funding was frontloaded and after the massive inflows of 2011, donations started to taper off. By the summer of 2012, nonprofit organizations throughout the disaster zone were talking about the declines they were already seeing in funding and the steeper drops they expected to come. To their credit, many of the large donors from the U.S. and elsewhere allocated their funds for multiple years. However, by the end of the second year, in early 2013, almost all U.S. groups were facing pressure from their boards, donors, and other stakeholders to finalize the allocation of their funds and prepare to exit the scene. This was especially true for the organizations that had strayed from their core missions in operating relief funds for Japan, which entailed virtually every major American group involved in the 3.11 response. These pressures were natural and even healthy, but they just further steepened the downward slope on the far side of the bubble, adding to the threat to the sustainability of all the new programs that had been launched in the disaster zone by Japanese NGOs.

## Lessons from 3.11

As with any crisis, there are many lessons to draw from the 3.11 response about both what to anticipate for future megadisasters in developed countries and how we might react more effectively next time. Fortunately, this has been a story with no villains, only heroes. All of the major protagonists comported themselves as best they could and many acted with remarkable compassion, dignity and wisdom. U.S. organizations typically went out of their way to respect the desires and prerogatives of local Japanese groups and they adapted their approaches repeatedly in a highly fluid and complex environment in order to better meet the real needs on the ground. Meanwhile, Japanese NGOs did more than seemed possible given their institutional limitations. Their leaders consistently made extraordinary personal sacrifices to sustain their organizations' responses, and most demonstrated considerable grace and patience in dealing with well-intentioned foreign donors whose preconceptions did not always align with realities on the ground.

Surprisingly, although it seems de rigueur for disaster responses, there have thus far not even been any major nonprofit scandals involving international donors; no NGO executives have been caught lining their pockets, and few major misuses of charitable funds have come to light.[31] In fact, the most prominent "scandal" involved a Japanese man who was arrested for posing as a doctor so that his grant application to a Japanese foundation would be more convincing. He reportedly had some medical training that he drew upon in providing basic treatment for disaster survivors in under-served neighborhoods in the Ishinomaki area: even the judge who presided over his trial was forced to concede that he was attempting to help evacuees, even if his behavior was reckless and callous.[32]

However, while NGOs overseas and inside of Japan did their best to respond, 3.11 exposed numerous systemic flaws in how we deal with international disasters in an increasingly globalized world. One initial lesson of 3.11 is that nongovernmental responses to massive disasters in other developed countries are likely to involve a larger and more diverse array of players than we are accustomed to seeing when there are humanitarian crises in the developing world. This is because developed countries tend to have more robust economic linkages and a richer set of grassroots ties to other developed countries. This makes it even more important to look beyond the "usual suspects" when thinking about what is happening with the overseas response.

3.11 also drove home the point that international responses to disasters in developed countries are fundamentally about philanthropy, not the direct provision of humanitarian assistance. As many disaster experts noted in the immediate days after March 11, there is a highly limited role for "boots on the ground" in a country like Japan; rather, the most effective thing that NGOs can do to help is to channel resources to local responders. The centrality of philanthropy to international responses to disasters like 3.11 elevates the importance of the craft of international grant-making and highlights the value of country expertise, capabilities that were underdeveloped at many of the U.S. organizations responding to the disaster. For instance, one key element in grant-making is an awareness of how to manage grantee expectations. In too many cases, already overstretched Japanese NGOs have felt that they were led on by U.S. donors who inadvertently built up their hopes and monopolized valuable time by asking for a wide range of documentation before eventually turning down their funding requests. A greater knowledge of Japanese nonprofit culture and a deeper appreciation of the funder-grantee relationship could have saved considerable time and effort on both sides. Similarly, simplifying application processes—and ideally instituting a culturally appropriate unified application format for multiple overseas donors—could have gone far in lightening the burden on Japanese NGOs scrambling to meet needs in the disaster zone.

The disaster also highlighted the importance of cultivating cross-border relationships between humanitarian groups and philanthropic intermediaries before a disaster strikes. To some extent, the paucity of ties between American and Japanese NGOs in the field of humanitarian assistance can be seen as a particularly Japanese problem, given the relative underdevelopment of the country's nonprofit sector. Still, it is easy to envision similar issues arising for U.S.-based NGOs when dealing with Korea's nongovernmental sector or with various European countries. This suggests that more effort needs to be put into building up international civil society linkages and nurturing habits of cooperation among overseas and domestic NGOs likely to be involved in disaster responses in developed countries. There is much that can be done to this end, including developing stronger ties between national coalitions of humanitarian assistance organizations; encouraging greater involvement by NGOs in Asia, the world's most disaster-prone region, in forums for international humanitarian assistance and development organizations; and nurturing familiarity and habits of international cooperation by engaging NGOs from developed countries like Japan in small-scale joint initiatives with U.S.-based groups in third countries.

Finally, 3.11 showed that coordination is even more challenging for disasters in developed countries. It seems natural for groups like InterAction, the umbrella organization for humanitarian assistance and development NGOs, to play a central role in disseminating information and facilitating donor coordination for overseas disasters in developed countries, just as they do for crises in developing countries. But given the likelihood that the response will be more of a grassroots phenomenon with a broader array of players, greater effort needs to be made to make more information and advice on the response easily accessible to NGO leaders outside of the field of humanitarian assistance. In particular, more needs to be done to connect humanitarian groups with the NGOs that have country-specific expertise, especially those outside of the Washington D.C. "beltway" where much of the public-private coordination involving humanitarian assistance organizations tends to take place. The same goes for philanthropic intermediaries that specialize in overseas giving. Bringing these circles closer together will not only enhance coordination, but also allow each to benefit from the others' unique insights and networks.

Similarly, if philanthropy is to be the core of the response, there are many steps that can be taken to share information on the recipient country's nonprofit sector: the preparation of background papers on the national nonprofit system, the dissemination of basic guides to the country's legal regulations, and the creation of databases that allow organizations to identify reputable local NGOs and see what they are doing in the disaster zone. These seemingly obvious resources were difficult to find in a timely manner in the case of Japan, despite efforts by various groups to provide them.[33]

Stronger coordination on the part of overseas donors can only go so far, though, without effective coordination within the country where the disaster strikes. This is a particular challenge for developed countries, which are unaccustomed to receiving outside assistance. In developing countries, donor clusters or roundtables that link international development NGOs, bilateral ODA agencies, UN agencies, and host governments can be repurposed to coordinate disaster aid, but, as 3.11 showed, often there are no equivalent mechanisms in place in rich countries. In Japan, the staff of overseas organizations were invited to join discussions convened by Japan Platform and JANIC, but limited institutional capacity and linguistic and cultural barriers kept these forums from living up to their potential despite admirable efforts by the host organizations.[34] Moreover, the domestic coordination mechanisms needed to bring together Japan's professional humanitarian assistance NGOs and local-level groups were sorely lacking. This was exacerbated by the fact that the Japanese NGOs with the capacity and know-how to provide disaster relief on a large scale were internationally oriented ones that normally worked on disasters outside Japan and thus had few connections to local authorities and limited experience navigating the politics of rural Japan.

The experience of 3.11 suggests that there is much work to do in developed countries to build the capacity to receive assistance from overseas NGOs when a megadisaster occurs. This ranges from big-picture issues to highly technical measures. There is a need to encourage organizations and coalitions that would be natural contact points for overseas donors to think through what is needed to take on the roles of being a neutral facilitator and a clearinghouse for information. Further, the feasibility of creating networks of volunteer translators who can assist in preparing documents for overseas organizations, particularly for countries like Japan, Korea, and others with uncommon languages, needs to be explored. Analysis is also required of domestic coordination networks to establish whether or not they are structured in such a way as to allow overseas organizations and even domestic organizations that normally have an international orientation, to take part easily.

*****

In a sense, the U.S. nongovernmental response to 3.11 was a portent of what we are likely to see in the future when large-scale disasters strike other developed countries. The extraordinary response by American NGOs and the U.S. public was surprising in its scope and complexity, and it suggests that the way we react to disasters abroad is being transformed by the advance of globalization, the revolution in communications technology, and changes in the nature of disaster philanthropy. Just as disasters are the sum of thousands of personal tragedies, the U.S. response to 3.11 proved to be the amalgamation of millions of people-to-people ties to Japan. In our increasingly interconnected world, this grassroots reaction is likely to become one of the defining traits of overseas responses to megadisasters in developed countries and it needs to be taken into account when we grapple with one issue that we have barely begun to master—how to effectively assist developed countries suffering from massive humanitarian crises.

## Notes

[1] Data from a Japan Center for International Exchange (JCIE) survey of 1,100 American and Japanese nonprofit organizations and corporate donors covering the two years from March 2011 to March 2013 (JCIE, "U.S. Giving for Japan Disaster Exceeds $710 Million. JCIE Special Report," *Civil Society Monitor*, March 8, 2013).

[2] Sources: Estimates for Japan come from JCIE, "U.S. Giving for Japan Disaster Exceeds $710 Million," JCIE Special Report, *Civil Society Monitor*, March 8, 2013. Other figures are from the University of Indiana's Center on Philanthropy.

[3] Michael Flint and Hugh Goyder, *Funding the Tsunami Response* (London, UK: Tsunami Evaluation Coalition, 2006), 15.

[4] Financial Tracking Service, UN Office for the Coordination of Humanitarian Affairs, "Haiti–Earthquakes–January 2010. Table B: Total Humanitarian Assistance per Donor," Table ref# R24. Data from the UN Office for the Coordination of Humanitarian Affairs (OCHA) Financial Tracking Service website. The service depends on self-reporting by donors, which is less accurate for nongovernmental donors than for the governments that are members of the UN system, as indicated by the fact that more comprehensive surveys of U.S. private giving by the University of Indiana's Center on Philanthropy have found $1.45 billion in American private donations for Haiti, considerably more than the $1.27 billion that UN OCHA estimates for all private donors worldwide.

[5] The data collected by OCHA, which is normally biased towards governmental funding, credits private giving with comprising 80 percent of total overseas aid for the 3.11 response. A better sense can be gained, however, by amalgamating data from several sources, including Japan's Ministry of Foreign Affairs and the analysis of that data for Japan's annual almanac of philanthropy, *Giving Japan, 2012*. Taken together, these suggest that nongovernmental sources provided roughly twice as much aid in monetary terms as governmental sources, highlighting how large a role overseas private giving played in this disaster.

As background, the Japanese Ministry of Foreign Affairs reports that there were 17.5 billion yen (US$184 million at US$1=95 yen) in cash donations by foreign governments, as well as a number of large in-kind donations. (The largest expenditures by foreign governments appear to be 40 billion yen [US $420 million] in oil donated by Kuwait, the $95 million that the U.S. Congressional Research Service estimates was expended for Operation Tomodachi, and another 10,000 tons each of gasoline and diesel fuel at a market price of approximately US$25–30 million that was donated by China.) Combined, the largest cash and in-kind donations from foreign governments total 67 billion yen, or roughly US$700 million, although these figures could be expected to increase by some 20 to 30 percent if the total costs of all in-kind goods and technical assistance could be quantified and included in the total.

In contrast, adding up the private giving from major donors surveyed by *Giving Japan, 2012* and JCIE's survey of U.S. donors—US$712.6 million (67.7 billion yen) from the U.S., approximately US$188 million (17.9 billion yen) from Taiwan, US$47 million (4.5 billion yen) from Korea, US$26 million (2.5 billion yen) from the UK, and US$252 million (24 billion yen) that was collected by Red Cross and Red Crescent Societies in other countries—indicates that at least 127 billion yen (roughly US$1.3 billion) originated with overseas private donors. As with government funds, these estimates could be expected to increase if more accurate counts were available.

For further information, see Financial Tracking Service, UN OCHA "Japan Emergencies for 2011: Total Humanitarian Funding per Donor in 2011" (Table ref# R24c); Ministry of Foreign Affairs of Japan, "Shogaikokura kara no bushi shien/kifukin" ["In-kind and Cash Donations from Various Foreign Countries"] December 28, 2012; Andrew Feickert and Emma Chanlett-Avery, "Japan 2011 Earthquake: U.S. Department of Defense (DOD) Response," *CRS Report for Congress*, No. 41690 (Washington DC: Congressional Research Service, 2011), 1; JCIE, March 8, 2013; and Japan Fundraising Association, *Kifu hakusho 2012* [*Giving Japan 2012*] (Tokyo, Japan: Japan Business Federation, 2012), 34–40.

[6] Feickert and Chanlett-Avery, 1.

[7] JCIE, "U.S. Giving…"; Feickert and Chanlett-Avery, 1.

[8] JCIE, "Database of U.S. Giving for 3.11," JCIE Web site, 2013. Of the 105 organizations that collected more than $100,000, thirty-nine had no prior experience working on disasters and only one-third defined themselves primarily as humanitarian assistance organizations.

[9] Two of the most prominent were essays on the Give Well blog (blog.givewell.org) and a widely circulated article by Reuters' commentator Felix Salmon entitled "Don't Donate Money to Japan" (March 14, 2011).

[10] *USA Today* blared "US Donations Not Rushing to Japan" (Oren Dorell and Cathy Lynn Grossman, March 17, 2011) and ABC News asked "Americans Less Generous in Disaster Relief?" (Devin Dwyer, *ABC News Online*, March 18, 2011).

[11] Toshihiro Menju and Atsuko Geiger, "Friendship across Borders: Nearly 100 U.S. Sister City Organizations Raise Relief Funds for Japan," JCIE Special Report, *Civil Society Monitor*, September 2012.

[12] JCIE, March 8, 2013.

[13] Estimates of funds raised in the U.S. as of March 2013. Some organizations raised additional funds outside of the U.S. (JCIE, March 8, 2013).

[14] Taiwanese media reports indicate that 90 percent, or approximately US$235 million, of the total US$260.64 million collected in Taiwan came from private donors ("Taiwanese Urged to Keep Helping Japanese Victims," *Taipei Times*, March 11, 2013).

[15] "Korean Red Cross Collects Record Amount of Donations for Japan Quake," *Yonhap News Agency*, March 28, 2011.

[16] Personal correspondence with Japan Society executive, March 15, 2013.

[17] See, for instance, Network for Good, *Impulse on the Internet: How Crisis Compels Donors to Give Online*, (Washington DC: Author, 2006).

[18] JCIE, "U.S. Giving in Response to Japan's March 11 Disaster Tops $630 Million," JCIE Survey, *Civil Society Monitor*, September 11, 2012.

[19] Japan Fundraising Association, 2012, 22. While there is an important place for cash grants-in-aid after a disaster, it is worth noting that there were many problems with these funds after 3.11. Intense public criticism arose over delays in distributing

the funds, but perhaps the most worrying phenomenon was the way that funds which were disbursed. The slow pace of finalizing local rezoning plans prevented people from investing in rebuilding homes and businesses, and so the distribution of large cash settlements instead fed an extraordinary boom in bars and *pachinko* gambling parlors.

[20] Ibid.

[21] JCIE, March 8, 2013b. Donations for nonprofit activities include giving for religious organizations, educational organizations and other similar organizations in the disaster zone that operate as nonprofit organizations. The Japanese Red Cross Society operates two major funds. Donations from within Japan and the general public overseas go into the first fund, to be used for cash grants-in-aid for disaster victims, and donations from overseas Red Cross and Red Crescent societies and a few other overseas groups have been allocated to a second fund for relief and reconstruction efforts directly implemented by the Japanese Red Cross Society as well as a handful of nonprofit partners. Only donations to the second fund are counted as going for nonprofit activities.

[22] Author's estimates based on JCIE's survey of U.S. giving for Japan. While U.S. donations are estimated to account for as much as one-quarter to one-third of all private pledges to Japanese nonprofits active in the disaster zone, one should keep in mind that they comprise a considerably smaller portion of overall income for these groups, as private giving is just one of several streams of funding, and government contracts and subsidies also cover a substantial portion of many organizations' budgets.

[23] John Cosgrove, *Synthesis Report: Expanded Summary. Joint evaluation of the International Response to the Indian Ocean Tsunami* (London, UK: Tsunami Evaluation Coalition, 2007), 16.

[24] JCIE, "Database…"

[25] Japanese embassy and consulate requests to avoid sending in-kind donations were initially reported by some media outlets as a Japanese refusal of all donations, but this was an obvious misunderstanding that arose out of faulty reporting. In fact, Japanese embassies quickly took the unprecedented step of accepting cash donations themselves, receiving millions of dollars which they forwarded on to the Japanese Red Cross.

[26] Author's recollection from the "Funding Conference on US-Japan Cooperation on Supporting the Japan Disaster Response" (July 21, 2011), which convened representatives from more than forty American and Japanese NGOs, foundations and corporations in New York to share information on challenges they were facing in their disaster responses. This was sponsored by JCIE, the Japan Foundation Center for Global Partnership and the Institute of International Education.

[27] Interview with a representative of a U.S. donor organization, March 14, 2013.

[28] Stacey White, "A Nation's Personal Journey," *The New York Times*, March 16, 2011, para. 4.

[29] Japan Fundraising Association, 2012, 23.

[30] Japan Business Federation, *Higashi daishinsai ni okeru keizaikai no hisaisha/hisaichi shien katsudo ni kansuru hokukusho* [Report on the Corporate

Sector's Support for Victims and the Disaster Zone after the Great East Japan Earthquake] (Tokyo, Japan: Author, 2012).

[31] In contrast, there were numerous embarrassing nonprofit scandals in the United States after the 9/11 attacks and the Hurricane Katrina response. (See, for example, "9/11 Charities Under Scrutiny for Failing to Raise Money for Victims," *Associated Press*, August 25, 2011; Adam Nossiter, "Katrina: US Raids New Orleans Agency in Scandal Over Housing Cleanup Program," *The New York Times*, August 11, 2008.) Likewise, there has been considerable press coverage of the misuse of funds after the Sichuan Earthquake by Chinese organizations and following the Haiti Earthquake by groups such as Wyclef Jean's Yele Haiti. (See Edward Wong, "An Online Scandal Underscores Chinese Distrust of State Charities," *The New York Times*, July 3, 2011, and Deborah Sontag, "In Haiti, Little Can be Found of a Hip-Hop Artist's Charity," *The New York Times*, October 11, 2012.)

In comparison, surprisingly few scandals have come to light in connection with the 3.11 response. On the U.S. side, in the first few weeks after 3.11, fraudsters were reported to have put up fake fundraising websites, most often claiming to be collecting funds for the Japanese Red Cross Society, but these were quickly discredited. Meanwhile, in Japan, there have been rumors in nonprofit circles of a few isolated incidents of accounting misconduct by NGOs in the disaster zone, for example, involving the submission of the same receipts to two different donors in order to double-bill certain direct expenses; however, this should be understood in the proper context. It appears that much of this double-billing is so that NGOs can cover other expenses necessary to carry out the programs they committed to implement, such as staff salaries and overheads, because many funders from Japan and elsewhere insist on paying only select direct expenses and ridiculously small amounts for salaries, plus there are few alternative funding sources for general operational support. So, while these NGOs are not abiding by the letter of the law, so to speak, what they are doing can be said to be in keeping with the overall spirit in which they were given funds.

[32] "Man Who Posed as Doctor in Tsunami-Hit Area Gets Suspended Sentence," *Japan Today*, June 9, 2012.

[33] For example, JCIE worked to create a public online database (www.jcie.org/311database) that would allow overseas donors to identify potential grantees working in the geographic and issue areas where they were focusing their funding and enable Japanese NGOs to identify which overseas organizations were providing funds. However, technical problems with the software design and limited staff capacity prevented the database from being launched until almost two years after the disaster.

[34] Within Japan, even the members of Japan Platform and JANIC had considerable difficulty in coordinating with government and local authorities. One illustrative example involved their main channel for consultations with the national government. They were accustomed to responding to overseas disasters and had developed a strong working relationship with the Japanese foreign ministry, which regularly organizes government-NGO consultative sessions. However, because this was a domestic disaster, a different agency, the Cabinet Office, was mandated to

take the lead, and it had much less appreciation of the role of NGOs in the response, plus there were no preexisting coordination mechanisms that could be activated for it to engage with NGOs.

## Bibliography

Cosgrove, John. *Synthesis Report: Expanded Summary. Joint evaluation of the International Response to the Indian Ocean Tsunami*. London, UK: Tsunami Evaluation Coalition, 2007.

Feickert, Andrew, and Emma Chanlett-Avery. "Japan 2011 Earthquake: U.S. Department of Defense (DOD) Response." *CRS Report for Congress*, No. 41690. Washington DC: Congressional Research Service, 2011.

Financial Tracking Service, UN Office for the Coordination of Humanitarian Affairs. "Haiti–Earthquakes–January 2010. Table B: Total Humanitarian Assistance per Donor." Table ref# R24. http://fts.unocha.org/reports/daily/ocha_R24_E15797___1303160211.pdf

—. Japan Emergencies for 2011: Total Humanitarian Funding per Donor in 2011." (Table ref# R24c). http://fts.unocha.org/reports/daily/ocha_R24c_C105_Y2011_asof___1303160211.pdf

Flint, Michael, and Hugh Goyder. *Funding the Tsunami Response*. London, UK: Tsunami Evaluation Coalition, 2006.

Japan Center for International Exchange (JCIE). "Database of U.S. Giving for 3.11." JCIE Web site. 2013. www.jcie.org/311database

—. "U.S. Giving for Japan Disaster Exceeds $710 Million." JCIE Special Report. *Civil Society Monitor*, March 8, 2013.

—. "U.S. Giving in Response to Japan's March 11 Disaster Tops $630 Million." JCIE Survey. *Civil Society Monitor*, September 11, 2012.

Japan Fundraising Association. *Kifu hakusho 2012 [Giving Japan 2012]*. Tokyo, Japan: Japan Business Federation, 2012.

Japan Business Federation. *Higashi daishinsai ni okeru keizaikai no hisaisha/hisaichi shien katsudo ni kansuru hokukusho [Report on the Corporate Sector's Support for Victims and the Disaster Zone after the Great East Japan Earthquake]*. Tokyo, Japan: Author, 2012.

"Korean Red Cross Collects Record Amount of Donations for Japan Quake." *Yonhap News Agency*, March 28, 2011. http://english.yonhapnews.co.kr/national/2011/03/28/3/0302000000AEN20110328003100315F.HTML (accessed March 15, 2013).

"Man Who Posed as Doctor in Tsunami-Hit Area Gets Suspended Sentence." *Japan Today*, June 9, 2012. http://www.japantoday.com/

category/crime/view/man-who-posed-as-doctor-in-tsunami-hit-area-gets-suspended-sentence (accessed March 20, 2013).

Menju, Toshihiro, and Atsuko Geiger. "Friendship across Borders: Nearly 100 U.S. Sister City Organizations Raise Relief Funds for Japan." JCIE Special Report. *Civil Society Monitor*, September 2012. http://jcie.org/311recovery/sistercities.html

Ministry of Foreign Affairs of Japan. "Shogaikokura kara no bushi shien/kifukin." ["In-kind and Cash Donations from Various Foreign Countries."] Ministry of Foreign Affairs, December 28, 2012. http://www.mofa.go.jp/mofaj/saigai/pdfs/bussisien.pdf

Network for Good. *Impulse on the Internet: How Crisis Compels Donors to Give Online*. Washington DC: Author, 2006. http://www.networkforgood.org/downloads/pdf/Whitepaper/20061009_crisis_compels_donors.pdf (accessed March 16, 2013).

"Taiwanese Urged to Keep Helping Japanese Victims." *Taipei Times*, March 11, 2013. http://www.taipeitimes.com/News/taiwan/archives/2013/03/11/2003556812

White, Stacey. "A Nation's Personal Journey." *The New York Times*. March 16, 2011. http://www.nytimes.com/roomfordebate/2011/03/15/what-aid-makes-sense-for-japan/a-personal-journey-for-japan

CHAPTER NINE

THE LANGUAGE OF LEADERSHIP IN THE AFTERMATH OF THE JAPANESE EARTHQUAKE

SHOJI AZUMA

## Introduction

On March 11, 2011, a massive earthquake known as the Great Eastern Japan Earthquake hit about 80 miles off the coast of the Japanese mainland of Honshu. The initial shock was a magnitude of 9.0 on the Richter scale, making it not only the most powerful earthquake ever to hit Japan but also one of the five most powerful earthquakes in the world since 1900. The quake was followed by a massive tsunami, which swept across the northeast coast of Japan. Not only was there catastrophic damage to public infrastructure, homes, and buildings, but more than 28,000 people are still being reported either dead or missing. Estimates for the cost of destruction reached as high as 17 trillion yen (about $170 billion), making it the most expensive natural disaster in Japanese history.[1] To make the situation worse, the tsunami caused the meltdown of three nuclear reactors in the Fukushima Daiichi nuclear power plant. The massive earthquake and tsunami, followed by the release of radiation from the nuclear power plant, represent one of the greatest disasters to strike the nation in modern history. It has indeed been a national crisis for Japan.

The language used by Japan's leadership as they dealt with this devastating national crisis guides the question for this paper. In his study of political speeches, Charteris-Black points out that

> the most important type of behavior by which leaders mobilize their followers is their linguistic performance. In democratic frameworks it is primarily through language that leaders legitimize their leadership.[2]

In the spirit of language as the central force in political persuasion, this study examines the relationship between language and leadership in this historically unprecedented period of national crisis in Japan. More specifically, the following questions will be addressed: What rhetorical strategies did the Japanese leadership use to speak to the nation in the aftermath of the disaster? How effective was the *persuasive power* of the language the leadership demonstrated (or failed to demonstrate) in the most difficult time for the country and the people? How successful was the leadership in encouraging those people affected by the disaster and leading the nation in the most critical days right after the earthquake?

This study uses the theoretical constructs of *rapport talk* versus *report talk*, which stem from Deborah Tannen's genderlect theory.[3] The basic tenet of the theory is that there are two distinctively different speech styles: one seeks connection, the other status. Rapport talk is a conversational style that seeks to establish connection with others. On the other hand, report talk is another conversational style that seeks to command attention, convey information, and win arguments. In analyzing the language of leadership, the theoretical constructs of rapport talk and report talk are useful tools.[4]

## Data

The data for this study come from the Prime Minister's address at a press conference held on March 12, 2011, the day after the earthquake.[5] The Prime Minister's speech at this press conference was one of the most significant speeches that the public heard right after the earthquake. This study also examines Emperor Akihito's historically unprecedented video address to the Japanese people on March 16, 2011.[6] Furthermore, to offer a comparative perspective, Emperor Hirohito's (Emperor Akihito's father) radio broadcast, which announced to the Japanese people the termination of the Second World War on August 15, 1945, is also examined.[7] In Japan's long history, these are the only two occasions when the Emperor has addressed the common people directly (albeit via a phonograph record or a video tape). Given that invisibility is a method used to establish and maintain the supreme authority of the Emperor in Japan, these direct speeches to the Japanese people are extremely rare and warrant close examination. In what follows, an examination of speeches by Prime Minister Kan (hereafter PM Kan) and the two Emperors is presented.

## Prime Minister Kan

When the earthquake hit Japan on March 11, 2010, the Prime Minister of Japan was Mr. Naoto Kan, then the leader of the ruling Democratic Party of Japan (hereafter DPJ). He succeeded Mr. Yukio Hatoyama, who had resigned after his bungled handling of a controversial U.S. base relocation in Okinawa prefecture and his involvement in a financial and political scandal. Mr. Kan became the twenty-ninth postwar Prime Minister of Japan on June 8, 2010, and stayed in office until September 2, 2011. Although he had actively engaged in civic grassroots movements and presented himself as a "champion of the people", PM Kan's approval rating eventually tumbled to 19 percent, the lowest since the ruling DPJ took power in September 2009 in a turnover that brought an end to an almost half-century of uninterrupted Liberal Democratic Party (LDP) rule in Japan.[8] Japan's political instability can be observed in the number of Prime Ministers who have gone through what has been called a "revolving door"; Prime Ministers take office but then resign after very short tenures. For example, PM Kan was the fifth Prime Minister in five years, and he himself held the office for little more than a year.

The day following the quake, PM Kan appeared in front of reporters at a press conference and gave a speech to the Japanese people, who were just then learning of the scale of the devastation, and were anxiously waiting for their political leader to address the nation with guidance and consolation. The speech was broadcast live to the entire nation by the major TV and radio stations.

Generally, as in any speech, it is crucial to set the tone, or *frame*, for what follows early on. Here the term frame is used in the sense discussed in Bateson and Goffman.[9] A frame is a conceptual or cognitive view of a particular situation. It identifies the meaning of a specific expression. For example, a certain utterance can be understood as joking or fighting, and this could be used as a frame to establish a guide for interpreting the remaining speech.

How did PM Kan frame his speech? Observe the following original Japanese utterance, accompanied by an English translation (this and all other translations are the author's).

Jishin ga hassei shite ichinichi han ga keika o *itashimashita.*
    Hisai o sareta minasan ni *kokoro kara omimai o mooshiagemasu* to tomo ni kyuuen, kyuushutsu ni atatte zenryoku o agete itadaite iru jieitai, keisatsu, shooboo, kaijoo hoanchoo, soshite kaku jichitai, kankei kakui no hontoo ni mi o oshimanai doryoku ni *kokoro kara kansha o mooshiagemasu.*

One and a half days have passed since the earthquake occurred. Along with my deepest sympathies to all who have suffered, (I) also want to thank from the bottom of (my) heart those who have been working quite selflessly on the rescue, including the Self-Defense Forces (JSDF), the Police, the Fire Agency, the Japan Coast Guard, and local governments.[10]

PM Kan starts his speech with a very formal and conventional greeting. After briefly offering sympathy to the suffering, he quickly turns to listing the various agencies and expressing formal gratitude, which is almost formulaic, being a very typical speaking style for government officials and bureaucrats. Furthermore, the humble forms of verbs such as *itashimashita* (did) and *mooshiagemasu* (express) indicate the formality which functions to expand the psychological distance between the speaker and the audience. The interpretive frame is that of a typical formal governmental report. There is no personal, *down-to-earth* expression to which the audience can easily relate.

Immediately after the formal opening of the speech, PM Kan continues:

*Watashi* wa honjitsu gozen rokuji ni jieitai no herikoputaa de genchi o shisatsu shimashita.
*I* inspected the area from aboard a JSDF helicopter at six o'clock this morning.[11]

After the formal, impersonal greeting at the beginning of the speech, PM Kan next talked about his own actions rather than the state of the suffering people. He accomplished this with the unusual overt pronoun of *watashi* (I). This overt first-person pronoun promoted PM Kan to a prominent position grammatically and semantically, emphasizing himself as the person in charge. Consequently, this relegated the audience to a much less significant position.

At this point, a few words about Japanese grammar, particularly subject deletion, are warranted. Unlike English and many other languages, grammatical subjects as well as objects are commonly deleted in Japanese. Thus, we get a sentence like the following: *Uketorimashita* ("[I] received [it]". The sentence consists of just the verb; both its grammatical subject and object are deleted. This type of deletion is frequently observed in Japanese and is a perfectly grammatical sentence. Furthermore, word order in Japanese is very flexible, with the only constraint being that a verb must terminate a sentence. In other words, the subject pronoun is not required at the initial position of the sentence, but it can be placed anywhere except the final position of the sentence (or it can be completely omitted), allowing the speaker to shift the focus of the sentence. Given these grammatical characteristics in Japanese, PM Kan's overt first-person pronoun in the initial prominent position of the sentence suggests that the speaker is firmly promoting himself to the focal position. In this sense, therefore, the utterance is characterized as *speaker-oriented*.

PM Kan continues his speaker-oriented speech and reports what he found through the inspection. Observe the following utterance:

> Konkai no jishin wa ookina tsunami o tomonatta koto ni yotte, taihen jindai na higai o oyoboshite iru koto ga akiraka ni narimashita.
>
> It has become clear that this earthquake, with the accompanying tsunami, has caused severe damage.[12]

He implies that the cause of the severe damage was discovered through his inspection. Here, the message is that PM Kan, as the person in charge, is *the* person capable of correctly understanding and reporting the situation to the Japanese people.

After trying to establish himself as a fully capable leader, PM Kan continues his speech by reporting his own actions and directives, citing numbers and figures. Consider the following utterances in English translation:

> The number of SDF members mobilized was increased from an original 20,000 members to 50,000.
>
> (We) are preparing the delivery of food, water, blankets, heaters, and toilets.[13]

PM Kan explains what he has done or is planning to do to cope with the damage caused by the earthquake and tsunami. Then, he continues and briefly touches upon the situation with the failing Fukushima Daiichi nuclear power plant. Consider the following English translation:

> With respect to the Fukushima Daiichi nuclear power plant, *a new situation* has developed. (I) will let the Chief Cabinet Secretary provide a detailed report on that later.[14]

PM Kan refers to the explosion at the nuclear power plant (and possible meltdown) as *a new situation*, an evasive understatement and noncommittal phrase that avoids details regarding the implications of the new situation. Although he claims that a detailed report will be provided by his Chief Cabinet Secretary, no such report was ever provided. Instead, the description later given by the Chief Cabinet Secretary was merely a vague phrase: "some kind of explosion-like phenomenon" (*"nanra ka no bakuhatsu teki jishoo"*).

PM Kan continues by stating what he has done from his perspective as the leader of the country. The noteworthy trait of PM Kan's speech is his utter silence regarding the people, how they have fared since the disaster struck, and what they are feeling, suffering, hoping, and expecting. The entire speech was, essentially, speaker-oriented report talk, describing what he and his government have done or have tried to do. As a further dismissal of his audience, his report talk wasn't even complete, lacking any detail regarding the ongoing disaster at the nuclear power plant. This speaker-oriented mode of speaking right after the disaster extended the sense of social distance between PM Kan and his people. He was unable to foster trust with his people, as evidenced by his extremely low approval rating. According to an NHK public opinion poll,[15] PM Kan's approval rating right after the earthquake was a mere 27 percent, with a disapproval rating of 59 percent. This trend of a low approval rating (and a high disapproval rating) continued throughout the rest of his tenure. For the remaining period, the average approval rate dropped to 22 percent, while the disapproval rate rose to 62 percent.[16] PM Kan was not able to restore public trust in the aftermath of the earthquake. *The Japan Times*, one of the country's most respected news organizations, reported that

> Mr. Kan's lack of leadership and of sound political judgment...deepened people's distrust of the DPJ government and government, per se.[17]

For any political leader, a national crisis is an opportunity to unite the nation and strengthen his/her leadership through language (e.g., President Bush during the 9/11 crisis). However, PM Kan's report talk did not suffice to secure the people's trust and establish his strong leadership when it was most needed.

## Emperor Akihito

The 1947 Constitution of Japan clearly defines the Emperor as *the symbol of the state*. Unlike royalty in other countries, the Emperor of Japan is not even the nominal head of state. As such, the present-day Emperor possesses no political power, serving merely as a social figurehead for formal and ceremonial functions. Although the Emperor makes occasional public appearances, he spends most of his time inside the Imperial Palace, invisible to the public eye. Usually, the only chance for people to hear the Emperor speak is during his New Year's speech or his birthday address on December 12. Both of these are highly ceremonial events, and his speeches are very brief, offering traditional, formulaic greetings and wishes of good health and blessings.

Emperor Akihito had not spoken directly to the common people until the devastating earthquake hit Japan. On March 16, 2011, the Emperor voluntarily decided to speak to the entire nation through a form of TV video message.[18] The video message was broadcast throughout the country by most major TV stations. This was the most unprecedented TV speech given by an Emperor since the radio speech given by his father, Emperor Hirohito, in 1945.

How did Emperor Akihito open his speech to the nation? Observe the following Japanese utterance, with its English equivalent:

> Kono tabi no toohoku chihoo taiheiyoo oki jishin wa magunichuudo 9.0 to iu rei o minai kibo no kyodai jishin de ari, hisaichi no hisan na jookyoo ni *fukaku kokoro o itamete imasu.*

> This earthquake off the Tohoku district in the Pacific Ocean is reportedly an unprecedented, enormous earthquake of magnitude 9.0, and [I] *am deeply hurt* by the grievous situation in the disaster-hit areas.[19]

From the outset, the Emperor sincerely expresses empathy for those affected by the earthquake by explicitly stating that he is *deeply hurt*. Recall that PM Kan's first remark was an official, formal greeting with only a brief formulaic acknowledgement of those suffering. PM Kan's speech began like any other government announcement read by a professional politician. The Emperor's address, on the other hand, establishes his special persona as one who is not afraid to express his own personal emotional state and who is willing to share his feelings with the people, despite the fact that he is expected to be detached from the people as *Tennoo Heika* (Heavenly Emperor). In the minds of many, the Emperor still maintains the symbolic power of the supreme authority, even though the claim to divinity was renounced by his father at the insistence of the American military forces right after the Second World War. The first line of the Emperor's speech sets a frame of personal connection and bond between him and the people. It is an official announcement by the Emperor, but it is not simply in the sense that rapport is embedded in the message. It goes much deeper into people's minds than the first line in PM Kan's speech because it expresses a personal, shared suffering, rather than a formulaic statement of sympathy.

The Emperor continues to express his inner feelings honestly as he describes his worries about the possible grave situations surrounding survivors and about the nuclear power plant. Observe the following Japanese utterance, along with its English equivalent:

> Nani nimo mashite kono daisaigai o ikinuki hisaisha to shite no mizukara o hagemashi tsutsu korekara no hibi o ikiyoo to shite iru hitobito no ooshisa ni *fukaku mune o utarete imasu*.

> Above everything, [I] *have been greatly moved* by the bravery of the survivors who are encouraging themselves in trying to live on through this enormous disaster.[20]

The expression of *fukaku mune o utarete* literally means "chest being hit deeply". It is not an expression of something remote and abstract; it makes the sentiment concrete, close, physical, and realistic. Possibly another expression such as *kandoo shite* ("be impressed") might be an expected alternative here. However, the Emperor went beyond the stale expression and deliberately chose the more heart-felt and emotionally rich expression of *mune o utarete*. The Emperor's speech is generally conceived as a gentle and graceful one, and indeed he has kept that tone throughout his speech; but here, in selecting this particular expression, he made sure that his true and sincere feelings were correctly conveyed to the people and that he was able to establish a connection with them. In other words, his speech is a clear example of rapport talk, which is not found in PM Kan's speech.

Interestingly, the Emperor is not just revealing his inner feelings or emotions; in his speech he is also evoking the metaphor of family, which represents bonds or connectedness among people. Consider the following Japanese utterance, along with its English equivalent:

> Korekara mo *mina ga aitazusae itawariatte* kono fukoo na jiki o norikoeru koto o chuushin yori negatte imasu.

> [I] hope from the bottom of (my) heart that *the people will, hand in hand, treat each other with compassion* and overcome these difficult times.[21]

The Emperor specifically talks about the spirit of helping each other by using the expression of *aitazusae*, which literally means to "mutually hold each other's hand". The term used to address his audience here is *mina* (you), which is strictly reserved for the Emperor (or any superior person) to use. It reminds us of a scene of family members holding each other's hands with the guidance of a father-like figure, in this case the Emperor.

In the following utterance, by including himself in this bond or circle of a family, the Emperor reinforces the idea of family unity:

> Hisaichi no korekara no kunan no hibi o *watashitachi mina* ga samazama na katachi de sukoshi demo ooku *wakachiatte iku* koto ga taisetsu de aroo to omoimasu.
>
> [I] believe that *we all* have to *share* with the victims as much as possible, in whatever way we can, their hardship in days ahead.[22]

The Emperor uses the plural first person pronoun *watashitachi mina* (we all), which includes himself. This is a crucial expression that tells the audience who he thinks he is. Being the Emperor, he can claim the loftiest of positions and offer words of consolation from his throne. However, the Emperor unmistakably descends, closing the social gap and joining the circle of the people by using the inclusive pronoun *we*. The Emperor, here, unequivocally declares that he is a member of the family, establishing a rather more reciprocal relationship with the public.

Interestingly, the Emperor makes his declaration while maintaining his authority as the Emperor. This task is accomplished by the expression *watashitachi mina*. The word *watashitachi* (we) is a typical plural second-person pronoun used by common people, but the word *mina* (all) is reserved for the Emperor to use to address people as subjects. By juxtaposing the two words, the Emperor skillfully performs the double task of maintaining his nobility while at the same time putting himself within the circle of the people. The expression *watashitachi mina* is an effective linguistic device that allows the speaker to claim his dual identity as the Emperor and a member of the family.

In concluding his speech, the Emperor talks about hope and the future. Again, the theme of family or unity is expressed. Consider the following utterance:

> Kokumin *hitori bitori* ga hisai shita kaku chiiki no ue ni korekara mo nagaku *kokoro o yose* hisaisha to tomo ni sorezore no chiiki no fukkoo no michinori o mimamori tsuzukete iku koto o kokoro yori negatte imasu.
>
> [I] implore [our] people to come *together as one*, to keep their *hearts* close to the afflicted areas, and continue watching over the victims on the long road to recovery.[23]

In the public mind, the memory of the impact and the tragedy of the earthquake might be eventually weakened as time goes by. However, the Emperor reminds the people of the importance of togetherness and watching out for those who were made victims by the earthquake. By *kokoro o yose* (literally "bring heart together"), the Emperor encourages the people to have not just mere sympathy, but empathy—the willingness

212                          Chapter Nine

to stand in someone else's shoes. Furthermore, the Emperor uses the metaphor of a journey (*michinori*, "road") to frame the recovery efforts. This metaphor of a journey reinforces the idea of going through a tough time together to reach the shared goal of recovery. The Emperor assures the people that while the present difficulties are tremendous and the road to recovery will be long and arduous, they will arrive at a better place, so long as people are united and take care of one another as a family.

In comparison with PM Kan's bureaucratic speaker-oriented report talk, the Emperor's speech is an artful example of rapport talk, focusing on the addressee and the connection between the speaker and the addressee, sharing their sorrow and encouraging everyone to work together. Public reaction to the Emperor's speech was overwhelmingly positive. A major newspaper reported that victims felt that the Emperor's message was "encouraging" and "convincing", and that his words made them feel inclined to stay "hopeful" despite the grave tragedy.[24] The newspaper cited one victim as saying, with tears in her eyes, that she was greatly encouraged by the words of the Emperor, who thought of victims first. An editorial of another major newspaper pointed out that the Emperor's speech was sinking more deeply into people's minds and was more persuasive than the politicians' speeches.[25] Yet another major newspaper wrote that people were greatly encouraged by the Emperor's thoughtful words and gentle manner of speaking.[26]

## Discussion

### *Politicians and Rapport Talk*

Here it could be argued that there are different expectations of the roles of Prime Minister and Emperor, to save face for PM Kan. Being the political leader, PM Kan is expected to focus on the details of the rescue and recovery mission (e.g., numbers and figures). On the other hand, the Emperor is not a political but a symbolic leader, a cultural figurehead. As such, he is not expected to go into the procedural details of recovery efforts. These differing roles could certainly have influenced the respective speech style differences between PM Kan's report talk and the Emperor's rapport talk.

However, one crucial point to acknowledge is the fact that PM Kan, aside from his one brief obligatory acknowledgement of the victims, failed to include important elements of rapport talk in his largely dull report talk. Perhaps PM Kan thought that it would be wrong to appeal to emotion and that report talk would be enough or even ideal in a political speech.

However, interestingly, in his study of political language, Lakoff states that

> emotion is both central and legitimate in political persuasion. Its use is not an illicit appeal to irrationality, as Enlightenment thought would have it. The proper emotions are rational.[27]

In a similar way, Westen argues that the political brain is an emotional brain.[28] Management studies on leadership also suggest the importance of emotion.[29] According to them, successful leaders are generally described as interactive, inspirational, empowering, and passionate, or, to use their term, *transformational*. In the present context, this is in accordance with the claim that rapport talk should be considered an integral part of any successful political speech.

### *President George W. Bush and the Inclusive* **We**

With respect to this point, it is intriguing to compare PM Kan's speech with U.S. President George W. Bush's speech on the occasion of the terrorist attacks, which was delivered as a televised address to the nation on September 11, 2001. Consider the opening lines of President Bush's speech:

> Today, our fellow citizens, our way of life, our very freedom came under attack in a series of deliberate and deadly terrorist acts. The victims were in airplanes or in their offices: secretaries, men and women, military and federal workers, moms and dads, friends and neighbors.[30]

The first part of Bush's speech is not about the speaker himself, but about the public and the victims, very much unlike PM Kan's speech. President Bush successfully brings the public into the spotlight and frames the speech as a narrative about the people. By characterizing the victims involved in the tragedy with their everyman roles, he personifies them and brings the tragedy closer to the audience. The bewilderment and sorrow the nation is feeling is not a narrative of someone else distant from themselves, but someone close to them, like *moms and dads* or *friends and neighbors*. The choice of the words let the audience experience the tragedy as their own tragedy, evoking empathy within the entire nation. In this sense, President Bush's speech is exemplary of rapport talk, persuasive and even inspirational, regardless of whether one agrees or disagrees with President Bush's politics. For example, Mika Brzezinski, a frequent critic of former President Bush, was working as a journalist for CBS and was at Ground Zero when the second tower collapsed on September 11, 2001, and now a liberal commentator and a co-host of MSNBC's "Morning Joe", commended Bush's 9/11 speech specifically for its leaderly compassion on October 30, 2012, the day after Hurricane Sandy slammed into New Jersey and New York City.[31] This very recent example shows that rapport talk successfully transcends political agenda or ideology, especially in times of disaster or tragedy and withstands even the harshest criticism.

Another interesting point about President Bush's speech is that he started the speech with *our fellow citizens* and not with a more usual *my fellow citizens*. The inclusive *we* (e.g., *we, our*) is a pronoun allowing the speaker to negotiate his/her relationship with the audience. To be more specific, it is a linguistic device used to establish connection and a sense of togetherness with the audience. It enhances rapport talk. In the speech, President Bush used the word *our*, the possessive form of the inclusive *we*, eighteen times, making it the single most frequently used word in his speech. Together with the five uses of the inclusive *we*, President Bush used forms of the inclusive *we* twenty-three times, while he used the singular first person pronoun *I* only seven times. The repeated use of the inclusive *we* shows that Bush's speech was a deliberate and effective example of rapport talk, evoking the ameliorating emotions of patriotism and togetherness among the people.

Interestingly, this inclusive *we* was skillfully used by President Obama in his 2008 campaign slogan "Yes We Can", while his unsuccessful opponent Hillary Clinton was shouting a slogan of "Yes I Can" using the exclusive pronoun *I*.

### *PM Kan and Exclusive* We

In PM Kan's speech there was no instance of inclusive *we*. There was one occasion where the plural first person pronoun *watashitachi* (we) was used; however, it was an instance of exclusive *we*, referring to PM Kan and his government, excluding those addressed in the speech. Consider the following utterance:

> *Watashitachi* to shite wa mazu juumin no minasama no anzen to iu koto o dai ichi ni kangaete saku o utte mairimashita
>
> *We as the government* took measures with the thought of residents' safety first.[32]

PM Kan could have used the inclusive *we* to negotiate a connection or sense of fellowship with the people, but he simply missed the opportunity. Recall that the Emperor was able to set a frame of fellowship by deftly juxtaposing the words *watashitachi* (we) and *mina* (you), unequivocally establishing a carefully nuanced instance of an inclusive *we*. Instead, PM

Kan's speech is characterized by the unidirectional style of the political leader, directed at the people. It is speaker-oriented, inviting no dialogue or shared bond between the speaker and addressee. Rather than bridging the distance between the officials and the public at this time of hardship, it was instead enlarged. Such unidirectionality resurfaced and was highlighted in the last utterance of PM Kan's speech. Observe the following final remark made by PM Kan:

> Watashi kara no kokumin no minasama e no onegai to sasete itadakimasu.
>
> Let me make this as a request to all of you from me.[33]

As PM Kan frames this speech, it is nothing but a request from him as Prime Minister to the nation as the governed to cooperate with the requests of his government.

The unidirectional nature of this speech is reflected by the frequency of each word used in Prime Minister's speech. By far the most frequently used word is *minasan* (all of you), mentioned twelve times. This is followed by *onegai* (request), mentioned eight times, then by *zenryoku* (in its full power), *shikkari* (firmly), *jishin* (earthquake), *genshiryoku hatsudensho* (nuclear power plant), each mentioned four times, and *watashi* (I), mentioned three times. The speech was an *onegai* (a request) to *minasan* (all of you) from the speaker.[34] The following is a representative utterance:

> 20 kiro ken no *minasan* ni taihi o *onegai* suru koto ni shimashita.
>
> [I] decided to request of all of you who are within 20 kilometers radius to evacuate.[35]

This utterance is typical of an announcement issued by a government official giving commands from an elevated position of authority. It may be effective report talk, but it lacks the important qualities of rapport talk that evokes cooperative pathos in a time of emergency.

Contrasting PM Kan's report talk with an analysis of Emperor Akihito's speech reveals notable differences in the types of words used and their frequencies. The three most frequently used words by the Emperor are *hitobito* (people) (eight times), *negatte* (hoping) (five times) and *hisaisha* (victims) (five times). Those words are followed by *fukaku* (deeply) (four times) and *kokoro* (heart) (four times). The Emperor was clearly talking about the people and the victims, expressing sincere hopes for their well-being. Notice also that the Emperor did not use the first-person pronoun as PM Kan did. Here, we see that the Emperor's audience-oriented speech clearly typifies rapport talk.

***Emperor Akihito and Over-Accommodation***

Interestingly, Emperor Akihito's rapport talk was visually observed by his body language, as well in the form of *over-accommodation*. Accommodation is a strategy whereby speakers adapt to another's communicative behavior in order to gain social approval. The behavior includes linguistic, prosodic, and non-verbal behaviors. If accommodation exceeds the socially expected degree, it is called over-accommodation.[36]

After the earthquake and tsunami, the Emperor and the Empress, who are rarely seen in public, visited evacuation shelters in the affected areas to console and encourage the victims. According to news reports and TV footage, the imperial couple were literally kneeling on the floors inside gymnasia used as evacuation shelters as they talked with evacuees.[37] The Emperor kneeling down was an instance of over-accommodation. After all, the imperial couple are accepted as "their Majesties", whose social status is elevated high above the common people. Through the gesture of kneeling down, the imperial couple literally descended to the position of the common people. However, the gesture of over-accommodation was met with psychological convergence on the part of the people; they accepted this with tremendous gratitude, and many people were seen wiping away tears. The act of kneeling down put the imperial couple *in the same shoes* as those affected by the disaster, instantly reducing the psychological (not to mention the physical) distance between them.

This instance of over-accommodation, along with the addressees' psychological convergence (or acceptance), can be also observed in the Emperor's utterances to victims during the visits. For example, the Emperor said the following on May 13, 2012: "***O**karada o daiji ni **ne***" ("Take care, please").[38] The Emperor used the prefix *o-* to *karada* (body), which indicates the speaker's respect for and politeness to the addressee. Furthermore, the sentence's final informal particle, *ne*, is used colloquially to solicit consensus, thus functioning to convey a sense of solidarity. Both linguistic items are not generally expected to be used by the Emperor. The utterance is an instance of over-accommodation in that the Emperor is converging downward to the addressee (the common person) by significantly reducing the hierarchical relationship between them. It was reported that the addressee was greatly moved and encouraged by this manifestation of the Emperor's concern.[39]

These linguistic items, body language, and gentle, caring tone of voice (what Gumperz calls *contextualization cues*[40]) contributed to framing the

Emperor as if he were a common person who genuinely cares for the victims. His deliberate frame of "ordinary" Emperor-hood was met with psychological convergence from the people. After all, in all of Japanese history, Emperor Akihito was the first never to be considered divinely descended, a status his father Emperor Hirohito was forced to reject by the U.S. in 1945. It appears that the desire to be connected with his people has been a theme throughout Emperor Akihito's life. He even became the first Crown Prince to marry a commoner when he married Michiko Shooda in 1959, breaking a thousand-year-old tradition.

***Emperor Hirohito: "I Am Always with You"***
Connection to the people is clearly observed in the language of the Emperor Akihito's video message, delivered directly to the people. Though formal, it is still fully modern Japanese, easily accessible to the people. This is a sharp contrast to the highly inaccessible formal classical Japanese used by his father, Emperor Hirohito, in the famous radio broadcast *Gyokuon Hoosoo* (Jewel Voice Broadcast) in which he announced to the Japanese people his acceptance of the Potsdam Declaration in 1945 after the atomic bombings of Hiroshima and Nagasaki.[41] The speech was a unidirectional announcement from the Emperor delivered to his subjects. The following is the first sentence of Emperor Hirohito's speech, which sets the frame of the formal announcement as report talk:

> *I announce to the loyal subjects* with the hope of settling the present situation by resorting to an extraordinary measurement after pondering the general trends of the world and the present situation of the empire.[42]

Emperor Hirohito used the archaic first-person singular pronoun *chin* (I), which is reserved exclusively for the Emperor to refer to himself. An analysis of the word frequency shows that the most frequently used word is this *chin* (I) (sixteen times), followed by *teikoku* (empire) (eight times), *shinmin* (subjects) (seven times), and *nanji* (you) (five times). Emperor Hirohito used the overtly archaic first-person pronoun frequently in order to frame himself as the figure who has the ultimate power and authority and that the decision to end the war was absolute and his alone. Emperor Hirohito's speech, being essentially report talk and clearly speaker-oriented, bears more resemblance to PM Kan's speech than his son's (Emperor Akihito's) video message.

However, it is interesting to note that Emperor Hirohito went further and included sympathetic remarks about the difficult situations engulfing his people at the end of the war. He overtly and explicitly stated the following:

> The welfare of the wounded and the war-sufferers and of those who have lost their homes and livelihood, are the objects of *my profound solicitude. I* am keenly aware of the innermost feelings of all of you.[43]

Emperor Hirohito revealed his own capacity for empathy and feeling for his people through the use of the first-person pronoun. This appeal to pathos through personal identification is an effective strategy to persuade the listeners to feel closer to the speaker. This affecting speech was reinforced by the following utterance:

> I have resolved to pave the way for a grand peace for all the generations to come by *enduring the unendurable and suffering what is unsufferable. I am always with you.*[44]

Emperor Hirohito here frames himself as someone who will endure the same hardships expected of his people. Even while maintaining his elevated status and using archaic, formal Japanese, the sense of unity, togetherness or rapport was effectively established. In the post-war years, after renouncing his divinity, Emperor Hirohito travelled throughout Japan to encourage the rebuilding of the nation, and throughout his reign he retained the affection of the Japanese people.[45]

Although their language is very different (i.e., Emperor Hirohito's classical Japanese versus Emperor Akihito's modern Japanese) and they belong in differing historical contexts, both Emperors use similar rapport talk. Both speeches were, similarly, gratefully received by the people. Unfortunately, PM Kan's speech, also given at a time of hardship, was rather lacking in rapport talk when people most sorely needed it.

## Conclusions

This study has shown evidence of the rhetorical value of rapport talk for public motivation and persuasion through the examination of speeches given by Japanese leaders immediately following the devastating earthquake and tsunami that hit Japan in March 2011. In particular, rapport talk, or language that establishes connectedness with the addressee by appealing to pathos, is crucial even for political leaders whose roles tend to be thought of as purely administrative, presenting figures, numbers, facts, logic, and policies; or, to put this differently, they often use report talk. Without emotionally connecting with people, all those hard numbers and facts carry little weight or importance. PM Kan's speech was largely unsuccessful at gaining the trust of the nation after the triple disaster because he failed to adopt this fundamental aspect of the language of persuasion, thus confirming Westen's assertion that there is a place for proper emotions in political speaking.[46] In short, effective rapport talk was altogether missing in PM Kan's speech.

On the other hand, Emperor Akihito's video message was extremely successful due to its appropriate use of rapport talk. People embraced the Emperor's speech with gratitude and enthusiasm. It was also shown that this use of rapport talk was, to a certain extent, shared by Emperor Akihito's father, Emperor Hirohito, in his historic "Jewel Voice Broadcast" in 1945. While the historical and social contexts surrounding them were remarkably different, the rhetorical impact was the same.

George Lakoff,[47] a cognitive linguist, claims that if we fully appreciate how the brain and the mind work, we will understand that "our brains evolved for empathy, for cooperation, for connection to each other and to the earth." In the context of this study, empathy, cooperation, and connection are all crucial ingredients of any successful rapport talk. With respect to the arts of persuasion through which leadership is performed, this study suggests that rapport talk is as essential in the East as it is in the West, where the theoretical concept was originally developed. Interestingly, this holds true even in the most transcendent and institutionalized discourse of the Japanese Imperial household.

# Notes

[1] Naikakufu [Cabinet Office, Government of Japan]. *Higashi Nihon Daishinsai ni Okeru Higaigaku no Suikei ni Tsuite* [On an Estimate of the Total Cost of Destruction from the Eastern Japan Great Earthquake.] 2011.
[2] Jonathan Charteris-Black, *Politicians and Rhetoric: The Persuasive Power of Metaphor* (New York, NY: Palgrave Macmillan, 2005), 1.
[3] Deborah Tannen, *Conversational Style* (Norwood, NJ: Ablex, 1984), *You Just Don't Understand* (New York, NY: Ballantine, 1990), *Gender and Discourse* (New York, NY: OUP, 1996).
[4] e.g., Shoji Azuma, *Senkyo Enzetsu no Gengogaku* (Kyoto, Japan: Minerva Shoboo, 2010), "Soapbox Speeches in the Summer of Seiken Kootai," *Japanese Language and Literature* 45(1), 141–67.
[5] Shushoo Kantei [Prime Minister of Japan and His Cabinet], *Toohoku Chihoo Taiheiyoo Oki Jishin ni Kansuru Kan Naikaku Soori Daijin Messeeji* [Prime Minister Kan's Message on the Eastern Japan Great Earthquake], March 12, 2011.
[6] Kunaichoo [Imperial Houschold Agency], *Toohoku Chihoo Taiheiyoo Oki Jishin ni Kansuru Tennoo Heika no Okotoba* [*Emperor's Speech on the Eastern Japan Great Earthquake*], March 16, 2011.

[7] NHK Senji Rokuon Shiryoo [Japan Broadcasting Corporation Wartime Archive], *Shoowa Tennoo, Shuusen no Gyokuon Hoosoo* [*Emperor Showa, Jewel Voice Broadcast on the Termination of War*], August 15, 1945.
[8] NHK Hoosoo Bunka Kenkyuujo [Japan Broadcasting Corporation Culture Research Institute], *Seiji Ishiki Getsurei Choosa 2011* [2011 Monthly Report on Political Opinion], 2011.
[9] Gregory Bateson, *Steps to an Ecology of Mind* (New York, NY: Ballantine Books, 1972), and Erving Goffman, *Frame Analysis* (New York, NY: Harper, 1974).
[10] Shushoo Kantei, 2011.
[11] Ibid.
[12] Ibid.
[13] Ibid.
[14] Ibid.
[15] NHK Hoosoo Bunka Kenkyuujo [Japan Broadcasting Corporation Culture Research Institute], Seiji Ishiki Getsurei Choosa 2010 [2010 Monthly Report on Political Opinion], 2010.
[16] NHK Hoosoo Bunka Kenkyuujo, 2011.
[17] "Leading a Nation in Crisis," *The Japan Times*, August 31, 2011.
[18] "*Hisaisha Anjiru Ryoo Heika ni Kandoo*" ["Impressed by the Emperor and Empress, Who Are Anxious about the Victims"], *The Asahi Shimbun*, July 5, 2012, 1.
[19] Kunaichoo, 2011.
[20] Ibid.
[21] Ibid.
[22] Ibid.
[23] Ibid.
[24] "*Heika no Okotoba, Hisaichi Hagemashi.*" ["Emperor's Words, Encouraging the Stricken Area."] *The Nihon Keizai Shimbun*, March 17, 2011.
[25] "*Kokumin to Tomo ni o Mune ni*" ["Together with the People"], *The Asahi Shimbun*, May 16, 2011.
[26] "*Hisaisha o Hagemasu Atatakai Okotoba*" ["Warmhearted Words Encouraging the Victims"], *The Yomiuri Shimbun*, April 28, 2011.
[27] George Lakoff, *The Political Mind* (New York, NY: Penguin Books, 2009), 8.
[28] Drew Westen, *The Political Brain* (New York: Public Affairs, 2007).
[29] e.g., Bernard M. Bass, "Does the Transactional-Transformational Leadership Paradigm Transcend Organizational and National Boundaries?" *American Psychologist* 52(1997), 130–9; Bass and Bruce J. Avolio, *Improving Organizational Effectiveness through Transformational Leadership* (Thousand Oaks, CA: Sage, 1994); Bass and Ronald E. Riggio, *Transformational Leadership* (Mahwah, NJ: Lawrence Erlbaum, 2006); and Michael Z. Hackman and Craig E. Johnson, *Leadership: A Communication Perspective* (Long Grove, IL: Waveland, 2009).
[30] President George W. Bush, televised address to the nation, NBC News, September 11, 2001, 0:15:00.
[31] Korson, 2012.
[32] Shushoo Kantei, 2011.
[33] Ibid.

[34] This general pattern of word frequency in PM Kan's speech was confirmed when five of his speeches (given on March 12, 13, 15, 18 and 25, 2011) were tabulated and word frequency was calculated. The most frequently used word is *minasan* (all of you) (fifty-two times), which is followed by *kokumin* (the people) (twenty-one times) and *onegai* (request) (fifteen times). *Watashi* (I) was used eleven times.
[35] Shushoo Kantei, 2011.
[36] e.g., Howard Giles and Peter F. Powesland, *Speech Style and Social Evaluation* (New York, NY: Academic Press, 1975); Giles, Justine Coupland and Nikolas Coupland, *Contexts of Accommodation: Developments in Applied Sociolinguistics* (New York, NY: CUP, 1991); Coupland, "Speech Accommodation," in *Society and Language Use*, eds. Jürgen Jaspers, Jan-Ola Östman, and Jef Verschueren, 21–27 (Philadelphia, PA: John Benjamin, 2010).
[37] e.g., "*Gokazoku wa, Omizu wa*" ["How about Family, How about Water"], *The Asahi Shimbun*, March 31, 2011; "Ryoo Heika, Okarada Daiji ni" [Emperor and Empress, Take Care, Please"], *The Asahi Shimbun*, April 26, 2011; "Ryoo Heika ga Hinanjo Omimai" ["The Emperor and Empress Visit an Evacuation Shelter"], *The Yomiuri Shimbun*, March 31, 2011; Nihon TV News, "Tennoo Koogoo Ryooheika Miyagi no Hisaisha Mimawareru" ["The Emperor and Empress Visiting Victims in Miyagi Prefecture"], April 27, 2011.
[38] "Sendai no Kasetsu Juutaku, Ryoo Heika Omimai" [The Emperor and Empress Pay a Visit to Evacuation Shelters in Sendai"], *The Asahi Shimbun*, May 14, 2011, 30.
[39] Ibid.
[40] John Gumperz, *Discourse Strategies* (New York, NY: CUP, 1982).
[41] NHK Senji Rokuon Shiryoo, 2012.
[42] Ibid.
[43] Ibid.
[44] Ibid.
[45] Shoji Azuma, "Speech Accommodation and Japanese Emperor Hirohito," *Discourse and Society* 8(2), 189–202.
[46] Westen, 2007.
[47] Lakoff, 267.

# Bibliography

Azuma, Shoji. "Speech Accommodation and Japanese Emperor Hirohito." *Discourse and Society* 8(2), 189–202.
—. *Senkyo Enzetsu no Gengogaku*. Kyoto, Japan: Minerva Shoboo, 2010.
—. "Soapbox Speeches in the Summer of Seiken Kootai." *Japanese Language and Literature* 45(1), 141–67.
Bass, Bernard M. "Does the Transactional-Transformational Leadership Paradigm Transcend Organizational and National Boundaries?" *American Psychologist* 52(1997), 130–9.

Bass, Bernard M., and Bruce J. Avolio. *Improving Organizational Effectiveness through Transformational Leadership*. Thousand Oaks, CA: Sage, 1994.
Bass, Bernard M., and Ronald E. Riggio. *Transformational Leadership*. Mahwah, NJ: Lawrence Erlbaum, 2006.
Bateson, Gregory. *Steps to an Ecology of Mind*. New York, NY: Ballantine Books, 1972.
Charteris-Black, Jonathan. *Politicians and Rhetoric: The Persuasive Power of Metaphor*. New York, NY: Palgrave Macmillan, 2005.
Coupland, Justine. "Speech Accommodation." In *Society and Language Use*. Edited by Jürgen Jaspers, Jan-Ola Östman, and Jef Verschueren. 21–27. Philadelphia, PA: John Benjamin, 2010.
Giles, Howard, Justine Coupland and Nikolas Coupland. *Contexts of Accommodation: Developments in Applied Sociolinguistics*. New York, NY: CUP, 1991.
Giles, Howard, and Peter F. Powesland. *Speech Style and Social Evaluation*. New York, NY: Academic Press, 1975.
Goffman, Erving. *Frame Analysis*. New York, NY: Harper, 1974.
"*Gokazoku wa, Omizu wa*." ["How about Family, How about Water."] *The Asahi Shimbun*, 30. March 31, 2011.
Gumperz, John. *Discourse Strategies*. New York, NY: CUP, 1982.
Hackman, Michael Z., and Craig E. Johnson. *Leadership: A Communication Perspective*. Long Grove, IL: Waveland, 2009.
"*Heika no Okotoba, Hisaichi Hagemashi*." ["Emperor's Words, Encouraging the Stricken Area."] *The Nihon Keizai Shimbun*, 1. March 17, 2011.
"*Hisaisha Anjiru Ryoo Heika ni Kandoo*." ["Impressed by the Emperor and Empress, Who Are Anxious about the Victims."] *The Asahi Shimbun*, 37, July 5, 2012.
"*Hisaisha o Hagemasu Atatakai Okotoba*." ["Warmhearted Words Encouraging the Victims."] *The Yomiuri Shimbun*, 13. April 28, 2011.
"*Kokumin to Tomo ni o Mune ni*." ["Together with the People."]. *The Asahi Shimbun*, 13. May 16, 2011.
Korson, Alex (Producer). *Morning Joe* [Television broadcast]. October 30, 2012. New York, NY. MSNBC. 3:0:0.
Kunaichoo [Imperial Household Agency]. *Toohoku Chihoo Taiheiyoo Oki Jishin ni Kansuru Tennoo Heika no Okotoba* [*Emperor's Speech on the Eastern Japan Great Earthquake*]. March 16, 2011. http://www.kunaicho.go.jp/okotoba/01/okotoba/tohokujishin-h230316-mov.html
Lakoff, George. *The Political Mind*. New York, NY: Penguin Books, 2009.
"Leading a Nation in Crisis." *The Japan Times*, August 31, 2011. p. 14.

Naikakufu [Cabinet Office, Government of Japan]. *Higashi Nihon Daishinsai ni Okeru Higaigaku no Suikei ni Tsuite* [On an Estimate of the Total Cost of Destruction from the Eastern Japan Great Earthquake.] 2011. http://www.bousai.go.jp/oshirase/h23/110624-1kisya.pdf#search='%E9%9C%87%E7%81%BD+%E6%90%8D%E5%AE%B3+%E9%A1%8D'

NHK Hoosoo Bunka Kenkyuujo [Japan Broadcasting Corporation Culture Research Institute]. *Seiji Ishiki Getsurei Choosa 2010* [2010 Monthly Report on Political Opinion]. 2010. http://www.nhk.or.jp/bunken/yoron/political/2010.html

—. *Seiji Ishiki Getsurei Choosa 2011* [2011 Monthly Report on Political Opinion.] 2011. http://www.nhk.or.jp/bunken/yoron/political/2011.html

NHK Senji Rokuon Shiryoo [Japan Broadcasting Corporation Wartime Archive]. *Shoowa Tennoo, Shuusen no Gyokuon Hoosoo* [*Emperor Showa, Jewel Voice Broadcast on the Termination of War*]. 2012. 0:04:42. http://cgi2.nhk.or.jp/shogenarchives/sp/movie.cgi?das_id=D0001410387_00000

Nihon TV News. "Tennoo Koogoo Ryooheika Miyagi no Hisaisha Mimawareru" ["The Emperor and Empress Visiting Victims in Miyagi Prefecture"]. April 27, 2011. http://www.news24.jp/articles/2011/04/27/07181777.html

"Ryoo Heika, Okarada Daiji ni." [Emperor and Empress, Take Care, Please."] *The Asahi Shimbun*, 11. April 26, 2011.

"Ryoo Heika ga Hinanjo Omimai." ["The Emperor and Empress Visit an Evacuation Shelter."] *The Yomiuri Shimbun*, 30. March 31, 2011.

"Sendai no Kasetsu Juutaku, Ryoo Heika Omimai." [The Emperor and Empress Pay a Visit to Evacuation Shelters in Sendai."] *The Asahi Shimbun*, 38. May 14, 2011.

Shushoo Kantei [Prime Minister of Japan and His Cabinet]. *Toohoku Chihoo Taiheiyoo Oki Jishin ni Kansuru Kan Naikaku Soori Daijin Messeeji* [Prime Minister Kan's Message on the Eastern Japan Great Earthquake]. March 12, 2011. http://www.kantei.go.jp/jp/kan/statement/201103/12message.html

Tannen, Deborah. *Conversational Style*. Norwood, NJ: Ablex, 1984.

—. *You Just Don't Understand*. New York, NY: Ballantine, 1990.

—. *Gender and Discourse*. New York, NY: OUP, 1996.

Westen, Drew. *The Political Brain*. New York: Public Affairs, 2007.

## Acknowledgment

This research was supported in part by the Hakuho Foundation Japanese Language Research Fellowship and MEXT/JSPS Grants-in-Aid for Scientific Research (Grant Number: 23520535).

# PART IV

# A GLOBAL SURVEY OF SUSTAINABLE DEVELOPMENT IN AREAS OF SOCIAL VULNERABILITY

# Chapter Ten

# Prison Labor, Education, and Recidivism: A Study of the Bolivian Prison System as a Possible Model for Effective Prisoner Rehabilitation

## Cristal Downing

### Introduction

Few communities are as socially vulnerable as prisoners, particularly in a developing country like Bolivia. This vulnerability is exacerbated by the fact that the Bolivian prison system receives so little funding from the State that prison maintenance, prisoner welfare and even prison security are the responsibility not of the penal authorities, but of the prisoners themselves. Incarcerated persons in Bolivia must pay for all living expenses in prison. This results in a need for steady income, something for which most prisoners are not skilled enough to sustain when they arrive in jail. Given that the State presence in the prisons is almost non-existent, NGOs work in the prisons to provide programs focused on education and skills training. These programs facilitate the improvement of the prisoners' literacy levels and their entry into skilled labor while they are incarcerated. The NGO programs also teach the prisoners financial and other skills necessary to participate in entrepreneurial ventures, either as the sole entrepreneur or as one of a few participants in a small business.

The uniqueness of the Bolivian prison system is based not only on the fact that prisoners must pay to be in prison, but also on the country's low recidivism rate. Bolivia demonstrates remarkably low numbers of former prisoners returning to jail as compared to other countries of both comparable and dissimilar economic and institutional strength. This paper examines the relationship between these two phenomena, and aims to explore the following question: could the underfunding and corruption of the Bolivian prison system have unintentionally generated education, skills training programs, and a prison labor system that results in successful prisoner rehabilitation? This paper hypothesizes that the Bolivian prison environment empowers prisoners to lead stable lives both inside prison and when they return to society outside. Bolivian prisons thereby provide an unexpected yet effective solution to problems of social vulnerability in the previously incarcerated community.

The paper is based on my experience of working in six prisons in the city of Cochabamba, Bolivia, in 2009. During that time, I provided support to an NGO called Ayni Ruway in the implementation of various education and skills training programs. I entered the prisons on a daily basis and became well-acquainted with the workings of Bolivian prison life. This knowledge and understanding provides the primary source for this paper. Secondary sources are taken from the broad literature on prisoner rehabilitation, education, and prison labor.

## The Bolivian Prison

The Bolivian penal system is unique in that prisoners must pay to live in prison. The State does not provide adequate funding to the prisons and has transferred the responsibility for the maintenance of prison buildings and prisoner welfare to the inmates themselves. The prison guards and other officials are underpaid and highly opportunistic with respect to accepting bribes and making other efforts to improve their own lot. These two entwined issues have long been deeply entrenched in the workings of the Bolivian prison system, and result in a series of both single and recurring payments to be made by inmates. These payments are used to maintain buildings; the guards and other members of prison authorities also receive payments for a variety of allowances they make to the prisoners. From the moment of entry to the prison, Bolivian prisoners immediately find it necessary to earn enough to cover rent, bribes, and other living expenses such as food and medical attention. They have therefore established relationships with NGOs who provide education and vocational skills training in order that the prisoners can sustain a variety of entrepreneurial ventures that provide them an income while in prison.

In order to understand how the prisoners incur expenses and how their entrepreneurial ventures function, it is first necessary to relate the social organization of the Bolivian prison and the different groups of people present within it. First, there are the inmates themselves. In the prisons of Cochabamba, the majority of prisoners are from poor rural backgrounds and have been accused of some crime related to the *Ley 1008* ("Law 1008"), which was imposed by the U.S. government as part of its anti-drug efforts in Andean countries in the 1980s. Most prisoners have no prior experience of formal education, as they have worked full-time from an early age, so the average level of literacy upon entry to the prisons is very low. The common length of sentences varies greatly, but most prisoners do not have legal representation and must wait indefinitely for their case to be processed; this sometimes takes years, as the judicial system in Bolivia is slow and dysfunctional.

Prisoners can reduce their sentence by being voted into office as a *delegado* ("delegate"), who serves on a leadership panel in one of a variety of areas related to the infrastructure and administration of the prison. These include the treasury, work, NGO relations, education, sports, food, events planning for celebrations such as that held on Prisoners' Day, and a variety of other areas. Perhaps the most noteworthy of the delegate positions other than prison treasurer is the discipline secretary, who is responsible for maintaining good conduct. The delegates are responsible for representing the interests of the prisoners to prison authorities in whatever area they serve. The position of delegate brings great responsibility: the delegates, as representatives of the prison population, also decide how the prisoners' money is spent and must maintain current balance sheets at all times.[1] Delegate elections are the most important times of the year, with campaigns and election-related events taking up a large portion of candidates' and voters' time. The voting is done by anonymous ballot. The delegate system is structured and effective, often lauded as the prisoners' successful effort to create a system in prison that is fairer than the legal system supposedly handling their cases.[2]

Also present in the prison system are the guards, though they hardly ever enter the prison itself and are limited to peripheral areas in the role of monitoring individuals entering and leaving the prison and with what belongings. Their function does not encompass the monitoring or prevention of violence between prisoners, which usually takes the form of community "justice" (often physical violence) for one prisoner committing a crime against another, or, in the case of sex offenders, for the crime for which the person was sent to prison.[3] The only time the guards enter the prison is to conduct the morning *lista*, where they check that all prisoners are present. The salary of a private guard—the lowest but most common rank of prison guard—was less than $100 per month in 2003 and has increased only negligibly since then.[4] This salary is insufficient to maintain a family in a Bolivian city, where the prisons are located. Underpayment has therefore resulted in corruption—mostly in the form of bribery—being commonplace.[5] The guards accept bribes from the prisoners for a range of "favors": allowing non-family members to stay in prison, allowing unauthorized items such as drugs and alcohol to enter the prison, and even allowing prisoners to leave the prison for a specified period of time, among other things.[6] In many cases, if the guards need money, they threaten to make life difficult for the prisoners in some way, a situation that can only be remedied by the payment of a bribe. The guards are supervised by the governor of the prison, whose function is limited almost entirely to listening to the delegates in whatever matters they choose to discuss with him. The governors are as corrupt as the guards and accept bribes from the prisoners for "favors" similar to those outlined above.

The first payment that some prisoners in Bolivia have to make is for their transport to the prison, if they are not detained within walking distance.[7] Many prisons do not have vehicles in which they can transport prisoners from the site of detention or the court to the prison itself, so arrested individuals and their guards take taxis to prison, in which case the prisoner is forced to pay. The next cost incurred by every prisoner upon entry to the Bolivian prison is the *ingreso* or "entrance fee". This payment is usually made to the guard at the door of the prison, in which case he or she will take a percentage of the fee as commission. If the prisoner is not able to pay the ingreso upon arrival, it can usually be paid within 24 hours to a prison delegate, in which case it will be slightly less because no commission is to be extracted. This amount ranges from 25 Bolivianos (about US$3.50) to 130 Bs depending on the prison and who is collecting the payment.[8] It is added to the communal fund administered by the delegates to support their various areas of work. If the ingreso cannot be paid within twenty-four hours of entry, its value can be compensated through cleaning or cooking duties.[9]

Living space, either rented or bought, is the second cost incurred by prisoners upon entry to the prison. Each cell has a property title which is a document that illustrates the details of the space and its transaction history. The owner of the cell holds one copy of the title and another copy is kept in the prison's communal records. The title is passed from one prisoner to another at the point of sale, which is usually when one prisoner is leaving jail and sells it to someone who has just arrived. At this time, a contract is drawn up and signed in the presence of a witness, usually a delegate.[10] Rent for a cell is paid to the owner of the cell, who is usually another inmate who had enough money to buy two or more cells and thereby augment his income by renting out the space he does not need. The prison population as an entity can own a cell, in which case the title is claimed by the communal fund and rent is paid into that account. However, this is not common because of the lack of prison space. Inmates who expect to spend years in prison can buy cells from inmates who are leaving or, on rare occasions, from the communal fund. Most cells are big enough for a single bed and a cupboard, and are often compartments of larger areas that have been divided with cardboard or scraps of corrugated metal. Some cells, especially in San Pedro prison in La Paz, are more like apartments with living rooms, bedrooms and fully equipped kitchens.[11] This is a result not only of the prison payment structure, which has allowed for more "luxury" sections of the prison to develop and cater for wealthier occupants, but also of the fact that prisoners must provide their own food, as the state provides only one bowl of soup per day, if at all.

Prisoners who cannot afford to pay for space in a cell are forced to sleep in hallways or even bathrooms. The real estate business in the prisons is one way for prisoners to make money—beginning with the real estate agents, who scout for potential buyers (newly imprisoned inmates) and charge a commission to the seller if their scouting is successful.[12] The delegates usually permit sellers to advertise their cells publicly so the entrance, restaurant areas, and other common areas in the Bolivian prisons are covered with signs advertising *celda(s) en venta* ("cell[s] for sale") and listing the amenities (microwave, TV, etc.) provided in the cell for sale.

The housing market in the prison is affected by internal and external factors relating to supply and demand, and prices increase and decrease accordingly. For example, sometimes the government proposes changes in law that will suddenly allow many inmates to leave prison. This usually happens as a result of overcrowding and pressure on the government by human rights groups to improve the conditions in the prisons. These proposals cause a decrease in cell prices because the demand for cells is expected to drop. The Bolivian government sometimes talks of building new prisons and demolishing the current buildings, and these discussions also lead to temporary drops in the prices of cells.[13] For the most part, however, cell prices are increasing due to growing overcrowding. In addition to the commission charged to the seller by the agent, there are also transaction fees charged to the buyer, which are paid into the communal fund.

In addition to payments for living space and food, prisoners must pay for medical attention, supplies, and all other daily expenses. The Bolivian government does provide prisoners with a tiny daily stipend, but it is nowhere near enough to cover their living expenses, especially if the prisoner's family lives in the prison. Family residency is permitted in most all-male, non-maximum security prisons in Bolivia, and is often preferable because it means that the family can stay together and avoid the upkeep of two homes—one in prison and one outside. In many cases it is the breadwinner of the family who is detained and the other family members suddenly find themselves unable to pay their monthly expenses. It therefore makes much more financial sense to keep the family in one "household", resulting in all family members, including children, living in the prison with the inmate. In the case of the women's prisons, children are permitted to live with their mothers, but their fathers are not allowed to live in the prison.

The Bolivian state gives each prisoner a meager 6.60 Bs per day—approximately 95 cents—but this is not enough to cover living expenses. There are six prisons in the Cochabamba area, and living expenses vary little from one prison to the next with the exception of the maximum-security prison of El Abra, the only purpose-built prison in Cochabamba; the others are not as comfortable as El Abra because they were built as halfway houses or markets.[14] Ayni Ruway's reports show that most prisoners in the Cochabamba area need approximately 650 Bolivianos (US$93) per month to live alone in prison and 1,950 Bolivianos (US$280) to support a family of four there. The State provides approximately 198 Bolivianos per month (US$29), resulting in a responsibility for 452 Bolivianos per month per prisoner living alone, and 1,752 Bolivianos per month per prisoner supporting a family of four. The average prisoner therefore needs more than four times what the state gives him to live alone in prison and about ten times what the state gives him in order to maintain an average family there. This does not take into account the single initial fee for the right to sleeping space nor the acquisition of a cell, occasional bribes and other payments to guards, and possible medical expenses. The need to maintain an income in prison is clear.

Prisoners in all parts of the country have found ways to maintain an income while in prison. Some are assisted by NGOs such as Ayni Ruway, which founded education and artisan micro-enterprise programs in the prisons of Cochabamba to facilitate the income of the prisoners. As part of these programs, the organization offers classes at a variety of levels from basic reading and writing through high-school-level instruction. The NGO also offers prisoners training in the production of various items that they may sell to the public, thereby gaining an income to contribute to their monthly expenses. The products they make and sell are displayed outside the prison, where the prisoners' family members sell them on behalf of their imprisoned relatives. The money is then given to the prisoners according to the payment structure they have established for their businesses, and they in turn pay the fees and expenses mentioned above. For example, in the city of Cochabamba everyone knows that to buy a well-made and reasonably priced *asado* (barbeque), you should go to San

Antonio prison. There, the barbeques are displayed on the pavement where a wife or other family member supervises sales. Similarly, many residents of Cochabamba use the laundry service provided by inmates in the women's prison. To buy furniture, one can visit San Sebastián men's prison or San Pedro de Sacaba prison.

Prisoners are also known to practice the professions they held before their detention. There are therefore doctors, accountants, cooks, pharmacists, barbers, and construction workers who offer their services to the prison population or are paid by the communal fund to work for the good of the community. They are also able to offer services to visitors who visit the prison either to socialize with family members or intentionally to take advantage of the low prices of these services as compared to outside.[15] In addition, there are the previously mentioned real-estate agents.

The cooks and shop owners are especially successful because, after finding funds to buy a second cell, they provide for inmates' basic needs in terms of food and other everyday items. Equally valuable to the prison community are those who provide medical attention and are therefore in frequent demand, as insanitary conditions in the prison often result in prisoners becoming ill. There is almost no medical attention available to prisoners other than assistance provided by any doctor or other medical professional who happens to be a prisoner at the time.[16] In fact, while I was working in Cochabamba, there was a case of tuberculosis in one prison. The prisoners were responsible for the sick man, who was attended by another prisoner who had worked as a medical assistant a few years previously. NGOs do hold "Health Days" every three or four months. On these days, doctors visit the prisons and conduct general check-ups and provide basic services to prisoners. Other prisoners find work in surprising ways, such as Thomas McFadden, to whose account of life as a prisoner in Bolivia this paper frequently refers. He established himself as a tour guide in the San Pedro prison in La Paz as a way to secure his income.

The inmates of San Pedro de Sacaba prison, which is representative of the four all-male, non-maximum-security prisons in the Cochabamba area, chose to learn how to manufacture the items listed below with the support of Ayni Ruway. The following is a table of the prices of the products sold by the inmates of this prison and how much profit is made from each product. This information was obtained in July 2009 directly from the prisoners who produce these items. It should be noted that although Ayni Ruway provides initial support to new prisoners, inmates sustain on-going businesses and complete independent transactions with suppliers outside the prisons. They are therefore able to buy the raw materials for these products and maintain the equipment necessary to fabricate them. The prisoners report that after acquiring these materials and selling their products, they have a 20 percent profit margin on average.

**Table 10.1. Income and Profit from Each Item Sold by Prisoners of San Pedro de Sacaba.**

| Product category | Product (cm) | Price (Bs) | Price (USD) | Profit Bs / USD |
|---|---|---|---|---|
| **Burnt engraving** | Picture 100 x 80 | 300 | 42.86 | 60 / 8.57 |
|  | Picture 80 x 60 | 120 | 17.14 | 24 / 3.42 |
|  | Picture 40 x 30 | 50 | 7.14 | 10 / 1.42 |
| **Macramé** | Large picture frame | 210 | 30 | 42 / 6 |
|  | Medium picture frame | 180 | 25.71 | 36 / 5.14 |
|  | Small picture frame | 100 | 14.28 | 20 / 2.85 |
|  | Pencil case | 110 | 15.71 | 22 / 3.14 |
|  | Bag with "corn weave" | 100 | 14.28 | 20 / 2.85 |
|  | Bag with "snail weave" | 135 | 19.28 | 27 / 3.85 |
| **Furniture**[17] | Bed frame 150 x 200 | 1300 | 185.71 | 260 / 37.14 |
|  | Chair | 80 | 11.42 | 16 / 2.28 |
|  | Table 80 x 60 | 140 | 20 | 28 / 4 |
|  | Table 70 x 40 | 100 | 14.28 | 20 / 2.85 |
|  | Foldable table w/ design | 160 | 22.85 | 32 / 4.57 |

It cannot be over-emphasized that the purpose of the work carried out by the prisoners is not to aid in their rehabilitation but rather to allow them to fulfill their financial responsibilities within the prison.[18] Similarly, the education and vocational training programs implemented by Ayni Ruway do not have the objective of contributing to prisoner rehabilitation, but rather aim to support them as they struggle to pay to live in prison. The Bolivian prison system is significant because prisoners there need money to live in prison in the same way that people outside prison have daily outgoings to cover. This necessity, however, may actually be instigating activities that play a role in successful prisoner rehabilitation.

## Prison Labor, Education, and Prisoner Rehabilitation

The question of "prison work" or "prison industry"—labor in which the prisoners are productively engaged and for which in some cases they are paid a wage—has been the subject of debate for decades. The idea that "idleness and inertia" lead to personal discontent and can result in other more serious societal problems is embodied in the Universal Declaration of Human Rights, in which Article 23 states "everyone has the right to work."[19] Other documents present the idea that unemployment "creates childlike dependence on others" and should therefore be discouraged.[20] In addition, a statistical relationship has been found between prolonged unemployment upon release and reconviction, demonstrating that vocational training and/or employment while in prison decreases the chance that the inmate will reoffend in the future. In fact, the more months of vocational training completed by the inmate (either as part of a productive work program, or not), the less likely he or she is to reoffend, though some studies have shown that this only begins to be true after one year of training or work.[21]

Prison labor is seen as rehabilitative for two reasons as defined by Grünhut: "Training for work, and training by work."[22] Either by encouraging independence or by training the inmate so that he or she could obtain a job upon release (or a combination of the two), work while in prison can be considered a positive experience. Problems with this theory began in the late 1800s when some prisons in the U.S. and England, where much of this discussion was taking place, became exploitative factories in which prisoners did not exercise freedom of work but rather were forced to work in whatever position was most needed at the time and in extremely denigrating conditions. In addition, economic factors undergoing change outside the prison affected the interior goings-on of the institution and penal policy overall. For example, a new emphasis on factories and industry provoked a change in penal policy to allow prisoners to take part in work similar to the manufacturing that was taking place in factories outside. This seemed absurd to some, because the purpose of the prison was not to support economic activity, but rather to protect society and rehabilitate criminals. In addition, the prisoners' productivity presented competition to outside workers: if prisoners were successful in their work and sold more than outsiders, they would bring in greater income than non-criminals outside the prison. This was considered unfair to non-criminal workers.[23]

More recent discussions of vocational activity and prison rehabilitation have debated the idea that prisoners who are part of a prison industry should pay a fee to defray the costs of their imprisonment. Some argue that this type of payment system should be encouraged because it forces the prisoner to think of how he or she will use wages earned and allows him or her to consider the difference between disposable income and regularly incurred expenses.[24] However, in most cases this fee would be minimal. It would fulfill the sole purpose of training the inmate to think of wages in relation to regular expenses, not of actually covering his or her living expenses. In addition, some have argued that it is ethical to pay prisoners because it demonstrates the value of their work and that by forcing them to pay for their own living expenses, they realize that they are capable of paying their own way in life. In this way, paid prison labor, combined with a system in which inmates pay a small fee, is considered by some to have rehabilitative value.

One point of contention related to prison industry is the free association and social interactions between the prisoners in the work context. Scholars argue that this contact detracts from the value of them being in prison. However, this social interaction also plays a role in the rehabilitation of the prisoner in that it allows him or her to maintain a feeling of being a social individual who can function in a group or society. In fact, work-release programs where prisoners are permitted to leave the prison for a certain amount of time per week in order to work have been lauded as effective work-related rehabilitative processes that lead to a drop in recidivism. Similarly, home furlough programs in which prisoners are permitted to spend time outside prison with their families for a few days per month have seen success in rehabilitation. This is largely because of the degree of normality—albeit small—that the prisoner feels by leaving the prison and as a result of the social interaction he or she experiences while outside.[25] This makes social interaction in the work and prison contexts very important in rehabilitation.

Social skills and individual interactions are also common themes in theories of prisoner education. Programs across the U.S. found that prisoners who participate in literacy and other education programs that aim to teach practical skills as well as contribute to emotional and psychosocial rehabilitation are 72 percent less likely to re-offend than those who had not participated in such programs.[26] Those who had access to literacy instruction and who were provided with educational programs they could apply to both prison and outside activities were more likely to make a positive transition to post-prison life. Effective prisoner education programs are therefore considered to be those that not only facilitate literacy and vocational skills learning, but that are also of use to life inside and outside prison. These programs result in lower recidivism levels.[27]

Other studies have shown that inmates are more likely to stay in basic and higher education programs if they see their companions work hard in these programs and subsequently find that those companions have been employed after leaving prison. This success reinforces the idea that education can provide opportunities for a "second chance" and a transition away from criminal activity. This motivates prisoners to continue their educational pursuits, increasing the chances that they will leave prison with a higher level of literacy and education than when they entered and will therefore be less likely to re-offend. Even among those prisoners who were considered "high-risk" (those who were repeat offenders and had spent most of their adult life in prison), there was a 30 percent improvement in recidivism rates after education programs that lasted for a period of two years or more.[28] Each of the other prisoner groups included in the study demonstrated between 30 and 36 percent improvement in recidivism rates. This shows the clear correlation between education and recidivism.[29]

In addition to these studies of prisoner education programs, there have been extensive reports by prisoners on their own experience of rehabilitation, and the centrality of education in that process. These prisoners recognize the doubts that some criminologists and prisoners have about the value of education as a correctional tool, but use their own lives and those of their companions as the basis of an argument that supports prisoner education in a variety of subjects. Many of these reports address the fact that most prisoners have not completed high school and describe education as something that assists them in improving literacy, gaining vocational skills and strengthening their self-esteem. These characteristics empower prisoners to persevere in acquiring the skills themselves, and in committing to using them in useful, productive work outside prison instead of returning to criminal behavior.[30]

Although debates over effective methods of prisoner rehabilitation have gone on for centuries, prison labor and educational programs are frequent topics of discussion in the field. The consensus is certainly that some sort of productive activity has a positive effect on prisoner rehabilitation. Opinions diverge with regard to what type of activity this should be, and the extent of the impact it can have on corrections, especially when dealing with repeat offenders who are considered more likely to return to prison after their release. Nevertheless, prison labor and educational programming in literacy, vocational training, and other applied skills provide the basis for many successful prisoner rehabilitation programs.

## Prison Labor and Education in Bolivian Prisons

In the six prisons of Cochabamba, Bolivia, vocational training is provided by Ayni Ruway. Ayni Ruway's other services—such as social work and legal advice—are focused on the prisoner's self-improvement and personal development for the better. However, vocational training is the focus of the NGO's work in the prisons and is based almost entirely on providing the prisoners with skills they can use while they are inside in order to earn a salary and pay their living costs. Ayni Ruway and the prisoners with whom the organization works do realize the value of learning new skills and becoming literate in order to improve employment possibilities after prison. However, the NGO established these vocational programs not for their rehabilitative value, but rather in direct response to the fact that the government forces prisoners to pay for their own living expenses while not providing them with any of the tools necessary to do so. Most of the inmates come to prison without ever having held a steady job and without having completed training in any area that would give them a useful skill. Therefore, Ayni Ruway's programs are essential to the survival of the prisoner within the Bolivian penal system, where he or she must earn a living wage.

Upon arriving at the prison, after finding accommodation at least on a temporary basis, a prisoner must begin to work if he or she is to live in a cell rather than in the bathroom or hallways. As previously mentioned, some prisoners continue the profession they held outside prison—hairdressing, construction, dentistry, accounting, or a variety of others—but these are a small minority. Most of the prisoners have no skill they can use in prison and therefore must learn a new skill with which to start a new job as soon as possible. These individuals usually work alone or in small groups, and are responsible for the production, marketing and sales associated with their business. They are considered to be small business entrepreneurs. In the Cochabamba area, these prisoners become part of Ayni Ruway's vocational training programs, where they are taught a variety of skills ranging from furniture or barbeque making to artisanal wood etching and macramé, depending on the prison. As entrepreneurs, they are also taught how to start and manage a small business, participating in programs that aim to teach marketing, basic financial management, and other skills relevant to entrepreneurship.

Inmates of all skill levels in these areas spend up to six days per week working in the space in the prison that has been allocated for this activity. Some of these spaces are actually supposed to be common or recreational areas but have been taken over by tools, wood, and other materials. Other spaces are rooms that have been converted into workshops. A teacher from Ayni Ruway visits the space once or perhaps twice per week to provide on-the-job training to recently incarcerated prisoners, to monitor the small businesses, give advice to prisoners, and to meet with the prison's delegate for work. In those meetings, delegates can make requests for new materials or even new skills classes on behalf of the prisoners, in which case the representative will in turn present the idea to Ayni Ruway staff. In the case of new classes, the delegate will also present the idea to the governor of the prison to make him aware of the new program.

Between these visits, the prisoners continue to produce and sell their products from the prison. Inmates choose which of the above-mentioned available trades to practice according to their interests and the Ayni Ruway training and classes available to them. They then use these newly acquired skills in their own entrepreneurial ventures or in collaboration with one or two others. These entrepreneurial ventures work independently without supervision between Ayni Ruway's visits. Ayni Ruway provides training as well as some initial tools and materials (wood, fabric, wool, etc.) so that they can establish themselves in the business. The proceeds from the sale of these items go directly to the prisoners to cover their living expenses and to pay for whatever materials they were originally loaned. From that point onwards, the prisoners make all transactions with outside suppliers and are therefore able to acquire materials and new tools independent of the NGO.

Ayni Ruway also provides literacy classes, basic science classes, and mathematics classes at a variety of levels depending on the population of the prisons in which they work. These also consist of weekly or bi-weekly visits by the teachers to conduct the class, after which they usually meet with the delegate for education to receive updates or respond to any queries or suggestions. If new classes are requested, they may be approved if resources permit, because training and education are considered positive influences that facilitate the inmates' work in the prison, despite the fact that the training and education sessions are not provided by the prison authorities themselves. Approximately 90 percent of prisoners in Cochabamba have no experience of formal education before they come to prison, and leave at a more advanced level than when they arrived. The prisoners who did not already have a profession they could practice inside prison also gain a new skill that can be used both inside and outside prison. Therefore, although the principal purpose of the vocational training programs provided by Ayni Ruway is to provide the inmates with a way to make a living while incarcerated, the prisoners are also inculcating skills that will be useful to them after their re-entry into society.

## Recidivism in Bolivia

Rates of recidivism are often used as an indication of the effectiveness of prisoner rehabilitation programs. They give the percentage of inmates who return to prison (in other words, who continue to commit crimes) and are usually measured as re-arrest within three years of release. It is important to take into account that the time period differs between countries and indices, and that the "stopping event" could be parole violation.[31] Reconviction, or the percentage of released inmates who are convicted again within a certain amount of time after their release, is also used to evaluate correctional programs. Re-offense is the rate at which prisoners commit a crime within a certain amount of time after their release, and is difficult to measure because it is possible that individuals commit crimes for which they are not arrested or convicted. In Bolivia, individuals who are arrested are sent directly to prison, not to a holding facility, and many are held in prison for more than six months without their case being processed. In some other countries, however, individuals in prison are there because they have been convicted of a crime. While aware of these differences, we can make a useful comparison between Bolivian recidivism rates and reconviction rates from other countries.

Recidivism data is not readily available from government authorities in Bolivia, and in many cases can only be found in secondary sources such as newspaper reports. In addition, it is extremely difficult to collect recidivism data at the institutional level for a number of reasons. First, due to an extreme lack of funding within the penal system itself, resources to keep track of individuals arrested and/or individuals in prison are scarce. Records usually only show the number of inmates in each prison and are kept by the prisons themselves. More detailed information with names, ages, and provenance of members of the prison population are seemingly non-existent, but the few that have been mentioned in conversations with prison authorities are not accessible to anyone outside the *Regimen Penitenciario* (Prison Authorities). In addition, most inmates arrive at prison without personal identification such as a birth certificate or national identification card. The majority of the prison population is from rural areas in which documentation such as this is not commonly issued or needed. In the four prisons of Cochabamba from which data was collected, the percentage of prisoners without personal identification ranged from 38 percent in one prison to 77 percent in another.

Despite these difficulties, it has been possible to obtain data from a variety of sources. The first is the prisoners themselves, who proffered the following information to me as part of my work with Ayni Ruway, which maintains excellent working relations with prisoners, especially the prison delegates. In addition, this data was supported by previous information collected by Ayni Ruway's lawyer, who is very popular among inmates because of his support regarding their cases. There is no apparent reason for prisoners to lie to Ayni Ruway or the NGO's lawyer regarding the number of times they have been in prison. In three of four prisons from which data was collected, 100 percent of the prisoners questioned were in prison for the first time. In the fourth, 96 percent were there for the first time.

There exist few other sources of recidivism data; however, the reports that have been found are as follows. In 2008, *El Deber* (a newspaper based in Santa Cruz, Bolivia) reported recidivism to be between 20 and 30 percent nationally, and at 36 percent in San Pedro prison in La Paz.[32] In 2004, Kathryn Ledepur, writing for the *Andean Information Network* in Cochabamba, cited an article from *La Razón* (based in La Paz), stating:

> remarkably, despite the lack of resources, judicial delay, and corruption, Bolivia has a re-offender rate of 22 percent. Other countries in Latin America have recidivist rates as high as 75 percent.[33]

Even the highest of these rates, which was the 36 percent recidivism rate reported in San Pedro, falls far below comparable rates in other Latin American countries. Argentina has a National Recidivism Registry and is economically and politically stronger and more organized than Bolivia.[34] However, the ex-Secretary of Criminal Policy and current National Delegate of the Civic Coalition, Patricia Bullrich, stated in an interview that Argentina's recidivism rate is 70 percent, making it comparable to other "bad" recidivism rates in other countries. She also stated that a "good" recidivism rate is around 30 percent.[35] Guatemala, which is similar to Bolivia economically and exhibits similar social ills and inequality, demonstrates a 60 percent recidivism rate. It should be noted in this case that recidivism data in Guatemala is scarce, probably because of the similarly weak institutions and lack of state funding for the penal system.[36] Not only are Argentina and Guatemala's recidivism rates significantly higher than Bolivia's, but they also do not force inmates to pay to be in prison.

The U.S. Bureau of Justice Statistics measures recidivism as re-arrest within three years, and its census of the U.S. prison population was in 1994. The resulting report documented a 67.5 percent recidivism rate nationwide.[37] Nine years later, in 2003, the Urban Institute conducted a study that found that seven out of ten previously incarcerated individuals return to prison within three years of their release.[38] In the UK, the adult reconviction rate is measured as the rate at which an individual is convicted of a crime within two years of leaving prison. This rate was 60 percent in 2005.[39] Neither the U.K. nor the U.S. penal systems force inmates to pay to be in prison, and both countries have invested significant amounts of money in improving prisoner rehabilitation.

Switzerland provides the greatest contrast to Bolivia in terms of wealth, economic strength, and institutional funding. It also exhibits some of the lowest levels of both poverty and inequality. The most recent relevant study was published in 2008, and found that the rate of reconviction within three years was 24.1 percent.[40] In comparing the above data, we can see that despite the fact that poverty levels are a contributing factor to crime and recidivism, Bolivia exhibits recidivism rates closer to comparable measurements in Switzerland than to those of Argentina, Guatemala, the U.S., or the U.K. Despite different measuring methods, this comparison is useful because in Bolivia one need only be arrested to be sent to prison, whereas in Switzerland one must be convicted. Taking these differences into account, it is possible to draw the conclusion that the Bolivian recidivism rate is unusually low for a country demonstrating such levels of poverty and such underfunded institutions.

## Bolivian Prison Labor: An Effective Rehabilitation Method?

As has been mentioned, prisoners in Bolivia are permitted to select the type of skill they wish to learn and therefore the type of work they are going to do. They are not only more free to work than prisoners elsewhere who cannot make such choices, but are also more independent, as their choices directly affect their welfare. "Idleness and inertia" are certainly not present in this context, where prisoners work at least six days per week to produce for and maintain their own entrepreneurial ventures. Freedom of and to work is therefore present in that the inmates can choose a type of work and are under the same obligation to work that is experienced outside prison—i.e., work is necessary in order to cover living expenses and support a family. There can be no "childlike dependence" on those around them, because upon entry to the prisons it becomes immediately necessary to sustain a steady and legitimate occupation. The work in the prison encourages a belief that the prisoner is capable of making those choices and sustaining work as a result of his or her own decisions. Being paid for that work also instills a sense of self-worth in the prisoner, making him or her understand the value of work in a steady and legal profession.

While some prisoner rehabilitation programs elsewhere have explored the idea of making the prisoner pay a small fee to be in prison in order to encourage inmates to think of how they spend their wages, the Bolivian penal system forces inmates to cover almost all living expenses. Though this is in many ways problematic, especially with respect to bringing family members to live in prison so as to avoid maintaining two homes, it does instill a more in-depth understanding of the relationship between paid wages, living expenses and disposable income. Financial administration is also an important task of the prison delegates, who are held responsible for prison funds by the rest of their community. In addition, in order to maintain their entrepreneurial ventures, prisoners are trained in and allocated the task of managing the cash flows of their businesses. Financial planning and budget management are therefore inherent to many aspects of prison life in Bolivia, contributing to preparing inmates to assume similar responsibilities after their departure from prison. After having conducted skills training and financial education programs with prisoners upon their entry to prison, Ayni Ruway does not find it necessary to continue anything more than occasional monitoring and advice needed for the ongoing production and operations associated with the inmates' small businesses. This indicates that inmates become adept both at production of the items they choose to make and at managing their business budget. Similarly, Ayni Ruway rarely hears reports of prisoners being unable to cover their living expenses, indicating that inmates are efficiently managing their family budgets and are therefore able to cover these payments. These skills are transferrable to life outside prison and could therefore contribute to the decreased likelihood that the prisoner will return to prison.

In addition, contrary to the arguments made against this type of correctional model elsewhere, economic factors outside the Bolivian prison do not affect penal policy or the activities within the prison, apart from the long-standing effect that the poor finances of the government has had on the penal system overall. Competition presented by the prisoners to workers outside does exist. Furniture makers within the prison, for example, can compete directly with furniture makers outside because they are both selling in the same market. However, individuals in Bolivian society outside the prisons do not often complain of this competition because they are accustomed to competition from within the prisons.

The Bolivian prison also provides the inmates with extensive social interaction, both with family members and workmates. This commonly debated characteristic of prison labor is present in both prisoner employment and in life outside work: they are permitted to socialize as freely as they choose with friends, workmates, and family members within the prison. This is apparent upon entering the prison and seeing prisoners working, talking, associating with family members, and conducting all manner of activities that allow them to interact with other individuals. The delegate system also provides structure to these interactions, as individual self-worth is instilled through the voting process and delegate candidates conduct campaigns in social environments. Inmates are also permitted—and sometimes are forced economically—to bring their families to live in prison with them, which, though problematic, again reinforces this characteristic of social interaction within the prison and adds another degree of normalcy to life inside the institution. This may also contribute to their rehabilitation. This idea is supported by a 1973 study of home furlough programs in the U.S., which showed that prisoners who were permitted to spend fourteen days per year at home were not as likely to reoffend as those who were not. This was attributed to the fact that the prisoner could maintain something resembling "normal" family relationships while incarcerated, and the maintenance of a family life contributes to the successful rehabilitation of the prisoner.

The Bolivian government has not instigated this system of prisoner payments and work due to a desire to rehabilitate incarcerated individuals effectively, even though the penal code does state that the purpose of the prison is prisoner rehabilitation. However, the idea of prison labor as a tool for rehabilitation does not always depend on the belief that prisons exist to rehabilitate inmates—the two ideas are not inseparable. This separation is exhibited in Bolivia, where the penal policy and other codes do not say that rehabilitation should be practiced in the form of a prison labor system or prisoners paying their own costs of living. In fact, governmental and prison authorities regularly make efforts to hide the reality of the situation—that the prison system is so underfunded that the responsibility for maintenance of almost every aspect of prison life has been passed to the prisoners themselves and that their families are in many cases permitted to live with them.

However, despite this hidden reality and the fact that this system is the result of the government's desperate financial situation rather than effective correctional planning, the Bolivian prison does seem to present what many would argue is an effective rehabilitation system. Evidence supporting the successful rehabilitation of prisoners in Bolivia comes from the low recidivism rates there. For some reason, prisoners in Bolivia generally do not return to prison—a great contrast to the U.S., the U.K., Argentina, Guatemala, and many other countries where around 60 or 70 percent of prisoners are likely to return to prison within three years of release. This low recidivism rate indicates that the aspects of the Bolivian prison system that differ from those of other countries—namely the prison labor activities and extensive educational programming—are causing successful prisoner rehabilitation.

This supports arguments for paid prison labor and high levels of social interaction, which not only allow the prisoners in Bolivia to exercise their right to work, but also give them a feeling of independence and self-worth. This connection between work and lower recidivism is in turn supported by the statistical relationship between prolonged unemployment and higher levels of prisoner return to prison. As unemployment is not an option for prisoners in Bolivia, their experience of employment in the prison is linked to the low recidivism rates there.

The Bolivian NGO educational programming in the penal system also combines with the low recidivism rate to support the argument that prison education contributes to successful prisoner rehabilitation. Just as the studies mentioned earlier found that prisoners who participated in education programs were 72 percent less likely to re-offend, in the study of the Bolivian prison we see extensive education programs and a low recidivism rate. The programs do not state an objective of rehabilitating prisoners, but rather are more geared towards providing the literacy and other skills prisoners need to work productively and manage their own businesses. However, the education programs of Ayni Ruway and other NGOs working in Bolivian prisons are unique due to the number of them in each prison and the fact that the prisoners are able to participate in selecting relevant and applicable curricula through their delegate for education. As 90 percent of the prisoners in Bolivia had less than primary levels of education when they arrived (and it can be assumed that those who did have levels above that were in the same group as the few who practiced their previous professions of law, accountancy, and other offices in prison), their literacy and education levels improve and they are better equipped to participate in the workforce both inside and outside the prison. It is significant to note that the studies of prison corrections mentioned above found a 30 to 36 percent decrease in recidivism rates in all study groups (high-achievers, high-risk, etc.) who participated in a prison education program. It is conceivable that this decrease accounts for the difference between Bolivia's approximate 36 percent (or lower) recidivism rate and the 60 or 70 percent rate of Guatemala, Argentina, and more developed countries which do not force inmates to pay to be in prison.

## Conclusion

The Bolivian prison system is unique. Due to government underfunding and corruption, the prisons are not provided with adequate resources to house the prisoners. Responsibilities such as prisoner welfare, maintenance of buildings and other associated expenses are therefore passed to the inmates themselves. This makes it immediately necessary for inmates in the Bolivian prison to earn a steady income from the moment they arrive in prison. The State does provide a meager stipend to prisoners, but they need four times that amount to cover their own expenses and ten times that amount to maintain a family of four—something that is common in the prisons because families cannot afford the upkeep of a home in prison and one outside. A variety of NGO programs exist in the prisons in Bolivia to support the inmates as they struggle to earn enough to cover their expenses.

One such NGO is Ayni Ruway, which works in the six prisons of Cochabamba as well as in other parts of Bolivia. This NGO's focus is on providing inmates with the literacy levels and skills they need to maintain small entrepreneurial ventures in the prisons. These range from furniture production outfits to laundry services and macramé artisans, among others. Ayni Ruway provides initial materials to incoming prisoners, teaches them the skills necessary to maintain their businesses, and provides a number of other basic education classes with the goal of enhancing the inmates' income-generating abilities in any way possible. After initial support, the NGO monitors and gives advice to these small businesses and finds that after initial training and support, prisoners earn enough to cover their expenses.

Another unique aspect of the Bolivian penal system is its low recidivism rate. The highest reported rate is 36 percent, meaning that just 36 percent of prisoners return to prison within three years. This contrasts greatly with Guatemala, which has a similar economic and political situation but a 60 percent recidivism rate, and with Argentina, the U.S., the U.K., and others. In fact, Bolivia's recidivism rate is closest to Switzerland's, where crime levels are much lower and socioeconomic indicators show a better quality of life than in Bolivia.

Extensive vocational training and education for a prison labor system accompany the unique need for income and give rise to the low recidivism rate in Bolivian prisons. Much literature exists linking prison education programs and prison labor to lower recidivism rates, yet there is a lot of debate over the effectiveness of these methods as part of prisoner rehabilitation. Although the Bolivian government implemented this system due to underfunding, not due to its potential as an effective rehabilitation method, the low recidivism rates in Bolivia indicate that prisoners there do experience successful rehabilitation. The Bolivian prison system therefore provides an unexpected yet fascinating example of how prison labor and education can play a central role in prisoner rehabilitation.

## Notes

[1] Juan Carlos Pinto Quintanilla, *Cárcel de San Pedro: radiografía de la injusticia* [*San Pedro Prison: Radiography of Injustice*] (La Paz, Bolivia: ISLI, 1995), 49.

[2] Ibid., 23.

[3] Thomas McFadden and Rusty Young, *Marching Powder: A True Story of Friendship, Cocaine, and South America's Strangest Jail* (New York, NY: St. Martin's Griffin, 2003), 177.

[4] Ibid., 302.

[5] Pinto Quintanilla, 49.

[6] McFadden and Young, 179.

[7] Ibid., 52.

[8] Pinto Quintanilla, 37.

[9] McFadden and Young, 53.

[10] Ibid., 82.

[11] Ibid., 68.

[12] Ibid., 81.

[13] Ibid., 106.

[14] Information obtained from previous investigations conducted by Edson Vargas, the lawyer of the Ayni Ruway staff, through informal interviews with prisoners, observing advertisements for the rent and sale of cells in the prisons and buying food and drink from kitchens in the prisons.

[15] McFadden and Young, 58, 134.

[16] Pinto Quintanilla, 44.

[17] These prices are averages of the prices of each item of furniture, which vary according to the wood used.

[18] Pinto Quintanilla, 22.

[19] Gordon Hawkins, "Prison Labor and Prison Industries," *Crime and Justice*, 5(1983), 85–127.

[20] Ibid.

[21] John Braithwaite, *Prisons Education and Work: Towards a National Employment Strategy for Prisoners* (Queensland, Australia: Australian Institute of Criminology / University of Queensland Press, 1980), 12.

[22] Max Grünhut, Penal Reform: A Comparative Study (Oxford: Clarendon Press, 1948).

[23] Hawkins.

[24] Ibid.

[25] Braithwaite.

[26] Ibid., 298.

[27] Ibid., 301–3.

[28] Stephen Duguid and Ray Pawson, "Education, Change and Transformation: The Prison Experience," *Evaluation Review* 1998 no. 4, 470–95.

[29] Ibid., 482–487.
[30] Tiyo Attallah Salah-EL, "Attaining Education in Prison Equals Prisoner Power," *Journal of Prisoners on Prisons* 4( ), 1–5; Ron Nissimov, "Prison with Education Best Rehabilitation, Inmates Say," *The Plain Dealer*, June 21, 1993, 1B.
[31] National Institute of Justice, "Measuring Recidivism," February 20, 2008.
[32] Javier Méndez Vedia, "Reincidencia. El precio de tener los ojos cerrados" ["Recidivism: The Price of Having Our Eyes Closed"], *El Deber*, June 22, 2008.
[33] Kathryn Ledepur, "Bolivia's Prisons and the Impact of the Law 1008," *Andean Information Network*, July 31, 2004.
[34] Registro Nacional de Reincidencia [National Recidivism Registry].
[35] Radio la Red Interview with Patricia Bullrich, February 15, 2011.
[36] "Sobrepoblación y reincidencia frenan reinserción social" ["Over-Population and Recidivism Hinder Social Reinsertion"]. *Great City Magazine*, 2013.
[37] Bureau of Justice Statistics, "Re-entry trends in the U.S," BJS Web site, 2013.
[38] Christy A. Visher and Jeremy Travis, "Transitions from Prison to Community: Understanding Individual Pathways," *Annual Review of Sociology*, 2003 no. 29, 89–113.
[39] Ministry of Justice, "Compendium of Reoffending Statistics and Analysis," *Ministry of Justice Statistics Bulletin*, November 4, 2010.
[40] Confédération Suisse, "Taux de récidive de Suisses jugés/libérés en 2008" ["Recidivism: Swiss Judged / Released in 2008"], Swiss Statistics Web site, n.d.

## Bibliography

Braithwaite, John. *Prisons Education and Work: Towards a National Employment Strategy for Prisoners*. Queensland, Australia: Australian Institute of Criminology / University of Queensland Press, 1980.
Bureau of Justice Statistics. "Reentry Trends in the U.S." BJS Web site, 2013. http://bjs.ojp.usdoj.gov/content/reentry/recidivism.cfm
Confédération Suisse. "Taux de récidive de Suisses jugés/libérés en 2008." ["Recidivism: Swiss Judged / Released in 2008."] Swiss Statistics Web site, n.d. http://www.bfs.admin.ch/bfs/portal/fr/index/themen/19/04/03/01/02/01.html
Duguid, Stephen and Ray Pawson. "Education, Change and Transformation: The Prison Experience." *Evaluation Review* 22(1998), 470–95.
Grünhut, Max. *Penal Reform: A Comparative Study*. Oxford, UK: Clarendon Press, 1948.
Hawkins, Gordon. "Prison Labor and Prison Industries." *Crime and Justice*, 5(1983), 85–127.
Ledepur, Kathryn. "Bolivia's Prisons and the Impact of the Law 1008." *Andean Information Network*, July 31, 2004. http://ain-bolivia.org/2004/07/bolivias-prisons-and-the-impact-of-law-1008/

McFadden, Thomas, and Rusty Young. *Marching Powder: A True Story of Friendship, Cocaine, and South America's Strangest Jail*. New York, NY: St. Martin's Griffin, 2003.

Méndez Vedia, Javier. "Reincidencia. El precio de tener los ojos cerrados." ["Recidivism: The Price of Having Our Eyes Closed."] *El Deber*, June 22 2008. http://www.eldeber.com.bo/extra/2008-06-22/nota.php?id=080621204837

Ministry of Justice. "Compendium of Reoffending Statistics and Analysis." *Ministry of Justice Statistics Bulletin*, November 4, 2010. https://www.justice.gov.uk/downloads/statistics/mojstats/compendium-of-reoffending-statistics-and-analysis.pdf

National Institute of Justice. "Measuring Recidivism." February 20, 2008. http://www.nij.gov/topics/corrections/recidivism/pages/measuring.aspx

Nissimov, Ron. "Prison with Education Best Rehabilitation, Inmates Say." *The Plain Dealer*, June 21, 1993, 1B.

Pinto Quintanilla, Juan Carlos. *Cárcel de San Pedro: radiografía de la injusticia*. [San Pedro Prison: Radiography of Injustice] La Paz, Bolivia: ISLI, 1995.

Radio la Red. Patricia Bullrich interviewed by Carlos Sylvestre. February 15, 2011. Radio broadcast, 0:13:2. http://www.radiolared.multimediosamerica.com.ar/mananasylvestre/noticia/4295

Registro Nacional de Reincidencia [National Recidivism Registry]. Web site. n.d. http://www.dnrec.jus.gov.ar/

Salah-El, Tiyo Attallah. 1992. "Attaining Education in Prison Equals Prisoner Power." *Journal of Prisoners on Prisons* 4(1), 1–5.

"Sobrepoblación y reincidencia frenan reinserción social." ["Over-Population and Recidivism Hinder Social Reinsertion."] *Great City Magazine*, 2013. http://www.gtcit.com/publicaciond.php?PublicacionId=42954&lang=es

Visher, Christy A., and Travis, Jeremy. "Transitions from Prison to Community: Understanding Individual Pathways." *Annual Review of Sociology*, 2003 no. 29, 89–113. DOI: 10.1146/annurev.soc.29.010202.095931

# Chapter Eleven

# The Seywiaka Project: Expanded Territory and Access to Education in a Displaced Indigenous Community in Colombia

## Cristal Downing

### Introduction

"From an ethnic perspective, poverty is the absence of territory."[1] Poverty is well known to indigenous populations in Colombia, who have long suffered varying degrees of territorial dispossession. Indigenous people make up around 1 percent of the Colombian population, but comprise approximately 25 percent of the internally displaced people (IDPs) there.[2] These IDPs, who number between 3.8 and 5.4 million, have been forced from their land due to the armed conflict that has plagued the country for almost fifty years.[3] In addition, socioeconomic indicators such as literacy rates and life expectancy show that the welfare of Colombia's indigenous population lags significantly behind that of the majority.[4] Part of the reason for this is that state-provided social services such as education are less accessible to populations in the rural areas where most Colombian indigenous groups live. These areas suffer not only from a lack of these services but also from weak overall state presence, which creates opportunities for illegal armed groups to take control of territory. Integrated development and peace-building projects related to the resolution of displacement, improved social services, and poverty alleviation present the Colombian government with opportunities to tackle literacy and health while increasing state presence in rural areas where illegal armed groups have taken control.[5]

One example of such a project is the village of Seywiaka. Internally displaced indigenous groups in the Sierra Nevada de Santa Marta requested in 2007 that the government support them in establishing this and other villages in the region as part of a collaborative effort between indigenous and non-indigenous NGOs and state agencies. These village development projects had three complementary goals, which represent the needs expressed by the indigenous community in their initial request: 1) to restore ancestral lands in the lower parts of the Sierra to the indigenous communities, contributing to the resolution of their displacement; 2) to create sustainable village development projects that enable the indigenous people to fulfill their traditional role as protectors of the mountains while allowing them access to state-provided services such as education; and 3) to facilitate a move away from coca and other illicit crop production in the Sierra Nevada de Santa Marta. This is the first group of villages in Colombia to be established as part of a collaborative development initiative at the request of indigenous groups with the support of government agencies and NGOs.[6] It could therefore set a precedent for similar projects with other indigenous communities affected by displacement.

Seywiaka is the result of the Kogi people's utilization of available political institutions to request the support of government agencies in the implementation of a development project that responds to their needs as displaced indigenous people. The process of Kogi re-territorialization was accompanied by their request for increased access to government-provided social services such as education in the form of an "ethno-educational center" ("EEC"). This paper first argues that this project was selected for government support because the Kogi people possess ecological and other types of legitimacy in the eyes of the Colombian government, demonstrate high levels of social cohesion and organization, and represent an opportunity for the government to establish a peaceful presence in a rural conflict-affected setting without diminishing indigenous sovereignty there. The paper goes on to discuss potential outcomes of the Seywiaka project, and examines external limitations that may be detrimental to the project's potential as a scalable model.

I conducted research in Seywiaka in March, June, and July of 2011, during which time I made a series of visits to Seywiaka to observe life in the village and in the school. The interviews I conducted with Seywiaka residents, though initially planned, could not be relied upon due to rigid restrictions placed on exchanges with outsiders. This made it impossible to draw reliable information from interviews. Therefore, this paper focuses on the actions and perspectives of the Kogi *cabildo* (a local political representative body) as the representative body of the Kogi people. The cabildo's propositions and consents are included in the primary sources used for the paper and are interpreted as being true to the needs and desires of the Kogi community. Primary sources in this paper comprise, for the most part, project contracts and other internal documentation related to the projects. These documents were collected in the offices of Fundación Pro-Sierra and Acción Social (the two entities with the closest relationship to the indigenous bodies involved). The content of the contracts is drawn from the request made by the indigenous people and details the project goals and the responsibilities of each entity involved. These contracts are collaborative products of the Kogi in conjunction with additional entities involved in project implementation. Internal documentation from Acción Social is produced by and for their offices. Documents from Fundación Pro-Sierra are also for use by and for their offices and were produced by teams from Pro-Sierra and the indigenous-led NGOs.

## The Kogi people and the Seywiaka Village Project

The Seywiaka village project addresses many of the issues being confronted by displaced indigenous groups and other poor rural populations in Colombia. It also represents an opportunity for the Colombian government to contribute to the resolution of many of the challenges it faces as it works to defeat violent insurgent forces and simultaneously improve the welfare of its poorest citizens. The village is nestled in the Sierra Nevada de Santa Marta mountain range on the Caribbean coast of Colombia, which has been home for centuries to the Kogi, Arhuaco, Wiwa, and Kankuamo indigenous groups and comprises a fertile watershed area. These groups number about 53,000 in total, with the Kogi comprising between 4,000 and 5,000 of that number. The groups share various cultural traits, such as a belief that the Sierra is the *Corazón del Mundo*—the Heart of the World.[7] This belief originates with the Tairona people, from whom these four groups descend,[8] and represents their recognition that the Sierra is so fertile: it contains one of the most diverse ecological systems in the world, supplies water to an area in which 2 million people now live, and is a mineral-rich terrain for agricultural production. The indigenous people believe not only that the Sierra is the center of the world, but also that they are responsible for protecting it. These groups are very protective of themselves and their culture, because in so doing they believe they are protecting the world itself.[9] This protectiveness often exhibits itself as hostility to contact with outsiders, which precluded the Tairona from being colonized by the Spanish to the same extent as most indigenous groups in the Caribbean and Andean regions. Therefore, the cultures of the indigenous groups in the Sierra before the armed conflict began were almost exactly as they were in pre-Columbian times.[10]

The history of the guerrilla presence in the Sierra is similar to that of many other traditionally indigenous and Afro-Colombian territories in Colombia, which possess significant natural resource wealth. The Sierra has seen intense conflict due mainly to the presence of the guerrilla group known as the *Ejército de Liberación Nacional* (ELN) and their quest for power and funding for their activities both in the Sierra and elsewhere. The ELN were attracted to the fertility of the land in the Sierra and resultant opportunities for strategic territorial control and production of coca.[11] This leaf is traditionally consumed by indigenous people throughout South America for medicinal, nutritional, and ceremonial purposes, but is also used to make the cocaine that funds much of the guerrilla activity in Colombia.[12] Indigenous communities in the Sierra suffered as targets of armed attack. They were subsequently victims of forced displacement as their land was taken and they retreated further up into the mountain range. After centuries of having been respected and protected by the indigenous people in the Sierra, the ecological balance was disturbed by the invasion of the illegal armed groups and the consequent fighting in the region.[13]

Indigenous groups are currently returning to the lower parts of Sierra and reclaiming the land that once belonged to them in the *cordón ambiental* or environmental band around the bottom of the mountain range. Particularly important in this re-territorialization is the land around the lower watershed, an important resource for their renewed agricultural production. The indigenous people of the Sierra have repeatedly expressed their desire that these lands be returned to them in order to sustain their way of life and to restore stability to their community after its displacement and other conflict-related disruptions. The resolution of displacement of indigenous groups is at the forefront of a range of both government and NGO projects in the area, of which Seywiaka is one.[14]

The Seywiaka development initiative returned ancestral lands to the Kogi people of the Sierra while providing state-funded culturally relevant health and education services. The village, inaugurated in July of 2010, is home to approximately 300 Kogi people who are living together for the first time after coming to the village from temporary Kogi settlements higher up in the Sierra. Overlooking the Palomino River on the border of the La Guajira and Magdalena Departments, the settlement comprises approximately fifty traditional-style houses, two ceremonial centers, and a meeting room. In addition to these buildings, the village has six one-room school buildings, four of which are used to hold classes, with two smaller buildings used for storage and other administrative purposes.[15]

The school itself is called a *Centro Etnoeducativo* or ethno-educational center (EEC). The curriculum is split between traditional Kogi learning topics related to agriculture practices, religious beliefs, and other aspects of their way of life, and "Western" components such as math, reading, and writing. Classes are conducted in the Kogi language for the first two years and then Spanish is taught as a second language from the third year onwards. Children from the village attend classes in the EEC while children from more remote indigenous villages further into the mountains sleep in boarding houses in Seywiaka and attend classes in the village as well. There is also a teachers' house and additional quarters for the nurse who works in Seywiaka's small health facility. At the time of this study, there were four teachers in Seywiaka: two were Kogi, one was white but had lived with indigenous communities in the Sierra for most of her life, and the other was Afro-Colombian. There is a communal kitchen and eating area beside the EEC where the women of the village cook breakfast and lunch for the children.

Seywiaka is one of ten villages that comprise the *Familias Guardabosques—Corazón del Mundo* (FG-CM) projects.[16] These settlements were created with funding from Acción Social, a department of government established by the administration of President Uribe (in office 2002–2010) as a state-run agency that focuses on an integrated approach to development and peace-building. Most of the programs themselves are directed towards assisting IDPs and others affected by the conflict.[17] Seywiaka and the other FG-CM villages are the first set of village development projects in Colombia to be established with state funding at the request of the target community. It is evident from project documentation that in establishing these new villages, Acción Social and the other entities involved were responding primarily to the indigenous people's need and right to return to their original territories, while also taking into account educational, environmental and other factors in planning and implementing the project. For example, the initial project contract written and signed by indigenous groups, Fundación Pro-Sierra, Acción Social, and others was based on the initial project request presented to the government by the indigenous groups.[18] In it, the four principal functions of the FG-CM villages were stated as being:

> 1) To stop the colonizing advances of outsiders into the higher parts of the Sierra; 2) To concentrate and disseminate the State's social programs to the middle and higher parts of the Sierra, in accordance with the traditions and customs of the indigenous communities; 3) To facilitate

cultural and spiritual exchange between the four indigenous groups of the Sierra; and 4) To strengthen and consolidate indigenous territories through the expansion and purification of the protected lands ("resguardos") and improved access to and management of sacred sites."[19]

These goals address not only the indigenous people's need to return to and maintain control over ancestral lands, but also their displacement due to encroachment by illegal armed groups and other outsiders and their concern about maintaining territorial sovereignty. The expansion of the protected land came about through the state's purchasing of land from *campesinos* (peasants) in the region, who had previously encroached upon indigenous territories.[20]

Indigenous people from all four ethnic groups of the Sierra collectively made the initial request for the project through their cabildos, which used associated political mechanisms to communicate with the national government. In their request, the four groups expressed their desire to return to their ancestral lands and construct peaceful sustainable communities with access to government services. Associated contracts reflect that NGOs in the Sierra region seconded these community-driven processes, particularly the Fundación Pro-Sierra Nevada de Santa Marta, which has conducted development-related research and projects with the indigenous community in the Sierra for decades.[21]

As the government body responsible for this type of project, Acción Social funded the establishment of the villages, including Seywiaka. However, their planning and implementation was a collaborative effort led by indigenous entities, including Organización Gonawindúa, which worked closely on Seywiaka. This NGO is managed by the Kogi people and works closely with the Kogi cabildo in political and economic matters. Fundación Pro-Sierra also played an integral role in all of the village projects and was a significant collaborator because of its productive thirty-year relationship with the indigenous communities in the Sierra. Acción Social was present in planning and implementation, but recognized indigenous participants as being the key agents in the endeavor. This is demonstrated in the following quotation from one of the internal documents used in the Acción Social offices, written during project implementation by employees of Acción Social:

> This project was not developed on the third or fourth floor of Acción Social: it is the result of long nights and early mornings chewing coca between bonfires that fill the air with smoke, which makes the eyes of the elders more beautiful and irritates ours because of the powerlessness of never having been there before.[22]

The FG-CM projects comprise a series of villages in the Sierra that were created to fulfill three specific goals identified by the indigenous communities. These objectives are outlined in the final project contract between all parties, the Fundación Pro-Sierra documents written with the indigenous cabildos, the finalized internal documentation used in Acción Social's offices, and on the Acción Social website. These objectives stem from the four previously mentioned project functions stated in the project request and initial contract, and are: 1) to establish villages on newly protected ancestral lands and therefore facilitate the expansion of indigenous territories and the resolution of indigenous displacement; 2) to enable the indigenous groups of the Sierra to continue their role as the protectors of the Heart of the World in sustainable development projects that allow them access to education and other social services; and 3) to decrease the cultivation of coca for non-traditional use in the Sierra.[23] This paper focuses on the first two objectives.

## Indigenous Participatory Development and Territorial Rights

There are two principal bodies of theory that propose that development initiatives "for" autonomous indigenous people cannot fulfill those communities' needs. The first places indigenous sovereignty and self-determination at odds with the concept of the nation-state. This argument proposes that indigenous efforts to voice their welfare needs to national governments forces indigenous people's participation in political systems that cannot by their nature satisfy their needs. Many scholars who make this argument state that Western-style political systems do not provide the mechanisms necessary for indigenous groups to implement "development" in the way they would choose, and therefore do not enable them to move away from land dispossession and territorial destitution.[24] This theory suggests that the only way for indigenous communities to resolve their welfare issues and maintain their sovereignty is for the governments of the nation-states in which they find themselves to discontinue contact with them, therefore avoiding the violation of the indigenous "sovereign right to exist without external exploitation or interference."[25] Any sort of indigenous political participation, even if the community initiates it, cannot happen on indigenous terms because they must operate in a Western-style political system that does not fulfill indigenous needs.

The second field of research states that state-funded social services such as education and health are not culturally relevant to indigenous communities. They not only interfere with indigenous sovereignty, but also result in a debilitation of indigenous culture and a Westernization of indigenous life.[26] Development initiatives that include education and health services are therefore unwelcome in indigenous communities because they represent efforts by the state to assimilate indigenous people into the general population. In the Americas, bilingual and bicultural education programs are increasingly common in indigenous communities, but issues still exist in relation to the state's role in curriculum design, selection of content, and implementation. Education, in particular, becomes the subject of much debate as a possible tool for the colonization of indigenous communities through psychological rather than physical means.[27] This body of theory is accompanied by calls for governments to withdraw from social service provision in indigenous communities and to allow these autonomous populations to determine their own schooling.

However, theory related to participatory development and the importance of the community voice in development projects allows for indigenous and other autonomous communities' interaction with government both through political mechanisms and in the provision of social services.[28] Participation in development-related politics as well as in the planning and implementation of projects that incorporate state social service provision can happen without infringing on the cultural rights and sovereignty of the target population. The community involved must be able to identify its own needs and the ways in which it experiences "poverty" (i.e., not necessarily as a money-metric deficiency). It must also be permitted the political and cultural forum in which to request, plan and implement the project(s) aiming to fulfill those needs. The target community's input and participation in the project must be considered of equal if not greater value than that of other planners. If this type of participation—in both the initiation and implementation of the project—is present, these theorists believe that a successful, culturally relevant development initiative can be implemented without sacrificing the sovereignty or self-determination of the indigenous target community.[29]

Expanding the land over which they hold sovereignty is also essential to indigenous welfare. In his paper entitled "Ecological Wealth Versus Social Poverty" (2005), Pablo Alarcón-Cháires identifies various dimensions of indigenous land claims that he believes should be formally institutionalized and thereby legitimized in countries throughout the Americas, in order that indigenous economic welfare be upheld and protected. He links institutions associated with environmental conservation to those related to land claims and autonomous political entities, and calls for an improved definition of institutions dealing with indigenous territories. This, he says, will allow indigenous populations to manage the natural resources on their land and improve their own welfare.[30] Indigenous economic activity is therefore directly linked to the use of land and to the protection of their right to occupy and exploit the natural resources to which they lay rightful claim.

The link between environmental politics and indigenous land claims is of particular importance because ancestral lands are often areas of rich biodiversity. Indigenous groups' economic reliance on the resource-rich land and traditional respect for its conservation gives dual purpose to the protection of their land rights. Various indigenous groups throughout the Americas have called upon this dual purpose as part of what has been called their "ecological legitimacy". This legitimacy stems from the "romanticized cultural heritages" or cultural assumptions that associate indigenous cultures with respect and care for the land they occupy, whether or not this is true.[31] Indigenous groups in various countries have used ecological legitimacy to strengthen arguments for improved rights and sovereignty, especially in relation to land.[32]

This legitimacy is further supported by strong collective identities connecting indigenous people to their land. Struggles for indigenous rights often focus on the need to create cohesive shared identities that facilitate the exercising of collective rights, including the right to claim and exploit territory. By identifying the characteristics that unite them, indigenous people can call on international legal institutions for support. For example, the UN Declaration on the Rights of Indigenous Peoples (UN-DRIP) stipulates that:

> Indigenous peoples have the right to own, develop, control and use the lands and territories…which they have traditionally owned or otherwise occupied or used.[33]

It goes on to say that traditional land-tenure and resource-management systems must be protected by legal institutions.[34] This is of particular importance in countries such as Colombia, where it has been shown that in areas where property rights are not institutionally protected and encroachment presents a constant threat, there is little economic activity. The economic welfare of the population is threatened by this insecurity.[35]

In addition to appearing at UN forums on indigenous rights, these issues were at the forefront of the 1989 International Labor Organization (ILO) Indigenous and Tribal Peoples Convention.[36] The ideas presented in the ILO document and the UN-DRIP were subsequently reflected in the Colombian Constitution of 1991, which explicitly acknowledges the multiethnic nature of the Colombian population and includes various laws addressing indigenous rights.[37] It also addresses further complications to indigenous territorial dispossession caused by the ongoing conflict in Colombia, as indigenous people have been disproportionately affected by displacement. Since the implementation of the Constitution of 1991, efforts to alleviate poverty, address displacement and other conflict-related issues, and to resolve environmental concerns, have recognized the disadvantaged condition of indigenous and other vulnerable groups. These efforts have encouraged the protection of indigenous interests not only as part of national diversity, but also as being essential to indigenous economic and political participation.[38]

## Expanded Lands and Access to Education: Actual Outcomes of the Seywiaka Project

In order to understand fully how the initial project documents came into existence, it is necessary to consider the political mechanisms used by the Kogi to initiate their re-territorialization and fulfill the goals they outlined in their initial project request. One such mechanism is Article 329 of the Constitution of 1991, a document that reaffirms and more explicitly defines social, economic, and political rights. This article confirms the inalienable right of indigenous communities in Colombia to exploit their own autonomous territories, stating that:

> "Resguardos" are collective property and are inextricable. The relations and coordination of these entities will be defined by the applicable laws.[39]

*Resguardos* are autonomous indigenous territories defined by law and claimed by right, thereby forming legitimate institutions that protect collective rights.[40] The resguardos are also protected as spaces in which indigenous communities maintain sovereignty and can govern in accordance with their traditions and customs, or *usos y costumbres*, and in their own language. These rights are restated in Article 21, Decree 2164 of 1995, which also considers resguardos to be somewhat similar to municipalities and therefore eligible to receive funding from the state.[41]

There are three resguardos in the Sierra region: the Kogui-Malayo-Arhuaco resguardo; the Arhuaco resguardo; and the Kankuamo resguardo.[42] The FG-CM villages were established as part of the expansion of the Kogui-Malayo-Arhuaco resguardo through government funding provided for the purchase of land from resident campesinos. Article 329's treatment of resguardos as similar to municipalities also led to the funding of the EEC in Seywiaka, whose presence corresponds to the second function stated in the project contract and the second objective of the villages: to augment state-funded social programming in the Sierra as part of sustainable village projects. The formation of the resguardo therefore played a key role in facilitating these outcomes, by allowing the Kogi people to apply for funding for social programs.

A further mechanism complements the increased protection of the resguardos. Decree 1088 of 1993 permits and regulates the establishment of "Asociaciones de Cabildos Indígenas" (or cabildos), which are

> autonomous forms of government recognized by the national government which can undertake social programs with resources transferred by the national government.[43]

Project contracts and documentation from Fundación Pro-Sierra demonstrate that the Kogi and other indigenous cabildos were at the forefront not only of the initial request for the villages, but also of implementation of the project with state services. The utilization of the cabildos per their purpose as stated in Decree 1088 was directly related to expansion of the Kogi resguardo as part of the Seywiaka project. It was also essential to the establishment of the EEC in Seywiaka with funding from the state. The project contract demonstrates that the Kogi cabildo not only administered the funding for this center, but also approved the bilingual, bicultural curriculum. The cabildo was also responsible for deciding which of the approximately 1,500 displaced Kogi people should be brought to Seywiaka to live. This decision was made based on where families were living, how many children they had, whether they wished to move to the new village, and other factors.

The cabildo also had the autonomous authority to allocate the new resguardo land to the families who came to live Seywiaka. Similar to most other indigenous land-tenure practices, families in Seywiaka participate in a communal *minga* system. This system is defined by a shared responsibility for cultivating land and therefore maintaining it as economically active to the collective benefit of the community.[44] Tenancy agreements can be issued if the cabildo chooses to do so, and are independent of the national government. The agreements may be accompanied by consent, either tacit or explicit, that the benefits of cultivating the land will be shared between community members in accordance with the minga system.[45] Indigenous minga land-tenure is therefore protected by law, as recommended by the UN-DRIP and the Colombian Constitution, and is practiced by indigenous people in communities such as Seywiaka.

In addition to protecting the right to claim and exploit land, these institutions create a conduit for indigenous political and economic participation. The opportunities presented by these institutions initially provoked widespread political and social reorganization of indigenous communities across Colombia. As they began to classify their land and identify the cultural traits that unified them and connected them to that land, they also began to make attempts to utilize these communication conduits to improve their economic and social welfare.[46] In establishing Seywiaka village and the other FG-CM villages, the Kogi and other indigenous groups of the Sierra were the first to use these conduits successfully to implement a village development project on their own terms. This could set a precedent for other indigenous communities in Colombia to do the same.

The Kogi people have always been protective of their traditions and culture and are relatively closed to outsiders. This self-isolation has contributed to the preservation of their culture and language, allowing them a strong collective identity and high levels of social cohesion. They have also always had a developed leadership structure and were ready to organize and establish autonomous local political institutions to legitimize their sovereignty when these laws were signed into effect. They now have not only a Kogi cabildo based in the city of Santa Marta, but also an associated NGO, Organización Gonawindúa. This allows the Kogi to receive financial support from both the state (through the cabildo) and other interested donors and gives them legitimacy within the national political system. The initial FG-CM project contract demonstrates that from the outset of the planning and implementation process of the Seywiaka project, the Kogi cabildo and NGO were considered to be

> special territorial entities that are legally able to enter into request processes for investment in their territory and whose experience, credibility and community support will facilitate the success of the [FG-CM] projects.[47]

In addition, the Kogi people were able to draw on their ecological legitimacy in the request for Seywiaka. This legitimacy and resultant support is reflected in the project contracts, which begin with a description of the Sierra as a UNESCO-protected ecosystem and the "principal source of water for the north coast of Colombia."[48] Similarly, the internal Acción Social document associated with the project places heavy emphasis on the fact that the restoration of these lands to the Kogi people will facilitate the resolution of many of the environmental issues currently harming the Sierra. The ecological legitimacy of the new Kogi residents of the village comes from the fact that their subsistence agriculture practices are non-invasive and do not damage the environment. In addition, their traditional belief that the Sierra is the Heart of the World and that they are the protectors of it provides further motivation for them to take responsibility for the environmental conservation of the Sierra. All associated documents therefore highlight the fact that in addition to benefitting the economic welfare of the community, Kogi settlement in Seywiaka is of ecological importance because it would stop degradation and improve environmental conditions.[49]

Ecological legitimacy, in combination with the Kogi's political organization and perceivable collective identity under the laws mentioned above, was crucial to their utilization of these channels of communication with the national government. Their ability to organize allowed them to negotiate the parallel political and social structures dictating the process by which they made the request for the village projects. This led to government support for their project and ultimately to the successful fulfillment of the first objective of the FG-CM villages: to resolve displacement and expand the resguardos of the indigenous groups in the Sierra. Their organization was also crucial to the second project outcome: improved access to state-funded education in the Sierra.

This evidence of successful indigenous participation further increases the significance of the project. A balance was struck whereby the state was permitted to expand its presence in the Sierra through culturally relevant education programming, while the Kogi people were able to resolve displacement, expand their resguardo, and positively impact their social welfare through the placement of a culturally relevant primary education center in Seywiaka. The suggestion of this balance sets this project apart from others in which the state is the main actor. In Seywiaka, the state has a defined role and its presence is felt. However, the indigenous community maintains ultimate authority over community matters. This implies that contrary to what many claim, it is possible for indigenous communities to participate in national political systems on their own terms and for those systems to fulfill indigenous needs. The interaction between government and indigenous communities in the implementation of the project also indicates a state response which contradicts arguments that assert that indigenous-state collaboration is always coercive. As it is the first such project, this interaction could set an example for other indigenous communities to utilize these political mechanisms to instigate similar initiatives.

## Education, Rural Welfare, and the State: Positive Potential Seywiaka Project Outcomes

Although it was hard to evaluate the "success" of the Seywiaka project when the village had been inhabited for less than two years, it is important to note aspects of planning and implementation that have been successful up to this point in time, and to highlight areas of potential future success. Though the objective of establishing a state-funded EEC in the village has been achieved, the presence of the school could continue to be significant in a number of ways. Projected outcomes could also be monitored and cited by other indigenous communities if they find themselves able to initiate a re-territorialization process using the political mechanisms described above.

Education is key to self-governance and the sustained peace of the community, as well as to facilitating productive communication with national government. It can emphasize rules and norms through nonviolent interaction, thereby underscoring the rule of law and encouraging productive and peaceful citizenship at the community level.[50] In indigenous communities that experience relative political autonomy as part of resguardos, this advantage can be applied in order to strengthen self-governance. The positive effects of bilingual, bicultural education on citizenship of the resguardo could be immediately reflected in daily life outside school, and can also contribute to interaction between the indigenous cabildo and national institutions.

One example of this is the bilingual, bicultural education programs implemented in Nasa indigenous communities in the Cauca department of southwest Colombia. The Nasa have a long history of violent intrusions onto their land by the FARC guerrilla group and have been insistent in their public calls to the Colombian government for assistance and increased rights to political autonomy. The Nasa people have implemented bilingual, bicultural education programs as part of community efforts to affirm their unified collective identity and strengthen their autonomous self-governance. They see education as an essential vehicle in working towards a complete "ethnic citizenship" of their resguardos within the Colombian nation-state. As the right to govern in their own language is part of the autonomy granted to resguardos, language fluency and preservation is an important part of maintaining sovereignty, as well as being a cultural signifier.[51]

The experiences of the Nasa people indicate that bilingual, bicultural education could be an essential tool in maintaining community solidarity and strengthening autonomous governance and collective identity for the

Kogi people as well. The village of Seywiaka was inaugurated in 2010 and the 300 inhabitants of the village have been living there since then. However, though residents are all from the Kogi ethnic group and had had contact with each other before they came to the village, many have not lived together before. It is essential that the new community of Seywiaka fosters a cohesive society in which everyone feels that he or she can contribute equally to community welfare. This cohesion and autonomous self-governance corresponds to the "ethnic citizenship" sought through education by the Nasa people.

The EEC also has the potential to provide the children with a unified, structured, and stable "social microenvironment",[52] an important benefit as stability and a feeling of connection to the community are a priority in supporting displaced children.[53] These social microenvironments can encourage children to think about their role in their community, reinforcing traditional values and attitudes that motivate children to participate in community welfare decisions and to act in a way that supports community bonds.[54] This is of great importance in the formation of a stable and cohesive society in the new village of Seywiaka. It ties directly to the Kogi content of the EEC curriculum, part of which teaches about agriculture and the community's responsibility to contribute to production as part of the collective minga system. In addition, the lives of the women and children of the village revolve around the EEC, as it houses a kitchen in which they cook and eat breakfast and lunch. The institution's function as the center of daily activity promises to unite the village and thereby assist in the process of creating a secure and permanent settlement, while bringing community members together and reinforcing necessary social cohesion.[55]

Thanks to the decentralization of the education system in Colombia, the curriculum in Seywiaka is divided between what is called a "traditional" component, which incorporates Kogi learning topics such as agricultural methods and religious beliefs, and a "Western" component, which teaches skills such as reading, writing, math, and Spanish. This curriculum is approved by the Kogi cabildo.[56] School is taught in the Kogi language for the first two years and then changes to teaching Spanish as a second language in the third year. The traditional values instilled as part of education in Seywiaka are of great importance in self-governance: as an indigenous community, rules and norms are based on traditional beliefs that have unified the community for centuries and continue to bring people together in the new village. This combination of state-provided services and traditional content was outlined in the four initial functions of the FG-

CM villages stated in the request and initial project contract. This function was

> to concentrate and disseminate the State's social programs to the middle and higher parts of the Sierra, in accordance with the traditions and customs of the indigenous communities

exactly as the EEC does.[57]

Elsewhere in the Sierra, in a village of Arhuaco people, bilingual, bicultural education was found to provide the space and the skills necessary to negotiate violent encroachments while strengthening community self-determination. In that context, the Arhuaco people "decolonized" their schools in the late 1990's, introducing bicultural, bilingual (but state-funded) education programs into educational facilities they also called EECs. These EECs incorporated Western topics such as math in addition to instructing students on Arhuaco beliefs and language. All of the four teachers at the school were Arhuaco and were trilingual in the Arhuaco language, Ika, and Spanish. Their understanding of both the languages and the cultures allowed them to teach content from both spheres. Similar to Seywiaka, schooling was conducted in the community language (in this case Ika) for the first two years, and then transitioned to Spanish in the third. Ika-language literacy was seen as part of the community's self-determination, something that would strengthen collective identity.[58]

Research demonstrated that this system of education allowed the children to operate comfortably in non-traditional contexts and with non-indigenous people, without losing their sense of unity and belonging in the community. Residents also felt that the EEC had provided the desired space necessary to strengthen autonomy and self-governance and that this had been engendered in the children.[59] The Arhuaco and Kogi experiences of encroachment and displacement in the Sierra have been similar and the Seywiaka project contracts demonstrate that their goals in expanding their resguardos with support from the state are very much aligned. It is therefore possible that bilingual, bicultural education will have similar effects in Seywiaka as it did in the Arhuaco community studied. Given the importance of a collective identity in legitimizing land claims and political participation, the potential for a strengthened collective identity resulting from bilingual, bicultural education is particularly significant to the Kogi people. The ability simultaneously to negotiate Western and indigenous social structures on indigenous terms would also be of great use in the future. These benefits would also be of value in other Colombian indigenous communities as they struggle to resolve their displacement, improve their welfare, and request support from the Colombian state.

In terms of the EEC's location, it is important to note that the government was invited to establish the center in Seywiaka itself: the proximity of this state-funded institution promises to "restore trust" in the government, as well as to increase the presence of the state in the Sierra. Both of these were project goals stated in the final contract. Indigenous children and adults in the Sierra had limited experience of government prior to the implementation of the projects. Specifically, the most constant state presence was the military—a reminder of the conflict. As rural Colombian society has been shown to trust educational institutions more than other representatives of government, the institutions' credibility enables schools and teachers to facilitate both public trust in government and the promotion of a positive image of the state. The EEC, as a peaceful and inclusive institution that is not associated with the conflict and over which the Kogi community has been assured ultimate authority, could help to promote trust in government while strengthening the rural presence of the state.[60]

This peaceful interaction, stronger collective identity, and increased trust in rural communities could be of particular value to the children who sleep in the boarding houses in Seywiaka but who are from remote villages: some of those villages are similar to the settlements previously occupied by the current residents of Seywiaka and were established as a result of internal displacement.[61] If and when further requests are made for new villages to be established in indigenous ancestral territories, the mutual understanding and trust promulgated by the children's schooling will be essential. If the presence of the EEC in the village is considered a success, requests for similar institutions in other indigenous communities may be more positively received by the state.

In requesting this state-funded EEC and specifying that this was the type of state presence they wanted in their new community, the Kogi recognized the need for a peaceful state presence in the Sierra as the violence in the region is suppressed. In addition, as an institution that members of the community approved and in which they can participate, it has the potential to position a positive representative of the government firmly within the social fabric of the village. It therefore addresses the Sierra's

> urgent need to implement a comprehensive emergency plan aimed at protecting fundamental rights; guaranteeing respect for economic, social and cultural rights; and re-establishing the real and effective presence of the state, taking into account the right of indigenous communities to consultation and decision making by consensus.[62]

The most significant aspect of it is that this presence has been established at the invitation of the target community and on their own terms, taking their *usos y costumbres* (traditions and customs) into account. The fact that it was the indigenous communities themselves who initiated the implementation of the FG-CM projects was also crucial to the collaboration that led to their implementation. This is of particular interest given the frequency of calls by poor communities for integrated approaches to participatory development projects that address violence, poverty, education, and other factors affecting welfare.[63]

## Seywiaka Project Limitations and Prospects for Scalability

Despite the positive impact of the Seywiaka project in fulfilling the indigenous community's goals of expanding the Kogi resguardo and increasing access to education in the Sierra, the project does exhibit some limitations in terms of the prospects of other indigenous groups to follow the same re-territorialization process as the Kogi. The Kogi's ecological legitimacy, political organization, and social cohesion all distinguish them from other indigenous groups in Colombia, and played a great role in their success in requesting support from the Colombian government. There are national-level issues surrounding the definition and legitimacy of indigenous identity that affect indigenous land rights and political participation which would make replicating the project in other internally displaced indigenous communities difficult or even impossible.

The Seywiaka project is significant because it demonstrates that indigenous communities can participate in national politics in order to meet their own needs, without sacrificing their autonomy and self-determination. The Colombian government had attempted to implement development projects "with" and "for" the indigenous people in the Sierra in the past, but these projects eventually failed because the indigenous target community felt that they were not adequately consulted. This was because of the government's lack of communication with the communities at whom the projects were directed and the perceived attempts to interfere with indigenous sovereignty and establish a state presence in the indigenous community without an invitation from the group itself. This resulted in the feeling that the indigenous people were being forced to participate in a project in which they were not consulted and therefore had no voice—in keeping with the argument that indigenous political and project participation is by nature coercive.[64]

If the government were to attempt to implement projects similar to Seywiaka and the FG-CM villages in other parts of Colombia, they may find that the projects' origins outside the community would hinder progress and prevent the re-territorialization process, education, and other government-provided services from being experienced. Instead of strengthening state presence in rural communities, replication of the FG-CM project without invitation from the target community may result in a decrease in trust in government and a further disengagement of rural citizens from the Colombian state. It would therefore be more effective for the government to examine specific aspects of the Seywiaka project to assess which elements could be adapted to other projects that are already founded on community participation.

The degree of political organization of the community will also affect its suitability for initiating this type of project. Political institutions in Colombia are structured to enable indigenous communities like the Kogi to act upon their belief in land as an integral part of their identity and welfare.[65] Other indigenous groups, however, did not have similar pre-existing social leadership structures or strong collective identities as did the Kogi, and have not been recognized as legitimate in the same way by the national government. A similar project therefore may not have the political foundation necessary to initiate the same processes as the Kogi.

One reason for this is the differing interpretations of the term "indigenous" and the fact that the groups are not self-defined but rather are designated by government as having indigenous status. The Mokaná people, for example, live on the Caribbean coast and in 1998 attempted to register as an indigenous group and form a legal cabildo in order to utilize the appropriate institutions to claim land. The government responded negatively, saying that supposed members of this group did not share a common language, way of dressing, and other cultural traits that would unify them in such a way as to qualify them as an indigenous group. They were not considered to have ecological or any other kind of legitimacy that would have allowed them to claim land as part of a resguardo. They continue to make efforts at self-determination, but are still considered a non-indigenous community. As a consequence, they are denied both the right to request governmental support in claiming land, and state-provided social services to fulfill their other welfare needs.[66]

The Mokaná are not as well-organized politically as the Kogi and have not been able to establish their own NGOs and cabildos. This is true of other indigenous groups in other parts of Colombia. They are therefore unable to go through the same re-territorialization process as the Kogi did, and to use cabildos to make requests of government. In many cases they also do not have a close relationship with NGOs such as Fundación Pro-Sierra, which provide additional support. Therefore, even though many of the driving ideas behind Seywiaka may be applicable to these communities, it is possible that the argument that national political systems do *not* serve the needs of indigenous communities would be applicable in other cases in Colombia.

This raises questions about who is able to define a community as "indigenous" and with what motivation. It also highlights some possible issues surrounding the responsiveness of institutions that apply to indigenous land claims in Colombia and to the possible scalability of Seywiaka as a re-territorialization project. Though these institutions seem to represent inclusive national political and economic participation and other relevant opportunities for indigenous populations, it is possible that in the case of the Mokaná people, the institutions are irrelevant because the people continue to be excluded. The political system does not function in a way that allows them to satisfy their needs by negotiating the mechanisms within it, thus supporting arguments that claim that indigenous participation in Western-style political systems is not possible. This exclusion could have detrimental consequences for indigenous people's welfare, for, as we have seen, the right to own and exploit land is essential to economic activity and movement away from poverty; access to social services such as education is crucial to political stability at the local and national levels.[67]

In addition, public investment for indigenous groups in projects like Seywiaka has recently been falling in real terms, and community economies are weak and cannot support a decent quality of life for their inhabitants.[68] This means that the likelihood of the Seywiaka project being replicated in any adapted form is diminishing. In addition, it is too early to tell if the Seywiaka community economy will be strong and sustainable. If it becomes weak, the government may designate the project as unsuccessful and be even more reluctant to respond to requests from other indigenous communities. In the same vein, if the community economy becomes strong and the villagers are able to maintain a high standard of living, this could encourage the government to seek ways to create opportunities for political participation in other indigenous communities and to work with those communities to adapt the Seywiaka project to their own customs and needs.

It has also been reported that the government has started to dedicate fewer resources to the purchase of land to expand resguardos, therefore limiting the amount of land the indigenous populations can claim.[69] The struggle to claim land is, in turn, inextricably linked to the fight against poverty in Colombian indigenous populations, who measure their wealth by the degree of autonomy they have over their territory and how much of it they control.[70] If the government does not support the indigenous populations in utilizing the political mechanisms necessary to go through a re-territorialization process, the tensions between national government and indigenous groups could be exacerbated. This increased tension contrasts greatly with the possibility of a stable relationship between the two being formed by projects like Seywiaka, in which representatives from both groups worked side by side. If an increase in the size of the resguardos is not permitted, the indigenous people will be more at risk of living in increasing levels of poverty and of further internal displacement. It is therefore important that the Colombian government continue to not only allow institutional support for indigenous land claims as part of resguardos, but also to provide financial support for those claims. Without this support, the welfare of indigenous groups in Colombia is unlikely to improve.

The interaction between the government EECs and the children of the Kogi Seywiaka community promises to contribute to mutual understanding and productive future collaboration. However, significantly, at the time of research, two of the four teachers in the school were Kogi, one was white but had lived with indigenous communities in the Sierra for most of her life, and the other was Afro-Colombian. In the Arhuaco community already mentioned, the inclusion of non-indigenous teachers in the EEC actually had a negative impact on the biculturalism of the curriculum, because the non-indigenous teacher resisted combining Western and traditional topics in class, and did not understand traditional topics enough to be able to incorporate them into the curriculum in the way the community desired. That teacher was eventually asked to leave the community and was replaced by an indigenous Arhuaco teacher.[71] Despite the efforts made to produce a complementary curriculum with components from both cultures, and the approval of the curriculum by the Kogi cabildo, the allocation of non-indigenous teachers to Seywiaka could be detrimental to the potential outcomes of bilingual, bicultural education there.

## Conclusion

The Seywiaka project has fulfilled the two objectives of allowing the Kogi people to reclaim some of their ancestral lands and expand their resguardo, and providing access to education and other government services in a permanent and peaceful community. The process of re-territorialization through which the Kogi and other indigenous groups of the Sierra passed in order to construct the project villages and expand their resguardos also brought about increased access to education in their community. This access was funded by the government at the request of the indigenous communities, who invited the state to establish a presence in the new villages while at the same time stating a need for colonizing advances into the indigenous resguardos to be stopped and reversed. This indicates a heightened understanding between the indigenous people of the Sierra and the Colombian state, and could set a precedent for future projects that promote collaboration between those entities on more equal terms. Seywiaka's participatory process is also significant because it provides the basis for a counter-argument to those who state that Western-style national political systems by their nature cannot provide the means for indigenous groups to satisfy their needs. The actual outcomes of the project indicate that the Kogi people were able not only to negotiate the Colombian national political system, but also to satisfy their needs successfully without losing sovereignty or control over project components such as education and the EEC.

There are a number of additional potential outcomes of the project that should be noted. The presence of an EEC in the village will not only contribute to increased literacy and provide the children with access to education, but also has the potential to support both the community's self-governance and the creation of a stable environment in which to live after displacement. By affirming their language and culture through its curriculum, the EEC could also strengthen the collective identity and self-determination that was so essential to the initiation of the Seywiaka project by the Kogi community. In addition, this educational facility is an invited representative of the government and therefore plays an important role in strengthening Colombia's fragile state and engaging the rural population in a peaceful way. The incorporation of culturally relevant education into the Seywiaka project is therefore hugely important at both the community and national levels.

In addition, increased access to education will facilitate further efforts by the Kogi people to request that the government support them in efforts to expand the territories to which they lay claim. Increased literacy will prepare them to make the requests, and the experience of interacting with state representatives on Kogi terms in their own village will allow the children to recognize differences and similarities between the two groups. This recognition will be especially relevant when they have political-level communication with the state in the future, and have to negotiate Kogi and national social and political systems simultaneously in order to collaborate.

The social cohesion and reinforcement of collective identity and self-determination resulting from the placement of the EEC in the village will also strengthen their legitimacy in the eyes of the government, therefore possibly facilitating future land claims. This point is especially important, as we have seen that the land rights of groups such as the Mokaná, where social cohesion is not as evident, are limited. As the state is reducing funding for indigenous-related projects and restricting the amount of land that can be claimed by the indigenous people, all of these factors will affect the Kogi people's future prospects of claiming more of their ancestral lands and furthering the resolution of their displacement.

If, as indications already show, this type of project is not to be supported in indigenous communities in the future, the precedent set by the project could be negated. In limiting the property rights of indigenous groups and their opportunities to participate in the political processes associated with re-territorialization, the Colombian government runs the risk of also limiting the probability that the displacement of those groups will be resolved. This will further affect indigenous welfare and indicates a possible continuation of state fragility in the form of a "lack of will or inability to meet basic human needs and to secure citizens from violent conflict and control of their territories."[72] In addition, the failure of the state to support the creation of new villages also prevents state acceptance of possible future requests for projects and associated invitations by indigenous populations to establish a peaceful presence in their communities, as happened with the requested education and health services in Seywiaka. If requests from other indigenous communities are not answered, access to education will continue to be restricted. This would perpetuate lower literacy rates in indigenous communities and contribute to a continued lack of interaction between those populations and non-military state representatives. It would also diminish the possibility of Colombia fostering multiple examples of successful indigenous political participation.

Overall, the Seywiaka project represents improved welfare in the Kogi community. Through their ecological and organizational legitimacy, social cohesion and strong collective identity, they were able to successfully request a development project that did not involve government interference in their affairs. It has allowed them to increase the size of their resguardo and establish a state-funded bilingual, bicultural EEC at their own request. Contrary to many arguments stating that this type of interaction must be coercive and involve a loss of sovereignty by the indigenous people involved, the Kogi people were not coerced to participate. Instead, they were able to initiate a re-territorialization process that was accompanied by their request to expand their resguardo and place a bilingual, bicultural EEC in the village. The Kogi people maintain sovereignty of the EEC and their village. The associated re-territorialization process and collaborative implementation of the Seywiaka project have potential benefits to the community itself and the national government, as these measures strengthen the fragile state of both.

When the project is placed in the context of current national affairs, we see the complications surrounding its replication. The Kogi may be unique in their self-isolation, legitimacy and social cohesion, so that other groups are not able to adapt the Seywiaka model to fulfill their needs. First, requests for a similar project would have to come from the community in which it was planned to take place, as community participation was key to the implementation of the Seywiaka project. That community would have to be socially cohesive and have an organized collective identity like the Kogi in order to be considered as a legitimate political body by the state and initiate a re-territorialization process. Second, in light of the fact that the Colombian government is providing less support for re-territorialization projects and is limiting the size of resguardos, it seems less likely that the state would respond positively to such a request. Given that at the time of writing the village had been established for less than two years, it is too early to know whether the government will recognize and respond to the potential of the village as an adaptable model to be used in response to similar requests. It is also too soon to be able to confirm whether the government would be willing to try to find ways to collaborate with indigenous communities to implement similar projects elsewhere. However, a precedent has been set by the Kogi and other indigenous people of the Sierra Nevada de Santa Marta for indigenous groups in other parts of Colombia to initiate similar processes. It is up to the state to respond positively, thereby continuing Colombia's progress towards the resolution of internal displacement, increased access to education, and a stronger, conflict-free state.

## Notes

[1] Author's translation. A. Carolina Borda Niño and Dario J. Mejía Montalvo, "Participación Política y Pobreza de las Comunidades Indígenas de Colombia," ["Political Participation and Poverty in Colombia's indigenous communities"] in *Pueblos Indígenas y Pobreza*, eds. Alberto Cimadamore, Robyn Eversole, and John-Andrew McNeish, 71–87 (Buenos Aires, Argentina: CLACSO, 2006), 83.
[2] Anastasia Moloney, "Colombia Awa Tribe at Risk of Disappearing," *Thompson Reuters Foundation*, October 19, 2011.

[3] Internal Displacement Monitoring Center, "Colombia," IDMC Web site, n.d.
[4] Maurice Bryan, "State of the World's Minorities and Indigenous Peoples 2011: Americas," MinorityRights.org, 2011.
[5] Fabio Velásquez, *Desarrollo institucional colombiano: retos para la construcción de un estado incluyente y participativo* [*Institutional Development in Colombia: Challenges to the Construction of an Inclusive and Participatory State*] (Madrid, Spain: FRIDE, 2010).
[6] Acción Social, Organización Gonawindúa, Fundación Pro-Sierra de Santa Marta, et al. *Initial Project Contract: Acuerdo de Entendimiento para hermanar esfuerzos que permitan de manera concertada, eficaz y rápida, la conformación del cordon ambiental y tradicional de la Sierra Nevada de Santa Marta*. [*Agreement to Join Efforts to Allow the Formation of the Environmental and Traditional Band of the Sierra Nevada de Santa Marta in a Coordinated, Efficient, and Rapid Way*] (Bogotá, Colombia: Acción Social, 2008).
[7] Londoño, J. and Kogi cabildo representatives. Presentation made in Fundación Pro-Sierra Nevada de Santa Marta, 2010.
[8] Gerardo Reichel-Dolmatoff, *Datos Historico-Culturales sobre las Tribus de la Antigua Gobernación de Santa Marta* [*Historic and Cultural Data on the Tribes of the Old Government of Santa Marta*] (Bogotá, Colombia: Imprenta del Banco de la República, 1951).
[9] Eduardo Uribe Botero, *Natural Resource Conservation and Management in the Sierra Nevada de Santa Marta: Case Study* (Bogotá, Colombia: CEDE / Universidad de los Andes, 2005).
[10] Reichel-Dolmatoff.
[11] Uribe Botero.
[12] "Antonil" [Anthony Henman], *Mama Coca* [*Mother Coca*] (London: Hassle-Free Press, 1978).
[13] Londoño and Kogi cabildo representatives, 2010.
[14] Ibid.
[15] Acción Social, *Seywiaka: Cordón Ambiental y Tradicional de la Sierra Nevada de Santa Marta. Cuenca Río Palomino, departamento de La Guajira* [*Seywiaka: Environmental and Traditional Band in the Sierra Nevada de Santa Marta, Palomino River Watershed, Department of La Guajira*] (Bogotá, Colombia: Author, 2010).
[16] Acción Social Website, www.accionsocial.gov.co
[17] Ibid.
[18] Acción Social, Organización Gonawindúa, Fundación Pro-Sierra de Santa Marta et al.
[19] Ibid., 2.
[20] Juana Londoño, *Pueblo cultural indígena de Sewiaja* [*Indigenous Cultural Village of Sewiaja*] (Santa Marta, Colombia: Fundacíon Pro-Sierra Nevada de Santa Marta, 2009).
[21] Acción Social, Organización Gonawindúa, Fundación Pro-Sierra de Santa Marta, et al., *Initial Project Contract: Acuerdo de Entendimiento para hermanar esfuerzos que permitan de manera concertada, eficaz y rápida, la conformación del cordon ambiental y tradicional de la Sierra Nevada de Santa Marta* .

[*Agreement to Join Efforts to Allow the Formation of the Environmental and Traditional Band of the Sierra Nevada de Santa Marta in a Coordinated, Efficient, and Rapid Way*] (Bogotá, Colombia: Acción Social, 2008).

[22] My translation. Acción Social, *Seywiaka: Cordón Ambiental...*, 2010, 2.

[23] Acción Social, Organización Gonawindúa, Fundación Pro-Sierra de Santa Marta, et al., *Final Project Contract: Acuerdo de Entendimiento para hermanar esfuerzos que permitan de manera concertada, eficaz y rápida, la conformación del cordon ambiental y tradicional de la Sierra Nevada de Santa Marta*. [*Agreement to Join Efforts to Allow the Formation of the Environmental and Traditional Band of the Sierra Nevada de Santa Marta in a Coordinated, Efficient, and Rapid Way*] (Bogotá, Colombia: Acción Social, 2008).

[24] Duane Champagne, "Rethinking Native Relations with Contemporary Nation-States," in *Indigenous Peoples and the Modern State*, eds. Duane Champagne, Karen Jo Torjesen, and Susan Steiner 3–23 (Oxford, UK: Rowman and Littlefield, 2005), 4.

[25] Andrew Gray, *Indigenous Rights and Development: Self-Determination in an Amazonian Community* (London, UK: Berghan Books, 1997), 297.

[26] Champagne, 5.

[27] Luz A. Murillo, "This Great Emptiness We Are Feeling: Toward a Decolonization of Schooling in Simunurwa, Colombia," *Anthropology and Education Quarterly* 40(4), 421–37.

[28] J. Arboleda, P. Petesch and J. Blackburn, *Voices of the Poor in Colombia: Strengthening Livelihoods, Families and Communities*. Washington DC: World Bank, 2004.

[29] Robert Chambers, "Participation and Poverty," *Development*, 50(2), 20–5; Samuel Hickey and Giles Mohan, *Participation: From Tyranny to Transformation? Exploring New Approaches to Participation in Development* (London, UK: Zed Books, 2004).

[30] Pablo Alarcón-Cháires, "Riqueza Ecológica Versus Pobreza Social" ["Ecological Wealth Versus Social Poverty"], in *Pueblos Indígenas y Pobreza*, [*Indigenous Peoples and Poverty*] eds. Alberto Cimadamore, Robyn Eversole and John-Andrew McNeish, 41–70 (Buenos Aires, Argentina: CLACSO, 2006).

[31] Anthony Bebbington, "Modernization from Below: An Alternative Indigenous Development?" *Economic Geography* 1193, no. 69, 274–92.

[32] Laura Pulido, "Ecological Legitimacy and Cultural Essentialism: Hispano Grazing in Northern New Mexico," *Journal of Capitalism, Nature and Socialism* 4(7), 28.

[33] Article 26, UN Declaration on the Rights of Indigenous Peoples.

[34] Ibid.

[35] Fazio A. Sánchez and M. López, "Land Conflicts, Property Rights and the Rise of the Export Economy during XIX Century in Colombia, 1850–1925," *Journal of Economic History* 70(2), 386.

[36] International Labor Organization. C169 Indigenous and Tribal Peoples Convention, 1989.

[37] Constitución Política de Colombia [Colombian Political Constitution], July 4, 1991.

[38] Borda Niño and Mejía Montalvo, 74.
[39] Author's translation. Artículo 329, Constitución Política de Colombia [Article 329, Colombian Political Constitution].
[40] Uribe Botero, 7.
[41] Borda Niño and Mejía Montalvo, 77.
[42] Londoño and Kogi cabildo representatives, 2010.
[43] Uribe Botero, 16.
[44] Jeanette Kloosterman, *Identidad Indígena: 'Entre romanticismo y realidad': El derecho a la autodeterminación y la tierra en el resguardo Muellamués, en el suroeste de Colombia* [*Indigenous Identity: "Between Romanticism and Reality": The Right to Self-Determination and Land in the Muellamués Resguardo in the South-West of Colombia*] (Amsterdam, the Netherlands: Thela Publishers, 1997), 115.
[45] Ibid., 116.
[46] Borda Niño and Mejía Montalvo, 78.
[47] My translation, pp. 1, Initial and Final Project Contracts.
[48] Initial and Final Project Contracts.
[49] Initial and Final Project Contracts; Londoño, 2009; Londoño 2010; Acción Social, 2010.
[50] Enrique Chaux and Ana Vásquez, "Peace Education in Colombia: The Promise of Citizenship Competencies," in *Colombia: Building Peace in a Time of War* ed. Virginia M. Bouvier, 159–72 (Washington DC: United States Institute of Peace Press. 2009).
[51] Manuel Ramiro Muñoz, "Education Needs and Forced Displacement in Colombia," DVV International Adult Education and Development 2008 no. 70; and Joanne Rappaport, *Intercultural Utopias, Public Intellectuals, Cultural Experimentation, and Ethnic Pluralism in Colombia* (Durham, SC: Duke University Press, 2005).
[52] Chaux and Velásquez, 160.
[53] Neil Boothby, "Displaced Children: Psychological Theory and Practice from the Field," *Journal of Refugee Studies*, 5(2), 15.
[54] Chaux and Velásquez.
[55] Council of Europe, *Education and Social Cohesion* (Strasbourg, France: Council of Europe Publishing, 2000).
56 Initial and Final Project Contracts.
[57] Initial Project Contract, 2.
[58] Murillo.
[59] Ibid.
[60] Chaux and Velásquez, 160.
[61] Londoño and Kogi cabildo representatives, 2010.
[62] Hector Fabio Henao Gaviria, "The Colombian Church and Peacebuilding," in *Colombia: Building Peace in a Time of War*, ed. Virginia M. Bouvier, 173–90 (Washington DC: United States Institute of Peace Press, 2009), 180.
[63] Arboleda et al., 5.
[64] Uribe Botero.
[65] Borda Niño and Mejía Montalvo, 77.
[66] Ibid., 80.

[67] Though obviously, in the event that they are not in fact an indigenous group, they should not be permitted to utilize indigenous political institutions to claim land, and therefore their possible poverty should not be attributed to not being excluded from the possible gains brought by those institutions.

[68] Marcelo Giugale, Olivier Lafourcade, and Connie Luff, *Colombia: The Economic Foundation of Peace* (Washington DC: World Bank Publications, 2003), 802–3.

[69] Borda Niño and Mejía Montalvo, 77.

[70] Ibid., 82.

[71] Murillo.

[72] Yolande Miller-Grandvaux, "Education and Fragility: A New Framework." *Journal of Education for International Development*, 4(1), 3.

# Bibliography

Acción Social. *Seywiaka: Cordón Ambiental y Tradicional de la Sierra Nevada de Santa Marta. Cuenca Río Palomino, departamento de La Guajira.* [*Seywiaka: Environmental and Traditional Band in the Sierra Nevada de Santa Marta, Palomino River Watershed, Department of La Guajira.*] Bogotá, Colombia: Author, 2010.

—. *Presentación de Videos y Entrevistas Asociados con el Pueblo de Seywiaka.* [*Presentation of Videos and Interviews Associated with Seywiaka Village.*] Bogotá, Colombia: Acción Social, 2010.

—. Acción Social Website. www.accionsocial.gov.co [accessed April 2012].

Acción Social, Organización Gonawindúa, Fundación Pro-Sierra de Santa Marta, et al. *Initial Project Contract: Acuerdo de Entendimiento para hermanar esfuerzos que permitan de manera concertada, eficaz y rápida, la conformación del cordon ambiental y tradicional de la Sierra Nevada de Santa Marta.* [*Agreement to Join Efforts to Allow the Formation of the Environmental and Traditional Band of the Sierra Nevada de Santa Marta in a Coordinated, Efficient, and Rapid Way.*] Bogotá, Colombia: Acción Social, 2008.

—. *Final Project Contract: Acuerdo de Entendimiento para hermanar esfuerzos que permitan de manera concertada, eficaz y rápida, la conformación del cordon ambiental y tradicional de la Sierra Nevada de Santa Marta.* [*Agreement to Join Efforts to Allow the Formation of the Environmental and Traditional Band of the Sierra Nevada de Santa Marta in a Coordinated, Efficient, and Rapid Way.*] Bogotá, Colombia: Acción Social, 2008.

Alarcón-Cháires, Pablo. "Riqueza Ecológica Versus Pobreza Social." ["Ecological Wealth Versus Social Poverty."] In *Pueblos Indígenas y*

*Pobreza* [*Indigenous Peoples and Poverty*]. Edited by Alberto Cimadamore, Robyn Eversole, and John-Andrew McNeish. 41–70. Buenos Aires, Argentina: CLACSO, 2006.

"Antonil" [Anthony Henman]. *Mama Coca.* [*Mother Coca.*] London: Hassle-Free Press, 1978.

Arboleda, J., P. Petesch and J. Blackburn. *Voices of the Poor in Colombia: Strengthening Livelihoods, Families and Communities.* Washington DC: World Bank, 2004.

Bebbington, Anthony. "Modernization from Below: An Alternative Indigenous Development?" *Economic Geography* 1193(69), 274–92.

Boothby, Neil. "Displaced Children: Psychological Theory and Practice from the Field." *Journal of Refugee Studies.* 5(2), 106–22.

Borda Niño, A. Carolina, and Dario J. Mejía Montalvo. "Participación Política y Pobreza de las Comunidades Indígenas de Colombia." ["Political Participation and Poverty in Colombia's Indigenous Communities."] In *Pueblos Indígenas y Pobreza* [*Indigenous Peoples and Poverty*]. Edited by Alberto Cimadamore, Robyn Eversole and John-Andrew McNeish. 71–87. Buenos Aires, Argentina: CLACSO. 2006.

Bryan, Maurice. "State of the World's Minorities and Indigenous Peoples 2011: Americas." 2011. MinorityRights.org. www.minorityrights.org/download.php?id=1011

Champagne, Duane. "Rethinking Native Relations with Contemporary Nation-States." In *Indigenous Peoples and the Modern State.* Edited by Duane Champagne, Karen Jo Torjesen, and Susan Steiner. 3–23. Oxford, UK: Rowman and Littlefield, 2005.

Chambers, Robert. "Participation and Poverty." *Development*, 50(2), 20–5.

Chaux, Enrique, and Ana Vásquez. "Peace Education in Colombia: The Promise of Citizenship Competencies." In *Colombia: Building Peace in a Time of War.* Edited by Virginia M. Bouvier. 159–72. Washington DC: United States Institute of Peace Press. 2009.

Constitución Política de Colombia [Colombian Political Constitution]. July 4, 1991. Available at http://web.presidencia.gov.co/constitucion/index.pdf

Council of Europe. *Education and Social Cohesion.* Strasbourg, France: Council of Europe Publishing, 2000.

Fundación Pro-Sierra Nevada de Santa Marta Web site. n.d. http://www.prosierra.org/

Giugale, Marcelo, Olivier Lafourcade, and Connie Luff. *Colombia: The Economic Foundation of Peace.* Washington DC: World Bank Publications, 2003.

Gray, Andrew. *Indigenous Rights and Development: Self-Determination in an Amazonian Community.* London, UK: Berghan Books, 1997.
Henao Gaviria, Hector Fabio. "The Colombian Church and Peacebuilding." In *Colombia: Building Peace in a Time of War.* Edited by Virginia M. Bouvier. 173–90. Washington DC: United States Institute of Peace Press, 2009.
Hickey, Samuel, and Giles Mohan. *Participation: From Tyranny to Transformation? Exploring New Approaches to Participation in Development.* London, UK: Zed Books, 2004.
Internal Displacement Monitoring Center. "Colombia." IDMC Web site. n.d. http://www.internal-displacement.org/countries/colombia
International Labor Organization. "C169 – Indigenous and Tribal Peoples Convention." ILO Web site. June 27, 1989. http://www.ilo.org/ilolex/cgi-lex/convde.pl?C169
Kloosterman, Jeanette. *Identidad Indígena: 'Entre romanticismo y realidad': El derecho a la autodeterminación y la tierra en el resguardo Muellamués, en el sur-oeste de Colombia.* [*Indigenous Identity: "Between Romanticism and Reality": The Right to Self-Determination and Land in the Muellamués Resguardo in the South-West of Colombia.*] Amsterdam, the Netherlands: Thela Publishers, 1997.
Londoño, Juana. *Pueblo cultural indígena de Sewiaja.* [*Indigenous Cultural Village of Sewiaja*] Santa Marta, Colombia: Fundacíon Pro-Sierra Nevada de Santa Marta, 2009.
Londoño, Juana, and Kogi cabildo representatives. Presentation made to Fundación Pro-Sierra Nevada de Santa Marta, June 2010. Santa Marta, Colombia.
Miller-Grandvaux, Yolande. "Education and Fragility: A New Framework." *Journal of Education for International Development*, 4(1), 1–14.
Moloney, Anastasia. "Colombia Awa Tribe at Risk of Disappearing." Thompson Reuters Foundation. October 19, 2011. http://www.trust.org/alertnet/news/feature-colombia-awa-tribe-at-risk-of-disappearing/
Muñoz, Manuel Ramiro. "Education Needs and Forced Displacement in Colombia." *DVV International Adult Education and Development* 70(2008). http://www.iiz-dvv.de/index.php?article_id=728&clang=1
Murillo, Luz A. "This Great Emptiness We Are Feeling: Toward a Decolonization of Schooling in Simunurwa, Colombia." *Anthropology and Education Quarterly* 40(4), 421–37.

Pulido, Laura. "Ecological Legitimacy and Cultural Essentialism: Hispano Grazing in Northern New Mexico." *Journal of Capitalism, Nature and Socialism* 4(7), 27–58.

Rappaport, Joanne. *Intercultural Utopias, Public Intellectuals, Cultural Experimentation and Ethnic Pluralism in Colombia.* Durham, SC: Duke University Press, 2005.

Reichel-Dolmatoff, Gerardo. *Datos Historico-Culturales sobre las Tribus de la Antigua Gobernación de Santa Marta* [*Historic and Cultural Data on the Tribes of the Old Government of Santa Marta*]. Bogotá, Colombia: Imprenta del Banco de la República, 1951.

Sánchez, Fazio A., and M. López. "Land Conflicts, Property Rights and the Rise of the Export Economy during XIX Century in Colombia, 1850–1925." *Journal of Economic History* 70(2), 378–399.

UN Declaration on the Rights of Indigenous Peoples. September 13, 2007. Available at http://www.un.org/esa/socdev/unpfii/documents/DRIPS_en.pdf

Uribe Botero, Eduardo. *Natural Resource Conservation and Management in the Sierra Nevada de Santa Marta: Case Study.* Bogotá, Colombia: CEDE / Universidad de los Andes, 2005.

Velásquez, Fabio. *Desarrollo institucional colombiano: retos para la construcción de un estado incluyente y participativo* [*Institutional Development in Colombia: Challenges to the Construction of an Inclusive and Participatory State*]. Madrid, Spain: FRIDE, 2010. http://www.fride.org/publication/879/colombian-institutional-development:-challenges-to-building-an-inclusive-and-participatory-state

# Chapter Twelve

## Empty Lots: Success or Failure of Sustainable Urbanization and Development against Flooding?

### Jennifer Trivedi

In Biloxi, Mississippi recovery and development since Hurricane Katrina have both been shaped by many factors, such as the rising cost of building and living in the flood zone (particularly the costs of "building up", that is, constructing homes and buildings elevated above ground level, sometimes by as much as ten to twenty feet) and the necessary costs to homeowners and flood insurance. Social and political debates have also played a role in deciding where homes and businesses—both new and reconstructed—can and will be built, as well as what types of potential temporary and permanent homes should be permitted in different areas. In the case of more temporary housing, this also includes when and for how long the structures can remain in place in certain areas. Both of these broader issues—cost and location—are influenced by a range of internal and external factors. How and where recovery and development occur and the speed with which they happen in Biloxi are ultimately influenced by a myriad of factors over which individuals, families, and groups affected by Katrina may not have any significant influence.

Internally, there are many factors that may affect recovery, reconstruction, and development, such as regulations and ordinances determined by the local government, the opinions of local residents, neighborhood identity and people's views of their own identity in the context of neighborhood identity, the state of the local economy, and individual and group class status. All of these can and do influence if, when, and where new homes may be built or rebuilt. Additional complications like the state of the local economy and the cost and availability of labor and material can also affect reconstruction. External factors play a role as well, including state and national government regulation and the national economy, which can affect the number of tourists visiting the area. Ultimately, the risk of future hurricanes has an effect, emerging at both the local level, with individual and group decisions about where to move to or rebuild, and beyond the local level, with government decisions about new regulations and both government and businesses' decisions about insurance rates and availability. We can consider these factors by looking at particular areas of the city, including especially hard-hit neighborhoods such as East Biloxi and areas with less destruction such as parts of northern Biloxi.

When looking at post-Katrina recovery and development in Biloxi, there are several questions we need to ask. Considering Katrina's devastation in the area, is underdevelopment a success or failure of sustainable urbanization and development against flooding? In addition to East Biloxi's underdevelopment, issues of rising rebuilding costs and debates about new construction have an effect on the city and its residents. What are the effects of such efforts on reconstruction, including population size, reconstruction of homes and businesses, and a tax base? And what are the effects on individuals and their perceptions of a community and their place within it? Businesses, particularly casinos, and some homes have returned to the area of East Biloxi, but many plots remain empty where homes once stood. These empty lots were particularly commonplace in the hardest-hit areas, even five years after the storm, standing in mute testimony to Katrina's destruction, but also to patterns of reconstruction and underdevelopment during recovery. This work is based on fieldwork conducted in 2006, 2010, and 2011, as well as historical document and media research conducted from 2006 through 2012. However, recovery, rebuilding, and development (and research on them) remain ongoing efforts in 2014.

While local residents continue to express ties to specific neighborhoods and areas of the city such as East Biloxi, there is an ongoing debate about whether or not people should rebuild in specific areas within those neighborhoods and how they should do it. Local residents and politicians have discussed potential new home construction in areas of the city like northern Biloxi, affected far less physically by the storm than East Biloxi. These discussions center largely on issues of identity and point to potential conflicts within the city. Combining quantitative and qualitative research including surveys, semi-structured interviews, document research (historical and media), and participant observation, I will show that discussions and actions that affect sustainable urbanization and development are not simply government decisions that draw lines on a map and establish regulations. Such debates illustrate how individuals and small groups strive to protect their own way of life and how often the desires or needs of a few are weighed against what is seen as a larger public good. The actions that emerge from these debates have real impacts on people's lives, homes and livelihoods.

## Biloxi and Katrina

Biloxi is a small town located in Harrison County, the middle of three coastal counties in the state of Mississippi. The city itself includes a peninsula and a larger area on the mainland. The peninsula is bordered by the Mississippi Sound of the Gulf of Mexico to the south and by the Bay of Biloxi (or, as it is often referred to, simply "Back Bay") to the north.[1] The city's geographic location among these waterways, as well as numerous rivers, lakes and bayous, puts it at particular risk to hurricanes. When Katrina came ashore near the Louisiana-Mississippi border, Biloxi—especially the particularly at-risk area of East Biloxi—was hit hard by the storm.[2] Entire blocks were flattened as homes up and down both sides of many streets were severely damaged or completely destroyed. Approximately fifty people in the area died. As one official reported at a city council meeting, nearly 5,000 single-family homes were completely destroyed or suffered more than 50 percent damage throughout the county. Apartments, condos and several public housing facilities, as well as businesses (including every one of the area's more than twelve legal casinos) were similarly damaged.

Biloxi's economy is built on three key components.[3] First is Keesler Air Force Base, home to military personnel and their families and employer to several thousand additional civilian employees. Military personnel have a long history of leaving the base and spending money at local businesses, further supporting the local economy. Second is the seafood industry, which has historically pushed economic development in the area. The industry includes fishermen on their boats bringing in fish, shrimp and oysters, as well as processing plants. Finally, there is the now-legal casino industry, which forms the foundation of the area's tourism industry. Vacationers have long come to the area for the water and the climate, later coming for first illegal, then legal gambling. In addition, like many other towns, the city hosts a variety of other businesses not directly related to any of these three fields, such as small local stores and restaurants and locations of regional or national chain businesses like Wal-Mart and Winn Dixie.

Biloxi's population both before and after Katrina was mostly white, but with sizable African-American and Asian communities. The Asian community is largely composed of Vietnamese immigrants and their descendants. The white community includes immigrants from and descendants of populations from a number of areas, including France, Eastern Europe (especially the southern area), Italy, Ireland, and Germany. Many individuals in the area identify themselves not only as white, but also by their particular ethnic or national heritage. A large part of minority populations, like African-Americans and Vietnamese individuals and families, lived in the East Biloxi area prior to the storm. However, Katrina has caused significant population shifts in the area that are revealed in both official data like censuses and in my own discussions with local residents in 2006 and again in 2010–2011. Local residents frequently pointed out the decreasing Vietnamese population and increasing Hispanic and Latino populations.

Data from the U.S. Census and the American Community Survey support these claims. Between 2000 and 2010, the city's African-American population decreased by about 10 percent. The city's white population decreased more substantially, by about 17 percent. However, the most significant decrease was in the Asian population, which dropped by 25 percent. At the same time, the Hispanic population increased by 208 percent. Local residents spoke with me about the population changes, including several individuals within the school system who described the changes they were seeing in student enrollment. They attributed the significant decrease in the Asian population to Vietnamese fishermen leaving for other waterfront cities that sustained less storm damage. The increase in Hispanic residents is attributed to a construction boom as rebuilding began and more workers brought their families with them. Whether or not these are the only reasons behind the population shifts is not clear and more research is needed on the matter.

Biloxi's population declined from 50,466 in 2000 to 44,054 in 2010, a loss of about 13 percent.[4] Estimates from the American Community Survey taken between 2005 and 2009 show a population of nearly 47,000, indicating that population loss since Katrina is an ongoing process.[5] Residents I spoke with in the last year pointed to ongoing recovery problems, such as finding and keeping work with the effects of Katrina, the 2010 BP Deepwater Horizon oil spill, and ongoing national economic problems. They attributed the population decline in large part to Katrina, but also cited the effects of the oil spill and economic downturn on the three components of the local economy. People described how five years after the storm, Keesler is still rebuilding.

The seafood industry suffered damage to local processing plants, harbors, bait shops, and boats, as well as the effects of the storm on the fish, shrimp, and oyster populations. In addition, after the destruction of infrastructure, local residents described to me how many fishermen, particularly Vietnamese fishermen, moved to other nearby cities. They have not left the Gulf Coast, but have left Biloxi. The industry also suffered from the BP Deepwater Horizon oil spill, with restrictions on fishing in certain waters and a decrease in sales that local residents attributed to public fear of buying potentially contaminated seafood. In addition, the general economic decline and increasing boat fuel costs are additional burdens for fishermen in the area. The tourism industry was similarly affected by ongoing problems. After changes to state law made by the Mississippi legislature, casinos did come back after Katrina, rebuilding on land instead of on barges over the water, as had been previously required. However, the return of the tourism industry has been affected by the general national economic decline, which has resulted in fewer visitors, and the BP Deepwater Horizon oil spill, which left many people reluctant to visit beaches on the Gulf Coast for a period after the spill.

Rebuilding efforts, hampered by issues such as the BP Deepwater Horizon oil spill and the economic downturn, have also been affected by the scale of Katrina's destruction. The reconstruction of homes by individuals and families has been slowed by the fact that local resources these people might have been able to rely on if their own home had been the only one affected have instead been spread thinly. One local resident I interviewed, "Sarah", pointed to such problems.[6] She suggested that there was often an institutional assumption that disasters affect individuals, not communities. This was not the case with Katrina or, indeed, with hurricanes in general on the coast. Those, she argued, affected everyone.

## Housing Relief after the Storm

In the aftermath of Katrina, many individuals and families had suffered significant damage to or complete destruction of their homes. For them, the most pressing housing concern was simply finding somewhere to stay immediately, even if they found more permanent housing solutions later on. I spoke with many such individuals while conducting fieldwork in Biloxi in 2010 and 2011, including several residents of the severely affected area of East Biloxi. Residents who had lost their homes entirely had to find somewhere else to live, while residents whose homes had been damaged often tried to find a way to stay in the home while doing repairs.

Both groups faced additional struggles in trying to apply for insurance funds and other sources of aid to support the recovery and rebuilding process financially.

Residents whose homes had been entirely destroyed by Katrina faced the question of where to live in the storm's aftermath, often while continuing the search for more permanent housing or efforts to rebuild their pre-storm homes. Many of these individuals and families found themselves living with friends, family members, and occasionally co-workers during this period. People who had evacuated in advance of Katrina often stayed with family members outside of the area, usually the same family members they stayed with during the storm. Eventually, sometimes months after the storm, residents who had lost their homes were able to get mobile homes to live in through the Federal Emergency Management Agency (FEMA).

These "FEMA trailers" were sometimes delivered to residents' private lots, often where their homes had stood before the storm, or to larger communities where residents could live in newly established neighborhoods. In some cases, residents chose to stay in these communities because of their proximity to job locations, as gas was expensive and roads were often still damaged or closed, making a longer commute difficult. "Laura" lived in a FEMA trailer in one such community. She described staying with family members in Georgia during and just after the storm. However, she needed to return to Biloxi for her job. Since her home had been completely destroyed by Katrina, Laura found herself staying with friends and co-workers in the area for several months before she was able to qualify for and have access to a FEMA trailer. While Laura noted that she heard many people complain about the trailers, for her it was a blessing, because it was finally her "own little space".

Residents' experiences with the FEMA trailer program and the trailers themselves were mixed. Some were grateful for the private space, the ability to move out of someone else's home and start piecing their own homes back together. Others had health concerns about the chemicals used in the trailers' production, often encouraged by media coverage. Further complicating matters was the fact that many residents had only a limited time to remain in the trailer. They had to rebuild their home or find other housing options in this time, a period relatively soon after the storm when housing shortages were still a problem, sometimes within a year after Katrina made landfall on the coast. Several residents, when describing looking for new housing during this time, spoke of their decision to move outside of Biloxi, often to nearby cities elsewhere on the coast, due to (1) being further from the water and therefore safer from flooding and (2) the lack of available and affordable housing in Biloxi itself. "Jessica" spoke of how she had been looking at cottages in the area before the storm, considering a move. She described the same homes selling at higher rates (at least $30,000 or more) immediately after the storm.

This cost increase created difficulties for many residents looking to buy new homes. Even if they had received insurance money for their home destroyed by Katrina or other funds from the federal government (such as SBA loans) or private organizations, the increasing cost of available homes often put them outside their price range. This was true even for residents looking at homes smaller than the ones they had lived in pre-Katrina, as was Jessica's case. Rising costs proved a substantial problem for many residents looking for new homes. Even in cases where people had damaged homes, not ones that were completely destroyed, rising costs proved problematic. Biloxians I spoke with in 2010 and 2011 remembered higher costs for supplies and labor needed to repair and rebuild homes, as well as sometimes expensive and fraudulent contractors. "Susan" described having to have her roof re-done due to storm damage. A contractor working on a neighbor's house quoted her an estimate and signed a contract, but after taking her deposit, was never heard from again.

## Renters

Biloxians who had been renting their home prior to Katrina often faced issues that homeowners did not. Renters I spoke with who had lived in hard-hit areas like East Biloxi prior to the storm found themselves not only without a home and their possessions, but with no aid to assist their efforts to find new housing. They themselves did not receive the funds to repair or rebuild the homes they had lived in, as the homeowners did. Relatively few organizations were providing funds to renters to find and rent new homes after the storm. Organizations and government agencies that offered funding to homeowners after the storm in the form of grants or low-rate loans did not always have equivalent programs to assist renters.

"Frank" described how, in the aftermath of Katrina, residents who had suffered losses often tried to get grant money to help cover expenses and recover. To qualify for such grants, though, residents had to own their own homes and have insurance for them, often leaving renters with no assistance. Renters, Frank noted, often "didn't get anything". Further complicating the situation was the fact that, prior to the storm, in poorer neighborhoods residents, especially older residents, often had to choose between paying their rent and paying for insurance to cover the loss of their possessions. When Katrina flooded, damaged, or destroyed their homes, often they not only did not receive funds to find a new place to live, but were left without any insurance to cover their personal losses of the contents of the home.

"Alice" was a renter in East Biloxi. She described some of the difficulties she faced after losing her rental home. As a renter, she noted, she got nothing for her losses. Not only was her home gone, but the land was sold to a casino, so there was no chance to return and rent the home again after its reconstruction. Despite the fact that Alice's story is like so many Biloxians', as a renter she did not qualify for the aid that homeowners received, and she did not have the same options of home repairs or reconstruction.

Despite these problems, a few groups did offer funds to help renters. However, it is important to note that the groups which residents remember as helping renters are not groups whose main purpose is to provide disaster relief or aid, but rather groups that are in the area providing other types of assistance, often to vulnerable populations. As Frank described to me, the NAACP distributed thousands of dollars in grant money to aid residents of Biloxi, particularly East Biloxi, to help them get back on their feet after the storm, including funds to cover rent.

## Costs of Rebuilding in the Flood Zone

The parameters of East Biloxi vary, including distinctions between younger and older residents, as well as insiders and outsiders. The area includes land in the city's Wards 1 and 2, east of Interstate 110. It is the oldest part of the city and has a large portion of low-lying land. The area has long been home to a racially and ethnically diverse population, with large numbers of African-Americans, Vietnamese, and immigrants from a variety of countries, some of them recent arrivals and some long established in the U.S. According to descriptions from local residents, the poorest residents were most likely to live in East Biloxi, one of the areas worst affected by Katrina. This is supported by outside reports, such as Delurey et al., who describe how, within a 2 $\text{mi}^2$ area of East Biloxi, 40 percent of residents had incomes under $15,000 before Katrina.[7] In part because of this poverty level, while the economic effects of Katrina, the oil spill, and the general economic decline have been felt across the city, they have had the deepest impact in East Biloxi.

The low-income population in East Biloxi is particularly vulnerable. As Frank described, before Katrina hit many residents in East Biloxi, particularly the elderly, were already struggling, forced to choose between homeowners, renters, or flood insurance that would help after a storm and daily needs like food, heat, and medication.[8] In the aftermath of Katrina, he continued, as they had been unable to afford insurance or home ownership before the storm, many found themselves unable to attain aid. According to Frank and others, insurance rates in Biloxi, especially East Biloxi, significantly increased rebuilding and living expenses. Residents describe insurance rates up to five times higher than they had been pre-Katrina. In an area where people were unable to afford insurance before the storm, higher insurance rates after the storm seemed unattainable to many. Frank noted that some residents had come back into the area but were living without insurance because they simply could not afford it. "It is hard to live on the peninsula now," he said.

In part, rebuilding difficulties are fueled by astronomically high insurance rates. However, it also stems from the high cost of simply rebuilding a home. Because of the destruction caused by Katrina, new flood zone maps had been drawn and new regulations put into place based on changing Federal Emergency Management (FEMA) requirements or "building up", as local residents often referred to it. Homes built in the flood zone must now be elevated above the depth of potential flood waters. Building up is expensive, particularly for elderly or disabled residents who must accommodate much longer wheelchair ramps or put in costly elevators. On top of the higher costs of such construction, some residents find themselves unable to fit these additions onto the small lots in the area. In East Biloxi, the average lot size is 5,000 square feet, just one-eighth of an acre.

The combination of high insurance rates and the high cost of rebuilding have resulted in relatively little development in East Biloxi since Katrina. This problem has not gone unnoticed by local residents or officials. Over and over I heard about the need for recovery in East Biloxi and how it was based largely on home construction in the area, followed for many by the need for schools, churches and local businesses. Despite these problems, efforts are being made to rebuild East Biloxi, largely emerging from the efforts of grassroots groups working with outside organizations. Other researchers have demonstrated the problems with outside organizations coming into a community, particularly after disasters. But the organizations working in East Biloxi that have received the most media attention and praise seem to be those working with local groups and residents. Such locally driven efforts, combined with outside aid, like the efforts through the Hope Community Center or Coastal Women for Change (CWC), play an important role in helping vulnerable and at-risk populations get back into homes and promote sustainable development—people who live closest to the water, low-income residents who may not be able to afford to rebuild on their own, and people who may have special needs that need to be accommodated in home construction (for example, disabled residents in wheelchairs).

Such efforts are working on the ground in East Biloxi, mitigating the cost of rebuilding in the area with outside experts, grant money and other resources. Architecture for Humanity has worked with groups like the Gulf Coast Community Design Studio (GCCDS) to design and build not only single-family homes for residents who need them, but to do so in a way that allows for future development. As the GCCDS described on their website,

> Architecture for Humanity's Model Homes Program worked to develop and construct seven model homes to find the most effective means of financing and construction of a new home in East Biloxi. This program tackled the issues facing many who are rebuilding their homes, such as elevating homes to new FEMA requirements, hurricane and flood risk, affordability and longevity. AFH is committed to creating sustainable homes using practices and materials that are environmentally responsible. The GCCDS was responsible for the design of the final project.[9]

This approach has also worked with local residents to figure out what they need specifically, accommodating disabilities and various family structures. While such an approach gives the opportunity for future development as a primary element of the architectural brief and has put a number of East Biloxi residents back in single-family homes, underdevelopment in the area remains a problem, in large part attributable to the cost of rebuilding. Residents who did not qualify for aid after the storm and who have been unable to get assistance from special groups like GCCDS are often unable to rebuild their own home, resulting in significant numbers of empty lots in the area, even five years after Katrina.

In addition to these largely locally driven reconstruction efforts, state-level response to Katrina has also had an effect on new housing emerging in East Biloxi. In an effort to move individuals and families out of FEMA trailers, the Mississippi Emergency Management Agency (MEMA) administered grant funding for the Mississippi Alternative Housing Project (MAHP).[10] The program led to the development, construction, and distribution of what is referred to as a MEMA or Katrina cottage, a small housing unit larger than the FEMA trailers with a small front porch, taking local housing styles into account. The unit is also wind-resistant up to 150 miles per hour.[11] The project initially began "to develop and produce a safer and more comfortable temporary housing unit for use after a disaster."[12]

Initially the MEMA trailers were considered by many to be semi-permanent housing solutions, homes for residents to move into instead of FEMA trailers. Over time residents and officials in Biloxi began considering the possibility of making the cottages more permanent. Beginning in 2010 the cottages were auctioned off by MEMA. During that time, the Biloxi City Council considered local legal changes that would allow residents to live in the cottages permanently in areas previously zoned for mobile homes. Several city officials and representatives noted that the cottages both looked more appealing than other mobile homes and were safer in the face of potential future hurricanes. While seemingly more affordable than new home construction, higher insurance rates and elevation expenses do remain a problem. Some city officials suggested working towards grants to support the elevation of the structures, continuing to argue that they were far safer than the alternative of regular mobile homes. Driving around the area in 2011, cottages were visible on lots in East Biloxi and even in mobile home parks further north and west in the city. They are clearly being used in the area, some seemingly as somewhat temporary shelters for residents rebuilding their homes on other parts of their lots and some seemingly as permanent residences.

Some of the MEMA cottages seem more permanent, as a number of residents in the East Biloxi area have elevated the cottages as required for residences in the area and put in stairs, ramps, or even elevators to access them. Across the coast, mobile home parks have MEMA trailers scattered throughout. The MEMA cottages are easily identifiable by their design, mimicking more traditional forms of coastal architecture and homes that existed before Katrina. While many residents may eventually move out of their MEMA trailers and into more permanent housing, other Biloxians and other coastal residents are clearly making the cottages into permanent shelters.

The use of other temporary housing for longer periods was more complicated than the situation with MEMA cottages. One local resident spoke before the City Council in the summer and fall of 2010. "Sam" had lost his home in Katrina, despite its elevation, and had received little insurance money for the loss. In the years after the storm, Sam had worked to make the most of the money he did have, designing and building his replacement home largely by himself, with some help as needed. During these efforts, Sam and his family were residing in a travel trailer on their property. However, when the matter was brought up before the city government, Sam was told his trailer did not meet the necessary requirements of a permanent shelter in the area, with concerns raised about the potential for severe winds and floods. Sam's arguments against these concerns included the fact that his temporary home was easily moved in advance of a storm; his desire to rebuild; the fact that being off-site would cause delays in rebuilding; and his concern that materials and equipment might be stolen if he were not on site.

The city argued in response, noting that they had allowed for such temporary shelters soon after the storm, but since it had been over five years, he should be further along in rebuilding. Other residents on the coast described living in such travel trailers after the storm while trying to rebuild their own homes. With many residents across the coast waiting for FEMA trailers, some individuals, like "Heather", had given up on the waiting list and dug into their own savings to buy travel trailers to live in until a home could be repaired or rebuilt. However, many of these residents rebuilt their homes fairly quickly, often thanks to grant money and assistance from various groups like local churches. While residents like Heather had been allowed to stay in such travel trailers as needed up to several years after the storm, the city eventually began restricting such usage, citing concerns about safety and potential insurance costs. The result was that, over five years after Katrina, despite making progress in the form of making plans and buying resources to rebuild, Sam was instructed to move his travel trailer to an RV park and travel to his home to work on its reconstruction. This restriction, Sam argued, would slow down his rebuilding even more and was thus problematic if the city wanted to encourage residents to rebuild, especially in hard-hit neighborhoods.

## Resources

Ultimately further complicating the high costs of building up and insurance in East Biloxi is the ongoing absence of the resources destroyed by Katrina. When I spoke to Frank, he noted that he had talked to a lot of people in East Biloxi and that such talk pointed to four important needs in the area for recovery: schools, a solid economy with businesses in the area, churches, and housing. People need to live in East Biloxi to bring it back, he argued. While most of the casinos that were in the area prior to Katrina have reopened, now on land, many small businesses that were destroyed by the storm have been struggling to rebuild. Even those businesses that have returned have struggled. "Steven" described his interactions with the owners of a small local bakery as they slept on the floor in the shells of their home and business, slowly cleaning, repairing and eventually reopening the business before beginning work on their own home.

Despite the reconstruction of local schools after the storm, several have now closed due to budget cuts at the state level (related to recent economic problems) and the reduction in the population in the area since the storm. One school closure, Nichols Elementary, has been particularly contentious, with accusations of favoritism and racism related to the school's history with its blue-ribbon status and connections to the first African-American school in the area. Local residents who wanted the school reopened began to look outside of the area for aid, eventually securing the promise of $1.5 million from the Kellogg Foundation for the school to reopen. This figure was based on what a local organization, Save Our Schools, had been told by officials that it would take to keep Nichols open: approximately $468,000 per year. However, the school remains closed as the funds were rejected by local school board officials. The debate around Nichols also served to underscore divisions between different parts of the city. As one man said at a public meeting, some East Biloxi residents felt that officials did not care, emphasizing that, "East Biloxi [...] *is* the city of Biloxi, the oldest part of the city."

Finally, the damage to roads caused by Katrina remains a problem. Over five years after the storm, reconstruction work on the roads had yet to begin. Plans for the repairs were ongoing, as described repeatedly in city council meetings, but did not begin at all until almost six years after Katrina. Local officials and consultants pointed to the problems they faced with getting funds from FEMA, which were made contingent on telescoping pipes in the area to look for PVC piping in damaged areas, the reasoning being that there was no sense in repairing and repaving roads if they would have to be torn up again to repair pipes. While seemingly a logical plan, local residents were often quick to point out—in public meetings and to me privately in interviews—that they had seen no such requirements in nearby cities like Gulfport, where the damaged streets had already been replaced. Residents remained frustrated with the process and noted their opinion that the state of the roads was further delaying redevelopment in East Biloxi, only supported by estimates that road repairs in East Biloxi were not likely to start for another year and would remain incomplete for at least two and a half years. When reconstruction efforts did start, the work first began largely in areas of northern Biloxi, rather than the hardest-hit areas of East Biloxi, a point that seemed to support further conflict and disagreements related to recovery between the two areas and their residents.

### Debates about Building Outside of the Flood Zone

In response to Katrina's destruction and in part due to the high cost of rebuilding in East Biloxi, some residents and officials began to look to moving outside the most at-risk flood zones, particularly to northern parts of the city. Construction in areas of northern Biloxi would potentially be significantly cheaper than rebuilding the same home in East Biloxi, both in the short term (not having to build up) and in the long term (significantly lower insurance rates). But such efforts have not been without difficulties, largely centered on issues of identity and class status.

Residents I spoke with in interviews and participant observation in 2006 and 2010–11 repeatedly referenced specific neighborhoods across Biloxi. For many, these neighborhoods were a key part of their own personal and family identities, as well as how they identified others. Among the most frequently referenced areas were East Biloxi, including neighborhoods within and adjacent to the area such as Point Cadet ("the Point") and Back Bay, and outside areas such as Woolmarket. It is important to note that the names used to refer to these areas and their borders have changed over time and are used differently by insiders and outsiders. The term "East Biloxi," for example, refers to a much larger geographic area for outsiders than for many residents, especially older individuals. As Schmidt wrote,

> the actual boundaries of the neighborhoods vary according to various sources, but all residents have a general understanding of what these boundaries are.[13]

Despite this potential confusion about the exact geographic boundaries, these neighborhoods frequently serve as a marker of identity. People often described themselves not only as Biloxians, but as from Back Bay, the Point, or Woolmarket. Moreover, this identity was maintained even among residents who had moved out of those neighborhoods, as was especially the case for the Point, which was largely flattened by Katrina. A strong sense of neighborhood identity complicates a consideration of insider/outsider status in the area. One may be a resident of Biloxi but still be to some extent an "other" from another neighborhood. This demarcation seemed particularly strong between residents of the oldest and newest areas of Biloxi, such as East Biloxi and the northern part of the city. Residents of each may consider residents of the other part of Biloxi, but still draw distinctions between their neighborhood and other areas.

East Biloxi, located on the eastern tip of the city's peninsula, is among the areas at greatest risk to hurricanes in the city. It includes significant amounts of low-lying land and is surrounded on three sides by water. The northern part of the city, in contrast, sits inland, north not only of the Gulf of Mexico and Back Bay, but, in some cases, north of the smaller local waterways, including lakes and rivers. Because of this geographic location, many viewed the annexation of a large land area now part of northern Biloxi as an avenue for future growth and development. Supported in part by the Mississippi Supreme Court decision, Edwards and Brewer v. Harrison County Board of Supervisors 2008-CA-01271-SCT (hereinafter "Edwards v. Harrison County"), this push to move north only strengthened after Katrina.

In the Supreme Court decision on Edwards v. Harrison County, the court affirmed the decision of the Circuit Court of Harrison County, First Judicial District, which in turn affirmed the decision of the Harrison County Board of Supervisors and the Planning Commission to allow rezoning to support the move northward. Justice Pierce (writing for the court) noted in procedural history that Bill Hessle, director of operations and property management, had "pointed out that the growth of the county is due north and that Hurricane Katrina has increased the growth in that direction."[14] Later in the decision, Pierce cited case law that states that to reclassify property, there must be proof,

> by clear and convincing evidence, that either: (1) a mistake in the original zoning occurred; or (2) a change occurred in the character of the neighborhood to justify rezoning and a public need,

later adding that "Edwards contends that no evidence was presented to show a change in the character of the neighborhood or public need. We disagree."[15] For Pierce, the court, and many others, Katrina marked a significant change in the area:

> Hurricane Katrina made landfall on August 29, 2005. The impact of this natural disaster on the State of Mississippi and, more significantly, on the Gulf Coast of Mississippi, is a phenomenon that cannot be ignored in the case before the Court today. Indeed, the whole world, let alone the Harrison County Board of Supervisors, was on notice of the devastation and destruction the citizens and land of the Mississippi Gulf Coast suffered from Hurricane Katrina.[16]

The court ultimately concluded that "Hurricane Katrina had significantly changed Harrison County on a number of levels" and it "jettisoned the growth of Harrison County from south of Interstate I-10 to north of Interstate I-10."[17]

Despite the ruling of the Mississippi Supreme Court, the case and related zoning laws remained contentious in the discussion of a potential new subdivision. One resident who opposed the new subdivision argued that attempts to rezone land in the area for the subdivision were nothing more than a part of the "post-Katrina mentality regarding codes, insurance, and regulations." This mentality, she argued, has held "us" back. Another resident countered the idea that Katrina and the Edwards v. Harrison County decision supported growth in the northern part of the area and rezoning, asking "isn't it time to stop using Katrina as an excuse?" Other residents speaking against the new subdivision in public meetings argued that their area had not seen a change in character, even with Katrina. Some argued that Katrina had not affected them at all.

In contrast, residents, the developer of the subdivision, and city officials and members of the public who supported the new subdivision focused on the need for affordable single-family homes since Katrina, especially ones further inland, and the fact that Katrina had changed the area as a whole. One resident specifically urged the council to consider how such changes would affect the city as a whole. One city official, who spoke repeatedly in favor of the subdivision, noted that Biloxi needed development, especially single-family homes. He said that housing took a severe hit with Katrina, going on to describe the situation in Harrison County and how nearly 5,000 homes suffered at least 50 percent damage or were completely destroyed by Katrina. He also added that since Katrina, the city had issued fewer than 800 permits for new single-family homes in the area, although he admitted they had issued permits for the construction of multi-family residences like apartment complexes and condos.

As the argument about whether or not to approve zoning changes to allow for the construction of the new subdivision progressed, statements related to class status and the economic status of current and potential new residents became increasingly frequent. Over and over again, opponents of the new subdivision claimed that it would include low-income or subsidized housing. When told repeatedly by the developer and city officials that the plans did not include such housing and that the change in zoning would not allow for low-income or subsidized housing, opponents continued to raise the issue. When one local resident raised the issue of low-income housing at a public meeting, she spoke specifically to the developer, saying that "I know you're saying you're not [putting in low-income housing] and I believe you," but went on to question if low-income housing would be a part of the subdivision. Almost immediately after reassurances from the developer and city officials that the subdivision would not include low-income housing, another local resident rose to speak, arguing that Biloxi "needs low-income housing. Can you guarantee us it won't become low-income housing?"

Even residents who spoke in favor of the new development did so with caveats about low-income housing, with one man saying that since it was not low-income or subsidized housing, he and others would be "proud to have [it] in our community." Such qualifications about not wanting low-income or subsidized housing in the area are especially problematic considering the concentration of vulnerable lower-income residents in areas that are at the greatest risk to hurricanes and least likely to be able to afford regular insurance, let alone the cost of rebuilding without it. The opposition to allowing such residents to rebuild in less at-risk areas places them in a position of either simply returning to a higher-risk area and pre-Katrina vulnerability or leaving them in limbo, unable to afford to rebuild in East Biloxi and unable to find housing in safer areas.

## The Casino Industry

While obviously not a direct housing issue, the importance of casinos in the local economy does play several roles in the reconstruction of Biloxi homes after Katrina. First and foremost is the availability of jobs and thus funding to rebuild homes, particularly for residents who did not get insurance money or other available aid. Second is the move of the casinos from water to land, located largely in severely affected areas like East Biloxi.

Katrina damaged or destroyed many local businesses in Biloxi. In particular, casinos in the area were hard hit. When legalized in the early 1990s, casino gambling in Mississippi had to occur on water. While the state government initially intended them to be placed on riverboats, supporters pushed and earned approval for the casinos to remain on barges near the shores of rivers and the Gulf of Mexico, anchored similarly to offshore oil barges. This placement made the casinos susceptible to hurricanes. Although many casino employees and local residents saw the limited effects of Hurricane Georges in 1998 on the casinos as a sign that they were able to withstand hurricanes, others began to voice concerns about their stability. These concerns included the physical ability of the casinos to withstand stronger hurricanes and the ability of the businesses and the local economy to rebound if the casinos were destroyed by such a storm.

Concerns about the casinos and their ability to withstand a more severe storm were supported by the importance of the casinos in the local economy. Biloxi's economy relies on three main components: the military (largely in the form of Keesler Air Force Base), the seafood industry (including both catching and canning), and tourism. While tourists come through the area to visit the beach, fish recreationally, and to see other sights, the casinos are a large draw. In 2004, the year before Katrina, Bernstein et al.'s report for the Mississippi Governor's Commission on Recovery, Rebuilding and Renewal (GCRRR) notes that 37 percent of the 30.7 million tourists to Mississippi visited the coast, spending $1.9 billion.[18] In Harrison County, where Biloxi is located, 28.7 percent of local jobs were tied to tourism in 2005.[19] The casinos clearly offer many jobs to residents of Biloxi and the surrounding area. The potential loss of those jobs is problematic, as it potentially leaves the area in a position of economic hardship.

When Katrina hit, it destroyed or severely damaged every casino in Biloxi. Bringing casinos back to the area was seen as a critically important endeavor, one needed to ensure that reconstruction was possible. As early as September 2005, less than a month after Katrina, the state legislature began to debate changing the law to allow casinos to rebuild on land. The changes to the law were passed, although the vote was close, and casinos were allowed to rebuild on land within 800 feet of the water.[20] It is impossible to tell whether or not the casinos would have actually rebuilt in the area had they not been allowed to rebuild on land. Residents I spoke with in 2006 saw the move as positive, arguing that it would help the casinos rebuild and increase both job options and available tax money during the difficult process of rebuilding.[21] While we cannot tell if residents' ideas that moving the casinos onto land is what encouraged rebuilding, it is clear is that the casinos came back. Bringing casinos back to the area brought jobs back to the area. Many residents I spoke with in 2006, 2010, and 2011 noted that they did not think that the recovery would be going as well as it was without those jobs. Moreover, they noted that without jobs and available funds, many more residents would be left without funds or homes and would have had to leave the area. For these residents, the reconstruction of casinos and the related return of jobs was necessary for repairing and rebuilding homes.

The casinos' return to the area, however, was not without its problems. While their return brought back jobs that were needed for some residents to fund the reconstruction of their homes, the move of casinos onto land eliminated space for some homes to rebuild. Furthermore, some Biloxians argue that it drove up the cost of land in the area. Some residents, even those who support the casinos in the area and their reconstruction, point to the problems they see with casinos being rebuilt and reopening quickly while home repair and reconstruction languished.

Other residents were left angry at the casinos and the focus placed on their reconstruction, which seemed to prioritize casinos ahead of home repairs and rebuilding. As Alice argued, residents needed their own plans and groups to promote their needs in reconstruction. She posited that if it was a situation of individuals versus the casinos, "the casinos win" and subsequently created a situation of "prosperity for the outsiders, not the insiders."

With new state laws that restrict casinos to land within 800 feet of waterways they were previously required to build over, especially combined with the fact that individual cities have to decide to allow casinos to build within their boundaries, the physical area in which casinos can be constructed is severely limited. Moreover, this land is predominantly made up of areas largely destroyed by Katrina. So, casinos had to be rebuilt on the land adjacent to the water which they owned before Katrina or in areas where homes and small businesses had been wiped out by the storm. In either case, the move potentially leaves casinos at risk to future storms, and with casinos buying up empty lots to build on, local residents saw the cost of land increase.

Complicating this potential cost increase, however, is the fact that residents who wanted to sell their land seem to have overestimated the increase. Nearly every resident I spoke with about the issue described people holding onto empty lots in the hope of getting more money for the land from casinos or condo developers. While no one admitted to such actions themselves, the discussion of land costs was widespread, even over five years after Katrina. In an interview with "Joe" in 2010, he noted that since casinos had purchased the initial land they bought at a premium "now everyone thinks they'll get that money," fueling the speculative cost of land in East Biloxi. These perceptions have pushed some residents to hold onto their land without rebuilding on it, leaving many areas looking abandoned and sometimes overgrown.

## Risk of a Future Storm

The risk of future hurricanes in the area raises additional complications for recovery and the repair and rebuilding of homes. This risk has effects at the local level, influencing individual decisions to repair, rebuild, or buy homes in the city. At the local level it also affects where and how businesses choose to build homes for sale. At the broader level, often including a significant influence of groups and organizations at the regional or national level, decisions about insurance rates and new regulations affect the potential for growth and recovery.

In 2010 and 2011 I spoke with residents who had lost their homes or suffered significant damage to their homes and were sometimes reluctant to rebuild or buy again in neighborhoods they had previously lived in, particularly the hard-hit areas like East Biloxi. Even if they had the funds and the opportunities to repair or rebuild their homes where they had previously stood, they expressed concerns about the potential for future hurricanes and the destruction they might cause. Some residents moved to or attempted to move to areas further inland that had escaped the most severe devastation from the storm, such as neighborhoods in northern Biloxi, or to other nearby cities that had also avoided the brunt of Katrina, often due to differences in geography. In some cases, such moves were also encouraged by the lower costs of insurance and homes available elsewhere. Other residents wanted to rebuild where their homes had once stood, but were unable to do so due to the high cost of rebuilding and insurance or their status as renters. Some residents were able to rebuild in the same or nearby locations by themselves or with the help of grassroots and outside organizations.

Businesses similarly often chose to place new development, including new homes, further inland. The debate about new housing in northern Biloxi and new development emerging in neighboring cities like D'Iberville are both examples of such efforts to reduce the potential risk to new homes and businesses. But, as demonstrated with the new subdivision example, such efforts were not as simple as placing new construction in areas at less risk to hurricanes. In reality, a variety of potential road blocks like the opinions of local residents and city regulations complicated such moves.

Concerns about the risk of future hurricanes and the potential problems these concerns can cause do not emerge only at the local level. Decisions like insurance rates or federal regulations often come from businesses outside the area or from the federal government. Both frequently include considerations for the risk of future disasters. Given Biloxi's historic pattern of repeated hurricane strikes, including several severe storms within the last 100 years, such as Hurricane Camille in 1969 and the 1947 Fort Lauderdale Hurricane, such adjustments are not unexpected. And while such adjustments make sense from a perspective of considering risk, they also have a profound impact on people on the ground and their ability to recover and rebuild after a disaster, a fact that should not be forgotten and must be better understood to prepare for future disasters.

## Underdevelopment: Success or Failure?

When we look at the situation on the ground in Biloxi over the five years after Katrina, several important facts emerge. East Biloxi remains largely underdeveloped. Future development is, to a significant extent, moving north. While development is moving, neighborhood identity and the location of various populations remain somewhat stagnant. East Biloxi, for example, remains a lower-income area, with large populations of racial and ethnic minorities. But all of this leads us to several questions. First, considering Katrina's devastation in the area, is this underdevelopment a success or a failure of sustainable urbanization and development against flooding? Second, in addition to East Biloxi's underdevelopment, the issues of rising rebuilding costs and debates about new construction have had an effect on the city as a whole and its residents. What are the effects of such efforts on a city's reconstruction, including population size, reconstruction of homes and businesses, and a tax base? Finally, what are the effects on individuals and their perceptions of a community and their place within it?

In response to the first question, we need to consider East Biloxi's underdevelopment since Katrina and its status as a success or a failure of sustainable urbanization and development against flooding. The area's underdevelopment means, in part, a lack of population and construction in the flood zone. As is perhaps somewhat obvious, buildings that do not exist cannot be destroyed by hurricanes. Based on my research in the area, I do not think that this necessarily makes the overall area an example of a success of sustainable urbanization or development against flooding. What construction has occurred in the area, focused on addressing local and individual housing needs, as well as meeting new disaster mitigation efforts, demonstrates that sustainable urbanization and development that protects against flooding is possible. However, such successes require a cooperative effort between different groups, outsider expertise, insider knowledge (of local housing needs and residents' desires), and funding sources. Examples such as the GCCDS show that such cooperative efforts are possible, at least on a small scale.

But while some development efforts in East Biloxi have proved successful, overall underdevelopment remains a problem. This has an effect not only in East Biloxi specifically, but in the city as a whole, as addressed in the second question. Underdevelopment in East Biloxi has an effect on the city in terms of a smaller population size overall, resulting in fewer homes and businesses rebuilt and a smaller tax base. In addition, given that much of Biloxi's tourism industry is centered in and near East

Biloxi, the appearance of underdevelopment may be problematic. Solutions for some of the area have been suggested, including efforts geared towards rebuilding homes, like those by GCCDS and even the Katrina cottages, as well as by efforts to revitalize public property in the area. Local and national organizations like the Salvation Army have purchased damaged properties and are working to refurbish them for public use. The city itself has used grant money and federal aid to build new public spaces in damaged areas, such as a new library and community center. The city has brought in outside advisers to help develop city and state properties in East Biloxi, hoping to create a public space suitable for both private businesses such as restaurants and joint public-private ventures such as the city farmer's market (housed under a bridge since Katrina destroyed the open-air structure it was previously held in) and local festivals. Many of these efforts, however, still remain in the construction or planning phases over five years after the storm. Until they are completed and prove useable by local residents, their beneficial effect on the area and its development remains somewhat questionable.

Finally, underdevelopment in East Biloxi and arguments over potential future development in areas further north in the city affect individuals, including their perceptions of their community and their place within it. For many residents I spoke with in East Biloxi, the future development in East Biloxi must go beyond simply rebuilding homes. For them, development must include local businesses, schools, and even churches, as Frank put it, "whatever their God may be." Development is, for these residents, not simply the physical act of rebuilding, but putting a community back together and helping it grow. In areas of northern Biloxi, residents voiced very different opinions about development, emphasizing that they did not oppose development in general, but did oppose rezoning land and allowing for development that did not, in their view, fit into the area. While their perception of development was different, seemingly based around their view that Katrina had not affected them as they had experienced a relative lack of physical destruction from the storm, the idea of community and keeping a sense of community identity intact remained an important component of the future and development.

Underdevelopment in East Biloxi has an effect on neighborhoods in the area, the city as a whole, and the neighborhoods' and city's populations. East Biloxi residents feel the need to rebuild their community, citing underdevelopment as one of the reasons long-term recovery remains an ongoing process. Other neighborhoods have been drawn into a discussion of East Biloxi's underdevelopment as developers, city officials, and some residents look to their areas in an effort to rebuild the city and its homes with less risk. City officials and local residents argue, even over five years after Katrina, about how to rebuild the area and rehouse its residents. The lack of housing in the area remains a problem for many. It is a problem the city has sought to address in various ways, including supporting development in other lower-risk areas and allowing for housing like the Katrina cottages, which emerged from state-sponsored projects geared towards developing safe housing for local residents. Business development in the city as a whole has been affected by the rebuilding of casinos, largely in East Biloxi and nearby areas. It is centered on the desire to bring in new businesses and encourage more pre-Katrina businesses to return in order to bring in jobs and revenues that may help the city in a time of economic problems and promote long-term development. Ultimately, underdevelopment in East Biloxi since Hurricane Katrina has affected local residents who continue to struggle to rebuild their own homes and businesses, their neighborhoods, their city, and their sense of community.

## Notes

[1] The phrase "Back Bay" is used both to refer to the body of water known as the Back Bay of Biloxi and to the neighborhood of Back Bay that borders the bay itself.

[2] Axel Graumann, Tamara Houston, Jay Lawrimore, David Levinson, Neal Lott, Sam McCown, Scott Stephens, and David Wuertz, "Hurricane Katrina: Building Back Better Than Ever," December 31, 2005, 2; Jennifer Trivedi, "Hurricanes Did Not Just Start Happening: Expectations of Intervention in the Mississippi Gulf Coast Casino Industry," in *The Political Economy of Hazards and Disasters*, eds. Eric C. Jones and Arthur D. Murphy, 295–312 (Lanham, MD: AltaMira Press, 2009), 295.

[3] Trivedi 2009.

[4] U.S. Census Bureau, Biloxi City, Mississippi: Census 2000 Demographic Profile, 2000, Biloxi City, Mississippi: Census 2010 Demographic Profile, 2010.

[5] American Community Survey, "Biloxi City, Mississippi: 2005–2009 American Community Survey 5-Year Estimates." 2009.

[6] Pseudonyms have been used throughout this essay to protect the identity of informants as much as possible.

[7] Michael Delurey, David Sulek, and Lawrence Frascella, "Convenors of Capability," *Strategy + Business* 2008(Spring), 3.

[8] Jennifer Trivedi, "Vulnerability, Agency, and Recovery: East Biloxi after Hurricane Katrina," *SfAA Newsletter*, 22(4), 39–41.

[9] Gulf Coast Community Design Studio (GCCDS), "A House for Louise," Mississippi State University College of Architecture and Design, 2008.

[10] Michael Beard, *Future Directions of FEMA's Temporary Housing Assistance Program* (Washington DC: Department of Homeland Security, 2011).

[11] Ibid, 11.
[12] Mississippi Emergency Management Agency, *2005–2008 Annual Report* (Jackson, MS: Author, 2008).
[13] Aimee Schmidt, "Down Around Biloxi: Culture and Identity in the Biloxi Seafood Industry (Part II)," *Mississippi Folk Life*, 28(2), 6–19.
[14] Edwards v. Harrison County Board of Supervisors, no. 2008-CA-01271-SCT (Miss. 2008), 4.
[15] Ibid.
[16] Ibid., 13.
[17] Ibid.,13–4.
[18] Bernstein, et al. *After Katrina: Building Back Better Than Ever* (Jackson, MS: Governor's Commission on Recovery, Rebuilding and Renewal, 2005), 78, 81; Trivedi, 2009, 299.
[19] Bernstein et al., 83.
[20] Geoff Pender and Tom Wilemon, "Biloxi Blues: Mississippi Economy Hit Hard by Casino Losses," *Tallahassee Democrat*, September 2, 2005, A4; Trivedi, 302.
[21] Trivedi 2009, 304.

# Bibliography

American Community Survey. "Biloxi City, Mississippi: 2005–2009 American Community Survey 5-Year Estimates." 2009. http://factfinder2.census.gov/faces/tableservices/jsf/pages/productview.xhtml?pid=ACS_09_5YR_DP5YR5&prodType=table

Beard, Michael. *Future Directions of FEMA's Temporary Housing Assistance Program*. Washington D.C.: Department of Homeland Security, 2011.

Bernstein, Mark, et al. *After Katrina: Building Back Better Than Ever: A Report to the Honorable Haley Barbour, Governor of Mississippi, from the Governor's Commission on Recovery, Rebuilding and Renewal*. Jackson, MS: Governor's Commission on Recovery, Rebuilding and Renewal, 2005.

Delurey, Michael, David Sulek, and Lawrence Frascella. "Convenors of Capability." *Strategy + Business* 2008(Spring), 1–8.

Graumann, Axel, Tamara Houston, Jay Lawrimore, David Levinson, Neal Lott, Sam McCown, Scott Stephens, and David Wuertz. Hurricane Katrina: Building Back Better Than Ever. December 31, 2005. www.governorscommission.com/final/Main.asp

Gulf Coast Community Design Studio (GCCDS). "A House for Louise." Mississippi State University College of Architecture and Design, 2008. http://www.gccds.org/projects/biloxi/_houses/louise/louise.php

Mississippi Emergency Management Agency (MEMA). *2005–2008 Annual Report*. Jackson, MS: Author, 2008.

Pender, Geoff, and Tom Wilemon. "Biloxi Blues: Mississippi Economy Hit Hard by Casino Losses." *Tallahassee Democrat*, September 2, 2005, A4.

Edwards v. Harrison County Board of Supervisors, no. 2008-CA-01271-SCT (Miss. 2008).

Schmidt, Aimee. "Down Around Biloxi: Culture and Identity in the Biloxi Seafood Industry (Part II)." *Mississippi Folk Life*, 28(2), 6–19. http://www.mississippifolklife.org/media/archive-issues/28.2_SF95.pdf (accessed June 12, 2011).

Trivedi, Jennifer. "Hurricanes Did Not Just Start Happening: Expectations of Intervention in the Mississippi Gulf Coast Casino Industry." In *The Political Economy of Hazards and Disasters*. Edited by Eric C. Jones and Arthur D. Murphy. 295–312. Lanham, MD: AltaMira Press, 2009.

—. "Vulnerability, Agency, and Recovery: East Biloxi after Hurricane Katrina." *SfAA Newsletter*, 22(4), 39–41.

U.S. Census Bureau. Biloxi City, Mississippi: Census 2000 Demographic Profile. 2000. http://factfinder2.census.gov/faces/tableservices/jsf/pages/ productview.xhtml?src=bkmk

—. Biloxi City, Mississippi: Census 2010 Demographic Profile. 2010. http://factfinder2.census.gov/faces/tableservices/jsf/pages/productview.xhtml?pid=DEC_10_DP_DPDP1&prodType=table

# CHAPTER THIRTEEN

# INDICATORS OF SOCIAL VULNERABILITY AND SUSTAINABLE DEVELOPMENT

# OLUWATOYIN OLATUNDUN ILESANMI

**Introduction**

Globally, many nations are prone to numerous types of disaster (natural and anthropogenic hazards) which entail risks of varying magnitudes. A disaster is the fulfillment of a risk on a given territory. The extent and costs of the damage caused by such disasters severely interrupts the functioning of the society occupying the territory in such a way that the human, material or environmental losses incurred cannot be overcome solely with the resources which the affected society has at its disposal.[1] Natural disasters are complex phenomena arising from the interaction between environmental hazards and human actions.[2] They pose a significant threat to sustainable development, particularly in developing countries.[3] The human and economic cost of natural disasters has risen steeply in recent decades, due primarily to a range of environmental socio-economic and demographic pressures that are making societies more vulnerable to hazards.[4] Anthropogenic hazards or man-made disasters refer to threats that have an element of human intent, negligence or error, or that involve the failure of a man-made system.[5]

Both natural and man-made disasters result in terrifying casualties and damage, often leading to disruption of normal functioning in the affected nations and communities, causing widespread human, material, economic, and environmental losses which often exceed the ability of the affected community to cope using its own resources. The number of casualties and damage caused by such disasters, while varying greatly from disaster to disaster, has been on the increase in recent decades[6] in both the developed (e.g., Japan) and less developed (e.g., Sudan) nations across the globe. A typical example of this is the recent earthquake and tsunami that occurred in Japan on Friday, March 11, 2011, which resulted in extremely high loss of lives and properties and a sharp drop of the value of the Japanese Yen.

Nigeria, which is the most populous developing nation in Africa, consisting of different tribal communities (Yoruba, Hausa and Ibo) is not immune to the social effects of disaster on vulnerable groups. The nation has witnessed the incidence of different types of hazards and disasters. These range from flood, fire, religious conflicts, inter-tribal conflicts, and political conflicts born of the struggle for the equal sharing of the national assets. In recent times, the spate of man-made disasters include terrorist activities, kidnappings, armed robberies, and pipeline vandalism, which exposes affected communities to destruction of lives and property through explosions. The major terrorist groups in Nigeria are the radical Islamic *Jama'atu ahlus Sunnah lid da'awati wal Jihad* sect, popularly called Boko Haram (see Figure 13.1) in the northeast, and the militant group in the Niger delta. Currently, the northern parts of Nigeria (especially Maiduguri, Jos, and Abuja) are subject to sporadic attacks of suicide bombing and violence assumed to be organized by Boko Haram. The group is assumed to be responsible for the series of suicide bombing attacks against the Force Headquarters in Abuja and churches and prisons in different cities and towns in the northern region of the nation.[7]

Figure 13.1. Boko Haram Members.[8]

Globally, vulnerability to disaster may be precipitated by the totality of the relationships in the social situation which constitute conditions that, in combination with environmental forces, produce disasters. Bankoff, Frerks, and Hilhorst[9] view this as a community's social vulnerability (SV) to multiple stressors and shocks, including natural or man-made disasters and hazards. In Nigeria, this includes both physical and social characteristics that contribute to decreased capacity and resilience. Etymologically the term "vulnerability" is derived from the Latin word *vulnerare* (to be wounded)[10] and denotes risk, fragility, and defenselessness as well as the potential to be harmed physically and/or psychologically. It is the reverse of resilience and the degree to which a system or unit (such as a human group or a place) is likely to experience harm due to exposure to perturbations or stresses.[11]

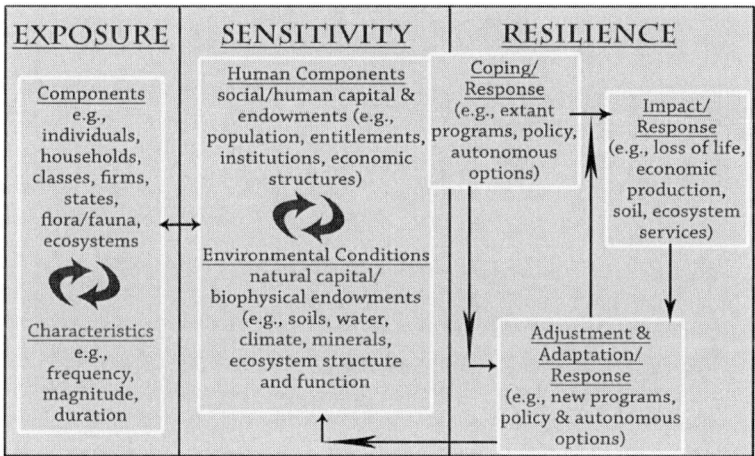

Figure 13.2. SEI / Clark University Vulnerability Framework. This framework distinguishes between three dimensions of vulnerability: exposure, sensitivity, resilience.[12]

Essentially, social vulnerability (SV) is the existing inherent defenselessness in social institutions, organizations and societies exposed to multiple hazards and disasters. According to Clark et al.,[13] SV is the differential incapacity of a group of people to deal with the adverse impacts of hazards (e.g., earthquakes and/or landslides), based on their position within both the physical and social worlds. Generally, a group of people, institutions or societies could be defenseless in the face of hazards, such as stresses, perturbations, and shocks; due to lack of sensitivity and capacity to anticipate and cope with them; as well as their lack resilience or ability to recover from the stress and to buffer themselves against and adapt to future stresses and perturbations.[14] Risk, in the context of vulnerability,

> is a function of the perturbation, stressor, or stress and the vulnerability of the exposed unit. It directs attention to the conditions that make exposure unsafe, leading to vulnerability and to the causes creating these conditions. Used primarily to address social groups facing disaster events, the application of the model emphasizes distinctions in vulnerability by different exposure units (e.g., class, ethnicity).[15]

Receptors are humans, animals, and plants that may be exposed to environmental stress.[16] As receptors, humans are often divided on the basis of age group—infants (0 to 6 months), toddlers (7 months to 4 years), children (5–11 years), teens (12–19 years), and adults (20+ years) —because certain age groups are more susceptible to the effects of certain types of hazards than others.[17]

In Nigeria, different living conditions, social standards, residential environments (rural, urban, or urban slum), social interactions, institutions, and systems of cultural values usually lead to people's different abilities or inabilities to prepare for and cope with disasters.[18] Therefore, an identification of the social forces and multiple stressors, such as marginalization or social inequalities,[19] which increase the ability of a community to respond to, cope with, recover from, and adapt to the impact of hazards will enhance the evolution of sustainable development in fragile states like Nigeria. However, within most developing societies, a search of the existing literature reveals that little or no attempt has been made to determine the social forces and or stressors that reinforce the overwhelming existence of social vulnerability.[20] Hence the need for this paper, which attempts to identify the social conditions and driving forces that transform natural hazards (e.g., floods, earthquakes, mass movements, etc.) into social disasters (who and what is vulnerable) through a review of literature on the theoretical basis of social vulnerability, the identification of at-risk people, and the identification of the nature, types, and sources of SV. This leads in turn to a consideration of the mental health implications of SV, and recommendations are offered concerning measures that could be taken to reduce SV in Africa.

## Theoretical Basis of Social Vulnerability

Numerous theories of social vulnerability have been proposed over the years.[21] These include the risk-hazard (RH) model,[22] the pressure-and-release model (PAR),[23] the hazards-of-place (HOP) model,[24] the exposure model,[25] and the political economy.[26] The RH model states that the impact of a hazard is a function of exposure to the hazardous event and the sensitivity of the entity exposed.[27] This model emphasizes exposure and sensitivity to perturbations and stressors[28] and works from hazard to impacts.[29]

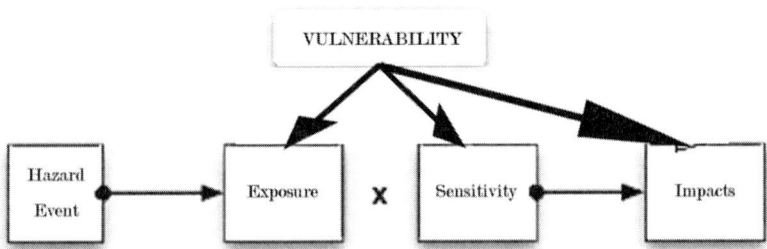

Figure 13.3. The Risk-Hazard (RH) Model. This model shows the impact of a hazard as a function of exposure and sensitivity. The chain sequence begins with the hazard, and the concept of vulnerability is noted implicitly, as represented by the arrows.[30]

The "crunch" model (hazard x vulnerability = disaster or risk of disaster) was first introduced in *Shelter after Disaster*,[31] was further refined by Blaikie, Cannon, Davis, and Wisner[32] in *At Risk: People's Vulnerability to Natural Disasters*, and became known as the pressure and release (PAR) model. This model illustrates the "Progression of Vulnerability" in three social developing stages: "Root Causes", "Dynamic Pressures", and "Unsafe Conditions",[33] and distinguishes them from natural hazards. It views disaster as the intersection between socio-economic pressure and physical exposure. It defines risk as a function of perturbation or stress and the vulnerability of the exposed unit.[34] Principal root causes include the "economic, demographic and political processes"[35] which affect the allocation and distribution of resources between different groups of people. Dynamic pressures are economic and political processes in local circumstances (e.g., migration patterns). Unsafe conditions are the specific forms in which vulnerability is expressed in time and space, such as those induced by the physical environment, local economy, or social relations.[36]

The HOP model of vulnerability[37] implies that SV is a multidimensional concept that helps to identify those characteristics and experiences of communities (and individuals) that enable them to respond to and recover from environmental hazards. The HOP model provides a place-based overview of both the physical event parameters (and their potential impacts) and the underlying socio-economic and demographic characteristics of the population residing within the hazard zone. It combines biophysical vulnerability (the physical characteristics of hazards and environment) and social vulnerability to determine an overall place vulnerability and it focuses more on the identification of at-risk and vulnerable populations.

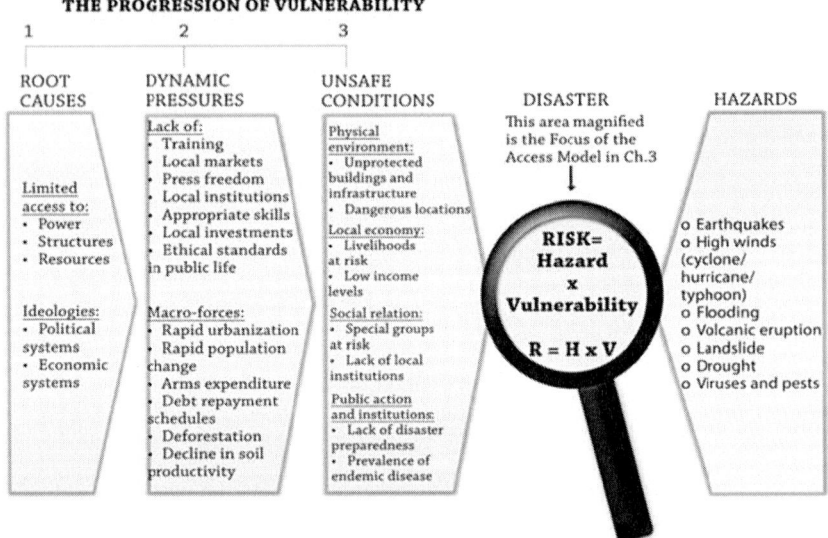

Figure 13.4. The Pressure and Release (PAR) Model. This model shows the progression of vulnerability. The diagram shows a disaster as the intersection between socio-economic pressures on the left and physical events (natural hazards) on the right.[38]

The exposure model[39] identifies conditions that make people or places socially vulnerable to extreme natural events. It assumes that vulnerability is a social condition, a measure of societal resistance, or resilience to hazards[40] as well as the integration of potential exposures and societal resilience, with a specific focus on particular places or regions.[41]

The political economy analysis theory of vulnerability posited by North[42] states that poverty, the use of resources, and the distribution of assets and income within a population are all institutionally determined. It attributes social vulnerability to the structural characteristics of the state and the economy, which determine how resources are distributed.[43] According to this perspective, the economic, political, and ideological structures create inequality by constructing and reconstructing factors like class, gender, race, and ethnicity as barriers.[44] These structural barriers limit people's opportunities and choices, thereby reducing their access to valued resources.[45] Ultimately this increases their vulnerability.[46]

Feminist theoretical perspectives on the issue of gender inequality state that women are disproportionately disadvantaged globally[47] and argue that gender inequality is supported by gender cultural systems that have ideological and material dimensions which are extremely resilient.[48]

Capacity and vulnerability analysis theory[49] views people's vulnerabilities and capacities in three broad interrelated areas: the access to or lack of physical/material resources, lands, climate, environment, health, skills and labor, infrastructure, housing, finance, technologies, and hazards; the existence or lack of social/organizational relations among people; and communities' attitude toward or motivation to create change. This theory distinguishes between vulnerability and needs, viewing vulnerability as a long-term factor that affects a community's ability to respond to events or make it susceptible to disaster, and needs as the immediate requirements for survival or recovery after disaster.

The structural social theory relating to the causes of vulnerability to hazards was developed by Hewitt,[50] who emphasized lack of access to resources (poverty and marginalization translate into vulnerability through the mechanisms of coping behavior and stress) as the cause of vulnerability to hazards.

## Who are the Most Vulnerable to Disasters?

The documentation of disaster experiences in Nigeria over the past centuries has revealed a consistent pattern of vulnerability for certain groups in the six geopolitical zones (north central, southeast, northwest, northeast, south and southwest) that persistently suffer from disaster impacts to a disproportionate degree. These are the unemployed, those stigmatized with illnesses (such as HIV/AIDS-affected individuals and the mentally ill), poor families, the elderly, people with disabilities, the self-employed (especially in rural areas), migrant workers, people in areas facing war or civil conflicts, displaced people, and refugees and workers in the informal economy—the majority of whom are women. The victims of official or cultural prejudice (such as ethnic or religious minorities) which leads to inequitable access to resources may also be categorized as vulnerable groups.[51]

## Nature, Type and Sources of Social Vulnerability

The nature of social vulnerability is always area-specific and complex;[52] while hazards may be international, regional, or national, vulnerabilities are by nature localized to certain specific communities, villages or towns. The complex nature of social vulnerability centers on the social, demographic, and economic conditions (such as gender, age, health status and disability, ethnicity or race or nationality, caste or religion, and socio-economic status) and the potentially political factors that are the root causes of the vulnerability of a specific group.[53] These are the fundamental pressures that create and drive the patterns of social vulnerability. Such root causes may be systemic "mega-forces" within a given society.

Furthermore, social vulnerability to hazards and disasters varies among different social groups over time and space, as indicated below.[54]

A. *Individual vulnerability.* This is determined by:
- Personal data, such as age, gender, race and ethnicity, employment status, literacy, and marital status;
- Personal disaster preparedness, such as social standards, knowledge about hazard and risks, access to information, and willingness to decrease susceptibility;
- Access to resources;
- Diversity of income sources; and
- Social status of individuals within a community.

B. *Family or household vulnerability.* This is determined by:
- Household characteristics, such as household size, tenure status, access to water, gas and power supply; and
- Housing conditions, such as residence type, building stock and building construction material.

C. *Neighborhood vulnerability.* This is determined by:
- Physical: proximity to hazard zones, relief/slope, abundance of transport infrastructure, road conditions, building density/proportion of built-up areas, roof material/size, distance to neighboring buildings, size and distribution of green spaces, commercial and industrial development, distance to city center (rural and urban);
- Social environment: supply of gas, water, and electricity, abundance of educational facilities, abundance of medical facilities and emergency management, and building codes.

D. *Collective vulnerability* of a nation, region or community in different forms and spheres. This is determined by:

- Institutional and market structures, such as the prevalence of informal and formal social security and insurance; and
- Infrastructure and income. Collective vulnerability is exacerbated by "exogenous" environmental changes which occur through climate change.

These aspects of vulnerability are obviously interlinked. At the community level, social vulnerability is affected by the relative distribution of income, access to and diversity of economic assets, and by the operation of informal social security arrangements.

## Indicators of Social Vulnerability (SV) and Capacities of Different Sectors

Indicators of SV, as shown in Table 13.1 below, are quantitative measures intended to represent the characteristics[55] of who and what is exposed to threat (hazard identification), the differential susceptibility (the potential for loss, injury, harm, and adverse impacts on livelihoods), and impacts of that exposure.

Over the years, researchers have identified multiple indicators for social vulnerability. For instance, Cutter, Mitchell, and Scott identified eleven factors of SV, including personal wealth, age, density of the built environment, occupation, household stock and tenancy, single-sector economic dependence, and infrastructure dependence, and three factors related to differences in race and ethnicity.[56] Evans, DeBonis, Krasilovsky, and Melton also recognized age, wealth, employment, and ethnicity as indicators of SV.[57]

The literature[58] shows that the indices of social vulnerability in developing nations like Nigeria consist of the following:

- Socio-economic status (income, political power and prestige), which affects the ability of individuals and communities to absorb losses and be resilient to hazard impacts.
- Poverty, which is a state of deprivation (lack of access) to key resources.[59] Poor people are more likely to live in substandard housing, which can be a major disadvantage when disasters occur.[60] During disasters, the poor are less likely to have access to critical resources and lifelines such as communications and transportation.[61]
- Disability and physical frailty status: people with mental and physical disabilities are at increased risk because they will require extra assistance.[62]

**Table 13.1. Indicators of Vulnerability and Capacities.**[63]

| Sectors | Vulnerabilities | Capacities |
|---|---|---|
| Social | * occupation of unsafe areas<br>* high-density occupation of sites and buildings<br>* lack of mobility<br>* low perceptions of risk<br>* vulnerable occupations<br>* vulnerable groups and individuals<br>* corruption<br>* lack of education<br>* poverty<br>* lack of vulnerability and capacity assessment<br>* poor management and leadership<br>* lack of disaster planning and preparedness | * social capital<br>* coping mechanisms<br>* adaptive strategies<br>* memory of past disasters<br>* good governance<br>* ethical standards<br>* local leadership<br>* local NGOs<br>* accountability<br>* well-developed disaster plans and preparedness |
| Physical | * at-risk buildings<br>* unsafe infrastructure<br>* unsafe critical facilities<br>* rapid urbanization | * physical capital<br>* resilient buildings and infrastructure that can cope with and resist extreme hazard forces |
| Economic | * mono-crop agriculture<br>* non-diversified economy<br>* subsistence economies<br>* indebtedness<br>* relief/welfare dependency | * economic capital<br>* secure livelihoods<br>* financial reserves<br>* diversified agriculture and economy |
| Environmental | * deforestation<br>* pollution of ground, water and air<br>* the destruction of natural storm barriers (such as mangroves)<br>* global climate change | * natural environmental capital<br>* the creation of natural barriers to storm action (such as coral reefs)<br>* natural environmental recovery processes (such as forests recovering from fires)<br>* bio-diversity<br>* responsible natural resource management |

- Gender inequality causes and perpetuates poverty and vulnerability, especially for women. Women often suffer the impacts of a disaster disproportionately.[64]
- Cultural, racial, and ethnic differences: the confluence of race and class (socioeconomic status) produces social inequalities.[65] Discrimination also plays a major role in increasing the vulnerability of racial and ethnic minorities.[66] Ethnic communities are often geographically and economically isolated from jobs, services and institutions.
- Age (Elderly + Children): both the young and the elderly may be unable to respond to disasters without outside support.[67] The elderly are more likely to lack adequate economic resources and the necessary physical ability to respond effectively to a disaster. They are more likely to suffer health problems and physical harm and to experience a slower recovery.[68] They also tend to be more reluctant to evacuate their homes in a disaster.[69]
- Employment loss: the potential loss of additional employment following a disaster increases the possible number of unemployed workers in a community. Such losses contribute to a slower recovery from the disaster.
- Underdevelopment of rural areas, as compared to the development of urban cities: rural residents may be more vulnerable because of lower incomes and more dependence on a locally based resource economy (e.g., farming or fishing). The commercial and industrial development of a community (infrastructure and lifelines) and the value, quality, and density of residential, commercial, and industrial buildings may provide indicators of the state of the economic health of a community, potential losses in the business community, and longer-term issues with recovery after an event.
- Family structure and population growth: families with large numbers of dependents and single-parent households often have limited wherewithal to outsource care for dependents and thus must juggle work responsibilities and care for family members.
- Educational status: poor literacy and language skills may cause disadvantages in responding to a disaster when seeking information, applying for assistance, or seeking post-disaster employment.[70]
- Health status: the public health literature shows that people with pre-existing illnesses may be at risk of death, illness, or injury in disaster settings. People with pre-existing cardiovascular and respiratory conditions who are exposed to smoke from forest fires may be more at risk of adverse health outcomes and may be

vulnerable to heart attacks during seismic activity. People living with mental or physical disabilities are less able to respond effectively to disasters and require additional assistance in preparing for and recovering from disasters.[71]
- Lack of proximate medical services: healthcare providers, including physicians, nursing homes, and hospitals, are important post-event sources of relief. The lack of proximate medical services lengthens the time needed to obtain short-term relief and achieve longer-term recovery from disasters.
- Special-needs populations (the infirm, institutionalized, transient, and homeless people and those who are totally dependent on social services for survival), who are already economically and socially marginalized and require additional support in the post-disaster period. Special-needs populations are difficult to identify, let alone measure and monitor.
- Resource dependency, which is constituted by reliance on a narrow range of resources leading to social and economic stresses within livelihood systems. Resource dependency relates to communities and individuals whose social order, livelihood, and stability are a direct function of its resource production and localized economy.[72]
- The social vulnerability context within which people pursue their livelihoods includes:
  o Trends (such as economic or resource trends);
  o Shocks (such as conflicts, economic shocks, health shocks, and natural shocks such as earthquakes);
  o Seasonality (seasonal fluctuations in prices, production, health, and employment opportunities).

## Mental Health Implications

The concept of social vulnerability has been associated with a number of indicators that bind the socioeconomic, environmental, cultural, and psychological factors to the exposure of poorer social groups to risks in areas prone to disaster (such as environmental degradation) and lack of public policy. Therefore all indicators of SV have a number of mental health implications for psychological interventions and counseling. First, the mental health, disability, and physical injury impacts of disaster and loss may negatively affect the victims' perceptions of themselves, their motivations, self-esteem, self-confidence, emotional, spiritual, or religious well-being and capacity, as well as the will to assert themselves and claim their rights (survival and resilience). It is therefore necessary to pay attention to the socially vulnerable groups in both rural and urban centers. Attention should be focused on the development of psychotherapeutic intervention programs which will enable them to improve their life chances and grant them the opportunity to function fully in society. Some of them may require basic psychological care without hospitalization; others may require hospitalization for life-threatening injuries and poor mental health.

In Nigeria, little or no attention is currently being paid to the psychological needs of the mentally ill. As a result, there is therefore a dearth of policies and advocacies focusing on this aspect of socially vulnerable groups, the implication of which is that everyone in Africa lives in highly volatile societies prone to vulnerability emanating from disaster, loss, hazards, and conflicts (ethnic, political, religious, or otherwise). It is therefore necessary to create enabling agencies (i.e., policy makers) that will interact with mental health service providers in order to establish an environment conducive to the development of pre- and post-disaster mental health services to care for socially vulnerable groups. This will greatly reduce the trauma of hazards in socially vulnerable societies like Africa.

In terms of location, people in rural areas in developing nations like Nigeria have lower levels of development and also face many challenges as a result of where they reside. Such challenges include less access to health and other social services. They therefore require better access to psychological health and social services for improved quality of life.

The impact of a disaster such as the complete destruction of a residence or the loss of employment may also have negative psychological implications for socially vulnerable groups in Nigeria. It may take them longer to recover. They may be forced into living on the streets, squatting, staying with friends and family, or staying in boarding houses and supported accommodation with no fixed address. They usually have lower incomes, are unemployed, and have limited or no access to safe, secure services and adequate housing. They may be exposed to many dangers in the society, such as antisocial environments and to violence that endangers them and increases their risk of developing physical and mental health problems (e.g., mental disorders, suicide, drug and substance abuse, self-harm, and cardiovascular disorders).

Additionally, policies and practices related to disaster response often assume that all residents of an area have the same information, the same resources, and the same ability to act upon information. Furthermore, they assume that all residents will react in the same way. However, social vulnerability factors in Nigeria can shape and influence access to and knowledge of resources (physical, financial and social), control of these resources, and perceived or real power within the larger community or society. They may also weaken the capacity of the individual or household to act. Consequently, the relationships between enabling agencies (policy makers), mental health service delivery agencies, and the poor need to function well to support the poor and their capacity to deal with indicators of social vulnerability. If these do not function effectively, both the aspirations and opportunities of the poor will be correspondingly reduced in developing nations. The emphasis and importance of their "coping strategies" to deal with vulnerability or "development" strategies to take advantage of market opportunities will also be negatively affected. The amount of choices available to them will be limited if failures in policies to support them and bad management of resources mean that they are forced to exploit their natural resource base in unsustainable ways. Such consequences will erode the livelihood asset base on which they depend. Vulnerability is all-embracing in Nigeria, affecting everything inside it: the poor, the assets they use, the agencies they deal with, their relationships, and the ways that processes influence those relationships. With good psychological tools, vulnerability factors can be managed and people can be helped to deal with them better.

## Recommendations: Measures to Reduce Social Vulnerability in Africa

Africa is a developing continent prone to a wide variety of natural and man-made hazards and disasters such as floods, hurricanes, earthquakes, tsunamis, droughts, wildfires, plagues, and pollution of the air and water. All of these cause extensive loss to livelihoods and property and claim many lives. It is a continent with a growing population which will continue to increase. Most African countries are poor, ill-equipped and ill-prepared to cope with the impacts of hazards and disasters. At present, disaster management in Africa is largely limited to emergency humanitarian assistance. Reducing disaster risk through preventive measures is a central concern for Africa's sustainable development. It is vitally important that its countries adopt cost-effective policies to lower risk and allocate appropriate resources for hazard and disaster mitigation.

Measures to reduce SV to disaster in Africa are therefore strategies for sustainable development, including measures to eradicate poverty and halt environmental degradation. These are individual or societal capacity or capability-building strategies to mitigate hazards, which require pre- and post-development targeted at access to: educational opportunities, communications and early warning, available means of risk mitigation (social and personal protection), economic surplus available for preparedness, social assets (networks) available for preparedness, and savings and other buffers, as well as social and personal resources for reconstruction and recovery.

Pre- and post-disaster development requires adequate knowledge of the social, economic, demographic, and housing characteristics that influence each community's ability to respond to, cope with, recover from and adapt to environmental hazards. Such knowledge will enhance the formulation of policy advocacy that will center on two main components of hazard risk and vulnerability reduction. The first component will support policies aimed at structural mitigation and the reduction of adverse effects to property using protective measures. The second component will support policies aimed at non-structural mitigation measures focusing on reducing the impacts of disasters through the betterment of those segments of society that are adversely impacted or at a high risk of impact from disaster events.

Furthermore, these strategic measures will necessitate the development of sustainable social protection strategies to guide and coordinate social protection interventions targeted at the poor, the disabled, the aged, children, widows, orphans, and other vulnerable groups in Africa. The strategies will ensure that the livelihoods of these vulnerable groups are secure enough to meet their basic needs and to protect them from the worst impacts of risks and shocks. Such sustainable social protection strategies will include:

- Post-disaster debris removal. Debris created in a disaster poses significant challenges to relief and recovery operations and to a rapid return to normal. Disaster debris needs to be removed from roads, homes, and public facilities before survivors can begin rebuilding normal lives. If in the haste to recover, disaster debris is disposed of improperly, it will cause future hardships for the disaster-affected population. Disasters often destroy physical infrastructure (buildings, roads, bridges) which has taken decades to create. Disaster debris can include: household items, vehicles, and personal possessions; damaged or destroyed buildings, including bricks, broken concrete, reinforcing iron, wood, roofing, electrical wiring and piping; materials from damage to roads, railways and other infrastructure; materials collected in irrigation canals, water ponds, lagoons and rivers; hazardous materials; and sand, gravel, wood, and other vegetative matter transported by disaster agents.

- Technological development. Africa is, in many ways, the continent most in need of scientific knowledge to provide solutions and assist its socio-economic development. However, investment in science, technology, and innovation (STI) is frequently a low priority for decision- and policy-makers, and scientific institutions have relatively weak infrastructures.
- Development of Human and Financial Resources. This is the building of human capital through the establishment of training workshops, outreach and advocacy programs, field workshops for economists and scientists from the continent, the widespread promotion of e-learning and IT application kits at lower levels of education, and establishment of support for young and emerging African scientists in all areas of quaternary research through a committed grants program for attendance at training workshops and meetings.
- Educational development. The scarcity and inaccessibility of knowledge is a key constraint for residents of vulnerable societies. Therefore, increased knowledge generation would necessitate the development and improvement of the education and training sector. This would require huge intellectual and financial resources, as well as political will and commitment, to rectify the situation in vulnerable societies.
- Incorporation of research findings into policies that will facilitate planning guides and training activities at all levels in African society.
- Development of sustainable energy. An increase in access to high-quality, reliable, and affordable energy in a sustainable manner.
- Building resilience strategies to deal with shocks and stresses through information and access to services and facilities, as well as increase of social capital by all stakeholders and partners.
- Improved understanding of the numbers and needs of poor households. Poor households are incapacitated households which have no adults fit to work or have such a high dependency ratio that maintaining the household is virtually impossible. Such households often have many elderly members and children and require long-term welfare support. They are more likely to be vulnerable to shocks and stresses such as HIV and AIDS, droughts and floods, and changes in agricultural policies and volatility in prices, any of which can damage the welfare and productivity of vulnerable households. Their capacity will improve only when the children grow up to become economically active.

## Conclusion

This presentation of the indicators of social vulnerability and sustainable developments contributes to a greater understanding of the nature and level of risks that vulnerable people experience in Nigeria; where these risks come from; who will be the worst affected; what measures are available at all levels to reduce the risks; and what initiatives can be undertaken both locally and internationally to reduce the vulnerability and strengthen the capacities of people at risk.

SV is the exposure of individuals or collective groups to livelihood stress as a result of the impacts of social and environmental climate extremes and climate change. A set of indicators of social vulnerability of any given set of individuals or social situations has been identified. The indicators of individual vulnerability are the incidence of poverty and the risk posed by extreme events to income sources. Changes in collective vulnerability are indicated through changes in the distribution of resources within a population and by institutional changes, which can either enhance security or exacerbate vulnerability.

## Notes

[1] Louis Bockel, Marie Thoreux, and Shelly D. Sayagh, *Resilience of Rural Communities to Climatic Accidents A Need to Scale Up Socio-Environmental Safety Nets (Madagascar, Haiti): Policy Brief* (Rome, Italy: FAO, 2009), 3–4.
[2] David Alexander, *Natural Disasters* (London, UK: Routledge, 2001).
[3] Mark Pelling, ed., *Natural Disasters and Development in a Globalizing World* (London, UK: Routledge, 2003).
[4] John Twigg, *Disaster Risk Reduction, Mitigation and Preparedness in Development and Emergency Programming*. Good Practice Review, Humanitarian Practice Network (HPN) (London, UK: ODI, 2004).
[5] "Anthropogenic Hazard," Wikipedia, December 11, 2013. http://en.wikipedia.org/wiki/Anthropogenic_hazard on 2nd April, 2012.
[6] Courtney G. Flint and E. A. Luloff, "Natural Resource-Based Communities, Risk, and Disaster: An Intersection of Theories," Society and Natural Resources 18(2005), 399–412.
[7] Adeola Balogun, Mustapha Salihu, and Adelani Adepegba, "Many Feared Dead as 20 Bomb Explosions Rock Kano," *Punch*, January 21, 2012, http://www.punchng.com/news/many-feared-dead-as-20-bomb-explosions-rock-kano-%E2%80%A2-police-confirm-7-dead/
[8] Image from "Boko Haram: Nigeria's Terrorist Insurgency Evolves," *Codewit World News*, December 19, 2011, http://www.codewit.com/boko-haram/2707-boko-haram-nigerias-terrorist-insurgency-evolves

[9] Gregg Bankoff, George Frerks, and Dorothea Hilhorst, eds., *Mapping Vulnerability: Disasters, Development and People* (London, UK: Earthscan, 2004).

[10] Kirsten Dow, "Exploring Differences in Our Common Future(s): The Meaning of Vulnerability to Global Environmental Change," *Geoforum* 23(1992), 417–36.

[11] Flint and Luloff.

[12] B. L. Turner II, Roger E. Kasperson, Pamela A. Matson, James J. McCarthy, Robert W. Corell, Lindsey Christensen, et al. "Science and Technology for Sustainable Development Special Feature: A Framework for Vulnerability Analysis in Sustainability Science," *Proceedings of the National Academy of Sciences of the United States of America PNAS* 100(14), 8077.

[13] George E. Clark, Susanne C. Moser, Samuel J. Ratick, Kirstin Dow, William B. Meyer, Srinivas Emani, Weigen Jin, Jeanne X. Kasperson, Roger E. Kasperson and Harry E. Schwarz, "Assessing the Vulnerability of Coastal Communities to Extreme Storms: The Case of Revere, MA., USA," *Mitigation and Adaptation Strategies for Global Change*, 3(1), 59–82.

[14] Lele Zou and Frank Thomalla, *The Causes of Social Vulnerability to Coastal Hazards in Southeast Asia* (Stockholm, Sweden: Stockholm Environment Institute, 2008), 20.

[15] Piers Blaikie, Terry Cannon, Ian Davis, and Ben Wisner, *At Risk* (London: Routledge, 1994), cited in Turner et al., "A Framework for Vulnerability Analysis in Sustainability Science, 100(14), p. 8074.

[16] Ibid.

[17] Health Canada. 2004. Canadian Handbook on Health Impact Assessment. Available online: http://www.hc-sc.gc.ca/ewh-semt/pubs/eval/handbook-guide/

[18] Jürgen Weichselgartner, "Disaster Mitigation: The Concept of Vulnerability Revisited," *Disaster Prevention and Management* 10(2), 85–94.

[19] Susan L. Cutter, Bryan J. Boruff and W. Lynn Shirley, "Social Vulnerability to Environmental Hazards," *Social Science Quarterly* 84(1), 242–61.

[20] Dennis Mileti, *Disasters by Design: A Reassessment of Natural Hazards in the United States* (Washington DC: Joseph Henry Press, 1999); Gilbert F. White and J. Eugene Haas, *Assessment of Research on Natural Hazards* (Cambridge, MA: MIT Press, 1975).

[21] Weichselgartner.

[22] B. L. Turner II, Roger E. Kasperson, Pamela A. Matson, James J. McCarthy, Robert W. Corell, Lindsey Christensen, Noelle Eckley, Jeanne X. Kasperson, Amy Luers, Marybeth L. Martello, et al., "A Framework for Vulnerability Analysis in Sustainability Science," *Proceedings of the National Academy of Sciences of the United States of America* (*PNAS*) 100(14), 8074–9.

[23] Piers Blaikie, Terry Cannon, Ian Davis, and Ben Wisner, *At Risk: Natural Hazards, People's Vulnerability, and Disasters* (London, UK: Routledge, 1994).

[24] Susan L. Cutter, "Vulnerability to Environmental Hazards," *Progress in Human Geography* 20(4), 529–39.

[25] Ian Burton, Robert W. Kates, and Gilbert F. White, *The Environment as Hazard*, 2nd ed. (New York, NY: Guildford Press, 1993).

[26] Douglass C. North, *Institutions, Institutional Change and Economic Performance* (Cambridge, UK: CUP, 1990).
[27] Turner et al.
[28] Robert W. Kates, Christoph Hohenemser, and Jeanne X. Kasperson, *Perilous Progress: Managing the Hazards of Technology* (Boulder, CO: Westview Press, 1985).
[29] Turner et al.
[30] diagram after Turner et al., http://upload.wikimedia.org/wikipedia/en/thumb/5/55/RH_model.svg/350px-RH_model.svg.png
[31] Jack McGraw, review of *Shelter after Disaster*, by Ian Davis, reprinted on the Mass Emergencies Web site, n.d. www.massemergencies.org/v3n4/Davis_Review_v3n4.pdf
[32] Blaikie et al.
[33] Joseph F. St. Cyr, "Review: At Risk: Natural Hazards, People's Vulnerability, and Disasters," *Journal of Homeland Security and Emergency Management* 2(2), Article 4.
[34] Blaikie, Piers, Terry Cannon, Ian Davis, and Ben Wisner, *At Risk: Natural Hazards, People's Vulnerability, and Disasters* (London, UK: Routledge, 1994).
[35] Blaikie et al.
[36] Ibid.
[37] Cutter, "Vulnerability to Environmental Hazards"; Susan L. Cutter, Jerry T. Mitchell, and Michael S. Scott, "Revealing the Vulnerability of People and Places: A Case Study of Georgetown County, South Carolina," *Annals of American Geographers* 90(4), 713–37; The H. John Heinz III Center for Science, Economics and the Environment, *Human Links to Coastal Disasters* (Washington DC: Author, 2002); Burton et al.
[38] Blaikie et al.; Ben Wisner, Piers Blaikie, Terry Cannon, and Ian Davis, *At Risk: Natural Hazards, People's Vulnerability and Disasters*, 2nd ed. (London, UK: Routledge, 2004).
[39] Mary B. Anderson, "Vulnerability to Disaster and Sustainable Development: A General Framework for Assessing Vulnerability," in *Storms* vol. 1, eds. Roger Pielke Jr. and Roger Pielke, Sr., 11–25 (London, UK: Routledge, 2000); Blaikie et al.
[40] Kenneth Hewitt, *Regions of Risk: A Geographical Introduction to Disasters* (Harlow, UK: Longman, 1997); Jeanne X. Kasperson, Roger E. Kasperson, and B. L. Turner II, eds., *Regions at Risk: Comparisons of Threatened Environments* (Tokyo, Japan: United Nations University Press, 1995).
[41] Cutter, Mitchell and Scott;
[42] North.
[43] James G. March and Johan P. Olsen, "Institutional Perspectives on Political Institutions," *Governance: An International Journal of Policy and Administration* 9(3), 247–64.
[44] Jill Quadagno, "Creating the Capital Investment Welfare State: The New American Exceptionalism," *American Sociological Review* 1999 no. 64, 1–11.
[45] Nancy Hooyman and H. A. Kiyak, *Social Gerontology: A Multidisciplinary Perspective* (Boston, MA: Pearson, 2005).

[46] Vern L. Bengtson, Elisabeth O. Burgess, and Tonya M. Parrott, "Theory, Explanation, and a Third Generation of Theoretical Development in Social Gerontology," *Journal of Gerontology, Social Sciences* 1997 no. 52B, 572–88; Steven Sanderson, "Political-Economic Institutions," in *Changes in Land Use and Land Cover: A Global Perspective*, eds. William B. Meyer and B. L. Turner, 329–355 (Cambridge, UK: CUP, 1994).

[47] Michael Thompson, "Security and Solidarity: An Anti-Reductionist Framework for Thinking about the Relationship between Us and the Rest of Nature," *Geographical Journal* 163(2), 141–49; Judith Lorber, *Gender Inequality: Feminist Theories and Politics* (Los Angeles, CA: Roxbury, 2005).

[48] Eudine Barriteau, "Theorizing Gender Systems and the Project of Modernity in the Twentieth-Century Caribbean," *Feminist Review* 1998 no. 59, 186–210.

[49] Cecilia L. Ridgeway and Shelley J. Correll, "Unpacking the Gender System: A Theoretical Perspective on Gender Beliefs and Social Relations," *Gender and Society* 2004 no. 18, 510–531; Mary B. Anderson and Peter J. Woodrow, *Rising from the Ashes: Development Strategies in Times of Disaster* (London, UK: IT Publications, 1998).

[50] Kenneth Hewitt, ed., *Interpretation of Calamity: From the Viewpoint of Human Ecology* (Boston, MA: Allen, 1983).

[51] International Social Security Association (ISSA), *Dynamic Social Security for Asia and the Pacific: The Integral Role of Social Security*, Social Policy Highlight 09, 2009.

[52] United Nations, "World Economic and Social Survey 2007: Development in an Ageing World." 2007; Asian Development Bank (ADB), *Social Protection Strategy* (Manila, Philippines: Author, 2003), http://www.adb.org/Social Protection/strat.asp; Ian Davis, "Social Vulnerability and Capacity Analysis: Report on ProVention Consortium International Workshop, Geneva, May 25–6, 2004," in *Social Vulnerability and Capacity Analysis (VCA): An Overview*, eds. Ian Davis, Bruno Haghebaert and David Peppiatt, 2, Discussion paper presented at the ProVention Consortium Workshop at IFRC Geneva, May 25–6, 2004.

[53] Ian Davis, Bruno Haghebaert, and David Peppiatt, "Social Vulnerability and Capacity Analysis (VCA): An Overview," Discussion paper presented at the ProVention Consortium Workshop at IFRC, Geneva, Switzerland, May 25–6, 2004, p. 9.

[54] Dow.

[55] Cutter, "Vulnerability to Environmental Hazards."

[56] Cutter, Mitchell, and Scott.

[57] A. Evans, M. DeBonis, E. Krasilovsky, and M. Melton, *Measuring Community Capacity to Resist and Repair After Wildfires* (Santa Fe, NM: The Forest Guild, 2007); Walter Gillis Peacock, Betty Hearn Morrow, and Hugh Gladwin, eds. *Hurricane Andrew and the Reshaping of Miami: Ethnicity, Gender, and the Socio-Political Ecology of Disasters* (Miami, FL: Florida International University / International Hurricane Center, 2000).

[58] Michael Masozera, Melissa Bailey, and Charles Kerchner, "Distribution of Impacts of Natural Disasters across Income Groups: A Case Study of New Orleans," *Ecological Economics* 63(2007), 299–306.; Alice Fothergill and L. A.

Peek, "Poverty and Disasters in the United States: A Review of Recent Sociological Findings," *Natural Hazards* 32(1), 89–110; Matthew S. Carroll, Patricia J. Cohn, David N. Seesholtz, and Lorie L. Higgins, "Fire as a Galvanizing and Fragmenting Influence on Communities: The Case of the Rodeo-Chediski Fire," *Society and Natural Resources* 18(2005), 301–20.

[59] Alecia P. Long, "Poverty is the New Prostitution: Race, Poverty, and Public Housing in Post-Katrina New Orleans," *Journal of American History* 94(3), 795–803.

[60] Nicole Dash, Betty Hearn Morrow, Juanita Mainster, and Lilia Cunningham, "Lasting Effects of Hurricane Andrew on a Working-Class Community," *Natural Hazards Review* 8(1), 13–21.

[61] Betty Hearn Morrow and Brenda Phillips, "What's Gender 'Got to Do with It'?" *International Journal of Mass Emergencies and Disasters* 17(1), 5–11.

[62] Susan L. Cutter, "The Forgotten Casualties: Women, Children, and Environmental Change." *Global Environmental Change* 1995 no. 5, 181–94.

[63] Davis, Haghebaert, and Peppiatt.

[64] Alice Fothergill, "Gender, Risk, and Disaster," *International Journal of Mass Emergencies and Disasters*, 14(1), 33–56.; Elaine Enarson and Betty Hearn Morrow, *The Gendered Terrain of Disaster: Through Women's Eyes* (New York: Praeger, 1998); Elaine Enarson, Alice Fothergill, and Lori Peek, "Gender and Disaster: Foundations and Directions," in *Handbook of Disaster Research*, eds. Havidan Rodriguez, Enrico L. Quarantelli, and Russell Dynes, 130–46 (New York, NY: Springer, 2006); Elaine Enarson, "Identifying and Addressing Social Vulnerabilities," in *Emergency Management: Principles and Practices for Local Government*, eds. William L. Waugh Jr. and Kathleen Tierney, 2nd ed., 257–78 (Washington DC: ICMA Press, 2007); Susan M. Bianchi and Daphne Spain, "Women, Work, and Family in America," *Population Bulletin*, 51(3), 1–48; Jerry Buckland and Maitur Rahman, "Community-Based Disaster Management during the 1997 Red River Flood in Canada," *Disasters* 23(2), 174–91.

[65] Hans-Martin Füssel, "Vulnerability: A Generally Applicable Conceptual Framework for Climate Change Research," *Global Environmental Change* 17(2), 155–67; Kent B. Germany, "The Politics of Poverty and History: Racial Inequality and the Long Prelude to Katrina," *Journal of American History* 2007 no. 97, 743–51; Peacock, Morrow, and Gladwin; Alice Fothergill, E. Maestras, and J. D. Darlington, "Race, Ethnicity and Disasters in the U.S.: A Review of the Literature," *Disasters* 23(2),156–73.

[66] R. Bolin, "Race, Class, and Disaster Vulnerability," in *Handbook of Disaster Research*, eds. Havidan Rodriguez, Enrico L. Quarantelli, and Russell Dynes, 113–29 (New York, NY: Springer, 2006); Ehren B. Ngo, "When Disasters and Age Collide: Reviewing Vulnerability of the Elderly," *Natural Hazards Review* 2(2), 80–9.

[67] The H. John Heinz III Center for Science, Economics and the Environment; William A. Anderson, "Bringing Children into Focus on the Social Science Disaster Research Agenda." *International Journal of Mass Emergencies and Disasters* 23(3), 159–75; Brenda D. Phillips and Paul L. Hewett, "Home Alone: Disasters, Mass Emergencies and Children in Self-Care," *Journal of Emergency*

*Management* 3(2), 31–5; Nilamadhab Kar, "Psychological Impact of Disasters on Children: Review of Assessment and Interventions," *World Journal of Pediatrics* 5(1), 5–11; Susan M. Smith, Mary Jane Tremethick, Peggy Johnson, and June Gorski, "Disaster Planning and Response: Considering the Needs of the Frail Elderly," *International Journal of Emergency Management* 6(1), 1–13; Ngo.

[68] Hugh Gladwin and Walter Gillis Peacock, "Warning and Evacuation: A Night for Hard Houses," in *Hurricane Andrew: Ethnicity, Gender, and the Sociology of Disasters*, eds. Walter Gillis Peacock, Betty Hearn Morrow and Hugh Gladwin, (London, UK: Routledge, 1997).

[69] Betty Hearn Morrow, "Identifying and Mapping Community Vulnerability," *Disasters* 23(1), 11–18.

[70] Lisa C. McGuire, Earl S. Ford, and Catherine Okoro, "Natural Disasters and Older US Adults with Disabilities: Implications for Evacuation," *Disasters* 31(1), 49–56.

[71] Gary E. Machlis, Jo Ellen Force, and Randy Guy Balice, "Timber, Minerals and Social Change: An Exploratory Test of Two Resource-Dependent Communities," *Rural Sociology* 55(3), 411–24.

[72] W. Neil Adger, "Sustainability and Social Resilience in Coastal Resource Use," Global Environmental Change Working Paper 97-23, Centre for Social and Economic Research on the Global Environment. University of East Anglia and University College London, 1997.

## Bibliography

Absher, James D., and Jerry. J. Vaske. "Understanding Obstacles to Firewise Implementation." In *The Proceedings of the Human Dimensions of Wildland Fire Conference*. Fort Collins, CO: International Association of Wildland Fire, 2007.

Adger, W. Neil. "Sustainability and Social Resilience in Coastal Resource Use." Global Environmental Change Working Paper 97-23, Centre for Social and Economic Research on the Global Environment. University of East Anglia and University College London. 1997.

Alexander, David. *Natural Disasters*. London, UK: Routledge, 2001.

Anderson, Mary B. "Vulnerability to Disaster and Sustainable Development: A General Framework for Assessing Vulnerability." in *Storms*, vol. 1. Edited by Roger Pielke Jr. and Roger Pielke Sr. 11–25. London, UK: Routledge, 2000.

Anderson, Mary B., and Peter J. Woodrow. *Rising from the Ashes: Development Strategies in Times of Disaster*. London, UK: IT Publications, 1998.

Anderson, William A. "Bringing Children into Focus on the Social Science Disaster Research Agenda." *International Journal of Mass Emergencies and Disasters* 23(3), 159–75.

Asian Development Bank (ADB). *Social Protection Strategy.* Manila, Philippines: Author, 2003. http://www.adb.org/SocialProtection/strat.asp

Bankoff, Gregg, George Frerks, and Dorothea Hilhorst, eds. *Mapping Vulnerability: Disasters, Development and People.* London, UK: Earthscan, 2004.

Barriteau, Eudine. "Theorizing Gender Systems and the Project of Modernity in the Twentieth-Century Caribbean." *Feminist Review* 1998 no. 59, 186–210.

Bengtson, Vern L., Elisabeth O. Burgess, and Tonya M. Parrott. "Theory, Explanation, and a Third Generation of Theoretical Development in Social Gerontology." *Journal of Gerontology, Social Sciences* 1997 no. 52B, 572–88.

Bianchi, Susan M., and Daphne Spain. "Women, Work, and Family in America." *Population Bulletin*, 51(3), 1–48.

Blaikie, Piers, Terry Cannon, Ian Davis, and Ben Wisner. *At Risk: Natural Hazards, People's Vulnerability, and Disasters.* London, UK: Routledge, 1994.

Bockel, Louis, Marie Thoreux, and Shelly D. Sayagh. *Resilience of Rural Communities to Climatic Accidents A Need to Scale Up Socio-Environmental Safety Nets (Madagascar, Haiti): Policy Brief.* Rome, Italy: Food and Agriculture Organization of the United Nations (FAO), 2009.

Bolin, R. "Race, Class, and Disaster Vulnerability." In *Handbook of Disaster Research.* Edited by Havidan Rodriguez, Enrico L. Quarantelli, and Russell Dynes. 113–29. New York, NY: Springer, 2006.

Buckland, Jerry, and Maitur Rahman. "Community-Based Disaster Management during the 1997 Red River Flood in Canada." *Disasters* 23(2), 174–91.

Burton, Ian. "Vulnerability and Adaptive Response in the Context of Climate and Climate Change." *Climatic Change* 36(1997), 185–96.

Burton, Ian, Robert W. Kates, and Gilbert F. White. *The Environment as Hazard.* 2nd ed. New York, NY: Guildford Press, 1993.

Busso, Gustavo. "Vulnerabilidad social: nociones e implicancias de políticas para Latinoamérica a inicios del siglo XXI." Paper Presented at the International Seminar on the Different Expressions of the Social Vulnerability in Latin America and the Caribbean. Santiago, Chile, 20–21 June, 2001.

Bustamante, Jorge A. [on the Vulnerability of Migrants as Subjects of Human Rights]. United Nations Working Paper E/CN.4/AC.46/1998/

5 October 8, 1998. http://www.unhchr.ch/Huridocda/Huridoca.nsf/0/ d3305c8038efc08a802566c0004f1581?Opendocument
Carroll, Matthew S., Patricia J. Cohn, David N. Seesholtz, and Lorie L. Higgins. "Fire as a Galvanizing and Fragmenting Influence on Communities: The Case of the Rodeo-Chediski Fire." *Society and Natural Resources* 18(2005), 301–20.
Clark, George E., Susanne C. Moser, Samuel J. Ratick, Kirstin Dow, William B. Meyer, Srinivas Emani, Weigen Jin, Jeanne X. Kasperson, Roger E. Kasperson and Harry E. Schwarz. "Assessing the Vulnerability of Coastal Communities to Extreme Storms: The Case of Revere, MA., USA." *Mitigation and Adaptation Strategies for Global Change*, 3(1), 59–82.
Cutter, Susan L. "The Forgotten Casualties: Women, Children, and Environmental Change." *Global Environmental Change* 1995 no. 5, 181–94.
—. "Vulnerability to Environmental Hazards." *Progress in Human Geography* 20(4), 529–39.
—. "A Research Agenda for Vulnerability Science and Environmental Hazards." *IHDP Update, Newsletter on the International Human Dimensions Programme on Global Environmental Change.* 2001. cited in The Vulnerability of Science and the Science of Vulnerability. Retrieved online from http://webra.cas.sc.edu/hvri/pubs/2003_TheVulnerabilityofScience.pdf
Cutter, Susan L., Lindsey Barnes, Melissa Berry, Christopher Burton, Elijah Evans, Eric Tate, and Jennifer Webb. "A Place-Based Model for Understanding Community Resilience to Natural Disasters." *Global Environmental Change* 18(4), 598–606.
Cutter, Susan L., Bryan J. Boruff and W. Lynn Shirley. "Social Vulnerability to Environmental Hazards." *Social Science Quarterly* 84 (1), 242–61.
Cutter, Susan L., Jerry T. Mitchell, and Michael S. Scott. "Revealing the Vulnerability of People and Places: A Case Study of Georgetown County, South Carolina." *Annals of American Geographers* 90(4), 713–37.
Dash, Nicole, Betty Hearn Morrow, Juanita Mainster, and Lilia Cunningham. "Lasting Effects of Hurricane Andrew on a Working-Class Community." *Natural Hazards Review* 8(1), 13–21.
Davis, Ian. "Social Vulnerability and Capacity Analysis: Report on ProVention Consortium International Workshop, Geneva, May 25–6, 2004." In Davis, Haghebaert and Peppiatt, p. 2.

Davis, Ian, Bruno Haghebaert, and David Peppiatt. "Social Vulnerability and Capacity Analysis (VCA): An Overview." Discussion paper presented at the ProVention Consortium Workshop at IFRC Geneva, May 25–6, 2004.

Dow, Kirsten. "Exploring Differences in Our Common Future(s): The Meaning of Vulnerability to Global Environmental Change. *Geoforum* 23(1992): 417–36.

Enarson, Elaine. "Identifying and Addressing Social Vulnerabilities." In *Emergency Management: Principles and Practices for Local Government.* Edited by William L. Waugh Jr. and Kathleen Tierney. 2nd ed. 257–78. Washington DC: ICMA Press, 2007.

Enarson, Elaine, Alice Fothergill, and Lori Peek. "Gender and Disaster: Foundations and Directions." In *Handbook of Disaster Research.* Edited by Havidan Rodriguez, Enrico L. Quarantelli and Russell Dynes. 130–46. New York, NY: Springer, 2006.

Enarson, Elaine, and Betty Hearn Morrow. *The Gendered Terrain of Disaster: Through Women's Eyes.* New York: Praeger, 1998.

Evans, A., M. DeBonis, E. Krasilovsky and M. Melton. *Measuring Community Capacity to Resist and Repair After Wildfires.* Santa Fe, NM: The Forest Guild, 2007.

Flint, Courtney G., and E. A. Luloff. "Natural Resource-Based Communities, Risk, and Disaster: An Intersection of Theories." Society & Natural Resources 18(2005), 399–412.

Fothergill, Alice. *Heads above Water: Gender, Class, and Family in the Grand Forks Flood.* Albany, NY: SUNY, 2004.

—. "Gender, Risk, and Disaster." *International Journal of Mass Emergencies and Disasters*, 14(1), 33–56.

Fothergill, Alice, E. Maestras, and J. D. Darlington. "Race Ethnicity and Disasters in the U.S.: A Review of the Literature." *Disasters* 23(2), 156–73.

Fothergill, Alice, and L. A. Peek. 2004. "Poverty and Disasters in the United States: A Review of Recent Sociological Findings." *Natural Hazards* 32(1), 89–110.

Füssel, Hans-Martin. "Vulnerability: A Generally Applicable Conceptual Framework for Climate Change Research." *Global Environmental Change* 17(2), 155–67.

Germany, Kent B. "The Politics of Poverty and History: Racial Inequality and the Long Prelude to Katrina." *Journal of American History* 2007 no. 97, 743–51.

Gladwin, Hugh, and Walter Gillis Peacock. "Warning and Evacuation: A Night for Hard Houses." In *Hurricane Andrew: Ethnicity, Gender, and the Sociology of Disasters*. Edited by Walter Gillis Peacock, Betty Hearn Morrow and Hugh Gladwin. pg 65. London, UK: Routledge, 1997.

Gómez, José Javier. *Vulnerabilidad y medio ambiente*. Santiago, Chile: Economic Commission for Latin America and the Caribbean (ECLAC), 2001.

H. John Heinz III Center for Science, Economics and the Environment, The. *Human Links to Coastal Disasters*. Washington DC: Author, 2002.

Health Canada. 2004. Canadian Handbook on Health Impact Assessment. Available online: http://www.hc-sc.gc.ca/ewh-semt/pubs/eval/handbook-guide/

Hewitt, Kenneth. *Regions of Risk: A Geographical Introduction to Disasters*. Harlow, UK: Longman, 1997.

—., ed. *Interpretation of Calamity: From the Viewpoint of Human Ecology*. Boston, MA: Allen, 1983.

Hooyman, Nancy, and H. Asuman Kiyak. *Social Gerontology: A Multidisciplinary Perspective*. Boston, MA: Pearson, 2005.

International Social Security Association (ISSA). *Dynamic Social Security for Asia and the Pacific: The Integral Role of Social Security*, Social Policy Highlight, 09. 2009.

Kar, Nilamadhab. "Psychological Impact of Disasters on Children: Review of Assessment and Interventions." *World Journal of Pediatrics* 5(1), 5–11.

Kasperson, Jeanne X., Roger E. Kasperson, and B. L. Turner II, eds. *Regions at Risk: Comparisons of Threatened Environments*. Tokyo, Japan: United Nations University Press, 1995.

Kasperson, Jeanne X., Roger E. Kasperson, Nick Pidgeon, and Paul Slovic. "The Social Amplification of Risk: Assessing Fifteen Years of Research and Theory." in *The Social Amplification of Risk*. Edited by N. F. Pidgeon, Roger E. Kasperson, and P. Slovic. 13–46. Cambridge, UK: CUP, 2003.

Kates, Robert W., Christoph Hohenemser and Jeanne X. Kasperson. *Perilous Progress: Managing the Hazards of Technology*. Boulder, CO: Westview Press, 1985.

Kumagai, Yoshitaka, Matthew S. Carroll, and Patricia Cohn. "Coping with Interface Wildfire as a Human Event: Lessons from the Disaster/Hazards Literature." *Journal of Forestry* 102(6), 28–32.

Leong, Karen J., Christopher A. Airriess, Angela Chia-Chen Chen, Verna M. Keith, Wei Li, Ying Wang, and Karen Adams. 2007a. "From Invisibility to Hypervisibility: The Complexity of Race, Survival, and

Resiliency for the Vietnamese-American Community in Eastern New Orleans." In *Through the Eye of Katrina: Social Justice in the United States*. Edited by Kristin A. Bates and Richelle S. Swan. 169–85. Durham, NC: Carolina Academic Press, 2007.

Leong, Karen J., Christopher A. Airriess, Wei Li, Angela Chia-Chen Chen, and Verna M. Keith. "Resilient History and the Rebuilding of a Community: The Vietnamese-American Community in New Orleans East." *Journal of American History* 94(3), 770–9.

Long, Alecia P. "Poverty is the New Prostitution: Race, Poverty, and Public Housing in Post-Katrina New Orleans." *Journal of American History* 94(3), 795–803.

Lorber, Judith. *Gender Inequality: Feminist Theories and Politics*. Los Angeles, CA: Roxbury Publishing, 2005.

Machlis, Gary E., Jo Ellen Force, and Randy Guy Balice. "Timber, Minerals and Social Change: An Exploratory Test of Two Resource-Dependent Communities." *Rural Sociology* 55(3), 411–24.

March, James G., and Johan P. Olsen. "Institutional Perspectives on Political Institutions." *Governance: An International Journal of Policy and Administration* 9(3), 247–64.

Masozera, Michael, Melissa Bailey, and Charles Kerchner. "Distribution of Impacts of Natural Disasters across Income Groups: A Case Study of New Orleans." *Ecological Economics* 63(2007), 299–306.

McGuire, Lisa C., Earl S. Ford, and Catherine Okoro. "Natural Disasters and Older US Adults with Disabilities: Implications for Evacuation." *Disasters* 31(1), 49–56.

Mileti, Dennis. *Disasters by Design: A Reassessment of Natural Hazards in the United States*. Washington DC: Joseph Henry Press, 1999.

Morrow, Betty Hearn. *Community Resilience: A Social Justice Perspective*. The Community and Regional Resilience Initiative Research Report 4. 2008. Available at: http://www.resilientus.org/library/FINAL_MORROW_9-25-08_1223482348.pdf

—. "Identifying and Mapping Community Vulnerability." *Disasters* 23(1), 11–18.

Morrow, Betty Hearn, and Brenda Phillips. "What's Gender 'Got to Do With It'?" *International Journal of Mass Emergencies and Disasters* 17(1), 5–11.

Ngo, Ehren B. "When Disasters and Age Collide: Reviewing Vulnerability of the Elderly." *Natural Hazards Review* 2(2), 80–9.

North, Douglass C. *Institutions, Institutional Change and Economic Performance*. Cambridge, UK: CUP, 1990.

Peacock, Walter Gillis, Betty Hearn Morrow, and Hugh Gladwin, eds. *Hurricane Andrew and the Reshaping of Miami: Ethnicity, Gender, and the Socio-Political Ecology of Disasters.* Miami, FL: Florida International University / International Hurricane Center, 2000.

Peacock, Walter Gillis, and Kathleen Ragsdale. "Social Systems, Ecological Networks and Disasters." *Hurricane Andrew: Ethnicity, Gender and the Sociology of Disasters.* Walter Gillis Peacock, Betty Hearn Morrow, and Hugh Gladwin. New York, NY: Routledge, 1997.

Peguero, Anthony A. "Latino Disaster Vulnerability." *Hispanic Journal of Behavioral Sciences* 28(1), 5–22.

Pelling, Mark, ed. *Natural Disasters and Development in a Globalizing World.* London, UK: Routledge, 2003.

Phillips, Brenda D. and Paul L. Hewett. "Home Alone: Disasters, Mass Emergencies and Children in Self-Care." *Journal of Emergency Management* 3(2), 31–5.

Quadagno, Jill. "Creating the Capital Investment Welfare State: The New American Exceptionalism." *American Sociological Review* 1999 no. 64, 1–11.

Ridgeway, Cecilia L., and Shelley J. Correll. "Unpacking the Gender System: A Theoretical Perspective on Gender Beliefs and Social Relations." *Gender and Society* 18(2004), 510–31.

Rhodes, Alan, and Sam Reinholtd. "Beyond Technology: A Holistic Approach to Reducing Residential Fire Fatalities." *The Australian Journal of Emergency Management*, 13(1), 39–45.

Sanderson, Steven. "Political-Economic Institutions." In *Changes in Land Use and Land Cover: A Global Perspective.* Edited by William B. Meyer and B. L. Turner. 329–355. Cambridge, UK: CUP, 1994.

Smith, Susan M., Mary Jane Tremethick, Peggy Johnson, and June Gorski. "Disaster Planning and Response: Considering the Needs of the Frail Elderly." *International Journal of Emergency Management* 6(1), 1–13.

St. Cyr, Joseph F. "Review: *At Risk: Natural Hazards, People's Vulnerability, and Disasters*," *Journal of Homeland Security and Emergency Management* 2(2), Article 4. http://www.geo.mtu.edu/volcanoes/06upgrade/Social-KateG/Attachments%20Used/AtRiskReview.pdf.pdf

Thompson, Michael. "Security and Solidarity: An Anti-Reductionist Framework for Thinking about the Relationship between Us and the Rest of Nature." *Geographical Journal* 163(2), 141–49.

Trujillo, Monica, Amado Ordonez, and Rafael Hernandez. *Risk-Mapping and Local Capacities: Lessons from Mexico and Central America.* Oxford: Oxfam, 2000.

Trujillo-Pagán, Nicole. "Katrina's Latinos: Vulnerability and Disasters in Relief and Recovery." In *Through the Eye of Katrina: Social Justice in the United States.* Edited by Kristin A. Bates and Richelle S. Swan. 147–68. Durham, NC: Carolina Academic Press, 2007.

Turner II, B. L., Roger E. Kasperson, Pamela A. Matson, James J. McCarthy, Robert W. Corell, Lindsey Christensen, Noelle Eckley, Jeanne X. Kasperson, Amy Luers, Marybeth L. Martello, et al. "A Framework for Vulnerability Analysis in Sustainability Science." *Proceedings of the National Academy of Sciences of the United States of America (PNAS)* 100(14), 8074–9. www.pnas.org_cgi_doi_10.1073_pnas.1231335100

Twigg, John. *Disaster Risk Reduction, Mitigation and Preparedness in Development and Emergency Programming.* Good Practice Review, Humanitarian Practice Network (HPN). London, UK: Overseas Development Institute (ODI), 2004.

United Nations Disaster Relief Organization. *Preliminary Study on the Identification of Disaster-prone Countries Based on Economic Impact.* Geneva, Switzerland: Author, 1990.

United Nations. "World Economic and Social Survey 2007: Development in an Ageing World." 2007. http://www.unngls.org/site/article.php3?id_article=296

United Nations. *World Population Ageing 2007.* New York, NY: United Nations Department of Social and Economic Affairs, Population Division, 2007. www.un.org/esa/population/publications/WPA2007/wpp2007.htm

Weichselgartner, Jürgen. "Disaster Mitigation: The Concept of Vulnerability Revisited." *Disaster Prevention and Management* 10(2), 85–94.

White, Gilbert F. and J. Eugene Haas. *Assessment of Research on Natural Hazards.* Cambridge, MA: MIT Press, 1975.

Wisner, Ben, Piers Blaikie, Terry Cannon, and Ian Davis. *At Risk: Natural Hazards, People's Vulnerability and Disasters.* 2nd ed. London, UK: Routledge, 2004.

Zou, Lele, and Frank Thomalla. *The Causes of Social Vulnerability to Coastal Hazards in Southeast Asia.* Stockholm, Sweden: Stockholm Environment Institute, 2008. http://www.sei-international.org/mediamanager/documents/Publications/Sustainable-livelihoods/social_vulnerability_coastal_hazards_thomalla.pdf

# CHAPTER FOURTEEN

# SOCIAL VULNERABILITY AND RESILIENCE IN LAGOS MEGACITY AND IBADAN URBAN FRINGE, NIGERIA

## ADETOKUNBO OLUWOLE ILESANMI

### Introduction

This study explores the issues of vulnerability and resilience framed in the case study contexts of Lagos megacity and the urban fringe of Ibadan, Nigeria. With more than half of the world's population living in urban areas, the twenty-first century has been described as "the urban century".[1] The majority of the world's population lives not just in cities, but in "megacities"—contiguous urbanized areas with populations above 10 million people.[2] In this league are Tokyo, New York City, Mexico City, Mumbai, São Paulo, Delhi, Shanghai, Kolkata, Dhaka, Buenos Aires, Los Angeles, Karachi, and Rio de Janeiro.[3] Megacities, as contemporary products of global urbanization, represent both spaces of opportunity and spaces of risk and potential disasters.

The paradox of megacities is that they simultaneously offer the sophisticated benefits of urbanity and the grimmest challenges of human security. They symbolize the apex of human ingenuity and creativity, accommodating most of the world's superlative mega-structures—the tallest and largest. Ironically, these vibrant urban settings also serve as tense hosts to a variety of vices: crime, violence, unemployment, poor infrastructure, and exposure to natural disasters; and they generate a complex diversity of processes that produce and exacerbate risks. Whether and to what degree these risks turn into disasters depends on the vulnerability of the exposed system and population. The capacity to anticipate or cope with risks, or to resist and recover from the impact of hazards, is determined not only as a direct function of the event but also in the context of increasing social inequality and poverty.[4]

A unique feature of the global urban trend is that more of the largest cities are now in the developing world; only a handful are in industrialized countries. By the end of the last century, the world's twenty most populous cities had switched from having a Euro-American focus to a developing world bias within a period of twenty years. Megacities in the developing nations are therefore particularly critical, given their size, pace of growth, high population density, social inequality and poverty.[5] Their vulnerabilities relate to natural hazards, environmental degradation, inadequate housing, and lack of access to basic services.

The first case-study—Lagos—is used to explore megacity vulnerability factors, particularly how the megacity contributes to the effects of environmental fragility on particular social groups. In the second case-study, the vulnerability implications of urbanization on the urban fringe areas of Ibadan will be examined. In the developing world, a large and growing proportion of the population lives in or around metropolitan areas, including the "urban fringe".[6] The current upsurge in sub-urbanization trends makes the urban fringe an area of unique interest and a topical issue in urban debates.[7]

By the year 2025, 61 percent of the world's population will be urban, most megacities will be in the "south clusters", and about 85 percent of these developments will occur in urban fringes.[8] Unlike the relatively fashionable notion of suburbs in the urban literature of developed nations, studies reveal a contrary view of the nature of urban fringes in developing countries.[9] Urban fringes are highly vulnerable to risks, similar to the city itself, and are potential zones of vulnerability due either to a lack of dependable formal institutions or the absence or failure of urban governance. Two pertinent research questions arise: what are the factors of vulnerability associated with the urban fringe, and what are the informal sector responses to the failures of urban governance?

Both case studies contribute to the understanding of how environmental, infrastructural, and institutional risk factors interact with social and economic factors to create unique forms of vulnerability and resilience. A conceptual overview in the next section is followed by the analysis of and discussions based on the case studies. Conclusions are drawn regarding reducing vulnerability and increasing resilience in the megacity and the urban fringe.

## Conceptual Overview

### Vulnerability and Resilience

The term "vulnerability" has varied meanings among distinct groups: academia, disaster-management agencies, and the climate change community.[10] Adger, however, identifies three key factors in defining vulnerability: the *exposure* to perturbation or external stresses, the *sensitivity* to perturbation, and the *capacity* to adapt to and/or cope with these.[11] Contemporarily, the concept of vulnerability implies that disasters do not simply result from natural processes, but rather are social products. Hansjürgens, Heinrichs and Kuhlicke trace its origin to two distinct but overlapping research areas: (a) hazard research and (b) poverty and development research.[12] However, researchers in developing countries have found the hazard paradigm less appropriate. They stress the need to acknowledge the political-economic context more rigorously in analyzing the conditions that reduce the ability of people and places to respond to environmental threats.[13] The focus becomes not just the hazard, but the production of vulnerable conditions. Wisner, Blaikie, Cannon and Davis thus distinguished between root causes, dynamic pressure, and unsafe conditions that put pressure on individuals and households.[14] This "livelihood approach" focuses on the assets and resources (physical, ecological, political, social and financial) of individuals and households that can be applied in dealing with a wide range of risks. The more assets people control, the less vulnerable they are, as assets increase their capacities to cope.[15]

Vulnerability has also been viewed as the predisposition of an element, system or community to be affected by or susceptible to damage; it is the internal risk factor, while hazards are the external risk factor.[16] Vulnerability results from three factors: *physical fragility or exposure*—susceptibility of settlements to be affected by natural or social phenomena due to location in hazard-prone areas; *socio-economic fragility*—predisposition to suffer harm due to marginalization, social segregation or poverty; and *lack of resilience*—the limitations of access to resources and the incapacity to absorb the impact of disaster.

Resilience refers to the capacity of a system to absorb disturbances and reorganize while undergoing change so as to retain essentially the same function, structure and identity.[17] Resilience has also been defined with specific applications to *social* systems; *natural and built* environments; and *social-ecological* systems.[18] Urban resilience refers to the degree to which cities are able to tolerate alteration before reorganizing around a new set of structures and processes. The concept of urban resilience describes a society that is flexible enough to adjust to uncertainty and capitalize on the positive opportunities that the future may bring.[19] Resilience Alliance defines resilience as: the amount of change a system can undergo and still retain the same controls on function and structure; the degree to which the system is capable of self-organization; and the ability to build and increase the capacity for learning and adaptation.[20] Resilience may relate to an urban system as a whole, or the specific resilience of components of the system. Cities need to be resilient to present challenges and future threats of natural hazards, disasters, terrorism, climate change, or economic or political instability.

Vulnerability and resilience are closely related concepts: one refers to persistence and sustainability, the other to the capacity to withstand and adapt. Resilience is often seen as the intrinsic ability of a system, element, or community to resist the impact of a natural or social event—the ability not to be affected by the event in the first place. Others consider resilience as the ability of the system or element to absorb the impact and cope with it successfully. Both notions infer a reciprocal relationship: a more vulnerable system should be less resilient, and a system is less vulnerable if it is more resilient. Addressing vulnerability conditions improves the capacity to respond and adapt, thus supporting the system's resilience.

*Megacities, Vulnerability and Resilience*

The conventional approach to defining megacities is the population size: usually a threshold of 10 million people. UN-Habitat adds the category of cities with 20 million inhabitants.[21] Another definition combines population and functional primacy, while a third approach relates to the "global city" or "world city", focusing on the city's nodal role and prominence in the global economic network.[22]

Hansjürgens et al. suggest that current definitions fail to reveal explicitly the specific conditions of megacities with respect to the production of and exposure to risks, so as to permit an analysis of social vulnerability.[23] They propose that the phenomenological conditions that turn megacities into distinct "places of risk" are their sheer size, the speed at which they experience change, and their complexity. An appropriate definition will therefore integrate the elements of size/scale, speed, and complexity as shaping megacity-specific vulnerabilities.

With specific reference to megacities in developing nations, a transformation of the urbanization process has been experienced in recent decades, producing different urban forms and social concerns. The massive dimensions, scale, and global connectedness of megacities, juxtaposed with a local disconnectedness, make them a new urban form. In contrast with the case when accelerated urbanization began in Western Europe and North America, this phenomenon is most notable in countries with the lowest levels of economic development rather than the highest. Megacities in developing countries host some of the poorest groups of people, often living in high-risk areas or crowded into slums at the edges of booming urban areas.[24]

Vulnerabilities of megacities assume a unique nature because, according to UN-Habitat, thirteen of the world's megacities, including Lagos, are situated along coastlines and are therefore vulnerable to catastrophic flooding due to rising sea levels.[25] Meanwhile, the importance of port cities in international trade has grown significantly, particularly in developing countries, as the volume of sea trade has more than doubled in the last three decades.[26] Port cities have therefore grown not only in terms of population but also in terms of asset value; hence the significance of their vulnerability.

Generally, megacity living offers some benefits: economic opportunities, better quality of life, easier access to basic services, and rich cultural diversity.[27] With increasing globalization-induced social polarization, however, the proportions of marginalized populations excluded from these benefits are increasing. These people are vulnerable to the effects of economic, social and political insecurity, exploitation, health crises, food insecurity, environmental pollution, and natural hazards. Their livelihoods are jeopardized by their informal legal status, which impedes their labor, tenure and political rights (formal/informal nexus); their poor living environment, which particularly affects their housing and health (social/ecological nexus); and their dependence on the cash economy, which makes them extremely susceptible to price rises and financial crises (global/local nexus).[28]

A contrasting (but increasingly accepted) view on megacities is that they also offer unique opportunities for increasing human security and enabling communities to buffer various types of shocks without the loss of livelihoods—a new quality of social resilience.[29] Far from being "mega-problem cities", megacities may be viewed as "laboratories" in which solutions for new urban challenges can be developed. The perception of megacities thus shifts from "global risk areas" towards "engines of global change" and resilient socio-ecological systems with a sustainable future.[30] In formulating a framework for vulnerability analysis in megacities, four vital processes that influence social vulnerability of megacity populations were identified as: inclusion/exclusion of citizens; coordination/synchronization; attraction/exposure; and resources intake/outflow.[31]

## *Urban Fringe, Vulnerability, and Resilience*

A growing proportion of populations in developing nations lives in the "urban fringe", which refers to the border zone between urban and rural landscapes, and is often a conflict zone that lies outside the corporate existence of the city and incorporates a hybrid of rural and urban features.[32] Given the persistent spate of urbanization trends in many developing countries, fringe areas are asserting greater influence on cities as either viable zones for regional economic development or zones of conflicts and vulnerability. Their growth may represent either an opportunity (they serve as buffers for future urban development) or a risk (their spread eats into rural farmlands and open spaces). The notable theoretical constructs on urban growth have evolved primarily in the context of American cities. Onokerhoraye and Omuta identified three classical theories of urban structure—concentric, sector and multiple nuclei—to explain urban land-use patterns.[33] In spite of the existence of these theoretical generalizations, no specific theory is known to address urban fringe issues.

The experience of cities in the developing world, which follow a different pattern from the classical models, makes a case for theoretical reversal. Many of these were pre-industrial cities, which were primarily administrative or religious centers in which the central area was the place of residence of the ruling elite, with the poor living in the city's fringe zones. Here, social class is invisibly related to distance from the center of the city. Vulnerability and resilience are important concepts in global change research.[34] Turner suggests that the two constitute different but complementary framings.[35] Vulnerability is associated with the weakest parts of systems prone to disturbances, while resilience represents the systemic characteristics that make systems more robust and able to manage disturbances.

Conceptualizing urban fringe development as an inherently dynamic process within social and ecological systems, the level of vulnerability will increase in direct proportion to the reduced level of resilience from the urbanization processes. The socio-spatial dialectic of interrelationships between people and physical and social environments infers that, as people work and live in urban space, they gradually impose themselves on the environment, modifying and adjusting it to suit their needs. Vulnerability is a vital aspect of urban fringe morphogenesis: as communities are created, maintained and modified, the values, attitudes and behavior of the inhabitants are simultaneously influenced by their surroundings. The vulnerability and resilience of the urban fringe can therefore be conceptualized within the context of man-environment interaction and the ability of individuals and social groups residing in this zone to respond, cope with, recover from, and adapt to external stress placed on their livelihoods and well-being by urbanization processes. Due to their proximity to the city, fringe areas experience much of the impact of urbanization processes. Moreover, the population pressure on them means that resources in such zones are often overexploited. Heterogeneous in social composition, urban fringe areas often accommodate a diversity of populations, especially lower-income groups that are particularly vulnerable to negative externalities of both rural and urban systems, such as risks to health, physical hazards related to occupying unsuitable sites, lack of access to basic services, and poor housing conditions. Environmental changes also impinge upon the livelihood strategies of these communities in terms of their limited access to different types of capital. Recent studies emphasize the importance of local assessments of vulnerability to capture the diversity in the social, economic and natural environment of communities.[36] Understanding vulnerability and resilience therefore requires localized studies that can help find specific answers to questions about *who* and *what* are vulnerable, what are they vulnerable to, how vulnerable they are, the causes of their vulnerability, and what responses can lessen their vulnerability.

## Case Study 1: Lagos Megacity

Lagos megacity—with its several slums, squatter settlements and marginalized coastal communities—reflects the three established vulnerability tensions. This section describes the context and positions the case study within the conjunction of the three tensions. Although Lagos, according to Mabogunje, is undeniably the only megacity in Nigeria, a few other urban centers—Kano, Port Harcourt, Ibadan and Kaduna—are already showing indications of growth towards megacity status.[37] Using the example of Lagos, early recognition could ensure that the challenges associated with megacities are addressed before they become too complex or costly.

### *Lagos: Historical, Physical, Social, Economic Characteristics*

The coastal city of Lagos, situated within 6°23'N and 6°41'N (lat.) and 2°42'E and 3°42'E (long.), is Nigeria's most rapidly urbanizing and populous conurbation (see Figure 14.1). Its growth has been phenomenal, demographically and spatially: from a population of about 25,000 in 1866, it grew to 300,000 in 1950, 665,000 by 1963 and over ten million in 2010, attaining the status of a megacity according to the UN definition. Although population figures are widely disputed, the UN projects a figure of 12.4 million by 2015.[38] The 2006 census figure for the metropolitan area of Lagos was 7.9 million, which, based on an annual growth rate of 6 percent, indicates that the population will reach about 12.7 million in 2015. The state government, however, regards the census figures as under-counted, claiming a population of over 17 million.[39] Lagos exemplifies the cities of the global south, which face an escalating crisis of inadequate provision of basic services. The striking irony is that the vast demographic explosion has occurred in a context of economic decline, portraying "the paradoxical characteristics of the contemporary African city as a dysfunctional yet dynamic urban form."[40]

Figure 14.1. Map of Nigeria Showing the States (Lagos and Oyo States Highlighted).

City conditions have been deteriorating since the post-independence euphoria of the early 1960s, through the era of the 1990s when Lagos assumed the dubious distinction of being regarded as one of the world's worst cities, up to its present transitional state. The history of Lagos in the closing decades of the twentieth century was marked by severe deterioration in quality of life: proliferation of slums; environmental degradation; congested roads; flooding; disrupted sewage networks; and increasing crime rates.[41] In terms of spatial expansion, from its original lagoon setting, the sprawling city has engulfed a vast expanse of surrounding areas, including over 100 different slums. The vitality of Lagos's economy and its nodal position in the national economy and transport networks explain its growth, despite the breakdown of many basic infrastructure services and the difficulties this has caused for both economic enterprises and individual residents.[42]

The genesis of Lagos' present dysfunctions has been traced to the failure of successive colonial administrations to tackle the problems of overcrowding, disease, and inadequate urban infrastructure, as well as the associated strategy of segregation between wealthy enclaves and the supposedly indifferent indigenous populations.[43] This, in part, led to the devastating public health crises that culminated in the bubonic plague outbreaks of the 1920s, the establishment of the Lagos Executive Development Board (LEDB), and subsequent clearance-driven urban renewal efforts. The immediate post-independence era was also characterized by inadequate technical and administrative expertise for the city's management and haphazard expansion.[44]

Two dominant approaches to analyzing the Lagos phenomenon have been identified.[45] First is an eschatological evocation of urban apocalypse, characterized by poverty, violence, disease, uncontrolled growth, lack of access to basic services, massive unemployment, and infrastructural collapse.[46] The second approach describes the novelties of the city's morphology, conceiving the seemingly chaotic aspects of its growth as a series of self-regulatory systems. Rather than focus on the shortcomings, it celebrates "the continued, exuberant existence of Lagos and other cities like it", and the "ingenious, alternate systems" which they generate.[47]

An alternate perspective has been offered which attempts to frame the experience of Lagos within a wider geopolitical arena of economic instability, petro-capitalist development, and regional internecine conflicts.[48] This historical view reveals how structural factors militated against any effective resolution to the city's worsening infrastructure crisis. The causative factors of the crisis are elucidated through a succession of urban evolutionary phases. The first phase—*colonial Lagos*—was characterized by "incomplete modernity" due to the inherited bifurcated systems of urban administration. The second phase—the *post-colonial metropolis*—evidenced initial optimism, with subsequent descent into despair as an already unstable urban system deteriorated under the combined pressures of political instability, accelerated rates of migration and the destabilizing effects of oil wealth, exacerbated by the 1967–70 civil war. Lagos, which at independence was the leading industrial center of Nigeria, from the mid-1970s onwards suffered from accelerating industrial decline. The forty-two slum communities or "blighted areas" identified in Lagos metropolis in 1981 by a World Bank Urban Renewal project have increased to about 100 due to the inadequacy of formal housing.[49] The genesis of these extensive slums has been linked to the city's failed industrialization strategy: they represent intense concentrations of human labor for which the promise of work and prosperity never materialized.[50] The third phase saw a succession of military regimes, interspersed with the global recession of the early 1980s, leading by the late 1990s to a near-complete breakdown in the public realm, pervasive political and economic crises and massive infrastructural collapse. The introduction of the structural adjustment programs intensified the spread of poverty, causing declining levels of public investment and many abandoned projects.[51] Lagos has largely developed independently of the efforts of city planners, through a process of "amorphous urbanism".[52] The colonial state apparatus and its postcolonial successors failed to establish a fully functional metropolis through investment in the built environment or the construction of integrated technological networks.

About 70 percent of the population live in slums, the majority being located in the oldest settled areas of mainland Lagos and in marshy areas near the lagoons.[53] Between eight and ten families live in single structures, sharing kitchen and sanitation facilities. Whilst facing the threats and challenges of poverty, violence, insecurity, unemployment, disease and poor infrastructure, Lagos continues to grow exponentially.[54] Moreover, Lagos experiences extreme weather events with increasing frequency, while its low-lying nature puts it at further risk from flooding, aggravated by inadequate refuse- and waste-disposal systems. The physical and social impacts of the floods include damage to roads and household properties, dirty environments, infrastructural damage, homelessness, lack of potable water, and the prevalence of malaria and other diseases.[55]

The summary of these qualitative data depict Lagos as a largely spontaneous evolution of uncoordinated and incremental assemblage of structures which gradually spread across all available space. It is in this milieu of social and infrastructural crisis, accentuated by the effects of global climate change, that its social vulnerabilities become highly visible.

***Vulnerability Analytical Framework***

The framework of Hansjürgens et al. is adapted in the analysis of the Lagos case study. The analysis reveals the presence of four identified processes, to varying degrees.[56]

*Inclusion/exclusion of citizens*: the slum dwellers and squatters who represent the majority of the megacity's inhabitants have relatively little entitlement to resources of health care, public infrastructure, legal rights, and tenure security to land and housing. Their shelters are at risk of sudden demolition and are generally ill-equipped to cope with natural hazards. In addition, many of the low-income people for whom the social housing schemes were initially designed have been marginalized and excluded by higher-income earners. The attention of the public housing agency—Lagos State Development and Property Corporation (LSDPC)— is now diverted to building for medium- and high-income earners for profit.

*Coordination/synchronization*: Lagos megacity has borne the brunt of political rivalry and lack of coordination between the federal and state governments, for example, with respect to the security of the fast-receding Atlantic coastline and the polluting effects of abandoned shipwrecks along the seashore. Notwithstanding the efforts of the National and State Emergency Relief Agencies, mitigation and rescue plans during past cases of local building collapses, the Lagos Armory explosion, petrol tanker and pipe-line explosions, and incessant flooding have not evidenced a coherent, optimal, horizontally integrated strategy among the relevant agencies.[57]

*Attraction/exposure*: large multitudes that migrate into endangered, flood-prone coastal settlements due to inaccessibility to land in better locations become exposed and vulnerable.[58] Lagos, like many African cities, lacks the infrastructure to withstand extreme weather conditions. Poor urban planning and urban governance challenges contribute to making urban slum dwellers the most at-risk population. Despite the environmental challenge posed by flooding due to storm surges and heavy rainstorms, which is exacerbated by urban development, the vulnerability of the urban poor has not been adequately considered in urban planning.

*Resources intake/outflow*: three valid cases are: (1) the large volume of pollutants and industrial waste discharged into the lagoon; (2) the inadequate sewage discharge and disposal systems for majority of the urban informal settlements; and (3) the pressure on land that has resulted in extensive reclamation works which invariably deplete the fauna and flora.

In terms of the "who", "where", and "when" of vulnerability, it was found that the poor homeless and low-income majority, particularly the frail elderly, disabled, women, and street children, are the most vulnerable to urban shocks. They are located in the many slums and squatter settlements in the core and particularly in the coastal peripheries and are most prone to floods, pipeline explosions and related hazards in the wet and dry seasons respectively.

***Tensions of Megacity Vulnerability and Resilience***

Attempts to capture the megacity's complexity, its vulnerability to varying disasters and stresses, and its capacity to be resilient could assume a combination of three approaches: the megacity shapes and is being shaped by processes on the global and the local scale, in formal-informal spheres, and within the socio-ecological system.[59]

*(a) Global-local.* Issues associated with megacities exist at several levels: the community, district, city, the megacity itself and beyond. Situations that appear to have a primarily local relevance can also have an impact at the global level. For example, the recent fatal floods in Lagos warranted the declaration of a holiday for workers and students in the state, with the attendant effects on commercial, economic, and international travel networks, inferring a wider scope of vulnerability than the immediate source of the hazard.[60]

*(b) Formal-informal.* The informal sector is growing and securing the livelihoods of multitudes in megacities of developing countries.[61] For the urban poor, informality, insecurity, and thus vulnerability are closely related.[62] On the one hand, the informality of these populations makes them more vulnerable to exploitation, state arbitrariness, and exposure to environmental hazards. On the other hand, they are not forced to rely primarily on the formal elements of urban governance. Informal activities are often more dynamic, flexible, and better able to cope with disturbances. This rapid adaptive capacity generates the opportunity for greater resilience in megacities. Lee, however, views the formality/informality nexus not as two polar extremes, but as a continuum of economic, social, and political processes at different stages and spatial levels.[63] Analysis of vulnerabilities and resilience in megacities cannot treat formal and informal elements as separate categories; there are always multiple linkages which can be strengthened in order to reduce vulnerability (e.g., through participatory governance and improved labor rights).[64]

*(c) Socio-ecological.* Megacities as dynamic systems require resources and energy to survive and meet the needs of their populations. Although the interrelation between the natural environment and the population is not as clear in a megacity as it is in a smaller city, because ecosystems in megacities are not very visible, a megacity is not self-contained; rather, it needs to be served by its surrounding ecosystem. This highlights the man-made nature of some risks and the need to consider social issues in building resilience.

## Case Study 2: The Urban Fringe of Ibadan

Nigeria has witnessed a drastic transition from rural to urban-oriented economies, accompanied by the increasing mobility of large segments of the population and economic activities to the urban fringes of major cities. Due to the urban bias of the nation's development policies, these zones experience much of the impact of the urbanization processes.[65] This second case study examines the vulnerability implications of urbanization on the urban fringe areas of Ibadan. Based on the literature and ongoing research, it analyzes the historical, physical, and social characteristics of Ibadan and traces the urbanization pattern and morphological transformation of the metropolis in the pre- and post-colonial eras in order to identify the vulnerability factors associated with the sprawling trend of urbanization.

### *Ibadan: Historical, Physical, Social and Economic Characteristics*

Ibadan, the capital of Oyo State, is Nigeria's second largest city, with a population of about 3.3 million people.[66] It is an inland city built on a ridge, with altitudes of 150 to 275 meters.[67] At longitude 7°2' and 7°40'E and latitude 3°35' and 4°10'N, Ibadan was founded in 1829 as a war camp, one of the new generation of fortified towns which emerged due to the pervading insecurity in Yorubaland in the nineteenth century. Initially occupied by immigrant warriors from Oyo, Ife, and Ijebu who moved into the city in search of security from the intra-Yoruba war (1825–1893) and the military jihad originating from the Sokoto Sultanate, it is now the largest indigenous city in tropical Africa. Ibadan is 128 km northeast of Lagos and 345 km southwest of Abuja, the federal capital.

Ibadan was originally a forest site with several ranges of hills that offered strategic defense opportunities. It began as a military city-state which became a large empire from the 1860s to the 1890s and was appropriately nicknamed *idi Ibon*, "butt of a gun", because of its unique military character. It emerged as a marketing center for traders and goods from both the forest and grassland areas. The economy of Ibadan primarily rested on agriculture, trade (slaves, palm oil, yams, and kola for export; shea butter, salt, horses, and weapons as imports) and craft (weapons, smithery, cloth, ceramics). The colonial period reinforced the position of Ibadan in the Yoruba urban network. After an initial boom in the rubber business (1901–1913), cocoa became the main produce of the region, attracting foreign firms and local traders whose activities embraced both the import of manufactured articles and the export of local agriculture produce.[68] The north-bound railway which reached Ibadan in 1901 and the convergence of Lagos-north road traffic made it a major center for bulk trade.

Centrally located and accessible from the then-capital city (Lagos), Ibadan became the headquarters of the Western Region in 1952. This change involved a substantial transfer of political power from the British Colonial Office to the nationals and led to a rapid expansion in the number of government buildings.[69] The city has grown, particularly through the establishment of institutions and the construction of transport networks. The founding of University College in 1948, which later became the premier University of Ibadan, and the establishment of University College Hospital—then the only teaching hospital in Nigeria—enhanced the city's importance. Ibadan has witnessed rapid growth in both area and population. From a built-up area of less than 40 km$^2$ in 1950, it had spread to over 400 km$^2$ by 2000.[70] Similarly, its estimated population of 60,000 in 1856 was 200,000 by 1890, 625,000 in 1963, almost 2 million by 2000, and is now about 3.3 million.[71]

Inter-city expressways and internal ring roads have generated an urban sprawl that encroaches into neighboring rural areas. The convergence of major trade routes on Ibadan, coupled with the railway and an expressway from Lagos, accelerated the city's growth. These stimulated growth in commerce and employment opportunities.[72] Following the introduction of the Structural Adjustment Program (SAP) in 1986, which was intended to encourage foreign investments, limit imports, and promote export-oriented industries, there was an increase in informal economic sector activities in Ibadan. A major change in the occupational structure involved the development of small-scale craft and petty trading activities, two activities which account for the increase in the informal sector employment and manifest urban poverty in the city.

The SAP-induced economic crisis and the decrease of public funds radically changed the city's social and physical landscapes, causing the general decay of urban infrastructure and social services. These had a strong impact on the emergence of slums based on the conjunction of two major factors: growing poverty on the one hand and an increase in property market and rental housing on the other, due partly to the relatively high price of building materials. The Ibadan-Lagos expressway encouraged many Lagos-based workers to live in cheaper housing in Ibadan. This new influx had a significant influence on the property market as demand rose, giving estate agents and landlords the opportunity to push up rents, which in turn lead the urban poor to find rooms in the cheapest areas, the inner city and the urban fringe slums.

## Morphological Transformation

Until 1970, Ibadan was the largest city in sub-Saharan Africa. The total area of the city was estimated at approximately 103.8 km$^2$ in 1952, with only 36.2 km$^2$ built up, the remaining 67 km$^2$ being devoted to non-urban uses such as farmlands, floodplains, forest reserves, and water bodies. These "non-urban land uses" largely disappeared in the 1960s: an aerial study in 1973 revealed that the urban landscape had spread over about 100 km$^2$. The developed land increased from only 12.5 km$^2$ in 1931 to 112 km$^2$ in 1973, 136 km$^2$ in 1981, 210–240 km$^2$ in 1988–89, and 400km$^2$ by the year 2000.[73] Overall, the built-up area during the latter half of the twentieth century multiplied ten-fold. In the 1980s the Ibadan-Lagos expressway generated the greatest urban sprawl (on the east and north), followed by the Eleiyele expressway (on the west), spreading the city further into neighboring local government areas.[74] Measured from the central business district, Ibadan had sprawled out to a radius of 12–15 km along the primary roads.

# Discussion

## Vulnerability-Based Definition of Megacities

This study adopted a definition of megacity for the analysis of vulnerability, based on the elements of size/scale, speed, and complexity. Using these phenomenological elements permits a more systematic view of the dynamic interaction between the material and social in mega-urban areas and a rediscovery of the mutual dependency of the human-environment system.[75] The approach views society and nature not as opposing entities but as interconnected spheres, and tries to understand vulnerability as a holistic concept, rooted in both natural and social systems. By no longer focusing simply on one physical trigger or the social production of vulnerable conditions, it becomes possible to develop a more systematic view of the dynamics of megacities and plan appropriate disaster-preparedness measures.

## Vulnerability, Urban Governance, Social Capital, Diversity and Resilience

Using the framework of Hansjürgens et al. in the analysis of the Lagos case study provided a deeper understanding of social vulnerability and its distribution across time, space, and social status.[76] It also highlights the crucial role of urban governance—both as problem and solution—in determining vulnerability and in mitigating or adapting to risks.[77] "Poor" governance performance, in terms of the failure to manage basic urban services such as the provision of efficient transport systems, affordable housing, water supply, sanitation, or regulation of pollution-generating industries, can create a hazardous situation for citizens and intensify vulnerability. Governance deficits are particularly obvious when inadequate response to risk events turns them into disasters. Thus, appropriate and adequate governance and well-designed strategies for both mitigation and adaptation are indispensable in the effort to limit vulnerability. The essential components of a resilience-strengthening agenda include: adaptation-enhancing information tailored to the conditions of vulnerable groups; improving the general coping capacities of affected people through access to services; and improving social capital in a context of lack of financial and physical capital.

The issue of social capital makes local community-based organizations crucial in reducing vulnerability. Megacities agglomerate people of diverse backgrounds, knowledge, and cultural heritage, engaging them in formal and informal social interaction and discourse. Within this context, megacities offer vast opportunities for groups of people to examine the risks they face and develop collective actions to manage these. Such actions are evident across the world in grassroots citizen efforts to combat environmental degradation, crime, and environmental shocks such as floods. Perhaps the greatest potential of megacities is the people inhabiting them—their social capital and social diversity—providing the ability to shape the risks they face together and giving an informal face to urban governance.

The Lagos example reveals that the very crisis of Lagos is the womb of its resilience: despite the exponential population growth and dearth of infrastructure, it continues to thrive. The largely informal populace seems to have invented an "ingenious alternative system" with which to deal with the myriads of challenges.[78] This inherent resilience that has enabled Lagos to survive in the face of adversity may be a source of lessons for other developing nations' cities. The strong resilience is perhaps based on the high levels of informality and social capital within the city. Resolution of the challenges of megacities may therefore hinge on the appreciation of the human scale and the avoidance of reactionary policies such as demolitions, repressive regulation of informal activities, and displacement of poor people by "mega-projects".

Vulnerability and resilience issues are often culture-specific, demanding the need to understand much more about the customs, cultural perceptions, needs, and resources of local communities to reduce risk in megacities. The re-emergence of democratic structures in Nigeria, for example, holds great potential for the rebirth of strategic policy-making, planning, and effective implementation. Lagos in particular is on the verge of a radical transformation. What is required is a strategy to transform the problem of the megacity into the potential success it can become. This demands the recognition of the complex and multi-faceted nature of the problems which need to be tackled in context: changing the burgeoning megacity into a sustainable city without injuring its social, cultural, and ecological dimensions.

### *Urbanization-Based Vulnerability Factors*

The issues germane to the discussion of the Ibadan case study, which also represent the factors of vulnerability identified as being associated with its urban fringe, are as follows: informal sector activities, proliferation of slums, inadequate water supply and waste management, vulnerability to flooding, and deficiencies in urban governance.

**Informal sector activities.** One of the most significant consequences of the structural adjustment programs and austerity measures instituted in the mid-1980s—arising partially from the diminished role of government vis-à-vis employment and social services—is the proliferation of informal sector economic activities outside of the formal market structure. This gave rise to a conceptual dichotomy between formal and informal sectors of the economy. Despite Nigeria's overall record of urban growth during the decades of reform, social disparities between urban and rural areas remained wide—a key driving force behind the large tide of suburbanization. Other authors have addressed the phenomenon of the informal sector in greater detail.[79] Of greater relevance, however, are the aspects of the informal sector that impact the urban fringe landscape and expose it to various risks.

The informal activities of Ibadan's urban fringe cover an array of activities characterized by heavy reliance on family or friends for capital to improve business and a relatively large proportion of low-level education.[80] Informal settlements are the principal features of the urban fringe landscape, many of which are not well integrated with the rest of the city. Groups of urban fringe migrants often aggravate existing socio-spatial segregation. On the other hand, some new migrants choose to live in ethnic- or economic-based clusters to help maintain previously established social relations networks and assert their group identity. They bring with them informal channels for the flow of capital, skills and social connections that can improve their economic opportunities and living experiences in the city.

**Proliferation of slums.** Ibadan has a large proportion of slums and poor informal settlements on the fringes, mainly because accommodation in the city has been priced beyond what many citizens can afford.[81] Poverty proliferates, and successive governments have not adequately addressed the issue of slums. Three types of slum have been identified according to their age, location, and size.[82] The oldest slum is the core area of the city, which covers the entire pre-colonial town. The second type is the small-scale slums and squatter settlements found at the margins of the city on illegally occupied land. The third category consists of the numerous slums along major roads or close to local labor markets, generally occupied by tenants on legal lands found on the fringes of the city. Their size, history, and socio-economic and cultural features differ from one to another. Our interest is in the latter two types, which are situated in the urban fringe areas and are of more recent origin. The development of unplanned urbanization along the major roads from the 1970s to the 1990s has resulted in notable slums in the north, east, and south of the city. Thirty percent of the derelict houses in Ibadan are found in the fringes of the city at more than 5 kilometers from the center: for example, Agbowo, close to the university and inhabited by students and junior staff of the university; Ojoo, a mixed Hausa-Yoruba settlement founded in the mid-1970s around the main transit market on the Lagos-Kano Road; and Sasa, another Hausa-Yoruba settlement close to the International Institute of Tropical Agriculture.[83]

**Inadequate water supply.** Ibadan is characterized by inadequate water supply. Water production is reported to be 107 million liters per day and is supplied principally from reservoirs on the Eleiyele and Asejire Rivers.[84] A recent project appraisal found that about 25 percent of the population have access to a "safe water supply"; unaccounted-for water (UFW) is reported to be more than 70 percent; while average daily hours of supply is four. Adeniji and Ogundiji give water access data for two informal settlements, Mapo (in the city center) and Apete (a peri-urban slum): in Mapo, about 68 percent of households used well water, about 4 percent drew their water from a communal standpipe; and about 4 percent depended on water vendors.[85] In Apete, about 91 percent used well water and the rest depended on boreholes, streams, rain water and/or water vendors.

**Inefficient sanitation and waste management.** Sanitation provision in Ibadan is grossly deficient: most people lack access to a hygienic toilet, and large amounts of fecal waste are discharged into the environment without adequate treatment. This is likely to have major impacts on the burden of infectious disease and on the quality of life. Waste generation in the city includes solid, liquid and industrial waste. Although the exact figures of solid waste generated are difficult to determine, it is generally agreed that enormous quantities are generated daily. Residential land use accounted for the bulk (70.1 percent) of the solid waste generated, followed by commercial land use (18.8 percent) and industrial land use (9.7 percent).[86]

The metropolis also faces dire challenges with the management of liquid waste. Except for micro-systems serving institutions such as the University College Hospital and private estates, there is no available evidence of formal sewerage or wastewater treatment systems in Ibadan. Fecal waste is disposed of largely by means of septic tanks, pit latrines and buckets, with the attendant risks of subterranean and ground-water pollution and public health hazards. In middle- and high-income areas, most households have pit latrines or septic tanks. In many low-income settlements, open defecation on refuse tips and wastelands or into open drains is reported to be widespread. In addition, toilets discharging directly to open drains are reported to be common.[87] Sanitation access data for Mapo and Apete indicate that in Mapo, about 54 percent of households had a flush toilet and 41 percent a pit latrine, while in Apete, about 97 percent had pit latrines.[88] The uncontrolled disposal of waste, especially in the unplanned fringe areas, poses serious health hazards. The unwholesome environment forces the populace to spend appreciable portions of their low income and time on improving their personal health, with adverse consequences for general economic well-being.[89]

Industries in Ibadan also generate a lot of toxic chemical waste and ash, but the exact quantities have not been measured. Due to the relatively high cost and shortage of land in the city core and the ineffective implementation of land-use planning, many industries are located in the fringe areas side-by-side with residential land uses. While some of these make private arrangements for disposal of their waste, others simply allow waste to discharge with little or no monitoring. The risk of ground-water pollution is rife, as companies fail to take proper precautions at disposal sites to ensure proper sanitary conditions.

The apparent failure of many programs for waste disposal in Ibadan has led to a continuous shift in responsibilities between agencies and the various tiers of government, as well as prompting some degree of privatization. The Environmental Protection Commission (EPC), the state arm of the Federal Environmental Protection Agency (FEPA), is involved in the physical execution of both the Ibadan Flood Control/Storm Drainage and the Ibadan Waste Management components of the World Bank-assisted Oyo State Urban Project. The EPC has identified new sanitary landfill sites mainly on the fringes, such as along the major roads entering Ibadan from Oyo, Iwo, Abeokuta, Old Lagos, Olojuoro, Akanran, and Ife.

In the absence of institutionalized waste-disposal facilities (or the unwillingness of people to use the few available), people employ various methods to dispose of their waste, with severe repercussions for the environment. The illegal dumping of refuse in open spaces, along roads, and in open gutters blocks drains and sewer holes. Refuse is usually burned in households, depots, and disposal sites, causing environmental pollution. Burning and disposing of ashes in drainage channels and open dumps, often unauthorized and with little chance of being cleared, is the preferred method of many inhabitants of the fringe areas. The large number of markets in Ibadan, the preponderance of street trading, and the unguided increase in informal sector activities contribute extensively to the invasion of all available spaces by petty traders who block access roads, thus increasing the generation of waste and complicating collection mechanisms. On a positive note, the introduction of monthly environmental sanitation days in the mid-1980s, an initiative that has been sustained by successive civilian governments, has increased people's participation in waste management.

***Vulnerability to flooding.*** Major river floods have caused severe damage in Ibadan, and flooding remains a potential risk in spite of efforts to channel the major Ogunpa River. There is no established institutional support for people who are affected by floods, as evidenced by recent city-wide flooding in July and August 2011, which forced whole communities to evacuate homes. Thousands of buildings were devastated and there were hundreds of fatalities (see Figures 14.2 and 14.3).

Figure 14.2. Floods in an Apete Neighborhood in Ibadan.[90]

Figure 14.3. Wreckage of Connecting Bridge and Queue on a Temporary Timber Bridge.[91]

*Deficiencies in urban governance.* Given governments' low level of investment in the informal sector, workers in this sector are perpetually marginalized, unable to contribute meaningfully to urban development, which makes resilience-building an uphill task. However, the people still endeavor to develop informal arrangements of maintaining social relations in the urban fringe. They try to bridge the social gap through local networks such as residents' and landlords' associations. There is also the problem of jurisdictional conflicts between local, state and federal agencies.

With existing infrastructure either in a state of decay or not expanding quickly enough to accommodate growing populations, the pace and quality of life in much of the urban fringe is often appalling. In some fringe communities, the suburban system reflects ethnic and income segregation mirroring urban socio-economic structures. There has been an increase in the number of non-natives establishing themselves in the fringe, thus complicating the dynamics of immigrant and indigenous cultures. Balancing this trend is the building of resilience, which largely depends on local social networks, mostly in informal settings.

The challenge of increasing resilience and reducing vulnerability in urban fringe areas is essentially a developmental issue. The fringe is highly vulnerable to various risks that could be anticipated from development processes and could be prevented through adequate planning. Since the informal sector constitutes the bulk of the economy, urban renewal projects cannot afford to ignore it. This necessitates participatory approaches to urban planning, development and governance, in order to reduce vulnerability, increase resilience, and improve quality of life in the urban fringe.

## Conclusion

This study explored the issues of vulnerability and resilience through the review of relevant literature, contextualized in the case studies of the megacity of Lagos and the urban fringe of Ibadan, Nigeria. The Lagos context assumed a definition of megacities which integrates size/scale, speed, and complexity, as these relate to vulnerabilities specific to megacities. The study highlighted how the megacity may represent either a space of opportunity or of risk and potential disasters. It also identified three tensions related to social vulnerability—the global/local, formal/ informal and social/ecological—examining Lagos within these coordinates.

The Ibadan context revealed the pertinent factors of vulnerability associated with the urban fringe. The challenge of mainstreaming risk and vulnerability in fringe areas is highly relevant to many developing countries with large informal sectors characterized by the failure of the state in urban governance. Given the accelerating pace of suburbanization and dynamics of social, economic, cultural, and political change, local social networks in fringe areas need to be strengthened. Local actors such as landlords, youth movements, and residents' associations may contribute a lot in building resilience and reducing the risks of disasters.

In attempting to push the frontiers of research concerning vulnerability-reduction and resilience-building, this study highlights the need to appropriate the diversity and human scale of megacities and social capital in urban fringes. Beyond analyzing individual case-studies, collaboration and partnership appears to be the key to building local resilience and reducing vulnerability. Future research should increasingly appreciate the multi-disciplinary character of vulnerability and resilience issues as reflected in the involvement of experts with backgrounds as diverse as architecture, ecology, economics, engineering, epidemiology, geography, hydrology, political science, sociology, and urban planning. It is imperative that the frameworks for coordinating international research efforts on vulnerability, resilience, and related concepts should be intensified in the pursuit of a more sustainable urban future.

## Notes

[1] UN-Habitat, *State of the World's Cities 2008/2009: Harmonious Cities* (London, UK: Earthscan, 2008).
[2] Doreen Massey, John Allen, and Steve Pile, eds., *City Worlds* (London and New York: Routledge, 1999); Frauke Kraas, "Megacities and Global Change: Key Priorities," *Geographical Journal* 173(1), 79–82.
[3] UN-Habitat, 2008, 6.

[4] Piers Blaikie, Terry Cannon, Ian Davis and Ben Wisner, *At Risk: Natural Hazards, People's Vulnerability and Disasters* (London, UK: Routledge, 1994).

[5] David Satterthwaite, ed., *The Earthscan Reader in Sustainable Cities* (London, UK: Earthscan, 1999).

[6] John O. Browder, James R. Bohland, and Joseph L. Scarpaci, "Patterns of Development on the Metropolitan Fringe—Urban Fringe Expansion in Bangkok, Jakarta and Santiago," *Journal of the American Planning Association* 61(3), 310–27.

[7] Richard E. Stren, "Urban Governance in Developing Countries: Experiences and Challenges," in *Governing Cities in a Global Era: Urban Innovation, Competition and Democratic Reform*, eds. Robin Hambleton and Jill Gross, 57–70 (New York, NY: Palgrave Macmillan, 2007).

[8] UN-Habitat, 2008.

[9] Véronique Dupont, *Peri-Urban Dynamics—Population, Habitat and Environment on the Peripheries of Large Indian Metropolises* (New Delhi, India: French Research Institutes, 2005).

[10] Juan Carlos Villangran de Leon, *Vulnerability: A Conceptual and Methodological Review*, SOURCE Publication Series of UNU-RHS, no.4 (Bonn, Germany: UNU Institute for Environment and Human Security, 2006).

[11] W. Neil Adger, "Vulnerability," *Global Environmental Change* 16(3), 268–81.

[12] Bernd Hansjürgens, Dirk Heinrichs, and C. Kuhlicke, "Mega-Urbanization and Social Vulnerability," in *Megacities: Resilience and Social Vulnerability*, eds. Hans-Georg Bohle and Koko Warner, SOURCE Publication Series of UNU-RHS, No. 10, 20–28 (Bonn, Germany: UNU Institute for Environment and Human Security, 2008).

[13] Susan L. Cutter, "Presidential Address: The Vulnerability of Science and the Science of Vulnerability," *Annals of American Geographers* 93(1), 1–12.

[14] Ben Wisner, Piers Blaikie, Terry Cannon, and Ian Davis, *At Risk: Natural Hazards, People's Vulnerability and Disasters*, 2nd ed. (London, UK: Routledge, 2004).

[15] Adger.

[16] Omar D. Cardona, "The Need for Rethinking the Concepts of Vulnerability and Risk from a Holistic Perspective: A Necessary Review and Criticism for Effective Risk Management," in *Mapping Vulnerability, Disasters, Development and People*, eds. Greg Bankoff, George Frerks, and Dorothea Hilhorst, 37–51 (London, UK: Earthscan Publications, 2004).

[17] Brian C. Walker, S. Holling, Stephen R. Carpenter, and Ann Kinzig, "Resilience, Adaptability and Transformability in Social–Ecological Systems," *Ecology and Society* 9(2), Article 5.

[18] Mark Pelling, *The Vulnerability of Cities. Natural Disasters and Social Resilience* (London, UK: Earthscan, 2003).

[19] Resilience Alliance, *A Research Prospectus for Urban Resilience: A Resilience Alliance Initiative for Transitioning Urban Systems Towards Sustainable Future* (Canberra, Australia: CSIRO Australia / Arizona State University / Stockholm University, 2007).

[20] Resilience Alliance, "Resilience," October 29, 2002, http://www.resalliance.org/576.php
[21] UN-Habitat, 2008.
[22] J. V. Beaverstock, R. G. Smith, and P. J. Taylor, "A Roster of World Cities," *Cities* 16(6), 445–58.
[23] Hansjürgens et al.
[24] Mike Davis, *Planet of Slums* (London, UK: Verso, 2006); Ian Douglas, Kurshid Alam, Maryanne Maghenda, Yasmin Mcdonnell, Louise Mclean, and Jack Campbell, "Unjust Waters: Climate Change, Flooding and the Urban Poor in Africa," *Environment and Urbanization* 20(1), 187–205; Gavin W. Jones and Pravin Visaria, *Urbanization in Large Developing Countries–China, Indonesia, Brazil and India* (Oxford, UK: Clarendon Press, 1997).
[25] UN-Habitat, 2008, 140.
[26] World Bank, *World Development Report, 2004: Making Services Work for People* (Washington DC: Author, 2004).
[27] Kraas.
[28] Sheilah Meikle, "The Urban Context and Poor People," in Rakodi and Lloyd-Jones, 37–51; Carole Rakodi and Tony Lloyd-Jones, eds., *Urban Livelihoods: A People-Centered Approach to Reducing Poverty* (London, UK: Earthscan, 2002); UN-Habitat, *Planning Sustainable Cities* (London, UK: Earthscan, 2009).
[29] Kraas.
[30] Resilience Alliance, 2007.
[31] Hansjürgens et al.
[32] Browder et al.
[33] Andrew G. Onakerhoraye and Gideon E. D. Omuta, *City Structure and Planning for Africa* (Benin City, Benin: The Benin Social Science Series, 1994).
[34] Kraas; Oran R. Young, "Institutional Dynamics: Resilience, Vulnerability and Adaptation in Environmental and Resource Regimes," *Global Environmental Change* 20(3), 378–85.
[35] B. L. Turner, "Vulnerability and Resilience: Coalescing or Paralleling Approaches for Sustainability Science?" *Global Environmental Change* 20(4), 570–6.
[36] Lilibeth Acosta-Michlik, Ulka Kelkar, and Upasna Sharma, "A Critical Overview: Local Evidence on Vulnerabilities and Global Environmental Change in Developing Countries," *Global Environmental Change* 18(4), 539–542.
[37] A. L. Mabogunje, "Reconstructing the Nigerian City: The New Policy on Urban Development and Housing," in *The City in Nigeria: Perspectives, Issues, Challenges and Strategies*, eds. Dolapo Amole, Ayo Ajayi, and Afolabi Okewole, 1–9 (Ile-Ife, Nigeria: Obafemi Awolowo University, 2002).
[38] UN-Habitat, *The State of African Cities 2010: Governance, Inequality and Urban Land Markets* (London, UK: Earthscan, 2010).
[39] Lagos State, *Household Survey, 2010 Edition* (Lagos Bureau of Statistics, Ministry of Economic Planning and Budget, the Secretariat, Alausa, Ikeja 2010).
[40] Matthew Gandy, "Planning, Anti-Planning and the Infrastructure Crisis Facing Metropolitan Lagos," *Urban Studies* 43(2), 374.

[41] Catherine Kehinde George, "Challenges of Lagos as a Mega-City," *AllAfrica*, February 10, 2010.

[42] Josephine Olu Abiodun, "The Challenges of Growth and Development in Metropolitan Lagos," in *The Urban Challenge in Africa: Growth and Management of Its Large Cities*, ed. Carole Rakodi, 192–222 (New York, NY: United Nations University Press, 1997).

[43] Ayodeji Olukoju, *Infrastructure Development and Urban Facilities in Lagos, 1861–2000* (Ibadan, Nigeria: Institut Francais dc Recherche en Afrique, 2003); Margaret Peil, *Lagos: The City Is the People* (London, UK: Belhaven, 1991).

[44] M. A. O. Ayeni, "Living Conditions of the Poor in Lagos," *EKISTICS*, 43(255), 77–80.

[45] Matthew Gandy, "Learning from Lagos," *New Left Review* 2005 no. 33, 36–52.

[46] George Packer, "The Megacity," *The New Yorker*, November 13, 2006; Pep Subiros, "Lagos: Surviving Hell," in *Africas: The Artist and the City*, 34–45 (Barcelona, Spain: Centre de Cultura Contemporania de Barcelona, 2001).

[47] Rem Koolhaas, Stefano Boeri, Stanford Kwinter, Nadia Tazi, and Hans-Ulrich Obrist, *Mutations* (Barcelona, Spain: Actar, 2001), 652.

[48] Gandy, 2006.

[49] Ibidun O. Adelekan, "Vulnerability of Poor Urban Coastal Communities to Climate Change in Lagos, Nigeria," paper presented at the Fifth Urban Research Symposium on Cities and Climate Change, Marseilles, France, June 28–30, 2009.

[50] Davis; UN-Habitat, *The Challenge of Slums* (London, UK: Earthscan, 2004).

[51] Adepoju G. Onibokun and Adetoye Faniran, *The Impact of Structural Adjustment on Housing, Environment and Urban Productivity in Nigeria* (Ibadan, Nigeria: CASSAD, 1995).

[52] Gandy, "Planning…".

[53] World Bank, "Project Appraisal Document: Lagos Metropolitan Development and Governance Project." June 7, 2006.

[54] Gandy, 2005.

[55] UN-Habitat, 2008.

[56] Hansjürgens et al.

[57] "Toll in Blast at Nigeria Armory Exceeds 1,000," *New York Times*, February 3, 2002; Patrick Sakdapolrak, Carsten Butsch, R. L. Carter, M.-D. Cojocaru, Benjamin Etzold, Nanda Kishor, Carmen Lacambra, Marquesa L. Reyes, and Saut Sagala, "The Megacity Resilience Framework," in *Megacities: Resilience and Social Vulnerability*, eds. Hans-Georg Bohle and Koko Warner, 10–19, SOURCE Publication Series of UNU-RHS no.10. (Bonn, Germany: UNU Institute for Environment and Human Security, 2008).

[58] Adelekan.

[59] Sakdapolrak et al.

[60] Joshua Bassey, Feyisipo, Austin Imhonlele, and Oluyinka Alawode, "Lagos Rains Kill 10 as Experts Predict More Downpour," *Businessday Online*, July 12, 2011.

[61] Meikle

[62] P. W. Daniels, "Urban Challenges: The Formal and Informal Economies in Mega-Cities," *Cities* 21(6), 501–11.

[63] Roger Lee, "Informal Sector," in *The Dictionary of Human Geography*, ed. Ron E. A. Johnston. 390–3 (Oxford, UK: Blackwell, 2000).
[64] Daniels
[65] Robert W. Taylor, "The Policy Context," in *Urban Development in Nigeria*, ed. Robert W. Taylor, 13–24 (Aldershot, UK: Avebury, 1993).
[66] Thomas Brinkhoff, *City Population: Population Statistics for Countries, Administrative Areas, Cities and Agglomerations—Interactive Maps—Charts*. n.d.
[67] Adepoju G. Onibokun and A. J. Kumuyi, "Ibadan, Nigeria," in *Managing the Monster: Urban Waste and Governance in Africa*, ed. Adepoju G. Onibokun, 49–100 (Ottawa, Canada: International Development Research Centre, 1999).
[68] A. L. Mabogunje, *Cities and African Development* (Ibadan, Nigeria: OUP, 1977).
[69] Ibid.
[70] Laurent Fourchard, "Urban Slums Reports: The Case of Ibadan, Nigeria," *Understanding Slums: Case Studies for the Global Report on Human Settlements*, UN-Habitat, 2003.
[71] Brinkhoff.
[72] Mabogunje, 1977.
[73] Onibokun and Kumuyi.
[74] Fourchard.
[75] Dorothea Hilhorst, "Complexity and Diversity: Unlocking Social Domains of Disaster Response," in *Mapping Vulnerability: Disasters, Development and People*, eds. Greg Bankoff, George Frerks, and Dorothea Hilhorst, 52–66 (London, UK: Earthscan, 2004).
[76] Hansjürgens et al.
[77] Pelling
[78] Koolhaas et al., 652.
[79] S. I. Abumere, B. C. Arima, and T. A. Jerome, *The Informal Sector in Nigeria's Development Process* (Canberra, Australia: Development Policy Centre, 1998).
[81] Grace Adeniji and Bukola Ogundiji, "Climate Adaptation in Nigerian Cities: Regularizing Informal and Illegal Settlements in Ibadan," paper presented at the Fifth Urban Research Symposium on Cities and Climate Change, Marseilles, France, June 28–30, 2009.
[82] Fourchard.
[83] Abumere.
[84] Grace Adeniji, "Natural Springs Project: Communities Initiatives for Water Resources Management in Ibadan, Nigeria," paper presented at the Seventh International Science Conference on the Human Dimension of Global Environmental Change, IHDP Open Meeting. Bonn, Germany, April 26–30, 2009.
[85] Adeniji and Ogundiji.
[86] Onibokun and Kumuyi.
[87] I. O. Olaseha and M. K. C. Sridhar, "Community Mobilization for Drainage Improvement: Experience from Three Communities in Ibadan, Nigeria," *International Quarterly of Community Health Education* 22(1), 77–85.
[88] Adeniji and Ogundiji.
[89] Onibokun and Kumuyi.

[90] Image reprinted from "Flood Rocks Ibadan Residents," *PM News*, August 28, 2011.
[91] "Dam Burst Kills over 100 in Nigeria," *China Daily*, September 1, 2011.

## Bibliography

Abiodun, Josephine Olu. "The Challenges of Growth and Development in Metropolitan Lagos." In *The Urban Challenge in Africa: Growth and Management of Its Large Cities.* Edited by Carole Rakodi. 192–222. New York, NY: United Nations University Press, 1997.

Abumere, Sylvester I., Ben C. Arima, and T. A. Jerome. *The Informal Sector in Nigeria's Development Process.* Canberra, Australia: Development Policy Centre, 1998.

Acosta-Michlik, Lilibeth, Ulka Kelkar, and Upasna Sharma. "A Critical Overview: Local Evidence on Vulnerabilities and Global Environmental Change in Developing Countries." *Global Environmental Change* 18(4), 539–542.

Adelekan, Ibidun O. "Vulnerability of Poor Urban Coastal Communities to Climate Change in Lagos, Nigeria." Paper presented at the Fifth Urban Research Symposium on Cities and Climate Change, Marseilles, France, June 28–30, 2009. http://siteresources.worldbank.org/INTURBANDEVELOPMENT/Resources/336387-1256566800920/6505269-1268260567624/Adelekan.pdf

Adeniji, Grace. "Natural Springs Project: Communities Initiatives for Water Resources Management in Ibadan, Nigeria." Paper presented at the Seventh International Science Conference on the Human Dimension of Global Environmental Change, IHDP Open Meeting. Bonn, Germany, April 26–30, 2009.

Adeniji, Grace, and Bukola Ogundiji. "Climate Adaptation in Nigerian Cities: Regularizing Informal and Illegal Settlements in Ibadan." Paper presented at the Fifth Urban Research Symposium on Cities and Climate Change, Marseilles, France, June 28–30, 2009. http//siteresources.worldbank.org/INTURBANDEVELOPMENT/Resources/336387-1256566800920/6505269-1268260567624/Adeniji.pdf (accessed 15.06.11).

Adger, W. Neil. "Vulnerability." *Global Environmental Change* 16(3), 268–81.

Ayeni, M. A. O. "Living Conditions of the Poor in Lagos." *EKISTICS*, 43(255), 77–80.

Bassey, Joshua, Feyisipo, Austin Imhonlere and Oluyinka Alawode. "Lagos Rains Kill 10 as Experts Predict More Downpour." *Businessday Online*, July 12, 2011. http://www.businessdayonline.

com/NG/index.php/news/76-hot-topic/24461-lagos-rains-kill-10-as-experts-predict-more-downpour

Beaverstock, Jonathan V., Richard G. Smith, and Peter J. Taylor. "A Roster of World Cities." *Cities* 16(6), 445–58.

Blaikie, Piers, Terry Cannon, Ian Davis and Ben Wisner. *At Risk: Natural Hazards, People's Vulnerability and Disasters*. 1st edition. London, UK: Routledge, 1994.

Brinkhoff, Thomas. *City Population: Population Statistics for Countries, Administrative Areas, Cities and Agglomerations—Interactive Maps—Charts*. n.d. http//www.citypopulation.de

Browder, John O., James R. Bohland and Joseph L. Scarpaci. "Patterns of Development on the Metropolitan Fringe—Urban Fringe Expansion in Bangkok, Jakarta and Santiago." *Journal of the American Planning Association* 61(3), 310–27.

Cardona, Omar D. "The Need for Rethinking the Concepts of Vulnerability and Risk from a Holistic Perspective: A Necessary Review and Criticism for Effective Risk Management." In *Mapping Vulnerability, Disasters, Development and People*. Edited by Greg Bankoff, George Frerks, and Dorothea Hilhorst. 37–51. London, UK: Earthscan Publications, 2004.

Cutter, Susan L. "Presidential Address: The Vulnerability of Science and the Science of Vulnerability." *Annals of American Geographers* 93(1), 1–12.

Daniels, Peter W. "Urban Challenges: The Formal and Informal Economies in Mega-Cities." *Cities* 21(6), 501–11.

"Dam Burst Kills Over 100 in Nigeria." *China Daily*, September 1, 2011. http://chinadaily.com.cn/2011-09/01/content_13594235.htm

Davis, Mike. *Planet of Slums*. London, UK: Verso, 2006.

Douglas, Ian, Kurshid Alam, Maryanne Maghenda, Yasmin Mcdonnell, Louise Mclean, and Jack Campbell. "Unjust Waters: Climate Change, Flooding and the Urban Poor in Africa." *Environment and Urbanization* 20(1), 187–205.

Dupont. Véronique. *Peri-Urban Dynamics—Population, Habitat and Environment on the Peripheries of Large Indian Metropolises*. New Delhi, India: French Research Institutes, 2005.

"Flood Rocks Ibadan Residents." *PM News*, August 28, 2011. http://www.pmnewsnigeria.com/2011/08/28/flood-rocks-ibadan-residents/comment-page-1/?replytocom=121185

Fourchard, Laurent. "Urban Slums Reports: The Case of Ibadan, Nigeria." *Understanding Slums: Case Studies for the Global Report on Human*

Settlements. UN-Habitat, 2003. http://www.ucl.ac.uk/dpu-projects/Global_Report/pdfs/Ibadan.pdf

Gandy, Matthew. "Learning from Lagos." *New Left Review* 2005 no. 33, 36–52.

—. "Planning, Anti-Planning and the Infrastructure Crisis Facing Metropolitan Lagos." *Urban Studies* 43(2), 371–96.

George, Cathcrine Kehinde. "Challenges of Lagos as a Mega-City." *AllAfrica*, February 10, 2010. http://www.allafrica.com/stories/201002221420.html

Hansjürgens, Bernd, Dirk Heinrichs, and Christian Kuhlicke. "Mega-Urbanization and Social Vulnerability." In *Megacities: Resilience and Social Vulnerability*. Edited by Hans-Georg Bohle and Koko Warner. 20–28. SOURCE Publication Series of UNU-RHS, No. 10. Bonn, Germany: UNU Institute for Environment and Human Security, 2008.

Hilhorst, Dorothea. "Complexity and Diversity: Unlocking Social Domains of Disaster Response." In *Mapping Vulnerability: Disasters, Development and People*, edited by Greg Bankoff, George Frerks, and Dorothea Hilhorst. 52–66. London, UK: Earthscan, 2004.

Jones, Gavin W., and Pravin Visaria. *Urbanization in Large Developing Countries–China, Indonesia, Brazil and India*. Oxford, UK: Clarendon Press, 1997.

Koolhaas, Rem, Stefano Boeri, Stanford Kwinter, Nadia Tazi and Hans-Ulrich Obrist. *Mutations*. Barcelona, Spain: Actar, 2001.

Kraas, Frauke. "Megacities and Global Change: Key Priorities." *Geographical Journal*, 173(1), 79–82.

Lagos State. 2010. *Household Survey 2010 Edition*. Lagos Bureau of Statistics (LBS), Ministry of Economic Planning and Budget. Ikeja, Lagos. http://www.lagosstate.gov.ng/HOUSEHOLD%202010.pdf

Lee, Roger. "Informal Sector." In *The Dictionary of Human Geography*. Edited by Ron E. A. Johnston. 390–3. Oxford, UK: Blackwell, 2000.

Mabogunje, Akin L. *Cities and African Development*. Ibadan, Nigeria: OUP, 1977.

—. "Reconstructing the Nigerian City: The New Policy on Urban Development and Housing." Conference Paper on the City in Nigeria. Abuja (2002).

Massey, Doreen, John Allen, and Steve Pile, eds. *City Worlds*. London, UK: Routledge, 1999.

Meikle, Sheilah. "The Urban Context and Poor People." In *Urban Livelihoods: a People-Centered Approach to Reducing Poverty*. Edited by Carole Rakodi and Tony Lloyd-Jones. 37–51. London, UK: Earthscan, 2002.

Olaseha, Isaac O., and M. K. C. Sridhar. "Community Mobilization for Drainage Improvement: Experience from Three Communities in Ibadan, Nigeria." *International Quarterly of Community Health Education* 22(1), 77–85.

Olukoju, Ayodeji. *Infrastructure Development and Urban Facilities in Lagos, 1861–2000*. Ibadan, Nigeria: Institut Francais de Recherche en Afrique, 2003.

Onibokun, Adepoju G., and Adetoye Faniran. *The Impact of Structural Adjustment on Housing, Environment and Urban Productivity in Nigeria*. Ibadan, Nigeria: CASSAD, 1995.

Onibokun Adepoju G., and A. J. Kumuyi. 1999. "Ibadan, Nigeria." In *Managing the Monster: Urban Waste and Governance in Africa*. Edited by Adepoju G. Onibokun. 49–100. Ottawa, Canada: International Development Research Centre, 1999.

Onakerhoraye, Andrew G., and Gideon E. D. Omuta. *City Structure and Planning for Africa*. Benin City, Benin: The Benin Social Science Series, 1994.

Packer, George. "The Megacity." *The New Yorker*, November 13, 2006. http://www.newyorker.com/archive/2006/11/13/061113fa_fact_packer

Peil, Margaret. *Lagos: The City Is the People*. London, UK: Belhaven, 1991.

Pelling, Mark. *The Vulnerability of Cities: Natural Disasters and Social Resilience*. London, UK: Earthscan, 2003.

Rakodi, Carole, and Tony Lloyd-Jones, eds. *Urban Livelihoods: A People-Centered Approach to Reducing Poverty*. London, UK: Earthscan, 2002.

"Resilience." Resilience Alliance website. 2002. http://www.resalliance.org/576.php (accessed 15.06.11).

Resilience Alliance. *A Research Prospectus for Urban Resilience: a Resilience Alliance Initiative for Transitioning Urban Systems Towards Sustainable Future*. Canberra, Australia: CSIRO Australia / Arizona State University / Stockholm University, 2007.

Sakdapolrak, Patrick, Carsten Butsch, R. L. Carter, M.-D. Cojocaru, Benjamin Etzold, Nanda Kishor, Carmen Lacambra, Marquesa L. Reyes and Saut Sagala. "The Megacity Resilience Framework." In *Megacities: Resilience and Social Vulnerability*. Edited by Hans-Georg Bohle and Koko Warner. 10–19. SOURCE Publication Series of UNU-RHS, No.10. Bonn, Germany: UNU Institute for Environment and Human Security, 2008.

Satterthwaite, David, ed. *The Earthscan Reader in Sustainable Cities*. London, UK: Earthscan, 1999.

Stren, Richard E. "Urban Governance in Developing Countries: Experiences and Challenges." In *Governing Cities in a Global Era: Urban Innovation, Competition and Democratic Reform.* Edited by Robin Hambleton and Jill Gross. 57–70. New York, NY: Palgrave Macmillan, 2007.

Subiros, Pep. "Lagos: Surviving Hell." In *Africas: The Artist and the City*, 34–45. Barcelona, Spain: Centre de Cultura Contemporania de Barcelona, 2001.

Taylor, Robert W. "The Policy Context." In *Urban Development in Nigeria.* Edited by Robert W. Taylor. 13–24. Aldershot, UK: Avebury, 1993.

"Toll in Blast at Nigeria Armory Exceeds 1,000." *New York Times*, February 3, 2002. http://www.nytimes.com/2002/02/03/world/toll-in-blast-at-nigerian-armory-exceeds-1000.html

Turner II, Billie L. "Vulnerability and Resilience: Coalescing or Paralleling Approaches for Sustainability Science?" *Global Environmental Change* 20(4), 570–6.

UN-Habitat. *The Challenge of Slums.* London, UK: Earthscan, 2004.

—. *State of the World's Cities 2008/2009: Harmonious Cities.* London, UK: Earthscan, 2008.

—. *Planning Sustainable Cities.* London, UK: Earthscan. 2009.

—. *The State of African Cities 2010: Governance, Inequality and Urban Land Markets.* London, UK: Earthscan, 2010.

Villangran de Leon, Juan Carlos. *Vulnerability: A Conceptual and Methodological Review.* SOURCE Publication Series of UNU-RHS, No.4. Bonn, Germany: UNU Institute for Environment and Human Security, 2006.

Walker, Brian, C. S. Holling, Stephen R. Carpenter, and Ann Kinzig. "Resilience, Adaptability and Transformability in Social–Ecological Systems." *Ecology and Society.* 9(2), Article 5. http://www.ecologyandsociety.org/vol9/iss2/art5/

Wisner, Ben, Piers Blaikie, Terry Cannon, and Ian Davis. *At Risk: Natural Hazards, People's Vulnerability and Disasters.* 2nd ed. London, UK: Routledge, 2004.

World Bank. *World Development Report, 2004: Making Services Work for People.* Washington DC: Author, 2004.

—. "Project Appraisal Document: Lagos Metropolitan Development and Governance Project." June 7, 2006. http://www-wds.worldbank.org/external/default/WDSContentServer/WDSP/IB/2006/06/19/000160016_20060619104001/Rendered/PDF/36433.pdf

Young, Oran R. "Institutional Dynamics: Resilience, Vulnerability and Adaptation in Environmental and Resource Regimes." *Global Environmental Change* 20(3), 378–85.

# CHAPTER FIFTEEN

## BEYOND THE CODE OF SILENCE: FINDING A BETTER PATH TO REBUILDING AND RECONCILIATION IN POST-INDEPENDENCE NAMIBIA

### NDUMBA J. KAMWANYAH

### Introduction

In 1999, the Caprivi Liberation Army—a separatist movement led by the former Democratic Turnhalle Alliance (DTA) President Mishake Muyongo—launched an attack in Katima (the regional capital of the Caprivi region), killing and destroying lives and property. The government of Namibia responded swiftly and indiscriminately by detaining, torturing, killing and sending many Caprivi-region residents, especially the Mafwe-speaking people, into exile in neighboring Botswana and abroad in Western countries, where they were given asylum status.[1]

The perceived ethnic marginalization of the Caprivian-speaking Namibians, the sense of not feeling included in *one Namibia, one nation*, was apparently at the center of their rationale for engaging in this heinous action. The validity of the Caprivi secessionists' claim is difficult to establish, but concurrent research and surveys (such as the National Housing Income and Expenditure Surveys [NHIES] of 1993/94 and 2003/2004 respectively; the Village-Level Participatory Poverty Assessments—Poverty Profiles published by the National Planning Commission [NPC] in 2000; and the 2006 and 2008 Millennium Development Goals [MDGs] reports) show a high level of extreme poverty in that part (the Caprivi region) of Namibia.[2] In addition, the Central Bureau of Statistics figures[3] also portray Namibia as the most unequal society in the world, with high rates of HIV/AIDS, unemployment and underdevelopment—all factors that exert greater impact on how citizens interact with and view each other in the new Namibia.

The Caprivi secession attempt, in the larger context, can largely be attributed to Namibia's colonial history, which created distrust among Namibians. Therefore it also reflects the failure of Namibia's post-independence reconciliation and nation-building project to reconcile and rebuild Namibia after 100 years of the man-made disaster of colonialism, which segregated Namibians, marginalized communities, and destroyed the societal and moral fabric of Namibia. It is true that the national liberation struggle, as an antithesis to colonialism, successfully mobilized and united Namibians against colonialism, but in terms of perceptions and the way people view and treat each other, the attainment of independence did not necessarily result in the decolonization of the Namibian mind, which was poisoned by divisive apartheid policies and the liberation struggle way of thinking.

Consequently, despite the current government's good intention to unify and rebuild the country, Namibian society continues to be polarized by old racial, ethnic, and political divisions. Past and recent events suggest that the South West Africa People's Organization (SWAPO)-led government's vision to reconcile (ethnically, racially, economically, and politically), unite, and rebuild Namibia is being undermined by the colonial and national liberation legacy of ethnic and racial stereotyping, social exclusion, prejudices, unquestioning loyalty, and group divisions.[4] Namibia's old racial, ethnic, and political divisions are probably exemplified by the current simmering ethnic tension between two groups: those who would prefer a non-Oshiwambo-speaking person to become the next president of Namibia after the incumbent president Pohamba's term expires in 2014, and those who view such a call as tribalism, divisive, and against the nation's slogan of *one Namibia, one nation*.

Although the ruling party, SWAPO, in comparison to opposition parties, appears to be a multicultural party consisting of members from all Namibia's ethnic and racial groups, its leadership structure is mainly dominated by the Oshiwambo-speaking ethnic group. Both the founding president Dr. Sam Nujoma and the current President Hifikepunye Pohamba are from the Oshiwambo ethnic group, and most of their cabinet ministers are also largely drawn from the Oshiwambo-speaking Namibians.

Is this Oshiwambo ethnic domination in the ruling party SWAPO structures and the government creating barriers to reconciliation and nation building, or is it merely a political domination at the elite level? Many political commentators on Namibian politics believe that this seemingly ethnic domination of the Namibian government by the

Oshiwambo-speaking Namibians is at the center of Namibia's simmering ethnic and political tension.[5] This ethnic tension is also believed to have prompted a recent New Year's Day ethnic slur by the deputy minister of mines and energy, Willem Isaack, against Namibian police officers at Berseba during a Hai/Khaua Traditional Authority meeting.[6] According to media reports, Isaack has denied the accusation, but this outburst follows that of another high-level SWAPO member, former Youth and Sport Minister Kazenambo Kazenambo, who is an Omuherero-speaking Namibian. He called his fellow ministers "stupid Owambos" with a "Boer" mentality in an interview with *Insight Magazine*'s Tileni Mongudhi in February 2012.[7] Seeing ethnicity and regionalism as barriers to Namibia's policy of reconciliation and national unity, President Pohamba and the SWAPO leadership were (rightly) displeased with Kazenambo and seized this opportunity to rally Namibians behind the country's policy of reconciliation and *one Namibia, one nation*.[8]

Other cases of tension threatening Namibia's cohesion, harmony and peace reported in local media include increasing tribal tensions over land between the Ondonga people and Oshikwanyama speakers; the tension between the Mbukush people and the Caprivians over the delimitation proposal; and the unresolved low-intensity war over land raging in the Kavango region between Oshikwanyama-speaking farmers and the Ukwangali traditional authority.[9] In a recent article in *The Namibian*, "We Are Each Other's Keepers: Diversity and Divergence," former Prime Minister Nahas Angula (now the Minister of Defense) summed up the situation in this way:

> The Delimitation Commission, drought and general poverty in the country seem to have triggered some kind of pent-up tension among communities. This and that community is demanding this and that in the name of whatever. It is clear, however, that these demands are motivated by underlying social tensions.[10]

The United Nation's 2008 report, "The Convention on the Elimination of all Forms of Racial Discrimination" ("CERD"), also found increased hate speech and verbal attacks on minority groups and oppositions by government officials and other sectors.[11] Some threats of violence and instances of political intolerance cited in the Namibian media throughout the past years since independence include the hate speech against the leaders and members of the Rally for Democracy and Progress Party in 2008 and the Congress of Democrats in 1989 after each of these parties split from the ruling party, SWAPO. Another example is the government's hostility towards and intolerance of *The Namibian* (especially its editor,

Gwen Lister, who is white). The newspaper was subsequently banned by former president Dr. Sam Nujoma in 2002 and remained silenced until 2011, when the ban was lifted by a cabinet decision. SWAPO's angry outburst about the launching of *Breaking the Wall of Silence* (1995), the book by the anti-apartheid activist Pastor Groth, is a further example, as is the hate speech against the Wall of Silence Movement (BWS), which was established to seek justice for ex-SWAPO detainees.[12]

To paraphrase the Namibian political scientist Joe Diescho, the situation got too close for comfort during the 2009 Presidential and Parliamentary elections (amidst political instability, name-calling, political intolerance, and threats of violence), making Namibia vulnerable to conflict again.[13] As an example, here one is reminded of an incident, which was widely reported in local and international media in 2009, where the founding president Nujoma (also referred to as the "Father of the Nation") reportedly told a political rally in the north, a region which is a stronghold of the SWAPO ruling party, that the whites should be beaten with hammers if they try to sabotage the progress made by Africans in Namibia or elsewhere in Africa.[14]

Against this background, is Namibia building a Tower of Babel? The columnist Kaure makes this apt analogy, as, twenty-three years into independence (despite peace, stability, and multi-party democracy), Namibians seem to be speaking in different tongues, unable to understand each other when it comes to reconciliation and national unity.[15] Is Namibia's racial and ethnic diversity a curse? What is the implication of this one national identity for diversity and pluralism? Does unity imply silence over differences, especially unpopular or dissenting views? Put differently, is diversity (racial, ethnic and political) a curse (in the sense of the Babylonian confusion)? Is Namibia's heterogeneity too high a barrier for the country's reconciliation and national unity, thus posing a danger for nation-building? Or, the other way round, is reconciliation being used by the SWAPO ruling party as a fig leaf for manipulation through the slogan of *one Namibia, one nation* in order to control politics in Namibia?

## Historical Context and Background

The achievement of political independence in March 1990 paved the way for Namibia to address the wounds of the past engendered by over 100 years of colonial rule and a bitter liberation struggle. Both colonialism (German and South African regimes) and the anti-colonial resistance (national liberation movements) left a trail of harrowing accounts of direct and indirect violence and injustice. Under the German and South African colonial powers, gross human rights violations and abuses of the dignity and freedoms of the country's inhabitants characterized Namibia's pre-independence era.[16] Equally, the same can be said about SWAPO's record in exile, when it comes to people it suspected and accused of working for the colonial regime of apartheid South Africa.

Known as South West Africa then, Namibia remained a German colony from 1884 until 1915, when German colonial rule was defeated by Union of South Africa troops during the First World War.[17] In 1920, the League of Nations, the predecessor of the United Nations, mandated that the Union of South Africa rule Namibia on behalf of His Majesty George V of England.[18] However, despite the UN's 1945 request to place Namibia under UN trusteeship for seventy-five years, South Africa, reneging on its promise to develop the country's inhabitants, occupied Namibia and extended its policy of apartheid and military occupation until independence in 1990.

Just like the Babylonian confusion, through its policy of apartheid South Africa used Namibia's ethnic and language diversity to confound, divide and conquer Namibians. The policy of apartheid—a policy developed to segregate and relegate (politically, economically, socially and psychologically) black Namibians and their South African counterparts to an inferior position—has confined black Namibians to the Bantu "homelands", denied them social justice through political repression, forced removals, and imposed land appropriation.[19] Just as in South Africa, South Africa's Truth and Reconciliation Commission (TRC) also uncovered shocking and gruesome evidence of apartheid South Africa's security forces' brutality against Namibians, especially SWAPO members/supporters. A case in point (which came up during the trial of apartheid-era germ warfare expert Dr. Wouter Basson in South Africa) is the poisoning and dumping of the bodies of 200 Namibians into the sea by a specially made South African security force aircraft.[20] By their own admission, Koevoet, a notorious counterinsurgency unit which operated in Namibia during the national liberation struggle, also claims to have killed about 3,800 SWAPO combatants.[21] Due to the general amnesty issued by Advocate Louis Pienaar (then Administrator General of SWA/Namibia and the South African Representative at the time of the implementation of UN Resolution 435) on the eve of the country's independence in 1990, the TRC had no mandate in Namibia, which does not have a TRC of its own. As a result, many questions about the apartheid South Africa regime's human rights abuses against Namibians (especially black Namibians) remain unanswered, with many innocent Namibians presumed dead, tortured, or simply vanished at the hands of apartheid security and armed forces.²² It is on the grounds of this very same general amnesty that the charge that Basson, dubbed Dr. Death, conspired in the murder and poisoning of 200 SWAPO detainees, was dismissed right at the beginning of his thirty-month trial in the Pretoria High Court. In South Africa, Basson's trial ended in his acquittal on forty-six charges brought against him. The Namibian government and SWAPO protested Basson's acquittal and threatened to have him extradited to Namibia to stand trial. However, at the time of this writing, no extradition charge has been brought against Basson.²³

As for German colonialism in Namibia, what is today known as the Herero genocide, approximately, 60,000 Herero, 10,000 Nama, and 17,000 Damara were slaughtered by the German army between 1904 and 1908 in retaliation for their rebellion against German colonial rule.²⁴ The Herero genocide remains not only one of the thorniest issues in the Namibian nation-building process, but is also a stumbling block in the bilateral relationship between the Namibian government and the German government because of Germany's refusal to pay reparations for the Namibian genocide. The Herero-speaking Namibians have been demanding reparations and continue to accuse the SWAPO-led government (which they perceive as an Oshiwambo-dominated government) of indifference when it comes to pressing the German government to apologize for their atrocities and to pay reparations for their colonial injustices against the Hereros and the Namas. Bemoaning the Namibian government's lack of political will to address the Herero genocide, Hengari had this to say:

> While the solemn reception of the skulls on Namibian soil played out in a symbolic manner that showed this part of our history as taking its rightful place in the historiography of the Republic of Namibia, certain caveats still remain. These caveats don't only relate to the controversies and insensitivities on the part of the German government, but they also relate to how the Namibian government has been dealing with these controversies over time.
>   It should be noted that Germany is less likely to confront its blood-drenched history against the Ovaherero and Nama outside the signals and texture of its bilateral relations with the Namibian government. In essence, if the Namibian government does not treat the genocide question as a priority theme in its bilateral relations with Germany, it is less likely that Berlin would treat demands for reparations in a manner that is respectful and urgent. The controversies surrounding the return of the skulls merely confirm the absence of this question on the Namibian government policy agenda with Germany. Since independence, there has been no official discourse on the genocide and reparations on the part of the Namibian government. Germany merely plays its negotiating

position on the basis of a policy vacuum on this question. After all, during the past two decades, there have been way too few senior government officials who had spoken openly in an official capacity about reparations, including the Ovaherero genocide (calling it as such), less so within the framework of liberation or "patriotic" history. Therefore government silence in the face of bad treatment during the skull-handover ceremony merely confirms a policy of looking the other way.

As a result, the manner in which the Namibian government treats this issue has taken on the sad allure of ethnicity. And for as long as government does not take an activist role in leading and crafting a coherent policy-framework encompassing some of the key demands of affected communities, minorities will be justified to see matters from a communitarian and ethnic point of view. It is a perception that a self-respecting government may not want to see perpetuated.[25]

To date, the Herero genocide remains unresolved, but on March 22, 2012, the German parliament reportedly debated a motion to acknowledge its brutal 1904–1908 genocide of the Nama and Herero peoples, as reported in the online newspaper *Pambazuka*.[26] This German parliament discussion followed the first-ever return and repatriation of human skulls of the genocide victims more than a century after they were illegally taken from Namibia to Germany.

In response to the colonial occupation, especially the South African colonial and military rule, the main Namibian national liberation movement, SWAPO, began to lobby and petition against South Africa's illegal occupation in the early 1960s.[27] After a strategic three-pronged approach of a military campaign (which culminated in twenty-three years of armed struggle), political mobilization, and intensive diplomacy, Namibia's independence emerged within the framework of free and fair elections in 1998 under the UN-supervised mandate Resolution 435.[28] SWAPO, now the ruling party, easily won the first election and formed a government dedicated to liberal democracy and constitutional supremacy.

However, despite SWAPO's insistence on the principles of freedom, justice, and solidarity as a national liberation movement, hundreds of Namibians who fled colonial oppression between the 1960s and 1980s to join SWAPO in exile were detained and tortured by the movement's military wing, the People's Liberation Army of Namibia (PLAN).[29] Apart from a few thousand survivors who returned home under the UN 435 agreement, hundreds more are believed to have been killed and dumped in a mountain crevasse near Lubango in Angola.[30] Some were arrested with the help of the host African countries' police and security forces, such as Tanzania, and there was also the

...Mboroma mass detention camp shooting in which four Namibians were killed and fifteen seriously wounded by Zambian soldiers on August 5 1976, allegedly on instructions from the top Swapo leadership in exile....[31]

As a result, the detainee issue, as it is known in Namibia, refuses to wither away as SWAPO hoped it would. Victims and survivors of the SWAPO detentions continue to demand a public apology from the SWAPO-led government, as Tsudao Gurirab recently summed up in *The Namibian*:

> ...it is no longer acceptable to say some got caught up in the crossfire without putting names and faces to those affected in different categories as either spy, victim of crossfire, etc. In an increasing[ly] intolerant environment in our country, it also raises the real concern for the citizens whether the culprits may become repeat offenders. For our continent remains a veritable graveyard of Constitutions with generously entrenched human rights but which end up failing the citizens. How can we trust them if "sorry" is the hardest word for them to say?[32]

As of the present, the detainee issue has culminated in the formation of a group (consisting of former SWAPO detainees) called Breaking the Wall of Silence (BWS), which has been advocating the TRC-type approach and calling for the SWAPO government to apologize and exonerate them. Recently it has also been reported in the local media that plans by the survivors of the SWAPO atrocities in exile to form a civic organization, to be referred as the Namibia Truth and Justice Association, are already at an advanced stage.[33] In addition (in parallel with the goal of seeking justice for victims of the colonial and liberation brutality in Namibia), for the first time since independence, a coalition for transitional justice was also established in 2009 to seek justice for past abuses. Nonetheless, despite demands for an apology and public debate about the past, SWAPO refuses to accept responsibility or apologize for its own past atrocities, because doing so is believed to be against the country's policy of reconciliation and national unity.

## Policy Goals, Objectives, and Assumptions

In an attempt "to overcome the racial, ethnic, social and political division in the country," the SWAPO-led government introduced the policy of national reconciliation at independence.[34] The overall goal of the policy of national reconciliation suggests that a shared Namibian identity be forged through national unity as expressed through the *one Namibia, one nation* slogan.

The assumptions underlying the Namibian Policy of National Reconciliation are: *Amnesia* → *National Unity* → *Reconciliation* → *Democratization*. Thus, to hypothesize: when Namibians avoid discussing the past or things that divide them, national unity would result. In turn, the presence of national unity would create the right milieu for Namibians to come together and reconcile as a nation. Finally, Namibia's stability and democracy would depend on a reconciled and united post-independence Namibia. This explanation is rooted in the theoretical assumption that disunity is not conducive to reconciliation and nation-building. But more importantly, the Namibian policy of national reconciliation is also rooted in the collective memory theory of post-conflict nation-state building, the notion that societies emerging from conflict should first establish stability through democratic political institutions to build the nation.[35] In the context of Namibia, this implies that reforming and improving Namibia's political institutions (such as the executive branch, judiciary and the legislative body) will ensure economic stability and build a more inclusive form of post-independence nation.

Generally, the Namibian reconciliation policy is understood to be constructed around three broad policy goals, namely: economic justice, race/ethnicity integration, and political reconciliation.[36] The construction of reconciliation and national unity as a political goal is aimed at facilitating the integration of former political enemies and building a foundation for a culture of tolerance, human rights and good governance through democratic political institutions, such as the executive, legislative, and judicial branches. As a result, over the past years, not only have free and fair elections been held at the national, regional and local levels, but the government has also succeeded in integrating former combatants from both sides of the conflict.[37]

The race/ethnicity goal involves bridging and healing racial and ethnic divisions created by years of divisive colonial policies and the war of national liberation. With the adoption of the constitution at the dawn of independence, stratification and discrimination based on skin color, ethnicity, and gender became obsolete. Instead, the government embarked on the integration of public service, most notably in the education sector, where schools were opened to all races and ethnicities. In addition, the hated apartheid homelands were replaced with thirteen political regions through the adoption of the Regional Councils Act of 1992.

On the other hand, the economic goal pertains to addressing past inequalities as a means of leveling the economic playing field, including provision of the most basic public services, such as sanitation, water, electricity, and health care. Many structures and programs, such as the

Affirmative Action (AA) policy and the Black Economic Empowerment (BEE) program, were put into place immediately after independence to address and correct the past economic imbalances.

To give credit where it is due, earlier research on Namibia's nation-building process suggests that symbolically the Namibian policy of national reconciliation has played an important role in overcoming the political, racial, and ethnic tensions immediately after independence.[38] However, at a substantive and practical level, twenty-three years into independence, the dream of *one Namibia, one nation* remains elusive due to the lack of clear mechanisms to address past abuses, political and ethnic marginalization, and poverty. Just like Adam Smith's invisible hand of the market (based on the theory that the market will correct itself without any intervention from the government), the Namibian Policy of National Reconciliation (NPNR) is based on a mechanical approach with no policy instrument to translate it into action. At best, post-independence Namibia's policy of reconciliation can be described as a code of silence and can be contrasted with neighboring South Africa's Truth and Reconciliation Commission, which employed truth-telling as a strategy to reconcile South Africans.[39] The two countries have a shared history of apartheid and oppression under the then-white rule of South Africa. Namibia became a colony of South Africa after the First World War as part of the mandate of the League of Nations awarded to the British Crown, which mandated South Africa to administer the territory on its behalf. The creation of an apartheid state in 1948 by the National Party not only introduced inhumane treatment, but also subjugated blacks in South Africa and Namibia to a white-controlled economy. Apartheid policy was predicated on separate development that implied inferior education, social services, and forced removals of blacks from their ancestral land. Apartheid policy utilized South African blacks and migrant laborers from neighboring countries such as Namibia, Botswana, Angola, and Zambia as a source of cheap labor. In an effort to liberate their respective countries from the racist South African occupation, Umkhonto Wesizwe, the military wing of the ruling party African National Congress (ANC) in South Africa, shared the same trenches with their comrades of PLAN, the military wing of SWAPO. Both the ANC and SWAPO ruling parties have been accused of violations of human rights on their own cadres suspected of spying for the apartheid regime. Lastly, after the fall of apartheid rule, both countries inherited societies that were fragmented and deeply divided along racial, ethnic, political and economic lines. In efforts to forge a collective national identity, the new governments in Namibia after independence and

South Africa after the fall of apartheid adopted policies of national reconciliation to heal the wounds of the past.

It is against this background, in contrast to South Africa, the Namibian policy of national reconciliation censors any discussions about the past and provides a blanket amnesty for past abuses committed by colonial governments (Germany and apartheid South Africa respectively), including Namibians who supported and benefited from colonialism, as well as SWAPO.[40] To date, the SWAPO-led government refuses to debate publicly the NPNR and refuses to set up a South African-style "truth commission", adamant that resurrecting the past would incite vengeance and promote divisions.[41] Instead, the government emphasizes the importance of eliminating all interpretations that may promote points of difference and divisions among Namibians.[42] But the other reason appears to be that SWAPO's refusal is motivated by a conscious effort to conceal its own history of human rights abuses committed in exile, especially on the people now referred to as SWAPO detainees.

Given Namibia's pre-independence history of distrust, unity is important for post-independence democracy and nation-building, but does the call for shared feelings under *one Namibia, one nation* mean that the vision of one Namibian identity is promoted to the exclusion of other identifications, especially dissenting or unpopular views?

## Macro Reconciliation at the National Level

*Reconciliation and Nationalism*

"Namibia cannot claim to be a 'United Nation' as citizens are not passionate about the country and its national symbols," reads the preamble to the Cabinet-approved "Nationhood and National Pride Campaign" launched to address the lack of nationalism and patriotism among Namibians.[43] Clearly the Western model of ethnically and linguistically homogenous nations has profoundly influenced the Namibian reconciliation and nation-building process. Patriotic sentiments—nationalism—towards an *imagined community* and a sense of collective suffering and common destiny are glues that help keep the nation-state together.[44] Therefore reconciliation—from the Latin for re-establishment of solidarity among people—serves an important nationalistic function of social harmony, cohesion, peace, and a feeling of unity among citizens. In other words, reconciliation is believed to have neutralizing effects that can help divided societies overcome past rivalries, live cooperatively, and resuscitate political values of human rights and democracy.[45]

Certainly, given Namibia's history of deep-rooted hatred and distrust left by colonialism and the bitter liberation struggle, these nationalistic characteristics of common suffering, collective identity and patriotic feelings apply to Namibia's post-independence reconciliation and national identity. In the language of Hage Geingob, the Prime Minister of Namibia, "we need to ensure that ethnicity never is allowed to be played up to replace national identity as the most important identity."[46] It is clear from Geingob's comment that the SWAPO-led government firmly believes that emphasizing the importance of unity mediates ethnic and political rivalries and repudiates any idea of differentiated citizenship.[47]

True to the Western model of ethnically and linguistically homogenous nation-statehood, at the dawn of independence Namibia abandoned Afrikaans (a colonial language) as its lingua franca and instead opted for English as a neutral language to promote a national identity that supersedes ethnicity and race, hallmark traits that defined pre-independence Namibia. Why? A homogenous language might serve the purpose of uniting a heterogeneous group of people.[48] In pre-independence Namibia, the colonial government used language and ethnic diversity to exercise control over the indigenous Namibians by dividing them and turning them against each other. As a symbol of superiority and unity, Afrikaans was elevated above all indigenous languages as Namibia's official language, whereas Namibians were discouraged from learning or studying each others' indigenous languages/cultures.

The Namibian government's choice of English as a reconciliation language is troublesome at two levels. Firstly, in terms of information and access to services, it has wide implications, because the majority of Namibians do not speak English. Secondly, at the level of public debate about the past, just like the apartheid regime of South Africa, which used Afrikaans and ethnicity to exercise control over Namibians, the government is using English (as an official language) and national identity as tools to censor diversity and difference. By implication, Namibia's model of reconciliation and national identity implies that were it not for colonialism and apartheid, Namibians would have been a united front at all levels of the Namibian society.

Therefore, against this backdrop, the objectives of Namibia's reconciliation and national unity is to move Namibian citizens away from old divisive identities created by the apartheid South Africa toward a shared national identity of *one Namibia, one nation*, a blind model of citizenship in which race, ethnicity, and political difference don't matter.[49] In other words, reconciliation becomes something that can be experienced as a natural order.

By making national unity a major theme of Namibia's post-independence nation-state, the creators of the Namibian policy of reconciliation and national unity highlight the assumption that unity is an important psychological ingredient for cooperation among Namibians. Put simply, disunity would have threatened Namibia's transitional process, thereby undermining the country's process of democratization.

*One Namibia, one nation* also means old grievances of the past simply cannot be discussed, because to do so would divide Namibians further. Why? The fear is that division would threaten the democratic community because it can undermine cohesion, increase the cost of cooperation, and cause moral damage to society.[50] This suggests that unity is an important element in reconciling divided societies. In its attempt to seek a consensus, however, reconciliation has serious implications for societal differences in terms of experience, interpretation, and definition.[51] Much of the scholarly literature points to the agreement that unity is an important psychological ingredient for reconciliation and nation-building, but in an important sense, unity and reconciliation are two different things. Where unity tends toward closure and final settlement, reconciliation is a means to an end—indeed a conflict process with overt and underlying tensions.[52] Therefore, inasmuch as Namibia's commitment to the shared identity of *one Namibia, one nation* is well-intended, the presupposition of unity as the precondition for Namibia's reconciliation is at odds with reconciliation as a process.

## Micro-Reconciliation at the Individual Level

Since the Namibian reconciliation and nation-building policy portrays an image of universality, obviously the SWAPO government sees ethnic, racial and political divisions as barriers to reconciliation and national unity. Writing in the Namibian newspaper in 2012, Elijah Ngurare, the SWAPO Youth League Secretary General, had this to say about the recent simmering ethnic and racial tension in the country:

> After independence, Namibia brought into operation the Regional Councils Act of 1992, which replaced the apartheid homelands with thirteen political regions.
> However, twenty-two years later, there is a tribally induced mystic wind blowing across the country. It can be heard, it can be felt, and, perceptively, it can be seen. The apartheid homelands are still present in our minds.
> The fashionable thing to say nowadays is that all development is going to the north and not to the south. In 2012 the minorities are promised, on a tribal basis, a chance to rule over the majority. The ascent

to power is clearly now being primarily motivated on tribal identity rather than on the content of a person's character or ability to run such a diverse country. At this rate, what legacy are we to leave for the younger and future generations: tribalism or nationalism? Clearly, the Constitution of Namibia does not prescribe that only a certain tribe must remain in power. Nor does it prescribe that no other tribe should come to executive power. Therefore, the individuals who are busy with schemes based on anti-Owambo politics lack a unifying character. What they are scheming with can work against the very ideals that we fought for (unity and prosperity) and promote the ideologies we wanted to destroy—which are segregation, regionalism, racism, etc.

It is regrettable that these sentiments are aired by people who are supposed to know better, symbols of unity and pillars of wisdom. One wonders how the same people advocating for this campaign will justify that their government would be inclusive and would not discriminate against Aawambo if they succeed.[53]

But Namibians (according to the key informants and respondents interviewed for my doctoral thesis) clearly have no problem with wanting to see reconciliation work across all races, ethnicities and political ideologies. They also have no problem identifying themselves through both ethnic and national identity, suggesting that the notion of *one Namibia, one nation* does not conflict with Namibia's multiethnic/racial/political identities. Instead the policy's lack of substance in improving and responding to the needs of a multicultural populace is what the citizens interviewed see as the greatest barrier to Namibian reconciliation and national unity. In reality, Namibia's policy of national reconciliation is broad and lacks clear mechanisms to achieve the set goals of reconciling and unifying the Namibians.[54] Namibia's policy of national reconciliation not only reflects the views and stories of SWAPO, the party that liberated the country (history written by the winners), but also imposes a patriotic sense of "belonging" to the exclusion of diversity and dissenting views.[55] The policy of national reconciliation has succeeded in forging ties between the economic and political elites, a process that has not only tilted the national identity towards elitism, but has also been seen to perpetuate pre-independence patterns of social differentiation, inequalities, divisions and distrusts.[56] Consequently, in a country where most people rely on indigenous political institutions, this policy's reliance on the Western notion of state/nationhood has created a wedge between the political elite of Namibia and ordinary Namibians, making Namibia's reconciliation and national unity a top-down process.[57]

## Barriers to Reconciliation and National Unity

Should it be *one Namibia in diversity* instead of *one Namibia, one nation*? It can be suggested that the notion of *one Namibia, one nation* is not mutually exclusive of other alternative modes of identification. Therefore, it is perhaps better for Namibia to view reconciliation and national identity in terms of what Schwerdt calls "multiple identities"[58] instead of one super-national identity because Namibians don't identify themselves exclusively as only Namibians, but also in terms of group identity, such as Herero, Nama, Damara, Afrikaner, Colored, and so forth.

Why am I phrasing reconciliation and national unity in terms of societal division or heterogeneity? Is this approach not similar to the hated Bantustan policy devised by the colonial and apartheid regime of South Africa, where citizens were grouped and categorized according to their ethnicity and race? Here is the answer: Reconciliation is inherently political, and like all things politics it is an interest-driven process that is susceptible to manipulation. Therefore, from the point of nation building, if colonialism and the apartheid regime of South Africa used Namibia's diversity to divide and rule, at the national level Namibia's post-independence policy of national reconciliation is being used as tool to control politics. Consequently, instead of valuing differences and criticisms of the country's policy of national reconciliation as resources for building a vibrant post-colonial Namibia, the Namibian reconciliation approach of national unity (with its cult-like discourse of a single Namibian nationhood script) not only treats reconciliation as an end (as opposed to viewing it as a means to an end), but also fixes the meaning of national identity to the exclusion of other alternative modes of identifications and interpretation.

The common dominator of both the apartheid/colonial and post-colonial approaches is the creation of citizens as subjects, as opposed to using Namibia's rich diversity as resource for vibrant citizenship, nation-building, and democracy. Therefore, while it is important for the country to have one common identity at the national level, other models of identification (when used positively) can also be of importance in promoting national attachment to the nation-state.

The caveat with the Namibian reconciliation and nation-building process is not only that it has been driven by a top-down approach, but it also relies heavily on its cult-like discourse about reconciliation and national identity—a single Namibian nationhood script—to the exclusion of dissenting views that speak against this monolithic understanding and conception of nation-building. In this way, the assumption underlying the

Namibian policy of national reconciliation falls within what scholars of nation/state-building see as post-colonial Africa's attempt to structure social and political life around one common national identity despite Africa's cultural heterogeneity.[59] Instead of valuing differences and critiques as resources for nation-building, the Namibian reconciliation approach not only treats reconciliation and national identity as an end (as opposed to viewing it as a means to an end), but it also freezes discussions related to reconciliation and national identity, which have resulted in a fixed meaning of what is meant by nation-building.

Thus the challenge for Namibia is to offer an alternative to the "difference-blind" model, a highly static and homogenizing model of nation building that characterizes post-independence Namibia's reconciliation and national identity in order to accommodate varying interpretations and meanings of reconciliation and nation-building as influenced by the following main factors. *First*, there is a tendency, especially by the ruling party officials, to judge and evaluate reconciliation and nation-building in terms of the peace and stability the country has been enjoying since independence, using peace and stability as tool to censor public debate about reconciliation and nation-building. In other words, Namibia's reconciliation and nation-building seem to be driven by the fear that discussing them could potentially reinforce past divisions through which the nation could relapse into conflict. *Second*, the perception of being disadvantaged and marginalized is making citizens question the virtue of the country's post-independence reconciliation and national unity. This is a factor connected to the relationship between injustice and nation-building that is reproduced by the citizens' lived experience of economic dependency, poverty, political domination, and discrimination. To address this would require social and economic mechanisms to manage the societal differences, equal treatment, fairness, and equal distribution of resources. *Third*, the country's highly partisan politics prevent citizens from engaging in issues pertaining to reconciliation and nation-building in a constructive manner. This would require a political environment characterized by what Opotow calls a "culture of inclusion"[60]—the need to involve and accommodate all citizens in the country's governing affairs at all levels of society. *Fourth*, the nationalistic lens (patriotic talk) through which reconciliation and nation-building are viewed and discussed is facilitating a culture of exclusion and therefore closing doors for genuine demands for openness, transparency and more democracy. In other words, patriotism is making it easy to exclude and dismiss those views which contrast SWAPO's version of reconciliation and nation-building. *Fifth*, the legacy of racial and ethnic tension among citizens is still making it easy for citizens to view and treat each other through a racial or ethnic lens. In this context, this article suggests that the problem is not merely the prevalence of racism and ethnocentrism, but is more connected to the process of reconciliation and nation-building in terms of equal opportunities, equal treatment, and resource distribution. *Sixth*, activism based on party politics contributes to an entrenched party-dominated system in which discussions pertaining to reconciliation and national unity are manipulated and controlled by SWAPO because it commands broad-base electoral support.

## Conclusion: Reconciling and Uniting Namibians

Opotow once wrote that reconciliation is a conflict-ridden process, meaning that reconciliation has many redeeming qualities that can shape a society positively.[61] But it also has the potential to be destructive. This means that when conducted in a transparent, open and inclusive way, reconciliation can build trust and legitimize the nation-building process. On the other hand, because reconciliation tends to emphasize cooperation and unity, it can also exclude, fix positions, and provide a basis for marginalizing other voices pertinent to reconciliation and the nation-building process, especially for those who do not fit the mainstream voice of nation-building.[62] This perspective is in line with Gibson's idea that building a nation through reconciliation is indeed a mini-theory of democracy in the sense that it requires openness, transparency, equitable distribution of resources, and broader citizenry participation.[63] The question for Namibia is how can Namibia foster reconciliation and unity in a more positive and democratic way? Therefore, here's what a successful model of Namibian reconciliation and nation-building, consisting of overlapping elements, should look like.

### *Common Destiny*

Scholarship is in agreement that the task of reconciling and unifying a nation has to do with finding commonalities—ties that bind people together. Unless Namibians realize that they are in this together, Namibia's post-independence reconciliation and nation-building are less likely to be effective. Therefore Namibia's bitter and divisive past (as a result of apartheid, colonialism and the bitter liberation struggle) could serve as a tie that binds together Namibians from all walks of life. The shared experience of colonialism and the national liberation struggle could provide an opportune educative experience for the nation to reflect on and to examine the actions being taken in order to build the nation's future based on common destiny.

On the other hand, it could be argued that a balance has to be maintained in the process of forging this collective path because interpretation and meaning of reconciliation and national unity varies due to the subjective nature of experience. This is because every individual has experienced colonialism, apartheid, and the liberation struggle differently.

*Peace and Stability*

Against the backdrop of Namibia's violent past during the colonial and national liberation struggles, a stable and peaceful post-independence environment is important for reconciling and uniting Namibians because it provides the right milieu for citizens to engage with each other in a peaceful and constructive manner. However, stability and peace should not privilege unity over differences, meaning that it should not be used as a tool to instill fear and to suppress and silence citizens' voices.

*More Democracy*

Another important element in reconciling and uniting Namibians has to do with Namibia's constitutional democracy, which has many redeeming qualities (democracy subjects citizens to universal standards of democratic principles) upon which reconciliation and nation-building could be based. For reconciliation and national unity to materialize, Namibians must be willing to accommodate each other as well as to subscribe to democratic principles and support political institutions in terms of pluralism, political tolerance, and civil public discourse.

However, democracy is one thing; how to implement it is another. Herein it can be argued that due to post-independence Namibia's culture of political centralism and political intolerance towards differing views, Namibia's democratization process has tilted towards a political system in which SWAPO has consolidated political power and entrenched its political domain.[64] As a result, SWAPO controls both the justification for reconciliation and national unity and the means to achieve them.

A look at Namibia's post-independent political culture reveals a militant notion of inclusion or exclusion as a key factor shaping the conception of reconciliation and nation-building. Due to the highly personalized political space in the country and the reality that the memory of colonialism is still fresh in the minds of most Namibians, SWAPO is not only relying on its solidified and unassailable electoral position in the country, but has also invented a militant notion of reconciliation that is rooted in arrogance, threats, and patriotic talks to silence its opponents, resulting in an institutional dominance of the reconciliation process that condones injustice when it comes to the past.[65] Why? Because Namibia is a product of the national liberation struggle, many of the issues pertaining to reconciliation and nation-building are expressed in the form of patriotism and nationalism. SWAPO is positively regarded as the party that brought independence and peace to the country; therefore any talks that contradict the party's views of national unity are likely to be inferred by most Namibians as a return to colonialism, pain and suffering.[66]

*Political Tolerance*

The action of reconciling and creating a national identity requires the willingness of Namibians to co-exist despite their differences and past divisions. The political scientist du Pisani asserts that post-independence Namibia suffers from a tolerance deficit due to the country's past of apartheid, colonialism, liberation struggle, and ethnic and political divisions.[67] Yet political tolerance is an important virtue that informs the outlook of post-independence Namibian political reconciliation.[68] Would Namibia's constitutional democracy lead to broader tolerance among Namibians? As compared to the colonial era, some Namibian political scholars suggest that there is as yet no emerging legitimacy crisis for the Namibian democracy because many Namibians are more convinced about the gains of independence, national unity and reconciliation.[69] But given post-independence Namibia's culture of political centralism (due to the concentration of power in the executive, the fusion of party and state, weak civil society, and the reality that the SWAPO-led government enjoys unquestioned broad-based public support), the question is for how long can Namibia fend off the legitimacy crisis? While SWAPO's broad-based support is important for institutional legitimacy, the unquestioning nature of such support is detrimental to reconciliation and nation-building. Thus political partisanship would play a big role in how the country legitimizes its reconciliation and nation-building in terms of who and what to include in the definition of a shared Namibian identity. Those who feel that the current conception of the national identity is not democratic are less likely to support the shared identity efforts. In other words, the democratic process and wider involvement of ordinary citizens in the conception of the national identity process would increase the support for a shared identity and therefore promote reconciliation and nation-building. Therefore, if apartheid and liberation politics were not fertile ground for political tolerance, post-independence Namibia's political environment seems (as this study indicates) not to nurture political tolerance.

The central assumption of the Namibian policy of national reconciliation is that support of and subscription to national identity and its political institutions would instill tolerance, and by implication reconcile Namibians. This means a call for an all-inclusive national identity in order to minimize the effects of hatred, divisions, and mistrust created by colonialism and the liberation struggle. However, while the question of how tolerant and accepting Namibians are towards each other and to their shared identity is important, both colonialism and the liberation struggle left a legacy of ethnic nationalism, social exclusion, patriotism, and loyalty, factors that may triumph over different conceptions of national unity and reconciliation.[70] Past scholarly comments and media reports about Namibia suggest that instances of intolerance against people who harbor different views of the reconciliation—especially opposition political parties, gay men and lesbian women, journalists, and academics—are widespread.[71]

*Multiple Interpretations*

Post-independence Namibia's attempt to promote common identification at the national level is crucial, but nation-building through reconciliation and national unity should not only privilege greater good at the national scale over difference (regardless of ethnic, racial and political belonging) at the individual, group and community levels. It is important to realize that reconciliation and/or unity are contested politics, therefore appreciating diversity as a resource for nation-building would militate against the current tendency to rely only on the macro politics of reconciliation and unity. In other words, the country's ongoing nation-building through reconciliation and unity should be a process that fosters citizen involvement, unfreezes positions, and decreases inter-group conflict. This will involve countering the tendency to silence both conflicting or dissenting views and different definitions of reconciliation and national identity.

This subjective interpretation of reconciliation and unity not only points to the need for the government to be accountable and transparent in dealing with reconciliation and national identity, but also suggests the need to manage differences. On the other hand, it is rather difficult (if not impossible) for a government to legislate for individual experiences through a policy because feelings are subjective. Nonetheless, the government can create an enabling environment where citizens can express their subjective views in a calm and safe environment. In this context, reconciliation and national unity would mean accepting and tolerating different ideologies/opinions, thereby managing differences in a diverse society without discrimination.

## *More Economic Development*

It is obvious that the framers of the Namibian policy of national reconciliation (the government in particular) see political, racial, and ethnic division as the main threats to post-independence Namibia's nation-building process. But various studies on Namibian politics suggest that economic disparities (poverty, unequal distribution of the nation's wealth, and natural resources) as they relate to ethnic, racial, and political identity are barriers creating misgivings about Namibia's reconciliation and national unity. The perception that the current reconciliation is only serving to strengthen existing inequalities in the country instead of challenging the status quo, land rights, unemployment, and corruption is one of the main factors creating tension among groups. In the context of Namibia, immediately after independence the Namibian government introduced economic policies and programs in order to forge reconciliation and national unity, including economic programs to integrate ex-combatants (both PLAN and SWAFT/Koevoet) such as DBC and SIPE, including the recent establishment of the Ministry of Veterans' Affairs in 2008. However, despite the Namibian government's good intention to address economic inequality, it is believed that the country's reconciliation process and the conception of

> one Namibian national identity is being marred by, among other things, the absence of broad socio-economic transformation characterized by the burning land question, Herero genocide reparation, allegations of widespread racial and gender discrimination, gross income disparities, joblessness and homelessness which affect especially the majority black and colored population.[72]

Socio-economic indicators suggest that post-independence Namibia's economic resources are unequally distributed and that there are clear ethnic differences in income between ethnic language groups.[73] Although Namibia is generally considered a middle-income country with a seemingly high GDP, the country's Gini coefficient of 0.60 suggests that Namibia is actually one of the world's leaders in high income inequality.[74] According to previous analysis, Namibia's dual economy (formal and informal economy), which was inherited from the colonial government, is partially what is perpetuating post-independent Namibia's economic disparity, with the richest few of the population, who are mostly white Namibians and a few black elites, controlling the country's wealth. Where there is inequality and poverty, there is also social exclusion, which prevents individuals or groups from participating in the society as full citizens.[75] Therefore, it goes without saying that the perceptions of being excluded as a racial, ethnic, or political group are likely to foment discontent when people realize that their group is not benefiting from the nation-building.

Therefore reconciling and uniting Namibians will require great effort and effective strategies to fight economic underdevelopment, alleviate poverty, eliminate corruption, and empower citizens in order to promote self-reliance at the individual, community and local levels.

## *A Non-Zero-Sum Identity*

The policy of *one Namibia, one nation* can and does serve the purpose of decreasing intergroup tension and therefore contributes to reconciliation and national unity, as citizens see themselves as Namibians rather than exclusively through a racial/ethnic lens. But, asks Schwerdt, can Namibians also see themselves as both Namibians and Herero or Afrikaner?[76] Theorists advise that identity is not a zero-sum game.[77] Given Namibia's multiculturalism, social, political, and economic factors are bound to influence the sense of belonging and identity.

## *Leadership*

Lack of leadership in terms of understanding the national questions and the implications of reconciliation and national identity is what is lacking in Namibian politics. As a result, not only has Namibia seen what Melber calls a "militant" notion of reconciliation,[78] but the country has also experienced the absence of a national leadership beyond political, racial and ethnic identities.

## *Citizenry Engagement*

For Namibia's policy of reconciliation and national identity to be forward-looking, it should provide a platform for citizens to learn from each other in the search for commonalities and differences. Namibia's current approach does not allow citizens to engage each other in a calm manner, but instead polarizes them into discussing reconciliation and nation-building using preconceived meanings and definitions.

Citizenry engagement is also connected to awareness and information —the need for informed participation. As the situation is now, there is no information system to stimulate and make citizens participate in reconciliation and nation-building. Politicians talk about reconciliation, but this information is highly political and not driven by an understanding of reconciliation in the bigger picture as a democracy-promoting activity. Instead it is driven by manipulation, patriotism, and intimidation.

*A Bottom-Up Approach*

Lastly, due to the failure of SWAPO to transform its hierarchy and decision-making channels, post-independence Namibia's reconciliation and national unity is a top-down process. Reconciling and uniting a nation is not only a function of government or politicians; therefore, there is a great need to transform the government and the ruling party's hierarchy and decision-making process to allow broader participation and citizen involvement. The assumption here is that when people have the opportunity to participate and shape the process, they are more likely to support and participate in the nation-building process. This means that the Namibian reconciliation and nation-building process has to take into account citizens' views about policies and political institutions instead of precluding difference through a top-down approach to defining Namibian identity.

# Notes

[1] For more background and current developments, see "Caprivi Treason Trial", Wikipedia, n.d., http://en.wikipedia.org/wiki/Caprivi_treason_trial; Catherine Sasman, "Caprivi Group Wants UN to Probe Treason Trial," *The Namibian*, September 26, 2012.

[2] such as the National Housing Income and Expenditure Surveys (NHIES) of 1993/94 and 2003/2004 respectively; the *Village-Level Participatory Poverty Assessments–Poverty Profiles*, published by the National Planning Commission (NPC) in 2000; and the 2006 and 2008 Millennium Development Goals (MDGs) reports.

[3] Central Bureau of Statistics, *National Household Income Survey 2003/2004* (Windhoek, Namibia: National Planning Commission, 2006).

[4] Andre du Pisani, "Liberation and Tolerance," in *Re-examining Liberation in Namibia: Political Culture since Independence*, ed. Henning Melber, 129–36 (Stockholm, Sweden: Elanders Gotab, 2003).

[5] John Grobler, "Insult Reflects Tribal Division in Namibia," *Mail and Guardian*, February 10, 2012, 12.

[6] Luqman Cloete, "Deputy Minister's 'Tribal Tirade' Investigated by Police," *AllAfrica*, January 16, 2013; see also Ndumba J. Kamwanyah, "Another Test for President Pohamba," *The Namibian*, January 11, 2013.

[7] See for example: Grobler; Ndumba J. Kamwanyah, "Namibia: Ethnic Tension in Presidential Succession Race," *AllAfrica*, March 2, 2012; Nico Smit, "KK on the Rampage," *The Namibian*, February 3, 2012.

[8] Festus Nakatana, "KK Loses His Head Again," *Namibian Sun*, February 03, 2012.

[9] "White Man Grabs Black's Land," *The Namibian*, May 31, 2013.
[10] Nahas Angula, "We Are Each Other's Keepers: Diversity and Divergence," *The Namibian*, May 10, 2013, para. 1.
[11] Christof Maletsky, "UN Report Lambastes Nam for Hate Speech," *The Namibian*, August 21, 2008.
[12] For example, see Lauren Dobell, "The Ulenga Moment, SWAPO and Dissent," *Southern Africa Report*, 13(4), 3–8; John S. Saul and Colin Leys, "Lubango and After: 'Forgotten History' as Politics in Contemporary Namibia," *The Next Liberation Struggle: Capitalism, Socialism and Democracy in Southern Africa*, ed. John S. Saul, 107–28 (New York, NY: Monthly Review Press, 2005).
[13] Joseph Diescho during his public lecture held in Windhoek, Namibia's capital, after the 2009 national and presidential election.
[14] "African Leader Warns of Race War," *Western Voices World News*, October 6, 2009.
[15] Alexactus T. Kaure, "Unity in Diversity: Myth or Reality?" *The Namibian*, June 27, 2008.
[16] Theo-Ben Gurirab, "The Genesis of the Namibian Constitution: The International and Regional Setting," in *Constitutional Democracy in Namibia—A Critical Analysis after Two Decades*, eds. Anton Bösl, Nico Horn, André du Pisani, 109–17 (Windhoek, Namibia: Konrad-Adenauer-Stiftung, 2010).
[17] Joseph Diescho, *The Namibian Constitution in Perspective* (Windhoek, Namibia: Gamsberg Macmillan, 1994); Eunice M. Iipinge and Debie LeBeau, *Beyond Inequalities: Women in Namibia* (Windhoek, Namibia: SARDC/UNAM, 2004).
[18] Iipinge and LeBeau; National Society for Human Rights, *Namibia Country Report: Victims of War, Torture and Organized Political Violence as Well as Issues of National Reconciliation and Justice* (Windhoek, Namibia: Author, 2002).
[19] Iipinge and LeBeau; Wade C. Pendleton, *Katutura: A Place Where We Stay* (Windhoek, Namibia: Gamsburg Macmillan, 1994).
[20] For more, see Southern African Documentation and Cooperation Centre (SADOCC), "South Africa: Wouter Basson Acquitted among Strong Protests," SADOCC Web site, April 22, 2002; Stephen Timm, "I'd Just Make Sure I Killed More of Them," *BDlive*, October 16, 2012.
[21] Timm; a Wikipedia entry defines Koevoet (pronounced [ku:fut]) as an Afrikaans and Dutch word for a crowbar, which is an allusion to Koevoet's mission of preying on insurgents from the local population.
[22] Paul Conway, "Truth and Reconciliation: The Road Not Taken in Namibia," *The Online Journal of Peace and Conflict Resolution* 5(1), 66–76.
[23] For more, see SADOCC, note 20 above.
[24] *A Report to the Namibian People: Historical Account of SWAPO Spy-Drama* (Windhoek, Namibia: Breaking the Wall of Silence Movement, 1997).
[25] Alfredo Tjiurimo Hengari, "The Republic Must Show Solidarity with the History of Genocide," *The Namibian*, July 10, 2011, paras. 3–5.
[26] See Eric Van Grasdorff, Nicolai Röscgert, and Firoze Manji, "Germany's Genocide in Namibia," *Pambazuka News*, March 20, 2012.
[27] Iipinge and LeBeau.

[28] Diescho, 1994; Iipinge and LeBeau. The signing of the tripartite accords (supervised by the United States and the former Soviet Union) on December 22, 1988, between South Africa, Cuba, and Angola made the implementation of the Resolution 435 possible (Diescho, 1994).

[29] Ndumba J. Kamwanyah, "In Times of Peace: Reconciliation and Public Debate about the Past in Namibia," *The UMASS Boston Dispute Resolution Newsletter*, 3(1), 6–7. SWAPO, then the main national liberation movement and now the ruling party in Namibia, has been accused of committing gross violations of human rights against its own cadres in the movement suspected of spying for apartheid South Africa. In order to reflect the organization's post-independence transformation from a liberation movement to a political party, the term Swapo Party will be used interchangeably with SWAPO.

[30] Christof Maletsky, "Hear Our Plea, BWS Urges Swapo," *The Namibian*, November 27, 2007; National Society for Human Rights, *Namibia Country Report: Victims of War, Torture and Organized Political Violence as Well as Issues of National Reconciliation and Justice* (Windhoek, Namibia: Author, 2002).

[31] Catherine Sasman, "Mboroma Killing Commemorated," *The Namibian*, August 7, 2012, para 1.

[32] Tsudao Gurirab, "Is it Hard to Say Sorry?" *The Namibian*, August 4, 2012, para. 3.

[33] Sasman, "Mboroma Killing Commemorated."

[34] Lauren Dobell, *Swapo's Struggle for Namibia, 1960–1991: War by Other Means* (Basel, Switzerland: P. Schlettwein, 2000); Jauch, 1998, 74.

[35] by extension, reconciliation can flourish. Theodore W. Adorno, "What Does Coming to Terms with the Past Mean?" in *Bitburg in Moral and Political Perspective*, ed. Geoffrey H. Hartman, 114–129 (Bloomington, IN: Indiana University Press, 1986); Barbara A. Misztal, "Memory and Democracy," *American Behavioral Scientist* 48(10), 1320–38.

[36] Dobell, 2000; Herbert M. Jauch, *Affirmative Action in Namibia: Redressing the Imbalances of the Past* (Windhoek, Namibia: New Namibia Books, 1998).

[37] Jauch.

[38] Lauren Dobell, "Silence in Context: Truth and/or Reconciliation in Namibia," *Journal of Southern African Studies*, 23(2), 373–82; Andre du Pisani, "Liberation and Tolerance," in *Re-examining Liberation in Namibia: Political Culture since Independence*, ed. Henning Melber, 129–36 (Stockholm, Sweden: Elanders Gotab, 2003); Phanuel Kaapama, Lesley Blaauw, Bernie Zaaruka, and Esau Kaakunga, *Consolidating Democratic Government in Southern Africa: Namibia* (Johannesburg, South Africa: EISA, 2007).

[39] Kamwanyah, "In Times of Peace…"

[40] Ibid.

[41] Dobell, "Review of Namibia's…"

[42] Minette E. Mans, "State, Politics and Culture: The Case of Music," in *Re-Examining Liberation in Namibia: Political Culture Since Independence*, ed. Henning Melber, 113–128 (Stockholm, Sweden: Elanders Gotab, 2003).

[43] The "Nationhood and National Pride" campaign, which commenced in 2010, was launched by the Ministry of Information and Communication Technology

(MICT) in conjunction with the Ministry of Education and other stakeholders. The campaign will be reviewed after five years.

[44] Brian Harlech-Jones, "Language, Nationalism and Modernization: Reflections from Namibia," in *Guardian of the Word: Literature, Language and Politics in SADC Countries*, eds. Brian Harlech-Jones, Ismael Mbise, and Helen Vale, (Windhoek, Namibia: The Association of University Teachers of Literature and Language, 2001); Jenny Schwerdt, "One Namibia–One Nation: A Qualitative Study of the Official Nation-Building Process and Experienced Participation among Rural San in Namibia," Master's thesis, University of Linköping, 2009.

[45] Priscilla B. Hayner, *Unspeakable Truths: Facing the Challenge of Truth Commissions* (New York, NY: Routledge / Kegan Paul, 2002); Thiven Reddy, "From Apartheid to Democracy in South Africa: A Reading of Dominant Discourses of Democratic Transition," in *History Making and Present-Day Politics: The Meaning of Collective Memory in South Africa*, ed. Hans Erik Stolten, 148–64 (Uppsala, Sweden: Nordic African Institute, 2007); Andrew Schaap, *Political Reconciliation* (New York, NY: Routledge, 2005).

[46] Hage Geingob, quoted in *The Namibian*, October 22, 1993, 2.

[47] Andre du Pisani and Guy Lamb, *The Role of the Military in State Formation and Nation-Building: An Overview of the European and Africa Experiences*, unpublished manuscript, n.d.

[48] Maria Ericson, *Reconciliation and the Search for a Shared Moral Landscape: An Exploration Based upon a Study of Northern Ireland and South Africa* (New York, NY: P. Lang, 2001).

[49] For more on the blind model of citizenship, see Bashir Bashir and Will Kymlicka, "Introduction: Struggles for Inclusion and Reconciliation in Modern Democracies," in *The Politics of Reconciliation in Multicultural Societies*, eds. Bashir Bashir and Will Kymlica, 1–24 (New York, NY: Oxford University Press, 2008).

[50] Misztal.

[51] Angela Pratt, Catriona Elder and Cath Ellis, "Papering over Difference," in *Reconciliation, Multiculturalism, Identities: Difficult Dialogues, Sensible Solutions*, eds. Mary Kalantzis and Bill Cope, 135–47 (Australia: Common Ground, 2001); Schaap.

[52] Susan Dwyer, "Reconciliation for Realists," *Ethics and International Affairs* 13(1), 81–98.

[53] Elijah Ngurare, "The Politics of Anti-Owambo: A National Dialogue Is Needed," *The Namibian* March 23, 2012, paras. 1–4.

[54] Diescho, 1994; Dobell, 2000; Saul and Leys, 2005.

[55] Saul and Leys, 2005. The SWAPO party is still positively regarded as the party that brought independence and peace in the country, and therefore any talks that contradict its views are likely to be inferred by its political power base (members and supporters) and most Namibians as a return to colonialism, pain and suffering.

[56] Diescho, 1994, "Reconciliation—The Good, the Bad and the Ugly," *The Namibian*, April 6, 1990, 6, and *Government and Opposition in Post-Independence Namibia: Perceptions and Performance* (Windhoek, Namibia: Namibia Institute for Democracy / Konrad Adenauer Foundation, 1996); Reinhart Kössler and

Henning Melber, "Political Culture and Civil Society: On the State of the Namibian State," in *Contemporary Namibia: The First Landmarks of a Post-Apartheid Society*, eds. Ingolf Diener and Olivier Graefe, 147–60 (Windhoek, Namibia: Gamsberg Macmillan, 2001); Chris Tapscott, "National Reconciliation, Social Equity and Class Formation in Independent Namibia," *Journal of Southern African Studies* 19(1), 29–39. The minority white population and black elites controlled the economy at the dawn of independence, a trend that still continues in post-independence Namibia. For both practical and political reasons, the new democratically elected SWAPO government opted for the policy of national reconciliation to prevent the flight of much-needed skills and capital as well as to minimize potential political destabilization by disaffected opponents. As a result, private property is constitutionally entrenched, and the old colonial public sector structure was left intact (Diescho, 1990, 1994; Tapscott).

[57] Harlech-Jones.

[58] Schwerdt.

[59] Samuel Gbaydee Doe, "Indigenizing Post-Conflict State Reconstruction in Africa: A Conceptual Framework," *African Peace and Conflict Journal* 1(4), 1–16.

[60] Susan Opotow, "Reconciliation in Times of Impunity: Challenges for Societal Justice," *Social Justice Research* 14(2), 149–70.

[61] Susan Opotow, "After Deadly Conflict: The Challenges of Social Reconciliation," *The UMASS Boston Dispute Resolution Newsletter*, 3(1), 2–3, 11.

[62] Schaap.

[63] James Gibson, *Overcoming Apartheid: Can Truth Reconcile a Divided Nation?* (New York, NY: Russell Sage Foundation, 2004).

[64] Gerhard Tötemeyer, "The Management of a Dominant Political Party System with Particular Reference to Namibia," paper presented at the conference on The Management of Dominant Political Parties, Friedrich-Ebert-Stiftung, Maputo, Mozambique, December 10–12, 2007.

[65] Henning Melber, "From Controlled Change to Changed Control: The Case of Namibia," in *Limits to Liberation in Southern Africa: The Unfinished Business of Democratic Consolidation*, ed. Henning Melber, 134–55 (Cape Town, South Africa: HSRC Publishers, 2003).

[66] Kamwanyah, "In Times of Peace…"

[67] du Pisani, 2003.

[68] Ibid.

[69] Kaapama et al.; Christiaan Keulder and Tania Wiese, *Democracy without Democrats? Results from the 2003 Afrobarometer Survey in Namibia*, Afrobarometer Paper no. 47 (Cape Town, South Africa: Idasa, 2003).

[70] du Pisani, 2003.

[71] Dobell, "The Ulenga Moment…"; Kamwanyah; Christo Lombard, "The Detainee Issue: An Unresolved Test Case for SWAPO, the Churches and Civil Society," in *Contemporary Namibia: The First Landmark of a Post-Apartheid Society*, eds. Ingolf Diener and Olivier Graefe, 161–84 (Windhoek: Gamsberg Macmillan, 2001); Maletsky, 2008; Melber, 2003.

[72] National Society for Human Rights, 1.

[73] Klaus Schade, "Poverty," in *Namibia. A Decade of Independence 1990–2000*, ed. Henning Melber, 211 (Windhoek, Namibia: Namibian Economic Policy Research Unit, 2000).
[74] Central Bureau of Statistics.
[75] Pempelani Mufune, "Youth in Namibia—Social Exclusion and Poverty," in *Namibia. Society. Sociology.*, eds. Volker Winterfeldt, Tom Fox, and Pempelani Mufune, 179–95 (Windhoek, Namibia: University of Namibia, 2002).
[76] Schwerdt.
[77] Gibson; Mai Palmberg, "Introduction," in *National Identity and Democracy in Africa*, ed. Mai Palmberg, 8–18 (Uppsala, Sweden: Nordic Africa Institute, 1999), 14.
[78] Henning Melber, "The Challenge of Reconciliation: Lessons for Namibia?" *The Namibian*, September 5, 2005.

# Bibliography

*A Report to the Namibian People: Historical Account of SWAPO Spy-Drama*. Windhoek, Namibia: Breaking the Wall of Silence (BWS) Movement, 1997.
Adorno, Theodore W. "What Does Coming to Terms with the Past Mean?" In *Bitburg in Moral and Political Perspective*. Edited by Geoffrey H. Hartman. 114–129. Bloomington, IN: Indiana University Press, 1986.
"African Leader Warns of Race War." *Western Voices World News*, October 6, 2009. http://www.wvwnews.net/story.php?id=7951
Angula, Nahas. "We Are Each Other's Keepers: Diversity and Divergence." *The Namibian*, May 10, 2013. http://www.namibian.com.na/indexx.php?archive_id=107933&page_type=archive_story_detail&page=314
Bashir, Bashir, and Will Kymlicka. "Introduction: Struggles for Inclusion and Reconciliation in Modern Democracies." In *The Politics of Reconciliation in Multicultural Societies*. Edited by Will Kymlicka and Bashir Bashir. 1–24. New York, NY: OUP, 2008.
Central Bureau of Statistics. *National Household Income Survey 2003/2004*. Windhoek, Namibia: National Planning Commission, 2006.
Conway, Paul. "Truth and Reconciliation: The Road Not Taken in Namibia." *The Online Journal of Peace and Conflict Resolution* 5(1), 66–76.
Cloete, Luqman. "Deputy Minister's 'Tribal Tirade' Investigated by Police." *AllAfrica*, January 16, 2013. http://allafrica.com/stories/201301180868.html
Diescho, Joseph. *Government and Opposition in Post-Independence Namibia: Perceptions and Performance*. Windhoek, Namibia:

Namibia Institute for Democracy / Konrad Adenauer Foundation, 1996.
—. *The Namibian Constitution in Perspective*. Windhoek, Namibia: Gamsberg Macmillan, 1994.
—. "Reconciliation—The Good, the Bad and the Ugly." *The Namibian*, April 6, 1990, p. 6.
Doe, Samuel Gbaydee. "Indigenizing Post-Conflict State Reconstruction in Africa: A Conceptual Framework." *African Peace and Conflict Journal* 1(4), 1–16. http://www.apcj.upeace.org/issues/APCJ_June2009_Vol2_Num1.pdf
Dobell, Lauren. *Swapo's Struggle for Namibia, 1960–1991: War by Other Means*. Basel, Switzerland: P. Schlettwein, 2000.
—."The Ulenga Moment, SWAPO and Dissent." *Southern Africa Report*, 13(4), 3–8.
—. "Silence in Context: Truth and/or Reconciliation in Namibia." *Journal of Southern African Studies*, 23(2), 373–82.
—. "Review of Namibia's Wall of Silence." *Southern Africa Report* 1(4), 30–3.
du Pisani, Andre. "Liberation and Tolerance." In *Re-examining Liberation in Namibia: Political Culture since Independence*. Edited by Henning Melber. 129–36. Stockholm, Sweden: Elanders Gotab, 2003.
du Pisani, Andre, and Guy Lamb. *The Role of the Military in State Formation and Nation-Building: An Overview of the European and Africa Experiences*. Unpublished manuscript, n.d.
Dwyer, Susan. "Reconciliation for Realists." *Ethics and International Affairs* 13(1), 81–98.
Ericson, Maria. *Reconciliation and the Search for a Shared Moral Landscape: An Exploration Based upon a Study of Northern Ireland and South Africa*. New York, NY: P. Lang, 2001.
Gibson, James. *Overcoming Apartheid: Can Truth Reconcile a Divided Nation?* New York, NY: Russell Sage Foundation, 2004.
Gurirab, Theo-Ben. "The Genesis of the Namibian Constitution: The International and Regional Setting." In *Constitutional Democracy in Namibia—A Critical Analysis after Two Decades*. Edited by Anton Bösl, Nico Horn, and André du Pisani. 109–17. Windhoek, Namibia: Konrad-Adenauer-Stiftung, 2010.
Gurirab, Tsudao. "Is it Hard to Say Sorry?" *The Namibian*, August 4, 2012. http://www.namibian.com.na/indexx.php?archive_id=98697&page_type=archive_story_detail&page=757

Grobler, John. "Insult Reflects Tribal Division in Namibia." *Mail and Guardian*, February 10, 2012. http://mg.co.za/article/2012-02-10-insult-reflects-tribal-division-in-namibia

Harlech-Jones, Brian. "Language, Nationalism and Modernization: Reflections from Namibia." in *Guardian of the Word: Literature, Language and Politics in SADC Countries.* Edited by Brian Harlech-Jones, Ismael Mbise and Helen Vale. Windhoek, Namibia: The Association of University Teachers of Literature and Language, 2001.

Hayner, Priscilla B. *Unspeakable Truths: Facing the Challenge of Truth Commissions.* New York, NY: Routledge / Kegan Paul, 2002.

Hengari, Alfredo Tjiurimo. "The Republic Must Show Solidarity with the History of Genocide." *The Namibian*, July 10, 2011. http://www.namibian.com.na/columns/full-story/archive/2011/october/article/the-republic-must-show-solidarity-with-the-history-of-genocide/

Iipinge, Eunice M., and Debie LeBeau. *Beyond Inequalities: Women in Namibia.* Windhoek, Namibia: SARDC/UNAM, 2004.

Jauch, Herbert M. *Affirmative Action in Namibia: Redressing the Imbalances of the Past.* Windhoek, Namibia: New Namibia Books, 1998.

Kaapama, Phanuel, Lesley Blaauw, Bernie Zaaruka, and Esau Kaakunga. *Consolidating Democratic Government in Southern Africa: Namibia.* Johannesburg, South Africa: EISA, 2007.

Kamwanyah, Ndumba J. "Another Test for President Pohamba," *The Namibian*, January 11, 2013, http://www.namibian.com.na/columns/full-story/archive/2013/january/article/another-test-for-president-pohamba/

—. "Namibia: Ethnic Tension in Presidential Succession Race," *AllAfrica*, March 2, 2012, http://allafrica.com/stories/201203021129.html

—. "In Times of Peace: Reconciliation and Public Debate about the Past in Namibia." *The UMASS Boston Dispute Resolution Newsletter*, 3(1), 6–7.

Kaure, Alexactus T. "Unity in Diversity: Myth or Reality?" *The Namibian*, June 27, 2008. http://www.namibian.com.na/indexx.php?archive_id=45341&page_type=archive_story detail&page=3549

Keulder, Christiaan, and Tania Wiese. *Democracy without Democrats? Results from the 2003 Afrobarometer Survey in Namibia.* Afrobarometer Paper no. 47. Cape Town, South Africa: Idasa, 2003.

Kotzé, Carol Ella. "A Social History of Windhoek, 1915–1939." PhD dissertation, University of South Africa. 1990.

Kössler, Reinhart, and Henning Melber. "Political Culture and Civil

Society: On the State of the Namibian State." In *Contemporary Namibia: The First Landmarks of a Post-Apartheid Society.* Edited by Ingolf Diener and Olivier Graefe. 147–60. Windhoek, Namibia: Gamsberg Macmillan, 2001.

Lombard, Christo. "The Detainee Issue: An Unresolved Test Case for SWAPO, the Churches and Civil Society." In *Contemporary Namibia: The First Landmark of a Post-Apartheid Society.* Edited by Ingolf Diener and Olivier Graefe. 161–84. Windhoek: Gamsberg Macmillan, 2001.

Maletsky, Christof. "UN Report Lambastes Nam for Hate Speech." *The Namibian*, August 21, 2008. http://www.namibian.com.na/indexx.php?archive_id=41758&page_type=archive_story_detail&page=3478

—. "Hear Our Plea, BWS Urges Swapo." *The Namibian*, November 27, 2007. http://www.namibian.com.na/indexx.php?archive_id=37646&page_type=archive_story_detail&page=3867

Mans, Minette E. "State, Politics and Culture: The Case of Music." In *Re-Examining Liberation in Namibia: Political Culture Since Independence.* Edited by Henning Melber. 113–128. Stockholm, Sweden: Elanders Gotab, 2003.

Melber, Henning. "From Controlled Change to Changed Control: The Case of Namibia." In *Limits to Liberation in Southern Africa: The Unfinished Business of Democratic Consolidation.* Edited by Henning Melber. 134–55. Cape Town, South Africa: HSRC Publishers, 2003.

—. "The Challenge of Reconciliation: Lessons for Namibia?" *The Namibian*, September 5, 2005. http://www.namibian.com.na/indexx.php?archive_id=47187&page_type=archive_story_detail&page=3667

Misztal, Barbara A. "Memory and Democracy." *American Behavioral Scientist* 48(10), 1320–38.

Mufune, Pempelani. "Youth in Namibia—Social Exclusion and Poverty." In *Namibia. Society. Sociology.* Edited by Volker Winterfeldt, Tom Fox, and Pempelani Mufune. 179–95. Windhoek, Namibia: University of Namibia, 2002.

Nakatana, Festus. "KK Loses His Head Again." *Namibian Sun*, February 03, 2012. http://www.namibiansun.com/content/national-news/kk-loses-his-head-again

Ngurare, Elijah. "The Politics of Anti-Owambo: A National Dialogue Is Needed." *The Namibian* March 23, 2012. http://www.namibian.com.na/indexx.php?archive_id=93253&page_type=archive_story_detail&page=1045

National Society for Human Rights. *Namibia Country Report: Victims of War, Torture and Organized Political Violence as Well as Issues of*

*National Reconciliation and Justice*. Windhoek, Namibia: Author, 2002.
Opotow, Susan. "After Deadly Conflict: The Challenges of Social Reconciliation." *The UMASS Boston Dispute Resolution Newsletter*, 3(1), 2–3, 11.
—. "Reconciliation in Times of Impunity: Challenges for Societal Justice." *Social Justice Research* 14(2), 149–70.
Palmberg, Mai. "Introduction." In *National Identity and Democracy in Africa*. Edited by Mai Palmberg. 8–18. Uppsala, Sweden: Nordic Africa Institute, 1999.
Pendleton, Wade C. *Katutura: A Place Where We Stay*. Windhoek, Namibia: Gamsburg Macmillan, 1994.
Pratt, Angela, Catriona Elder and Cath Ellis. "Papering over Difference." In *Reconciliation, Multiculturalism, Identities: Difficult Dialogues, Sensible Solutions*. Edited by Mary Kalantzis and Bill Cope. 135–47. Australia: Common Ground, 2001.
Reddy, Thiven. "From Apartheid to Democracy in South Africa: A Reading of Dominant Discourses of Democratic Transition." In *History Making and Present-Day Politics: The Meaning of Collective Memory in South Africa*. Edited by Hans Erik Stolten. 148–64. Uppsala, Sweden: Nordic African Institute, 2007.
Sasman, Catherine. "Mboroma Killing Commemorated," *The Namibian*, August 7, 2012, para 1. http://www.namibian.com.na/indexx.php?archive_id=98445&page_type=archive_story_detail&page=768
—. "Caprivi Group Wants UN to Probe Treason Trial." *The Namibian*, September 26, 2012. http://www.namibian.com.na/indexx.php?archive_id=100398&page_type=archive_story_detail&page=662
Saul, John S., and Colin Leys. "Lubango and After: 'Forgotten History' as Politics in Contemporary Namibia." *The Next Liberation Struggle: Capitalism, Socialism and Democracy in Southern Africa*. Edited by John S. Saul. 107–28. New York, NY: Monthly Review Press, 2005.
Schaap, Andrew. *Political Reconciliation*. New York, NY: Routledge, 2005.
Schade, Klaus. "Poverty." In *Namibia. A Decade of Independence 1990–2000*. Edited by Henning Melber. 211. Windhoek, Namibia: Namibian Economic Policy Research Unit, 2000.
Schwerdt, Jenny. "One Namibia–One Nation: A Qualitative Study of the Official Nation-Building Process and Experienced Participation among Rural San in Namibia." Master's thesis, University of Linköping, 2009. ISRN: LiU-ISV/SKA-A--19/09—SE.

Smit, Nico. "KK on the Rampage." *The Namibian*, February 3, 2012, http://www.namibian.com.na/indexx.php?archive_id=91137&page_type=archive_story_detail&page=1142

Southern African Documentation and Cooperation Centre (SADOCC). "South Africa: Wouter Basson Acquitted among Strong Protests." SADOCC Web site. April 22, 2002. http://www.sadocc.at/news2002/2002-126.shtml

Tapscott, Chris. "National Reconciliation, Social Equity and Class Formation in Independent Namibia." *Journal of Southern African Studies* 19(1), 29–39.

Timm, Stephen. "I'd Just Make Sure I Killed More of Them." *BDlive*. October 16, 2012. http://www.bdlive.co.za/life/books/2012/10/16/id-just-make-sure-i-killed-more-of-them

Tötemeyer, Gerhard. "The Management of a Dominant Political Party System with Particular Reference to Namibia." Paper presented at the conference on The Management of Dominant Political Parties, Friedrich-Ebert-Stiftung, Maputo, Mozambique, December 10–12, 2007. http://library.fes.de/pdf-files/bueros/namibia/05913.pdf

Van Grasdorff, Eric, Nicolai Röscgert, and Firoze Manji. "Germany's Genocide in Namibia." *Pambazuka News*, March 20, 2012. http://www.pambazuka.org/en/category/features/80911

"White Man Grabs Black's Land." *The Namibian*, May 31, 2013. http://allafrica.com/stories/201306010081.html

# Contributors

**Adenrele Awotona** is the founder and director of the Center for Rebuilding Sustainable Communities after Disasters, University of Massachusetts Boston. Through research, consultancy and teaching, Professor Awotona has professional experience in several countries in Europe, Africa, Asia, the Middle East, South America, and the Caribbean. He earned his Doctorate degree from the University of Cambridge, UK, a certificate from Harvard University's Institute of Management and Leadership in Education, and two certificates from Cornell University, one in Managing Performance in Higher Education and another from the Administrative Management Institute. Professor Awotona has published extensively on community rebuilding after disasters.

**Shoji Azuma** is a Professor of Japanese at the University of Utah, U.S., where he teaches Japanese language and linguistics. His research interests include political discourse and sociolinguistics. His recent work includes *Senkyo Enzetsu no Gengogaku* ("*Linguisitcs of Political Speeches*") (Minerva Shobo, 2010) and "Soapbox speeches in the summer of Seiken Kootai" (*Japanese Language and Linguistics*, 45 no. 1, 2011, 141–167).

**Qin Bo** is Associate Professor and Deputy Head of the Department of Urban Planning and Management, Renmin University of China. He received his Ph.D. degree (2007) from the Department of Real Estate, National University of Singapore, his M.Sc. degree (2003) from the Department of Geography, Beijing University, and his B.Eng. degree (2000) from the Department of Architecture, Wuhan University. His research interests include urban internal spatial restructuring in Chinese cities, application of GIS and spatial statistics in urban studies, and urban sustainable development in China. His recent work includes research on the spatial pattern of firms in transitional Shanghai, a research project on *Low-Carbon Beijing* supported by the National Science Foundation of China (NSFC), and planning projects in Chengduo, Shenzhen, and Beijing.

**Charles Bonner** has taught courses in philosophy at a number of universities in Europe and the U.S. His recent publications focus on questions of ontology in relation to our present age of information. He has worked at research institutes and universities in Vienna, Prague, St Petersburg, Budapest, and Boston. He was trained in the natural sciences and engineering at Northwestern University and studied philosophy at Boston University, where he completed his doctoral degree in 1995. He is currently teaching environmental philosophy and biomedical ethics at Providence College in Providence, Rhode Island.

**Cristal Downing** is currently completing an M.Sc. in Political Science at the Universidad de los Andes in Bogotá, Colombia, where her research encompasses topics related to children and conflict. She also holds an M.A. in Latin American and Caribbean Studies from New York University, where her focus was on violence, development and Inter-American Relations with a geographic focus on the Andean region. Originally from London, UK, Cristal completed her Bachelor's degree cum laude at the University of Pennsylvania and since then has accrued more than six years of development and policy experience in Colombia, Guatemala, Argentina and Bolivia. There, she spent six months working with a local NGO to evaluate and strengthen their Human Rights and Development projects in the prisons of the city of Cochabamba. In Colombia she is involved in a number of projects related to education and conflict with local and international organizations.

**John H. Dreher**, B.A. cum laude, Yale University, and Ph.D. Indiana University, is currently an associate professor of philosophy at the University of Southern California (dreher@usc.edu). He is formerly director of the USC McNair Scholars Program (1997–2001), Associate Dean of the Graduate School of the University of Southern California (1997–2004), and Director of the School of Philosophy of the University of Southern California (1985–1997). His interests include the history of modern philosophy, as well as contemporary ethics and political philosophy. Recent contributions include work presented at sessions of the Oxford Round Table in 2011 and 2012: "Evolution and the Goal of Environmentalism," *Forum on Public Policy-e*, August 2011, and "Environmental Sustainability as a Culturally Invariant Value," *Forum on Public Policy-e*, August 2012. He also presented "The Circle, from Descartes' Point of View" to the Early Modern Circle of Southern California in June, 2012, and delivered "Implementing Global Standards of Global Justice and the Common Good," in November 2012 at the University of Paris, as part of a program sponsored by the University of Paris, District 8 and the USC/Levin Institute for Ethics.

**James Gannon** is the executive director of Japan Center for International Exchange (JCIE/USA) and oversees a wide range of programs designed to strengthen the underpinnings of U.S.-Japan relations and encourage deeper international cooperation in responding to regional and global challenges. Building on its long history of facilitating philanthropic giving between Japan and the U.S., JCIE has been especially active in responding to the March 11 disaster in Japan, operating funds to channel American donations to Japanese relief and recovery organizations, advising overseas humanitarian organizations on how to best respond, and facilitating coordination among a wide range of philanthropic and nonprofit organizations in both countries. Before joining JCIE in 2001, Jim was a researcher with the Japan Bank for International Cooperation and taught English in rural Japanese middle schools as part of the Japan Exchange and Teaching Program. He received a BA from the University of Notre Dame, conducted graduate research at Ehime University in Japan, and has a Master's degree from Columbia University's School of International and Public Affairs. He is co-editor of *A Growing Force: Civil Society's Role in Asian Regional Security* (2013) and has written about philanthropy, disaster relief, U.S.-Japan relations, and Asia's evolving regional order for a wide range of publications.

**Yumei Han** is a PhD candidate in the area of comparative education in the Faculty of Education of Southwest University, Chongqing, China, and she is currently a visiting scholar through the China Scholarship Council-sponsored Joint PhD Program at the Department of Leadership in Education, College of Education and Human Development at University of Massachusetts Boston. Her research focuses include educational policy, comparative education, teacher evaluation, and rural education. In recent years Yumei Han has published more than ten articles in well-recognized Chinese journals in the educational research field.

**Yuping Han** is a lecturer and PhD candidate at the College of Economics and Management of Southwest University, Chongqing, China. She obtained a grant from the China Scholarship Council and worked as a visiting scholar at Wilfrid Laurier University. Her research interests include post-disaster reconstruction, agricultural education, urbanization and agricultural structural transformation, rural labor mobility, and social support systems. She published more than ten articles and book chapters, and has received research grants from both the university and the provincial levels.

**Adetokunbo Oluwole Ilesanmi** lectures at the Department of Architecture, Obafemi Awolowo University, Ile-Ife, Nigeria. He obtained his BSc in Architecture (First Class Honors) in 1983 and was awarded the Faculty Prize for the Best Overall Student in the Faculty of Environmental Design and Management; he earned his MSc in Architecture in 1985. He engaged in private architectural practice until 1999, when he resumed his academic career. He obtained his PhD in Architecture in 2006 from the Obafemi Awolowo University, Ile-Ife. His post-doctoral research interests include: sustainable housing, housing satisfaction and quality; housing and health; urban design and disasters; building evaluation; and built-environment education. He teaches architectural design, urban design, and housing-related courses at the undergraduate and postgraduate levels. Dr. Ilesanmi is a member of the Nigerian Institute of Architects (NIA), the Association of Architectural Educators in Nigeria (AARCHES), and is registered with the Architects' Registration Council of Nigeria (ARCON).

**Oluwatoyin Olatundun Ilesanmi** studied clinical psychology at the University of Ibadan, Nigeria (2005). She is a research fellow at the Centre for Gender and Social Policy Studies, Obafemi Awolowo University, Ile-Ife, Nigeria (toytundun@yahoo.com, phone: +0234-8052236377). She previously worked with Redeemer's University, Redemption Camp, Ogun State, Nigeria, from 2006 to 2011. Dr. Ilesanmi obtained professional training in Dispute and Conflict Analysis (2007), Gender Perspectives in United Nations Peacekeeping Operations (2009), Civil-Military Coordination (CIMIC) (2009), and Global Terrorism (2009) at the Peace Operations Training Institute, and genetic counseling (2009) at the Sickle Foundation, Nigeria. She is a member of the Nigerian Association of Professional Negotiators and Mediators. As a gendered psychotherapist and genetic counselor, Dr Ilesanmi is concerned with taking care of people with sickle-cell disease, the prevention and control of sickle-cell disease through awareness creation, information dissemination, psycho-education, screening, and genetic counseling.

**Hao Kai** is studying for an MA at the Department of Urban Planning and Management, Renmin University of China, from which he received his BA in Management with an Excellent College Graduates' Award. His academic interests focus on public administration and planning policy in China. He has been participating in many planning projects as a research assistant in cities such as Shanghaimiao, Qingshuihe, and Chengduo.

**Ndumba J. Kamwanyah**, a native of Namibia in southern Africa, is a public policy consultant currently working on an Outreach and Case Management System for HIV-positive offenders for Miriam Hospital/Lifespan Inc., U.S. He is also a public policy PhD candidate at the University of Massachusetts Boston. Ndumba holds an MSc in Public Policy, an MA in Conflict Studies from the University of Massachusetts Boston, and a BA in Social Work and Psychology from the University of Namibia.

Focusing on the intersection between policy and politics, Ndumba writes a weekly column for *The Namibian* newspaper and serves as an

Africa Blogger for the Foreign Policy Association, where he provides an in-depth perspective and analysis on the latest news, politics, policy discussions, and everything African.

A certified mediator, Ndumba provides capacity building through training, research and social impact analysis. Earlier in his career, Ndumba completed a consulting assignment in Liberia in support of the UN Mission in Liberia (UNMIL); taught traditional justice and indigenous African political institutions in sub-Saharan Africa at the Rhode Island College Anthropology Department (as an Adjunct Professor); and consulted on juvenile justice in Namibia and Uganda.

**Bandana Kar** is a geographer specializing in Geographic Information Science (GIScience) and hazard research. Her research agenda is to bridge the gap between GIScience and hazards. Her interest lies in: 1) advancing the concepts of GIScience, developing algorithms and applying them to models, and investigating the implications of social-physical interaction of environments; 2) exploring the impacts of spatial and temporal scales of analysis on modeled outcomes; 3) investigating the legal implications of location-based services in terms of location privacy violation; and 4) developing tools and techniques to visualize and disseminate modeled outcomes to broader audiences.

**Haifeng Li** is a lecturer in college English in the Rongchang College of Southwest University in China. He received his MA from Sichuan International Studies University. He also learned German as a second foreign language. His research interests include comparative education between China, the U.S., and Germany, educational policy, post-disaster reconstruction in the educational field, and agricultural education. He has published several papers in Chinese journals such as *China Agricultural Education*. In 2009 and 2011 he was elected as the leader of the translation service team for the Chongqing animal husbandry science and technology forum.

**Ling Li** is currently a professor at the Faculty of Education of Southwest University, Chongqing, China. She obtained her PhD from the University of Toronto. She joined Southwest University in 2008 and for the past five years she has been very productive in educational research. Her research interests include educational policy, urbanization and education, social support for educational reform, transdisciplinary research, and qualitative research methodology. She has published over thirty articles in the top-ranked Chinese and U.S. journals in the educational field. She has also received around fourteen research grants, both from China's top national research funds such as the Ministry of Education's major philosophy and social sciences research and development project funds, and from international sponsors such as the Social Sciences and Humanities Research Council of Canada and the Delta Kappa Gamma Women's International Society for Key Women Educators. She is currently honored as one of the hundred academic leaders and excellent overseas talents of the Chongqing municipality and serves as the chair of several key national research projects.

**Xinzhi Liu** has served as an associate professor at the College of Economics and Management of Southwest University, Chongqing, China, for six years. He received his PhD in economics from Northeast Normal University in China. He teaches courses in regional economics, agricultural economics, logistics, and other subjects. He is a well-recognized lecturer by both students and teachers, and he has received honors for excellent teaching at both the university and provincial levels. His research interests include regional economics, rural human capital development, agricultural education, urbanization, and education. He has published around twelve articles, edited or translated seven books, and received more than ten research grants from national, provincial and university funds in the field of economics in the past six years.

**Hans Skotte** is an Associate Professor in the Department of Urban Design and Planning Faculty of Architecture and Fine Art at the Norwegian University of Science and Technology (NTNU), Trondheim, Norway.

**Jennifer Trivedi** is a doctoral candidate in the University of Iowa's Anthropology Department. She is currently working on her dissertation on post-Katrina recovery in Biloxi, Mississippi. She earned her MA in Anthropology from the University of Iowa in 2007 and her BA in History from the University of Georgia in 2004. Mrs. Trivedi studies disaster recovery and preparation, Hurricane Katrina, emergency management responses and agencies in the U.S., as well as issues of perception, memory, vulnerability, risk, and uncertainty after disasters. Her MA research was published in the SEA volume *The Political Economy of Hazards and Disasters* as "'Hurricanes Did Not Just Start Happening': Expectations of Intervention in the Mississippi Gulf Coast Casino Industry." She has written entries for the *Encyclopedia of Disaster Relief* and the *Encyclopedia of Crisis Management* has forthcoming entries in *Disasters and Tragic Events and How They Changed American History*.

**Yu Wang**, a PhD candidate at the Department of Urban Design and Planning at the Norwegian University of Science and Technology, earned his postgraduate degree in Design and Theory of Architecture in 2007 from the School of Architecture, Xi'an University of Architecture and Technology (XAUAT), and his undergraduate degree in Architecture in

1998 from the School of Architecture, Shijiazhuang Railway Institute. From 2007 to 2009 he was a lecturer in Architecture, School of Architecture, Xi'an University of Architecture and Technology (XAUAT); from 2007 to 2009, a Project Architect, Shaanxi Provincial Conservation Engineering Institute of Monuments and Sites, XAUAT; and from 2011 to 2012, he was a part-time teacher in the Department of Urban Design and Planning, NTNU.

**Wenfan Yan** is Professor and Chair of the Department of Leadership in Education at the College of Education and Human Development of University of Massachusetts Boston. He received his PhD from the State University of New York at Buffalo. His research interests have been focused on the area of policy analysis around state, national, and international educational issues in equity, access, effectiveness and assessment of P–16 education. Dr. Yan has received a research grant from the American Educational Research Association, supported by the National Science Foundation and the National Center for Education Statistics. His recent research grant on Chinese education reform and service learning was supported by the Chinese government. His research program integrated both quantitative and qualitative methodologies and a variety of statistical analysis techniques, including complex analysis procedures such as multilevel modeling.

**Gui Yanli** is an Associate Professor at Renmin University of China. She obtained her Bachelor's degree from Nanjing University in 1992, then worked for Jilin Urban-rural Planning Academy and Urban Construction Academy in China and joined the Department of Urban Planning and Management, Renmin University of China in 2008, serving as Deputy Head. Her research focuses on urban and regional planning theory and post-disaster planning practices. As a scholar with practical expertise in planning, she has completed more than thirty planning projects in different regions as team leader, including the one in Chengduo County reported in her chapter in this book.

**Xinyue Ye** is an Assistant Professor of GIS and economic geography at Bowling Green State University, Ohio. He is an Associate Editor of *Stochastic Environmental Research and Risk Assessment* (SCI Journal). His work on comparative space-time analytical implementation won the national first-place award for "research and analysis" from the University Economic Development Association in 2011. He received the Association of American Geographers' Regional Development and Planning Specialty Group emerging scholar award in 2012. Dr. Ye earned his BS in Urban Planning from Zhejiang University, his MA in Human Geography from University of Wisconsin-Milwaukee, his MS in GIS from Eastern

Michigan University, and his PhD in Geography/Spatial Analysis from University of California, Santa Barbara and San Diego State University.

# INDEX

Adolescents – see Children
Advocacy 321, 323–4
Africa 310, 312, 321–4, 346, 349, 351, 353, 372, 374, 378, 386. See also specific countries.
Afrikaners 385, 392
Agriculture 3, 5–6, 10–1, 13–4, 48, 53–4, 57n., 62, 65–71, 74–5, 77, 114–5, 118, 140, 252–5, 262, 265, 318–9, 324, 344, 351, 353, 373
Aid 20, 27, 83, 87, 91, 175–8, 180, 187, 189, 192, 195
   Domestic 175
   Financial 77, 83, 141, 152, 155, 198n., 199n., 288–92, 295, 299, 304
   Foreign / International 12–3, 175, 197n.
   Medical 15, 31
   see also Charitable organizations, NGOs
Aircraft 35, 176, 213, 375
Akihito, Emperor of Japan 204, 208–19
Angola 377, 380
Angula, Nahas, Prime Minister of Namibia 373
Animals 31, 37, 62, 66, 68–9, 77, 144, 312
Antibiotics – see Health
Apartheid 372, 374–5, 379–83, 385, 387–9, 395n.
Apartments – see Housing
Arhuaco – see Indigenous peoples
Architecture – see Housing
Argentina 241–2, 244–6
Army – see Military

Asia 14, 113, 144, 178, 181–2, 194, 286. Individual countries listed by name.
Basson, Dr. Wouter 375–6
Biodiversity 66, 113–4, 259
Biology 6, 11, 37, 61, 131
Boko Haram 310. See also Nigeria; Terrorism.
Bolivia 227–48
   Cochabamba 228, 232–3, 237–41, 246
   La Paz 231, 233, 241
   Santa Cruz 241
Botswana 371, 380
Bulgaria 95
Bush, George H. W., President of the United States 180
Bush, George W., President of the United States 180, 208, 213–4
Businesses 13, 53–4, 69–70, 73, 75, 181, 186, 192, 198–9n., 227, 231–3, 238–9, 243, 245–6, 283–5, 291, 294, 299, 301–5, 319, 351–3, 355, 358
Canada 149
Capitalism 11–5, 347
Caribbean 253, 269
Casinos 299–301
Casualties 3–4, 85–6, 92, 95, 114, 131, 135, 310, 317, 319–21, 375
Catastrophes – see Disasters
Central America – see Latin America
Charity 20, 25, 174, 182
Charitable organizations 92, 177, 185, 191–3, 200n.
   Adventist Development and Relief Agency (ADRA) 191

Americares 184
Caritas Japan 191
Catholic Relief Services 184, 191
China Charity Federation 95
Church World Service 184
Direct Relief International 184
Give2Asia 178, 182, 184
Global Giving 177–8, 182, 184
International Rescue Committee 184
Kids in Distressed Situations (KIDS) 184
Latter-Day Saints Charities 184, 191
Mercy Corps 177, 184, 191
Peace Winds Japan 191
Operation Blessing International 184
Red Crescent 198n., 199n.
Red Cross Societies 198n.
　American Red Cross 143, 177, 184, 191
　Chinese Red Cross 95
　Japanese Red Cross 199n., 200n.
Salvation Army 184, 304
Samaritan's Purse 184
Save the Children, USA 184, 191
United Methodist Committee on Relief 184
United Way Worldwide 177, 178, 184, 190
World Vision 177, 184, 191
Children 25, 83, 95, 183, 232, 255, 261, 265–7, 271–2, 312, 319, 323–4, 349, 360
China 30, 45–169, 197n., 200n.
　Beijing 89, 95–7, 114
　Chengdu 61, 66
　Chengduo 61–79
　Chengwen 61
　Children's Foundation of China 95
China Earthquake Administration (CEA) 148
Chinese Academy of Sciences (CAS) 86
Chinese Architectural History Research Institute (CAHRI) 50–1
Chongqing 99n.
Communist Party (ruling party) (CPC) 87–8, 98
Emergency Management Office (EMO) 147–9
Gaduo 61, 71
Gaduojuewu 71
Guangdong 94
Guangzhou 114
Haikou 95
Hainan Province 95
Hangzhou 114
Headquarters for Earthquake Fighting and Disaster Relief (HEFDR) 88–9
ICOMOS 51
Jiegu 65
Labu 61, 71
Ministry of Civil Affairs (MCA) 147–8
Ministry of Construction 90–1
Ministry of Education 87, 90–1, 94
Ministry of Finance and State Administration of Taxation 148
Ministry of Health (MOH) 147
Ministry of Public Security (MPS) 148
Ministry of Water Resources (MWR) 148
National Bureau of Statistics 85
National Civil Defense (NCD) 148
National Development and Reform Commission 91

National Disaster Reduction Center (NDRC) 147
National Earthquake Administration – see China Earthquake Administration (CEA) 148, 153
National Disaster Reduction Center (NDRC) 147
National Workplace Emergency Management Center (NWEMC) 147, 153
Panxi 85
Policy Bureau of China 47
Qiang 46–8, 51–2, 54–5, 57n.
Qinghai 62–3, 67–8
Qinghai-Tibet Plateau 61
Qingshuihe 61, 70, 75
Qumalai 70
River Basin Commission (RBC) 148
Sanjiangyuan National Nature Reserve 61–2, 66, 69–70, 73, 75, 77
Shifang 96–7
Shanghai 89, 114, 339
Shangzhuang 64–5
Shenzhen 114
Sichuan 45–59, 70, 81–110, 200n.
State Council 47, 49–50, 88–90, 93, 148
Suzhou 114
State Administration of Cultural Heritage of China (SACH) 45, 48–50
State Administration of Work Safety (SAWS) 147–8, 153
Taoping 45–59
Tianjin 114
Tibet 61–79
Tongtianhe River 61, 67, 69, 72
Xiazhuang 64–5
Xiewu 61, 70, 75
Xining 70
Xiqu River 74
Yangtze River 121
Yushu 61–3, 65, 70–1, 77. See also Earthquakes
Zhaduo 61, 70, 75
Zhenqin 61, 71
Cities 70, 75, 77, 85, 89, 94, 112–6, 121, 183, 286–8, 295, 301–2, 310, 315, 319, 339–51, 353–4, 360
Civic organizations 205, 378
Civil defense programs 141–2, 153
Civilians 143, 285
  Government 358
  Mitigation efforts 142
Climate 3, 25, 111, 285, 315
  Climate change 6, 14, 17, 24, 26, 28–32, 111, 113, 132, 149, 317–8, 325, 341–2, 348
Clinton, Hillary Rodham 214
Clinton, William Jefferson, President of the United States 180
Coastal areas 12–3, 14, 30, 112, 114, 138, 142, 144, 151–2, 154, 176, 203, 253, 262, 269, 285, 287–8, 293–4, 297, 299–300, 343, 345, 349.
Coca 252, 254, 256–7
Colombia 21, 29, 251–281
  *Ejército de Liberación* (ELN) 254. See also Terrorism
  Ethno-educational center (EEC) ("Centro Etnoeducativo") 252, 255, 260–1, 264–7, 271–4
  *Fuerzas Armadas Revolucionarias de Colombia* (FARC) 264. See also Terrorism
  *Familias Guardabosques— Corazón del Mundo* (FG-CM) 255, 257, 260, 262, 263, 265–6, 268–9
  Palomino River 254

Colonialism 253, 255, 258, 266, 272, 347–8, 351–2, 356, 372, 374–82, 385–91, 396n., 397n.
Commercial development (infrastructure) 53, 316, 319, 350, 352, 357
Compensation for the effects of disasters and disaster mitigation 29, 77, 98, 117, 121, 187
Conservation 31, 45–8, 50–1, 55–6, 66–7, 74, 77, 115, 258–9, 263
Consumption
  of energy 113
  of resources 6, 11, 115
Crime 228–9, 240–2, 246, 339, 347, 354. See also Prison; Violence; War.
Recidivism 227–49
Crops – see Agriculture
Dhaka, Bangladesh 339
Disabilities 95, 291–2, 315–7, 320, 323, 349
Disasters 6–7, 13, 18, 86, 113, 203, 343
  Man-made disasters:
    Nuclear disasters 3, 6, 26–7, 30, 32, 36, 141
      Fukushima Daaichi nuclear disaster – see Japan
    BP Deepwater Horizon oil spill 17, 286–7, 290
  Natural disasters:
    Avalanches 131
    Droughts 322, 324, 373
    Earthquakes 3, 5, 10, 20, 23–4, 26, 32–3, 131, 140, 142, 145, 148–9, 152–3, 154, 311–2, 320, 322
      3/11 (Great Tohoku) 173–224, 309–10
      Operation Tomodachi 175, 197n.
      Great Hanshin Earthquake (1994) 185
      Haiti (2010) 31, 174–5, 180, 182, 200n.
      Hegben Lake, Montana (1959) 141
      Lisbon (1755) 7
      Loma Prieta (1989) 143
      Northridge (1994) 142–3
      Wenchuan (2008) 45–59, 81–110, 150–1
      Yushu (2010) 73–9
    Fires 35, 39n., 74, 140, 142, 149, 153, 310, 318–9, 322
    Floods 3–4, 6, 20, 32–3, 74, 131, 134, 140–4, 148–9, 151–3, 155, 283–307, 310, 312, 322, 324, 343, 347–50, 353–5, 357–9
    Hurricanes 3, 5, 10, 14, 24, 32, 113, 140, 154, 322
      Agnes (1972) 141
      Andrew (1996) 142
      Betsy (1965) 141
      Carla (1962) 141
      Camille (1969) 141, 302
      Donna (1960) 141
      Fort Lauderdale (1947) 302
      Georges (1998) 299
      Great Atlantic Hurricane (1938) 154
      Hugo (1990) 142–3
      Irene (2011) 154

Katrina (2005) 35, 144, 150, 152, 154, 174, 200n. 283–307
Sandy (2012) 14, 31, 35, 144, 150, 154, 214
Landslides 131, 311
Tornadoes 23, 32
Tsunamis 3, 5, 23, 26, 322
Indian Ocean tsunami (2004) 12–4, 174–5, 180, 182, 187–8
3/11 tsunami 30–1, 173, 186, 203, 207, 216, 218, 309–10. See also Earthquakes.
Typhoons 145
Volcanoes 3, 17
Krakatoa 17
Pompeii 7
Economic issues 5–6, 12–4, 24–5, 29–30, 33–4, 37, 39n., 62, 70, 89, 112–8, 135–7, 145, 155–6, 186, 194, 227, 235, 241, 243, 246, 251, 256, 258–63, 267, 270, 283–6, 294, 298–9, 309, 313–20, 323–4, 340–3, 345–8, 350–2, 355–7, 359–60, 372, 375, 380, 384, 386, 391–2, 397n.
Economies affected by disasters 3–4, 12, 14, 17, 53, 73, 299
Economic losses following disasters 3–4, 18, 85, 112, 131, 286–7, 290, 295, 300, 305, 309
Economic prosperity (growth) 5–6, 10, 13, 39n., 62, 69, 74, 77, 111–4, 116, 121–2, 140, 145, 154, 242, 270, 323–4, 343–4, 379–80, 391

Economic response to disasters (assistance) 12–3, 24, 35, 76, 92, 319
Ecosystems 6, 21, 27, 31, 34, 37, 38n., 62–3, 65–70, 74–5, 77–8, 111–30, 136, 252–4, 258–9, 262–3, 268–9, 273, 341, 343–4, 350, 355, 360
Damage to 7, 10, 132
Ecosystem Services Valuation (ESV) 112, 116–8, 120–2
Education 75, 81–110, 227–49, 251–81. See also Colombia, Ethno-educational center; Children
Elderly 74, 290–1, 315, 319, 323–4, 349
Emergency management (EM) 134–5, 137–8, 140–5, 147–56, 316
Employment 35, 62, 67, 71, 73–4, 77, 83, 113, 153, 173, 175, 190, 213, 227–49, 285–6, 288, 315–7, 319–21, 339, 344, 347–8, 350, 352, 355, 359, 372, 391
Energy 11, 29–31, 39, 75, 77, 113, 115, 197n., 287, 324, 347, 350, 373
England – see United Kingdom
Environmental legislation
in China 147–56
in the U.S. 140–4, 147–56
Europe 7, 194, 286, 343
FAFO Institute for Applied International Studies, the 50
France 30, 286
Gulf Coast Community Design Studio (GCCDS) 292, 303–4
Geingob, Hage, Prime Minister of Namibia 382
Germany 286, 376–7, 381
Geographical Information Services (GIS) 118, 122
Guatemala 241–2, 244–6
Gulf of Mexico (Gulf Coast) 144, 152, 154, 285, 287, 297, 299

Gurirab, Hage, Prime Minister of Namibia, 382
Health 23, 30, 74, 82–3, 87, 114, 147, 149, 153, 233, 251, 254, 257–8, 273, 288, 315–6, 319–21, 343, 345, 347, 349, 357, 380
    Antibiotics 25, 31
    Disease 7, 32, 37, 347–8, 356
    Doctors 13, 193, 233, 320
    Doctors without Borders 176
    Drugs 228–30, 321
    Epidemics 3, 24, 27
        HIV/AIDS 31, 315, 324, 371
        Influenza 31
        SARS 147, 149–50
        Tuberculosis (TB) 31, 233
    Facilities 74, 255, 320
        Hospitals 35, 74, 320–1, 352, 357
    Insurance 33
    Mental / psychological health 83, 94–6, 312, 320–2
        Post-traumatic stress disorder (PTSD) 3, 86
    Sanitation 54, 73, 149, 153, 207, 233, 348, 254, 256–8, 356–7, 380
    Vaccination 25, 31
Hirohito, Emperor of Japan, 204, 209, 317–9
Homelessness 47–8, 57n., 320, 348–9, 391
Housing 10, 23, 29, 45, 48, 50, 53–6, 73–4, 83, 86, 95, 141, 144, 184, 192, 199n., 203, 216, 218, 231, 238, 243–4, 246, 283–5, 287–94, 296, 298–305, 319–21, 323, 349, 355–6, 358
    Apartments 231, 285, 298
    Architecture 11, 47, 50, 65, 73, 75–6, 292–3, 360
    Condominiums 285, 298, 301

    ("Katrina") Cottages 289, 292–3, 304–5
Human Rights 5, 231, 235, 378–9, 382, 395n.
    Violations of 375, 378, 380–1
Hungary 95
Hunger 3, 37
International Labor Organization (ILO) 259
International Monetary Fund (IMF) 12
India 112
    Delhi 339
    Kolkata 339
    Mumbai 339
Indigenous peoples 75–6, 251–81
    Arhuaco (Colombia) 253, 260, 266, 271
    Bantu (Africa) 375
    Bantustan policy 385
    Damara (Namibia) 376, 385
    Hausa (Nigeria) 310, 356
    Herero (Namibia) 376–7, 385, 391–2
    Herero genocide 376–7
    Ibo (Nigeria) 310
    Ife (Nigeria) 351
    Ijebu (Nigeria) 351
    Kangba (China) 62, 70, 73
    Kankuamo (Colombia) 253, 260
    Kogi (Colombia) 252–7, 260–9, 271–4
    Mokaná (Colombia) 269–70, 273
    Mbukush (Namibia) 373
    Nama 376–7, 385
    Nasa 264–5
    Ondonga (Namibia) 373
    Tairona (Colombia) 253
    Ukwangali (Namibia) 373
    Wiwa (Colombia) 253
    Yuri (Colombia) 21
    Yoruba (Nigeria) 310, 351, 356
    See also United Nations, Declaration on the Rights of

Indigenous Peoples (UNDRIP)
Indonesia 14, 82
International Labor Organization (ILO) 259
  Indigenous and Tribal Peoples Convention (1989) 259
Ireland 286
Italy 132, 286
Japan 29–31, 82 173–224, 309–10
  Atomic bombing of Hiroshima and Nagasaki 217
  Democratic Party of Japan (DPJ) 205, 208
  Fukushima Daiichi nuclear disaster 18, 30, 35, 173, 186, 203, 207
  Honshu 203
  Ishinomaki
  Japan NGO Center for International Cooperation (JANIC) 178, 182, 195, 200n.
  Japan Platform 178, 182, 195, 200n.
  Japanese Self-Defense Forces (JSDF) 206
  Kobe 185
  Liberal Democratic Party (LDP) 205
  Okinawa 205
  Tokyo 173, 175, 182, 339
  See also Disasters, Man-made; Disasters, Natural
Jiabao, Wen, Premier of China 87
Jintao, Hu, President of China 87
Kan, Naoto, Prime Minister of Japan 204–8, 212, 214–6
Kazenambo, Kazenambo, Youth and Sport Minister of Namibia 373
Kumaratunga, Chandrika, President of Sri Lanka 12
Language 5, 12, 179, 196, 260, 264, 269, 272, 319, 375, 382, 391
  Afrikaans 382, 394n.
  Arhuaco 266
  Chinese 64
  English 179, 206, 382
  Ika 266
  Japanese 203–224
  Kogi 255, 262, 265
  Mafwe 371
  Omuherero 373
  Oshikwanyama 373
  Oshiwambo 372–3
  Spanish 255, 265–6
  Tibetan 64
Latin America 112, 241, 254
Land Use/Land Cover (LULC) 111–2, 115, 118, 120
Mexico City, Mexico 339
Military 376
National Association for the Advancement of Colored People (NAACP) 290
Namibia 371–403
  Berseba 373
  Breaking the Wall of Silence (BWS) 374, 378
  Caprivi region and people 371–3
  Central Bureau of Statistics 371
  Congress of Democrats 373
  Delimitation Commission, the 373
  Katima 371
  Kavango 373
  Koevoet 375, 391, 394n.
  Ministry of Veterans' Affairs 391
  Namibian Policy of National Reconciliation (NPNR) 380–1
  Rally for Democracy and Progress Party 373
  Regional Councils Act (1992) 379, 383
  South West African People's Organization (SWAPO) 372–8, 380–4, 386–9, 393, 395n., 396n., 397n.

New Zealand 46
Non-Governmental Organizations (NGOs) 95, 173–202, 227–9, 252–4, 256, 269–70, 318
  Acción Social 253, 255–7, 262
  Ayni Ruway 228, 232–5, 237–41, 243, 245–6, 247n.
  Fundación Pro-Sierra 253, 255–7, 261, 270
  Japan Center for International Exchange 184
  Organización Gonawindúa 256, 262
  Sasakawa Peace Foundation USA 184
  See also Charitable organizations
Ngurare, Elijah, SWAPO Youth League Secretary General 383. See also SWAPO
Niger delta 310
Nigeria 310, 312, 315, 317, 321–2, 325, 339–70
  Abuja 310, 351
  Apete 356–8
  Asejire River 356
  Eleiyele River 356
  Federal Environmental Protection Agency (FEPA) 357
    Environmental Protection Commission (EPC) 357
  Ibadan 339–70
  Ife 357
  Iwo 357
  Jos 310
  Kaduna 345
  Kano 345, 356
  Lagos 339–70
    Lagos Executive Development Board (LEDB) 347
    Lagos State Development and Property Corporation (LSDPC) 349
  Maiduguri 310
  Mapo 356–7
  Port Harcourt 345
  Ogunpa River 358
  Ojoo 356
  Olojuoro 357
  Oyo 346, 351, 357
  Sasa 356
  Structural Adjustment Program (SAP) 352
Nujoma, Sam, President of Namibia 372, 374
Obama, Barack, President of the United States 180, 214
Pakistan 112
  Karachi 349
São Paulo, Brazil 339
Philanthropy – see Charitable organizations
Pienaar, Louis 375
Pohamba, Hifikepunye, President of Namibia 372–3
Political autonomy 89, 94, 257–8, 260–2, 264–6, 268, 271
Pollution 6, 19, 28–9, 37, 39n., 66, 77, 112–5, 148, 318, 322, 343, 349, 354, 357–8
Potsdam Declaration, the 217
Poverty 20, 33, 132, 136, 155, 178, 182, 187, 228, 242–3, 251, 253, 258, 260, 268, 270–1, 278n., 289–90, 314–5, 317–25, 339–41, 343–5, 347–50, 352–5, 371, 373, 380, 386, 391–2
Prison 35, 227–49, 310
Racial issues 2, 47, 61, 251, 255–6, 264–5, 286, 271, 303, 314–7, 319, 321, 355, 359, 371–6, 378–87, 389–92, 397n.
  Racism 295, 319, 373, 379, 384, 386–7, 391
  Segregation 341, 347, 359, 372, 375, 384
Refugees 47–8, 315
Religion 3, 5, 7–8, 11, 13, 15, 21, 23, 36–7, 65, 72, 77, 182, 191, 199n., 255, 265, 310, 315–6, 320–1, 344

Resilience 134–7, 142–3, 150, 154–5, 311, 314–5, 317–8, 320, 324, 339–70
Rio de Janeiro, Brazil 349
Russia 95
South Africa 374–7, 380–2, 385, 395n.
   African National Congress (ANC) 380
      Umkhonto Wesizwe 380
   Pretoria 376
   Truth and Reconciliation Commission (TRC) 375, 380–1
South America – see Latin America
South Korea 185, 194, 196
Sri Lanka 12–4
Sudan 309
Sustainability 14, 56, 57n., 70, 74, 82, 112–6, 118, 121–2, 135–7, 148, 150–1, 154–6, 178, 191, 193, 252, 254, 256–4, 261, 264, 270, 284, 286, 291–2, 303, 309, 312, 322–5, 342–3, 355, 360
Switzerland 242, 246
Taiwan 185, 197n., 198n.
Tanzania 378
Technology 3, 7–15, 324
Terrorism 3, 143
   Suicide bombings 310
Tibet – see China
Tourism 13–4, 53–4, 62, 65, 69–73, 77, 284–5, 287, 300, 303
Tribes – see Indigenous peoples
Tsunamis 3, 5, 23, 26, 322
   Fukushima 30, 31, 173, 186, 188, 203–224, 309–10
   Indian Ocean tsunami (2004) 7, 12–3, 174–5, 180, 182, 187
Turkey 112
United Kingdom 48, 198n., 241
   England 235, 375
United Nations (UN) 137, 175, 195, 197n., 198n., 345–6, 375, 377
   Children's Fund (UNICEF) 184
   Convention on the Elimination of all Forms of Racial Discrimination (CERD) 373
   Declaration on the Rights of Indigenous Peoples (UNDRIP) 259, 261
   Earth Summit (1992) 136
   Educational, Scientific and Cultural Organization (UNESCO) 46, 48, 262
   Inter-Agency Secretariat of the International Strategy for Disaster Reduction (UNISDR)
   International Decade for Disaster Reduction (IDNDR) 136–7, 142, 147–8
   Habitat 342–3
   Hyogo Framework for Action (2005) 137, 151, 154
   Millennium Declaration 28
   Universal Declaration of Human Rights (1948) 235
   *Yokohama Strategy and Plan of Action for a Safer World, The* (1994) 137
Uribe, Álvaro, President of Colombia 255
United States, the 21, 55, 134, 143, 173–7, 180–92, 193, 196, 197n., 198n., 199n., 209, 258–9, 340, 343–344
   African-Americans 286, 290, 295
   Agency for International Development (USAID) 181
   Bureau of Justice 241
   Bureau of Public Roads 140
   Chamber of Commerce Business Civic Leadership Center 181
   Control of Electromagnetic Radiation (CONELRAD) system 151

Department of Homeland Security (DHS) 143–4
Department of Housing and Urban Development (HUD) 142
Emergency Alert System (EAS) 151–2, 155
Emergency Broadcast System (EBS) 152
Federal Civil Defense Administration 141
Federal Communications Commission 152
Federal Emergency Management Agency (FEMA) 142–4, 150, 152–4, 156, 288, 291–2, 295
    FEMA trailers 288, 293–4. See also Housing
Federal Insurance Administration 142
Fire Administration (USFA) 153
General Services Administration 142
Geological Survey 152, 155
Homeland Security Act (HSA) (2002) 143
    Homeland Security Presidential Directives (HSPDs) 143, 153
Integrated Public Alert and Warning System (IPAWS) 152
    Commercial Mobile Alert System (CMAS) 152
Japan-America Society of Hawaii 184
National Commission for Disaster Reduction 153
National Fire Academy (NFA) 153
National Fire Prevention and Control Administration (NFPCA) 142
National Oceanic and Atmospheric Administration (NOAA) 138
Nuclear Regulatory Commission, the 142
Office of Emergency Preparedness (OEP) 141
Patriot Act (2001) 143
States:
    California 29, 33, 175, 184
        Japanese Cultural and Community Center of Northern California 184
    Georgia 288
    Louisiana 33, 285
    Mississippi 152
        Back Bay (Bay of Biloxi) 285, 296–7, 305n.
        Biloxi 283–305, 305n.
            Woolmarket 296
        Mississippi Emergency Management Agency (MEMA) 292–3
        Mississippi River 140
        D'Iberville 302
        Gulfport 295
        Harrison County 285, 297–8, 300
        Keesler Air Force Base 285–6, 300
        Mississippi Alternative Housing Project (MAHP) 292
        Vietnamese communities 152, 155, 286–7, 290
    New Jersey 144, 154, 214
    New York 21, 181, 199n.
        Japan Society of New York 184–5

New York City 21,
181–2, 184–5, 199n.,
214, 349
Tennessee Valley
Authority (TVA), the
140
Washington D.C. 12,
181
Tone Alert Radio (TAR)
152
Venice Charter for the Conservation
and Restoration of Monuments
and Sites, the 45
Violence 36, 229, 253, 264, 266,
267–8, 273, 310, 321, 339,
347–8, 373–4
Vulnerability 5–6, 89, 99, 134, 136–
8, 143, 152, 156, 227–8, 260,
290–1, 299, 309–70

Biophysical 314
War 251–2, 254–5, 260, 267, 273–
4, 310, 315, 320–1, 344, 347,
374–5, 379, 383–4, 386–7,
390–1
War crimes 376, 378
Women 83, 213, 232–3, 255, 265,
291, 315, 319, 349, 390
Feminism 315
Work – see Employment
World Bank, the 12, 348, 357
World Health Organization
2002 Budapest Declaration 46
World Heritage Convention (WHC)
46
Youth – see Children
Zambia 378, 380